T0140368

Lecture Notes in Computer Science   13286

More information about this series at https://link.springer.com/bookseries/558

Paolo Rosso · Valerio Basile · Raquel Martínez ·
Elisabeth Métais · Farid Meziane (Eds.)

Natural Language Processing and Information Systems

27th International Conference on Applications
of Natural Language to Information Systems, NLDB 2022
Valencia, Spain, June 15–17, 2022
Proceedings

Springer

Editors
Paolo Rosso 🄳
Universitat Politècnica de València
Valencia, Spain

Valerio Basile 🄳
University of Turin
Torino, Italy

Raquel Martínez 🄳
Universidad Nacional de Educación
a Distancia
Madrid, Spain

Elisabeth Métais 🄳
Conservatoire National des Arts et Métiers
Paris, France

Farid Meziane 🄳
University of Derby
Derby, UK

ISSN 0302-9743   ISSN 1611-3349 (electronic)
Lecture Notes in Computer Science
ISBN 978-3-031-08472-0   ISBN 978-3-031-08473-7 (eBook)
https://doi.org/10.1007/978-3-031-08473-7

This Springer imprint is published by the registered company Springer Nature Switzerland AG
The registered company address is: Gewerbestrasse 11, 6330 Cham, Switzerland

Preface

This volume contains the papers presented at NLDB 2022, the 27th International Conference on Applications of Natural Language to Information Systems held during June 15–17, 2022, as a hybrid conference at the Universitat Politècnica de València, Spain. We received 106 submissions for the conference. Each paper was assigned to at least three reviewers, taking into account preferences expressed by the Program Committee members as much as possible. After the review deadline, Program Committee members were asked to complete missing reviews. In addition, the Program Committee and the General Chairs acted as meta-reviewers, completing missing reviews, writing additional reviews for borderline papers, and acting as moderators for submissions with considerably conflicting reviews. At the end of the process, each paper had received at least three reviews. On the basis of these reviews, the Program Chairs decided to accept papers with an average score of approximately 0.5 or above as full papers and papers with a slightly lower score as short papers. The confidence score indicated by the reviewers played a role in deciding borderline cases, as well as the content of the reviews and the topic of the papers with respect to the conference scope. The final acceptance rate counting the number of full papers according to NLDB tradition was 26 percent (28 out of 106), similarly competitive in comparison to previous years. In addition, 20 submissions were accepted as short papers. For the first time, and in line with most leading conferences, an industry track was created, and submissions were sought. Among those acceptances, six long papers and one short paper were from the industry track. Full papers were allowed a maximum of 12 pages and short papers a maximum of 8 pages. Two papers were withdrawn during the revision process. In addition to the reviewed papers, there were three invited talks at NLDB 2022:

- Eneko Agirre, University of the Basque Country/HiTZ Centre on Language Technology
- Lucie Flek, University of Marburg
- Ramit Sawhney, Tower Research Capital (Industry Keynote)

The NLDB conference, now a well-established conference, attracted submissions and participants from all over the world. The conference has evolved from the early years when most of the submitted papers were in the areas of natural language, databases, and information systems to encompass more recent developments in the data and language engineering fields. The content of the current proceedings reflects these advancements.

The conference organizers are indebted to the reviewers for their engagement in a vigorous submission evaluation process, as well as to the sponsors: Symanto, AI Zwei, and Google Research.

June 2022

Paolo Rosso
Valerio Basile
Raquel Martínez
Elisabeth Métais
Farid Meziane

Organization

General Chairs

Paolo Rosso   Universitat Politècnica de València, Spain
Elisabeth Métais   Conservatoire des Arts et Mètiers, France
Farid Meziane   University of Derby, UK

Program Chairs

Valerio Basile   University of Turin, Italy
Raquel Martínez   Universidad Nacional de Educación a Distancia, Spain

Program Committee

Jacky Akoka	Cnam and TEM, France
Luca Anselma	University of Turin, Italy
Ahsaas Bajaj	University of Massachusetts Amherst, USA
Mithun Balakrishna	Limba Corp, USA
Somnath Banerjee	University of Milano-Bicocca, Italy
Imene Bensalem	University of Constantine 1, Algeria
Claudia Borg	University of Malta, Malta
Cristina Bosco	University of Turin, Italy
Martin Braschler	ZHAW School of Engineering, Switzerland
Davide Buscaldi	Université Sorbonne Paris Nord, France
Elena Cabrio	Université Côte d'Azur, Inria, CNRS, I3S, France
Tommaso Caselli	Rijksuniversiteit Groningen, The Netherlands
Luis Chiruzzo	Universidad de la República, Uruguay
Alessandra Cignarella	University of Turin, Italy
Philipp Cimiano	Bielefeld University, Germany
Danilo Croce	University of Rome "Tor Vergata", Italy
Walter Daelemans	University of Antwerp, Belgium
Agustín Delgado	Universidad Nacional de Educación a Distancia, Spain
Liviu Dinu	University of Bucharest, Romania
Antoine Doucet	La Rochelle University, France
Elisabetta Fersini	University of Milano-Bicocca, Italy
Komal Florio	University of Turin, Italy

Vladimir Fomichov	Moscow Aviation Institute, Russia
Tommaso Fornaciari	Bocconi University, Italy
Marc Franco	Symanto, Germany/Spain
Flavius Frasincar	Erasmus University Rotterdam, The Netherlands
Yaakov Hacohen-Kerner	Jerusalem College of Technology, Israel
Helmut Horacek	DFKI, Germany
Dino Ienco	INRAE, France
Carlos A. Iglesias	Universidad Politécnica de Madrid, Spain
Ashwin Ittoo	University of Liege, Belgium
Epaminondas Kapetanios	University of Hertfordshire, UK
Zoubida Kedad	UVSQ, France
Christian Kop	University of Klagenfurt, Austria
Anna Koufakou	Florida Gulf Coast University, USA
Rim Laatar	University of Sfax, Tunisia
Mirko Lai	University of Turin, Italy
Deryle W. Lonsdale	Brigham Young University, USA
Cédric Lopez	Emvista, France
Natalia Loukachevitch	Moscow State University, Russia
Thomas Mandl	University of Hildesheim, Germany
Paloma Martínez	Universidad Carlos III de Madrid, Spain
Patricio Martínez	Universidad de Alicante, Spain
Abir Masmoudi	LIUM, University of Le Mans, France
Alessandro Mazzei	University of Turin, Italy
Luisa Mich	University of Trento, Italy
Nada Mimouni	Conservatoire des Arts et Métiers, France
Jelena Mitrović	University of Passau, Germany
Soto Montalvo	Universidad Rey Juan Carlos, Spain
Manuel Montes y Gómez	INAOE, Mexico
Johanna Monti	L'Orientale University of Naples, Italy
Rafael Muñoz	Universidad de Alicante, Spain
Debora Nozza	Bocconi University, Italy
Muhammad Okky-Ibrohim	University of Turin, Italy
Lucia Passaro	University of Pisa, Italy
Viviana Patti	University of Turin, Italy
Davide Picca	Columbia University, USA
Laura Plaza	Universidad Nacional de Educación a Distancia, Spain
Francisco Rangel	Symanto, Germany/Spain
Antonio Reyes	Autonomous University of Baja California, Mexico
Mathieu Roche	Cirad, TETIS, France
Horacio Saggion	Universitat Pompeu Fabra, Spain

Contents

Applications

Language Resources and Evaluation

Sentiment Analysis and Social Media

An Ensemble Approach for Dutch Cross-Domain Hate Speech Detection

Ilia Markov[1]([✉]) [iD], Ine Gevers[2] [iD], and Walter Daelemans[2] [iD]

[1] CLTL, Vrije Universiteit Amsterdam, Amsterdam, The Netherlands
i.markov@vu.nl
[2] CLiPS, University of Antwerp, Antwerp, Belgium
ine.gevers@student.uantwerpen.be, walter.daelemans@uantwerpen.be

Abstract. Over the past years, the amount of online hate speech has been growing steadily. Among multiple approaches to automatically detect hateful content online, ensemble learning is considered one of the best strategies, as shown by several studies on English and other languages. In this paper, we evaluate state-of-the-art approaches for Dutch hate speech detection both under in-domain and cross-domain hate speech detection conditions, and introduce a new ensemble approach with additional features for detecting hateful content in Dutch social media. The ensemble consists of the gradient boosting classifier that incorporates state-of-the-art transformer-based pre-trained language models for Dutch (i.e., BERTje and RobBERT), a robust SVM approach, and additional input information such as the number of emotion-conveying and hateful words, the number of personal pronouns, and the length of the message. The ensemble significantly outperforms all the individual models both in the in-domain and cross-domain hate speech detection settings. We perform an in-depth error analysis focusing on the explicit and implicit hate speech instances, providing various insights into open challenges in Dutch hate speech detection and directions for future research.

Keywords: Hate speech · Dutch · Cross-domain · Ensemble

1 Introduction

With the rise in popularity of social media platforms that offer anonymity in online debates and the associated increase in the amount of hateful content online, the issue of automatically detecting hate speech and related concepts, such as abusive and offensive language, toxicity, and cyberbullying, amongst others, has become a growing challenge for governmental organizations, social media platforms, and the research community.[1] Robust hate speech detection systems may provide valuable information to support moderators in effectively

---

[1] In this work, we use hate speech as an umbrella term to cover all related concepts.

I. Markov—Work done while at CLiPS, University of Antwerp.

P. Rosso et al. (Eds.): NLDB 2022, LNCS 13286, pp. 3–15, 2022.
https://doi.org/10.1007/978-3-031-08473-7_1

countering this phenomenon in online discussions and promoting healthy online debates [10].

Despite the variety of recently proposed approaches to tackle hate speech online and advances in the field of natural language processing (NLP), the task of automated hate speech detection remains challenging from multiple perspectives. These challenges – along with defining the concept itself due to the inherent subjectivity of the phenomenon [23] – include implicit hate speech detection, i.e., hate speech that is not explicitly expressed by means of profanities, slurs or insults [14], and the performance of hate speech detection systems under cross-domain conditions[2]: while the most widely used source of data is Twitter [28], there is a substantial drop in performance when evaluating hate speech detection approaches on out-of-domain datasets [18,21]. Another issue is that most of the hate speech-related research has been conducted on English data, while substantially less attention has been paid to languages other than English [23,28]. Our work intents to address these shortcomings by providing new insights into cross-domain hate speech detection in Dutch.

Due to a large amount of user-generated content available on social media and the arrival of transformer-based pre-trained language models, the accuracy of automated hate speech detection systems has increased significantly [31]. While pre-trained language models such as BERT [7] and RoBERTa [15] achieve impressive results for hate speech detection and are considered the best-performing models for this task [12,31], ensemble learning enables to further improve upon the best-performing individual models due to its ability to select the best-performing classifier for a particular message [1,17,20]. In recent shared tasks on detecting hate speech and related concepts, e.g., OffensEval [31] and TRAC [12] that provided multilingual datasets, most of the top-ranked teams used pre-trained language models as part of ensembles, e.g., [26,30].

In this work, we exploit two recent social media datasets for hate speech detection research in Dutch: LiLaH[3] [18] and DALC [2], composed of Facebook comments and tweets, respectively. On these datasets we evaluate state-of-the-art models both under in-domain and cross-domain (training on one dataset and testing on another) conditions and present an ensemble of state-of-the-art classifiers. By conducting cross-domain experiments we aim to examine whether state-of-the-art models are able to generalize well across different domains (social media platforms and topics), which is essential for the systems to be useful in real-world applications [21].

While previous work on cross-domain hate speech detection has dealt with the Dutch language as part of multilingual studies [18,27], to the best of our knowledge, the performance of state-of-the-art hate speech detection models for Dutch has not been investigated under cross-domain conditions. To fill in this gap, we evaluate transformer-based pre-trained language models for Dutch (i.e., BERTje [29] and RobBERT [6]) and a robust SVM approach (described

---

[2] Following previous work, e.g., [21], the domain term is used to cover both platforms and topical focuses.

[3] https://lilah.eu/.

in detail further in this paper), and combine them within a gradient boosting ensemble. We propose additional features to encode input information: the number of emotion-conveying words in a message, the number of hateful words, the number of personal pronouns, and the length of the message in terms of both words and characters. We perform an in-depth error analysis on the ensemble's output highlighting the open challenges in Dutch hate speech detection research that most of the state-of-the-art approaches share.

2   Methods and Ensemble

In this section, we describe the deep learning and machine learning approaches used in this study, as well as the proposed ensemble strategy.

BERTje. We use the monolingual Dutch pre-trained language model, BERTje [29], from the Hugging Face transformers library[4]. The model was pre-trained using the same architecture and parameters as the original BERT model [7] on a dataset of 2.4 billion tokens. The model is fine-tuned for one epoch with the default parameters. Hyperparameter optimisation (batch size, learning rate, and the number of epochs) provided marginal variation in the obtained results. The implementation was done using the simple transformers library[5].

RobBERT. We use the Dutch version of the RoBERTa model [15], RobBERT [6], available through the Hugging Face transformers library[6]. The model was pre-trained using the RoBERTa training regime on a corpus of 6.6 billion words. The model is fine-tuned for one epoch with the default parameters using the simple transformers library implementation.

SVM. The Support Vector Machines (SVM) algorithm [3] is widely used for the hate speech detection task due to its near state-of-the art performance and the possibility for an explicit feature engineering [17]. We adapt the stylometric and emotion-based approach proposed in [18], which relies on part-of-speech tags, function words, and emotion-conveying words and their associations from the LiLaH emotion lexicon for Dutch [4,16]. We enrich the approach by incorporating additional features: hateful words from the POW hate speech lexicon [5], word unigrams, and character n-grams (with n = 1–6), considering only those n-grams that appear in ten training messages (min_df = 10). We use *tf-idf* weighting scheme and the liblinear scikit-learn [22] implementation of SVM with optimized parameters (we selected the optimal liblinear classifier parameters: penalty parameter (C), loss function (loss), and tolerance for stopping criteria (tol) based on grid search under cross-validation).

---

[4] https://huggingface.co/GroNLP/bert-base-dutch-cased.
[5] https://simpletransformers.ai/.
[6] https://huggingface.co/pdelobelle/robBERT-base.

Ensemble. The ensemble approach relies on the predictions of individual models, additional features to represent input information and their weights to select the optimal classifier for a given feature combination. Following the ensemble strategy proposed in [13], we train the models described above under stratified 5-fold cross-validation and produce the predictions for each message in the training data and in the test set. Subsequently, we train the gradient boosting classifier [9] (scikit-learn implementation) on the predictions obtained by the individual models. To encode input information, we propose the following additional features: (1) the number of emotion-conveying words in a message, extracted from the Dutch LiLaH emotion lexicon [16], which has proven to be indicative features for hate speech detection [18, 25]; (2) the number of hateful words from the POW hate speech lexicon [5]; (3) the number of first-person personal pronouns, which are often used as features for hate speech detection to distinguish between 'us' and 'them' [24]; (4) message length in terms of words and (5) message length in terms of characters.

3   Experiments and Results

We present a suite of experiments designed to evaluate the performance of the state-of-the-art models and the ensemble approach described in Sect. 2 both under in-domain and cross-domain hate speech detection conditions.

3.1   Data

We carry out our experiments on two recent Dutch social media datasets composed of Facebook comments and tweets, as well as utilize this data to examine models' generalizability in cross-domain hate speech detection settings. In more detail, we use the following datasets for hate speech and abusive language detection research in Dutch:

LiLaH. The LiLaH dataset [18] is composed of Facebook comments extracted from prominent Flemish online newspapers, manually annotated for fine-grained types (e.g., violence, threat, offensive speech) and targets (e.g., community, journalist, commenter) of hate speech directed against the following minority groups: LGBT community and migrants. We focus on the coarse-grained (binary) hate speech classes: hate speech vs. non-hate speech, and use the training and test partitions, where the training and test sets are split by post boundaries to avoid within-post bias, i.e., comments under the same post are in the same subset.

DALC. The Dutch Abusive Language Corpus, or DALC v1.0 [2], is a manually annotated dataset of tweets for abusive language detection. Each tweet in the data was annotated following a three-level hierarchical scheme: denoting abusive language (abusive or not abusive), the category of abusive language (explicit or implicit), and the target of abusive language (individual, group, other). The dataset covers a variety of topics related to events occurred between 2015 and

2020, e.g., the Paris Attack in 2015, the Black Lives Matter protests in 2020. The training, development, and test partitions were split in such a way that there is no overlap for time periods and seed users. In this work, we merge the training and development subsets, fine-tuning the models on this combined training data. We focus on the binary classification setting: abusive vs. not abusive.

Both datasets feature an imbalanced class distribution, shown in Table 1, which is considered an inherent challenge for hate speech detection approaches [28]. For the cross-domain experiments, we merge the training and test subsets of the datasets. We train the models on one dataset and test on another, and vice versa.

Table 1. Statistics of the datasets used.

		LiLaH		DALC	
		# messages	%	# messages	%
Train	HS	3,753	43.8	1,252	20.0
	non-HS	4,821	56.2	5,003	80.0
Test	HS	949	44.0	637	33.5
	non-HS	1,209	56.0	1,264	66.5
Total		10,732		8,156	

3.2 Results and Discussion

The performance of the models described in Sect. 2 in terms of precision, recall, and F1-score (macro-averaged), both in the in-domain and cross-domain settings, is shown in Table 2. For the cross-domain experiments, we provide the results both on the test set used in the in-domain setup (test) in order to quantify the cross-domain drop, as well as on the entire dataset (entire) to have more data for the manual error analysis described further in Sect. 4.

As a reference point, we provide a majority class baseline. Statistically significant gains of the ensemble approach over the best-performing individual model for each setting according to McNemar's statistical significance test [19] with $\alpha < 0.05$ are marked with '*'.

The in-domain results show that all the examined models outperform the majority class baseline by a large margin. While BERTje and RobBERT achieve the highest results on the both datasets, and the result for BERTje on the DALC test set is similar to the F1-score of 74.8% reported in [2], the SVM approach performs well too, outperforming both the SVM approach proposed in [18] on the LiLaH dataset (75.3% vs. 74.7%), as well as the dictionary and the SVM approaches [2] on the DALC dataset (71.3% vs. 68.5% and 65.5%, respectively).

When the domains of the training and test corpora are disjoint, there is a large drop in performance for all the examined models, as evidenced by the cross-domain results. The drop is much higher (around 20 F1 points) when training on the DALC dataset (tweets) and testing on the LiLaH dataset (Facebook comments). We can observe that in this setting, the drop is mainly caused by

Table 2. In-domain and cross-domain results for the baseline, individual models and ensemble. The best results are highlighted in bold typeface.

In-domain

Model	LiLaH			DALC		
	Precision	Recall	F1	Precision	Recall	F1
Majority baseline	28.0	50.0	35.9	33.2	50.0	39.9
SVM	75.3	75.3	75.3	81.0	69.5	71.3
BERTje	77.6	77.1	77.3	82.5	72.7	74.7
RobBERT	77.4	75.7	76.0	82.7	73.3	75.3
Ensemble	**78.8**	**78.2**	**78.4***	**84.9**	**75.0**	**77.2***

Cross-domain

Model	Train DALC, test LiLaH (test)			Train LiLaH, test DALC (test)		
	Precision	Recall	F1	Precision	Recall	F1
SVM	70.7	59.4	55.5	67.7	69.4	67.9
BERTje	77.0	62.1	58.6	70.0	72.2	69.9
RobBERT	75.2	60.4	56.2	70.2	72.3	70.4
Ensemble	**76.3**	**62.5**	**59.3**	**74.0**	**76.8**	**74.0***

Model	Train DALC, test LiLaH (entire)			Train LiLaH, test DALC (entire)		
	Precision	Recall	F1	Precision	Recall	F1
Majority baseline	28.1	50.0	36.0	38.4	50.0	43.5
SVM	69.1	59.2	55.6	64.0	69.1	63.6
BERTje	**74.4**	61.7	58.5	66.2	72.7	64.6
RobBERT	72.5	60.0	56.2	65.9	72.2	64.4
Ensemble	74.1	**63.0**	**60.6***	**68.1**	**75.2**	**66.9***

substantially lower recall values, while when training on LiLaH and testing on DALC the main cause for the overall drop is lower precision. The asymmetric drop in performance across the two datasets is mainly due to the size and the distribution of classes in the training data: the LiLaH dataset is larger and there are twice as many hate speech instances. We carried out an additional experiment training on a subset of the LiLaH dataset of the same size and with the same class distribution as the DALC corpus, and testing on the DALC test set, observing that in this case there is a significant drop in recall as well, i.e., 58.1% instead of 69.4% for the SVM approach, resulting in 57.3% F1-score, similar to the DALC–LiLaH (test) setting. While the large drop in the DALC – LiLaH (test) setting is partially related to the smaller size of the DALC dataset used for training in comparison to the LiLaH corpus, the result in the LiLaH – DALC (test) setting demonstrates that even when all the available data is used for training, there is a substantial drop for all the models under cross-domain conditions.

The observed cross-domain drop cannot be explained by the length of the messages in the datasets nor by the lexical overlap: though Twitter is a microblogging platform that features a character limitation, the median length of the messages in terms of characters is similar across the two datasets: 125.6

(LiLaH) and 128.5 (DALC); moreover, the descriptive analysis showed that the Jaccard similarity coefficients [11] for the cross-domain training and test sets are similar across the different settings, that is, 14.7% for DALC – LiLaH (test) and 15.1% for LiLaH – DALC (test) (for the in-domain training and test sets these coefficients are 19.0% for LiLaH and 19.4% for DALC). The observed cross-domain drop could be related to other peculiarities of the datasets, such as different annotation guidelines and possible bias introduced by annotators. The manual error analysis presented below sheds more light on the nature of the misclassified instances.

In the in-domain and cross-domain (both when testing on the test set and on the entire dataset) settings, the ensemble approach outperforms the best-performing individual models by a significant margin. An ablation study showed that all the ensemble components contribute to its performance both under in-domain and cross-domain conditions, while the models incorporated into the ensemble produce uncorrelated predictions (measured using the Pearson correlation coefficient).

4   Error Analysis

Through a detailed error analysis of the ensemble results, we intend to get insights into common errors that most of the state-of-the-art approaches share. We perform a manual error analysis of the cross-domain results when training on the LiLaH dataset and testing on the entire DALC corpus.

The confusion matrices for the individual models and the ensemble approach presented in Fig. 1 demonstrate that the ensemble performs better than the individual models in terms of both false positives and false negatives. The only exception is the SVM approach, which shows the lowest number of false positives. A good SVM performance in terms of false positives compared to deep learning methods has been observed in previous studies on hate speech detection [17].

Moreover, the ensemble approach performs better with respect to both explicit and implicit hate speech instances, as shown in Table 3. It can also be noted that implicit hate speech instances are more challenging for all the examined models, which has been observed in previous research as well, e.g., [14].

Table 3. The number and percentage of correctly identified explicit and implicit hate speech instances by each model.

Explicitness	SVM	BERTje	RobBERT	Ensemble
Explicit (out of 1,229)	936 (76%)	1,070 (87%)	1,046 (85%)	1,113 (91%)
Implicit (out of 660)	401 (61%)	481 (73%)	481 (73%)	490 (74%)

We proceed to a manual error analysis of the erroneous false negative (both explicit and implicit) and false positive predictions. We focus on all 286 cases of false negatives, and select a random sample of 300 false positive examples.

4.1 False Negatives

First, we focus on the false negatives – hateful messages that were missed by the algorithm – and explore error classes that are frequent for both explicit and implicit instances, then we proceed to error classes specific to explicit and implicit hate speech instances.

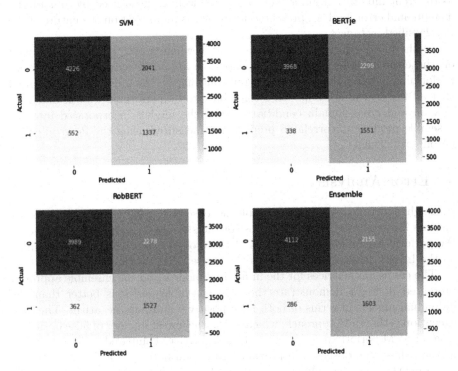

Fig. 1. Confusion matrices for the individual models and the ensemble approach when training on the LiLaH dataset and testing on the entire DALC corpus.

Questionable label We note that the majority of explicit and implicit instances fall under the questionable label category, that is, we doubt the annotators' decision on the label. This class also includes messages containing only an URL.

E.g.: *LITTLE NOTE FROM X - To Y URL* 'BRIEFJE VAN X - Aan Y URL'[7]

In the case of explicit false negatives, the number of instances within this category goes as high as 40%. This is partly due to the high number of messages containing only an URL (14%). In the implicit category, 34% of the messages belong to this category.

---

[7] Proper names are anonymized.

Sarcasm and irony As has been shown in multiple studies, e.g., [8], hateful messages containing sarcasm or irony are problematic for detection. Even though this only occurs in 3% and 4% of the explicit and implicit categories respectively, it is worth pointing out. These messages are often accompanied by laughing emojis and quotation marks.

E.g.: *The number of bankruptcies increases again. But according to #Rubberrug @USER @USER the #LyingHollander it is going 'great' in the Netherlands and EVERYONE is better 'off'. URL* 'Aantal faillissementen neemt weer toe. Maar volgens #Rubberrug @USER @USER de #LiegendeHollander gaat het 'fantastisch' in Nederland en gaat IEDEREEN er op 'vooruit'. URL'

The following three classes are specific for explicit false negatives:

Idiosyncratic and rare words van Aken et al. [1] observed that these words may cause errors in classification. In our analysis, we encountered misspellings, alternative swear words, such as *hat* 'muts', and swearing in another language. 23% of the messages belong to this class.

E.g.: *I'm blocking all souhailas you're all stupid* 'Ik blok alle souhailas jullie zijn allemaal stupid'

No swear words In 12% of the messages, hate speech was misclassified, likely because it was expressed without the use of swear words.

E.g.: *@USER @USER Youth care is a business model, they don't care about children, only about the money it makes.* '@USER @USER Jeugdzorg is een verdienmodel, geven geen donder om kinderen, wel om het geld wat het oplevert.'

Presence of targets Some messages were hateful, but the lack of a (clear) target may have hindered correct classification (see example). We observe this phenomenon in 4% of the messages. On the other hand, we note that some messages were misclassified as they refer to specific targets, e.g., individuals.

E.g.: *@USER I hate people animals>people* '@USER ik haat mensen dieren >mensen'

Next class is specific for implicit false negatives.

Metaphors and comparisons 14% of the implicit messages were misclassified as they rely on world knowledge to understand the content.

E.g.: *Really have trouble not to demolish every headscarf or hatebeard I encounter...* 'Heb echt moeite om elke hoofddoek of haatbaard die ik tegenkom niet te slopen...'

4.2   False Positives

Questionable label Similarly to false negatives, false positives – not hateful messages erroneously classified as hateful – also contain instances with a questionable label. However, this rate is lower (17%) than for false negatives.

E.g.: *@USER @USER Given your comment you're a radical troll yourself...* '@USER @USER Gezien jouw commentaar ben je zelf een radicale trol...'

Headlines of news articles We observed that headlines of news articles followed by an URL can be misclassified as hate speech, whereas the headline simply reports current affairs. This accounts for 11% of the instances. These news headlines are often related to targets who are frequently associated with hate speech, such as ethnical minorities.

E.g.: *Deported asylum seeker increasingly returns home independently URL* 'Uitgewezen asielzoeker steeds vaker zelf naar huis URL'

Use of hashtags/lexicon/references when referring to targets often associated with hate speech In our analysis, 20% of the false positives are messages that mention social groups that are often figure as the target of hate speech. These messages often distinguish 'us' and 'them'. The mentioned social groups are, e.g., members of LGBT or religious communities. We point out that these messages frequently use lexical items referring to death, killing or aggression.

E.g.: *@USER and #PVV make Muslims an almost bigger victim of the attacks than the people who were killed on Friday.* '@USER en #PVV maken dat moslims een bijna nog groter slachtoffer van de aanslagen zijn dan de mensen die vrijdag zijn afgemaakt.'

Counter narratives We note that messages condemning hate speech or countering hateful messages are often classified as hate speech. This class accounts for 10% of the messages.

E.g.: *Isn't it unbelievable that Muslims are being blamed for the actions of ISIS who are slaughtering Muslims in Syria and Iraq? How stupid?!* 'Het is toch ongelooflijk dat moslims de schuld krijgen van acties van ISIS die in Syrië en Irak moslims afslachten? Hoe dom?!'

Usage of swear words Instances containing swear words represent a part of the false positives in our analysis (7%).

E.g.: *Fuck the job, I just need money :sleeping_face: want to become sleeping rich.* 'Fuck een baan, ik heb gewoon geld nodig :sleeping_face: wil slapend rijk worden.'

5   Conclusions

The task of automatic hate speech detection has recently gained popularity and traction within the natural language processing community due to an increased need for moderation of such content online, which is only possible at large scale by applying automated methods. In this work, we evaluated state-of-the-art deep learning and conventional machine learning approaches for in-domain and cross-domain hate speech detection in Dutch social media. We showed that when the training and test corpora are from different platforms and cover different topics, there is a substantial drop in performance for all the examined models. We also showed that when these models are combined into an ensemble and input information is represented using additional features, such as emotion-conveying and hateful words, personal pronouns, and the length of the message, a significant boost in performance is observed both under in-domain and cross-domain hate speech detection conditions. Our error analysis of the ensemble results highlighted open challenges in Dutch cross-domain hate speech detection, confirming previous findings from research on English data that a large source of errors comes from questionable labels, the usage of figurative language, idiosyncratic and rare words, and swear words in non-hateful messages. Focusing on these challenges will enable to further enhance the performance of Dutch hate speech detection systems.

Acknowledgements. This research has been supported by the Flemish Research Foundation through the bilateral research project FWO G070619N "The linguistic landscape of hate speech on social media". The research also received funding from the Flemish Government (AI Research Program).

References

1. van Aken, B., Risch, J., Krestel, R., Löser, A.: Challenges for toxic comment classification: an in-depth error analysis (2018). arXiv/1809.07572
2. Caselli, T., et al.: DALC: the Dutch abusive language corpus. In: Proceedings of the 5th Workshop on Online Abuse and Harms, pp. 54–66. ACL (2021)
3. Cortes, C., Vapnik, V.: Mach. Learn. Support-vector networks **20**(3), 273–297 (1995)
4. Daelemans, W., et al.: The LiLaH Emotion Lexicon of Croatian, Dutch and Slovene, slovenian language resource repository CLARIN.SI (2020)
5. De Smedt, T., Voué, P., Jaki, S., Röttcher, M., De Pauw, G.: Profanity & offensive words (POW): Multilingual fine-grained lexicons for hate speech. Technical report TextGain (2020)
6. Delobelle, P., Winters, T., Berendt, B.: RobBERT: a Dutch RoBERTa-based language model (2020). arXiv/2001.06286
7. Devlin, J., Chang, M.W., Lee, K., Toutanova, K.: BERT: Pre-training of deep bidirectional transformers for language understanding. In: Proceedings of the 2019 Conference of the North American Chapter of the Association for Computational Linguistics: Human Language Technologies, ACL, pp. 4171–4186 (2019)
8. Frenda, S.: The role of sarcasm in hate speech. a multilingual perspective. In: Proceedings of the Doctoral Symposium of the XXXIV International Conference of the Spanish Society for Natural Language Processing, CEUR, pp. 13–17 (2018)
9. Friedman, J.H.: Greedy function approximation: a gradient boosting machine. Annal. stat. **29**(5), 1189–1232 (2001)
10. Halevy, A., et al.: Preserving integrity in online social networks (2020). arXiv/2009.10311
11. Jaccard, P.: Étude comparative de la distribution florale dans une portion des Alpes et des Jura. Bulletin de la Société vaudoise des sciences naturelles **37**, 547–579 (1901)

12. Kumar, R., Ojha, A.K., Malmasi, S., Zampieri, M.: Evaluating aggression identification in social media. In: Proceedings of the Second Workshop on Trolling, Aggression and Cyberbullying, ELRA, pp. 1–5 (2020)
13. Lemmens, J., Burtenshaw, B., Lotfi, E., Markov, I., Daelemans, W.: Sarcasm detection using an ensemble approach. In: Proceedings of the Second Workshop on Figurative Language Processing, ACL, pp. 264–269 (2020)
14. Lemmens, J., Markov, I., Daelemans, W.: Improving hate speech type and target detection with hateful metaphor features. In: Proceedings of the Fourth Workshop on NLP for Internet Freedom: Censorship, Disinformation, and Propaganda, ACL, pp. 7–16. (2021)
15. Liu, Y., et al.: RoBERTa: a robustly optimized BERT pretraining approach (2019). ArXiv/1907.11692
16. Ljubešić, N., Markov, I., Fišer, D., Daelemans, W.: The LiLaH emotion lexicon of Croatian, Dutch and Slovene. In: Proceedings of the Third Workshop on Computational Modeling of People's Opinions, Personality, and Emotion's in Social Media, ACL, pp. 153–157 (2020)
17. Markov, I., Daelemans, W.: Improving cross-domain hate speech detection by reducing the false positive rate. In: Proceedings of the Fourth Workshop on NLP for Internet Freedom, ACL, pp. 17–22 (2021)
18. Markov, I., Ljubešić, N., Fišer, D., Daelemans, W.: Exploring stylometric and emotion-based features for multilingual cross-domain hate speech detection. In: Proceedings of the Eleventh Workshop on Computational Approaches to Subjectivity, Sentiment and Social Media Analysis, ACL, pp. 149–159 (2021)
19. McNemar, Q.: Note on the sampling error of the difference between correlated proportions or percentages. Psychometrika $12(2)$, 153–157 (1947)
20. Melton, J., Bagavathi, A., Krishnan, S.: DeL-haTE: a deep learning tunable ensemble for hate speech detection. In: Proceedings of the 19th IEEE International Conference on Machine Learning and Applications, pp. 1015–1022. IEEE (2020)
21. Pamungkas, E.W., Basile, V., Patti, V.: Towards multidomain and multilingual abusive language detection: a survey. Pers. Ubiquitous Comput. $25(4)$, 1–27 (2021). https://doi.org/10.1007/s00779-021-01609-1
22. Pedregosa, F., et al.: Scikit-learn: machine learning in Python. J. Mach. Learn. Res. 12, 2825–2830 (2011)
23. Poletto, F., Basile, V., Sanguinetti, M., Bosco, C., Patti, V.: Resources and benchmark corpora for hate speech detection: a systematic review. Lang. Resour. Eval. $55(2)$, 477–523 (2021). https://doi.org/10.1007/s10579-020-09502-8
24. Qureshi, K.A., Sabih, M.: Un-compromised credibility: social media based multiclass hate speech classification for text. IEEE Access 9, 109465–109477 (2021)
25. Rajamanickam, S., Mishra, P., Yannakoudakis, H., Shutova, E.: Joint modelling of emotion and abusive language detection. In: Proceedings of the 58th Annual Meeting of the ACL, ACL, pp. 4270–4279 (2020)
26. Risch, J., Krestel, R.: Bagging BERT models for robust aggression identification. In: Proceedings of the Second Workshop on Trolling, Aggression and Cyberbullying, ELRA, pp. 55–61 (2020)
27. Smedt, T.D., et al.: Multilingual cross-domain perspectives on online hate speech (2018). arXiv/1809.03944
28. Vidgen, B., Derczynski, L.: Directions in abusive language training data: Garbage in, garbage out (2020). arXiv/2004.01670
29. de Vries, W., van Cranenburgh, A., Bisazza, A., Caselli, T., van Noord, G., Nissim, M.: BERTje: A Dutch BERT model (2019). arXiv/1912.09582

30. Wiedemann, G., Yimam, S.M., Biemann, C.: UHH-LT at SemEval-2020 task 12: fine-tuning of pre-trained transformer networks for offensive language detection. In: Proceedings of the 14th Workshop on Semantic Evaluation, ICCL, pp. 1638–1644 (2020)
31. Zampieri, M., et al.: SemEval-2020 task 12: multilingual offensive language identification in social media. In: Proceedings of the 14th Workshop on Semantic Evaluation, ICCL, pp. 1425–1447 (2020)

Convolutional Graph Neural Networks for Hate Speech Detection in Data-Poor Settings

Gretel Liz De la Peña Sarracén[1,2(✉)] and Paolo Rosso[1]

[1] Universitat Politècnica de València, Valencia, Spain
gredela@posgrado.upv.es, prosso@dsic.upv.es
[2] Symanto Research, Valencia, Spain

Abstract. Hate speech detection has received a lot of attention in recent years. However, there are still a number of challenges to monitor hateful content in social media, especially in scenarios with few data. In this paper we propose HaGNN, a convolutional graph neural network that is capable of performing an accurate text classification in a supervised way with a small amount of labeled data. Moreover, we propose Similarity Penalty, a novel loss function that considers the similarity among nodes in the graph to improve the final classification. Particularly, our goal is to overcome hate speech detection in data-poor settings. As a result we found that our model is more stable than other state-of-the-art deep learning models with few data in the considered datasets.

Keywords: Hate speech detection · Data-poor settings · Convolutional graph neural networks

1 Introduction

Hate speech detection is a prominent task in the Natural Language Processing and other disciplines. According to [5], which is a reference survey in the area, hate speech can be defined as a language that attacks or diminishes, that incites violence or hate against groups, based on specific characteristics such as physical appearance, religion, gender identity or other, and it can occur with different linguistic styles, even in subtle forms or when humour is used. Due to its negative real life implications, a number of proposals to face the problem have emerged in the last years. Among them, deep learning has gained significant traction, highlighting the state-of-the-art performance of the Transformer-based models [6]. However, hate speech is a complex phenomenon and human annotation is not straightforward, since there is not uniformity across all demographics. Then, expert-based datasets are usually small, especially in low-resource languages.

In order to deal with this limitation, we use a strategy based on graph neural networks (GNNs) which have been effective at tasks thought to have a rich relational structure, since they can preserve global structure information of a

P. Rosso et al. (Eds.): NLDB 2022, LNCS 13286, pp. 16–24, 2022.
https://doi.org/10.1007/978-3-031-08473-7_2

graph in embeddings [12]. In this sense, our idea is to represent the texts from a dataset as nodes in a graph, and learn embeddings in terms of neighbourhood aggregation. Thus, we do not need a large amount of data, such that we make use of limited labeled data by allowing information propagation through our automatically constructed graph.

The motivation derives from the strong representation learning capability of GNNs, which have gained practical significance in several applications. In general, GNNs generalize the deep neural network models to graph structured data, providing a way to effectively learn representations for graph-structured data either from the node level or the graph level. In [10], the authors provide a practical overview of the different types of GNNs by presenting a taxonomy which divides them into four categories: recurrent graph neural networks, convolutional graph neural networks, graph auto-encoders, and spatial-temporal graph neural networks. We focus on convolutional graph neural networks (CGNNs) which re-define the notion of convolution for graph data [7]. The main idea is to generate a representation for each node by aggregating its features and the features of its neighbors. Then, high-level node representations are extracted by stacking multiple graph convolutional layers. The use of this type of GNN is inspired by [11] that proposed a graph representation of documents and words together, and showed an improvement of GNNs over other methods with small training sets.

Our Contributions: The novelty of this work is three-fold. First, we propose a model based on CGNNs for text classification in a data-poor setting. Particularly, we study the case of hate speech detection where it is often difficult to obtain an expert-based large dataset due to the complexity of the task. Secondly, we propose a loss function to improve the final embeddings of the nodes in the graph by penalizing the closeness among nodes of different classes. Finally, we provide a comparison of HaGNN and other models. We show that our model is robust with a small amount of data, outperforming state-of-the-art models in these few data scenarios[1].

2   HaGNN Model

In this section, we formalize CGNNs and describe the way we use it in our system, followed by other details of our proposed loss function.

2.1   Hate Speech Detection

In this work we formalize hate speech detection as a binary classification, such that the task involves the classes hate and not-hate. The data comprises N samples, where each sample is given by $\{t_i, y_i\}$. The set $\{t_i\}_{i=1}^{N}$ is composed of texts that are represented with numeric feature vectors $\{x_i\}_{i=1}^{N}$. In order to generate these feature vectors we use the universal sentences encoder (USE)[2]

---

[1] We will make our codes freely available by the publication date of this work.

[2] https://tfhub.dev/google/universal-sentence-encoder/4.

[2], which encodes text into high-dimensional vectors. The model was optimized for greater-than-word length texts, such as sentences or short paragraphs. It was trained on several data sources and tasks to dynamically adapt a wide variety of natural language understanding tasks. The input is an English text of variable length and the output is a 512 dimensional vector. The set $\{y_i\}_{i=1}^{N}$ is composed of the labels 0 and 1, which indicate the presence or not of hate in each of the texts in $\{t_i\}_{i=1}^{N}$. Then, the aim of the task is to detect hateful content by assigning one of the labels to each t_i by using x_i.

Our goal is to obtain an accurate performance in hate speech detection when N is small. We address the issue by adapting CGNNs from a node level classification. Following, we describe the CGNN model and the loss function used.

2.2   Background: Convolutional Graph Neural Networks

Graph neural networks are models based on deep learning for graph-related tasks in an end-to-end manner. In particular, a CGNN re-defines the notion of convolution for graph data. This is a multi-layer neural network that operates directly on a graph and induces the embedding vectors of nodes based on the properties of their neighbors. Formally, let $G = (V, E)$ be a graph, where V and E represent the set of nodes and edges respectively. Let $X \in \mathbb{R}^{|V| \times d}$ be a matrix containing the features of the nodes, such that the i-th row is a d-dimensional feature vector of the i-th node. Moreover, let $A \in \mathbb{R}^{|V| \times |V|}$ be a matrix representation with a representative description of the graph structure, such as the adjacency matrix.

Then, CGNN takes as input the matrices X and A to learn a function of features on G and produces a node-level output ϕ. That is, a $|V| \times d'$ feature matrix, where d' is the number of output features per node. A hidden layer in a CGNN can be defined as a function $H_i = f(H_{i-1}, A))$, where $H_0 = X$, $H_L = \phi$, L being the number of layers, and $f(\cdot, \cdot)$ is a propagation rule. Thus, the feature vectors become more abstract at each consecutive layer.

Authors of [7] introduced the propagation rule (1). Where W_i is the weight matrix for the i-th layer and $\sigma(\cdot)$ is an activation function. The matrix $\hat{A}$ contains self-connections to aggregate, for each node, not only the information from its neighbors but also the node itself. It is done by adding the identity matrix I, that is $\hat{A} = A + I$. Furthermore, the matrix D is the diagonal node degree matrix of $\hat{A}$, which is used for a symmetric normalization to deal with the problem of changing the scale of the feature vectors.

$$f(H_{i-1}, A) = \sigma(D^{-\frac{1}{2}} \hat{A} D^{-\frac{1}{2}} H_i W_i) \tag{1}$$

2.3   Our Model

In order to generate the input for the model, we build the matrix X with the set of numeric feature vectors $\{x_i\}_{i=1}^{N}$, such that each vector is a row in X. On the other hand, we build the edges among nodes, to generate the matrix A, based on the inner product of the feature vectors. Then, the weight of each edge is defined by the inner product between the original vectors. We only add edges between node pairs with values higher than a threshold.

Once the matrices are generated, we feed our model. This consists of 2 convolutional layers with the propagation rule (1) and the ReLU as the activation function. Moreover, we add a normalization layer after each convolutional layer. Finally, we add two linear transformation layers and a softmax to obtain the nodes classification, as Eqs. (2), (3) and (4), where $A^* = D^{-\frac{1}{2}}\hat{A}D^{-\frac{1}{2}}$.

$$H_1 = ReLU(A^*XW_0) \tag{2}$$

$$H_2 = ReLU(A^*H_1W_1)W_1^L \tag{3}$$

$$Z = softmax(H_2W_2^L) \tag{4}$$

In each case W_i corresponds to the parameters of the convolutional layers and W_i^L are the parameters of the linear layers.

2.4 Proposed Loss: Similarity Penalty

The loss function is defined using the binary cross-entropy $\mathcal{CE}$ over the labeled samples. In addition, we introduce a novel loss function which is a combination of the $\mathcal{CE}$ and a function $\mathcal{DP}$ that considers the closeness among nodes in the graph. Equation (5) presents this combination, where θ represents the set of all the parameters of the model. The idea with $\mathcal{DP}$ is to penalize each pair of nodes from different classes with a high similarity between their generated embeddings. We use as the generated embedding ϕ the output of the last convolutional layer, and the cosine function to calculate the similarity between vectors. As Eq. (8) illustrates, we rely on the function $g(x) = 1 - log(x + 1)$ which is positive and decreasing in the interval of the similarity values. The term $|y_i - y_j|$ ensures only penalize for the pair of nodes from different classes by multiplying by zero the cases of pairs of vectors from the same class.

$$\mathcal{L}(\theta) = m\_\mathcal{CE} + m\_\mathcal{DP} \tag{5}$$

$$m\_\mathcal{CE} = \frac{1}{N}\sum_n \mathcal{CE}(\theta, x_n, y_n) \tag{6}$$

$$m\_\mathcal{DP} = \frac{2}{N(N-1)}\sum_i \sum_{j>i} |y_i - y_j| log\_dist(x_i, x_j) \tag{7}$$

$$log\_dist(x_i, x_j) = 1 - log(dist(\phi(x_i), \phi(x_j)) + 1) \tag{8}$$

2.5   Training the Model

The training is also based on [7] which describes a semi-supervised classification. In this sense, we divide the data into labeled (90%) and unlabeled (10%) texts. The aim is to make use of both labeled and unlabeled examples. That is, the training knows all the nodes, but not all the labels. Then, CGNN produces latent feature representation of each node by aggregating both the labeled and unlabeled neighbors of each node during convolution and the weights shared across all nodes are updated by propagating backwards the loss calculated from the labeled examples.

3   Experiments

We illustrate the performance of our HaGNN model with two datasets built for hate speech detection: HatEval [1] and CONAN [3]. The second one has the characteristic that non-hateful texts are counter-narrative to hate speech, which makes it interesting to discover how CGNNs can separate both types of texts.

HatEval was the Task 5 in SemEval 2019 about the detection of hate speech against immigrants and women in Spanish and English tweets. The corpus is composed of 10,000 tweets for English. The tweets was collected by three strategies: monitoring potential victims of hate accounts, downloading the history of identified haters and filtering tweets with three groups of terms: neutral keywords, derogatory words against the targets, and highly polarized hashtags. The first task was to detect hate speech and then to identify further features in hateful content such as whether each text was aggressive or not.

CONAN is a large-scale and multilingual corpus of hate speech/ counter-speech pairs. This corpus contains texts in English, French, and Italian and the pairs were collected through nichesourcing to three different non-governmental organizations. Both the hate speech and the responses are expert-based. We only use the 3864 pairs in English that we downloaded from the web.[3]

For hyperparameters setting we searched in the set $\{16, 32, 64\}$ for the size of both convolutional and linear layers, in $\{0.3, 0.5, 0.7\}$ for the threshold used in the generation of the matrix A, and in $\{0.0001, 0.001, 0.01, 0.1\}$ for the learning rate. Finally, we set the threshold to 0.5, the size of the hidden layers to 32, and we use the Adam optimizer with 0.01 of learning rate. We trained the model with 200 epochs and the strategy of early stopping with patience 10. We report the results obtained with this last configuration of hyperparameters, using the cross-validation strategy with 3 partitions. Moreover, we evaluated different number of convolutional layers and observed an improvement by using two layers instead of only one. However, we observed that the results remained similar for a number of layers greater than two as Fig. 1 shows.

In order to compare with other models we evaluated other classifiers. The first one is based on BERT [4] and the other one is based on ALBERT [8].

---

[3] https://github.com/marcoguerini/CONAN.

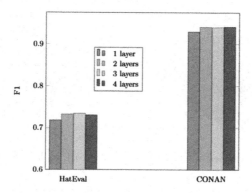

Fig. 1. Varying number of layers

These are Transformer-based models with state-of-the-art results, not only in text classification, but also in many other tasks. Furthermore, we evaluated a feedforward neural network (FFNN) of 2 layers with the same input that we use for HaGNN. We aim to analyze if the performance improvement is attributed to the proposal beyond the sentence embedding.

4 Results

In order to analyze the embeddings generated with the CGNN, Figs. 2(a) and 2(b) illustrate a visualization of CONAN, and 2(c) and 2(d) for HatEval with t-SNE [9, 9]. We observe the effectiveness of the convolutions, since in the last layer (2nd) the embeddings are more distinguishable between classes than between the original vectors. Similar variations in embeddings representations are obtained for HatEval. On the other hand, Table 1 shows the average of F1 and standard deviation obtained with our model. The results of classification are slightly higher, but not significant for CONAN by using our loss function. However, for HatEval, we can see an important improvement. Moreover, we observe an improvement in comparison to FFNN, where we use the same sentence embedding but changing the model. This shows the suitability of our proposal.

Table 1. F1 and standard deviation of HaGNN.

Model	HatEval	CONAN
HaGNN	$0.7320_{0.0165}$	$0.9407_{0.0302}$
HaGNN + DP	$0.7500_{0.0170}$	$0.9499_{0.0231}$
FFNN	$0.7094_{0.0204}$	$0.8925_{0.0319}$
BERT	$0.7200_{0.0189}$	$0.9354_{0.0204}$
ALBERT	$0.7208_{0.0248}$	$0.931_{0.02505}$

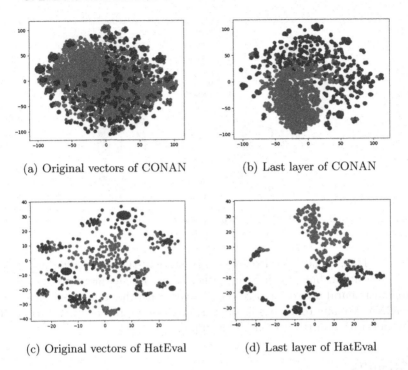

(a) Original vectors of CONAN

(b) Last layer of CONAN

(c) Original vectors of HatEval

(d) Last layer of HatEval

Fig. 2. Embeddings

Furthermore, Figs. 3(a) and 3(b) show a comparison among HaGNN, BERT and ALBERT for HatEval and CONAN respectively. We note that HaGNN obtains a better F1 with few data. Such that, with only 100 samples, it achieves 0.8148 in CONAN, while the other models obtain less than 0.62. In HatEval, the results obtained by HaGNN with 100 samples are not so high, although are higher than the results of the other models. Moreover, we can see that as the data size increases, Bert and Albert have better performance. Such that, around the size 500 the approaches are closer.

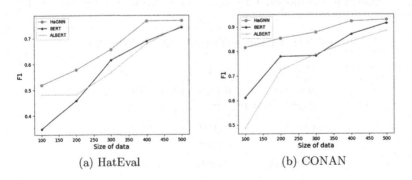

(a) HatEval

(b) CONAN

Fig. 3. F1 score for different sizes of data

5   Conclusions and Future Work

In this work, we propose the HaGNN model to address hate speech detection in scenarios with few data. The model is based on convolutional graph neural networks and we proposed a new loss function to penalize nodes from different classes with close generated embeddings. We show that HaGNN is robust in small datasets, outperforming state-of-the-art models in these scenarios. As future work, we attempt to extend this model for handling multimodal datasets.

Acknowledgments. This research work was partially funded by the Spanish Ministry of Science and Innovation under the research project MISMIS-FAKEnHATE on Misinformation and Miscommunication in social media: FAKE news and HATE speech (PGC2018-096212-B-C31). The first author gratefully acknowledges the support of the Pro^{2}Haters - Proactive Profiling of Hate Speech Spreaders (CDTi IDI-20210776) and XAI-DisInfodemics: eXplainable AI for disinformation and conspiracy detection during infodemics (MICIN PLEC2021-007681) R&D grants. The work of the first author was also partially funded by the Centre for the Development of Industrial Technology (CDTI) of the Spanish Ministry of Science and Innovation under the research project IDI-20210776 on Proactive Profiling of Hate Speech Spreaders - PROHATER (Perfilador Proactivo de Difusores de Mensajes de Odio). Moreover, the work of the second author was partially funded by the Generalitat Valenciana under DeepPattern (PROMETEO/2019/121).

References

1. Basile, V., et al.: Semeval-2019 Task 5: multilingual detection of hate speech against immigrants and women in twitter. In: 13th International Workshop on Semantic Evaluation, pp. 54–63. Association for Computational Linguistics (2019)
2. Cer, D., Yang, Y., et al.: Universal Sentence Encoder (2018). CoRR abs/1803.11175. http://arxiv.org/abs/1803.11175
3. Chung, Y.L., Kuzmenko, E., Tekiroglu, S.S., Guerini, M.: CONAN-counter narratives through nichesourcing: a multilingual dataset of responses to fight online hate speech. In: Proceedings of the 57th Conference of the Association for Computational Linguistics, ACL 2019, Florence, Italy, vol. 1 (Long Papers), pp. 2819–2829. Association for Computational Linguistics, 28 July-2 August 2019 (2019)
4. Devlin, J., Chang, M.W., Lee, K., Toutanova, K.: BERT: pre-training of deep bidirectional transformers for language understanding. In: Proceedings of the 2019 Conference of the North American Chapter of the Association for Computational Linguistics: Human Language Technologies, vol. 1 (Long and Short Papers), pp. 4171–4186. Association for Computational Linguistics (2019). https://www.aclweb.org/anthology/N19-1423
5. Fortuna, P., Nunes, S.: A survey on automatic detection of hate speech in text. ACM Comput. Surv. (CSUR) **51**(4), 1–30 (2018)
6. Isaksen, V., Gambäck, B.: Using transfer-based language models to detect hateful and offensive language online. In: Proceedings of the Fourth Workshop on Online Abuse and Harms, pp. 16–27 (2020)
7. Kipf, T.N., Welling, M.: Semi-supervised classification with graph convolutional networks. In: Proceedings of the 5th International Conference on Learning Representations, ICLR 2017 (2017)

8. Lan, Z., Chen, M., Goodman, S., Gimpel, K., Sharma, P., Soricut, R.: ALBERT: a lite BERT for self-supervised learning of language representations. In: International Conference on Learning Representations (2020), https://openreview.net/forum?id=H1eA7AEtvS

9. Pezzotti, N., Lelieveldt, B.P.F., Maaten, L.v.d., Höllt, T., Eisemann, E., Vilanova, A.: Approximated and user steerable tSNE for progressive visual analytics. IEEE Trans. Visual. Comput. Graphics **23**(7), 1739–1752 (2017). https://doi.org/10.1109/TVCG.2016.2570755

10. Wu, Z., Pan, S., Chen, F., Long, G., Zhang, C., Yu, P.S.: A comprehensive survey on graph neural networks. IEEE Trans. Neural Netw. Learn. Syst. **32**(1), 4–24 (2021). https://doi.org/10.1109/TNNLS.2020.2978386

11. Yao, L., Mao, C., Luo, Y.: Graph convolutional networks for text classification. In: Proceedings of the AAAI Conference on Artificial Intelligence, vol. 33, pp. 7370–7377 (2019)

12. Zhou, J., et al.: Graph neural networks: a review of methods and applications. AI Open **1**, 57–81 (2020)

Network Analysis of German COVID-19 Related Discussions on Telegram

Valentin Peter, Ramona Kühn$^{(\boxtimes)}$, Jelena Mitrović , Michael Granitzer ,
and Hannah Schmid-Petri

University of Passau, Innstraße 41, 94032 Passau, Germany
valentin.peter@hotmail.de,
{ramona.kuehn,jelena.mitrovic,michael.granitzer,
hannah.schmid-petri}@uni-passau.de

Abstract. We present an effective way to create a dataset from relevant channels and groups of the messenger service Telegram, to detect clusters in this network, and to find influential actors. Our focus lies on the network of German COVID-19 sceptics that formed on Telegram along with growing restrictions meant to prevent the spreading of COVID-19. We create the dataset by using a scraper based on exponential discriminative snowball sampling, combining two different approaches. We show the best way to define a starting point for the sampling and to detect relevant neighbouring channels for the given data. Community clusters in the network are detected by using the Louvain method. Furthermore, we show influential channels and actors by defining a PageRank based ranking scheme. A heatmap illustrates the correlation between the number of channel members and the ranking. We also examine the growth of the network in relation to the governmental COVID-19 measures.

Keywords: Corpus creation · Community detection · Network analysis · Covid-19 · Telegram · Querdenker · Social media

1 Introduction

A global pandemic started in 2020 after the outbreak of the SARS-CoV-2 virus that causes a disease named COVID-19. Governments all over the world implemented restrictions such as curfews, contact restrictions, and the obligation to wear medical masks. A group of people rejecting those measures inevitably formed, denying the existence of the virus and the risks associated with it. In Germany, this movement is called "Querdenken" (*lateral thinking*) and its members "Querdenker" (*lateral thinker*). They show a mistrust towards the established media [7] and are sceptical towards the governmental restrictions related to COVID-19. We will refer to them as COVID-19 sceptics in the following. They are a heterogeneous group, ranging from intellectuals, members of rightwing movements, supporters of alternative medicine, to mothers who are worried about their children [7,9].

P. Rosso et al. (Eds.): NLDB 2022, LNCS 13286, pp. 25–32, 2022.
https://doi.org/10.1007/978-3-031-08473-7_3

Protests are mainly organized via the messenger service Telegram[1] [5]. Telegram is known for its support of freedom of speech and the lack of censoring. However, Telegram does not provide features for collecting data for research purposes such as Twitter. Telegram offers 1:1 (private chats), 1:n (channels), and n:n (groups) communication. It offers end-to-end encryption and automatic deletion of messages. A group is either public or private and can have up to 200,000 members, while channels allow an unlimited number of members, but only one person to send messages. Channels and groups can reference each other by mentions ("@Person"), forwards ("Forwarded from ..."), or sharing Telegram links ("t.me/*"). Those references help to discover similar groups/channels and to unveil network structures and communities. We will use the terms groups and channels interchangeably, as their structure does not affect our methods.

We present how to efficiently sample relevant data from Telegram. Furthermore, we show how neighbouring channels can be detected. Our focus lies on channels that can be attributed to the COVID-19 sceptics movement in Germany. We create a dataset of 1979 distinct channels and cluster them into communities. Then, we investigate the channels to find influential actors in the German Querdenker movement. The channels are ranked using the PageRank algorithm. With our approach, we provide helpful insights into the organization and evolution of German COVID-19 sceptics' social network actions. Furthermore, we want to facilitate the process of creating datasets from Telegram for other researchers. Following research questions are guiding our work:

- RQ1: How can data from Telegram be sampled for further studies?
- RQ2: What are the major communities in the Telegram network of the German COVID-19 sceptics movement?
- RQ3: What are the most influential Telegram channels or actors of the German COVID-19 sceptics movement?
- RQ4: Is the growth of the German COVID-19 sceptics' network related to the governmental measures against COVID-19?

2   Related Work

The Querdenken movement in Germany has been mainly studied from a sociological perspective to understand who participates at the demonstrations. Those studies are based on online and offline surveys [5,7,9]. However, the authors remark that it is likely that the protesters at demonstrations do not reveal their true intentions as they fear legal consequences. In Telegram, opinions can be exchanged more freely without fearing any sanctions or negative reputation. However, the challenge is to detect relevant channels/groups here.

Some implementations of scrapers exist, e.g., the TeleGram-Scraper[2], focusing on information about group members. Telescrape[3] is similar to our implementation, with a greater focus on third party comment apps and media files.

---

[1] https://telegram.org/.

[2] https://github.com/th3unkn0n/TeleGram-Scraper.

[3] https://github.com/PeterWalchhofer/Telescrape.

For ranking nodes in networks, Jalili and Perc [6] present different measurements for node centrality and cascade models (e.g., PageRank). Kwak et al. [8] investigate on Twitter whether users are more influential if their messages are often reposted or mentioned by others. They count the followers and then use the PageRank algorithm on the followers' network allowing them to rank channels by their total number of retweets. Dargahi et al. [2] try to rank channels on Telegram using the `mention` graph to predict the number of participants. Their conclusion is that there is no relationship between the "degree of nodes in the Telegram mention graph and its number of followers". They found out that channels with many followers have the lowest PageRank. The authors point out that an algorithm that properly ranks Telegram channels is needed. In this paper, we will present an effective way for achieving that.

3   Dataset Creation with Exponential Discriminative Snowball Sampling

Data sampling on Telegram is more complicated than on other platforms, as it does not offer straight-forward features to scrape data and due to its structure and a variety of third-party plugins, it is more difficult to find connections between groups/channels. We answer RQ1 by first creating a list of channels (called seed) that serves as a starting point. From those channels, we identify relevant links to other channels with a ranking score. Channels with less than 10 messages are neglected as they are irrelevant.

To retrieve messages from a certain channel, the Telegram API endpoint `channels.getMessages` is used. The endpoint `channels.getFullChannel` provides information about a channel, e.g., number of participants. Global search results can be obtained via the endpoint `contacts.search`. To extract and sample data from Telegram, a scraper[4] is implemented that is based on the Telethon[5] library. The data is parsed to a custom data format containing 23 attributes per message (e.g., channel name, datetime, etc.) and saved to a CSV file. To avoid unnecessary requests, every downloaded message is persisted, so only new messages need to be downloaded. For each scraped channel, the complete history up to the 16th August 2021 is sampled.

Exponential discriminative snowball sampling is a well-known technique to sample hard-to-reach populations and to find relevant channels on Telegram [5,13]. A channel points to other channels by `links/forwards/mentions`. For exponential discriminative snowball sampling one has to first define how to generate the seed/where to start the sampling, second how to evaluate the next potential scraping candidates. The seed generation can bias the sample if one channel is used as starting point, as all of the following channels originate from only one source. Nevertheless, previous studies started with only one channel [5,13]. Similar to Dargahi et al. [2], we will start with a list of channels as seed.

---

[4] https://github.com/vali101/telegraph.
[5] https://pypi.org/project/Telethon/.

This list is created by the combination of three different methods: First, we use the Telegram `contacts.search` function to retrieve channels with the keywords "impfen" (*vaccination*), "maske" (*mask*), "corona" (*covid*), "pandemie" (*pandemic*), or "querdenken" (*German COVID-19 sceptics*). Second, we select channels that are mentioned by e.g., newspapers, famous bloggers, conspiracy news pages, etc. Third, we extract the links to the Telegram groups from the official register of the Querdenken movement.[6] A list of 231 distinct channels is generated that is our starting point for the scraping.

Now, we need to choose the next channels: Holzer [5] starts from one channel and selects the 25 most prominent channels based on `forwards/mentions/links`. He stops after two iterations, resulting in 51 distinct channels. This method does not work well when scraping >100 channels as the scraper starts drifting to channels with other topics or languages, as large channels (>1 million messages) heavily influence the ranking. Urman et al. [13] avoid this problem by counting how many distinct channels reference the channel instead of how often the channel is referenced in total to smooth out the influence of big channels. We will combine both approaches: the ranking score of each channel is determined by the number of distinct channels which refer to it. In each iteration, 200 channels are evaluated and persisted. In the end, our dataset consists of 1979 distinct channels with about 50 million messages in total.

4 Community Detection, Classification, and Ranking of Channels

A community is a combination of different channels that have shared topics, interests, or goals. Grouping the various channels of COVID-19 sceptics into smaller communities can help to better understand the heterogeneous groups. We use the well-established Louvain method for community detection [1]. For the implementation of the Louvain method, we use the Python library Python-Louvain.[7] To construct the network, `forwards`, `mentions`, and `links` can be used. In our dataset, every 5th message is a `forward` from another channel. `Mentions` only occur in 7% of the messages. We will therefore only use `forwards` to construct the network as they are more popular.

To define the most influential channels and communities, we do not assume that a high number of participants leads automatically to a high influence, as bots and fake accounts can be members. For each community that the Louvain method defined, we rank the top 5 channels using the PageRank algorithm both on `mentions` and `forwards`. This algorithm is a variant of the eigenvector centrality measure and was initially introduced to determine the importance of web pages and to rank them. It mimics a random surfer [10]. With PageRank, we identified the top 20 general channels. High PageRank means that many messages from this channel were forwarded by other influential channels. Based on a

---

[6] https://app.querdenken-711.de/initiatives-directory.

[7] https://python-louvain.readthedocs.io/en/latest/api.html.

codebook, we manually code the most prominent channels with the two properties `category_content` and `actor_type`. The `category_content` describes the topics that are discussed in the channel. It is quite challenging to define a category for the discussed topics as they are as heterogeneous as the group of the Querdenker itself. A big German newspaper defined four categories for the topics of the Querdenker [3]. We extend those four categories with two additional ones:

- *COVID-19 sceptic:* Topics about COVID-19 restrictions, conspiracies about the pandemic, criticism of the politics and established media.
- *QAnon:* Topics about QAnon conspiracy theories.[8]
- *Far-Right:* Channels with members of the far-right movement, official channels of right-wing media/movements. Topics: immigration, nationalism, etc.
- *Conspiracy:* Channels sharing all kinds of conspiracy theories, but no special focus on QAnon conspiracy theories.
- *Spiritual* (New): Channels sharing inspirational quotes, flower images, etc.
- *Alternative* (New): Channels sharing alternative news, often fake or influenced by conspiracy theories.

The `actor_type` expresses the role of the channel owner/members: *alternative media, news aggregator, influencer, political actor,* or *political initiative.* E.g., all channels from the Querdenken register were coded with `category_content= COVID-19 sceptics, actor_type=political initiative`. We also identified the language of the channels with the Polyglot Detector package[9] by using a random sample of 200 messages from each channel. To answer RQ2, we only consider the seven communities that represent 95% of all channels. The biggest community with 49% node share are the COVID-19 protesters, followed by conspiracy theorists/QAnon (17%) and Trump fanatics (17%). Community 4 (5%) are spiritual channels, community 5 (2%) far-rights in Britain, while community 6 and 7 (both 1%) have mixed topics.

We split the PageRank and number of participants into groups using equal frequency binning. Heatmaps show the correlation. In contrast to Dargahi et al. [2], we see a correlation between the number of participants and the PageRank, both for `mentions` (cf. Fig. 1a) and for `forwards` (cf. Fig. 1b). The identified influential channels in the German COVID-19 sceptics network are shown in Table 1, answering RQ3. Completeness can never be guaranteed as private channels cannot be considered or found.[10]

5   Growth of the Network and Evolution of Measures

To answer RQ4, we want to investigate how the network evolved compared to the measures against the pandemic. The number and severity of restrictions can be expressed by the Stringency Index: It was developed by Hale et al. [4] and is a COVID-19 Government Response Tracker to compare the different policies

---

[8] E.g., that "the world is run by Satan-worshipping pedophiles" [11].

[9] https://polyglot.readthedocs.io/en/latest/Detection.html.

[10] In the dataset, about 8000 invite links to private channels were found.

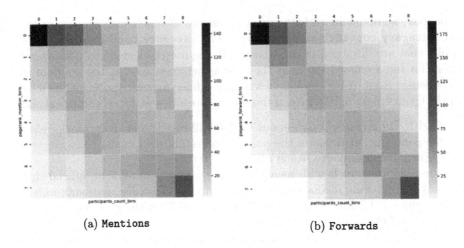

(a) Mentions   (b) Forwards

Fig. 1. Correlation between number of participants and PageRank.

Table 1. Most influential channels in the German COVID-19 sceptics network.

Channel name	Rank	Community	category_content	actor_type	Participants
reitschusterde	0.0283	1	Covid sceptic	Media	166,449
epochtimesde	0.0140	2	Alternative	Media	45,498
NTDDeutsch	0.0114	2	Alternative	Media	11,762
EvaHermanOffiziell	0.0109	1	Conspiracy	Influencer	183,440
SchubertsLM	0.0107	1	Other	News aggregator	47,207

against COVID-19 around the globe. They calculate the strictness of the measures using all original containment and closure policy indicators,[11] plus an indicator recording public information campaigns. Figure 2a illustrates the relation between message frequency in the German speaking COVID-19 sceptics channels and the stringency index, representing governmental COVID-19 measures. The first peak in the number of messages is reached when the Reichstag was stormed, the second peak when the lockdown and restrictions were extended. After this peak, both the stringency index and the number of messages move sideways. The growth of the Telegram network is expressed by an increasing number of new nodes and the sum of edges in a given time frame [13]. Figure 2b shows the number of new channels/groups joining the network per month.

---

[11] School/workplace closing, stay at home requirements, travel restrictions, etc.

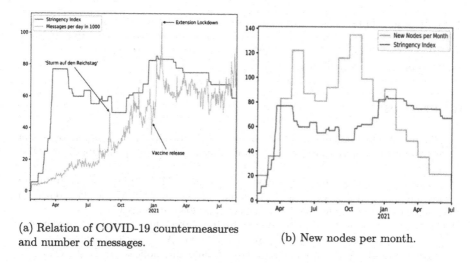

(a) Relation of COVID-19 countermeasures and number of messages.

(b) New nodes per month.

Fig. 2. Relation of COVID-19 restrictions and network activities.

6   Unknown Recommendation Problem

We want to discuss why the approach of Dargahi et al. [2] led to unsatisfactory results, while we achieved good results with the same method. In Telegram, it is unknown who forwarded a message or who mentioned it. One has to find all channels that reference the analysed channel. Unknown channels can stay undetected. We call this the **"Unknown Recommendation Problem"**. Furthermore, we notice a strong correlation (0.55) between the `forward` PageRank and the number of participants. In contrast, Dargahi et al. did not find enough neighbouring channels, and calculated the PageRank on the `mention` graph. Due to their diverse seed and the small number of channels, they discovered channels with many participants but did not collect information about their neighbouring channels.

7   Conclusion

We presented a way how to sample data from relevant channels on the messenger platform Telegram. Two different approaches were combined for sampling. The sampling bias was reduced by generating a large seed. We created the largest known dataset of the German COVID-19 sceptics movement on Telegram. We identified communities with the Louvain method and influential channels by using PageRank. We detected a correlation between the number of channel members and the ranking of the channel. In addition, we showed how activities increased in line with governmental COVID-19 measures. Future research can focus on intra-channel or intra-group communication. As some governments blame Telegram for the protests and want to ban it [12], its investigation becomes even more relevant.

Acknowledgements. The project on which this report is based was funded by the German Federal Ministry of Education and Research (BMBF) under the funding code 01—S20049. The author is responsible for the content of this publication.

References

1. Blondel, V.D., Guillaume, J.L., Lambiotte, R., Lefebvre, E.: Fast unfolding of communities in large networks. J. Stat. Mech. Theory Exp. **2008**(10), P10008 (2008)
2. Dargahi Nobari, A., Reshadatmand, N., Neshati, M.: Analysis of telegram, an instant messaging service. In: Proceedings of the 2017 ACM on Conference on Information and Knowledge Management, pp. 2035–2038 (2017)
3. Ebitsch, S., Kruse, B.: Wer den Hass verbreitet (2021). https://www.sueddeutsche.de/digital/steckbriefe-akteure-telegram-1.5278290. Accessed 3 Mar 2022
4. Hale, T., et al.: A global panel database of pandemic policies (Oxford COVID-19 government response tracker). Nat. Hum. Behav. **5**(4), 529–538 (2021)
5. Holzer, B.: Zwischen Protest und Parodie: Strukturen der "Querdenken"-Kommunikation auf Telegram (und anderswo) (2021)
6. Jalili, M., Perc, M.: Information cascades in complex networks. J. Complex Netw. **5**(5), 665–693 (2017)
7. Koos, S.: Die "Querdenker". Wer nimmt an Corona-Protesten teil und warum?: Ergebnisse einer Befragung während der "Corona-Proteste" am 4.10. 2020 in Konstanz (2021)
8. Kwak, H., Lee, C., Park, H., Moon, S.: What is twitter, a social network or a news media? In: Proceedings of the 19th International Conference on World Wide Web, pp. 591–600 (2010)
9. Nachtwey, O., Frei, N., Schäfer, R.: Politische Soziologie der Corona-Proteste (2020)
10. Page, L., Brin, S., Motwani, R., Winograd, T.: The PageRank citation ranking: Bringing order to the web. Technical Report Stanford InfoLab (1999)
11. Rose, K.: What is QAnon, the viral pro-Trump conspiracy theory? (2021). www.nytimes.com/article/what-is-qanon.html. Accessed 25 Feb 2022
12. Stempfle, M.: Was kann der Staat gegen Telegram machen? (2021). https://www.tagesschau.de/inland/telegram-verfassungsschutz-corona-leugner-101.html. Accessed 10 Mar 2022
13. Urman, A., Katz, S.: What they do in the shadows: examining the far-right networks on Telegram. Inf. Commun. Soc. 1–20 (2020)

Text Classification

Using Pseudo-Labelled Data for Zero-Shot Text Classification

Congcong Wang[1] , Paul Nulty[2] , and David Lillis[1]( )

[1] School of Computer Science, University College Dublin, Dublin, Ireland
congcong.wang@ucdconnect.ie, david.lillis@ucd.ie
[2] Department of Computer Science and Information Systems, Birkbeck,
University of London, London, UK
p.nulty@bbk.ac.uk

Abstract. Existing Zero-Shot Learning (ZSL) techniques for text classification typically assign a label to a piece of text by building a matching model to capture the semantic similarity between the text and the label descriptor. This is expensive at inference time as it requires the text paired with every label to be passed forward through the matching model. The existing approaches to alleviate this issue are based on exact-word matching between the label surface names and an unlabelled target-domain corpus to get pseudo-labelled data for model training, making them difficult to generalise to ZS classification in multiple domains, In this paper, we propose an approach called P-ZSC to leverage **p**seudo-labelled data for **z**ero-shot text **c**lassification. Our approach generates the pseudo-labelled data through a matching algorithm between the unlabelled target-domain corpus and the label vocabularies that consist of in-domain relevant phrases via expansion from label names. By evaluating our approach on several benchmarking datasets from a variety of domains, the results show that our system substantially outperforms the baseline systems especially in datasets whose classes are imbalanced.

Keywords: Text classification · Zero-Shot Learning · Weakly-supervised learning

1 Introduction

Recent years have seen numerous studies achieving great success in applying neural network models to text classification [3,5,21,22]. However, most are based on supervised learning, requiring human annotation for the training data. To mitigate the annotation burden, attention has been increasingly paid to seeking semi-supervised or unsupervised learning approaches for classification tasks via model training that uses minimal or no annotated data from the target task. Zero-shot learning (ZSL) is one example of this [14,16,17,27,29]. Yin et al. [28] define ZSL as having two categories: *label-partially-unseen* and *label-fully-unseen*. The former refers to a situation where a classifier is learnt from labelled examples from a set of known classes and tested on the union of these previously-seen classes and a set of unseen classes. The latter restricts a classifier from seeing any task-specific labelled data in its model development. It is a more challenging problem. Our work falls in the context of *label-fully-unseen* ZSL.

P. Rosso et al. (Eds.): NLDB 2022, LNCS 13286, pp. 35–46, 2022.
https://doi.org/10.1007/978-3-031-08473-7_4

In the context of *label-fully-unseen* ZSL, a matching model is commonly trained to capture the semantic similarity between text pairs. At training time, the text pair usually consists of a document and a label. This approach does not rely on any task-specific labelled data for model training. Semantic matching between general text pairs can then be transferred to downstream tasks. However, an example needs to be paired with every candidate label to pass forward through the matching model. This results in inefficiencies at inference time, especially with many possible labels.

In order to alleviate this problem, we present a classifier-based ZSL. Inference is more efficient because the classifier outputs a single class distribution given a single text as the input. Classifier-based ZSL, which is sometimes described as a type of extremely weakly-supervised learning [12,13,23], generates pseudo-labelled data for model training using label names only[1]. Existing work [12,13,23] generate the pseudo-labelled data based on exact-word matching between the label names and an unlabelled (task-specific) corpus. For corpora that have a heavy class imbalance, this can lead to minority classes without any pseudo-labelled examples. Hence, we propose P-ZSC: a simple yet effective approach for zero-shot text classification. In our approach, we propose a technique based on sentence embeddings (semantic matching) for label phrase expansion. To get the pseudo-labelled data, we use a confidence-based algorithm that assigns a label to an example based on a matching score between the label's expanded phrases and the example text. We pre-train the classifier on the pseudo-labelled data at document level and then self-train the classifier on the remaining unlabelled corpus. The results show that our system outperforms baseline systems by a large margin on a variety of datasets with different characteristics.

2   Related Work

As our work focuses on label-fully-unseen classifier-based ZSL. we examine related work on **Label-fully-Unseen ZSL** and **Weakly-supervised classification**.

2.1   Label-Fully-Unseen ZSL

For label-fully-unseen ZSL, most work has explored the problem through indirect (or distant) supervision from other problems. Pushp and Srivastava [17] propose three neural networks to learn the relationship between text pairs consisting of news headlines along with their SEO tags. Yin et al. [28] propose an entailment approach that applies pre-trained BERT to learn the relationship between text pairs that consist of the premises and hypotheses from three textual entailment datasets. Muller et al. [14] apply siamese networks and label tuning to tackle inefficiency issue at inference time in the entailment approach. Puri et al. [16] achieve zero-shot model adaptation to new classification tasks via a generative language modelling task. Other similar works using indirect supervision can be found in [9] and [15], who study zero-shot relation extraction by transforming it into a machine comprehension and textual entailment problem respectively. However, most of these works fall into the matching-based ZSL category.

---

[1] Since the label surface names are available at testing time with no need for human supervision, we describe it as classifier-based ZSL. In addition, no task-specific labelled data is used, thus meeting the definition of *label-fully-unseen* ZSL in [28].

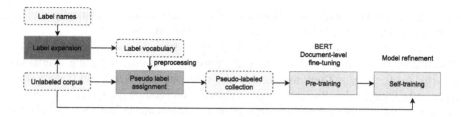

Fig. 1. The architecture of our system

2.2 Weakly-Supervised Classification

Due to the inefficiency of matching-based ZSL, another line of work has looked into achieving classifier-based ZSL via label names in a weakly-supervised fashion. WeST-Class is a framework for weakly-supervised learning neural text classification [12]. In [11], some metadata entities (e.g., authors, venues) are used as a source of weak supervision for text classification (META). ASTRA uses a few labeled data along with a self-training procedure on the (task-specific) unlabelled data for text classification [4]. ConWea uses a few human-provided seed-words to enrich the raw label names for pseudo-labelling data [10]. Despite weak supervision for offering seed words or a few labelled data, human effort is still involved in these approaches. The most recent works similar to ours are LOTClass [13] and X-Class [23], which use only label names for text classification, known as extremely weakly-supervised learning. LOTClass obtains pseudo-labelled data via a masked category prediction (MCP) task of BERT [3] at the token level. X-Class first leverages pre-trained BERT to obtain class-oriented document representations and then pseudo-labels data by applying clustering to the representations. However, both are exact-word matching based approaches, bringing difficulty in generalising to domains where the label names do not usually appear in the raw corpus. One goal of the P-ZSC proposed in this paper is to overcome these limitations.

3   Method

Formally, the problem that our system aims to solve is defined as follows: for a text classification task $\mathcal{T}$, given n label names $\mathcal{Y} : \{y_1, y_2, ...y_n\}$ and an unlabelled corpus $\mathcal{D} : \{d_1, d_2, ...d_m\}$ containing m documents from this task domain, the objective is to train a model f that can assign one or more labels from $\mathcal{Y}$ to an example x based on its probability estimation over $\mathcal{Y}$, namely, $f(x) : p(y_1|x), p(y_2|x), ..., p(y_n|x)$.

As illustrated in Fig. 1, our system has three stages: **label expansion**, **pseudo label assignment, pre-training and self-training**.

3.1   Label Expansion

In a typical classification task, the label names are only one or two words, which are insufficient to convey their potentially broad meaning. To enrich a label's meaning, we propose a simple **label expansion (LE)** algorithm to find the most semantically-similar words or phrases to the label from the unlabelled in-domain corpus $\mathcal{D}$.

Given $\mathcal{Y}$ and $\mathcal{D}$, first we combine all examples from $\mathcal{D}$ and split them into n-gram phrases consisting of all 1-grams, 2-grams and 3-grams (including overlaps): $\mathcal{G} : \{g_1, g_2, g_3, ..., g_L\}$. Then, we calculate the similarity between $\mathcal{Y}$ and $\mathcal{G}$ via a sentence embedding model. Basically, given a sentence embedding model E,[2] the matching score $\hat{s}_{i,j}$ between a label y_i and an n-gram g_j is calculated by the cosine similarity between the label's embedding and the n-gram's embedding:

$$\hat{s}_{i,j} = \text{cosine}(E_{avg}(y_i), E_{avg}(g_j)) \tag{1}$$

For any y_i or g_j with more than one token, E_{avg} takes the average pooling as the output embedding. After this, each label maintains a vocabulary of expanded phrases ranked by the similarity score. The vocabulary for each label y_i is denoted by $\hat{\mathcal{V}}_i$: $\{(\hat{v}_{i,k}, \hat{s}_{i,k})\}|_{k=1}^{\hat{K}}$ where $\hat{v}_{i,k}$ represents the kth expanded phrase in the vocabulary and $\hat{s}_{i,k}$ is the corresponding matching score.

Label vocabulary pre-processing: To maintain the quality of the label vocabulary, we include a further pre-processing step to optimise the original vocabulary $\hat{\mathcal{V}}_i$ and we denote a label's pre-processed vocabulary as: $\mathcal{V}_i : \{(v_{i,k}, s_{i,k})\}|_{k=1}^{K}$. We select only those phrases in $\hat{\mathcal{V}}_i$ where $\hat{s}_{i,k} \geq 0.7$, maintaining a minimum of 2 phrases and maximum of 100 per label[3]. We then apply a discounting on the phrases that co-occur across different labels, which is calculated by

$$s_{i,k} = \hat{s}_{i,k} * log_e \left(\frac{n}{LF(v_{i,k})} \right) \tag{2}$$

where n is the number of labels and $LF(v_{i,k})$ is the frequency of phrase $v_{i,k}$ across the vocabularies of all labels.

3.2   Pseudo Label Assignment

After expansion, we next construct a labelled collection (pseudo-labelled data) for model training. Due to the lack of annotated data, the alternative is to construct the collection via the process of **pseudo label assignment (PLA)**. We adopt a simple approach for PLA, which is described as follows:

A document $d_j \in \mathcal{D}$ is matched with a label's vocabulary $\mathcal{V}_i : \{(v_{i,k}, s_{i,k})\}|_{k=1}^{K}$ (from the previous section) through a cumulative scoring mechanism. To assign a label y_i to a document d_j, a matching score between them is first calculated by

$$s_{j,i}^* = \sum_{k=0}^{K} s_{i,k}[v_{i,k} \in G_j] \tag{3}$$

where G_j is the set of n-grams of d_j. For consistency with what was used in label expansion, here the n-grams also range from n=1 to n=3. With $s_{j,i}^*$, we denote $s_j^* : \{s_{j,i}^*\}|_{i=0}^{n}$

---

[2] We use the deepset/sentence_bert breakpoint from Huggingface model hub [18,24].

[3] The similarity threshold was chosen through preliminary experimentation on a another dataset.

as the matching score of d_j with every label from $\mathcal{Y}$. To decide if d_j is assigned one or more labels, a threshold ϵ is defined. For single-label tasks, if the maximum value of s_j^* at index i is greater than ϵ, then y_i is assigned to d_j. For multi-label tasks, if the value of s_j^* at any index is larger than ϵ, then the label at that index is assigned to d_j. Thus only the examples achieving high matching scores (high-confidence) with the labels are likely to be pseudo-labelled.

At this point, we get a pseudo-labelled collection denoted as $\hat{\mathcal{D}}$: $\{(x_i, y_i)\}|_{i=1}^N$ where N is the number of pseudo-labelled examples. To ensure the quality of $\hat{\mathcal{D}}$, the threshold ϵ should be chosen carefully. It will generate poor quality pseudo-labelled data if it is too low, but will result in zero examples for some labels if it is too high. Since the matching score $s_{i,k}$ is normalised by Eq. 2, we set ϵ to be $log_e n$. However, this value can lead to zero pseudo-labelled examples for insufficiently-expanded labels (e.g., their vocabularies contain few phrases: particularly common in class-imbalanced datasets). Hence, we reduce ϵ by half when the label with fewest expanded phrases has fewer than 10.

3.3 Pre-training and Self-training

With $\hat{\mathcal{D}}$ as the supervision data, the next step fits the model f to the target classification task by learning from the pseudo-labelled data. Instead of training from scratch, we use the pre-trained `bert-base-uncased` [3] as the base model (f_θ^*) and this can be replaced by other pre-trained language models easily [24]. To be specific, for a task $\mathcal{T}$, we add a classification head on top of the base model. The classification head takes the `[CLS]` output (denoted as $h_{[CLS]}$) of the base model as input and outputs the probability distribution over all classes:

$$h = f_\theta^*(x)$$
$$p(\mathcal{Y} \mid x) = \sigma(W h_{[CLS]} + b) \qquad (4)$$

where $W \in \mathbb{R}^{h \times n}$ and $b \in \mathbb{R}^n$ are the task-specific trainable parameters and bias respectively and σ is the activation function (softmax if $\mathcal{T}$ is a single-label task, or sigmoid for a multi-label task). In model training, the base model parameters θ are optimized along with W and b with respect to the following cross entropy loss (on the pseudo-labelled data):

$$\mathcal{L}_{pt} = -\sum_{i=0}^{n} y_i \log p(y_i \mid x) \qquad (5)$$

Since $\hat{\mathcal{D}}$ is a subset of $\mathcal{D}$, there are many unlabelled examples not seen in the model's pre-training. As indicated in LOTClass [13], the unlabelled examples can be leveraged to refine the model for better generalisation via **self-training**. Hence, we subsequently use $\mathcal{D}$ for model self-training. We first split $\mathcal{D}$ into equal-sized portions (assume each portion has M examples) and then let the model make predictions for each portion in an iteration with the predictions denoted as the target distribution Q. In each iteration, the model is trained on batches of the portion with the current distribution as P. The model is then updated with respect to the following KL divergence loss function [13]:

$$\mathcal{L}_{st} = \text{KL}(Q \| P) = \sum_{i=1}^{M} \sum_{j=1}^{n} q_{i,j} \log \frac{q_{i,j}}{p_{i,j}} \qquad (6)$$

In deriving the target distribution Q, it can be applied with either soft labeling [26] or hard labeling [8]. As soft labeling overall brings better results [13], we derive Q with the soft labeling strategy:

$$q_{i,j} = \frac{p_{i,j}^2 / p_j^*}{\sum_{j'} \left(p_{ij'}^2 / p_{j'}^* \right)}, p_j^* = \sum_i p_{i,j} \qquad (7)$$

$$p_{i,j} = p(y_j \mid x_i) = \sigma(\boldsymbol{W}(f_{\boldsymbol{\theta}}^*(x_i))_{[\text{CLS}]} + \boldsymbol{b})$$

This strategy derives Q by squaring and normalising the current predictions P, which helps boost high-confidence predictions while reducing low-confidence predictions.

4   Experiments

Having described the system components, next we conduct extensive experiments to demonstrate its effectiveness. This section reports the experimental details the results.

4.1   Datasets

Table 1 lists four datasets chosen for evaluation: **Topic** [30], **Situation** [25], **UnifyEmotion** [7] and **TwiEmotion** [19]. The former three are the benchmarking datasets used in [28]. **Situation** is a multi-label dataset and only **Topic** is class-balanced. We also include **TwiEmotion**, which is another emotion dataset that does not overlap with **UnifyEmotion**. Overall, these datasets are varied in their domains, types (single-label or multi-label), class distributions (class-balanced or imbalanced) and label abstractness.[4] Following [28], we choose *label-wise weighted F1* as the primary evaluation metric for all datasets except for **Topic**, for which *accuracy* is reported, as it is class-balanced.

Table 1. Datasets used. Avg len. is the average number of words in training examples.

	Type	# Train	# Test	Class dist.	Avg len.	Label surface names
Topic	Single	1300000	100000	Balanced	107.6	{Education & Reference, Society & Culture, Sports, Entertainment & Music, Politics & Government, Computers & Internet, Family & Relationships, Science & Mathematics, Health, Business & Finance}
Situation	Multi	4921	1789	Imbalanced	16.5	{shelter, search, water, utilities, terrorism, evacuation, regime change, food, medical, infrastructure, crime violence}
UnifyEmotion	Single	34667	14000	Imbalanced	47.5	{surprise, guilt, fear, anger, shame, love, disgust, sadness, joy}
TwiEmotion	Single	16000	2000	Imbalanced	19.2	{sadness, joy, love, anger, fear, surprise}

---

[4] Emotion labels like "joy", "sadness" are more abstract than topic labels like "sports" and "politics & government.".

4.2   Experimental Details

As generalisation is crucial, we avoid our system being dependent on any specific target dataset. Thus a separate dataset [1] was initially used for exploratory experiments to investigate configuration options for our system (e.g. the value for ϵ, selection and pre-processing of phrases). This was done before the system was exposed to any examples from any of the target testing datasets.

The training set of each target dataset is used as the unlabelled corpus $\mathcal{D}$ and the surface names (see Table 1) as the label set $\mathcal{Y}$. For model pre-training on the pseudo-labelled data, we fine-tune BERT-base-uncased on batch size of 16 using Adam [6] as the optimiser with a linear warm-up scheduler for increasing the learning rate from 0 to $5e-5$ at the first 0.1 of total training steps and then decreasing to 0 for the remaining steps. For self-training, we follow the hyper-parameters used in [13], with batch size 128 and update interval 50, which results in the number of training examples in each iteration (namely, M) being 50×128. As guided by the average example length in Table 1, we set the maximum input length for model pre-training and self-training to be 256 for **Topic** and 128 for the remaining three datasets.

4.3   Baselines

In experiments, we compare our system to multiple baselines, described as follows.

Label similarity [20] uses pre-trained embeddings to compute the cosine similarity between the class label and every 1-gram to 3-gram of the example. For single-label tasks, the label with the highest similarity score is chosen. For multi-label tasks, any label with a similarity score greater than 0.5 is chosen.

Entail-single and **Entail-ensemble** correspond to the best *label-fully-unseen* ZSL single and ensemble results reported in [28]. As **TwiEmotion** was not used in that paper, we followed their methodology to create a similar setup by fine-tuning three variants of BERT on three inference datasets (RTE/MNLI/FEVER). We choose the best of these in each category to report as "entail-single" and "entail-ensemble".

ConWea is a contextualised weakly-supervised approach for text classification, which uses few human-provided seed words for label expansion [10]. In our experiments, we feed at least 3 seed words per class to this approach. As a comparison, weak human supervision (few seed words) entails this approach unlike ours using label names only.

X-Class [23] uses label names only by building class-oriented document representations first and then using GMM to obtain the pseudo-labelled data. In our experiments, we use the pseudo-labelled data by X-Class for model fine-tuning (bert-base-uncased) and report the performance on the fine-tuned model.

WeSTClass is the system proposed in [12]. Although it is configurable to accept up to three sources of supervision, we run this system using label names as the only supervision resource so to be consistent with our study.

LOTClass is another text classification approach using only label names [13].

Entail-Distil [2] attempts to overcome the inference inefficiency issue of the entailment matching-based models [27]. The training data is pseudo-labelled first by the matching model (bert-base-uncased fine-tuned on MNLI) and then the pseudo-labelled data is used for downstream model fine-tuning (bert-base-uncased).

Sup. BERT is included so that a comparison with a fully-supervised approach can be done. This uses bert-base-uncased, fine-tuned on the training sets. A ZSL approach will be unlikely to match the performance of a fully-supervised approach, it is important to illustrate how large that performance gap actually is and to illustrate the degree to which our approach contributes towards closing it.

4.4 Results and Discussion

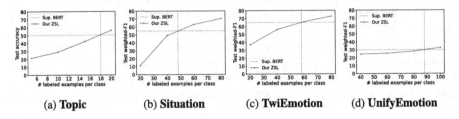

(a) **Topic**   (b) **Situation**   (c) **TwiEmotion**   (d) **UnifyEmotion**

Fig. 2. (a), (b), (c) and (d): The performance of P-ZSC is close to that of BERT trained on 18, 48, 58 and 88 labelled documents per class from **Topic**, **Situation**, **TwiEmotion**, and **UnifyEmotion** respectively.

In this section, we compare our system (P-ZSC) with the baselines in ZS text classification. We also dissect each component of P-ZSC by conducting an ablation study and investigate the quality of the pseudo-labelled data it generates.

Comparing to the Baselines. In comparing our system with the baselines (Table 2), P-ZSC substantially outperforms the semantic matching based runs including Label similarity, Entail-single and Entail-ensemble.

We found label similarity is a strong baseline. Although it is a simple matching between the sentence embeddings of label names and document phrases, interestingly, it outperforms the entailment runs for all datasets except **Topic**. This indicates that semantically matching a document's phrases with the label names can help determine the document's class. It should also be noted that the matching-based runs are around n (number of the labels) times slower than the classifier-based runs. Regarding the effectiveness of the classifier based runs, ours outperforms WeSTCLass and Entail-Distil. Entail-Distil achieves similar scores to ours on **UnifyEmotion** but the difference is substantially wider for the other datasets. Comparing to ConWea that uses seed words for label expansion, we find that our system outperforms it across the four datasets. For the more recent label-names-only approach X-Class, it performs well in the class-balanced dataset **Topic** while not in the rest of datasets as compared to our approach.

Likewise, it is interesting that LOTCLass performs well in **Topic** but exhibits poorer performance in the other datasets, suggesting that LOTCLass does not generalise particularly well. By analysis, to expand labels, LOTCLass identifies unlabelled examples with exact-word matches to label names. These are then expanded using BERT

Table 2. Performance of all methods on test sets of four datasets. Metrics shown are label-wise weighted F1 for all datasets except Topic, for which accuracy is used.

	Topic	Situation	UnifyEmotion	TwiEmotion
Semantic matching based runs				
Label similarity [20]	34.62	40.75	26.21	56.03
Entail-single [28]	43.80	37.20	24.70	49.60
Entail-ensemble [28]	45.70	38.00	25.20	50.16
Classifier based runs				
ConWea [10]	49.81	25.91	21.39	47.34
X-Class [23]	48.12	39.27	15.19	42.21
WeSTClass [12]	34.96	28.40	15.45	22.54
LOTClass [13]	**52.07**	5.85	7.19	16.82
Entail-Distil [2]	44.47	37.85	29.43	48.87
P-ZSC	50.68	**55.02**	**30.22**	**64.47**
Sup. BERT [3]	74.86	85.27	40.10	92.02

masked language modelling (MLM). Masked Category Prediction (MCP) is then used to pseudo-label the unlabelled examples at the token level. For some tasks, this works well since the label names (e.g. "education", "sports") are straightforward and usually have enough exact-word matches within unlabelled examples. Thus LOTClass performs well in the **Topic** dataset. However, for datasets like Situation or Emotion detection, classes such as "utilities" and "sadness" are more abstract and have a more unbalanced distribution, and are not contained directly in unlabelled examples. This leads to few examples in the label name data subsequently used by MLM and MCP. Thus LOTClass obtains relatively poor results for **Situation**, **UnifyEmotion** and **TwiEmotion**. As a comparison, our approach overall performs well across the datasets with different characteristics, indicating strong generalisability. Despite this, there is still a gap between our unsupervised runs and the supervised BERT run. This suggests that although our results indicate substantial progress, zero-shot (label-fully-unseen) text classification of multiple domains remains challenging and cannot yet be considered to be a solved problem.

Table 3. Ablation study. Metrics shown are label-wise weighted F1 for all datasets except Topic, for which accuracy is used.

	Topic	Situation	UnifyEmotion	TwiEmotion
P-ZSC	50.68	55.02	30.22	64.47
- Self-training	44.18	50.51	25.35	59.83
- PLA	49.83	46.20	29.86	56.35
- PLA + LE	46.33	43.26	20.97	48.59

Ablation Study. To examine the contribution of each component of our system, we conducted an ablation study, with the results reported in Table 3. This shows the performance of the entire P-ZSC system, and also separate results with the self-training step omitted, with the pseudo-label assignment (PLA) omitted and with both PLA and label expansion (LE) omitted. In each case, the removal of any phase results in a decline in performance for all datasets. Although this decrease is minor in some situations, the system performance suffers dramatically for at least one dataset in every case. This indicates that all phases are important to maintain peak effectiveness.

Pseudo-Labelled Data Quality In our system, the only "supervision" resources for the downstream model training is from the pseudo-labelled data that is obtained via LE and PLA. In the pipeline of our system, pseudo-labelled data is obtained without any human supervision, using only the label names and an unlabelled corpus of the target task. Given the importance of the pseudo-labelled data in the final performance, we construct the pseudo-labelled data that is a subset of the unlabelled corpus (i.e., only the high-confidence ones are pseudo-labelled). To quantify the quality of pseudo-labelled data, we follow a similar methodology to [13]. We compare P-ZSC with the Sup. BERT run fine-tuned on different numbers of actually-labelled examples per class. From Fig. 2, we notice that our pseudo-labelling can equal the performance of 18, 48 and 58 and 88 actually-labelled documents per class on **Topic**, **Situation**, **TwiEmotion** and **UnifyEmotion** respectively. This shows that there is some room to improve the pseudo-labelled data on datasets like **Topic**. This motivates us to explore adaptive PLA approaches on dataset characteristics (e.g., label abstractness) for generating better quality pseudo-labelled data for multi-aspect ZS text classification in the future.

5   Conclusion

Having identified drawbacks of existing ZS approaches, either in inference efficiency or in the classification of multiple domains, we have proposed a novel classifier-based approach that uses label expansion from the label names and pseudo-label assignment (PLA). Four datasets with different characteristics were selected, along with a number of benchmarks from recent state-of-the-art ZSL works. The experimental results show that our system (P-ZSC) can outperform the baselines and overall generalise well to zero-shot text classification of multiple domains. Although the pseudo-labelled data constructed by our system represents high quality in some aspects, there remains some room to improve it, such as combining with a few annotated examples in a semi-supervised learning fashion, PLA at the document level with confidence control and adaptive PLA approaches on more domain characteristics (e.g. label abstractness).

References

1. Alam, F., Qazi, U., Imran, M., Ofli, F.: Humaid: human-annotated disaster incidents data from twitter with deep learning benchmarks. In: Proceedings of the International AAAI Conference on Web and Social Media, vol. 15, pp. 933–942 (2021)

2. Davison, J.: Zero-shot classifier distillation (2021). https://github.com/huggingface/transformers/tree/master/examples/research_projects/zero-shot-distillation

3. Devlin, J., Chang, M.W., Lee, K., Toutanova, K.: BERT: Pre-training of deep bidirectional transformers for language understanding. In: Proceedings of the 2019 Conference of the North American Chapter of the Association for Computational Linguistics: Human Language Technologies, vol. 1 (Long and Short Papers), pp. 4171–4186. Association for Computational Linguistics, Minneapolis (June 2019). https://doi.org/10.18653/v1/N19-1423

4. Karamanolakis, G., Mukherjee, S., Zheng, G., Hassan, A.: Self-training with weak supervision. In: Proceedings of the 2021 Conference of the North American Chapter of the Association for Computational Linguistics: Human Language Technologies, pp. 845–863 (2021)

5. Kim, Y.: Convolutional neural networks for sentence classification. In: Proceedings of the 2014 Conference on Empirical Methods in Natural Language Processing, EMNLP, pp. 1746–1751. Association for Computational Linguistics, Doha (October 2014). https://doi.org/10.3115/v1/D14-1181

6. Kingma, D.P., Ba, J.: Adam: a method for stochastic optimization. In: Proceedings of the 3rd International Conference for Learning Representations, San Diego (2015)

7. Klinger, R., et al.: An analysis of annotated corpora for emotion classification in text. In: Proceedings of the 27th International Conference on Computational Linguistics, pp. 2104–2119 (2018)

8. Lee, D.H., et al.: Pseudo-label: the simple and efficient semi-supervised learning method for deep neural networks. In: Workshop on challenges in representation learning, ICML (2013)

9. Levy, O., Seo, M., Choi, E., Zettlemoyer, L.: Zero-shot relation extraction via reading comprehension. In: Proceedings of the 21st Conference on Computational Natural Language Learning, CoNLL 2017, pp. 333–342. Association for Computational Linguistics, Vancouver (August 2017). https://doi.org/10.18653/v1/K17-1034

10. Mekala, D., Shang, J.: Contextualized weak supervision for text classification. In: Proceedings of the 58th Annual Meeting of the Association for Computational Linguistics, pp. 323–333 (2020)

11. Mekala, D., Zhang, X., Shang, J.: Meta: metadata-empowered weak supervision for text classification. In: Proceedings of the 2020 Conference on Empirical Methods in Natural Language Processing, EMNLP, pp. 8351–8361 (2020)

12. Meng, Y., Shen, J., Zhang, C., Han, J.: Weakly-supervised neural text classification. In: Proceedings of the 27th ACM International Conference on Information and Knowledge Management, CIKM 2018, vol. 2018 (2018)

13. Meng, Y., et al.: Text classification using label names only: a language model self-training approach. In: Proceedings of the 2020 Conference on Empirical Methods in Natural Language Processing, EMNLP, pp. 9006–9017. Association for Computational Linguistics (November 2020). https://doi.org/10.18653/v1/2020.emnlp-main.724

14. Müller, T., Pérez-Torró, G., Franco-Salvador, M.: Few-shot learning with siamese networks and label tuning (2022). arXiv preprint, arXiv:2203.14655

15. Obamuyide, A., Vlachos, A.: Zero-shot relation classification as textual entailment. In: Proceedings of the First Workshop on Fact Extraction and VERification, FEVER, pp. 72–78 (2018)

16. Puri, R., Catanzaro, B.: Zero-shot text classification with generative language models (2019). CoRR, abs/1912.10165

17. Pushp, P.K., Srivastava, M.M.: Train once, test anywhere: zero-shot learning for text classification (2017). CoRR, abs/1712.05972

18. Reimers, N., Gurevych, I.: Sentence-bert: sentence embeddings using siamese bert-networks. In: Proceedings of the 2019 Conference on Empirical Methods in Natural Language Processing and the 9th International Joint Conference on Natural Language Processing, EMNLP-IJCNLP, pp. 3973–3983 (2019)

19. Saravia, E., Liu, H.C.T., Huang, Y.H., Wu, J., Chen, Y.S.: Carer: contextualized affect representations for emotion recognition. In: Proceedings of the 2018 Conference on Empirical Methods in Natural Language Processing, pp. 3687–3697 (2018)

20. Veeranna, S.P., Nam, J., Mencıa, E.L., Fürnkranz, J.: Using semantic similarity for multi-label zero-shot classification of text documents. In: Proceeding of European Symposium on Artificial Neural Networks, Computational Intelligence and Machine Learning, pp. 423–428. Elsevier, Bruges (2016)

21. Wang, C., Lillis, D.: A comparative study on word embeddings in deep learning for text classification. In: Proceedings of the 4th International Conference on Natural Language Processing and Information Retrieval, NLPIR 2020, Seoul, South Korea (December 2020). https://doi.org/10.1145/3443279.3443304

22. Wang, C., Nulty, P., Lillis, D.: Transformer-based multi-task learning for disaster tweet categorisation. In: Adrot, A., Grace, R., Moore, K., Zobel, C.W. (eds.) ISCRAM 2021 Conference Proceedings – 18th International Conference on Information Systems for Crisis Response and Management, pp. 705–718. Virginia Tech., Blacksburg (2021)

23. Wang, Z., Mekala, D., Shang, J.: X-class: text classification with extremely weak supervision. In: Proceedings of the 2021 Conference of the North American Chapter of the Association for Computational Linguistics: Human Language Technologies, pp. 3043–3053 (2021)

24. Wolf, T., et al.: Transformers:state-of-the-art natural language processing. In: Proceedings of the 2020 Conference on Empirical Methods in Natural Language Processing: System Demonstrations, pp. 38–45. Association for Computational Linguistics (October 2020). https://doi.org/10.18653/v1/2020.emnlpdemos.6

25. Xia, C., Zhang, C., Yan, X., Chang, Y., Philip, S.Y.: Zero-shot user intent detection via capsule neural networks. In: Proceedings of the 2018 Conference on Empirical Methods in Natural Language Processing, pp. 3090–3099 (2018)

26. Xie, J., Girshick, R., Farhadi, A.: Unsupervised deep embedding for clustering analysis. In: International Conference on Machine Learning, PMLR, pp. 478–487 (2016)

27. Ye, Z., et al.: Zero-shot text classification via reinforced self-training. In: Proceedings of the 58th Annual Meeting of the Association for Computational Linguistics, pp. 3014–3024 (2020)

28. Yin, W., Hay, J., Roth, D.: Benchmarking zero-shot text classification: datasets, evaluation and entailment approach. In: Proceedings of the 2019 Conference on Empirical Methods in Natural Language Processing and the 9th International Joint Conference on Natural Language Processing, EMNLP-IJCNLP, pp. 3905–3914 (2019)

29. Zhang, J., Lertvittayakumjorn, P., Guo, Y.: Integrating semantic knowledge to tackle zero-shot text classification. In: Proceedings of the 2019 Conference of the North American Chapter of the Association for Computational Linguistics: Human Language Technologies, vol. 1 (Long and Short Papers), pp. 1031–1040 (2019)

30. Zhang, X., Zhao, J., LeCun, Y.: Character-level convolutional networks for text classification. In: Proceedings of the 28th International Conference on Neural Information Processing Systems, vol. 1, pp. 649–657 (2015)

On-Device Language Detection and Classification of Extreme Short Text from Calendar Titles Across Languages

Rajasekhara Reddy Duvvuru Muni[1]([✉]), Devanand Jayakumar[1],
Tadi Venkata Sivakumar[1], ChangKu Lee[2], YoungHa Hwang[2],
and Karthikeyan Kumaraguru[1]

[1] Samsung R & D Institute India-Bangalore, Bengaluru 560037, India
raja.duvvuru@samsung.com
[2] Samsung Digital City, R3 building 25F, Suwon, Korea

Abstract. Smartphones have become indispensable part of day-to-day human life. These devices provide rapid access to digital calendars enabling users to schedule their personal and professional activities with short titles referred as event titles. Event titles provide valuable information for personalization of various services. However, very nature of the event titles to be short with only few words, pose a challenge to identify language and exact event the user is scheduling. Deployment of robust machine learning pipelines that can continuously learn from data on the server side is not feasible as the event titles represent private user data and raise significant concerns. To tackle this challenge, we propose a privacy preserving on-device solution namely Calendar Event Classifier (CEC) to classify calendar titles into a set of 22 event types grouped into 3 categories using the fastText library. Our language detection models with accuracies of 96%, outperform existing language detection tools by 20% and our event classifiers achieved 92%, 94%, 87% and 90% accuracies across, English, Korean and German, French respectively. Currently tested CEC module architecture delivers the fastest (4 ms/event) predictions with <8 MB memory footprint and cater multiple personalization services. Taken together, we present the need for customization of machine learning models for language detection and information extraction from extremely short text documents such as calendar titles.

Keywords: Language detection · Short text classification · Event classification · fastText

1 Introduction

Growing adoption of smartphones across geographies is enabling rapid access to the digital calendars and wider usage. Digital calendars from smartphones are widely used to schedule reminders of daily activities ranging from very personal to professional events for efficient time management. The digital calendar is an

P. Rosso et al. (Eds.): NLDB 2022, LNCS 13286, pp. 47–59, 2022.
https://doi.org/10.1007/978-3-031-08473-7_5

indispensable resource for many to manage daily professional routines, such as office related work (e.g. meetings to attend, reports to complete, etc.), daily family routines (e.g. dropping kids to school, etc.,) and scheduling recurring events (e.g. anniversaries, health checkups) to name a few. In addition to time management, digital calendars are being explored as smart aids for elderly care, health recommendations and drive medical interventions to name a few [1].

Digital calendars maintain wealth of information related to professional and personal life of the users in the form of event title, date, start time and end time [2]. With such user specific information, digital calendars provide valuable data, to deliver personalized services such as emoji suggestion, personalized reminders and serving relevant ads etc. The calendar titles hold important information such as event type (birthday, hospital appointments, etc.) and relationship (father, spouse etc.) to name a few. Extracting such information from calendar titles is crucial for personalization of smartphones and other associated services.

Information extraction from text is a well know Machine Learning (ML)task in natural language processing [3]. This information extraction may involve multiple steps such as language detection for the input text, classification of text into respective classes, etc. Language detection task deals with automatic detection of the language(s) in which the document content is written [4]. In its broader sense of natural language processing for information extraction, text classification (supervised) refers to a task of automatic categorization of a group of documents into one or more predefined classes [5]. Natural language texts/documents from multiple languages have been successfully used to develop machine learning models for language detection and diverse classification tasks like event detection, author assignment and sentiment classification to name a few. However, unlike other text, calendar titles are extremely short, often limited to few words and pose challenges, for language detection and event classification.

Besides the challenges associated with development of classifiers, server side solutions, using robust data and continuous learning cannot be used for calendar titles, given the sensitivity of the user data and privacy concerns. These challenges motivated us to build an on-device hybrid solution, which enables, real time language detection and event classification while preserving user privacy.

2   Related Work

In this section we present the work related to the calendar information driven personalization, machine learning based solutions for language identification and text classification.

Smartphone associated calendars are driving a diverse set of user experiences. Some of the most prominent personalization services include health recommendation, elderly care [1] and scheduling assistants [6]. However, most of the applications researched so far have been limited to only a few classes related to health care and exploitation of date and time aspects of calendar information [6]. To further extract, information such as actual event scheduled hidden in the calendar titles, research is required similar to the language identification and event classification using the calendar titles.

In natural language processing, language identification and text classification are extensively studied. Automatic identification of language in which, given text is written using machine learning is well researched with prominent solutions [7]. Over the last decade or so, with the advent of social media systems such as twitter, documents (tweets) with short text have become widely prominent. These short text documents posed specific challenges to language identification. Researchers have used features such as bag-of-words, character n-grams along with personal user information for language detection in short texts [8]. In an attempt to re-create the language detection module used by Apple's smart phone and computers, authors were able to achieve an overall accuracy of 98.93% with modified neural nets namely Long Short Term Memory (LSTM) architectures outperforming other state of the art language identifiers [9].

An off-the-shelf standalone python tool namely langid.py was developed by Lui and Baldwin which can identify 97 languages with consistent high accuracy across the text corpora [10]. Similarly, Joulin et al., [11] developed and distributed a fastText model that can identify 176 languages. In addition to these tools that can identify specific languages (monolingual), Zhang et al., developed a language identifier (gcld3) that can identify languages from text that has code switched instances where a single sentence may contain multiple languages [12]. We used these tools to assess their performance on calendar titles for language identification.

Various forms of text classification challenges have been extensively studied for solving many real world challenges [13]. Supervised machine learning methods gave outstanding classification performance across multitude of categories such as sentiment, mood, hate, based on manually labelled curated data [14]. On the contrary, to the normal text classification, short text classification has obtained much attention from NLP experts due to the challenges associated such as extreme short length of the documents often characterized by no more than a dozen words and less than 100 character length [15]. However, the number of classes to be classified with respect to the average length of document is far below the current research problem. These challenges and solutions available across domains enabled us to take up this task and evaluate the performance with respect to limited device resources available on a mobile device.

3   Methodology

Recent achievements in natural language processing prompted us to explore machine learning based solutions especially in the direction of supervised classification techniques. Like others, our experiments began with collection of data.

3.1   Data Set

The clean labelled data representing real world data is primary requirement for success of any ML task. Hence, we compiled a corpus of calendar titles from four languages namely, English (EN), Korean (KR), German (DE) and French (FR) from the users who gave consent for personalization and access to data. With the help of language experts, we annotated language labels and event categories for each calendar title. Briefly each title has been annotated with pre-defined event categories by two experts with none as a valid class. Titles with event annotation disagreement are moved to "none" class. Event categories considered in this study are broadly grouped into three categories. Details of the data set is provided in Table 1.

Table 1. Data summary. Titles per language and event class

Event type	Data summary - total entries per label			
	Event class	EN	KR	DE	FR
Annual event	Birthday	10202	2428	6074	2568
	Biztrip	25	0	0	0
	Reunionday	88	367	193	119
	Trip	883	651	5657	2180
	Weddinganniversary	178	122	201	63
	Yearendparty	163	357	56	38
Daily event	Exercise	1302	902	0	551
	Hospital	2398	1873	6152	3578
	Institute	681	355	2073	830
	Meal	2080	2366	2551	1920
	Meeting	3483	3179	9328	3071
	Nightlife	296	24	567	342
	Shopping	647	537	1631	841
	Watchingmovie	40	293	542	280
	Watchingshow	100	594	5208	958
Life event	babybirth	70	72	139	48
	Graduation	162	151	97	26
	Marriage	294	1097	340	159
	Movinghome	91	238	354	101
	Prom	87	16	9	6
	Schoolentrance	36	66	56	34
	None	29841	40989	26817	12704
	Total	53147	56677	68045	30417

3.2   Pre-processing

Document or text pre-processing is crucial step for text classification applications. Most of the textual data contains unnecessary content such as stop words, misspelling, emoji's, special characters, etc. This unnecessary information will adversely affect classifier performance. We begin our text processing with tokenization, which refers to the process of breaking down long textual sentences into words, phrases, symbols and other meaningful items namely tokens [16]. Followed by tokenization, individual words or tokens are analyzed for their meaningfulness. Most of the languages have huge set of words, repeated multiple times (ex. A, an, the etc.) without any significant contribution towards classification task often referred to as stop words [17]. These stop words are analyzed using standard language specific corpus along with custom entries into the corpus and are removed from calendar titles [18]. Followed by stop word removal, we cleaned the corpus, for punctuation marks and capital letters, which are absolute requirement for human understanding of meaning but are of little or no value to ML classifiers [19]. All the punctuation marks are eliminated along with the special characters and all the letters were converted to small case. Next critical pre-processing step in text cleaning is stemming. Stemming refers to the process of consolidating different forms of a word (plural, tense etc.) into the same feature space by removing the unnecessary characters that do not contribute to the semantic meaning of the words [20]. All the pre-processing steps were performed using the Natural Language Tool Kit [NLTK] [21].

3.3   Model Building and Evaluation

Labelled data has been split into training (80%) and test sets (20%) using stratified sampling as employed in Scikit-learn [22]. The fastText developed and released by Facebook [11], is the simplest architecture that requires moderate resources for complex text classification tasks similar to our calendar titles with multiple classes. We used fastText, to train a multi-class classifier with four language classes (Language identification) and four (one for each language) multiclass classifiers with 24 event classes (Event Classification).

The fastText uses skip gram method for developing character level n-gram features from the labelled training data. From these features, a linear classifier is built using the fully connected neural network that will transform features from embeddings and a softmax function for calculation of probability distribution of classes and/or a hierarchical softmax in case of large number of classes. Data imbalance is crucial aspect that will adversely impact ML classifier performance and should be taken care [23]. As the number of titles per class are highly imbalanced, we tried sampling techniques such as Synthetic Minority Over Sampling Technique (SMOTE) and built a customer corpus de-noising algorithm to improve classifier performance. For model evaluation, we used standard evaluation metric such as Accuracy, Precision, Recall and F1 score.

3.4   Engine Architecture

Our calendar title language detection and event classification engine is a hybrid architecture, with some of its components running on the device and some being accessed on-demand from the server as shown in Fig. 1. Text pre-processor and language detection models run on device. Once a language is detected, the client communicates with the server and downloads the respective language event classification model. Once the model is downloaded, respective event is detected. This type of architecture is chosen to preserve the privacy of user data and optimize the device resources.

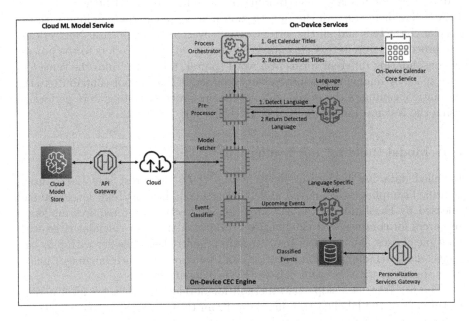

Fig. 1. System design for on-device language detection and event classification.

4   Results

Our language detector and event classifier should be able to perform across user languages. Keeping this in mind, we collected data from native speakers of English, Korean, German and French languages. A total of 208,286 event titles were collected and manually labelled across languages with language and event titles with the help of language experts. A closer look at the event titles indicates that, on an average more than 50% of the titles in calendar have less than five words Table 2.

4.1   Language Detection

We first evaluated the performance of different open source language identification tools for identification of language of given calendar title. We have chosen the fastText, Langid.py and GCLD3 as they support our target languages. The results of this analysis are summarized in Fig. 2. From the results, it is evident that, except for Korean language for all the other three languages, for the language detection of calendar titles there is scope for improvement.

For the development of a language detection model, we split our pre-processed data into training and test data sets with 168,446 and 42,111 respectively. Using the fastText, we trained a Language Detector (LD) model and assessed performance with test data set. Final model achieved an average training accuracy of 96% and an average test accuracy of 91%.

Table 2. Average number of tokens in calendar titles

Language	Total # of tokens	Total titles	Average tokens
EN	157516	53147	3
KR	145846	56677	3
DE	174254	68045	3
FR	98573	30417	3

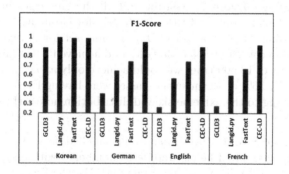

Fig. 2. Language detection benchmark.

Of all the four languages, as expected we achieve a highest test accuracy of 94% for Korean language and lowest test accuracy of 87% for German language owing to the nature of the feature extraction adopted by fastText. In summary, our model (CEC-LD), which is developed in the present work, with training from short text calendar titles, outperforms other state of the art models for language detection task of calendar titles.

4.2 Event Classification

For event classification task, due to the highly imbalanced nature of the data, overlapping words across languages and considering relevant deployability on-device we opted to have separate classifiers for each language.

English Language Event Classifier: Labelled English language data consisted 53,147 titles with 22 categories including "none" category. Our training set had 42,518 number of titles with a maximum number of 10,202 titles in category birthday and minimum number of 25 titles in "biztrip". Quantized fastText model trained using this data could achieve 98% accuracy and the model could give 93% accuracy on test data. Of all the categories, category "biztrip" has least performance and more than 70% of the events have an F1 score above 0.8.

Korean Language Event Classifier: Korean data has 56,677 labelled titles with 21 categories including "none" category. There were no titles related to re-union day. The fastText quantized model developed with 45,342 titles gave an overall accuracy of 98% and when validated with a test set of 11,335 titles gave an overall accuracy of 94%. Of all the event classes, nightlife event has the least classification performance and approximately 62% of the event classes had more than 0.8 F1 score.

German Language Event Classifier: Of all the languages in our dataset, we had the maximum number of titles i.e. 68,045 for German language with 22 categories including "none" category. Our training set for developing calendar event classification consisted of 54,436 titles and achieved a 94% accuracy. However, with the test of 13,609 titles we could achieve only an accuracy of 87%. Of all the events, only 36% of all the event classes were having F1 score higher than 0.8, probably owing to the extreme skewed distribution across the event classes.

French Language Event Classifier: In our labelled dataset of calendar data set French language related labels were least numbered with only 19 categories (Biz-trip, Prom and Re-union day were missing). For the French language, only a total of 30,417 titles were available. Of these total number of titles, 24,334 titles were used to build a quantized event classification model and achieved an overall accuracy of 97%. This model gave an accuracy of 90% with a test set of 6,083 titles. Approximately only more than 50% of events had an F1 score greater than 0.8 of all the 19 categories (Table 3).

Table 3. Final Event classification model performance with the test data set across languages and event classes

Language	EN				KR				DE				FR			
Train accuracy	0.98				0.98				0.94				0.97			
Test accuracy	0.93				0.94				0.87				0.9			
Event class	Precision	Recall	F1-score	Support	Precision	Recall	F1-score	Support	Precision	Recall	F1-score	Support	Precision	Recall	F1-score	Support
Babybirth	1.00	0.86	0.92	14	0.77	0.71	0.74	14	0.74	0.89	0.81	28	0.83	0.50	0.63	10
Birthday	0.99	0.99	0.99	2040	0.98	0.98	0.98	486	0.98	0.97	0.97	1215	0.99	0.97	0.98	514
Biztrip	1.00	1.00	1.00	5	N.A	N.A	N.A	N.A	N.A	N.A	N.A	N.A	N.A	N.A	N.A	N.A
Exercise	0.84	0.83	0.83	260	0.87	0.85	0.86	181	N.A	N.A	N.A	N.A	0.80	0.72	0.76	110
Getajob	1.00	0.41	0.58	17	0.87	0.87	0.87	15	0.92	0.80	0.86	45	0.81	0.68	0.74	19
Graduation	0.93	0.88	0.90	32	0.97	0.93	0.95	30	0.64	0.74	0.68	19	0.67	0.40	0.50	5
Hospital	0.87	0.85	0.86	480	0.93	0.93	0.93	375	0.91	0.90	0.90	1231	0.94	0.92	0.93	716
Institute	0.76	0.66	0.71	136	0.86	0.92	0.88	71	0.79	0.75	0.77	415	0.77	0.75	0.76	166
Marriage	0.95	0.97	0.96	59	0.97	0.96	0.97	220	0.90	0.90	0.90	68	1.00	0.94	0.97	32
Meal	0.91	0.89	0.90	416	0.94	0.93	0.94	473	0.82	0.81	0.81	510	0.92	0.86	0.89	384
Meeting	0.92	0.92	0.92	697	0.94	0.94	0.94	636	0.73	0.79	0.76	1866	0.77	0.83	0.80	614
Movinghome	1.00	0.67	0.80	18	0.81	0.81	0.81	48	0.85	0.73	0.79	71	0.87	0.65	0.74	20
Nightlife	0.77	0.69	0.73	59	1.00	0.40	0.57	5	0.76	0.81	0.79	113	0.83	0.87	0.85	68
None	0.94	0.96	0.95	5934	0.97	0.98	0.98	8178	0.87	0.80	0.83	5379	0.87	0.89	0.88	2667
Prom	0.94	0.94	0.94	17	1.00	1.00	1.00	3	1.00	0.00	0.00	2	1.00	1.00	1.00	1
Resignation	1.00	0.67	0.80	6	0.80	0.57	0.67	7	0.98	0.87	0.92	45	0.82	0.82	0.82	11
Reunionday	1.00	0.83	0.91	18	0.92	0.93	0.93	73	0.69	0.74	0.72	39	0.69	0.75	0.72	24
Schoolentrance	0.67	0.57	0.62	7	0.90	0.69	0.78	13	0.57	0.73	0.64	11	0.75	0.43	0.55	7
Shopping	0.87	0.68	0.77	129	0.84	0.79	0.81	107	0.61	0.71	0.66	326	0.72	0.70	0.71	168
Trip	0.86	0.75	0.80	177	0.90	0.86	0.88	130	0.70	0.79	0.74	1131	0.77	0.77	0.77	436
Watchingmovie	0.88	0.88	0.88	8	0.97	0.95	0.96	59	0.85	0.67	0.75	108	0.86	0.68	0.76	56
Watchingshow	0.86	0.90	0.88	20	0.90	0.92	0.91	119	0.75	0.84	0.79	1042	0.82	0.72	0.76	192
Weddinganniversary	0.94	0.92	0.93	36	1.00	0.96	0.98	24	1.00	0.88	0.93	40	0.93	1.00	0.96	13
Yearendparty	0.96	0.73	0.83	33	0.99	0.93	0.96	71	1.00	0.91	0.95	11	0.71	0.71	0.71	7
Accuracy	0.94	0.94	0.94	0.94	0.96	0.96	0.96	0.96	0.82	0.82	0.82	0.82	0.86	0.86	0.86	0.86
Macro avg	0.91	0.81	0.85	10618	0.92	0.86	0.88	11338	0.82	0.77	0.77	13715	0.83	0.76	0.79	6240
Weighted avg	0.94	0.94	0.94	10618	0.96	0.96	0.96	11338	0.83	0.82	0.82	13715	0.86	0.86	0.86	6240

4.3   Model Optimization for Data Imbalance

When event classes in training data set are imbalanced, standard machine learning classifiers tend to bias towards majority class. The imbalance in a given data set is represented by imbalance ratio, which is nothing but the ratio of number of titles in the majority class upon the number of titles in the minority class. Generally a data set is considered to be imbalanced when the imbalance ratio is bigger than 1.5. In our calendar titles data set, these ratios were 1193.64, 2561.81, 2979.67 and 2117.33 for EN, KR, DE and FR, respectively. Hence, it is evident that, the data distribution across the event classes is highly imbalanced.

```
Function NoiseRemoval(features, labels, nn_threshold,
bad_count_threshold):
    foreach feature label ∈ {features, labels} do
        nn_data = get_neighbors( feature, features, nn_threshold)
        bad_count = 0
        foreach nn_element, nn_label ∈ nn_data do
            if nn_label ≠ label then
                bad_count = bad_count + 1
        end
        if bad_count ≥ bad_count_threshold then
            Remove feature from features
    end
    return
```

Fig. 3. Pseudo-code for denoising algorithm.

As fastText deals with "word n-grams" and hierarchical split over well defined classes, data imbalance is not a problem. However, given the extreme imbalance in our data set, we want to evaluate the performance of fastText models for event classification with a popular sampling based method i.e. Synthetic Minority Over sampling Technique (SMOTE) and a data pre-processing (denoising) method developed in this work namely corpus-pruning. We compared these methods with the no balancing adopted classifier as baseline. As a data pre-processing method, our corpus-pruning algorithm is designed to remove the text documents that are overlapping (noise) between classes. This algorithm can be used for text filtering, when the input data is noisy with respect to documents and labels. Briefly, algorithm identifies the noisy titles to be eliminated from majority class i.e. none class using variety of clustering algorithms over the fastText title embeddings. The noise removal algorithm is flexible to the noise threshold we define Fig. 3.

First, we identify the nearest neighbors for every data point in the data set. Then we identify if the nearest neighbors belong to the same event class or different. We can define the noise threshold as the number of different event classes in the nearest neighbors that we tolerate for a given data point. We have a trade off in selecting the noise threshold. The stringent we select the noise threshold, the more data that might be eliminated. This will reduce our training set samples. Using this algorithm and keeping a threshold of 2, we lost as little as 7,469 titles from "none" event category and increase the overall performance of classifier. The impact of denoising algorithm on the class separation is depicted with t-SNE plot Fig. 4. For demonstration purpose we have removed the "none" class from plotting the t-SNE plots. Using this pre-processed data, when we trained our classifier model the overall model performance improved significantly from 82% to 89% in the case of German language and to our surprise did not had any effect on the French language Fig. 5. However, SMOTE based over-sampling has improved the classifier performance in English and Korean

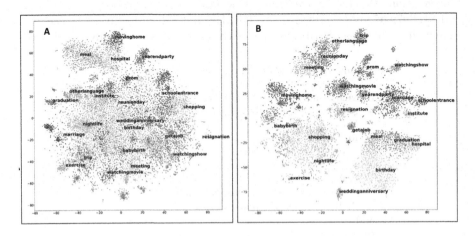

Fig. 4. T-SNE plots depicting the impact of denoising on label class separation A. Before noise removal and B. After noise removal.

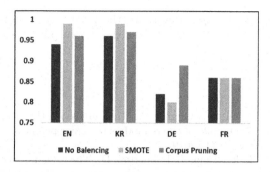

Fig. 5. Impact of different balancing techniques on event classification across languages.

language titles and has negatively affected the classifier performance in German language. For French language, there is no impact on the classifier performance. Taken together all these results indicate that, it is good practice to combine a set of pre-processing, sampling based methods to improve the classification performances when building the fastText based text classifiers with multiple language corpus [23].

4.4   On-Device Performance Evaluation

One of the critical factors in realizing the value of such information extraction engine is their deployability in production environment to protect the user privacy while maintaining the optimal performance of the client devices. To this end, we have tested our engine architecture on android studio. Our quantized language detection model was of size 477 KB and language specific event classification models were of 318, 206, 284 and 369 KB for EN, KR, DE and FR respectively. Run time analysis indicates that our engine uses a memory of 8MB at peak with a prediction run time of 4 ms occupying 70 KB of ROM on an average. These runtime estimates provide the efficient deploability of these models on resource constrained devices such as mobiles and tablets.

5   Conclusion

We presented the challenges and opportunities associated with language detection and event classification of the extreme short texts such as calendar titles with less than 3 words on an average. We also emphasize the need for adoption of sampling based methods and corpus pruning by noise removal to handle the class imbalance in building short text classification models using fastText. Overall, our models and architecture are lightweight in size, computations and are suitable for deploying on devices such as mobiles and tablets to drive personalization of customer experiences. Due the company policy and privacy we are not able to share data/model/code, but if anyone is interested to know more details they can contact the authors directly. In the future we would like to further refine and improve our noise removal algorithm for corpus pruning based model performance improvements.

References

1. Baric, V., Andreassen, M., Öhman, A., Hemmingsson, H.: Using an interactive digital calendar with mobile phone reminders by senior people-a focus group study. BMC Geriatr. **19**(1), 1–11 (2019)
2. Lovett, T., O'Neill, E., Irwin, J., Pollington, D.: The calendar as a sensor: analysis and improvement using data fusion with social networks and location. In: Proceedings of the 12th ACM International Conference on Ubiquitous Computing, UbiComp 2010, pp. 3–12. Association for Computing Machinery, New York (2010)
3. Singh, S.: Natural language processing for information extraction. arXiv preprint arXiv:1807.02383 (2018)
4. Jauhiainen, T., Lui, M., Zampieri, M., Baldwin, T., Lindén, K.: Automatic language identification in texts: a survey. J. Artif. Intell. Res. **65**, 675–782 (2019)
5. Kadhim, A.I.: Survey on supervised machine learning techniques for automatic text classification. Artif. Intell. Rev. **52**(1), 273–292 (2019). https://doi.org/10.1007/s10462-018-09677-1
6. Bank, J., Cain, Z., Shoham, Y., Suen, C., Ariely, D.: Turning personal calendars into scheduling assistants. In: Extended Abstracts on Human Factors in Computing Systems, CHI 2012, pp. 2667–2672 (2012)
7. Woo, J.H., Choi, H.: Systematic review for AI-based language learning tools. arXiv preprint arXiv:2111.04455 (2021)
8. Balazevic, I., Braun, M., Müller, K.R.: Language detection for short text messages in social media. arXiv preprint arXiv:1608.08515 (2016)
9. Toftrup, M., Sørensen, S.A., Ciosici, M.R., Assent, I.: A reproduction of Apple's bidirectional LSTM models for language identification in short strings. arXiv preprint arXiv:2102.06282 (2021)
10. Lui, M., Baldwin, T.: langid.py: an off-the-shelf language identification tool. In: Proceedings of the ACL 2012 System Demonstrations, pp. 25–30 (2012)
11. Joulin, A., Grave, E., Bojanowski, P., Mikolov, T.: Bag of tricks for efficient text classification. In: Proceedings of the 15th Conference of the European Chapter of the Association for Computational Linguistics: Volume 2, Short Papers, pp. 427–431 (April 2017)
12. Zhang, Y., Riesa, J., Gillick, D., Bakalov, A., Baldridge, J., Weiss, D.: A fast, compact, accurate model for language identification of codemixed text. In: Proceedings of the 2018 Conference on Empirical Methods in Natural Language Processing (EMNLP) (2018)
13. Kowsari, K., Jafari Meimandi, K., Heidarysafa, M., Mendu, S., Barnes, L., Brown, D.: Text classification algorithms: a survey. Information **10**(4), 150 (2019)
14. Hartmann, J., Huppertz, J., Schamp, C., Heitmann, M.: Comparing automated text classification methods. Int. J. Res. Mark. **36**(1), 20–38 (2019)
15. Zhu, Y., Li, Y., Yue, Y., Qiang, J., Yuan, Y.: A hybrid classification method via character embedding in Chinese short text with few words. IEEE Access **8**, 92120–92128 (2020). https://doi.org/10.1109/ACCESS.2020.2994450
16. Gupta, G., Malhotra, S.: Text document tokenization for word frequency count using rapid miner (taking resume as an example). Int. J. Comput. Appl. **975**, 8887 (2015)

17. Saif, H., Fernández, M., He, Y., Alani, H.: On stopwords, filtering and data sparsity for sentiment analysis of Twitter (2014)
18. Pahwa, B., Taruna, S., Kasliwal, N.: Sentiment analysis-strategy for text pre-processing. Int. J. Comput. Appl. **180**, 15–18 (2018)
19. Gupta, V., Lehal, G.S.: A survey of text mining techniques and applications. J. Emerg. Technol. Web Intell. **1**(1), 60–76 (2009)
20. Singh, J., Gupta, V.: Text stemming: approaches, applications, and challenges. ACM Comput. Surv. (CSUR) **49**(3), 1–46 (2016)
21. Bird, S., Klein, E., Loper, E.: Natural Language Processing with Python: Analyzing Text with the Natural Language Toolkit. O'Reilly Media, Inc. (2009)
22. Pedregosa, F., et al.: Scikit-learn: machine learning in Python. J. Mach. Learn. Res. **12**, 2825–2830 (2011)
23. Padurariu, C., Breaban, M.E.: Dealing with data imbalance in text classification. Procedia Comput. Sci. **159**, 736–745 (2019)

Transformer-Based Models for the Automatic Indexing of Scientific Documents in French

José Ángel González[1]([✉]) [iD], Davide Buscaldi[2] [iD], Emilio Sanchis[1] [iD], and Lluís-F. Hurtado[1] [iD]

[1] Valencian Research Institute for Artificial Intelligence (VRAIN), Camino de Vera, s/n, 46022 Valencia, Spain
{jogonba2,esanchis,lhurtado}@dsic.upv.es
[2] Laboratoire d'informatique de Paris-Nord (LIPN), CNRS UMR 7030, 99 Av. Jean Baptiste Clément, 93430 Villetaneuse, France
buscaldi@lipn.fr

Abstract. Automatic indexing is a challenging task in which computers must emulate the behaviour of professional indexers to assign to a document some keywords or keyphrases that represent concisely the content of the document. While most of the existing algorithms are based on a select-and-rank strategy, it has been shown that selecting only keywords from text is not ideal as human annotators tend to assign keywords that are not present in the source. This problem is more evident in scholarly literature. In this work we leverage a transformer-based language model to approach the automatic indexing task from a generative point of view. In this way we overcome the problem of keywords that are not in the original document, as the neural language models can rely on knowledge acquired during their training process. We apply our method to a French collection of annotated scientific articles.

Keywords: Automatic indexing · Keyword generation · Transformers

1 Introduction

Automatic indexing is the task of identifying a set of keywords (e.g. words, terms, proper names) that describe the content of a document. The keywords can then be used, among other things, to facilitate information retrieval or navigation in document collections. The literature in the field tends to show that automatic indexing does not satisfactorily emulate manual indexing by professionals. The development of automatic methods to perform this task remains a major challenge. This is particularly true in the case of scientific literature: the amount

Supported by: the AMIC-PoC project (PDC2021-120846-C44), funded by MCIN/AEI/ 10.13039/501100011033 and the European Union "NextGenerationEU"/"PRTR", a public grant overseen by ANR as part of the program "Investissements d'Avenir" (reference: ANR-10-LABX-0083) and the Vicerrectorado de Investigación de la Universitat Politècnica de València (PAID-11-21).

P. Rosso et al. (Eds.): NLDB 2022, LNCS 13286, pp. 60–72, 2022.
https://doi.org/10.1007/978-3-031-08473-7_6

of research works is growing continuously thanks to the proliferation of digital archives, posing a challenge for IR due to the complex information needs that require different approaches than known from, e.g., Web search, where information needs are simpler in many cases [6]. Indexing scientific articles represents a task that is still hard to tackle, and current models rely only on a small portion of the articles (title and abstract) and on author-assigned keyphrases, when available [4], instead of the full content. Moreover, it has been shown that keyphrases that do not occur in the documents account for about half of the manually assigned keyphrases [10], a number that increases up to ~58% of the total when scholarly data are considered [17].

This poses a major challenge as most of the existing methods are based on an extractive select-and-rank strategy, which cannot identify keywords that are not contained in the text. For this reason, in this work we leverage a transformer-based language model to approach the task from a generative point of view: the document in input is a "seed" for the generation of words by the model, which is able not only to reproduce parts of the document, but also keywords that are not in the document but were learnt during the construction of the model itself. The approach has many similarities with the solutions used for text summarization.

2   Related Work

Automatic indexing and automatic keyword extraction have been the object of many research works in the past. Three broad categories can be identified: statistical methods, graph-based methods, and supervised methods. Among the statistical methods, one of the most known and used ones, tf.idf, consists in using term and document frequencies to represent the specificity of terms [22]. More recent works use term co-occurrence matrices [19] or a combination of co-occurrence and frequency information [7]. Graph-based methods build graph of words extracted from documents depending on proximity information [5,18], sometimes combining the graph to statistical information [20]. Finally, supervised methods usually consider the task as a binary classification one: a list of candidate keywords is prepared, and a machine learning method decides which keywords should be included in the index and which ones should be discarded. These methods have been pioneered by [23], and more recent proposals are based on Neural Networks [12,17].

Typically, extraction algorithms carry out the keyword or keyphrase extraction in two steps: first, they generate a list of candidates with heuristic methods; then, the candidates are ranked according to some score that can be calculated in an unsupervised or supervised way. Some algorithms have been proposed for the indexing of scientific literature. HUMB [14] extracts all n-grams up to size 5, excluding those beginning or ending with stopwords, and then applies a conditional random field (CRF) classifier to determine the appropriateness of the keyword or not. Kleis [11] is also based on CRF for the second step but selects the candidates that match certain part-of-speech tag patterns (e.g., nouns, adjectives) that are learned on a labelled corpus [2]. To avoid the issues represented by the use of part-of-speech tagger, [13] select the keywords using document frequency information and TextRank [18]. [24] use word embeddings to obtain a semantic representation of the keywords that is passed as input to a classifier. [15] exploit the presence of citations in scientific papers to estimate the importance of words depending on their distribution not only in the text but also in the references. [12] apply Named Entity Recognition and a neural network based on a bi-LSTM based CRF to select and classify keywords, respectively. LSTMs are also used by the model presented by the AI2 institute [1] which was ranked first at the SemEval ScienceIE challenge [2]. Finally, [17] use Recurrent Neural Networks (RNNs) paired with a copy mechanism [25]. The main difference of our work with respect to [17] is that our model is based on pre-trained Transformers instead of RNNs.

3 The DEFT 2016 Task

Since 2005, in the context of the French national conference in Natural Language Processing, TALN, various text mining challenges ("Défi Fouille de Texte" or DEFT) have been organized every year, with different and original research themes. For the 2016 edition, the proposed challenge was the problem of indexing scientific documents in French [8]. The task consists in providing for a bibliographic record (composed by a title and an abstract) the keywords that best characterise it. The data used in the task cover four specialist areas: linguistics, information sciences, archaeology and chemistry. The team that was ranked first [16] exploited matrix factorization applied on term-document matrices. Similar methods were applied also by other teams with less success.

Table 1. Example from the domain Linguistique of the DEFT corpus. The keywords highlighted in green are extractive keywords and those highlighted in blue are novel keywords.

Document	Les eaux mêlées. La tradition rhétorique argumentative s'intéresse aux ensembles discursifs produits dans des situations où les opinions divergent. L'A. fait une analyse rhétorique du discours politique puis aborde les autres domaines d'études de l'argumentation.
Domain	Linguistique
Keywords	discours politique; persuasion; sémiotique discursive; rhétorique; argumentation

Table 1 illustrates an example from the DEFT corpus. For each domain, there are train, validation and test partitions that contain the 60%, 10%, and 30% of the samples respectively. Table 2 show some statistics of corpus. In this table, "Novel keywords" represents the percentage of keywords that do not appear in the sources i.e. the lower bound of the error of extractive systems if evaluated on exact matches. It should be noted that the evaluation in DEFT involves stemming on the reference and predicted keywords, which reduces the lower bound (% novel stems). The minimum Novel keywords value (45.20% in Archeologie) is still high: extractive approaches will fail at least the 45.20% of times in this domain. Extractive approaches will struggle, at least, the 64.45% of the times on the DEFT corpus.

Table 2. Statistics of the DEFT corpus.

	#samples	#keywords	#unique keywords	#keywords per sample	#words (keywords)	%Novel keywords	%Novel stems	#sentences (source)	#words (source)
Archeologie	718	11889	3044	16.56	21.35	41.31	37.44	7.37	208.86
Chimie	782	10005	4176	12.79	27.72	79.14	74.35	4.07	100.41
Linguistique	715	6191	1511	8.66	15.04	66.27	61.49	5.50	150.52
Sciences Inf	706	6010	1587	8.51	14.73	71.06	67.77	4.58	113.93

Some domains are intrinsically more difficult than others for extractive approaches: Chemistry (Chimie) > Information Sciences (Sciences Inf) > Linguistics (Linguistique) > Archaeology (Archeologie). The most difficult one is chemistry since many keywords refer to specific chemical compounds that either do not appear exactly in the sources or they are rewritten from the source in complex ways e.g. "methylene-3 perhydro cis-benzofurannone-2" could be written as "benzofurannone-2(methylene-3 perhydro)". Also, the chemistry domain has the largest number of unique keywords, and the sequences of keywords are the longest ones among all the domains (#words (keywords)). All these characteristics make the DEFT-2016 corpus a very challenging one, which constitutes an excellent test bed for automatic indexing methods.

4   Proposed Models

As discussed in the previous section, extractive approaches seem to not be the best choice for the DEFT task due to the high percentage of novel keywords in all the domains. For this reason, we propose to address DEFT as a text generation task, using generative systems to generate the sequence of keywords given the source. We used a pre-trained encoder-decoder model with a Transformer backbone as the main model in our experimentation: MBartHez [9], a French model that yields state-of-the-art results in other tasks. We hypothesize that due to the reduced number of samples and the task's difficulty, it could be beneficial to move the weights of the pre-trained model towards a better region for the DEFT task before finetuning on DEFT. To this aim, we do task-specific further pre-training using two different pre-training corpora, as described in Subsect. 4.1.

Since at least 20% of the keywords are extracted from the source in all the domains, we consider that the copy behavior of the model could play an important role, especially in mainly extractive domains like archaeology. To try to improve the trade-off between copying and generation of the model, we developed a copy mechanism for Transformer architectures to be used with MBartHez. The **copy enhanced model** is described in Subsect. 4.2.

After preliminary experiments, we observed that due to the differences among domains, finetuning a single model on all the domains at once degraded the results. So, we finetuned the models for each domain independently. Some of the finetuned models can be accessed through this link.

4.1 Task-Specific Further Pre-trained Models

Starting from the pre-trained MBartHez model, we further pretrained it on a keyword generation task that resembles the DEFT task. To this aim, we collected two different corpora of (source, target) pairs, where the source is a text excerpt and the target is a sequence of keywords: the **Wiki** corpus and the **HAL** corpus. Figure 1 shows the web page of one example of each corpus.

Fig. 1. Web page of examples from the **Wiki** and **HAL** corpora. The red boxes refers the source and the blue boxes refers the targets of each corpus. The examples are drawn from Wikipedia and HAL.

On the one hand, the **Wiki** corpus was extracted from the French dump of Wikipedia[1]. Since the sources of the DEFT dataset are the titles and the abstracts of bibliographic records, we used the titles and the lead paragraph of the Wikipedia articles as sources in the **Wiki** corpus. The lead paragraph of Wikipedia can be considered as an abstract, as it generally define the subject matter as well as emphasize the interesting points of the article. The targets of the **Wiki** corpus are the categories found at the bottom of the Wikipedia articles. It should be noted that these categories are not exactly keywords, but topics to link similar articles under a hierarchy. We removed the samples of the **Wiki** corpus whose source has less than 50 words and whose target has less than 4 categories.

On the other hand, the **HAL** corpus was extracted from "L'archive ouverte pluridisciplinaire (HAL)"[2]. The multidisciplinary open archive HAL is intended for the archival and the diffusion of scientific research articles and theses, published or not, originating mainly from French public and private research institutions. This means that the content of the archive is quite heterogeneous and includes documents written in various formats and languages (English content represents 66% of the total number of documents, with 30.7% of documents in

---

[1] https://dumps.wikimedia.org/frwiki/20211220/.

[2] https://hal.archives-ouvertes.fr/.

French). To create a corpus comparable in type and structure to the one proposed at DEFT, we selected a subset of papers that respected the following conditions: first, they had to be written in French; second, they had both title and abstract, and finally they had keywords associated. We started from the 2019-01-01 dump from the official HAL triple stores repository in RDF format[3], from which we selected all the files matching the above criteria, obtaining $271,126$ articles with title, abstract and keywords.

Statistics of both corpora are shown in Table 3. **HAL** is the pre-training corpus most similar to DEFT in terms of percentage of novel keywords and stems, and in terms of number of sentences in the source. Furthermore, it is the one which covers more categories of DEFT, and contains the largest number of unique categories and samples. **Wiki** is much more abstractive than **HAL** and DEFT, showing 10% more novel categories than the more abstractive domain in DEFT (chimie), and 36% more than **HAL**. Also, it only covers the 15% of the keywords of DEFT. These differences are interesting to observe to what extent the further pre-training can improve the performance of a model in lack of data that exactly resembles the downstream keyword generation task. Both pre-training corpora have a similar number of keywords per sample, generally being this number lower than in DEFT. The length of the keyword sequences is more than twice as long in **Wiki** than in **HAL**.

Table 3. Statistics of the **Wiki** and **HAL** corpora.

	#Samples	#keywords	#unique keywords	% coverage DEFT keywords	#keywords per sample	#words (keywords)	%Novel keywords	% Novel stems	#sentences (source)	#words (source)
Wiki	166,698	1,154,006	214,094	14.82	6.92	29.11	91.29	90.56	2.99	85.76
HAL	271,126	1,709,547	474,212	57.86	6.31	12.40	55.25	50.04	7.43	238.46

We further pretrained MBartHez during 3 epochs using the two pre-training corpora independently, and then we finetuned them for each domain of the DEFT task. We call these models as **MBartHez+Wiki** and **MBartHez+HAL**.

4.2 Copy Enhanced Model

We extended MBartHez with a copy mechanism and we further pre-trained it on the HAL corpus in the same way than **MBartHez+HAL**. Later, the further pre-trained copy-enhanced MBartHez is finetuned for each domain of the DEFT task. We call this model as **MBartHez+HAL+Copy**.

The copy mechanism combines a generation distribution, P_{vocab}, and a copy distribution P_{copy}, by weighting them using a switch to trade-off between generation and copy behaviors, p_{gen}. Both the distributions P_{vocab} and P_{copy}, and the switch p_{gen} are computed from the sequence of encoder hidden states and

---

[3] https://data.archives-ouvertes.fr/backup.

the decoder output at each step. We adapted the copy mechanism from [21] to be used with MBartHez, inspiring us on the work of [25].

Let x be the sequence of subwords used as input for the encoder, y the sequence of target subwords, h be the sequence of encoder hidden states, and s_t the decoder output on the step t, the copy mechanism is defined as follows. First, a context vector c_t is computed based on the additive attention of [3]:

$$e_{t,i} = v^\top \mathrm{GELU}(h_i + s_t) \tag{1}$$

$$\alpha_t = \mathrm{softmax}(e_t) \tag{2}$$

$$c_t = \sum_i \alpha_{t,i} h_i \tag{3}$$

where $e_{t,i}$ is the score for the hidden state h_i on the step t, v is a vector of learnable weights, and α_t is a probability distribution over the hidden states on the step t (attention weights). Differently from [25], we do not transform h_i and s_t in Eq. 1, since our approach is based on a pre-trained Transformer model whose capacity should be sufficient to transform the outputs in a proper way for computing the context vector. In this way, we do not over-parameterize the model, which helps to attribute the changes in the performance to the copy strategy and not so to the parameters added to the model.

The generation distribution over all the subwords in the vocabulary, P_{vocab}, is computed from the context vector c_t and the decoder output h_t. The probability of a subword w in P_{vocab} is computed as follows:

$$P_{vocab}(w) = \mathrm{softmax}(W_v s_t + W_v c_t)_{i(w)} \tag{4}$$

where W_v are the weights of the language modeling head in the underlying pre-trained Transformer decoder, and $i(w)$ is the index of the subword w in the vocabulary. We reuse the language modeling head to also transform the context vector since we observe slow convergence using a randomly initialized weight matrix to this aim. As previously, this also helps to not over-parameterize the model.

The copy distribution over all the subwords in the vocabulary, P_{copy}, is computed from the attention weights of the encoder hidden states. In this distribution, only the subwords w of the encoder input x can have a probability higher than zero, and it is the sum of the attention weights of the encoder states for w. The probability of a subword w in P_{copy} is computed as follows:

$$P_{copy}(w) = \sum_{i:x_i=w} \alpha_{t,i} \tag{5}$$

The P_{vocab} and P_{copy} distributions are combined by using a generate-copying switch to compute the final distribution P. Equation 6, shows how to compute the final probability of a ground-truth target subword y_t:

$$P(y_t) = p_{gen} P_{vocab}(y_t) + (1 - p_{gen}) P_{copy}(y_t) \tag{6}$$

The p_{gen} switch is computed by using the context vector, and the decoder outputs at steps t and $t-1$, as shown in Eq. 7:

$$p_{gen} = \mathrm{sigmoid}(w_g^\top c_t + u_g^\top s_t + v_g^\top s_{t-1}) \tag{7}$$

where w_g, u_g, and v_g are learnable weight vectors.

The source code of the copy enhanced model is released through this link. Its copy mechanism can be used with any pre-trained MBart model of the HuggingFace library, and easily extended to other encoder-decoder models.

5 Results

The results of our models and the systems that participated in the competition are presented in Table 4. We see that **MBartHez** obtains on average an F_1 score almost identical to the two best systems in the competition (Exensa and EBSI). It is interesting since both Exensa and EBSI systems combine strategies to copy keywords from the source and generate novel keywords from a controlled vocabulary (the DEFT ontology). So, it shows that an encoder-decoder model that can naturally copy or generate novel keywords not limited to the ontology of the task is competitive enough against robust, carefully designed systems for DEFT.

Table 4. Results of the models for each domain in the test set of DEFT. The second half of the table refers to the systems that participated in the competition. MBH is short for MBartHez.

	Archeologie			Chimie			Linguistique			Sciences Inf			Average		
	P	R	F1	P	R	F1	P	R	F1	P	R	F1	P	R	F1
MBH	43.76	33.61	36.60	19.97	22.76	20.28	29.85	31.70	30.28	32.61	28.89	29.94	31.55	29.24	29.27
MBH+Wiki	41.91	42.74	40.83	21.16	23.69	21.34	31.86	31.98	31.50	32.35	33.42	31.85	31.82	32.96	31.38
MBH+HAL	44.33	44.93	43.11	24.13	27.25	**24.36**	**35.70**	31.63	33.00	34.27	**35.72**	**34.09**	34.61	34.88	33.64
MBH+HAL+Copy	44.45	45.77	43.47	23.60	26.30	23.75	35.56	**37.75**	**35.95**	35.96	33.29	33.65	**34.89**	**35.78**	**34.21**
Exensa	43.48	**52.71**	**45.59**	**24.92**	21.73	21.46	23.28	32.73	26.30	21.26	30.32	23.86	28.24	34.37	29.30
EBSI	30.77	43.24	34.96	19.67	25.07	21.07	30.26	34.16	31.75	31.03	28.23	28.98	27.93	32.67	29.19
LINA	–	–	40.11	–	–	18.28	–	–	24.19	–	–	21.45	–	–	26.01
LIMSI	**55.26**	38.03	43.26	18.19	14.90	15.29	15.67	16.10	15.63	13.83	12.01	12.49	25.73	20.26	21.64
LIPN	33.93	31.25	30.75	10.88	**30.25**	15.31	13.98	30.81	19.07	11.72	23.54	15.34	17.63	28.96	20.12

When task-specific further pre-training is applied, better results than Exensa and EBSI are obtained. Specifically, the more the task-specific pre-training corpora resembles DEFT, the better the obtained results are. In the case of **MBartHez+Wiki**, despite the categories used in pre-training are not exactly keywords, it is already enough to improve, on average, on the Exensa and EBSI systems. **MBartHez+HAL** even improves on the performance of **MBartHez+Wiki**, obtaining the best results in the two domains with the highest percentage of novel keywords (Chimie and Sciences Inf).

The inclusion of the copy mechanism (**MBartHez+HAL+Copy**) allows improving the performance in the two most extractive domains (Archeologie and Linguistique) in comparison to **MBartHez+HAL**, especially on Linguistique. However, its results on Chimie and Sciences Inf are worse than those of **MBartHez+HAL**. On average, for all the metrics, **MBartHez+HAL+Copy** is the best system for all the domains of the DEFT task.

We obtain the best results in all the domains, with increments of between 2.9 and 5.11 F_1 scores, except in the Archeologie domain. In this domain, **MBartHez+HAL+Copy** outperforms all the systems of the competition except the Exensa system.

6   Analysis

We perform two different analyses to understand our systems' behavior, emphasizing their capabilities to copy keywords or generate novel ones.

On the one hand, we observed that **MBartHez** prioritized the generation of novel keywords compared to copying the keywords from the source, even on the most extractive domains. So, in order to study this behavior, we analyze to what extent the models are copying keywords from the source. Table 5 shows the percentage of generated keywords that exactly appear in the sources of the test set.

Table 5. Percentage of copy of the MBARTHez-based models in each domain of the test set. Δ refers to the difference between the percentage of copy in the generated keywords and the percentage of copy in the reference keywords. MBH is short for MBartHez.

	Archeologie	Chimie	Linguistique	Sciences Inf
MBH	44.71 (Δ-18.61)	20.18 (Δ-3.19)	23.61 (Δ-7.25)	27.60 (Δ+0.43)
MBH+Wiki	44.11 (Δ-19.21)	22.71 (Δ-0.56)	29.65 (Δ-1.21)	29.61 (Δ+2.44)
MBH+HAL	51.61 (Δ-11.71)	28.13 (Δ+4.86)	34.42 (Δ+3.56)	35.07 (Δ+7.90)
MBH+HAL+Copy	54.03 (Δ-9.29)	27.88 (Δ+4.61)	39.99 (Δ+9.13)	37.77 (Δ+10.60)

A general trend can be observed to increase the percentage of copy if task-specific further pre-training is performed. The more similar is the pre-training corpus to the DEFT corpus, the more percentage of copied keywords. It is interesting that, even though the **Wiki** corpus has 91% of novel keywords, further pre-training **MBartHez** with this corpus increases its copy capacity. **MBartHez** is the least extractive model, while **MBartHez+HAL+Copy** the most. The models further pre-trained on **HAL** exceed the percentage of copy of the reference in all the domains except Archeologie. The system that best fits the percentage of copy of the reference (sum of absolute deltas) is **MBartHez+Wiki**, and the one that worst fits that percentage is **MBartHez+HAL+Copy**.

In Archeologie (the most extractive domain), all the models copy fewer keywords than the reference, between 10% and 20%. **MBARTHez+HAL** and **MBARTHez+HAL+Copy** copy approximately a 10% less than the reference, but their results are similar to the best system. It could indicate that they are good at generating novel keywords in this domain. Increasing the percentage of copy in Archeologie seems to be a key factor to improve the results, and a 10% is still a large gap.

The copy mechanism increases the percentage of copy in all domains except in the domain with the highest percentage of novel keywords (Chimie). Its extractive behavior in the most extractive domains (Archeologie and Linguistique), compared to **MBartHez+HAL**, seems to be the cause of the improvements in the results. In the most abstractive domains, its performance is lower than **MBartHez+HAL**. Especially in Sciences Inf, the increment in the percentage of copy seems to be the cause of the reduction in the results.

On the other hand, we perform an **error analysis** to observe what errors of **MBartHez** are solved by using task-specific further pre-training and the copy mechanism. We consider two types of errors: **precision errors** (generated keywords not in the reference), and **recall errors** (reference keywords not in the generation). To this aim, Fig. 2 shows the 5 most common errors of **MBartHez** and **MBartHez+HAL+Copy** along with their frequency. It should be noted that these errors are stemmed keywords as in the DEFT evaluation.

In Fig. 2, we observe almost always the same errors for both the domains and models, but with lower frequency in **MBartHez+HAL+Copy** than in **MBartHez**. There are some exceptions where errors of **MBartHez** go out from the top 5 (and also from the top 10) in **MBartHez+HAL+Copy**. In the case of precision errors: *paléolith moyen* (Archeologie), *métal transit compos* (Chimie), *sémiot discurs* (Linguistique), and *relat utilis intermédiair* (Sciences Inf). In the case of recall errors: *paléolith supérieur* (Archeologie), *compos minéral* (Chimie), *linguist appliqu* (Linguistique)). Deeper analyses are required to determine why **MBartHez+HAL+Copy** improves more on these keywords than on the rest of the top keywords. There are still some errors that, if solved, would lead to significant increases in performance since they appear in a large number of samples in the test set, for instance, *etud expérimental* (Chimie), *europ* (Archeologie and Sciences Inf), and *pragmat* (Linguistique).

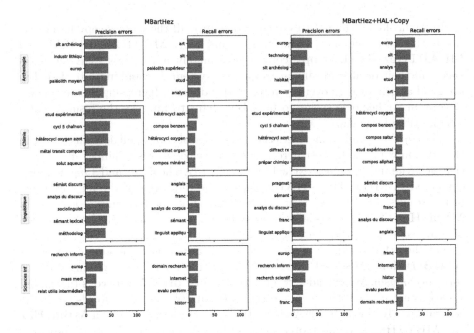

Fig. 2. The 5 most frequent errors of MBartHez and MBartHez+HAL+Copy in each domain. The x-axis is the frequency and the y-axis represents the errors.

7   Conclusion and Future Work

We approached a task on automatic indexing French scientific literature (DEFT) from a generative point of view by leveraging a pre-trained transformer-based language model (MBartHez). We showed that vanilla MBartHez does not improve previous approaches in the competition. Still, it can be improved by addressing task nuances through task-specific further pre-training and a copy mechanism. We explored two different corpora for task-specific further pre-training, showing that the more similar is the pre-training corpus to DEFT, the better the results. Even with a pre-training corpus that slightly resembles the keywords of DEFT, we also observed improvements on this task. The copy mechanism improved the performance in the most extractive domains. Finally, through an analysis of the copy capabilities, we observed that vanilla MBartHez prioritizes the generation of novel keywords even in the most extractive domains, but this can be alleviated with task-specific further pre-training and copy mechanisms.

As future work, we plan to incorporate the relevance of each token inside the attention mechanisms, focusing on aspects like centrality or TF-IDF to help the models to copy relevant keywords from the source. Regarding the task-specific further pre-training, it could be useful to cluster the **Wiki** and **HAL** corpora into DEFT domains and do further pre-training for each domain specifically.

References

1. Ammar, W., Peters, M., Bhagavatula, C., Power, R.: The AI2 system at SemEval-2017 Task 10 (ScienceIE): semi-supervised end-to-end entity and relation extraction. In: Proceedings of the 11th International Workshop on Semantic Evaluation, SemEval-2017, pp. 592–596 (2017)
2. Augenstein, I., Das, M., Riedel, S., Vikraman, L., McCallum, A.: SemEval 2017 Task 10: ScienceIE - extracting keyphrases and relations from scientific publications. In: Proceedings of the 11th International Workshop on Semantic Evaluation, SemEval-2017, pp. 546–555 (2017)
3. Bahdanau, D., Cho, K., Bengio, Y.: Neural machine translation by jointly learning to align and translate. In: 3rd International Conference on Learning Representations, ICLR 2015 (January 2015)
4. Boudin, F., Daille, B., Jacquey, É., Nie, J.: The DELICES project: indexing scientific literature through semantic expansion. arXiv arXiv:abs/2106.14731 (2020)
5. Bougouin, A., Boudin, F., Daille, B.: TopicRank: graph-based topic ranking for keyphrase extraction. In: International Joint Conference on Natural Language Processing (IJCNLP), pp. 543–551 (2013)
6. Cabanac, G., Frommholz, I., Mayr, P.: Scholarly literature mining with information retrieval and natural language processing: preface. Scientometrics **125**(3), 2835–2840 (2020). https://doi.org/10.1007/s11192-020-03763-4
7. Campos, R., Mangaravite, V., Pasquali, A., Jorge, A., Nunes, C., Jatowt, A.: YAKE! keyword extraction from single documents using multiple local features. Inf. Sci. **509**, 257–289 (2020)
8. Daille, B., Barreaux, S., Bougouin, A., Boudin, F., Cram, D., Hazem, A.: Automatic indexing of scientific papers presentation and results of DEFT 2016 text mining challenge. Inf. Retrieval Doc. Semant. Web **17**(2), 1–17 (2017)
9. Eddine, M.K., Tixier, A.J.P., Vazirgiannis, M.: BARThez: a skilled pretrained French sequence-to-sequence model. arXiv preprint arXiv:2010.12321 (2020)
10. Hasan, K.S., Ng, V.: Automatic keyphrase extraction: a survey of the state of the art. In: Proceedings of the 52nd Annual Meeting of the Association for Computational Linguistics (Volume 1: Long Papers), pp. 1262–1273 (2014)
11. Hernandez, S.D., Buscaldi, D., Charnois, T.: LIPN at SemEval-2017 Task 10: filtering candidate keyphrases from scientific publications with part-of-speech tag sequences to train a sequence labeling model. In: Proceedings of the 11th International Workshop on Semantic Evaluation, SemEval-2017, pp. 995–999 (2017)
12. Huang, H., Wang, X., Wang, H.: NER-RAKE: an improved rapid automatic keyword extraction method for scientific literatures based on named entity recognition. Proc. Assoc. Inf. Sci. Technol. **57**(1), 71–91 (2020)
13. Li, G., Wang, H.: Improved automatic keyword extraction based on TextRank using domain knowledge. In: Zong, C., Nie, J.-Y., Zhao, D., Feng, Y. (eds.) NLPCC 2014. CCIS, vol. 496, pp. 403–413. Springer, Heidelberg (2014). https://doi.org/10.1007/978-3-662-45924-9_36
14. Lopez, P., Romary, L.: HUMB: automatic key term extraction from scientific articles in GROBID. In: Proceedings of the 5th International Workshop on Semantic Evaluation, Uppsala, Sweden, July 2010, pp. 248–251. Association for Computational Linguistics (2010)
15. Lu, Y., Li, R., Wen, K., Lu, Z.: Automatic keyword extraction for scientific literatures using references. In: Proceedings of the 2014 International Conference on Innovative Design and Manufacturing (ICIDM), pp. 78–81. IEEE (2014)

16. Marchand, M., Fouquier, G., Marchand, E., Pitel, G.: Document vector embeddings for bibliographic records indexing. Inf. Retrieval Doc. Semant. Web **17**(2) (2017)

17. Meng, R., Zhao, S., Han, S., He, D., Brusilovsky, P., Chi, Y.: Deep keyphrase generation. In: 55th Annual Meeting of the Association for Computational Linguistics, Proceedings of the Conference, ACL 2017. vol. 1, pp. 582–592 (2017)

18. Mihalcea, R., Tarau, P.: TextRank: bringing order into text. In: Proceedings of the Conference on Empirical Methods in Natural Language Processing, pp. 404–411 (2004)

19. Rose, S., Engel, D., Cramer, N., Cowley, W.: Automatic keyword extraction from individual documents. In: Text Mining: Applications and Theory, vol. 1, pp. 1–20 (2010)

20. Rousseau, F., Vazirgiannis, M.: Graph-of-word and TW-IDF: new approach to Ad Hoc IR. In: Proceedings of the 22nd ACM International Conference on Information & Knowledge Management, pp. 59–68 (2013)

21. See, A., Liu, P.J., Manning, C.D.: Get to the point: summarization with pointer-generator networks. In: Proceedings of the 55th Annual Meeting of the Association for Computational Linguistics (Volume 1: Long Papers), Vancouver, Canada, July 2017, pp. 1073–1083. Association for Computational Linguistics (2017)

22. Spärck Jones, K.: A statistical interpretation of term specificity and its application in retrieval. J. Doc. **28**, 11–21 (1972)

23. Turney, P.D.: Learning algorithms for keyphrase extraction. Inf. Retrieval **2**(4), 303–336 (2000)

24. Wang, R., Liu, W., McDonald, C.: Using word embeddings to enhance keyword identification for scientific publications. In: Sharaf, M.A., Cheema, M.A., Qi, J. (eds.) ADC 2015. LNCS, vol. 9093, pp. 257–268. Springer, Cham (2015). https://doi.org/10.1007/978-3-319-19548-3_21

25. Xu, S., Li, H., Yuan, P., Wu, Y., He, X., Zhou, B.: Self-attention guided copy mechanism for abstractive summarization. In: Proceedings of the 58th Annual Meeting of the Association for Computational Linguistics, July 2020, pp. 1355–1362. Association for Computational Linguistics (2020). Online

Uncertainty Detection in Historical Databases

Wissam Mammar Kouadri[1], Jacky Akoka[1,2], Isabelle Comyn-Wattiau[3], and Cedric du Mouza[1(✉)]

[1] CEDRIC-CNAM, Paris, France
dumouza@cnam.fr
[2] IMT-BS, Paris, France
[3] ESSEC Business School, Cergy, France

Abstract. Historians analyze information from diverse and heterogeneous sources to verify hypotheses and/or to propose new ones. Central to any historical project is the concept of uncertainty, reflecting a lack of confidence. This may limit the scope of the hypotheses formulated. Uncertainty encompasses a variety of aspects including ambiguity, incompleteness, vagueness, randomness, and inconsistency. These aspects cannot be easily detected automatically in plain-text documents. The objective of this article is to propose a process for detecting uncertainty, combining dictionary-based approaches, and pattern identification. The process is validated through experiments conducted on a real historical data set.

Keywords: Uncertainty · Automatic detection · Historical data · Dictionary · Pattern

1 Introduction

Historians base their work on different sources of information. These are of three types: primary sources, secondary sources, and tertiary sources. A primary source is an original document that provides direct information about the subject of the research. This document is most often from the time when the event(s) reported took place. Primary sources can be letters, texts, images, reports, records, etc. Secondary sources are documents that use primary sources, and often consultation of other secondary sources, as an analysis, synthesis, explanation, or evaluation. Examples of secondary sources are biographies or historical research publications. A tertiary source is a selection and compilation of primary and secondary sources. Bibliographies, library catalogs, directories, recommended reading lists, and review articles are examples of tertiary sources.

Historical data refer to past information and are therefore generally associated with some uncertainty. Several classifications have been proposed for uncertainty, most notably the URREF classification [4], in which the term uncertainty encompasses various aspects of imperfect knowledge, including ambiguity, incompleteness, vagueness, randomness, and inconsistency. Ambiguity characterizes a situation where the information does not have complete semantics. For example,

P. Rosso et al. (Eds.): NLDB 2022, LNCS 13286, pp. 73–85, 2022.
https://doi.org/10.1007/978-3-031-08473-7_7

"Adam d'Artois made a gift of 5 crowns to his relative". "His relative" can refer to his father, his mother or any other member of his family. Therefore, ambiguity can be defined as a phrase that has more than one meaning. Incompleteness reflects a lack of information, such as the statement *"Reginaldus Agni studied for his licentiate in theology at the Sorbonne between ? and 1377"*. Vagueness corresponds to a situation characterized by an incomplete knowledge of the facts and events considered. The phrase *"the archbishop is in his first years of priesthood"* or *"Félix Esculi was born in the vicinity of Reims"* are two examples. Randomness characterizes the absence of order or pattern. In general, randomness expresses the lack of predictability of an event. It can be considered as representing the variability of observed natural phenomena. Finally, inconsistency characterizes a situation in which two or more pieces of information cannot be true at the same time. For example, *"the archbishop is 85 and 93 years old"*. Almost all historical data contain some type of uncertainty. Input data may be ambiguous or unclear. Knowledge of events may be questionable and takes the form of plausibility, probability and/or possibility.

Uncertainty is strongly related to the nature of the source. A primary source is more likely to be ambiguous and incomplete. A secondary or tertiary source will more often be vague when it proposes a synthesis and interpretation of a set of ambiguous and incomplete primary sources. It is important for the historian exploiting these sources and build his/her hypotheses to know if they are certain. Uncertainty is sometimes indicated explicitly, encoded for example by a question mark (e.g. between 1357 and ?, May 18, 1475 ?, etc.) or by a keyword ("unknown", "not known", etc.). However, the analysis of real historical data shows that uncertainty is often expressed directly in the text by a choice of terms, phrases or by the conjugation (time and mode) of verbs. Due to the amount of texts available in many historical projects, it becomes crucial to implement automatic processes to capture the information contained in these texts, structure them in a database so that historians can query them and verify their hypotheses. Therefore, automatic uncertainty detection in natural language analysis is required. It is a complex task.

The objective of this paper is to present a process for automatic uncertainty detection in plain-text historical data, combining dictionary and pattern-based approaches.

We present in Sect. 2 the related work. Section 3 introduces the uncertainty features of historical data. In Sect. 4 we describe our process to detect uncertainty combining a dictionary and a pattern-based approach. We present in Sect. 5 a discussion about the characteristics of historical data and the efficiency and limits of our approach. Finally Sect. 6 concludes the paper.

2   Related Work

Uncertainty or, more generally, hedging or speculation are linguistic strategies used to express doubt and vagueness when authors are not entirely sure of their claims and want to weaken the strength of statements. Therefore, identifying speculation in text, especially in scientific writing (including historical texts), involves defining the reliability, accuracy, and confidence of the information. Particularly for knowledge extraction, the degree of speculation in the sentence can serve as a score for the uncertainty of the extracted knowledge.

Many research works [1,3,5,5–9,11–13,15,17–21,23,24] have addressed uncertainty identification in text, proposing interesting tools and algorithms. The shared task in CoNLL-2010 [9] has classified uncertainty identification into two levels, extracting uncertainty from the text and identifying the scope of the uncertainty.

The straightforward method for uncertainty extraction from texts is to build a dictionary containing words and phrases that express uncertainty, then apply a matching scheme between the dictionaries and the text. For example, [11] proposed a web service for extracting uncertainty from French news. They propose a dictionary-based approach with linguistic patterns to detect uncertainty in the text. Likewise, [3] studied the presence of uncertainty in biomedical and physics research papers by considering a set of manually sourced speculative expressions. [5] evaluated uncertainty in radiological reports based on dictionary of uncertainty words sourced manually. Finally, [6] proposed a new method for uncertainty detection in scientific publications by extending a dictionary of uncertainty words using word2vec models. These methods are efficient with controlled language, like the case of radiological reports [15]. However, uncertainty is domain-dependent like the case of historical texts, where phrases could express uncertainty only in some contexts. To illustrate this issue, let us consider the following two sentences: S1 and S2. Due to homonyms, a given word in S1 may express uncertainty, while in S2, it expresses ability. Moreover, the large variety of phrases to express uncertainty can hardly be represented in dictionaries.

Therefore, studies published in [7,19,23,24] proposed machine learning methods for uncertainty expressions detection in text. For instance, [7] proposed a supervised method based on LSTM and CRF for uncertainty and uncertainty scope extraction. The model is trained on a French biomedical dataset labeled manually. [24] proposed a supervised method for detecting uncertainty in software requirements expressed in natural language. This method is based on a CRF model to extract the speculation cues, and proposed a rule-based heuristic to determine the scope of speculation. Authors of [23] conducted a study on uncertainty in Hungarian texts. They manually labeled an uncertainty corpus for Hungarian and used it to train a CRF model for uncertainty detection. Finally, in [19], the authors analyzed the performance of uncertainty extraction in different domains using different models.

As we can notice, most researches focus on speculation detection in English texts. Nevertheless, to the best of our knowledge, there is a limited number of studies dedicated to French texts. Moreover, the existing studies concern primarily biomedical data, which is different from historical data.

In the next section, we present different challenges related to uncertainty detection in historical data in the French language and we illustrate these problems using a real-life data sample taken from the Studium database [10].

3   Uncertainty in Historical Data

In history, much of the literature that researchers work with is fraught with uncertainty [14]. Whether primary or secondary sources, facts are recorded, in natural language, with the associated imprecision and uncertainty. For example: *"Absalon de Sancto-Victore was probably a student at the University of Paris around 1327."* The uncertainty is represented here in natural language by the word "probably" and the imprecision by "around". The interpretation of the facts by historians is also tainted by this uncertainty. For example: *"Hence, he must have obtained a master's degree between 1330 and 1335."* Uncertainty is embedded in "must have" and imprecision in "between 1330 and 1335". Furthermore, unlike some areas such as biomedicine mentioned in the state of the art, natural language is not controlled in history. Historians usually use expressions and metaphors to express the uncertainty of statements, making it challenging for humans and machines to capture and gauge this uncertainty. Thus, capturing all historical information in databases available to researchers requires taking into account this uncertainty embedded in natural language, to avoid erroneous reasoning.

Without loss of generality, in this article, we illustrate the uncertainty in prosopographic databases, which are very structuring tools in historical research. Prosopography is a field of the digital humanities, which consists in analyzing information about sets of individuals in the context of historical societies through a collective study of their lives [22]. It focuses on the common characteristics of large groups of individuals that appear in historical sources, usually poorly documented. It aims to represent and interpret historical data from texts describing the lives of historical figures. As with historical data in general, prosopography deals with information that is often incomplete, imprecise, and contradictory. To our knowledge, existing prosopographic databases do not encode uncertainty. Moreover, they are manually populated. To illustrate our approach, we present in this paper several examples relying on the prosopographic conceptual model proposed in [2]. We present below an extract of this conceptual model encompassing the main objects of prosopographic databases which are: factoids, persons, time, places, objects, and sources (Fig. 1).

A factoid can be considered as an event taken in a broad sense including all the facts that characterize individuals. A factoid involves *persons*, occurs at a given *place* and *time*, as mentioned in a *source* and may have an impact on *objects*. For example, *"The Italian Faustus Andrelinus, living in the 14th or 15th century, obtained a doctorate in Bologna after studying in Paris."* This sentence contains three factoids relating, respectively, to the period of life (time is 14th or 15th century) of Faustus Andrelinus (person), to his first studies in Paris (place) and then his studies in Bologna (place). The uncertainty here lies in the period of life spanning two centuries. Finally, the conceptual model integrates the management of uncertain information in four forms: incomplete data leading to null values, ambiguous information due to linguistic terms (e.g. about, probably, not far from, etc.), vague information (membership degree, importance degree, etc.), and inconsistent assertions.

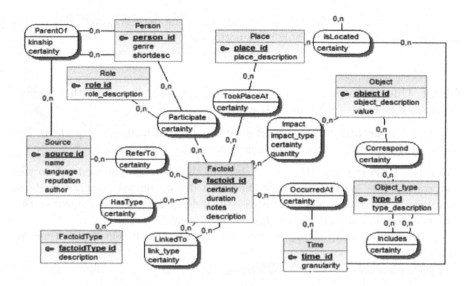

Fig. 1. Conceptual model capturing historical information - an excerpt [2]

To demonstrate the feasibility and challenges of detecting uncertainty from historical data, we consider the Studium Parisiense database, a prosopographic database describing members of Paris' schools and university from the twelfth century until the end of sixteenth century [10]. Studium database contains 20,000 files that are semi-structured (contains text fields). It contains sometimes question marks representing ambiguous or unsure values to encode the uncertainty. However, in most cases, it uses natural language comments to express the uncertainty.

To assess the uncertainty in the Studium database, we sampled files set randomly with a confidence level of 99% and an error within ±5%. The sample size we analyzed contains 896 files, which satisfied the requirement which is 638 or more. Statistics about the Studium database are depicted in Table 1.

Table 1. Statistics about Studium

Measures	Values
Number of files	896
Number of fields	53537
%structured fields	45.1%
% text fields	54.9%
Average number of words by field	10,279
% Fields with question marks	3.8%

Uncertainty in structured fields of the Studium database is expressed with "?". By analyzing the values of Table 1, we notice that most fields are unstructured. Moreover, by analyzing them, we find that they are replete with three different uncertainty types described below.

Direct Uncertainty: This uncertainty is expressed directly with common expressions or words from French language.

Pattern Uncertainty: This uncertainty is expressed using given patterns for uncertainty expression. More details are given in the next section.

Complex Uncertainty: The uncertainty, in this case, is expressed within the text context like in the sentence: "There is a debate on his presence in Paris university." The uncertainty, in this case, is understood from the context of the sentence since debate not always implies uncertainty.

In the next section, we present how we extract the different types of uncertainty from text.

4   Uncertainty Detection Process of Historical Data Expressed in French Language

Since the uncertainty is not encoded in dedicated fields, we must detect it by analyzing plain-text fields. This implies a parsing of the text and an application of NLP approaches. In this paper we propose two complementary approaches: first a dictionary based method and then a pattern based one. A specificity of our work is to focus on uncertainty automatic detection in French language which has been little studied so far.

4.1   Dictionary Based Method

To identify uncertainty in the Studium database, we have sourced a set of French linguistic resources (books, websites, other research works) that list expressions and words used to express speculation and uncertainty. Additionally, we translated to French a list of English words expressing uncertainty listed in [6]. The resulted dictionary contains 65 uncertainty indicators categorized into nouns, verbs, adjectives, adverbs, and expressions.

Then, we extended this seed (the dictionary of words) using all synonyms of the 65 indicators found in Wonef [16], the French translation of Wordnet. We added the list of synsets for each word of the list and repeated the operation for each newly added word until convergence, *i. e.* no new word is added to the list. Finally, we validated the list of generated words manually and retained only those that expressed the uncertainty.

Table 2 presents a sample from the resulted dictionary (column 2). Statistics about the initial uncertainty dictionary are displayed in column 3 while column 4 show statistics about the final uncertainty dictionary obtained after synsets extension.

Table 2. Sample and statistics of the French dictionary for uncertainty detection

	Examples	Size seed	Size dictionary
Adjectives	Douteux, incertain, probable, vraisemblable, possible, présumé, envisageable, imaginable	11	57
Adverbs	Approximativement, grossièrement, rudement, brutalement, souvent, presque	6	24
Nouns	Incertitude, probabilité, estimation, doute, hasard, possibilité	9	29
Verbs	Penser, croire, douter, hésiter, paraître, sembler, estimer	9	50
Expressions	Plus ou moins, avec brusquerie, à peu près, l'hypothèse que	30	30
Total		65	190

We checked the efficiency of the dictionary approach on a sample of data extracted from Studium. On the one hand we automatically attempted to detect uncertainty with dictionary words detection while parsing the text. On the other hand, we manually pointed out the uncertain data within the different files. Results of the uncertainty evaluation using a dictionary-based approach are presented in Table 3.

Table 3. Results of dictionary based approach applied to Studium database sample

Dictionary based approach	
Accuracy_score	0.70
Precision	0.95
Recall	0.24
F1_score	0.39

Our results show that this method provides very few false positives, thus it has a good precision. However it delivers many false negatives, leading to a very poor recall, *i.e.*, most uncertain data are not detected. Therefore the use of this method alone is not satisfactory. Observation of undetected uncertainty revealed the existence of patterns used to express it. In the following section we describe these patterns and evaluate the improvement obtained by taking them into account for uncertainty detection.

4.2 Pattern Based Method

The patterns were designed based on the data analysis of the Studium database. We sampled a set of files randomly and extracted the unstructured plain-text sections of the files. Then we carefully checked the data to extract frequent linguistic patterns used by historians in Studium to express uncertainty.

We classify the patterns that we identified into the following six categories:

Time and Place Uncertainty Patterns
This pattern is one of the most frequent patterns in the Studium database since historians cannot certify with certainty the precise date or place of a fact. Regarding datation they can often only situate the event in a time interval or in a relation to a reference date. For instance, in Studium we found the following sentences: *"il est né vers"* and *"il est né aux alentours de"*. These expressions mean that *"he was born around"*. Thus they reflect the fact that the historian who wrote these files is not sure about the person's birth date and cannot be more precise for this instant event (birth). We observe that the patterns for the dates are of the form

$$<ADV><NOUN> \text{ or } <ADV><NUM>$$

where <ADV> is a position adverb (*before, after, around, approximately, etc.*) and <NOUN> is a date (more or less precise, for instance referring to a special day by its name *e.g.* Eastern, Christmas, the King Coronation, etc., or by a precise date), and <NUM> is numerical value representing a year.

Similarly, for locations, we use <ADV><NOUN> patterns to express the uncertainty. For instance in the sentence *"il est né à côté de Paris"*, which means *"he was born near Paris"*, we do not know the exact birthplace, therefore we express this uncertainty using an area around the city of Paris.

As a consequence, to detect such patterns we must first extract the parts of the sentence corresponding to the form <ADV><NOUN> or <ADV><NUM>. Then, we check whether the <NOUN> corresponds to a place or date using a named entity recognition tool.

Choice Patterns
This type of pattern is used when the historian hesitates between two (or more) statements. For instance, we found in Studium database: *"Il est originaire du Pays de Galles ou du Herefordshire"* which means *"He is from Wales or Herefordshire"*. The author is not sure about the person's origin and expresses this uncertainty with a choice between two hypotheses.

These choice patterns are of the forms

$$<NP><CC><NP> \text{ or } <VB><CC><VB>$$

Where <NP> denotes a nominal group, <VB> a verbal group, and <CC> a choice conjunction (in the French language mainly "ou" or "soit", which means "or").

Precision Patterns
When a piece of information is lacking, the historians either state this lack of information explicitly, or estimate its value. Here again there exist patterns

which correspond to this situation. For instance, we found in Studium database several expressions like *"Datation arbitraire"* and *"Date estimée"* which means respectively *"Arbitrary dating"* and *"Estimated date"*. Here the author does not have an exact value for the date; therefore, she expresses this doubt by giving either a random or an estimated value.

This pattern has the form

$$<NOUN><ADJ>$$

where <NOUN> is a noun and <ADJ> is an adjective that expresses approximation.

Uncertainty Expressed with Conditional Mode
Conditional is a mode that expresses either wishes, hypothetical sentences or politeness in the interrogative form. Since the facts reported in the historical databases refer to a more or less distant past, and appear in more or less reliable sources, historians often use the conditional tense to express their doubts about a date, the course of a fact, the presence of a person, the authorship of a publication, etc. Consequently we make the assumption that all forms of conditional correspond to hypothetical sentences.

To detect the use of the conditional we inspect the verbal ending of the conditional (*e.g.* "erait", "iraient", etc., in French) and check that the prefix corresponds to a verbal radical.

Epistemic Uncertainty
Epistemic uncertainty is mainly expressed with the verb *"pouvoir"* ("can" in French). However, the main difficulty is that this verb has other semantics, like the expression of ability. For instance, *"ce personnage peut être le même que Laurence HOUSOM"* or *"il se peut que ce personnage soit le même que Laurence HOUSOM"* which means *"this person may be the same as Laurence HOUSOM"* reflects the uncertainty. Oppositely a sentence like *"il a pu assister au procès"* (it means "he was able to attend the trial") expresses a capability. We especially focus on the *"il se peut"* expression, largely used in our dataset. This use of the "pouvoir" verb has only an uncertainty meaning.

We observe that this pattern could be modeled as

$$<PRON><VERB> \text{ or } <PRON><PRON><VERB>$$

where <PRON> is a third-person pronoun (singular or plural) and <VERB> is a form of the verb "pouvoir".

Interrogative form Patterns
One of the most repeated uncertainty patterns on the Studium database is the uncertainty expressed in the interrogative form like the case of the following sentence *"Mais n'est-ce pas un frère de la province de Sienne?"* which means *"But isn't he a brother from the province of Siena?"*. In this example, the author expresses the uncertainty with a question form about the statement.

This pattern is easily detected by the presence of a question mark in the text.

The Pattern-Based Approach
To extract the uncertainty using the patterns, we parsed the text and searched for different patterns in the text. We also analyzed the uncertainty using both the dictionary defined in Subsect. 4.1 and the patterns depicted above. The results are presented in Table 4.

Table 4. Results of uncertainty analysis on the Studium database using pattern based approach (Patterns) and a combined approach (Dict + patterns)

Metric	Patterns	Dict + patterns
Accuracy_score	0.76	**0.8**
Precision	**0.9**	0.89
Recall	0.48	**0.59**
F1_score	0.62	**0.71**

Our results exhibit that using patterns improved the recall score compared to the simple dictionary approach (0.48 versus 0.24). In other words it means that the use of patterns allows us to detect more uncertain data. The precision remains high (0.9), which indicates that we have few false positives.

Finally, we combined both mechanisms (dictionary and patterns). Our results show that the joint use of patterns and dictionary permits to capture even more uncertain data (a precision of 0.59 compared to 0.48) at the cost of a small decrease of the precision (0.89).

5   Discussions and Challenges

Our experimental results show that extracting uncertainty from French historical data is challenging. As anticipated, our first experiment using a dictionary-based method revealed an excellent precision score indicating that this approach has significantly few false positives, compared to a poor recall indicating that this approach misclassifies a critical portion of uncertain data.

Further, we have analyzed a sample of data and extracted relevant patterns for uncertainty. With the pattern-based method, we have noticed a significant improvement in the recall and the F1-score, indicating that we are detecting, more uncertainties using the patterns. Using a hybrid approach that combines both dictionary and patterns has led to better results.

However, the hybrid approach misclassified 20% of the uncertainties, representing a critical portion of information. This result may be explained by the nature of the historical data in French. For instance, examples such as:
Date sujette à caution which means *Date subject to caution* and

Il est désigné comme «Anglicus» par la première source contemporaine qui le mentionne which means *He is referred to as "Anglicus" by the first contemporary source that mentions him* are frequent in Studium database. Patterns or dictionaries can not handle them since the uncertainty, in this case, may be understood only within the context of the sentence. Hence, the usefulness of machine learning methods.

The challenge, in this case, is that these methods are data greedy, need high-quality massive data for training, and require high cost for labeling. These findings open promising research doors for both NLP and database communities to propose new uncertainty extraction methods for knowledge extraction.

6 Conclusion

This paper described a first study aiming at automatically detecting uncertainty embedded in historical information sources expressed in French natural language. We combined a dictionary-based approach with patterns. The latter were deduced from previous papers and enriched with different techniques. Combining dictionary and patterns allowed us to improve the recall. However, complex uncertainty is sometimes expressed within the text. Future research will consist in enriching the approach with machine learning techniques with the aim of improving the automatic detection of the uncertainty.

This study is dedicated to prosopographic databases where source is available in French natural language. However, the techniques proposed may be applied to other domains of historical information and to other languages. It is another avenue of future research.

Acknowledgements. This research has been partly funded by a national French grant (ANR Daphne 17-CE28-0013-01).

References

1. Adel, H., Schütze, H.: Exploring different dimensions of attention for uncertainty detection. arXiv preprint arXiv:1612.06549 (2016)
2. Akoka, J., Comyn-Wattiau, I., Lamassé, S., du Mouza, C.: Modeling historical social networks databases. In: Bui, T. (ed.) 52nd Hawaii International Conference on System Sciences, HICSS 2019, Grand Wailea, Maui, Hawaii, USA, 8–11 January 2019, pp. 1–10. ScholarSpace (2019). http://hdl.handle.net/10125/59714
3. Atanassova, I., Rey, F., Bertin, M.: Studying uncertainty in science: a distributional analysis through the imrad structure. In: WOSP-7th International Workshop on Mining Scientific Publications at 11th edition of the Language Resources and Evaluation Conference (2018)
4. Blasch, E., Laskey, K.B., Jousselme, A.L., Dragos, V., Costa, P.C., Dezert, J.: URREF reliability versus credibility in information fusion (STANAG 2511). In: Proceedings of the 16th International Conference on Information Fusion, pp. 1600–1607. IEEE (2013)

5. Callen, A.L., et al.: Between always and never: evaluating uncertainty in radiology reports using natural language processing. J. Digit. Imaging **33**(5), 1194–1201 (2020)
6. Chen, C., Song, M., Heo, G.E.: A scalable and adaptive method for finding semantically equivalent cue words of uncertainty. J. Informet. **12**(1), 158–180 (2018)
7. Dalloux, C., Claveau, V., Grabar, N.: Speculation and negation detection in French biomedical corpora. In: Recent Advances in Natural Language Processing, RANLP 2019, pp. 1–10 (2019)
8. De Marneffe, M.C., Manning, C.D., Potts, C.: Did it happen? The pragmatic complexity of veridicality assessment. Comput. Linguist. **38**(2), 301–333 (2012)
9. Farkas, R., Vincze, V., Móra, G., Csirik, J., Szarvas, G.: The CoNLL-2010 shared task: learning to detect hedges and their scope in natural language text. In: Proceedings of the 14th Conference on Computational Natural Language Learning - Shared Task, pp. 1–12 (2010)
10. Genet, J.P.: Studium parisiense, un repertoire informatisé des ecole de l'université de paris. Annali di Storia delle università italiane **21**(1), 25–74 (2017)
11. Goujon, B.: Uncertainty detection for information extraction. In: Proceedings of the International Conference RANLP-2009, pp. 118–122 (2009)
12. Islam, J., Xiao, L., Mercer, R.E.: A lexicon-based approach for detecting hedges in informal text. In: Proceedings of the 12th Language Resources and Evaluation Conference, pp. 3109–3113 (2020)
13. Mirzapour, M., Abdaoui, A., Tchechmedjiev, A., Digan, W., Bringay, S., Jonquet, C.: French FastContext: a publicly accessible system for detecting negation, temporality and experiencer in French clinical notes. J. Biomed. Inform. **117**, 103733 (2021)
14. Moghaz, D., Hacohen-Kerner, Y., Gabbay, D.: Text mining for evaluating authors' birth and death years. ACM Trans. Knowl. Discov. Data (TKDD) **13**(1), 1–24 (2019)
15. Peng, Y., Wang, X., Lu, L., Bagheri, M., Summers, R., Lu, Z.: NegBio: a high-performance tool for negation and uncertainty detection in radiology reports. In: AMIA Summits on Translational Science Proceedings 2018, p. 188 (2018)
16. Pradet, Q., De Chalendar, G., Desormeaux, J.B.: WoNeF, an improved, expanded and evaluated automatic French translation of WordNet. In: Proceedings of the 7th Global Wordnet Conference, pp. 32–39 (2014)
17. Saurí, R., Pustejovsky, J.: Are you sure that this happened? Assessing the factuality degree of events in text. Comput. Linguist. **38**(2), 261–299 (2012)
18. Sinha, M., Agarwal, N., Dasgupta, T.: Relation aware attention model for uncertainty detection in text. In: Proceedings of the ACM/IEEE Joint Conference on Digital Libraries in 2020, pp. 437–440 (2020)
19. Sinha, M., Dasgupta, T.: Detecting uncertainty in text using multi-channel CNN-TreeBiLSTM Network. In: Companion Proceedings of the Web Conference 2020, pp. 92–93 (2020)
20. Szarvas, G., Vincze, V., Farkas, R., Móra, G., Gurevych, I.: Cross-genre and cross-domain detection of semantic uncertainty. Comput. Linguist. **38**(2), 335–367 (2012)
21. Theil, C.K., Štajner, S., Stuckenschmidt, H.: Word embeddings-based uncertainty detection in financial disclosures. In: Proceedings of the 1st Workshop on Economics and Natural Language Processing, pp. 32–37 (2018)
22. Verboven, K., Carlier, M., Dumolyn, J.: A short manual to the art of prosopography. In: Prosopography Approaches and Applications. A Handbook, pp. 35–70. Unit for Prosopographical Research (Linacre College) (2007)

23. Vincze, V.: Uncertainty detection in Hungarian texts. In: Proceedings of COLING 2014. The 25th International Conference on Computational Linguistics: Technical Papers, pp. 1844–1853 (2014)
24. Yang, H., De Roeck, A., Gervasi, V., Willis, A., Nuseibeh, B.: Speculative requirements: automatic detection of uncertainty in natural language requirements. In: 2012 20th IEEE International Requirements Engineering Conference (RE), pp. 11–20. IEEE (2012)

Revisiting the Past to Reinvent the Future: Topic Modeling with Single Mode Factorization

Normand Peladeau[✉] [iD]

Provalis Research, Montreal, Canada
npeladeau@provalisresearch.com

Abstract. This paper proposes reexamining ancestors of modern topic modeling technique that seem to have been forgotten. We present an experiment where results obtained using six contemporary techniques are compared with a factorization technique developed in the early sixties and a contemporary adaptation of it based on non-negative matrix factorization. Results on internal and external coherence as well as topic diversity suggest that extracting topics by applying factorization methods on a word-by-word correlation matrix computed on documents segmented into smaller contextual windows produces topics that are clearly more coherent and show higher diversity than other topic modeling techniques using term-document matrices.

Keywords: Topic modeling · Topic coherence · Topic diversity · Latent semantic analysis · Matrix factorization

1 Introduction

Topic Modeling (TM) is an unsupervised machine learning technique that is used to extract the hidden semantic structure in a collection of documents in the form of topics. Those topics are typically represented as lists of words displayed in descending order of their relevance or probability. Initially developed in computer science for applications in information sciences, this technique has been adopted by many researchers in other disciplines, including biology and medicine, social sciences and the digital humanities, in crime analysis, communication studies, among others [8, 17].

Many authors will trace the origin of TM back to David Blei's paper [5] on Latent Dirichlet Allocation (LDA). While there have been many alternatives or extensions to LDA proposed by researchers in computer and information sciences, it remains the de facto standard against which those extensions are being measured. More recent contributions are attempting to address limitations of LDA by improving its computational efficiency or scalability, increasing its predictive value, or reducing its variability.

However, the question of the interpretability of the extracted topics has become an important focus of research in this area. It is no longer sufficient to obtain models that improve document retrieval or classification, it is also important for those topics to be easily interpreted by humans. This preoccupation with coherence has its origin from the observation that some of the topics obtained through TM techniques are difficult

P. Rosso et al. (Eds.): NLDB 2022, LNCS 13286, pp. 86–97, 2022.
https://doi.org/10.1007/978-3-031-08473-7_8

to interpret, containing words that seem disparate, what we may call "junk topics", or that some relatively coherent topics may still contain unrelated words, creating "contaminated topics". For [4], the fact that most TM techniques still rely on a bag-of-words representation of documents, ignoring the semantic and syntactic relationship of those words within the document, may explain the low coherence of some of the obtained solutions. Such a weakness is also likely at the origin of efforts to reintroduce semantic or syntactic information into TM methods by the integration of language model techniques [4, 26] or some forms of word-embedding [11] computed either on the learning dataset or on an external corpus.

It is our position that such an imperfect initial representation of the word semantics may be partly attributed to the almost universal practice of using a term-by-document matrix as the initial input for topic extraction. Its conventional usage can be traced back to Latent Semantic Indexing (LSI) [10]. A careful reading of this paper is needed to understand the rationale at the origin of this practice. It also allows the reader to be reminded of the pioneering works on automatic indexing and retrieval methods using clustering, latent class analysis, and especially the work of Borko [6, 7] using factor analysis (FA), which, by the nature of its results, can be considered an ancestor of modern TM techniques. None of those precursors used term-by-document matrices but started either with document-by-document similarity or term-by-term correlation matrices. LSI was proposing to move beyond the separate analysis of document similarities or term co-occurrences by explicitly representing both terms and documents in a single space of choosable dimensionality. By applying single value decomposition on a term-by-document, one obtains in a single operation three matrices: a term-by-topic matrix allowing one to assess how terms are related to each topic, a topic-by-topic matrix quantifying how topics relate to one another, and a topic-by-document matrix that characterizes the distribution of the various topics in all documents. Such an approach, explicitly named by their authors as a "two-mode factor analysis", positions itself in clear opposition to what we may call "single-mode factorization" (SMF) techniques as performed previously by Borko [6, 7], but also by other researchers in psychology [15, 18], communications [16] and literary studies [24, 25]. For an insightful review of the use of factor analysis for topic extraction, see [14].

The LSI paper identifies several shortcomings of prior studies using FA such as the fact that this statistical technique is computationally expensive, that too few dimensions are being extracted, and that extracted factors were characterized using only a few "significant" terms rather than the entire loading vectors. One has to recognize that the last two limits are clearly not inherent to FA itself but to its implementation by Borko. And while we agree that FAs can be computationally expensive, our own experiment suggests that it may still outperform some advanced TM techniques. From a strictly computational standpoint, LSI may be very attractive, yet we are not aware of any comparative study establishing its superiority over prior SMF methods in terms of the quality of the obtained topical categories used for indexation.

Technically speaking, TM using single-mode factor analysis is performed by applying principal component analysis (PCA) on a word-by-word correlation matrix. The obtained factor solution is then transformed using a Varimax orthogonal rotation to increase its interpretability by creating factors that are more independent from each other. It is also important to mention that historically, the correlation matrices used in SMF are rarely derived from word co-occurrence computed at the document level but are obtained instead on smaller units such as pages, paragraphs, or other forms of document segments [18, 24]. Such a practice was based on the observation that analyzing smaller segments of long documents tends to provide better topics. Interestingly, this idea of using a smaller contextual window, whether it is the sentence, the paragraphs, or a window of words, is underlying many of the proposed metrics for assessing topic coherence [1, 20]. It is also an inherent principle of several forms of word embedding and language models, where the context of a word is determined by its surrounding words such as in continuous skip-grams or continuous bag-of-words models. Finally, an obvious benefit from such a procedure, when compared to other topic modeling techniques, is its stability, since this statistical approach is, by nature, non-probabilistic. A recent study [22] comparing TM using factor analysis and LDA found that the former method generates topics viewed by human raters as more coherent than those obtained using LDA.

However, as suggested by [10], factor analysis suffers from scalability issues, and may be time consuming when more than a few thousand vocabulary items are being processed. A more efficient alternative would be to process the computed term-by-term correlation matrix using non-negative matrix factorization (NMF), allowing faster processing and handling of much larger datasets. While NMF has been used as a topic modeling technique [3], its conventional application has consisted of the factorization of the typical term-by-document matrix (see [27] for a notable exception). An SMF version of NMF can be implemented directly on a term-by-term correlation matrix in which negative values are first transformed into zeros. This produces a nonnegative term-by-topic matrix W and a second nonnegative topic-by-term matrix H. Both matrices may then be combined to create a single matrix of k topic weights for each term t using the following formula:

$$\text{Weight}_{tk} = \sqrt{W_{tk} \times H_{kt}}$$

It is important to remember that the obtained weight relates to the probability that such a topic is present in a paragraph rather than in the entire document. While our own single mode implementation of NMF seemed to generate easily interpretable topic solutions, such a variation has never been the subject of a systematic comparison with other TM techniques. The current paper will thus include this single mode variation of NMF along with the more traditional single mode FA version.

2   Experimental Investigation

2.1   Models

This section briefly describes all the TM techniques used in this comparison as well as the settings used for the topic extraction. While several of those methods allow one to integrate pre-trained embedding or other forms of resources from external knowledge base, we enabled this kind of computation solely under the condition that it was performed on the learning dataset. The rationale was that since almost any TM could potentially benefit from such a combination of an external knowledge base, an initial assessment should ideally be performed under a "knowledge poor" condition.

- **Latent Dirichlet Allocation (LDA)** [5] remains the de facto standard against which most TM techniques are still being compared today. We used the Gensim[1] implementation of LDA with alpha set to 50/k and the remaining default parameters.
- **Non-negative matrix factorization (NMF)** [3] is a technique commonly used for extracting topic. While two other TM techniques in the current study make use of NMF as part of their analytics process, the current designation will be restricted to the application of NMF on a term-by-document matrix. Gensim[1] implementation of NMF was used with default settings.
- The **Biterm** technique [27] also uses NMF but on a term-by-term association matrix obtained by computing the cosine similarity on the vectors of a matrix of positive point mutual information measures. Its relative similarity with the proposed SMF version justifies its inclusion in this experiment. The method was implemented using the Bitermplus python package[2] with the default parameters.
- **ProdLDA** is a neural network model based on a black-box autoencoding variational Bayes method. It uses a product of experts, rather than a mixture of multinomials to extract topics. According to [26], ProdLDA consistently produces more coherent topics than LDA. We used the AVITM implementation through the OCTIS python library.[3]
- **Embedded Topic Model (ETM)** [11] combines word-embedding and topic modeling. Topic proportions are derived using an amortized variational inference algorithm. The embeddings were learned on each dataset using a continuous bag-of-words approach. We used the ETM original implementation through the OCTIS python library (see Footnote 3).
- **Combined TM (CTM)** uses a Bidirectional Encoder Representations from Transformer (BERT) as an extension to the neural network model of ProdLDA in order to produce more coherent and more diverse topics [4]. The sentence embedding was trained directly on each dataset using paraphrase-distilroberta-base-v1.[4]
- **SM-FA** is a single mode factor analysis applying principal component analysis on correlation matrices derived from word co-occurrences within paragraphs [22]. The obtained results are then transformed using a Varimax orthogonal rotation. WordStat[5] implementation of this technique was used with default settings.
- **SM-NMF** consists of applying non-negative matrix factorization on the same correlation matrix as the one used for SM-FA after transforming all negative correlations to zero. WordStat (see Footnote 5) implementation was used with default settings.

2.2 Datasets

Three datasets have been chosen for comparing modeling techniques. The **20 Newsgroups** corpus consisted of 18,199 messages from which headers, footers, and quotations have been removed. The two additional datasets were chosen in an attempt to reflect

---

[1] https://radimrehurek.com/gensim/.

[2] https://pypi.org/project/bitermplus/.

[3] https://github.com/MIND-Lab/OCTIS.

[4] https://github.com/MilaNLProc/contextualized-topic-models.

[5] https://provalisresearch.com/products/content-analysis-software/.

typical conditions of applications of TM by social scientists and data scientists working in a business or commercial environment.[6] The **Airline Reviews** dataset consisted of 50,426 reviews of airline trips posted by travelers between 2016 and 2019 on the Trip Advisor web site. Finally, the much smaller **Election 2008** dataset consists of 243 political speeches delivered by six Democrats and four Republican candidates during the 2008 US Presidential race. Those speeches vary a lot in length with an average of 2,390 words per speech. They also vary a lot in the number of issues being raised and discussed. For all three corpora, we removed stop words and non-alphabetic characters and set the vocabulary for the topic extraction task to the 2000 most frequent words. No stemming or lemmatization was applied.

For the 20 Newsgroups and the Airline Reviews datasets, 20 and 100 topics were extracted using all eight techniques. For the Election 2008 dataset, we made the decision to extract 20 and 50 topics, based on the much smaller size of the corpus as well as the challenges it represented for some techniques to extract that many topics on such a small dataset. To take into account the topic variability of probabilistic TM models, we averaged results over five runs, with the exception of SM-FA, this non-probabilistic method yielding identical topic solutions every time.

2.3 Metrics

Each topic solution was assessed on two dimensions: diversity and coherence. Topic diversity was measured by computing the proportion of unique terms over the total possible number of top 10 terms for a topic solution. Better topic solutions should show higher proportions of unique terms in their solution. For measuring external topic coherence, a total of six metrics were selected. Each of them was computed using the Palmetto[7] application using Wikipedia as the reference corpus.

- C_{UMass} – Proposed by [19], this metric measures coherence by computing for the top-n words of each topic the sum of the conditional probability of a pair of words being drawn randomly from the same document. It relies on the assumption that a coherent topic will extract words that tend to occur in the same documents. It has been found to correlate with human evaluation scores on an intrusion test.
- C_{UCI} – Proposed by [20], this metric uses a sliding window of 10 words over the entire Wikipedia corpus to obtain the co-occurrence of all word pairs in a topic top-n words and computed the PMI on those co-occurrences.
- C_{NPMI} and C_A - Using Wikipedia as the external reference corpus, [1] found that computing a normalized version of the pointwise mutual information (NPMI) on a window ± 5 words around topic words, yield higher correlations to human judgments than the C_{UCI} or C_{UMass}. They also found that computing the distributional similarity between the top-n words in a topic using the cosine measure on the computed NPMI metric, further increased this correlation. This second metric will be referred as the C_A metric.

---

[6] The two additional datasets are available from https://provalisresearch.com/tm/datasets.zip.

[7] https://github.com/dice-group/Palmetto.

- C_V and C_P – Proposed by [23], the C_V combines the indirect cosine measure with the NPMI computed on a sliding window of 110 words and C_P which measures co-occurrence using the Fitelson's confirmation measure compute on a sliding window of 70 words. Both metrics were found to outperform other existing measures of coherence at predicting human ratings of topic coherence.

A recent review [12] suggests that existing coherence metrics may lack the necessary robustness to measure interpretability or to inform topic model selection. They found that the choice of a metric and aggregation method may favor some TM techniques while other metrics or aggregation methods will declare other techniques as winners. [13] also point that some metrics may be inappropriate for assessing newer topic models relying on neural networks or when analyzing specialized collections such as Twitter data. Until further investigation is done on the relative values of various metrics, we believe it would be unwise to select just a few coherence metrics.

Three of those metrics were also computed on the training dataset as measures of internal coherence: the C_{UMass}, the C_{UCI} and the C_{NPMI}. Those last two were computed on a Boolean contextual window of ± 10 words. The decision to use a contextual window twice as large as originally proposed [1] is justified by the fact that this computation was performed on unprocessed documents while computation of those metrics by other authors have been performed on transformed documents from which stop words have been removed.

3   Experimental Results

For each technique, except one, we computed average diversity and coherence scores across all 30 experiments (3 datasets $\times$ 2 sizes $\times$ 5 runs). The SM-FA being a deterministic statistical approach to TM yielding identical results at every run, averaging scores on a single run in all six conditions (3 datasets $\times$ 2 sizes) was performed. Variations between conditions will be mentioned when needed.

Taking into account topic diversity while interpreting topic coherence is crucial since some topic solutions may be highly coherent yet with a very limited number of words, typically frequent ones, appearing in many topics. Figure 1 positions all eight methods on scatterplots with topic diversity on the horizontal axis, going from the least diverse topic solution on the left to the most diverse on the right. Internal coherence scores are positioned on the vertical axis. The best performing models should thus be located in the upper right corner of the graphs. Because most coherence metrics are expressed on non-comparable scales, their scores have been standardized and are thus expressed in standard deviations from the overall mean. Scales of all plots have also been standardized facilitating comparisons across coherence metrics.

If we focus for now solely on the position on the horizontal axes, which represents topic diversity, it clearly shows that the two proposed SMF techniques produce topic models with the highest diversity scores reaching an average proportion of 0.91 and 0.92 unique terms. LDA comes third with an average score of 0.69, while ETM takes the last position with a diversity score of only 0.26. The observed poor diversity of this method seems to confirm prior observation made by [4].

Close examination of models with low diversity scores reveals two distinct patterns. For the 100 topic solutions on the Airline Reviews dataset, the lack of diversity of Biterm ($d = 0.15$) is caused by the inclusion of high-frequency words in multiple topics. For example, the word "flight" is found in 99% of the topics, "service" in 65%, "time" in 59%, and so on. While ETM ($d = 0.11$) also suffers from such an issue, the problem is exacerbated by the presence of many topics composed by the exact same top 10 words, often presented in different orders. In the worst case, a collection of the exact 10 words was used in seven of the topics in a model.

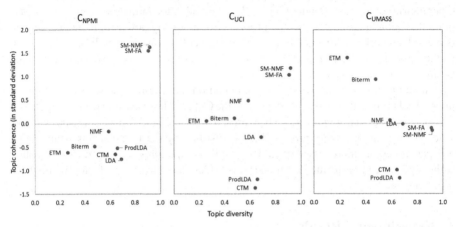

Fig. 1. Internal topic coherence by topic diversity for 8 topic modeling techniques

If we now consider the position on the vertical axes, we can see that both C_{NPMI} and C_{UCI} scores clearly favor the two SMF techniques, positioning them clearly far from the other, in the upper-right corner of the graphs. The high score on C_{NPMI} is consistent under all experimental conditions, varying between 1.38 and 1.73 standard deviations above the mean. Results on the C_{UCI} while not as high are also quite consistent with scores between 0.60 to 1.66 standard deviations above the mean. In fact, the two SMF methods occupy the first top two positions for 5 of the 6 experiments. The C_{umass} metric draws quite a different picture, positioning these two methods below the mean, clearly favoring models with low diversity scores.

An objection that may be raised with the use of the training set as the source to compute topic coherence is that it may simply measure the tendency of some TM techniques to overfit the data used for the learning. One must also remember that the SMF modeling techniques we proposed has been implemented on documents segmented into paragraphs rather than on the full documents. This may very well explain why the proposed two variations perform consistently better on the C_{NPMI} and C_{UCI} metrics, which rely on the analysis of a small contextual window. It would also be consistent with the mixed results obtained on the C_{UMass} that is based instead on cooccurrence at the document level. For those reasons, the use of an external source to validate the coherence, such as Wikipedia, should theoretically provide a more independent benchmark for assessing topic coherence.

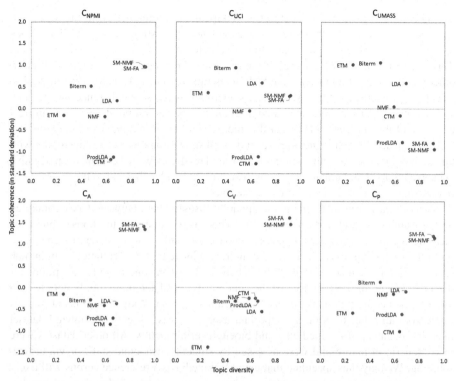

Fig. 2. External topic coherence by topic diversity for 8 topic modeling techniques

Figure 2 presents the scores obtained on all six external coherence measures computed on Wikipedia pages. It allows us to reject the overfitting hypothesis and confirm instead the previous findings that SMF techniques produce more coherent topics, occupying the first and second positions on four of the six metrics, namely, the C_{NPMI}, the C_A, the C_V, and C_P. Again, scores on the C_{UMass} contradict results from other metrics, positioning the two SMF methods as the least coherent while clearly favoring the methods with the lowest diversity scores. If the C_{UCI} metric computed internally clearly favors the two SMF modeling techniques, it is less clear when the same metric is computed using Wikipedia as the reference corpus. They are still positioned above the mean with average scores of 0.27 and 0.30 standard deviation, yet they are surpassed by three techniques, namely ETM, Biterm, and LDA. While, their relative scores remain positive for the 20 Newsgroups and the Election 2008 datasets, results obtained on the Airline Reviews data contradict those obtained on the learning dataset itself. Under this condition, both SMF methods achieved coherence scores well above all other ones, yet they perform poorly when computed on Wikipedia, with values always below the mean, ranging from -0.70 to -0.08. While one could point out the poor diversity of some models achieving high scores on this metric (e.g., Biterm and ETM), this divergence of conclusion when computing C_{UCI} internally or externally need further investigation.

Whether using the training dataset or Wikipedia as a reference corpus to assess the coherence of topic solutions, there is strong evidence suggesting that both SMF methods produce more coherent topics than other TM techniques included in this comparison. This is true for almost all coherence metrics except for the C_{UMass} which contradicts other results, suggesting instead that SMF techniques produce the least coherent topics. This C_{UMass} is still used in TM studies, sometimes as the sole coherence metric [11], so it is important to address such a contradiction. One should point out that empirical evidence of the correlation between this metric and human judgments of coherence is inconsistent at best. While the original study [19] shows that it correlates positively with human judgment scores, other studies have found relatively weak [23] and even negative [1] correlations with human judgments. The current results also add to the necessity of reassessing its values as a measure of coherence.

A more intriguing outcome is the apparent disagreement between C_{UCI} computed on the training dataset and on Wikipedia. There is a propensity to choose coherence measures computed on external knowledge bases. A study [23] often mentioned to support this, found that, overall, coherence metrics achieve higher correlation with human ratings when computed on Wikipedia. There is, however, one notable exception: for the TREC-Genomic dataset, four of the coherences correlated more highly with human ratings when computed on the dataset itself rather than on Wikipedia. This dataset differed from all other ones on an important aspect: it was a highly specialized dataset rated by members of the medicine and bioengineering faculty. All other datasets were more generic in nature and were assessed by students, academic staff, or via crowd-sourcing. We may thus speculate that using Wikipedia as a reference corpus will likely favor the identification of more generic topics or areas of knowledge that are familiar to most people but may fail to account for the specificity of a specialized corpus. To test this hypothesis, we ranked all 4,320 topics obtained on Airline Reviews, the most specialized dataset in our experiment, on both versions of the C_{UCI}. Then, we identified topics achieving very high scores when computed internally, but very low scores when computed on Wikipedia. Table 1 shows five topics from the same SM-FA model with the highest differences in raking.

Table 1. Ranking of five topics on internal and external C_{uci} coherence (out of 4,320 topics)

Topic words	Internal	External
toothbrush socks mask toothpaste plugs eye ear blanket kit pack	11th	4,012th
resort rep inclusive transat vacation reps package sunwing vacations mexico	55th	4,220th
blanket pillow neck mask headphones eye option cushion priority earphones	64th	4,261st
lighting mood dreamliner windows dark boeing window wall cool lights	116th	3,915th
pilot weather turbulence snow captain storm conditions landing delay bumpy	195th	3,580th

The first topic is a comprehensive description of the content of the vanity kit one gets when traveling first-class on a long-haul flight. It received the 11th highest internal coherence score but ranks 4012th when assessed using Wikipedia. The second one makes references to two Canadian airline companies (Air Transat and Sunwing) offering charter flights to vacation destinations and all-inclusive vacation packages. The third one concerns elements involved in the attempt to sleep during a night flight. The fourth topic perfectly reflects the passenger's impression of the LED lighting system and electronic window shades of the Boeing Dreamliner as described in a Wired article [21]. As for the fifth one, we are confident most travelers will have no problem making sense of it. On the other end of the spectrum, topics with high external coherence scores but low internal scores were characterized by the presence of the same high-frequency words such as airlines, flight, air, service, etc. Such examples seem to confirm that computing coherence metrics using an external knowledge base such as Wikipedia may fail to grab part of the specificity of the text corpus being analyzed. It also reminds us that coherence measures can hardly be considered by themselves without taking into account other metrics such as topic diversity or word frequency.

4   Conclusion

The significant influence of the original LSI paper [10] on subsequent research in information sciences may have given birth to a sort of "scientific paradigm" that had a lasting influence on the way topic modeling is being studied today. The idea to use a term-by-document matrix as the starting point for extracting topics and indexing documents in a single operation may have been justified by the objective of improving the efficiency of the indexing and retrieval of documents. Their use of the notion of "dual-mode factor analysis" positioned their work as a better alternative to prior usage of factor analysis in information sciences [6, 7]. However, the growing popularity of TM and its application outside the realm of information science for either descriptive, predictive, or comparative purposes amplify the relevance of topic coherence. The seductive idea behind LSI of extracting topics and indexing documents in a single step is not as relevant if it is done at the cost of less comprehensible topics.

In this regard, results of our study suggest that extracting topics by applying factorization methods on a word-by-word correlation matrix computed on documents segmented into smaller contextual windows produces topics that are more coherent and show higher diversity than many popular topic modeling techniques. Furthermore, this method seems to yield consistently better results whether it is being used to analyze relatively small numbers of long documents, as in the Elections 2008 dataset or large quantities of short comments, as in the Airline Reviews dataset.

We just hope that this paper will encourage researchers to revisit methods such as SMF that may have been forgotten or neglected, put them to the test and, if they are found to perform as well as in this present study, further develop them. Our proposal should not be considered as a nostalgic call for the use of old techniques, but as a guide for new research opportunities to improve on those techniques using modern approaches of machine learning and natural language processing. The methods we proposed already share a lot of similarities with current approaches in the development of language models or word-embedding and are also close in design to the research on the development of coherence metrics, so we are confident of the potential of such combinations for improving the way we do topic modeling today.

We should also mention potential limits of the current paper. In most cases, we used default options for each TM package. With a few exceptions, no systematic attempt has been made to optimize hyperparameters for the methods we tested. In some cases, we did test different settings when we expected a better performance could be achieved and selected those that appeared to produce better results. For this reason, the current comparison may be seen more as a baseline representative of what one would get when applying existing topic models with only a few minor adjustments.

As mentioned before, our focus was on two dimensions of topic models: coherence and diversity. While we found SMF techniques to be much more stable (not presented here), we didn't test other properties such as topic significance [2], topic coverage, or model perplexity. We also focused in this paper on "knowledge poor" modeling techniques relying exclusively on the analysis of the training dataset without the assistance of external linguistic or semantic resources such as pre-trained word-embedding or language models, even if some of the TM methods we tested did provide such capabilities. Those "knowledge rich" approaches consist of some forms of blending of co-occurrence analysis on the training dataset with data obtained from a model pretrained on external resources. For this reason, we thought that achieving good quality topic solutions on the text corpus currently under investigation could only contribute positively to such a combination. A comparison of SMF techniques with those "knowledge-rich" topic modeling techniques could be the object of such a study. We also believe that a closer examination of the properties and behavior of various topic coherence measures is warranted. Using different metrics sometimes yields contradicting conclusions at the topic as well as at the method level. A more in-depth qualitative analysis of topics scoring high on some measures but low on other ones, like we did for the two C_{UCI} metrics may provide some insights on their respective values.

References

1. Aletras, N., Stevenson, M.: Evaluating topic coherence using distributional semantics. In: IWCS, vol. 13, pp. 13–22 (2013)
2. AlSumait, L., Barbará, D., Gentle, J., Domeniconi, C.: Topic significance ranking of LDA generative models. In: Buntine, W., Grobelnik, M., Mladenić, D., Shawe-Taylor, J. (eds.) ECML PKDD 2009. LNCS (LNAI), vol. 5781, pp. 67–82. Springer, Heidelberg (2009). https://doi.org/10.1007/978-3-642-04180-8_22
3. Arora, S., Ge, R., Moitra, A.: Learning topic models - going beyond SVD. In: IEEE 53rd Annual Symposium on Foundations of Computer Science, pp. 1–10. IEEE (2012)
4. Bianchi, F., Terragni, S., Hovy, D: Pre-training is a hot topic: contextualized document embeddings improve topic coherence. In: 59th Annual Meeting of the Association for Computational Linguistics and the 11th International Joint Conference on Natural Language Processing (Volume 2: Short Papers), pp. 759–766. ACL (2021)
5. Blei, D.M., Ng, A.Y., Jordan, M.I.: Latent Dirichlet allocation. J. Mach. Learn. Res. 3, 993–1022 (2003)
6. Borko, H.: The construction of an empirically based mathematically derived classification system. In: Proceedings of the Spring Joint Computer Conference, vol. 21, pp. 279–289 (1962)
7. Borko, H., Bernick, M.: Automatic document classification. J. Assoc. Comput. Mach. 10, 151–162 (1963)
8. Boyd-Graber, J.L., Hu, Y., Mimno, D.M.: Applications of topic models. Found. Trends Inf. Retrieval 20(20), 1–154 (2017)

9. Chang, J., Gerrish, S., Wang, C., Boyd-Graber, J.L., Blei, D.M.: Reading tea leaves: how humans interpret topic models. In: Advances in Neural Information Processing Systems, vol. 22, pp. 288–296 (2009)
10. Deerwester, S., Dumais, S.T., Furnas, G.W., Landauer, T.K., Harshman, R.: Indexing by latent semantic analysis. J. Am. Soc. Inf. Sci. **41**(6), 391–407 (1990)
11. Dieng, A.B., Ruiz, F.J.R., Blei, D.M.: Topic modeling in embedding spaces. Trans. Assoc. Comput. Linguist. **8**, 439–453 (2020)
12. Doogan, C., Buntine, W.: Topic model or topic twaddle? Re-evaluating semantic interpretability measures. In: Proceedings of the 2021 Conference of the North American Chapter of the Association for Human Language Technologies, pp. 3824–3848 (2021)
13. Hoyle, A., Goel, P., Hian-Cheong, A., Peskov, D., Boyd-Graber, J., Resnik, P.: Is automated topic model evaluation broken? The incoherence of coherence. In: Advances in Neural Information Processing Systems, vol. 34 (2021)
14. Iker, H.P.: An historical note on the use of word-frequency contiguities in content analysis. Comput. Humanit. **13**(2), 93–98 (1974)
15. Iker, H.P., Harway, N.I.: A computer approach towards the analysis of content. Behav. Sci. **10**(2), 173–183 (1965)
16. Jandt, F.E.: Sources for computer utilization in interpersonal communication instruction and research. Today's Speech **20**(2), 25–31 (1972)
17. Jelodar, H., et al.: Latent Dirichlet allocation (LDA) and topic modeling: models, applications, a survey. Multimedia Tools Appl. **78**(11), 15169–15211 (2018)
18. Klein, R.H., Iker, H.P.: The lack of differentiation between male and female in Schreber's autobiography. J. Abnorm. Psychol. **83**(3), 234–239 (1974)
19. Mimno, D., Wallach, H.M., Talley, E., Leenders, M., McCallum, A.: Optimizing semantic coherence in topic models. In: Proceedings of the 2011 EMNLP Conference, pp. 262–272. ACL (2011)
20. Newman, D., Lau, J.H., Grieser, K., Baldwin, T.: Automatic evaluation of topic coherence. In: Human Language Technologies: 2010 Annual Conference of the North American Chapter of the Association for Computational Linguistics, pp. 100–108. ACL (2010)
21. Paur, J.: Boeing's 787 is as innovative inside and outside. Wired. Conde Nast, 24 December 2009
22. Peladeau, N., Davoodi, E.: Comparison of latent Dirichlet modeling and factor analysis for topic extraction: a lesson of history. In: 51st Hawaii International Conference on System Sciences (HICSS), pp. 615–623. IEEE (2018)
23. Röder, M., Both, A., Hinneburg, A.: Exploring the space of topic coherence measures. In: Proceedings of the 8th ACM International Conference on Web Search and Data Mining. pp. 399–408 (2015)
24. Sainte-Marie, P., Robillard, P., Bratley, P.: An application of principal components analysis to the works of Molière. Comput. Humanit. **7**(3), 131–137 (1973)
25. Sowa, C.A., Sowa, J.F.: Thought clusters in early Greek oral poetry. Comput. Humanit. **8**(3), 131–146 (1972)
26. Srivastava, A., Sutton, C.: Autoencoding variational inference for topic models. In: Proceeding of the 5th International Conference on Learning Representations (2017)
27. Yan, X., Guo, J., Liu, S., Cheng, X., Wang, Y. Learning topics in short texts by non-negative matrix factorization on term correlation matrix. In: SIAM International Conference on Data Mining. Society for Industrial and Applied Mathematics (2013)

Active Few-Shot Learning with FASL

Thomas Müller[1], Guillermo Pérez-Torró[1], Angelo Basile[1,2],
and Marc Franco-Salvador[1(✉)]

[1] Symanto Research, Valencia, Spain
{thomas.mueller,guillermo.perez,angelo.basile,marc.franco}@symanto.com
[2] PRHLT Research Center, Universitat Politècnica de València, Valencia, Spain
https://www.symanto.com

Abstract. Recent advances in natural language processing (NLP) have led to strong text classification models for many tasks. However, still often thousands of examples are needed to train models with good quality. This makes it challenging to quickly develop and deploy new models for real world problems and business needs. Few-shot learning and active learning are two lines of research, aimed at tackling this problem. In this work, we combine both lines into FASL, a platform that allows training text classification models using an iterative and fast process. We investigate which active learning methods work best in our few-shot setup. Additionally, we develop a model to predict when to stop annotating. This is relevant as in a few-shot setup we do not have access to a large validation set.

Keywords: Few-shot learning · Active learning · Siamese networks

1 Introduction

In recent years, deep learning has lead to large improvements on many text classifications tasks. Unfortunately, these models often need thousands of training examples to achieve the quality required for real world applications. Two lines of research aim at reducing the number of instances required to train such models: Few-shot learning and active learning.

Few-shot learning (FSL) is the problem of learning classifiers with only few training examples. Recently, models based on natural language inference (NLI) [4] have been proposed as a strong backbone for this task [10,30–32]. The idea is to use an NLI model to predict whether a textual premise (input text) entails a textual hypothesis (label description) in a logical sense. For instance, *"I am fully satisfied and would recommend this product to others"* implies *"This is a good product"*. NLI models usually rely on cross attention which makes them slow at inference time and fine-tuning them often involves updating hundreds of millions of parameters or more. Label tuning (LT) [20] addresses these shortcomings using Siamese Networks trained on NLI datasets to embed the input text and label description into a common vector space. Tuning only the label embeddings yields a competitive and scalable FSL mechanism as the Siamese Network encoder can be shared among different tasks.

© The Author(s), under exclusive license to Springer Nature Switzerland AG 2022
P. Rosso et al. (Eds.): NLDB 2022, LNCS 13286, pp. 98–110, 2022.
https://doi.org/10.1007/978-3-031-08473-7_9

Active learning (AL) [28] on the other hand attempts to reduce the data needs of a model by iteratively selecting the most useful instances. We discuss a number of AL methods in Sect. 2.1. Traditional AL starts by training an initial model on a seed set of randomly selected instances. In most related work, this seed set is composed of at least 1,000 labeled instances. This sparks the question whether the standard AL methods work in a few-shot setting.

A critical question in FSL is when to stop adding more annotated examples. The user usually does not have access to a large validation set which makes it hard to estimate the current model performance. To aid the user we propose to estimate the normalized test F1 on unseen test data. We use a random forest regressor (RFR) [11] that provides a performance estimate even when no test data is available.

FASL is a platform for active few-shot learning that integrates these ideas. It implements LT as an efficient FSL model together with various AL methods and the RFR as a way to monitor model quality. We also integrate a user interface (UI) that eases the interaction between human annotator and model and makes FASL accessible to non-experts.

We run a large study on AL methods for FSL, where we evaluate a range of AL methods on 6 different text classification datasets in 3 different languages. We find that AL methods do not yield strong improvements over a random baseline when applied to datasets with balanced label distributions. However, experiments on modified datasets with a skewed label distributions as well as naturally unbalanced datasets show the value of AL methods such as *margin sampling* [14]. Additionally, we look into performance prediction and find that a RFR outperforms stopping after a fixed number of steps. Finally, we integrate all these steps into a single uniform platform: FASL.

2   Methods

2.1   Active Learning Methods

Uncertainty sampling [14] is a framework where the most informative instances are selected using a measure of uncertainty. Here we review some approaches extensively used in the literature [28]. We include it in three variants, where we select the instance that maximizes the corresponding expression:

- **Least Confidence**: With $\hat{y}$ as the most probable class: $-P(\hat{y} \mid x)$
- **Margin**: with $\hat{y}_i$ as ith most probable class: $-[P(\hat{y}_1 \mid x) - P(\hat{y}_2 \mid x)]$
- **Entropy**: $H(Y) = -\sum_j P(y_j \mid x) \log P(y_j \mid x)$

Where $P(Y \mid X)$ denotes the model posterior. While *uncertainty sampling* depends on the model output, *diversity sampling* relies on the input representation space [5]. One approach [21] is to cluster the instances and use the cluster centroids as a heterogeneous instance sample. We experiment with three different methods: K-medoids [22], K-means [16] and agglomerative single-link clustering

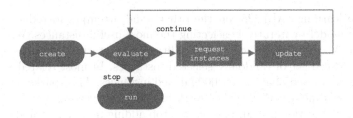

Fig. 1. FASL API diagram.

(AC). K-medoids directly finds cluster centroids which are real data points. For the others, we select the instance closest to the centroid.

Other research lines have explored different ways of combining both approaches. We adapt a two steps process used in computer vision [3]. First, we cluster the embedded instances and then sample from each group the instance that maximizes one of the uncertainty measures presented above. We also implemented contrastive active learning (CAL) [19]. CAL starts with a small labeled seed set and finds k labeled neighbors for each data point in the unlabeled pool. It then selects the examples with the highest average Kullback-Leibler divergence w.r.t their neighborhood.

2.2 Few-Shot Learning Models

We experiment with two FSL models. The first model uses the zero-shot approach for Siamese networks and label tuning (LT) [20]. We encode the input text and a label description – a text representing the label – into a common vector space using a pre-trained text embedding model.

In this work, we use Sentence Transformers [24] and, in particular, *paraphrase-multilingual-mpnet-base-v2*[1] a multilingual model based on *roberta XLM* [15]. The dot-product is then used to compute a score between input and label embeddings. LT consists in fine-tuning only the label embeddings using a cross-entropy objective applied to the similarity matrix of training examples and labels. This approach has three major advantages: (i) training is fast as the text embeddings can be pre-computed and thus the model just needs to be run once. As only the label embeddings are fine-tuned (ii) the resulting model is small and (iii) the text encoder can be shared between many different tasks. This allows for fast training and scalable deployment.

The second model is a simple logistic regression (LR) model. We use the implementation of *scikit-learn* [23]. As feature representation of the text instances we use the same text embeddings as above. In the zero-shot case, we train exclusively on the label description.

---

[1] https://tinyurl.com/pp-ml-mpnet.

2.3   System Design and User Interface

We implement the AL platform as a REST API with a web frontend. Figure 1 shows the API flow. The Appendix contains screenshots of the UI.

The user first creates a new model (create) by selecting the dataset and label set and label descriptions to use as well as the model type. They can then upload a collection of labeled examples that are used to train the initial model. If no examples are provided the initial model is a zero-shot model.

Afterwards the user can either request instances (request instances) for labeling or run model inference as discussed below. Labeling requires selecting one of the implemented AL methods. Internally the platform annotates the entire unlabeled dataset with new model predictions. The bottleneck is usually the embedding of the input texts using the underlying embedding model. These embeddings are cached to speed up future iterations. Once the instances have been selected, they are shown in the UI. The user now annotates all or a subset of the instances. Optionally, they can reveal the annotation of the current model to ease the annotation work. However, instance predictions are not shown by default to avoid biasing the annotator.

The user can now upload the instances (update) to the platform which results in retraining the underlying few-shot model. At this point, the user can continue to iterate on the model by requesting more instances. When the user is satisfied with the current model they can call model inference on a set of instances (run).

2.4   Performance Prediction

A critical question is how the user knows when to stop annotating (evaluate). To ease their decision making, we add a number of metrics that can be computed even when no test instances is available, which is typically the case in FSL. In particular, we implemented cross-validation on the labeled instances and various metrics that do not require any labels. We collect a random sample T of 1,000 unlabeled training instances. After every AL iteration i we assign the current model distribution $P_i(Y \mid X)$ to these instances. We then define metrics that are computed for every instance and averaged over the entire sample:

- **Negative Entropy**: $-H_i(Y) = \sum_j P_i(y_j \mid x) \log P_i(y_j \mid x)$
- **Max Prob**: $P_i(\hat{y} \mid x)$, with $\hat{y}_i$ as the most probable class
- **Margin**: $[P_i(\hat{y}_{i,1} \mid x) - P_i(\hat{y}_{i,2} \mid x)]$, with $\hat{y}_{i,k}$ as kth most probable class
- **Negative Update Rate**: $\delta(\hat{y}_{i-1}(x), \hat{y}_i(x))$, with δ as the Kronecker delta
- **Negative Kullback-Leibler divergence**: $-D_{\mathrm{KL}}(P_i \parallel P_{i-1})$

Entropy, max prob and *margin* are based on the uncertainty measure used in AL. The intuition is that the uncertainty of the model is reduced and converges as the model is trained. The *update rate* denotes the relative number of instances with a different model prediction as in the previous iteration. Again we assume that this rate lowers and converges as the model training converges. The *KL divergence* provides a more sensitive version of the update rate that considers the entire label distribution.

We also experiment with combining these signals in a random forest regressor (RFR) [11]. For every iteration i the model predicts the normalized test F1. In general, it is hard to predict the true F1 for an unknown classification problem and dataset without even knowing the test set. Therefore, we normalize all target test F1 curves by dividing by their maximum value (Fig. 3). Intuitively, the RFR tells us how much of the performance that we will ever reach on this task we have reached so far.

The feature set of the model consists of a few base features such as the number of instances the model has been trained with, the AL method used and the number of labels. Additionally, for each of the metrics above, we add the value at the current iteration i as well as of a history of the last $h = 5$ iterations.

3 Related Work

Active Learning Methods. We evaluate AL methods that have been reported to give strong results in the literature. Within *uncertainty sampling, margin sampling* has been found to out-perform other methods also for modern model architectures [18,27]. Regarding methods that combine *uncertainty* and *diversity sampling*, CAL [19] has been reported to give consistently better results than BADGE [1] and ALPS [33] on a range of datasets. A line of research that we exclude are Bayesian approaches such as BALD [12], because the requirement of a model ensemble makes them computationally inefficient.

Few-Shot Learning with Label Tuning. Our work differs from much of the related work in that we use a particular model and training regimen: label tuning (LT) [20]. LT is an approach that only tunes a relative small set of parameters, while the underlying Siamese Network model [24] remains unchanged. This makes training fast and deployment scalable. More details are given in Sect. 2.2.

Cold Start. Cold start refers to the zero-shot case where we start without any training examples. Most studies [1,19] do not work in this setup and start with a seed set of 100 to several thousand labeled examples. Some work [8,18,27] uses few-shot ranges of less than thousand training examples but still uses a seed set. One study [33] approaches a zero-shot setting without an initial seed set but it differs from our work in model architecture and training regimen.

Balanced and Unbalanced Datasets. Some studies have pointed out inconsistencies on how AL algorithms behave across different models or datasets [17]. It is further known in the scientific community that AL often does not out-perform random selection when the label distribution is balanced.[2] There is work [6] that focuses on unbalanced datasets but not with a cold start scenario. To fill this gap, we run a large study on AL in the under-researched few-shot-with-cold-start scenario, looking into both balanced and unbalanced datasets.

---

[2] https://tinyurl.com/fasl-community.

Table 1. Dataset statistics. train and test sizes of the splits. $|L|$ is the cardinality of the label set L. U quantifies the uniformness: $\sum_{l \in L} \left| f(l) - \frac{1}{|L|} \right|$, where $f(l)$ is the relative frequency of label l. $U = 0$ indicates that the data is distributed uniformly. Note that the generic datasets are balanced while the others are skewed.

	Dataset	Train	Test	$|L|$	$U_\%$
Generic	gnad [2]	9,245	1,028	9	34.4
	AG-news [9]	120,000	7,600	4	0.0
	hqa [29]	4,023	2,742	6	2.8
	azn-de [13]	205,000	5,000	5	0.0
	azn-en	205,000	5,000	5	0.0
	azn-es	205,000	5,000	5	0.0
Unbalanced	gnad	3,307	370	9	92.9
	AG-news	56,250	3,563	4	60.0
	hqa	1,373	927	6	82.9
	azn-de	79,438	1,938	5	74.8
	azn-en	79,438	1,938	5	74.8
	azn-es	79,438	1,938	5	74.8
Offense	hate [7]	8,703	2,000	2	77.8
	solid [25]	1,887	2,000	2	45.6

4 Experimental Setup

We compare a number of active learning models on a wide range of datasets.

4.1 Datasets

Generic Datasets. We run experiments on 4 generic text classification datasets in 3 different languages. AG News (AG-news) [9] and GNAD (gnad) [2] are news topic classification tasks in English and German, respectively. Head QA (hqa) [29] is a Spanish catalogue of questions in a health domain that are grouped into categories such as medicine, biology and pharmacy. Amazon Reviews (azn) [13] is a large corpus of product reviews with a 5-star rating in multiple languages. Here we use the English, Spanish and German portion.

Unbalanced Datasets. All of these datasets have a relatively even label distribution. To investigate the performance of AL in a more difficult setup, we also create a version of each dataset where we enforce a label distribution with exponential decay. We implement this by down-sampling some of the labels, without replacement. In particular, we use the adjusted frequency $n'(y) = n(\hat{y})^{-2 \cdot \text{rank}(y)}$, where $n(y)$ is the original frequency of label y, $\hat{y}$ is the most frequent label and rank(y) is the frequency rank with rank$(\hat{y}) = 0$.

Offensive Language Datasets. We also evaluate on the Semi-Supervised Offensive Language Identification Dataset (solid) [25] and HateSpeech 2018 (hate) [7]. These dataset are naturally unbalanced and thus suited for AL experiments.

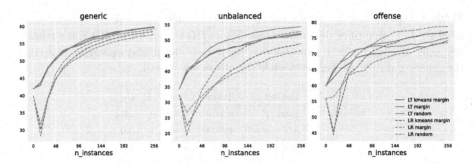

Fig. 2. Average test macro F1 score on the generic, unbalanced and offensive datasets. LT and LR denote label tuning and logistic regression, respectively.

Table 1 provides statistics on the individual datasets. Note that – following other work in few-shot learning [26, 30] – we do not use a validation set. This is because in a real world FSL setup one would also not have access to any kind of evaluation data. As a consequence, we do not tune hyper-parameters in any way and use the defaults of the respective frameworks. The label descriptions we use are taken from the related work [20, 30] and can be found in the Appendix.

4.2   Simulated User Experiments

It is common practice [17] in AL research to simulate the annotation process using labeled datasets. For every batch of selected instances, the gold labels are revealed, simulating the labeling process of a human annotator. Naturally, a simulation is not equivalent to real user studies and certain aspects of the model cannot be evaluated. For example, some methods might retrieve harder or more ambiguous examples that will result in more costly annotation and a higher error rate. Still we chose simulation in our experiments as they are a scalable and reproducible way to compare the quality of a large number of different methods. In all experiments, we start with a zero-shot model that has not been trained on any instances. This sets this work apart from most related work that starts with a model trained on a large seed set of usually thousands of examples. We then iteratively select batches of $k = 16$ instances until we reach a training set size of 256. The instances are selected from the entire training set of the respective dataset. However, to reduce the computational cost we down-sample each training set to at most 20,000 examples.

As FSL with few instances is prone to yield high variance on the test predictions we average all experiments over 10 random trials. We also increase the randomness of the instance selection by first selecting $2k$ instances with the respective method and later sampling k random examples from the initial selection.

5   Results

Active Learning Methods. Figure 2 shows the AL progression averaged over multiple datasets. For improved clarity only the best performing methods are shown.

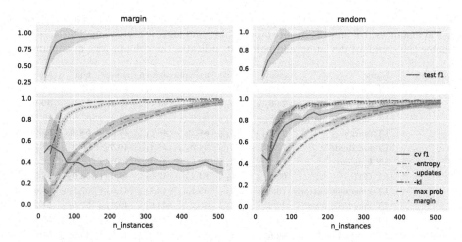

Fig. 3. Training metrics for AG-news for the *random* and margin AL methods. The upper plot shows the true average normalized test F1 (blue curve) as well as the average error of the regressor model (blue shade). The lower plot shows the raw training metrics. (Color figure online)

Plots for the individual dataset can be found in the Appendix. On the comparison between Label Tuning (LT) and Logistic Regression (LR) we find that LT outperforms LR on the generic datasets as well as the unbalanced datasets. On the offense datasets the results are mixed: LR outperforms LT when using *margin*, but is outperformed when using *random*.

With respect to the best performing selection methods we find that *random* and *margin* perform equally well on the generic datasets when LT is used. However, when using LR or facing unbalanced label distributions, we see that *margin* gives better results than *random*. On the offense datasets we also find substantial differences between *margin* and *random*.

Regarding *kmeans-margin*, we see mixed results. In general, *kmeans-margin* does not outperform *random* when LT is used but does so when LR is used. In most experiments *kmeans-margin* is inferior to *margin*.

Table 2 shows results by dataset for the 10 best performing methods. For each set of datasets we include the 10 best performing methods of the best performing model type. We find that uncertainty sampling (such as *margin* and *least-confidence*) methods outperform diversity sampling methods (such as *kmeans* and *kmedoids*). Hybrid methods such as (*CAL* and *kmeans-margin*) perform better than pure diversity sampling methods but are in general behind their counterparts based on importance sampling.

Test F1 Prediction Experiments. We test the F1 regression models with the *margin* and *random* AL method. We trained the LR model with $k = 16$ instances per iteration until reaching a training set size of 512. As for the AL experiments above we repeat every training run 10 times. We then train a prediction model for each of the 12 datasets used in this study (leaving out one dataset at a time).

Table 2. Average test macro F1 score on the generic, unbalanced and offense datasets for 256 instances. LT and LR denote label tuning and logistic regression. The subscript denotes the standard deviation and bold font indicates the column-wise maximum.

Generic	Name	gnad	azn-de	ag-news	azn-en	azn-es	hqa	Mean
	LT random	$72.3_{1.4}$	$\mathbf{47.7_{0.6}}$	$85.3_{1.0}$	$48.3_{1.1}$	$46.4_{1.5}$	$57.7_{1.6}$	59.6
	LT kmeans margin	$74.6_{1.1}$	$47.5_{1.6}$	$86.0_{0.4}$	$46.7_{1.4}$	$45.9_{1.7}$	$58.5_{0.9}$	$\mathbf{59.9}$
	LT kmedoids margin	$73.8_{1.5}$	$45.9_{1.9}$	$86.0_{0.5}$	$48.3_{1.3}$	$46.3_{1.3}$	$57.8_{1.4}$	59.7
	LT margin	$\mathbf{74.9_{1.5}}$	$45.5_{1.3}$	$\mathbf{86.2_{0.7}}$	$46.6_{1.4}$	$46.0_{1.4}$	$\mathbf{58.6_{0.9}}$	59.7
	LT kmedoids	$70.9_{2.5}$	$47.5_{1.2}$	$84.9_{1.0}$	$48.1_{1.1}$	$\mathbf{46.7_{1.6}}$	$56.9_{1.1}$	59.1
	LT k-means	$70.9_{1.2}$	$47.4_{1.7}$	$82.8_{1.2}$	$\mathbf{48.6_{0.9}}$	$46.0_{1.3}$	$55.4_{1.2}$	58.5
	LT CAL	$69.5_{2.3}$	$47.0_{1.4}$	$84.4_{0.7}$	$47.9_{1.6}$	$46.0_{1.1}$	$56.0_{2.4}$	58.5
	LT kmedoids entropy	$73.3_{1.2}$	$41.1_{2.6}$	$85.1_{0.6}$	$43.2_{2.6}$	$41.6_{2.1}$	$57.7_{1.5}$	57.0
	LT kmedoids least	$72.4_{1.3}$	$42.6_{2.0}$	$85.2_{0.5}$	$43.9_{1.8}$	$40.3_{2.6}$	$57.5_{1.3}$	57.0
	LT entropy	$72.1_{2.1}$	$40.2_{2.3}$	$84.7_{0.7}$	$41.3_{2.5}$	$39.9_{2.2}$	$56.5_{1.9}$	55.8
Unbalanced	LT random	$62.6_{6.6}$	$38.8_{2.4}$	$81.9_{1.0}$	$39.2_{2.5}$	$42.5_{3.0}$	$45.5_{2.0}$	51.8
	LT margin	$70.7_{2.2}$	$40.5_{2.4}$	$\mathbf{83.7_{0.8}}$	$41.6_{2.9}$	$41.8_{2.4}$	$47.9_{1.5}$	$\mathbf{54.4}$
	LT CAL	$65.2_{3.4}$	$\mathbf{41.1_{2.9}}$	$82.0_{1.1}$	$\mathbf{43.8_{1.5}}$	$\mathbf{42.9_{2.2}}$	$48.4_{1.8}$	53.9
	LT entropy	$\mathbf{70.8_{1.7}}$	$40.5_{1.9}$	$82.5_{1.3}$	$38.5_{3.1}$	$39.7_{1.4}$	$47.6_{2.7}$	53.2
	LT kmedoids least	$65.4_{2.8}$	$39.2_{2.1}$	$83.2_{0.9}$	$42.5_{2.1}$	$39.2_{3.0}$	$48.0_{1.5}$	52.9
	LT least confidence	$69.1_{2.4}$	$38.4_{2.1}$	$83.5_{0.7}$	$39.7_{2.0}$	$38.8_{1.5}$	$46.4_{2.4}$	52.7
	LT kmedoids margin	$62.0_{5.0}$	$40.5_{3.0}$	$83.6_{0.5}$	$40.8_{1.6}$	$40.6_{2.4}$	$47.4_{1.9}$	52.5
	LT kmedoids entropy	$64.1_{2.9}$	$39.0_{2.6}$	$82.6_{1.0}$	$39.6_{1.8}$	$40.4_{1.1}$	$47.6_{2.4}$	52.2
	LT kmeans margin	$66.8_{5.1}$	$37.4_{2.8}$	$82.4_{1.3}$	$39.9_{2.0}$	$38.8_{1.7}$	$47.0_{1.5}$	52.1
	LT kmedoids	$59.5_{6.8}$	$37.6_{3.3}$	$81.0_{1.6}$	$41.3_{1.7}$	$41.6_{2.4}$	$44.8_{1.6}$	51.0
Offense	Name	Hate	Solid					Mean
	LR random	$61.8_{4.6}$	$85.2_{1.9}$					73.5
	LR margin	$\mathbf{69.1_{1.8}}$	$\mathbf{88.3_{0.6}}$					$\mathbf{78.7}$
	LR least confidence	$68.9_{2.2}$	$87.8_{0.5}$					78.3
	LR entropy	$68.8_{2.2}$	$87.8_{0.6}$					78.3
	LR CAL	$68.3_{2.6}$	$87.2_{0.9}$					77.7
	LR kmedoids least	$66.7_{2.1}$	$87.5_{0.9}$					77.1
	LR kmedoids margin	$66.4_{2.4}$	$87.3_{1.0}$					76.9
	LR kmeans margin	$66.3_{1.9}$	$87.4_{0.9}$					76.8
	LR kmedoids entropy	$66.1_{2.2}$	$87.6_{0.7}$					76.8
	LR kmedoids	$64.8_{3.7}$	$86.8_{0.9}$					75.8

Figure 3 shows the model trained for AG-news. We see that the cross-validation F1 computed on the labeled instances (cv f1) has a similar trend as the test F1 when we use random selection. However, when using AL with margin selection the curve changes drastically. This indicates that CV is not a good evaluation method or stopping criterion when using AL. The uncertainty based metrics (max prob, margin and -entropy) correlate better with test F1 but still behave differently in terms of convergence. Negative KL divergence (-kl) and update rate (-updates) on the other hand show a stronger correlation. With regard to the regressor model we can see that the average error (shaded blue area) is large in the beginning but drops to a negligible amount as we reach the center of the training curve.

Table 3. Results on the prediction of the test F1: Mean squared error (MSE in ‰), Area under curve (AUC), precision ($\mathcal{P}$), recall ($\mathcal{R}$) and $\mathcal{F}_1$ as well as average test F1, error and number of training instances reached at a threshold of $\tau = 0.95$. *baseline i* indicates a baseline that predict 0 for every step $j : j < i$ and 1 otherwise. *base* is the base feature set discussed in Sect. 2.4. *all* uses all features. *forward* and *backward* denote ablation experiments with forward selection from *base* and backward selection from *all*, respectively. h indicates the size of the history and is 5 by default.

Model	MSE	AUC	$\mathcal{F}_1$	$\mathcal{P}$	$\mathcal{R}$	Test F1	err	Instances
Baseline 272	3483.2	86.6	80.4	81.2	**86.8**	94.3	2.0	272.0
Baseline 288	3759.8	86.3	80.0	83.1	84.0	94.6	1.8	288.0
Baseline 304	4038.8	85.9	79.4	85.1	81.1	**95.2**	1.4	304.0
Base	73.5	**97.3**	76.5	83.1	80.1	93.9	2.5	284.6
Forward cv-f1	56.5	96.9	80.7	84.0	83.8	94.5	1.8	**271.8**
Forward -entropy	70.8	96.4	79.1	84.5	80.9	94.3	2.1	283.5
Forward -updates	61.1	96.6	80.2	86.0	81.1	94.7	1.5	284.4
Forward -kl	77.1	96.6	75.0	84.3	76.0	94.3	2.3	295.1
Forward max-prob	59.9	96.9	80.4	86.0	80.4	95.0	1.4	288.1
Forward margin	59.4	96.9	79.2	**86.7**	78.3	95.0	1.4	294.2
All	65.9	97.1	80.4	86.2	81.6	95.1	**1.3**	287.3
All h=0	**56.0**	97.1	79.7	84.7	81.3	94.3	2.0	277.1
All h=1	57.4	97.1	80.7	85.4	82.4	94.5	1.7	276.6
Backward cv-f1	66.7	96.7	80.6	84.7	82.8	94.7	1.7	280.2
Backward -entropy	57.0	97.0	80.7	86.1	81.9	95.0	1.3	285.5
Backward -updates	64.5	97.1	80.4	86.3	81.1	95.0	1.4	288.6
Backward -kl	68.0	**97.2**	**81.2**	**86.7**	82.4	**95.2**	**1.2**	287.9
Backward max-prob	65.7	97.1	80.3	86.5	81.2	95.0	1.3	288.6
Backward margin	63.8	97.1	80.2	86.1	81.0	95.0	1.4	289.8

For evaluating the model, we compute a range of metrics (Table 3). Mean squared error (MSE) is a standard regression metric but not suited to the problem as it overemphasizes the errors at the beginning of the curve. Therefore we define $\tau = 0.95$ as the threshold that we are most interested in. That is, we assume that the user wants to train the model until reaching 95% of the possible test F1. With τ we can define a binary classification task and compute AUC, recall ($\mathcal{R}$), precision ($\mathcal{P}$) and $\mathcal{F}_1$.[3] Additionally, we compute the average test-F1, error (err) and training set size when the model first predicts a value $> \tau$.

In the ablation study with forward selection, we find that all features except *-entropy* and *-kl* lower the error rate (err) compared to *base*. For backward

---

[3] Note $\mathcal{F}_1$ is the F1-score on the classification problem of predicting if the true test-F1 is $> \tau$, while test-F1 is the actual F1 score reached by the FSL model on the text classification task.

selection, only removing *cv f1* causes a bigger increase in error rate compared to *all*. This might be because the unsupervised metrics are strongly correlated. Finally, reducing the history (Sect. 2.4) also causes an increase in error rate.

In comparison with the simple baselines (baseline *i*), where we simply stop after a fixed number of instances *i*, we find that *all* gives higher *test-f1* (95.1 vs 94.6) at comparable instance numbers (287 vs 288). This indicates that a regression model adds value for the user.

6   Conclusion

We studied the problem of active learning in a few-shot setting. We found that margin selection outperforms random selection for most models and setups, unless the labels of the task are distributed uniformly. We also looked into the problem of performance prediction to compensate the missing validation set in FSL. We showed that the normalized F1 on unseen test data can be approximated with a random forest regressor (RFR) using signals computed on unlabeled instances. In particular, we showed that the RFR peforms better than the baseline of stopping after a fixed number of steps. Our findings have been integrated into FASL, a uniform platform with a UI that allows non-experts to create text classification models with little effort and expertise.

Acknowledgements. The authors gratefully acknowledge the support of the Pro²Haters - Proactive Profiling of Hate Speech Spreaders (CDTi IDI-20210776), XAI-DisInfodemics: eXplainable AI for disinformation and conspiracy detection during infodemics (MICIN PLEC2021-007681), and DETEMP - Early Detection of Depression Detection in Social Media (IVACE IMINOD/2021/72) R&D grants.

Appendix

The repository at https://github.com/symanto-research/active-few-shot-learning contains the label descriptions, UI screenshots and additional plots and results for AL and performance prediction.

References

1. Ash, J.T., Zhang, C., Krishnamurthy, A., et al.: Deep batch active learning by diverse, uncertain gradient lower bounds. arXiv preprint arXiv:1906.03671 (2020)
2. Block, T.: Ten thousand German news articles dataset (2019). https://tblock.github.io/10kGNAD/
3. Boney, R., Ilin, A.: Semi-supervised few-shot learning with prototypical networks. arXiv preprint arXiv:1903.02164 (2017)
4. Bowman, S.R., Angeli, G., Potts, C., et al.: A large annotated corpus for learning natural language inference. In: EMNLP, pp. 632–642 (2015)
5. Dasgupta, S.: Two faces of active learning. Theoretical CS, pp. 1767–1781 (2011)
6. Ein-Dor, L., Halfon, A., Gera, A., et al.: Active learning for BERT: an empirical study. In: EMNLP, pp. 7949–7962 (2020)

7. de Gibert, O., Perez, N., García-Pablos, A., et al.: Hate speech dataset from a white supremacy forum. In: ALW, pp. 11–20 (2018)
8. Grießhaber, D., Maucher, J., Vu, N.T.: Fine-tuning BERT for low-resource natural language understanding via active learning. In: Coling, pp. 1158–1171 (2020)
9. Gulli, A.: AG's corpus of news articles (2005). http://groups.di.unipi.it/~gulli/ AG_corpus_of_news_articles.html
10. Halder, K., Akbik, A., Krapac, J., et al.: Task-aware representation of sentences for generic text classification. In: Coling, pp. 3202–3213 (2020)
11. Ho, T.K.: Random decision forests. In: Proceedings of 3rd International Conference on Document Analysis and Recognition, pp. 278–282. IEEE (1995)
12. Houlsby, N., Huszár, F., Ghahramani, Z., et al.: Bayesian active learning for classification and preference learning. arXiv preprint arXiv:1112.5745 (2011)
13. Keung, P., Lu, Y., Szarvas, G., et al.: The multilingual amazon reviews corpus. arXiv preprint arXiv:2010.02573 (2020)
14. Lewis, D.D., Gale, W.A.: A Sequential Algorithm for Training Text Classifiers. In: SIGIR 1994. pp. 3–12. Springer, London (1994). https://doi.org/10.1007/978-1-4471-2099-5_1
15. Liu, Y., Ott, M., Goyal, N., et al.: Roberta: a robustly optimized BERT pretraining approach. arXiv preprint arXiv:1907.11692 (2019)
16. Lloyd, S.: Least squares quantization in PCM. IEEE Trans. Inf. Theory **28**, 129–137 (1982)
17. Lowell, D., Lipton, Z.C., Wallace, B.C.: Practical obstacles to deploying active learning. In: EMNLP (2019)
18. Lu, J., MacNamee, B.: Investigating the effectiveness of representations based on pretrained transformer-based language models in active learning for labelling text datasets. arXiv preprint arXiv:2004.13138 (2020)
19. Margatina, K., Vernikos, G., Barrault, L., et al.: Active learning by acquiring contrastive examples. In: EMNLP, pp. 650–663 (2021)
20. Müller, T., Pérez-Torró, G., Franco-Salvador, M.: Few-shot learning with siamese networks and label tuning. In: ACL (2022). https://arxiv.org/abs/2203.14655
21. Nguyen, H.T., Smeulders, A.W.M.: Active learning using pre-clustering. In: ICML (2004)
22. Park, H.S., Jun, C.H.: A simple and fast algorithm for k-medoids clustering. Expert Syst. Appl. **36**, 3336–3341 (2009)
23. Pedregosa, F., Varoquaux, G., Gramfort, A., et al.: Scikit-learn: machine learning in Python. J. Mach. Learn. Res. **12**, 2825–2830 (2011)
24. Reimers, N., Gurevych, I.: Sentence-bert: sentence embeddings using siamese bert-networks. In: EMNLP (2019)
25. Rosenthal, S., Atanasova, P., Karadzhov, G., et al.: A large-scale semi-supervised dataset for offensive language identification. arXiv preprint arXiv:2004.14454 (2020)
26. Schick, T., Schütze, H.: Exploiting cloze-questions for few-shot text classification and natural language inference. In: EACL, pp. 255–269 (2021)
27. Schröder, C., Niekler, A., Potthast, M.: Uncertainty-based query strategies for active learning with transformers. arXiv preprint arXiv:2107.05687 (2021)
28. Settles, B.: Active learning literature survey. In: Computer Sciences Technical Report. University of Wisconsin-Madison (2009)
29. Vilares, D., Gómez-Rodríguez, C.: HEAD-QA: a healthcare dataset for complex reasoning. In: ACL, pp. 960–966 (2019)
30. Wang, S., Fang, H., Khabsa, M., et al.: Entailment as few-shot learner. arXiv preprint arXiv:2104.14690 (2021)

31. Yin, W., Hay, J., Roth, D.: Benchmarking zero-shot text classification: Datasets, evaluation and entailment approach. In: EMNLP, pp. 3914–3923 (2019)
32. Yin, W., Rajani, N.F., Radev, D., et al.: Universal natural language processing with limited annotations: try few-shot textual entailment as a start. In: EMNLP, pp. 8229–8239 (2020)
33. Yuan, M., Lin, H.T., Boyd-Graber, J.L.: Cold-start active learning through self-supervised language modeling. In: EMNLP (2020)

Identifying Fake News in Brazilian Portuguese

Marcelo Fischer, Rejwanul Haque$^{(\boxtimes)}$ [ID], Paul Stynes, and Pramod Pathak

National College of Ireland, Dublin, Ireland
x20118872@student.ncirl.ie,
{marcelo.fischer,rejwanul.haque,paul.stynes,pramod.pathak}@ncirl.ie

Abstract. Spread of fake news and disinformation may have many profound consequences, e.g. social conflicts, distrust in media, political instability. Fake news identification is an well-established area of natural language processing (NLP). Given its recent success on English, fake news identification is currently being used as a tool by a variety of agencies including corporate companies and big media houses. However, fake news identification still possesses a challenge for languages other than English and low-resource languages.

The bidirectional encoders using masked language models, e.g. bidirectional encoder representations from Transformers (BERT), multilingual BERT (mBERT), produce state-of-the-art results in numerous natural language processing (NLP) tasks. This transfer learning strategy is very effective when labeled data is not abundantly available especially in low-resource scenarios. This paper investigates the application of BERT for fake news identification in Brazilian Portuguese. In addition to BERT, we also tested a number of widely-used machine learning (ML) algorithms, methods and strategies for this task. We found that fake news identification models built using advanced ML algorithms including BERT performed excellently in this task, and interestingly, BERT is found to be the best-performing model which produces a F1_score of 98.4 on the hold-out test set.

Keywords: Fake news identification · Deep learning · Fact checking

1 Introduction

Fake news is not a new term or trend; it roots back to the 1600s with the name of 'propaganda' [6]. In short, fake news can be described as the act of knowingly or intentionally publishing distorted or false news content usually online. In fact, in many cases, where real news and fake news cannot be easily distinguished, society could possibly find itself in the brink of collapse as it would no longer be possible to hold value in truth. This is in fact a concerning matter to us.

The twenty-first century evidenced the proliferation of AI-based technologies in social network-based platforms; however, its downsides are also seen as such

P. Rosso et al. (Eds.): NLDB 2022, LNCS 13286, pp. 111–118, 2022.
https://doi.org/10.1007/978-3-031-08473-7_10

technologies are also easily exploited to impersonate or falsify individuals and damage their public image [17]. In many cases, fake news are seen to be so convincing that they can result in damaging actions towards specific individuals and/or the society. As an example, in 2016, a man is seen to threaten people with guns as a result of the spread of fake news [12]. We refer the readers to an interesting paper, [21], who pointed out that fake news influenced the 2016 presidential elections in the US.

Over the past few years, there have been a swathe of papers that focused in developing ML models to identify fake news with a common expectation which is to prevent fake news being published and spread online. Despite many challenges, to a certain extent, there have been successes in automatic fake news identification [3,7,9]. The literature in fact includes a wide range of papers that exploited a variety of machine learning algorithms (e.g. linear regression, random forests, SVM, hybrid neural networks), investigated different feature extraction methods and demonstrated different frameworks for fake news identification [5,10,13]. However, studies are primarily limited to high-resource languages, especially in English. The main reason for this is the scarcity of labeled datasets in low-resourced languages, which are needed to train classifiers in order to filter out fake news documents.

Recently, [16] investigated fake news identification problem in Brazilian Portuguese, and created a gold-standard reference corpus[1] for this task. They obtained a F1_score of 89.0% with their best-performing classifier that was built using support vector machine (SVM) algorithm.[2] Over the last five years, we witnessed a large volume of works that made use of large-scale pre-trained language model in NLP, e.g. BERT [1]. BERT, which makes use of the Transformer [20] architecture, provides context-aware representation from an unlabeled text by jointly conditioning from both the left and right contexts within a sentence. Considering the recent success of BERT in text classification (e.g. fake news identification [4]), we used BERT for fake news identification in Brazilian Portuguese. In addition to this, we tested a number of machine learning models and strategy (e.g. ensemble and stacking) in order to further investigate this line of research, i.e. identification of fake news in Brazilian Portuguese. This work presents more competitive baseline models for comparison as far as this task is concerned. In other words, our work can be seen as a direct extension of the work of [16].

2   Methodology and Experimental Setup

2.1   BERT for Fake News Identification Task

Vaswani et al. [20] introduced Transformer as an efficient alternative to recurrent or convolutional neural networks. Transformer which uses attention mechanism learns contextual relations between words in a text. The encoder-decoder

---

[1] Fake.Br Corpus [https://github.com/roneysco/Fake.br-Corpus].

[2] The authors used LinearSVC implementation in Scikit-learn [https://scikit-learn.org/stable/] with its default parameters.

architecture with attention mechanism has shown promising results on machine translation tasks.

Based on the Transformer architecture, Devlin et al. [2] proposed a powerful NN architecture – BERT – for a variety of NLP tasks including text classification such as sentiment analysis. BERT is a multi-layer bidirectional Transformer encoder architecture which provides context-aware representations from an unlabeled text by jointly conditioning from both the left and right contexts within a sentence. More specifically, BERT is made of a stack of encoders where each encoder consists of two sub-layers; the first sub-layer is a multi-head attention layer and the second sub-layer is a simple feed forward network. It can also be used as a pre-trained model with one additional output layer to fine-tune downstream NLP tasks, such as sentiment analysis, and natural language inferencing. For fine-tuning, the BERT model is first initialized with the pre-trained parameters, and all of the parameters are fine-tuned using the labeled data from the downstream tasks. There were two steps in BERT training: *pre-training* and *fine-tuning*. During pre-training, the model is trained on unlabeled data. As for fine-tuning, it is first initialized with the pre-trained parameters, and all of the parameters are fine-tuned using the labeled data from the downstream tasks (e.g. sentiment analysis). This strategy has been successfully applied to fake news identification task [11,14]. Likewise, in this work, we focused on investigating this state-of-the-art method for identifying fake news in Brazilian Portuguese. Furthermore, we compare BERT with different classical classification models. We employ the following classical supervised classification algorithms and techniques: Logistic Regression, Decision Tree, Random Forest, K-Nearest Neighbour, Linear Support Vector Classifier (LSVC), SVM, Naïve Bayes, Stacking, XGBoost, CNN, Gated Recurrent Unit (GRU), and LSTM.

2.2   Dataset

As pointed out above, [16,19] created a dataset for fake news detection in the Brazilian Portuguese language, namely Fake.Br. For this, they followed the annotation guidelines proposed by [8,18], and adopted a semi-automatic approach to create this corpus. First, the authors collected a total of 3,600 fake news. Then they crawled real news from trusted Portuguese sources. In order to crawl genuine news whose text would be similar to those of fake news, they used keywords from the previously collected fake news. Again, 3,600 genuine news articles were chosen based on cosine lexical similarity. They also manually verified the collected genuine news themselves to assure that they were at least topic related to the paired fake news. Note that [16,19] did not consider any news that were half true, and the collected news are from a wide range of domains (e.g. politics, religion, economy). The final dataset consists of 7,200 news articles which are equally distributed across two classes.

Since Fake.Br consists of real news articles that were collected from the web, they contain URLs which carry no useful information in their texts. However, presence of an URL in a text might be a pattern to help distinguishing between fake and real news. We used a placeholder to represent URLs. Emails were also treated similarly. Alphanumeric and noisy characters were removed. As for feature extraction from cleaned data, we investigated three different techniques, e.g. term-frequency (TF), term-frequency times inverse document frequeny (TF-IDF) and dense vector representation (i.e. word-embedding vectors). The TF and TF-IDF techniques were implemented using the SciKit-Learn library's *CountVectorizer* and *TfidfVectorizer* functions, respectively. For building deep learning models (e.g. LSTM), we used dense word vector which is a representation of a word into a numerical vector of some predefined length. In order to measure performance of our classification models, we used a range of evaluation metrics, i.e. Accuracy, Precision, Recall, and F1_score.

3   Results and Discussion

As pointed out above, we carried out our experiments using bag-of-words (BoW) approach. In case of deep learning models, an embedding layer was added to the network, which turns words into numerical vectors. The true news in the Fake.Br corpus are usually much longer in size than that of the fake news (cf. Table 1). This is usually seen in other fake news identification datasets too. In order to see whether the size of a text has any impact in predictions, we tested two different scenarios: full and truncated texts.

Table 1. Average length of texts in each class (real and fake).

Label	Average length (in characters)
Real	6674
Fake	1124

Table 2 presents the evaluation results obtained with the TF feature extraction technique. The bold values in the table indicate the best scores. When considering full texts, the best individual classifier overall is LinearSVC which is able to correctly classify 97.15% (i.e. accuracy) of fake news (corresponding to an F1_score of 97.14) of the test set. Therefore, in this scenario, the meta classifier in our stacking model was chosen as LinearSVC. As can be seen from Table 2, the stacking model outperforms all individual models and produces a F1_score of 97.49.

As for the truncated texts, each input was limited to 200 tokens, and results are shown in the right columns of Table 2. We see from Table 2 that the best individual classifier overall was LinearSVC and it even surpassed the performance of stacking model. Here, the meta classifier used in the stacking model was linear regression, and this setup provided us best results for the stacking. In summary, nearly all models built on the dataset of truncated texts were worse compared to those that were built on datasets of full texts. This indicates that the length of the news texts impacts the performance.

We choose the best-performing model (stacking model) and applied our second normalisation technique, i.e. TF-IDF. The results are shown in Table 3.

Table 2. Evaluation results using TF (full and truncated texts)

	Full text				Truncated text			
	Accuracy	Precision	Recall	F1_score	Accuracy	Precision	Recall	F1_score
Stacking	**0.9750**	**0.9766**	0.9735	**0.9749**	0.9674	0.9719	0.9624	0.9671
LinearSVC	0.9715	0.9656	0.9777	0.9716	**0.9715**	**0.9734**	0.9694	**0.9714**
LR	0.9715	0.9721	0.9708	0.9714	0.9632	0.9586	0.9680	0.9633
SVC	0.9660	0.9639	0,9680	0.9659	0.9646	0.9638	0.9652	0.9645
RF	0.9542	0.9441	0.9652	0.9545	0.9569	0.9659	0.9471	0.9564
DT	0.9444	0.9506	0.9373	0.9439	0.9438	0.9505	0.9359	0.9432
KNN	0.9319	0.8904	**0.9847**	0.9352	0.9472	0.9224	**0.9763**	0.9486
NB	0.8625	0.9290	0.7841	0.8505	0.7840	0.8246	0.7201	0.7688

Table 3. Evaluation results for stacking models with TF-IDF.

	Accuracy	Precision	Recall	F1_score
TF-IDF stacking full text	**0.9681**	**0.9719**	**0.9638**	**0.9678**
TF-IDF stacking truncated text	0.9625	0.9703	0.9540	0.9621

As stated above, performance of classification models is worse when the size of the text is truncated. We see the same trend here too. Interestingly, we see from Table 3 that use of the IDF normalization caused a drop in the performance of the stacking model. The fake news usually contain more slang and misspelled words in comparison to the real news which are collected from trustworthy sources. This is also true for Fake.Br. As far as fake news detection is concerned, IDF dilutes the importance of frequently occurring words which in fact can be a strong signal for a news being fake. This signal is lost when the frequencies are normalized using IDF. This could be the reason for the drop in performance when used IDF.

When comparing our approaches with those presented in [19], we see that performance of our stacking models are quite similar to those in [19]. This indicates that adding more complex feature to the stacking model may not improve its performance. This findings suggests that the simpler approach (e.g. [19] and ours) in stacking method could be better as far as text classification is concerned.

Table 4. Evaluation results obtained for the XGBoost models.

	Accuracy	Precision	Recall	F1_score
TF XGBoost - full text	**0.9667**	0.9745	**0.9582**	**0.9663**
TF-IDF XGBoost - full text	0.9667	**0.9772**	0.9554	0.9662
TF XGBoost - truncated text	0.9618	0.9662	0.9568	0.9615
TF-IDF XGBoost - truncated text	0.9562	0.9672	0.9443	0.9556

Table 4 presents the results for the XGBoost ensemble models. As in above, we see from Table 4 that the models trained on truncated texts are again worse than those trained on full texts. TF is found to be the best feature engineering technique this time too. If we compare evaluation scores presented above with the scores of Table 4, we can clearly see that stacking models (with TF and truncated) and LinearSVC outperforms models built using XGBoost ensemble technique. Although XGBoost is very powerful ensemble technique, it is highly dependent on hyper-parameter tuning. In our case, we performed random search in order to optimize hyper-parameters. Naturally, it was not possible to use all combinations of the grid for the search.

Now, we present the results obtained with our deep learning models. In case of deep learning, we considered a truncated texts with 300 tokens and each token was represented by an embedding vector with 100 dimensions. Two different setups were tested: with stopwords and removing stopwords. As above, we evaluated our deep-learning models on the test set and reported the evaluation scores in Table 5.

Table 5. Evaluation result for deep-learning models.

	Without stopwords				With stopwords			
	Accuracy	Precision	Recall	F1_score	Accuracy	Precision	Recall	F1_score
CNN	**0.9514**	**0.9513**	0.9513	**0.9513**	**0.9188**	0.9574	**0.8760**	**0.9149**
GRU	0.9368	0.9219	0.9540	0.9377	0.9118	0.9668	0.8524	0.9060
LSTM	0.9278	0.9008	**0.9610**	0.9299	0.9139	**0.9685**	0.8552	0.9083

The results for the deep learning models go against the findings of [19]. The removal of stopwords is helpful and improves the prediction power of the networks. This might be due to the fact that neural networks are more powerful in learning and finding patterns in complex data [15]. Therefore, removing less informative entities such as stopwords enables the models to learn highly informative patterns only. However, we see from [19] that the best-performing deep learning model (i.e. CNN) could not surpass the performance of best individual model, LinearSVC, and the stacking model.

As discussed above, we considered investigating state-of-the-art text classification algorithm, i.e. multilingual BERT, in our task. We tested BERT with the following setup: truncated texts with 128 token and keeping stopwords. As can be seen in Table 6, this state-of-the-art algorithm outperformed all the previous models and was able to achieve a F1_score of 98.40. The BERT model also provided us with the highest recall and accuracy when compared to the other models.

Table 6. Performance of BERT in fake news identiifcation.

	Accuracy	Precision	Recall	F1_score
BERT	0.9840	0.9750	0.9940	0.9840

4   Conclusion and Future Work

Fake news identification is an well-established area of NLP and this line of research is primarily limited to high-resource languages, especially in English. There is a handful of studies that focused on fake news identification in Brazilian Portuguese. This paper presented a comprehensive study on identification of fake news in Brazilian Portuguese. This work can be seen as a direct extension of [16,19] that presented state-of-the-art performance (i.e. F1_score of 89.0% using SVM algorithm) on a standard benchmark dataset (i.e. Fake.Br). Given the success of BERT in text classification, we tested it in this task (i.e. on fake news identification in Brazilian Portuguese). We also tested a number of machine learning models, techniques and strategy (e.g. ensemble and stacking). We were able to achieve a F1_score of 98.40 on hold-out test data using BERT and this is found to be the best-performing model in the task. In other words, we provided a number of competitive baselines on a standard dataset and this can be seen a new benchmark performance (i.e. BERT) as far as fake news identification in Brazilian Portuguese is concerned.

We aim to extend this work further by (i) performing a wider grid search for the XGBoost model, (ii) using a stacking model that includes both machine learning and deep learning models, and (iii) applying multi-stage fine-tuning on BERT.

References

1. Devlin, J., Chang, M.-W., Lee, K., Toutanova, K. Bert: pre-training of deep bidirectional transformers for language understanding. arXiv preprint arXiv:1810.04805 (2018)
2. Devlin, J., Chang, M.-W., Lee, K., Toutanova, K.: BERT: pre-training of deep bidirectional transformers for language understanding. arXiv preprint arXiv:1810.04805 (2018)
3. Fung, Y., et al.: InfoSurgeon: cross-media fine-grained information consistency checking for fake news detection. In: Proceedings of the 59th Annual Meeting of the Association for Computational Linguistics and the 11th International Joint Conference on Natural Language Processing (Volume 1: Long Papers), Online, August 2021, pp. 1683–1698. Association for Computational Linguistics (2021)
4. Glazkova, A., Glazkov, M., Trifonov, T.: g2tmn at Constraint@AAAI2021: exploiting CT-BERT and ensembling learning for COVID-19 fake news detection. In: Chakraborty, T., Shu, K., Bernard, H.R., Liu, H., Akhtar, M.S. (eds.) CONSTRAINT 2021. CCIS, vol. 1402, pp. 116–127. Springer, Cham (2021). https://doi.org/10.1007/978-3-030-73696-5_12

5. Goldani, M.H., Momtazi, S., Safabakhsh, R.: Detecting fake news with capsule neural networks. Appl. Soft Comput. **101**, 106991 (2021)
6. Gravanis, G., Vakali, A., Diamantaras, K., Karadais, P.: Behind the cues: a benchmarking study for fake news detection. Expert Syst. Appl. **128**, 201–213 (2019)
7. Hansen, C., Hansen, C., Lima, L.C.: Automatic fake news detection: are models learning to reason? In: Proceedings of the 59th Annual Meeting of the Association for Computational Linguistics and the 11th International Joint Conference on Natural Language Processing (Volume 2: Short Papers), Online, August 2021, pp. 80–86. Association for Computational Linguistics (2021)
8. Hovy, E., Lavid, J.: Towards a 'science' of corpus annotation: a new methodological challenge for corpus linguistics. Int. J. Transl. **22**(1), 13–36 (2010)
9. Hu, L., et al.: Compare to the knowledge: graph neural fake news detection with external knowledge. In: Proceedings of the 59th Annual Meeting of the Association for Computational Linguistics and the 11th International Joint Conference on Natural Language Processing (Volume 1: Long Papers), Online, August 2021, pp. 754–763. Association for Computational Linguistics (2021)
10. Jiang, T., Li, J.P., Ul Haq, A., Saboor, A., Ali, A.: A novel stacking approach for accurate detection of fake news. IEEE Access **9**, 22626–22639 (2021)
11. Jwa, H., Oh, D., Park, K., Kang, J.M., Lim, H.: exbake: automatic fake news detection model based on bidirectional encoder representations from transformers (bert). Appl. Sci. **9**(19), 4062 (2019)
12. Kang, C., Goldman, A.: In Washington Pizzeria Attack, Fake News Brought Real Guns. New York Times 5 (2016)
13. Kaur, S., Kumar, P., Kumaraguru, P.: Automating fake news detection system using multi-level voting model. Soft Comput. **24**(12), 9049–9069 (2019). https://doi.org/10.1007/s00500-019-04436-y
14. Liu, C., et al.: A two-stage model based on BERT for short fake news detection. In: Douligeris, C., Karagiannis, D., Apostolou, D. (eds.) KSEM 2019. LNCS (LNAI), vol. 11776, pp. 172–183. Springer, Cham (2019). https://doi.org/10.1007/978-3-030-29563-9_17
15. Mandical, R.R., Mamatha, N., Shivakumar, N., Monica, R., Krishna, A.N.: Identification of fake news using machine learning. In: 2020 IEEE International Conference on Electronics, Computing and Communication Technologies (CONECCT), pp. 1–6. IEEE (2020)
16. Monteiro, R.A., et al.: Contributions to the study of fake news in Portuguese: new corpus and automatic detection results. In: Villavicencio, A., et al. (eds.) PROPOR 2018. LNCS (LNAI), vol. 11122, pp. 324–334. Springer, Cham (2018). https://doi.org/10.1007/978-3-319-99722-3_33
17. Newman, N.: Journalism, media and technology trends and predictions (2021)
18. Rubin, V.L., Chen, Y., Conroy, N.K.: Deception detection for news: three types of fakes. Proc. Assoc. Inf. Sci. Technol. **52**(1), 1–4 (2015)
19. Silva, R.M., Santos, R.L.S., Almeida, T.A., Pardo, T.A.S.: Towards automatically filtering fake news in Portuguese. Expert Syst. Appl. **146**, 113199 (2020)
20. Vaswani, A., et al.: Attention is all you need. arXiv preprint arXiv:1706.03762 (2017)
21. Vosoughi, S., Roy, D., Aral, S.: The spread of true and false news online. Science **359**(6380), 1146–1151 (2018)

Unsupervised Ranking and Aggregation of Label Descriptions for Zero-Shot Classifiers

Angelo Basile[1,2], Marc Franco-Salvador[1(✉)], and Paolo Rosso[2]

[1] Symanto Research, Valencia, Spain
{angelo.basile,marc.franco}@symanto.com
[2] PRHLT Research Center, Universitat Politècnica de València, Valencia, Spain
prosso@dsic.upv.es

Abstract. Zero-shot text classifiers based on label descriptions embed an input text and a set of labels into the same space: measures such as cosine similarity can then be used to select the most similar label description to the input text as the predicted label. In a true zero-shot setup, designing good label descriptions is challenging because no development set is available. Inspired by the literature on Learning with Disagreements, we look at how probabilistic models of repeated rating analysis can be used for selecting the best label descriptions in an unsupervised fashion. We evaluate our method on a set of diverse datasets and tasks (sentiment, topic and stance). Furthermore, we show that multiple, noisy label descriptions can be aggregated to boost the performance.

Keywords: Learning with disagreements · Zero-shot classification · Generative models

1 Introduction

Recently, large Language Models (LMs) such as BERT [4] have pushed the boundaries of NLP systems and have enabled a transition from the supervised learning paradigm, where an input text is processed together with a ground-truth label, to a *pre-train, prompt and predict* paradigm [10], where a pre-trained LM is fed the input data to be processed and a description of the task to be performed. This paradigm shift has lead to zero-shot models that require no ground-truth labels. With a good task description, zero-shot models have been shown to be effective at many challenging NLP tasks [2]. However, LMs are highly sensitive to how a task description is framed [8] and, without a large development set, finding a good task description is hard. In this work we address this problem, focusing on zero-shot models based on Siamese BERT-Networks (SBERT) [16]. These networks embed both the input text and a description of the target labels in the same semantic space using a pre-trained LM; in this space, similarity measures are then applied to map the most similar label description to the most probable

© The Author(s), under exclusive license to Springer Nature Switzerland AG 2022
P. Rosso et al. (Eds.): NLDB 2022, LNCS 13286, pp. 119–126, 2022.
https://doi.org/10.1007/978-3-031-08473-7_11

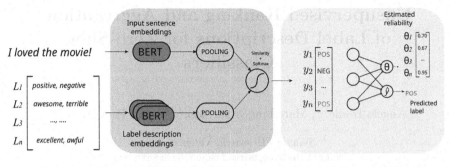

a) SBERT Zero-Shot Classifier   b) Probabilistic model aggregation

Fig. 1. Overview of the proposed method for a sentiment analysis task with two possible output labels, negative (NEG) and positive (POS). An unlabeled corpus with T documents is embedded through a) SBERT together with a set of n label descriptions L. A softmax classifier on top of the SBERT cosine similarity scores provides n predicted labels y, one for each item in the label description set. These predictions are then passed as input to b) the probabilistic aggregator, which outputs $\hat{y}$, a best guess of a single final predicted label for each document T and θ, a reliability score for the whole corpus for each label description y.

labels. As with prompting, a good label description is key to obtaining good performance. For instance, in the context of binary sentiment analysis, the words *awesome, perfect, great* and *bad, terrible, awful* are all potentially good descriptions for the labels *positive* and *negative*, respectively. How do we filter out the sub-optimal descriptions without having access to labelled data? We study the Learning with Disagreements literature [22], particularly, the item-response class of models, and show that methods developed for analysing crowd-sourced annotations can be transferred to the problem of description selection for zero-shot models. It has been shown that these models achieve high performance in two tasks related to disagreement analysis. First, they usually outperform majority voting at retrieving the gold truth. Second, they can identify which annotators are more reliable and which are spammers. In this work, we look at how we can use these models in the domain of model-based zero-shot classification. Figure 1 shows an illustration of the proposed method.

2   Zero-Shot Classification with SBERT

Zero-Shot classification models can tackle a task using no training data. Starting from a pre-trained LM, different architectures enable zero-shot classification using different strategies, such as prompting [2,10] or Natural Language Inference (NLI) for label entailment [27]. In this work, we focus on zero-shot classifiers based on Siamese Networks. They have recently been shown to perform on par with other methods while being highly efficient at inference time [12]. As discussed in [16], pre-trained LMs such as BERT can be modified to use Siamese networks and encode two inputs independently: when this architecture is coupled with a symmetric score function, the inference runtime requires only $O(n)$ computations for n instances regardless of the number of labels. In contrast, the runtime of standard cross-attention encoders would scale linearly with the number of labels. While the natural applications of SBERT Networks are clustering and search-related tasks, they can be used for zero-shot classification by providing the text to be classified as a first input and the possible labels (or label descriptions) as the second input: the output is a matrix of similarity measures, which can be transformed in a probability distribution through a softmax function application. For the details on the SBERT classification architecture, we refer to the original work [16].

Label Descriptions. Label descriptions are the key component that make it possible to turn a semantic similarity model in a zero-shot classifier. We experiment with four sets of label descriptions. First, we define as a baseline a *null hypothesis* (NH) label, which we set to be equal to the class name it describes: for example, in the context of sentiment analysis, we define the words *positive* and *negative* as label descriptions for the class POSITIVE and NEGATIVE, respectively. Second, as a first source of variation, we experiment with a set of *patterns* for turning a null hypothesis label into a proper sentence: for example, for the IMDB movie review dataset, we experiment with the pattern *The movie is* {`positive`, `negative`}. Third, for each dataset we manually write multiple variations over the null hypothesis (e.g., {*positive, negative*} → {*great, terrible*}). Finally, we experiment with automatically generated variations of the null hypothesis: under the assumption that the representation of a word in different languages can be a useful source of additional information for a multilingual encoder, we use a machine translation system to automatically translate the null hypothesis labels into three different languages, which can be directly fed to a multilingual pretrained SBERT model (see Sect. 4 for more details). Table 1 shows the label descriptions used for the IMDB movie review dataset.

3 Bayesian Label Description Analysis

From Crowdsourcing to Zero-Shot Classifiers. Bayesian inference provides a natural framework for dealing with multiple sources of uncertain information. This framework is successfully used in the context of analysing crowdsourced annotations as a robust alternative to: *i*) inter-annotator agreement metrics for identifying biases and potential reliability issues in the annotation process, and *ii*) majority voting for retrieving the gold truth label. In this work, we argue that this framework can be directly applied to the problem of prompt and label description selection and we use the word *annotator* to denote human annotators, zero-shot classifiers and actual label descriptions.

In NLP, a popular Bayesian annotation model is the Multi-Annotator Competence Estimation (MACE) model [7]. MACE is a generative, unpooled model. It is *generative* because it can generate a dataset starting from a set of priors,

Table 1. Overview of the label descriptions used for the IMDB movie review dataset. The null hypothesis (NH) labels (*positive, negative*) describe the class `positive` and `negative` respectively. The rows MANUAL and PATTERN have been manually compiled, while row AUTO shows the label descriptions generated automatically by translating the null hypothesis.

	POSITIVE	NEGATIVE
NH	Positive	Negative
MANUAL	Great	Terrible
	Really great	Really terrible
	A masterpiece	Awful
AUTO	Optimo	Terribile
	Grande	Terrivel
	Genial	Negativo
PATTERN	{}	
	It was {}	
	All in all, it was {}.	
	Just {}!	
	The movie is {}.	

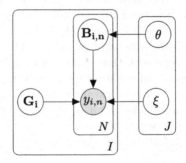

Fig. 2. The model plate for MACE. Given I instances and N annotators, the observed label $y_{i,n}$ is dependent on the gold label G_i and $B_{i,n}$, which models the behaviour of annotator n on instance i.

and the assumptions that produce a specific outcome can be represented as a graph, as shown in Fig. 2. Thanks to its *unpooled* structure, it models each annotator (or label description) independently and provides a trustworthiness score θ_j for each annotator j: we use this parameter for ranking the label descriptions assuming that high θ values lead to higher f1-scores. Given n label descriptions and i instances, the zero-shot model outputs n predicted labels y: MACE models each label $y_{i,n}$ for instance i from a label description n as being dependent on the true, unobserved gold label G_i and the behaviour $B_{i,n}$ of the zero-shot model with label description i on the instance n. The variable B was originally introduced in MACE for modelling the spamming behaviour of crowd-workers. Key

Table 2. Spearman ρ rank correlation with true f1-score for both the θ parameter of the MACE model and the baseline Cohen's κ score.

	$\rho(\theta, f1)$	$\rho(\kappa, f1)$
Ag News	**0.58**	0.38
Cola	**0.12**	0.08
Imdb	**0.94**	0.87
StanceCat	**0.66**	0.39
SubJ	0.09	**0.20**
Yelp	**0.83**	0.76
Yelp Full	0.16	**0.43**

of this work is that, in the context of zero-shot classifiers, B correlates strongly with the true f1-score of different label descriptions. As a consequence, it can be used to rank the label descriptions and eventually discard the sub-optimal ones. We refer to the original MACE paper [7] for additional details on the model.

4   Experiments and Results

4.1   Setup

For implementing the zero-shot classification module, we use the Python package `sentence-transformers` [16]. For our experiments on the English corpora, we use the pre-trained model `paraphrase-MiniLM-L3-v2` [17], which has been trained on a variety of different datasets. We evaluate our proposed method on a battery of popular text classification datasets: IMDB [11], Yelp Review [28], Yelp Polarity Review [28], AG's News Corpus [6], Cola [24]. In addition, we include StanceCat [20], a stance detection dataset for which non-aggregated annotations are available. For the null hypothesis (NH) label descriptions, we re-use the prompts that we could find in the literature on prompting [12,23,26] and manually crafted the rest.[1] We manually wrote the variations on the null hypothesis based on our intuitions. For the automatic generation of new label descriptions, we translated the English null hypothesis into French, Italian and Spanish using a pre-trained MarianMT model [9] through the `transformers` library [25]. Specifically, we used the `opus-mt-en-roa` model [21] .

We conduct our experiments using the Stan-based implementation [14] of MACE, trained with VB.

4.2   Results

Ranking. Table 2 shows the rank correlation scores with the true f1-score for different datasets. As a baseline, we use the average of Cohen's κ [1] computed

---

[1] The complete of the label descriptions used can be found at https://anonymous. 4open.science/r/zsla-1C75/.

Table 3. Macro-averaged F1 scores for the experiments with label aggregations.

Method	Aggregation	Ag News	Cola	Imdb	StanceCat	SubJ	Yelp	Yelp Full
NH	-	10.9	38.7	66.2	32.4	52.1	66.8	31.3
PATTERN	Mace	8.2	41.9	68.1	30.8	54.5	73.3	7.4
	Majority	8.1	40.6	67.2	31.4	51.7	72.3	**34.7**
MANUAL	Mace	9.7	38.7	66.3	**33.1**	**55.2**	69.8	33.5
	Majority	9.9	38.7	66.2	28.0	50.0	68.3	31.0
AUTO	Mace	10.3	**47.3**	**68.7**	31.5	43.3	**74.9**	7.4
	Majority	**24.8**	47.1	66.5	31.0	45.7	72.5	34.0

between each pair of label descriptions. For most of the datasets, the MACE's θ parameter, which models the trustworthiness of an annotator, outperforms the baseline. Medium to strong correlation between MACE's θ parameters and the true f1-score suggests that a model-based analysis using zero-shot classifiers can be used to effectively select the best performing label descriptions and discard the sub-optimal ones, i.e., by ranking the different label descriptions according to the θ values, the low-scoring labels can be safely left out.

Aggregation. Table 3 shows the results of the label aggregation experiments. In all of the cases, aggregating multiple label descriptions outperforms the Null Hypothesis (NH) baseline. In addition, MACE usually outperforms majority voting, excluding the cases where the label space contains more than two labels (i.e., Ag News and Yelp Full). On average, the automatically generated label descriptions outperform both the manually written label descriptions and the pattern variations: this suggests that human involvement is not necessarily needed for finding better performing label descriptions.

5   Related Work

The idea of using the meaning of a category for building dataless classification systems has first been explored already in pre-neural times [3]. Within the *pretrain, prompt and predict* paradigm [10], automatic prompt generation and ensembling has been investigated in [8]. [18] train a classifier on top of the soft-labels provided by an ensemble of zero-shot models for successfully cancelling the effect of poorly-performing prompts.

The idea of modelling ambiguity and disagreement in annotation as signal more than noise, has recently gained traction in the NLP community [5,15,22]. The closest source to our paper is probably [19], who use a Bayesian model to combine multiple weak classifiers in a better performing system. [13,14] highlight the benefits of Bayesian models for NLP specifically.

6   Conclusion

We set out to address two research questions: first, we looked at the problem of unsupervised ranking of different label descriptions by their estimated trustworthiness on different text classification datasets; second, we investigated whether the output of zero-shot models built with different label descriptions can be aggregated in order to obtain overall higher classification performance. We found that Bayesian models of annotations such as MACE can provide a good solution for both problems. Furthermore, we have found that automatically translated label descriptions outperform manually written ones. We focused on Siamese zero-shot models because their inference runtime is not affected by the number of label descriptions. When put all together, these findings suggest that zero-shot model performance can potentially be improved by automatically generating more label descriptions and aggregating their output with a probabilistic model.

Acknowledgements. We gracefully thank the support of the Pro^{2}Haters - Proactive Profiling of Hate Speech Spreaders (CDTi IDI-20210776), XAI-DisInfodemics: eXplainable AI for disinformation and conspiracy detection during infodemics (MICIN PLEC2021-007681), DETEMP - Early Detection of Depression Detection in Social Media (IVACE IMINOD/2021/72) and DeepPattern (PROMETEO/2019/121) R&D grants. We also thank the two anonymous reviewers for their helpful feedback.

References

1. Artstein, R., Poesio, M.: Survey article: inter-coder agreement for computational linguistics. Comput. Linguist. 555–596 (2008)
2. Brown, T., Mann, B., Ryder, N., et al.: Language models are few-shot learners. Adv. NIPS 1877–1901 (2020)
3. Chang, M.W., Ratinov, L.A., Roth, D., et al.: Importance of semantic representation: dataless classification. In: AAAI, pp. 830–835 (2008)
4. Devlin, J., Chang, M.W., Lee, K., et al.: BERT: pre-training of deep bidirectional transformers for language understanding. In: Proceedings of the 2019 Conference of the North American Chapter of the Association for Computational Linguistics: Human Language Technologies, Volume 1 (Long and Short Papers), pp. 4171–4186 (2019)
5. Fornaciari, T., Uma, A., Paun, S., et al.: Beyond black & white: leveraging annotator disagreement via soft-label multi-task learning. In: Proceedings of the 2021 Conference of the North American Chapter of the Association for Computational Linguistics: Human Language Technologies, pp. 2591–2597 (2021)
6. Gulli, A.: AG's corpus of news articles (2005). http://groups.di.unipi.it/~gulli/AG_corpus_of_news_articles.html
7. Hovy, D., Berg-Kirkpatrick, T., Vaswani, A., et al.: Learning whom to trust with MACE. In: Proceedings of the 2013 Conference of the North American Chapter of the Association for Computational Linguistics: Human Language Technologies, pp. 1120–1130 (2013)
8. Jiang, Z., Xu, F.F., Araki, J., et al.: How can we know what language models know? Trans. Assoc. Comput. Linguist. 423–438 (2020)

9. Junczys-Dowmunt, M., Grundkiewicz, R., Dwojak, T., et al.: Marian: fast neural machine translation in C++. In: Proceedings of ACL 2018, System Demonstrations, pp. 116–121 (2018)
10. Liu, P., Yuan, W., Fu, J., et al.: Pre-train, prompt, and predict: a systematic survey of prompting methods in natural language processing. arXiv preprint arXiv:2107.13586 (2021)
11. Maas, A.L., Daly, R.E., Pham, P.T., et al.: Learning word vectors for sentiment analysis. In: ACL, pp. 142–150 (2011)
12. Müller, T., Pérez-Torró, G., Franco-Salvador, M.: Few-shot learning with siamese networks and label tuning. In: ACL (2022)
13. Passonneau, R.J., Carpenter, B.: The benefits of a model of annotation. Trans. Assoc. Comput. Linguist. 311–326 (2014)
14. Paun, S., Carpenter, B., Chamberlain, J., et al.: Comparing Bayesian models of annotation. Trans. Assoc. Comput. Linguist. 571–585 (2018)
15. Plank, B., Hovy, D., Søgaard, A.: Linguistically debatable or just plain wrong? In: ACL, pp. 507–511 (2014)
16. Reimers, N., Gurevych, I.: Sentence-BERT: sentence embeddings using Siamese BERT-networks. In: EMNLP, pp. 3982–3992 (2019)
17. Reimers, N., Gurevych, I.: The curse of dense low-dimensional information retrieval for large index sizes. In: ACL, pp. 605–611 (2021)
18. Schick, T., Schütze, H.: Exploiting cloze-questions for few-shot text classification and natural language inference. In: EACL, pp. 255–269 (2021)
19. Simpson, E., Roberts, S., Psorakis, I., et al.: Dynamic Bayesian combination of multiple imperfect classifiers. In: Decision Making and Imperfection, pp. 1–35 (2013)
20. Taulé, M., Martí, M.A., Rangel, F.M., et al.: Overview of the task on stance and gender detection in tweets on catalan independence at ibereval 2017. In: 2nd Workshop on Evaluation of Human Language Technologies for Iberian Languages, IberEval 2017 (CEUR-WS), pp. 157–177 (2017)
21. Tiedemann, J., Thottingal, S.: OPUS-MT - Building open translation services for the World. In: Proceedings of the 22nd Annual Conference of the European Association for Machine Translation (EAMT), Lisbon, Portugal (2020)
22. Uma, A., Fornaciari, T., Dumitrache, A., et al.: SemEval-2021 task 12: learning with disagreements. In: Proceedings of the 15th International Workshop on Semantic Evaluation (SemEval-2021), pp. 338–347 (2021)
23. Wang, S., Fang, H., Khabsa, M., et al.: Entailment as few-shot learner. arXiv preprint arXiv:2104.14690 (2021)
24. Warstadt, A., Singh, A., Bowman, S.R.: Neural network acceptability judgments. arXiv preprint arXiv:1805.12471 (2018)
25. Wolf, T., Debut, L., Sanh, V., et al.: Transformers: state-of-the-art natural language processing. In: EMNLP, pp. 38–45 (2020)
26. Yin, W., Hay, J., Roth, D.: Benchmarking zero-shot text classification: datasets, evaluation and entailment approach. In: EMNLP, pp. 3914–3923 (2019)
27. Yin, W., Rajani, N.F., Radev, D., et al.: Universal natural language processing with limited annotations: try few-shot textual entailment as a start. In: EMNLP, pp. 8229–8239 (2020)
28. Zhang, X., Zhao, J., LeCun, Y.: Character-level convolutional networks for text classification. Adv. NIPS (2015)

Metric Learning and Adaptive Boundary for Out-of-Domain Detection

Petr Lorenc[1]([⊠]), Tommaso Gargiani[1], Jan Pichl[1], Jakub Konrád[1], Petr Marek[1], Ondřej Kobza[1], and Jan Šedivý[2]

[1] Faculty of Electrical Engineering, Czech Technical University in Prague, Prague, Czechia
{lorenpe2,gargitom,pichljan,konrajak,marekp17,kobzaond}@fel.cvut.cz
[2] Czech Institute of Informatics, Robotics and Cybernetics, Czech Technical University in Prague, Prague, Czechia
jan.sedivy@cvut.cz

Abstract. Conversational agents are usually designed for closed-world environments. Unfortunately, users can behave unexpectedly. Based on the open-world environment, we often encounter the situation that the training and test data are sampled from different distributions. Then, data from different distributions are called out-of-domain (OOD). A robust conversational agent needs to react to these OOD utterances adequately. Thus, the importance of robust OOD detection is emphasized. Unfortunately, collecting OOD data is a challenging task. We have designed an OOD detection algorithm independent of OOD data that outperforms a wide range of current state-of-the-art algorithms on publicly available datasets. Our algorithm is based on a simple but efficient approach of combining metric learning with adaptive decision boundary. Furthermore, compared to other algorithms, we have found that our proposed algorithm has significantly improved OOD performance in a scenario with a lower number of classes while preserving the accuracy for in-domain (IND) classes.

Keywords: Conversational agent · Out-of-domain · Metric learning

1 Introduction

Conversational interfaces built on top of Alexa or Siri mainly depend on dialogue management, which is responsible for coherent reacting to user utterances and sustaining the conversational flow [13]. The dialogue management is typically based on Natural Language Understanding (NLU) classifications [14]. Nevertheless, based on the open-world assumption [9], the system cannot be prepared for all possible utterances. The utterances not taken from the train distribution are called out-of-domain (OOD). An example of a conversation with the critical necessity for OOD detection is shown in Table 1. Therefore, we focus on an algorithm for OOD detection in conversational domain. Our algorithm is based on a simple but efficient approach of combining metric learning with

P. Rosso et al. (Eds.): NLDB 2022, LNCS 13286, pp. 127–134, 2022.
https://doi.org/10.1007/978-3-031-08473-7_12

Table 1. Example of the difference between in-domain (IND) and out-of-domain (OOD) utterances for a geographical conversational agent

User:	What is the population of Italy? (IND)
Agent:	About 60 million
User:	Great. Is there any news about the Italian prime minister? (OOD)
Agent:	I am afraid that I cannot answer it. My knowledge is in geography!

adaptive decision boundary. To the best of our knowledge, we have not seen the proposed combination previously. Beside that, our algorithm also preserves performance for In-Domain (IND) classification as the two are usually performed together [10]. Additionally, our algorithm does not require collecting OOD data (Out-of-domain Data Independent) and outperforms a wide range of current state-of-the-art algorithms for OOD detection on publicly available datasets.

2 Related Work

Out-of-Domain Data Dependent. If we get access to OOD data specific to our IND classes, we can find a threshold that optimally separates IND and OOD examples as shown in [11]. The threshold is a trade-off between IND accuracy and OOD performance. The same paper shows that we can set OOD examples as $n + 1$ class and train the classification model with other IND classes. The aforementioned approaches can be used on artificially created OOD instances from IND training examples [17] or enlarge known OOD training data [3] with the help of a pretrained language model.

Out-of-Domain Data Independent. The collection of OOD data is a resource-intensive process. Therefore, recent research also focuses on detecting OOD without the need to specify OOD data.

An example of metric learning for OOD detection is in [12]. They learn deep discriminative features by forcing the network to maximize interclass variance and minimize intraclass variance. Contrary to our approach, they learn features with a recurrent neural network and focus solely on OOD detection without focusing on IND performance.

The decision boundary for OOD was introduced in [18]. Their algorithm uses a post-processing step to find proper decision boundaries around IND classes. Contrary to our approach, they select the threshold for each IND class-based statistical distribution of the model's confidences. Another example of decision boundary is used in [21]. They proposed that the bounded spherical area greatly reduces the risk of treating OOD as IND in high-dimensional vector spaces. However, their method depends on fine-tuning BERT [5], which is computationally demanding [15].

3   Proposed Algorithm

Let $D_{ID} = \{(x_1, y_1), ..., (x_n, y_n)\}$ be a dataset , where x_i is vector representation of input utterance and $y_i \in T$ is its class. Then $T = \{C_1, ...C_i\}$ is a set of seen classes. Furthermore, n_i is the number of examples for i-th class.

The first step includes learning the transformation function $T(x)$, which maximizes interclass variance and minimizes intraclass variance. After application of $T(x)$ on every x vector it increases the point density of each class C_i around its centroid c_i:

$$c_i = \frac{1}{n_i} \sum_{x_i \in C_i} T(x_i) \tag{1}$$

where n_i is the number of examples for i-th class C_i.

The following step searches for decision boundary r_i specific to each i-th class. To select best boundary r_i, we mark i-th class C_i as IND class C_{IND} and all other C_s, where $s \neq i$, as OOD class C_{OOD}. Then, for chosen i-th class C_i, we obtain the best threshold value r_i balancing the $d(x_{IND}, c_i)$ and $d(x_{OOD}, c_i)$, where $d(x, y)$ is the normalized euclidean distance between vector x and y, $x_{IND} \in C_{IND}$ and $x_{OOD} \in C_{OOD}$. Altogether, we define the stopping criterion $F(C_{IND}, C_{OOD}, r_i)$ as:

$$F(C_{IND}, C_{OOD}, r_i) = \frac{\sum_{x \in C_{OOD}} (d(x, c_i) - r_i)}{\sum_{\forall s, s \neq i} n_s} + \frac{\sum_{x \in C_{IND}} (d(x, c_i) - r_i)}{n_i} * \beta_i \tag{2}$$

where β_i is a hyper-parameter to normalize the importance of OOD performance. We have empirically observed that lower values of β are better for lower numbers of IND classes and we suggest to use:

$$\beta_i = \frac{\sum_{\forall s, s \neq i} n_s}{n_i} \tag{3}$$

for i-th IND class C_{IND} to counter the imbalance between the number of OOD and IND examples.

Then, we minimize $max(F(C_{IND}, C_{OOD}, r_i), 0)$ by iteratively increasing the threshold value r_i and evaluating the stopping criterion. We stop searching when we reach the minimum or when the number of steps exceeds the maximum iteration limit.

4   Experiments

This section introduces datasets, experimental setting and results. We also discuss ablation experiments.

4.1   Datasets

Following [21], we used two publicly available datasets – BANKING77 [1] and
CLINC150 [11]. The BANKING77 dataset contains 77 classes and 13,083 customer service queries.

The CLINC150 dataset contains 150 classes, 22,500 in-domain queries and
1,200 out-of-domain queries. An example of such queries is shown in Table 2.

Table 2. Example of customer service queries in CLINC150 [11]

Intent name	Utterance
Change_speed	Will you please slow down your voice
Shopping_list	Show everything on my to buy list
OOD	What is the name of the 13th president

4.2   Experimental Setting

Following [21], we randomly select set of IND classes from the train set and integrate them into the test set as OOD. It results in various proportions between
IND and OOD utterances – 1:4 (25% of IND and 75% of OOD), 1:2 (50% of
IND and 50% of OOD) and 3:4 (75% of IND and 25% of OOD). The accuracy
and macro F1-score were computed as the average over 10 runs. The following
pretrained sentence embeddings were used – **Universal Sentence Encoder**
(USE)[1] by [2] and **Sentence-BERT** (SBERT) by [15]. As learning objectives
for transformation function $T(x)$ we choose—Triplet Loss [8] and Large Margin
Cosine Loss (LMCL) [20]. Both learning objectives attempt to maximize interclass variance and minimize intraclass variance. All hyper-parameters of LMCL
were set to values suggested by [20], and the hyper-parameters of Triplet Loss
were set to the default value of its Tensorflow implementation. According to [21],
we compare our approach to several models: Maximum softmax probability [7]
(MSP), OpenMax [16], Deep Open Classification [18] (DOC), Adaptive Decision
Boundary [21] (ADB), and ODIST [17]. MSP calculates the softmax probability
of known samples and rejects the samples with low confidence determined by
threshold. OpenMax fits Weibull distribution to the outputs of the penultimate
layer, but still needs negative samples for selecting the best hyper-parameters.
DOC uses the sigmoid function and calculates the confidence threshold based
on Gaussian statistics. ADB learns the adaptive spherical decision boundary for
each known class with the aid of well-trained features. In addition, ODIST can
create out-of-domain instances from the in-domain training examples with the
help of a pre-trained language model. All computations were run on a virtual
instance[2].

---

[1] Deep Average Network (**DAN**) and with Transformer encoder (**TRAN**).

[2] AWS ml.m5.4xlarge.

Table 3. Results on CLINC150 dataset. (1) - Results taken from [21] (2) - Results taken from [17]. (3) - Mean of own measurements based on USE-TRAN where ± is standard deviation

| Method | 25% Known ratio | | 50% Known ratio | | 75% Known ratio | | Note |
	Accuracy	F1	Accuracy	F1	Accuracy	F1	
MSP	47.02	47.62	62.96	70.41	74.07	82.38	(1)
DOC	74.97	66.37	77.16	78.26	78.73	83.59	(1)
OpenMax	68.50	61.99	80.11	80.56	76.80	73.16	(1)
DeepUnk	81.43	71.16	83.35	82.16	83.71	86.23	(1)
ADB	87.59	77.19	86.54	85.05	86.32	88.53	(1)
ODIST	89.79	UNK	88.61	UNK	87.70	UNK	(2)
Our$_{LMCL}$	**91.81** ± 0.11	**85.90** ± 0.08	88.81 ± 0.15	89.19 ± 0.09	**88.54** ± 0.05	**92.21** ± 0.10	(3)
Our$_{Triplet}$	90.28 ± 0.07	84.82 ± 0.14	**88.89** ± 0.03	**89.44** ± 0.04	87.81 ± 0.11	91.72 ± 0.17	(3)

Table 4. Results on BANKING77 dataset. (1) - Results taken from [21] (2) - Results taken from [17]. (3) - Mean of own measurements based on USE-TRAN where ± is standard deviation

| Method | 25% Known ratio | | 50% Known ratio | | 75% Known ratio | | Note |
	Accuracy	F1	Accuracy	F1	Accuracy	F1	
MSP	43.67	50.09	59.73	71.18	75.89	83.60	(1)
DOC	56.99	58.03	64.81	73.12	76.77	83.34	(1)
OpenMax	49.94	54.14	65.31	74.24	77.45	84.07	(1)
DeepUnk	64.21	61.36	72.73	77.53	78.52	84.31	(1)
ADB	78.85	71.62	78.86	80.90	81.08	85.96	(1)
ODIST	81.69	UNK	80.90	UNK	82.79	UNK	(2)
Our$_{LMCL}$	**85.71** ± 0.13	**78.86** ± 0.10	**83.78** ± 0.14	**84.93** ± 0.08	**84.40** ± 0.21	**88.39** ± 0.11	(3)
Our$_{Triplet}$	82.71 ± 0.34	70.02 ± 0.18	81.83 ± 0.15	83.07 ± 0.15	81.82 ± 0.08	86.94 ± 0.09	(3)

4.3 Results

Our measurement, shown in Table 3 and Table 4, revealed a significant difference between different types of embeddings. USE-TRAN shows outstanding performance in all measurements. The combination of USE-TRAN with LMCL outperforms the current state-of-the-art approach in the majority of evaluations. We can also observe how different ratios of examples influence the performance of the models and conclude that our algorithm is more superior in scenarios with

Table 5. Results on CLINC150 dataset. (1) - Results taken from [21] (2) - Results taken from [17]. (3) - Own measurement with different embeddings (USE-DAN/USE-TRAN/SBERT).

| Method | 25% Known ratio | | 50% Known ratio | | 75% Known ratio | | Note |
	F1 (OOD)	F1 (IND)	F1 (OOD)	F1 (IND)	F1 (OOD)	F1 (IND)	
MSP	50.88	47.53	57.62	70.58	59.08	82.59	(1)
DOC	81.98	65.96	79.00	78.25	72.87	83.69	(1)
OpenMax	75.76	61.62	81.89	80.54	76.35	73.13	(1)
DeepUnk	87.33	70.73	85.85	82.11	81.15	86.27	(1)
ADB	91.84	76.80	88.65	85.00	83.92	88.58	(1)
ODIST	93.42	79.69	**90.62**	86.52	**85.86**	89.33	(2)
Our$_{LMCL}$	93.2/**94.5**/92.7	83.0/**85.6**/81.0	86.5/88.9/85.2	86.2/89.2/83.6	74.7/78.4/71.4	90.0/**92.3**/87.7	(3)
Our$_{Triplet}$	91.6/93.3/91.1	80.7/84.6/78.8	84.6/89.0/84.2	85.3/**89.4**/84.1	70.2/76.6/69.2	89.0/91.8/87.2	(3)

Table 6. Results on BANKING77 dataset. (1) - Results taken from [21] (2) - Results taken from [17]. (3) - Own measurement with different embeddings (USE-DAN/USE-TRAN/SBERT).

Method	25% Known ratio		50% Known ratio		75% Known ratio		Note
	F1 (OOD)	F1 (IND)	F1 (OOD)	F1 (IND)	F1 (OOD)	F1 (IND)	
MSP	41.43	50.55	41.19	71.97	39.23	84.36	(1)
DOC	61.42	57.85	55.14	73.59	50.60	83.91	(1)
OpenMax	51.32	54.28	54.33	74.76	50.85	84.64	(1)
DeepUnk	70.44	60.88	69.53	77.74	58.54	84.75	(1)
ADB	84.56	70.94	78.44	80.96	66.47	86.29	(1)
ODIST	87.11	72.72	81.32	81.79	71.95	87.20	(2)
Our$_{LMCL}$	87.5/**89.9**/89.7	74.6/**78.4**/76.7	82.4/**83.9**/82.9	82.9/**84.9**/82.6	67.0/**73.1**/69.3	86.9/**88.7**/87.0	(3)
Our$_{Triplet}$	87.5/88.0/87.3	66.8/69.1/72.9	77.5/81.9/81.2	64.6/83.0/82.1	64.5/66.8/65.9	84.7/87.2/85.4	(3)

a lower number of IND classes. This can be beneficial for conversational agents like [6] or [14].

4.4   Ablation Study

How does the number of examples influence the performance? – Since the collection of IND training data can be an expensive process, we evaluate the performance of our proposed algorithm under a scenario with a limited number of training examples. Our evaluation focused on accuracy and macro F1-score over all classes. We compare our results with the best performing results of ADB and ODIST. The results indicate that our method is very efficient even with a small fraction of train data. The results shown in Fig. 1 were performed with a random limited selection of train sentences in the CLINC150 dataset. Shown performance is the average from 5 runs.

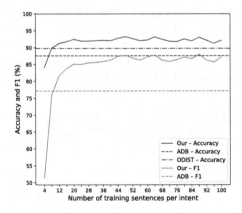

Fig. 1. Influence of the number of training sentences on the accuracy of the CLINC150 dataset. Only 25% of classes are taken as IND

What is the difference in performance between IND and OOD? Similar to [21], we also evaluate F1 over OOD and over IND, respectively. The results shown in Tables 5 and 6 have demonstrated the superior performance of our algorithm in a scenario where we classify into a smaller number of classes. This scenario is typical for conversational agents [10].

5   Conclusion

In summary, we proposed a novel algorithm for OOD detection with a combination of metric learning and adaptive boundary. The present findings might help solve the problem of OOD detection without the need for OOD training data. The theoretical part is focused on metric learning and the creation of adaptive boundaries, the crucial parts of our two-step algorithm. We describe our improvements over existing approaches and introduce our novel stopping criterion. The strengths of our work are then verified in a controlled experiment. The comparison on different datasets shows that the algorithm achieves superior performance over other state-of-the-art approaches. We showed that our algorithm finds the best decision boundary concerning IND accuracy and OOD performance, together with feasible computational requirements. We release all source code to reproduce our results[3].

5.1   Future Work and Usage

There is a rising group of other possibilities for loss functions used in the metric learning step. The Circle loss [19] or Quadruplet Loss [4] represent the next possible improvement of our algorithm. They show superior performance over LMCL. We want to investigate if improved metric learning will also increase the performance of our algorithm. With that in mind, we propose that our suggestion for a two-step algorithm is ready for usage in many scenarios concerning user input, such as a conversational agent or searching for information over a finite set of documents. In all these situations, there is a possibility that the user query is impossible to answer, leading to the fallback scenario.

Acknowledgments. This research was partially supported by the Grant Agency of the Czech Technical University in Prague, grant (SGS22/082/OHK3/1T/37).

References

1. Casanueva, I., Temcinas, T., Gerz, D., Henderson, M., Vulic, I.: Efficient Intent Detection with Dual Sentence Encoders. Association for Computational Linguistics (2020)
2. Cer, D., et al.: Universal sentence encoder. arXiv preprint arXiv:1803.11175 (2018)

---

[3] https://github.com/tgargiani/Adaptive-Boundary.

3. Chen, D., Yu, Z.: Gold: improving out-of-scope detection in dialogues using data augmentation. In: Empirical Methods in Natural Language Processing, pp. 402–434 (2021)

4. Chen, W., Chen, X., Zhang, J., Huang, K.: Beyond triplet loss: a deep quadruplet network for person re-identification. In: Conference on Computer Vision and Pattern Recognition (CVPR), pp. 1320–1329 (2017)

5. Devlin, J., Chang, M.W., Lee, K., Toutanova, K.: Bert: pre-training of deep bidirectional transformers for language understanding. In: North American Association for Computational Linguistics, pp. 68–94 (2019)

6. Finch, J.D., et al.: Emora: an inquisitive social chatbot who cares for you. In: Alexa Prize Processing, vol. 3 (2020)

7. Hendrycks, D., Gimpel, K.: A baseline for detecting misclassified and out-of-distribution examples in neural networks (2016)

8. Hoffer, E., Ailon, N.: Deep metric learning using triplet network. In: Feragen, A., Pelillo, M., Loog, M. (eds.) Similarity-Based Pattern Recognition, pp. 84–92 (2015)

9. Keet, C.M.: Open World Assumption, pp. 1567–1567. Springer, New York (2013). https://doi.org/10.1007/978-1-4419-9863-7_734

10. Konrád, J., et al.: Alquist 4.0: towards social intelligence using generative models and dialogue personalization. In: Alexa Prize Proceeding, vol. 4 (2021)

11. Larson, S., et al.: An evaluation dataset for intent classification and out-of-scope prediction. In: Proceedings of the 2019 Conference on Empirical Methods in Natural Language Processing and the 9th International Joint Conference on Natural Language Processing (2019)

12. Lin, T.E., Xu, H.: Deep unknown intent detection with margin loss. In: Proceedings of the 57th Annual Meeting of the Association for Computational Linguistics, pp. 5491–5496 (2019)

13. Moore, R.J., Arar, R.: Conversational UX design: an introduction. In: Moore, R.J., Szymanski, M.H., Arar, R., Ren, G.-J. (eds.) Studies in Conversational UX Design. HIS, pp. 1–16. Springer, Cham (2018). https://doi.org/10.1007/978-3-319-95579-7_1

14. Pichl, J., Marek, P., Konrád, J., Lorenc, P., Ta, V.D., Sedivý, J.: Alquist 3.0: Alexa prize bot using conversational knowledge graph. In: Alexa Prize Processing, vol. 3 (2020)

15. Reimers, N., Gurevych, I.: Sentence-Bert: sentence embeddings using Siamese Bert-networks. In: Proceedings of the 2019 Conference on Empirical Methods in Natural Language Processing. Association for Computational Linguistics (2019)

16. Shafaei, A., Schmidt, M., Little, J.J.: A less biased evaluation of out-of-distribution sample detectors. In: BMVC, p. 3 (2019)

17. Shu, L., Benajiba, Y., Mansour, S., Zhang, Y.: Odist: open world classification via distributionally shifted instances. In: Empirical Methods in Natural Language Processing (2021)

18. Shu, L., Xu, H., Liu, B.: Doc: deep open classification of text documents. In: Empirical Methods in Natural Language Processing, pp. 2911–2916 (2017)

19. Sun, Y., et al.: Circle loss: a unified perspective of pair similarity optimization. In: Conference on Computer Vision and Pattern Recognition (CVPR), pp. 6397–6406 (2020)

20. Wang, H., et al.: Cosface: large margin cosine loss for deep face recognition. In: CVPR, pp. 5612–5634 (2018)

21. Zhang, H., Xu, H., Lin, T.E.: Deep open intent classification with adaptive decision boundary. In: Proceedings of the AAAI Conference on Artificial Intelligence, vol. 35, pp. 14374–14382 (2021)

Classifying Documents by Viewpoint Using Word2Vec and Support Vector Machines

Jeffrey Harwell[(✉)] [iD] and Yan Li [iD]

Claremont Graduate University, Claremont, CA 91711, USA
{jeffrey.harwell,yan.li}@cgu.edu

Abstract. Ensuring viewpoint diversity in mass media is a historical challenge and recent political events, and the ever-increased use of the Internet, have made it an increasingly critical and contentious issue. This research explores the relationship between semantic structures and viewpoint; demonstrating that the viewpoint diversity in a selection of documents can be increased by utilizing extracted semantic and sentiment features. Small portions of documents matching search terms were embedded in a semantic space using word vectors and sentiment scores. The resulting features were used to train a support vector machine to differentiate documents by viewpoint in a topically homogeneous corpus. When evaluating the top 10% most probable predictions for each viewpoint, this approach yielded a lift of between 1.26 and 2.04.

Keywords: Viewpoint diversity · Word2vec embedding · Internet search · Sentiment · Machine learning · NLP

1 Introduction

The increased polarization of many societies, the deep concerns about misinformation, the rise of populist movements, and most recently the COVID-19 pandemic, raise critical questions about the role of information technology in public life and discourse. Viewpoint diversity is historically recognized as being critically important to sustaining healthy democratic societies, but it is difficult to measure [1]. And structural changes to mass media, caused in part by the rise of digital media [2], as well as political turmoil in America and Europe, have brought new urgency to this old issue. While it is naive to think that simply exposing people to diverse viewpoints will lead to engagement, understanding, and empathy [3, 4], or that all viewpoints are ethically equal, the inability to transparently account for the effect of algorithms on viewpoint diversity during content distribution has led to fears of viewpoint bias and filter bubbles [2, 5]. More concerning is the claim that, despite the vast number of sources available on the Internet, there is an underlying paucity of viewpoint diversity [6]. This research contributes a first step in investigating the relationship between semantic structures and viewpoint from a natural language processing (NLP) perspective and presents an algorithm that can detect and increase viewpoint diversity.

P. Rosso et al. (Eds.): NLDB 2022, LNCS 13286, pp. 135–143, 2022.
https://doi.org/10.1007/978-3-031-08473-7_13

Cognitive schema theory gives us a starting point to understand how viewpoint "exists" in a document. McGarry [7] uses Schema Theory to model the cognitive process of understanding the viewpoint of a document as a hierarchy of interacting frames. Language features (word choice, first person, possessives, passivization, etc.) activate frames in a certain order resulting in the foregrounding or backgrounding of certain information and indicating to the reader where they should feel empathy. This theory situates important components of viewpoint in the features of the text surrounding the subject. We show that by extracting these immediate contexts and representing the semantics in a vector space, it is possible to train a support vector machine (SVM) to detect viewpoint diversity.

2   Related Research

Extensive work has been done on the topic of diversity within the field of Information Retrieval (IR), but it has been focused on topical diversity; ensuring that all topics that could be relevant to a query are represented in the search results. Carbonell and Goldstein proposed the concept of Maximal Marginal Relevance (MMR), adding documents to search results based on relevance and dissimilarity to the documents already retrieved [8]. Akinyemia et al. conceptualized the task of increasing diversity as giving a balanced set of results to a topically ambiguous query. Wikipedia titles and faceted query expansion were employed to return results from potentially relevant topics [9].

To the best of our knowledge, Skoutas et al. [10] was the only study that took up viewpoint diversity explicitly. They noted that selecting the most dissimilar document results in an extreme, rather than representative, set of results. The authors proposed an LDA-based algorithm to select relevant documents that are also most like other clusters of documents in the corpus such that the entire corpus is well represented by the result set. Document similarity was to be measured by using min-hash and Jaccard similarity. This algorithm was not implemented, so its effectiveness is unknown. LDA was evaluated in this research, and it was not useful in identifying viewpoints within a corpus.

3   Method

As shown in Fig. 1 this research proceeds through five phases: (1) corpus creation, (2) text preprocessing, (3) context extraction, (4) feature engineering, and (5) viewpoint classification. Each phase is described in detail below.

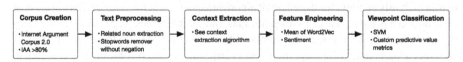

Fig. 1. Method overview

3.1 Phase 1: Corpus Creation

The Internet Argument Corpus 2.0 (IAC 2.0) [11] was selected for this research because it provides a large corpus of texts labeled by viewpoint. The full corpus contains approximately 482,000 posts collected from three online debates sites. This research used posts from 4forums.com where the inter-annotator agreement (IAA) regarding the author's stance was greater than 80%. Posts containing less than 4 tokens were excluded. Table 1 lists the stances and search keywords and Table 2 details the corpus statistics.

Table 1. Topics, stances, and keywords

Topic	Stance 1	Stance 2	Keywords
Gun control	Prefers strict gun control	Opposes strict gun control	Strict, gun, control
Abortion	Pro-life	Pro-choice	Abortion, pro-life, pro-choice
Evolution	Evolution occurs via purely natural mechanisms	Evolution involves more than purely natural mechanisms (intelligent design)	Evolution, natural, mechanism, intelligent, design
Existence of God	Atheist	Theist	Atheist, theist, God, exist

Table 2. Corpus Statistics

Topic	Number of posts (IAA > .8)	Average post length in words	Average sentence length	Stance 1 authors	Stance 2 authors
Gun control	2,842	141.0	7.5	80	180
Abortion	6,778	116.4	7.0	151	189
Evolution	4,582	151.6	7.2	201	100
Existence of God	2,696	134.7	7.3	119	115

3.2 Phase 2: Text Preprocessing

The corpus was parsed using a standard parser that includes tokenization and the removal of punctuation and stopwords. The words 'no', 'nor', and 'not' were not removed because preserving negation is theoretically important for viewpoint detection.

The search keywords (see Table 1) were only present in a small number of documents in the corpus (e.g., only 32% of the documents in the abortion forum corpus contained one of the keyword terms). To increase the number of documents that matched a search term, each set of keywords was augmented with a list of related nouns that occurred within a range of each keyword. Experimentation found that a range of four resulted in 90% of the documents in the corpus containing either a keyword or a related noun. The number of related nouns extracted for topics of gun control, abortion, evolution, and the existence of God was 2676, 2346, 2600, and 2434, respectively.

3.3 Phase 3: Context Extraction

In this phase, the context of each keyword and related noun was extracted from each matching document in the corpus. Because viewpoint is a document trait, more than one sentence of context was needed. A context size of 12 words (6 before and 6 after) was chosen, which is almost twice the length of the average sentence in the corpus after removing stopwords, punctuations, and spaces (see Table 2). Figure 2 describes the context extraction algorithm in detail.[1]

```
D_p = {parsed documents extracted from IAC 2.0}
K = {keyword terms}
R = {related nouns}
C_kd = {} // contexts for keywords extracted from document d
C_rd = {} // contexts for related nouns extracted from document d
C_id = {} // set of all beginning and ending indexes for contexts from document d

FUNCTION extract_context(S, C_d, C_id)
   FOR each term s in S
      s_s = stem s
      FOR each document d in D_p
         d_cleaned = remove stopwords, spaces, punctuation
         FOR each token t in d_cleaned
            t_s = stem of t
            t_i = index of t
            IF t_s = s_s THEN
               IF t_i not in any range in C_id THEN
                  C = all tokens ± 6 from t
                  store C in C_d
                  store beginning and ending index of C in C_id
               ENDIF
            ENDIF
         ENDFOR
      ENDFOR
   ENDFOR
END FUNCTION

extract_context(K, C_kd, C_id)
extract_context(R, C_rd, C_id)
```

Fig. 2. Context extraction algorithm

---

[1] Source code is available at https://github.com/jeffharwell/viewpointdiversity.

3.4   Phase 4: Feature Engineering

Word2vec
The semantics of a document represent an important dimension of a document's viewpoint relative to a topic. Word2vec was selected because of its effectiveness in representing semantics [12]. Computing the mean of word2vec feature vectors is an established method of representing a document [13] and is competitive with approaches such as doc2vec on small texts [14]. The keywords and related nouns represent the search topic, and they are the common element across the extracted contexts. Thus, these words were discarded before calculating the document vectors from the extracted contexts.

For each document, the mean of the word2vec representations for all tokens extracted from the search contexts was calculated, resulting in a single vector representing the search contexts. An identical operation was conducted to compute a single vector from the related noun contexts. If the document had no contexts extracted for either search or related nouns a zero vector was used to represent that context.

Sentiment
While word2vec captures the semantic similarity of the extracted contexts, semantic relatedness alone is not sufficient to differentiate viewpoint. For example, a set of product reviews could be semantically similar while representing opposite viewpoints. Sentiment analysis is effective at separating different opinions on a single topic [15] and sentiment analysis derived features are employed here to differentiate viewpoint.

To create the sentiment feature for a document three sentiment scores were calculated for each extracted context: a polarity score using Nltk Vader [16], and a polarity score and a subjectivity score using TextBlob [17]. Once again, the keyword or related noun itself was not included in the sentiment calculation. The minimum, maximum, and average of each of these sentiment scores for keyword contexts and related noun contexts was computed, and then the keyword sentiment scores, and related noun sentiments scores, were averaged to create a final nine sentiment feature for each document.

Final Feature Vector
To create the final feature vector for each document, the word2vec mean for all keyword contexts was appended to the word2vec mean for all related noun contexts. Experimental results showed that appending the two vectors resulted in better discrimination of viewpoints than averaging them. It seems that the context of related nouns interacts with the context of keywords in a way that is beneficial to differentiating viewpoints, whereas a simple average of the two vectors does not capture that interaction. The final feature vector includes 609 dimensions - 300 for keyword contexts, 300 for related nouns contexts, and 9 for sentiment features.

3.5   Phase 5: Viewpoint Classification

Support Vector Machines (SVM) find a hyperplane separating two classes in a high dimensional space making them well suited for the task of separating documents embedded in a high dimensional vector space. SVMs have a proven record in natural language processing and information retrieval and they have been used successfully in text classification tasks using word vector derived features [18]. Logistic regression was evaluated but it was mostly unable to separate the viewpoints in the feature space and so it was not employed against the full data set. It is possible that a pre-trained transformer would also be effective, but the aim of this research was to demonstrate the feasibility of the approach, and so this would be a subject of future research.

Our goal is to return documents that represent the most distinct viewpoints, i.e., posts with the highest posterior probabilities for each class. The traditional classification metric, binary classification based on the posterior probability of 50%, is not suitable for this task. Instead, we created a custom metric (see Fig. 3) that maximized the number of correct classifications in the top 10% of the posterior probabilities for each class.

p_i = {top 10% most probable predictions for class i}
a_i = {correct answer for predictions in p_i}
t_i = {correct predictions for class i given p_i and a_i}
f_i = {incorrect predictions for class i given p_i and a_i}

$PPV = t_1 / (t_1 + f_1) // i = 1$ for the positive class
$NPV = t_0 / (t_0 + f_0) // i = 0$ for the negative class

imbalance penalty $= abs((PPV - NPV) / 2)$

custom metric value $= \log_e (PPV + 1) + \log_e(NPV + 1)$ - imbalance penalty

Fig. 3. Custom metric definition

The Scikit-learn [19] SVM implementation was used with a radial basis function kernel. The data was scaled and trained using 80%/20% stratified sampling. A grid search was performed using the training data to find an optimal C and γ. Fivefold stratified cross-validation was used during the grid search and the relative class percentages were preserved for each fold.

4 Results

Three different pre-trained word vectors were evaluated; 300d GloVe vectors pre-trained based on Wikipedia, Common Crawl, and Twitter [20], 300d fastText subword vectors pre-trained based on Wikipedia, UMBC Web Based, and the statmt.org news dataset [21], and the 300d word2vec vectors pre-trained based on the Google News corpus [12]. The best model, presented in Table 3, used word2vec.

The assignment of a viewpoint to the "positive" class or the "negative" class is arbitrary and both viewpoints are equally important. Any application of the model will require a selection of true negative and true positive documents. Precision, Recall, and hence F1, do not consider true negatives and so they do not provide a full picture of effectiveness. It is necessary to consider the negative predictive value (NPV) and lift for both classes to understand how the model performs in identifying viewpoints.

The abortion topic had a more balanced number of documents for each viewpoint (41%/59%) and the model delivered a lift of 1.76 and 1.46 for the positive and negative classes respectively. The gun control and evolution topics both had a significant imbalance of viewpoint in the corpus. In both cases the models delivered low lift for the majority viewpoint, 1.06 and 1.22 for the evolution and gun control topics respectively, but a significant lift for the minority viewpoint, 2.00 and 2.04, respectively. In both cases, the model accomplishes the design goal of identifying the minority view effectively. On the existence of God topic, the model did not perform as well, delivering a low PPV of .58 for the minority class (positive in this case) and a preference for the majority viewpoint over the minority viewpoint.

Table 3. Results

Topic	Parameters	N	Performance[a]
Evolution	$C = 1$ $\gamma = 0.01$	Class 1 = 642 (0.71) Class 0 = 265 (0.29)	PPV = .75 NPV = .58 Lift Class 1:0 = 1.06:2.00
Abortion	$C = 1$ $\gamma = 0.001$	Class 1 = 552 (0.41) Class 0 = 786 (0.59)	PPV = .72 NPV = .86 Lift Class 1:0 = 1.76:1.46
Existence of God	$C = 100$ $\gamma = 0.001$	Class 1 = 244 (0.46) Class 0 = 289 (0.54)	PPV = .58 NPV = .83 Lift Class 1:0 = 1.26:1.54
Gun control	$C = 5$ $\gamma = 0.001$	Class 1 = 161 (0.28) Class 0 = 404 (0.72)	PPV = .57 NPV = .88 Lift Class 1:0 = 2.04:1.22

[a] PPV, NPV, and Lift were calculated on the combined top 10% of results for each class as ranked by posterior probability. Class 1 is positive.

5 Conclusions and Future Research

In this research, we have demonstrated that extracting the immediate contexts of a search term and embedding those contexts in a word2vec vector space along with sentiment features allows an SVM to effectively distinguish viewpoints within a topic. This is an important discovery which demonstrates that viewpoint can be represented by semantic structures extracted from documents. It is likely that additional features, such as reading level, negations, and the presence of questions, would further improve performance. These features will be investigated in future work.

The approach in its present form would not generalize well to unseen topics. An SMV trained on one topic would not effectively distinguish viewpoints when applied to a different topic because viewpoints within different topics are embedded in different parts of the semantic space. It is not clear if every topic has a unique viewpoint topology inherent in its embedding or if there are features within an embedding that correspond to viewpoint differences in a more general way. Work is underway to investigate the relationship in the feature space between pairs of documents that have the same or opposite viewpoints.

References

1. Napoli, P.M.: Deconstructing the diversity principle. J. Commun. **49**, 7–34 (1999)
2. Webster, J.G.: The Marketplace of Attention: How Audiences Take Shape in a Digital Age. The MIT Press, Cambridge (2014)
3. Putnam, R.D.: E pluribus unum: diversity and community in the twenty-first century the 2006 Johan Skytte prize lecture. Scand. Polit. Stud. **30**, 137–174 (2007)
4. Haidt, J., Rosenberg, E., Hom, H.: Differentiating diversities: moral diversity is not like other kinds. J. Appl. Soc. Psychol. **33**, 1–36 (2003)
5. Pariser, E.: The Filter Bubble: What the Internet is Hiding From You. Penguin UK (2011)
6. Ognyanova, K.: Intermedia agenda setting in an era of fragmentation: applications of network science in the study of mass communication. University of Southern California (2013)
7. McGarry, R.G.: The Subtle Slant: A Cross-Linguistic Discourse Analysis Model for Evaluating Interethnic Conflict in the Press. Parkway Publishers, Inc. (1994)
8. Carbonell, J., Goldstein, J.: The use of MMR, diversity-based reranking for reordering documents and producing summaries. In: Proceedings of the 21st Annual International ACM SIGIR Conference on Research and Development in Information Retrieval, pp 335–336. ACM (1998)
9. Akinyemi, J.A., Clarke, C.L., Kolla, M.: Towards a collection-based results diversification. In: Adaptivity, Personalization and Fusion of Heterogeneous Information, pp. 202–205. Le Centre de Hautes Etudes Internationales d'Informatique Documentaire (2010)
10. Skoutas, D., Minack, E., Nejdl, W.: Increasing diversity in web search results. Raleigh, North Carolina, United States (2010)
11. Abbott, R., Ecker, B., Anand, P., Walker, M.: Internet argument corpus 2.0: an SQL schema for dialogic social media and the corpora to go with it. In: Proceedings of the Tenth International Conference on Language Resources and Evaluation (LREC 2016), pp. 4445–4452 (2016)
12. Mikolov, T., Chen, K., Corrado, G., Dean, J.: Efficient estimation of word representations in vector space. In: Proceedings of Workshop at ICLR, Scottsdale, AZ (2013)
13. Pantel, P., Lin, D.: Discovering word senses from text. In: Proceedings of the eighth ACM SIGKDD International Conference on Knowledge Discovery and Data Mining, pp. 613–619 (2002)
14. Lau, J.H., Baldwin, T.: An empirical evaluation of doc2vec with practical insights into document embedding generation. In: Proceedings of the 1st Workshop on Representation Learning for NLP, pp. 78–86 (2016)
15. Jebaseeli, A.N., Kirubakaran, E.: A survey on sentiment analysis of (product) reviews. Int. J. Comput. Appl. **47** (2012)
16. Hutto, C., Gilbert, E.: VADER: A parsimonious rule-based model for sentiment analysis of social media text. In: Proceedings of the International AAAI Conference on Web and Social Media (2014)
17. Loria, S.: TextBlob Documentation. Release 0.16 (2020). http://textblob.readthedocs.io. Accessed 19 Apr 2022
18. Lilleberg, J., Zhu, Y., Zhang, Y.: Support vector machines and word2vec for text classification with semantic features. In: 2015 IEEE 14th International Conference on Cognitive Informatics & Cognitive Computing (ICCI* CC), pp. 136–140. IEEE (2015)

19. Pedregosa, F., Varoquaux, G., Gramfort, A., et al.: Scikit-learn: machine learning in Python. J. Mach. Learn. Res. **12**, 2825–2830 (2011)
20. Pennington, J., Socher, R., Manning, C.D.: GloVe: global vectors for word representation. In: Empirical Methods in Natural Language Processing (EMNLP), pp. 1532–1543 (2014)
21. Mikolov, T., Grave, E., Bojanowski, P., et al.: Advances in pre-training distributed word representations. In: Proceedings of the International Conference on Language Resources and Evaluation (LREC 2018) (2018)

Applications

Extracting and Understanding
Call-to-actions of Push-Notifications

Beatriz Esteves[1](✉) , Kieran Fraser[2] , Shridhar Kulkarni[2] ,
Owen Conlan[2] , and Víctor Rodríguez-Doncel[1]

[1] Ontology Engineering Group, Universidad Politécnica de Madrid, Madrid, Spain
beatriz.gesteves@upm.es, vrodriguez@fi.upm.es
[2] ADAPT Centre, Trinity College Dublin, Dublin, Ireland
{kieran.fraser,shridhar.kulkarni,owen.conlan}@adaptcentre.ie

Abstract. Push-notifications are a communication tool leveraged by
many apps to disseminate information, engage with their user base and
provide a means of encouraging users to take particular actions. The
nuanced intent behind a push is not always distinguishable to the end-
user at moments of delivery. This work explores the text content of notifications pushed by a number of prominent apps in the marketplace over
the period of 463 days. We present a new ontology that defines notification Call-to-action (CTA) labels in use today. This facilitates greater
understanding behind a push and is a step towards standardisation for
marketing teams. Subsequently, we then present results of a notification
dataset annotated with our CTA labels and propose and evaluate a CTA
text classification task, which could facilitate improved solutions for both
users subscribed to, and marketers creating, push-notifications.

Keywords: Push-notification · Call-to-action · Ontology engineering ·
Multi-label classification · Marketing

1 Introduction

In recent years, push-notifications have grown from a mechanism alerting users
to new information to being a key persuasive weapon in a brand's arsenal for
enticing engagement, increasing purchases and achieving many other Key Performance Indicators (KPIs), on which business success is measured. Users of technology subscribe to receiving communication from brands when they download
their app and/or opt-in via their platform (e.g. mobile vs web push). However,
many of these subscribers, at the point of opt-in, are unaware of the actions these
brands will subsequently try and nudge them to make through the medium of
push-notification. Consent dialogue boxes have been predominantly used since
the introduction of the GDPR, however, it has been shown that these do not
facilitate a sufficient understanding of usage to end-users and actually tend to
manipulate actions [17]. Persuasive Technology research [5,6] has uncovered techniques leveraged in mobile app messaging and how effective they are at nudging
users into a particular pattern of behaviour or taking a particular action.

P. Rosso et al. (Eds.): NLDB 2022, LNCS 13286, pp. 147–159, 2022.
https://doi.org/10.1007/978-3-031-08473-7_14

With advances in Natural Language Processing research and its deployment in commercial applications, a number of platforms have appeared which aid marketing teams create text content which is personalized and tailored for maximizing engagement. *Phrasee*[1] and *Copy.ai*[2] are such examples of this. Whilst the text generated from these platforms is widely distributed, there is no consensus on, or taxonomy for, the types of Call-to-action (CTA) that are embedded in the subsequent copy pushed at subscribers, particularly with respect to push-notifications, which have limited character space and therefore can be less transparent with respect to the action they are encouraging. This paper addresses this by examining push-notification copy, forming a taxonomy of CTA labels and facilitating CTA prediction.

2 Background

Fig. 1. Visual representation of the components of a common mobile push-notification.

Mobile push-notifications have been a subject of study since their conception by Blackberry's Research in Motion team [15]. Push-notifications give app owners and marketing teams a direct communication channel to subscribers. The visual representation of a push-notification, illustrated in Fig. 1, differs slightly depending on the platform, but it is generally composed of a text title, ticker text (i.e. descriptive text up to 240 characters on Android devices) and icon. Rich-media notifications, introduced in 2016[3], further support images, videos and interactive elements, creating a multi-modal experience. Research has studied numerous aspects of push-notifications and their impact on subscribers – from timing [8], frequency [16] and alert modality [4] to subscriber location [9], content preferences [14] and receptivity [1], amongst many others. In recent years, emphasis has been placed on push-notification transparency as dark patterns have been identified and poor notification management has been shown to negatively impact end-users [3,10].

Mehrotra et al. created PrefMiner [13] to identify patterns of notification types delivered in varying contexts and visualize if-then rules to aid understanding of how and when notifications were being pushed in-the-wild. In contrast, Liu et al. [12] took an offensive approach toward finding notification delivery patterns that were untoward by crawling app UI elements, autonomously triggering notifications and subsequently categorizing them with respect to their

---

[1] https://phrasee.co/.

[2] https://www.copy.ai/.

[3] https://www.adjust.com/blog/a-decade-of-push-notifications-with-braze/.

aggressive behavior using a novel taxonomy. It was concluded that aggressive notifications could be found across numerous app categories and called for the community to "take actions to detect and mitigate apps involving aggressive push notifications". This paper contributes toward the transparency of push-notification content by providing clear definitions of call-to-actions embedded in the text content of notifications which can be used to inform subscribers of what they are being nudged to do.

Push-notification text content has also previously been studied. Li et al. [11] autonomously identified and extracted text templates within push-notification content, Fraser et al. [5] studied persuasive aspects of the text and the impact on notification engagement, Mehrotra et al. [13,14] studied the titles of notifications and i) categorized them with respect to sender relationship and ii) clustered the notifications delivered from individual apps. Kanjo et al. [20] studied the frequency and positioning of emojis in the content of mobile notifications. Yet, to our knowledge, no research has addressed Call-to-actions associated with the text content of mobile push-notifications, nor could a taxonomy for such be found. The closest related work identified was that of the IAB Tech Lab who developed an "Audience Taxonomy"[4] with the main purpose of describing and segmenting the target audiences of data management platforms and analytics' providers, into three core pillars for audience segmentation: (i) demographic characteristics, e.g., gender or financial status; (ii) purchase intent; and (iii) interests, e.g., sports or literature preferences. Whilst this taxonomy provides detail on how notification subscribers could be segmented by apps/marketers and sent differing types of notification content, it does not provide detail about the subsequent actions which each segment are commonly nudged to perform through notifications. This work bridges this gap by providing a taxonomy for notification Call-to-actions.

3   Methodology

This section outlines the methodology proposed and implemented for: curating a mobile notification dataset (Sect. 3.1); extracting and defining CTA labels of mobile notifications (Sect. 3.2); annotating mobile notifications with CTA labels (Sect. 3.4); creating an ontology for the Annotation of Push-Notifications (APN) (Sect. 3.3). The output of this work contributes to aiding classification and transparency of mobile push-notifications with respect to their intention to nudge subscribers for particular actions, and subsequently also better informs marketing teams as to what combination of text features provides optimal clarity for a particular CTA.

3.1   Collecting Real-Time Push-Notification Data

The notification dataset discussed in this work was collected via a social listening tool created by EmPushy[5]. A purpose built Android application was developed

---

[4] https://iabtechlab.com/standards/audience-taxonomy/.

[5] https://www.empushy.com.

to observe notifications delivered in real-time. This push-aware application was deployed on an Android emulator running 24/7 over the period of 463 days from October 2020 to January 2022. During this time, 432 applications, spanning all category of application type, were installed on the emulator device from the Google Play Store[6]. Once installed, the push-aware application began logging notification content (such as title and ticker text) and associated metadata (such as the posting app, notification category and time of delivery) in real-time. This enabled time-sequenced notification data to be collected and stored for analysis. In total, 82,362 notifications were logged.

Alternative methods of collecting notifications have been demonstrated in related research [9,13,21]. Researchers have developed applications which observe incoming notifications, but in contrast to the approach presented in this paper, these apps were deployed *in-the-wild* on end-user devices. Limitations of this approach include the necessity to: recruit participants to download and use the notification-logging application; motivate participants to remain engaged over an extended period of time and ensure sensitive data is not collected. Using end-user devices also creates a limitation on the number of apps which can be monitored, as installation of apps is at the end-user's discretion. As the emulator does not contain any specific user information or sensitive data and as engagement with applications installed on the device can be simulated constantly over a long period of time, the proposed method addresses limitations found with *in-the-wild* approaches.

3.2   Understanding Call-to-actions in Mobile Push

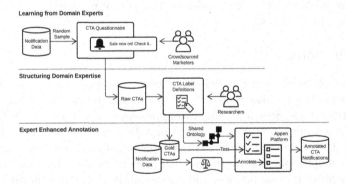

Fig. 2. An overview of the approach for expert-informed annotation of mobile push-notifications

The notification collection method facilitated the subsequent analysis of live push-notification campaigns and their intended CTAs. Figure 2 illustrates the approach taken to leverage domain knowledge for defining CTAs which subsequently informed the development of a push-notification ontology and provided

---

[6] Full app details available on the project website: https://empushy.github.io/nldb22.

clear label definitions for the crowdsourced annotation of push-notifications. The process was executed as follows:

1. **Learning from Domain Experts**
   During this phase, a questionnaire was created to collect opinions from marketers on aspects of the notifications. For each notification, the text content was displayed and a free-text field facilitated collection of the associated CTA. The questionnaire was presented to a crowd of experienced marketers sourced using the Prolific Academic platform[7]. In total, 66 marketers expressed an opinion, in their own words, regarding the associated perceived call-to-action for 10 distinct (non-overlapping) notifications each.

2. **Structuring Domain Expertise**
   During this phase, the dataset of 660 notifications, which included associated CTAs, was used to inform the creation of a high level taxonomy of CTA labels. The first 3 authors took 220 notifications each and, in isolation, created a high level taxonomy of labels using the marketers opinions and additional features of the notification (such as app category and app type) as an aid. All 3 researchers then consolidated their taxonomies into a final set of CTA labels, informed by marketing experts, and updated the 660 notifications to reflect the associated agreed CTA label. In addition, the final CTA definitions were used to create a computer ontology (discussed in Sect. 3.3) to be shared with the research community.

3. **Expert Enhanced Annotation**
   During this phase, a crowdsource annotation platform, Appen[8], was used to further label notifications with CTAs at scale. The gold-standard notification dataset with CTA labels and the shared ontology expressing the CTA definitions were used to educate and inform the annotation crowd. The output was an annotated notification dataset used for classifying CTAs in mobile push-notifications.

3.3   Creating an Ontology to Annotate Notifications

In order to determine the extent of the ontology, formal competency questions were made using the methodology described by Suárez-Figueroa [19] and the collected requirements are presented in the Ontology Requirement Specification Document (ORSD)[9]. Once the requirements were specified, and using the labels generated through the questionnaires made to crowdsourced marketers, as specified in Fig. 2, the Chowlk Visual Notation tool [2] was used to generate the ontology's diagram and RDF specification.

3.4   Annotating Call-to-actions in Mobile Push

On completion of the APN, an annotation task was created to annotate mobile push-notifications at scale. The Appen platform was used to launch the task due

---

[7] Crowdsource research platform: https://www.prolific.co/.

[8] Crowdsource annotation platform: https://appen.com/.

[9] Available at: https://w3id.org/apn/#orsd.

to its global workforce and self-service dashboard enabling maximum control over task creation and execution. APN was used to inform workers of the label definitions and the gold-standard CTA dataset was used to educate and evaluate workers as they proceeded with the task. Workers were required to annotate 20 notifications sampled from the gold-standard dataset before they could proceed. If they did not achieve (and maintain throughout the task) a *trust score* of 70% or above, they were unable to proceed. Each notification was annotated by at least 3 workers, however, if a confidence score threshold (of 0.7) was not achieved after 3 annotations, further workers were permitted to annotate the notification (a maximum annotation limit of 4 per notification was set). The confidence score, as defined by Appen, describes the level of agreement between workers and is weighted based on the *trust score* each worker maintains whilst answering test questions. The notification CTA labels are not mutually exclusive, therefore workers could select multiple CTAs for a single notification (e.g. a notification could be nudging the user to both "claim" a discount while making a "purchase").

Of the 82,362 notifications logged through EmPushy's social listening tool, 9,461 notifications were uploaded to the Appen platform for crowd annotation. These notifications represented the most diverse set whilst maintaining a balance between the category of app (as defined by the Google Play Store) and also a balance between notifications pushed by distinct apps in each category. Additionally, the text content of each notification was cleaned and notifications which were found to contain empty, null, non-english or duplicate text values were dropped. For apps which pushed a large number of notifications, the most diverse set was chosen by converting the text of each notification to sentence embedding [18] and ranking by cosine similarity – the notifications that were least similar to all others were first candidates for inclusion. In total, 1,569 workers from 26 different countries participated in the annotation task, of which 854 maintained a trust score of 70% or higher and annotated, on average, 30 notifications each. On completion of the task, 1,334 (14%) notifications required just 3 annotations to reach a confidence threshold of 0.7 – the collective confidence score of this group was 0.83. The remaining 8127 (85%) reached the limit of 4 annotations and collectively had a confidence score of 0.625–1,711 of these achieving confidence of 0.7 or higher. Kruskal-Wallis tests revealed annotator agreement was statistically significantly different between the CTA categories, $\chi^2(10) = 961.509, p < .001$, and between app types posting the notifications $\chi^2(32) = 257.947, p < .001$. This suggests that some notification CTAs are easier to identify than others and that this also varies depending on the type of app category pushing the notification.

4   APN – An Ontology for the Annotation of Push-Notifications

The ontology for the Annotation of Push-Notifications (APN) aims to provide a tool that can be used to model different aspects of push-notifications. The scope of this ontology is limited to the definition of a set of parameters that can be used to classify push-notification data, in particular its text content, with the end goal of creating a service which pushes more empathetic content to subscribers[10]. In this context, APN provides five taxonomies to categorize push-notifications in terms of their call-to-action, its urgency to be delivered, the presence of information that can be used to infer personal data, its target audience and the marketing campaign type. As this article focus on the understanding and prediction of CTAs in push-notification text, the authors will focus on CTA categories' definitions as the others are out of scope for this particular work.

The base concepts specified by APN are shown in Fig. 3 as boxes, with properties represented as arrows. Apart from the categorizations mentioned above, push-notifications can be annotated with its ID, `apn:notificationID`, and the time of delivery, `apn:pushedOn`, and can be associated with information related to application that pushed them. Aside from the usual app metadata, e.g. information about number of downloads (`apn:numberOfDownloads`), reviews (`apn:numberOfReviews`), stars (`apn:stars`) or install date (`apn:installDate`), information about the application type is also stored using the Google Play Store categories list[11].

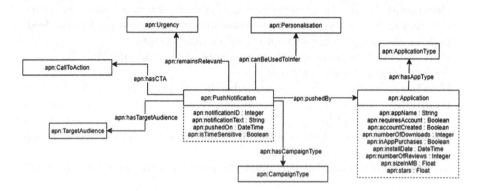

Fig. 3. Base concepts of the APN ontology.

The different types of CTA labeled in APN are specified in Fig. 4. As previously mentioned, these labels were established by the authors as a result of a consultation study where crowdsourced marketers were asked to label a random sample of push-notification texts from the collected dataset.

The definitions of CTAs specified by APN are presented below and examples of APN-annotated notifications are available in the ontology documentation[12].

– **Account Management:** Notifications that encourage subscribers to create and/or log into an account to take advantage of a certain feature.

---

[10] Online documentation for this ontology is available at: https://w3id.org/apn/.

[11] App categories: https://shorturl.at/xyAFI.

[12] Annotated notification examples: https://w3id.org/apn/#x9-examples.

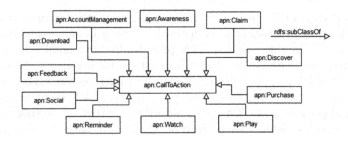

Fig. 4. APN taxonomy for the categorization of call-to-actions.

- **Awareness:** Notifications that make subscribers aware of information that does not need further investigation by the subscriber, e.g., a new feature, upcoming holiday, weather, stock price, or score of a match.
- **Claim:** Notifications that encourage the subscribers to click and claim some prize or reward from the application.
- **Discover:** Notifications that tease the content of the information itself to generate curiosity on the users and lead them to engage with the app.
- **Download:** Notifications to get the subscriber to download some resource.
- **Feedback:** Notifications to get the subscriber to provide some form of feedback or response, for instance on the app's functionalities.
- **Play:** Notifications related with gaming apps, where the subscriber is encouraged to re-engage with the game.
- **Purchase:** Notifications to get the subscriber to purchase a product.
- **Reminder:** Notifications that serve as a reminder or alert to the users or provide advice and tips.
- **Social:** Notifications that encourage the subscriber to engage with social tools e.g. share, like, comment, reply.
- **Watch:** Notifications that encourage the subscriber to watch some content.

5   Understanding Notifications and Call-to-actions

Following the collection and annotation of mobile notifications a number of classifiers were created and evaluated at predicting call-to-actions given notification text content. Feature engineering was applied to the notification dataset to better understand the individual elements of push-notifications that have a significant impact on CTAs. Three general feature categories were defined: **app-metadata**, which describes public information regarding the app pushing notifications; **noti-object**, which describes parameters of the notification that pertain to its state when delivered to a device; and **noti-text**, which describes individual elements of the text content which was pushed. The full table of features used can be found on the project website. Additional semantic features were added to the noti-text category of the annotated CTA dataset using Codeq's NLP API[13]. The

---

[13] https://api.codeq.com/.

NLTK, TextBlob, advertools and holiday python packages were used to engineer additional features from the dataset. In total, 198 unique features were used for analysis.

5.1 Pre-annotation Findings

Of the 432 apps installed during the active period, 346 (80%) were found to push notifications. *Sports, News* and *Shopping* category apps accounted for the majority of notifications pushed (41%, 20% and 12% respectively) with categories such as *Comics, House & Home* and *Photography* pushing less frequently. On average, apps tended to push 0.6 notifications per day throughout this period. Thursdays were the most popular day to push notifications whilst Mondays the least popular and notifications were sent more frequently in the afternoon (12h-17h) and early evening (18h-19h) as opposed to early morning (5h-8h) and early night (22h-23h).

Goodman and Kruskal's λ [7] was run to determine whether delivery date features of a notification (month of year, day of week, time of day) could be better predicted using knowledge of the type of app pushing the notification. Goodman and Kruskal's λ was statistically significant $p < .001$ for month (2.1% reduction in error of prediction), day (3.8%) and time (2.5%), highlighting that the specific time and date of a pushed notification could be better predicted when the category of app is known. A Kruskal-Wallis test was used to determine if there were differences in text content between notifications pushed by different app categories. Text features such as the number of stop words, number of emojis, average word length, number of sentences etc. were used to describe the text content. Statistically significant ($p < .001$) differences were found between app categories for all 24 features describing the text content. For example, the notification text content of entertainment apps had a significantly higher frequency of emoji use (mean rank = 49924) than that found in medical apps (mean rank = 26740). This illustrates the diversity of text used within notifications across market domains and suggests marketers within each app category abide by unique structures. This aligns with the work of Li et al. [11] which autonomously extracted notification templates used by apps associated with different categories, such as *social* or *shopping*.

Table 1. Findings from annotated CTA dataset.

(a) Goodman and Kruskal's λ results

Feature	Reduced err	p
app type	9.7%	<.001
num. app downloads	2.5%	<.001
Position emoji	1%	<.001
Position numeric char	3%	<.001
Position currency	3.7%	<.001

(b) Kruskal Wallis H Test results

Feature	χ^2	p
Count stopwords	151.9	<.001
Count emojis	287.1	<.001
Sentence length	156.4	<.001
Sentiment	80.6	<.001

5.2   Post-annotation Findings

All 11 call-to-action labels were found to be represented in the annotated noti-fication dataset. The labels were not mutually exclusive, therefore a number of instances were tagged with multiple labels. Goodman and Kruskal's λ was used to determine whether the CTA could be better predicted through use of app-meta, noti-object and noti-text features. Results, illustrated in Table 1a, show statistically significant reductions in error of prediction of CTA when consid-ering multiple notification features, all of which are available at the moment of delivery, thus potentially facilitating edge devices to tag notifications with CTAs in real-time and flag them to mobile subscribers, increasing transparency and explainability. Similarly, Table 1b depicts significant results from Kruskal Wallis H tests which were run to determine whether there were differences in text features between CTA categories. Findings suggests the use of stop words, emojis and sentiment do differ between CTA categories as does the length of the notification content itself. This analysis provides useful insight to the features, both present in the notification object and engineered from the notification text content, that can be used to predict notification CTAs.

5.3   Evaluating CTA Classification

Push-notification CTA inference, in the scope of this work, was defined as a multi-label classification problem and 6 algorithms were applied to set perfor-mance benchmarks for this task. Scikit-learn implementations of Random Forest, Decision Tree, Support Vector Machine, Gradient Boosting and XGBoost clas-sifiers were trained and evaluated on the task. Input features were comprised of app-metadata, noti-object and noti-text features – 198 in total. Categorical features were one-hot encoded and numeric features scaled to unit variance. Due to the large number of features and the subsequent sparse input vector (of length 345), dimensionality reduction was applied using Principal Component Analysis (PCA) to further optimize input. It was found that 80 principal components accounted for 85% of the variance. The data was split into subsets of training (80%), validation (10%) and test (10%). Training and validation sets were cre-ated using k-fold (k = 3) cross-validation. Model parameters were tuned to find the best estimator in each case. Table 2 illustrates the F1, precision, recall and ROC scores achieved by each model on the held-back test set.

Table 2. Push-notification multi-label CTA inference benchmark performance.

Model	F1	Precision	Recall	ROC
Random Forest	0.74	0.99	0.61	0.80
Decision Tree	0.64	0.67	0.69	0.81
SVM (sigmoid)	0.29	0.20	0.59	0.59
SVM (RBF)	0.75	0.98	0.64	0.82
Gradient Boosting	0.74	0.94	0.65	0.82
XGBoost	0.74	0.91	0.67	0.82

The Support Vector Machine (with RBF kernel) achieved the highest average F1 score (0.75), closely followed by Random Forest, Gradient Boosting and XGBoost classifiers. These models also achieved high precision scores meaning that, if applied to aid marketers creating a notification for a particular CTA, the probability of the model to predict a False Positive is low (e.g. mistakenly inferring the CTA as a *purchase* when it is not, potentially reinforcing false confidence in the marketer and causing them to push a notification with a CTA unaligned with their intended purpose). Future work will focus on improving the recall and overall F1 measure for push-notification CTA classification.

6 Conclusions

Push-notifications are sent by different apps with different intents. This paper has studied the text sent by 346 apps over 463 days, with the following results: (i) an ontology of push-notifications, including 11 categories of Call-to-action labels; (ii) a dataset of notifications annotated with these labels and (iii) a first exploration of the performance of standard text classification techniques, with very reasonable results, that can facilitate improved transparency and clarity of actions embedded in, and encouraged by, push-notifications.

This work is also an important advance in relation to the current labeling of push-notifications, as it represents a step towards standardizing their categorization. With this solution, marketers can provide more personalized services and subscribers have a basis for specifying what types of notifications they want to receive. Whilst there are some notifications not captured by the collection method proposed in this work, such as notifications related to certain app engagement behaviour, it does inform future work in which an *in-the-wild* approach including real user data (and proper anonymization methods) would provide a more extensive and balanced dataset. Additionally, other Linked Open Data sources, such as DBpedia, WikiData or the EU Open Data Portal, can in the future be leveraged to enrich the notification dataset and provide additional features to the classification tasks.

Funding Acknowledgements. This research has been supported by the European Union's Horizon 2020 research and innovation programme under the Marie Skłodowska-Curie grant agreement No 813497 (PROTECT) as well as with the financial support of Enterprise Ireland, the European Regional Development Fund (ERDF) under Ireland's European Structural and Investment Funds Programme 2014–2020 and Science Foundation Ireland under Grant Agreement No. 13/RC/2106_P2 at the ADAPT SFI Research Centre at Trinity College Dublin.

References

1. Avraham Bahir, R., Parmet, Y., Tractinsky, N.: Effects of visual enhancements and delivery time on receptivity of mobile push notifications. In: Extended Abstracts of CHI 2019, pp. 1–6 (2019)

2. Chávez-Feria, S., García-Castro, R., Poveda-Villalón, M.: Converting UML-based ontology conceptualizations to OWL with Chowlk. In: Verborgh, R., et al. (eds.) ESWC 2021. LNCS, vol. 12739, pp. 44–48. Springer, Cham (2021). https://doi.org/10.1007/978-3-030-80418-3_8

3. Elhai, J.D., Levine, J.C., Dvorak, R.D., Hall, B.J.: Fear of missing out, need for touch, anxiety and depression are related to problematic smartphone use. Comput. Hum. Behav. **63**, 509–516 (2016)

4. Exler, A., Günes, Z., Beigl, M.: Preferred notification modalities depending on the location and the location-based activity. In: UbiComp/ISWC 2019 Adjunct Proceedings, pp. 1064–1069 (2019)

5. Fraser, K., Conlan, O.: Enticing notification text & the impact on engagement. In: UbiComp/ISWC 2020 Adjunct Proceedings, pp. 444–449 (2020)

6. Fraser, K., Yousuf, B., Conlan, O.: Scrutable and persuasive push-notifications. In: Oinas-Kukkonen, H., Win, K.T., Karapanos, E., Karppinen, P., Kyza, E. (eds.) PERSUASIVE 2019. LNCS, vol. 11433, pp. 67–73. Springer, Cham (2019). https://doi.org/10.1007/978-3-030-17287-9_6

7. Goodman, L.A., Kruskal, W.H.: Measures of association for cross classifications. In: Measures of Association for Cross Classifications. Springer Series in Statistics, pp. 2–34. Springer, New York (1979). https://doi.org/10.1007/978-1-4612-9995-0_1

8. Ho, B.J., Balaji, B., Koseoglu, M., Srivastava, M.: Nurture: notifying users at the right time using reinforcement learning. In: UbiComp/ISWC 2018 Adjunct Proceedings, pp. 1194–1201 (2018)

9. Komninos, A., Simou, I., Frengkou, E., Garofalakis, J.: Discovering user location semantics using mobile notification handling behaviour. In: Chatzigiannakis, I., De Ruyter, B., Mavrommati, I. (eds.) AmI 2019. LNCS, vol. 11912, pp. 219–234. Springer, Cham (2019). https://doi.org/10.1007/978-3-030-34255-5_15

10. Lee, Y.K., Chang, C.T., Lin, Y., Cheng, Z.H.: The dark side of smartphone usage: psychological traits, compulsive behavior and technostress. Comput. Hum. Behav. **31**, 373–383 (2014)

11. Li, Y., Yang, Z., Guo, Y., Chen, X., Agarwal, Y., Hong, J.I.: Automated extraction of personal knowledge from smartphone push notifications. In: 2018 IEEE International Conference on Big Data (Big Data), pp. 733–742 (2018)

12. Liu, T., Wang, H., Li, L., Bai, G., Guo, Y., Xu, G.: DaPanda: detecting aggressive push notifications in android apps. In: 2019 34th IEEE/ACM International Conference on Automated Software Engineering (ASE), pp. 66–78 (2019)

13. Mehrotra, A., Hendley, R., Musolesi, M.: PrefMiner: mining user's preferences for intelligent mobile notification management. In: UbiComp 2016 Proceedings, pp. 1223–1234 (2016)

14. Mehrotra, A., Musolesi, M., Hendley, R., Pejovic, V.: Designing content-driven intelligent notification mechanisms for mobile applications. In: UbiComp 2015 Proceedings, pp. 813–824 (2015)

15. Middleton, C.A., Cukier, W.: Is mobile email functional or dysfunctional? Two perspectives on mobile email usage. EJIS **15**(3), 252–260 (2006)

16. Morrison, L.G., et al.: The effect of timing and frequency of push notifications on usage of a smartphone-based stress management intervention: an exploratory trial. PloS ONE **12**(1), e0169162 (2017)

17. Nouwens, M., Liccardi, I., Veale, M., Karger, D., Kagal, L.: Dark patterns after the GDPR: scraping consent pop-ups and demonstrating their influence. In: 2020 CHI Conference Proceedings, pp. 1–13 (2020)

18. Reimers, N., Gurevych, I.: Sentence-BERT: sentence embeddings using Siamese BERT-networks. In: EMNLP-IJCNLP 2019 Proceedings (2019)
19. Suárez-Figueroa, M.C., Gómez-Pérez, A., Villazón-Terrazas, B.: How to write and use the ontology requirements specification document. In: Meersman, R., Dillon, T., Herrero, P. (eds.) OTM 2009. LNCS, vol. 5871, pp. 966–982. Springer, Heidelberg (2009). https://doi.org/10.1007/978-3-642-05151-7_16
20. Tauch, C., Kanjo, E.: The roles of emojis in mobile phone notifications. In: UbiComp/ISWC 2016 Adjunct Proceedings, pp. 1560–1565 (2016)
21. Weber, D., Voit, A., Kollotzek, G., Henze, N.: Annotif: a system for annotating mobile notifications in user studies. In: Proceedings of the 18th International Conference on Mobile and Ubiquitous Multimedia, pp. 1–12 (2019)

Automated Bug Triaging in a Global Software Development Environment: An Industry Experience

Arthur Batista, Fabricio D'Morison Marinho, Thiago Rocha,
Wilson Oliveira Neto, Giovanni Antonaccio, Tainah Chaves, Diego Falcão,
Flávia de S. Santos, Felipe T. Giuntini, and Juliano Efson Sales[✉]

Sidia Research Institute, Manaus, Brazil
{arthur.batista,fabricio.marinho,thiago.rocha,wilson.neto,
giovanni.antonaccio,tainah.chaves,diego.falcao,flavia.santos,
felipe.giuntini,juliano.sales}@sidia.com

Abstract. Bug triaging is a crucial task in development and maintenance of software projects. In this context, the ability to quickly assign bug reports to specialized technical groups (TG) is essential to save time, reduce costs and gain competitiveness. An issue wrongly assigned increases the risk of negative impact in a project's budget and schedule. This paper presents an analysis of automated approaches to recommend specialized TGs to fix a new bug. The experiments show the effectiveness of the analyzed method in finding the target TG in the first rank positions, improving the *Accuracy@1* in 7% and the Mean Reciprocal Rank (MRR) in 3% compared with our previous work. More significantly, the new method reduces the model's training time from 5 h to 22 min. These results were validated in a real-world dataset composed of 410,631 bug reports obtained from the projects of a global smartphone manufacturer.

Keywords: Bug triaging · Technical group recommendation · Industry experience

1 Introduction

The level of dependency the global economy has on software puts its development tasks at great importance for companies of any size. Large companies operating in the global market frequently maintain a distributed network of software development units spread over different countries, which put them closer to key clients, besides the gain of diversity of talents and cultural perspectives on strategic and organizational decisions [11,12].

These advantages come with the cost of management. While, controlling project development is challenging, coordinating the distributed effort to solve bugs is even challenger [13].

Large applications and systems are frequently developed by different groups throughout their life cycle, using a complex set of technologies in such a manner

P. Rosso et al. (Eds.): NLDB 2022, LNCS 13286, pp. 160–171, 2022.
https://doi.org/10.1007/978-3-031-08473-7_15

that identifying the best team to analyze and fix a bug report is a non-trivial task [7]. In a context of hundreds of groups, any attempt to execute this task manually demands large efforts by experienced developers, being a timing-consuming and expensive task.

The unprecedented improvement achieve by machine learning algorithms and the high availability of data in the recent decade has allowed the construction of models that are able to both analyze patterns and make quicker and more precise recommendations in many fields [9].

The literature has presented a fair number of initiatives focused on automating the bug triaging for large projects given special attention to the description of the bug report [1,3,5–7,20,21].

In this paper, we analyze the use of the off-the-shelf `fastText` classifier in the problem of bug triaging. We aim at recommending bug reports to appropriate *technical groups* (TG) composed of developers and testers specialized in investigating and solving them. We evaluate the classifier in the context of a system developed at global scale, whose bug reports are written in different languages. To serve as a baseline, we compare the performance of the classifier with the LC25F method, a BM25 implementation, which showed promising results [3].

2 Related Work

As the recent literature suggests, there is an increasing interest in applying machine learning methods to the task of bug triage.

Jonsson et al. [7] proposed a method of automatic recommendation of issues to technical groups in large-scale projects using ensemble classifiers. The proposed method uses both textual and non-textual information and obtains an accuracy between 0.50 to 0.89 for five different systems using a 10-fold cross-validation approach, and between 15% and 65% for time-sorted evaluations using continuous new data.

Xia et al. [19] uses techniques of topic modeling as a bridge between a word representation schema from the bug report and the developers. The authors named the technique multi-feature topic model, which is built on the top of Latent Dirichlet Allocation, associated to a new learning method that uses some inference rules.

In the use case of a mobile industry, Pahins et al. [3] employs a combination of `fastText` [2] and information retrieval classification functions, reaching up to 89.7% of overall accuracy using the LC25F with K-Nearest Neighbors (KNN) with Reservoir sampling [18]. This setting outperforms other isolated approach, i.e. LC25F (87.9%), KNN (up to 83.5%), Ramson Forest (62.6%), SVM (85,4%), and MLP (80.4%).

Sarkar et al. (2019) [14] recently reviewed a large set of research approaches, evaluating them in nine bug report datasets from Ericsson's internal projects. In their context, a simple logistic regression classifier is able to present good results. The authors also propose a new method that shows better accuracy in a more controlled scenario, which is more adequate for an effective use in production.

Guo et al. [6] present a new automatic bug triaging solution based on convolutional neural networks (CNN) combined with batch normalization, and fully connected methods and learns from a `word2vec` [10] word vector representation of known fixes' bug reports. The proposed approach was evaluated in three open-source datasets of the projects, namely, Eclipse, Mozilla, and Net Beans with respectively 0.57, 0.37, and 0.79 of accuracy.

Yadav et al. [20] proposed a two-stage bug classifier based on the developers' profiles. Each developer profile is built based on her/his contribution and some performance evaluation metrics. The authors analyze the developer's contribution and performance in historical data to calculate the developer's weighted score, which indicates the level of experience in fixing and resolving recently reported bugs. This approach was tested in two open-source projects, Eclipse and Mozilla. The results are validated using precision, recall, F-score, hit ratio, tossing length, and fit-ratio, showing that the proposed method achieves a significantly higher F-score of up to 90% in both projects an F-score up to 90,6% in assigning the developer specialization.

Analysing the problem in a Turkish private bank, Aktas and Yilmaz [1] propose the *issueTAG* for team recommendation, instead of individual developers, because, according to the authors, individual recommendation does not consider different aspects as the workload of the teams, the individual developer status and the team's changes. The dataset is composed of issues whose features are its creation timestamp, a one-line summary, and a description written in Turkish. To classify, the author employs a linear support vector classifier (SVC) and obtain an F-measure of 0.80.

Tahir et al. [16] describes a hybrid method that associate a LSTM network with content-base filter. Contrary to the other initiatives, the authors aimed at solving two problems simultaneously, i.e., bug prioritization and assignment.

Zhang [21] also argues recommending a bug to a topic or group is more suitable than individual developers, as developers can change their roles and projects in the industry. His proposed approach uses deep neural network techniques, whereas the description of the issue and list of developers from a group act as features. This approach achieves between 64.8% and 86.3% of recall for TG recommendation in different evaluation scenarios.

From a different perspective, in order to minimize the time to execute the maintenance, Etemad et al. [5] propose an approach based on the temporal behavior of the team and the developers' schedule. The approach is implemented as a multi-objective algorithm and is evaluated on two case studies (JDT and Platform datasets) that showed superior performance in 71% and 74% of the cases, respectively.

Table 1 summarizes the literature discussed in this section, highlighting the data set, the representation of features, the type of the issue recommendation/assignment and the primary approach used.

In the Sect. 4 we present our instantiation of an off-the-shelf `fastText`-based classifier. Before presenting the classifier, we formalize in the next section the problem and how the data is structured.

Table 1. Summary of related works. TG stands for Technical Group, and Dev for Developer.

Author	Data domain	Text Represent.	Assignment Type	Main Approach
Jonsson et al. (2016)	Telecom and Automation	TF-IDF	TG	Stacked Generalization
Xia et al. [19]	GCC, OpenOffice, Mozilla, Netbeans and Eclipse	N/A	Developer	LDA and topic modeling
Pahins et al. (2019)	Mobile	Word embedding	TG and Dev	SVM, LC25F and KNN
Aktas and Yilmaz (2020)	Bank	TF-IDF	TG	SVC
Guo et al. (2020)	Mozila, Eclipse and Netbeans	Word embedding	Developer	CNN
Yadav and Sigh (2020)	Eclipse and Mozila	not inform	Developer	Heuristic counting the similarities between data corpora
Zhang (2020)	Multiple sources	not inform	TG and Dev	Deep Neural Network
Etemadi et al. (2021)	JDT and Platform	N/A	Developer	Scheduling-driven
Tahir et al. (2021)	Eclipse, CDT and JDT	N/A	Developer	LSTM with Content-based filtering

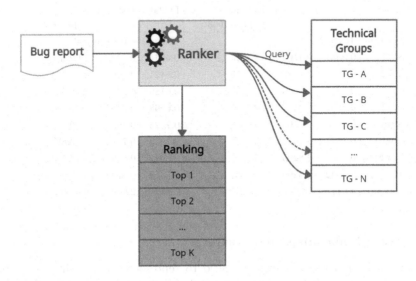

Fig. 1. A graphical depiction of the bug triaging problem.

3   Problem Formalization

We formalize the target problem as follows. Let G be a set of *technical groups* (TG) each of them associated with an institution. Let B be a set of k historical bug reports $(b_1, b_2, ..., b_k)$. Let $b_i = (t, d, r, n, z, u)$ be an element of B, where t is its title, d is its description, r are its steps of reproduction, n is its module name, z is its module detail, and u is its reporter department. Whereas t, d and r form the set of textual attributes, the remaining attributes, namely n, z and u, represent the categorical ones. Let A be a set of pairs $(b_i, g_i)|b_i \in B, g_i \in G$ and g_i is an appropriate technical group to address the bug report b_i. Let $B'|B' \cap B = \emptyset$ be a set of new but reports for which there is no technical group associated. The problem of bug triaging aims at define an automatic ranking method $f(A, G, b')$, that, supported by the historical data A, and the set of technical groups G, returns an ordered list R of technical groups, whose element's position is associated with its level of appropriateness to solve the new bug report b'.

Figure 1 depicts a graphical overview of the bug triaging problem.

4   A fastText-Based Approach

To address the problem of bug triaging, we trained and analyzed the performance of a fastText classifier, whose method to represent texts is described in the next section.

Table 2. Accuracy, MRR and Runtime of LC25F and fastText

Approach	LC25F	fastText	Relative improvement	LC25F	fastText	Relative improvement
Attributes	Textual			Textual + Categorical		
Acc@1	0.3551	0.4104	15.57%	0.4044	0.4328	7.02%
Acc@2	0.4755	0.5387	13.29%	0.5421	0.5663	4.46%
Acc@3	0.5411	0.6063	12.05%	0.6185	0.6332	2.38%
Acc@4	0.5863	0.6497	10.81%	0.6668	0.6737	N/A
Acc@5	0.6206	0.6805	9.65%	0.7028	0.7033	N/A
Acc@10	0.7177	0.7627	6.27%	0.7939	0.7837	−1.28%
Acc@20	0.8	0.8295	3.69%	0.8642	0.8491	−1.75%
MRR	0.4742	0.5299	11.75%	0.5353	0.5534	3.38%
Runtime	4 h 20 m	26 m	90.02%	5 h 39 m	22 m	93.52%

4.1   Word Embeddings and fastText

In natural language processing, we need to represent the meaning of a word or text in a computable model, whose state-of-the-art is currently achieve by *word embedding models*. A word embedding model is a statistical method that generates vectors to represent words by analyzing their co-occurrence in large text corpora [17]. Word vectors were initially computed by an explicit approach that takes into account the number of co-occurrence of pair of words to produce a large matrix, which is later submitted to factorization method to generate same-size vectors for all words, typically 300 [17].

Mikolov et al. [10] later proposed the skip-gram method, which uses a neural network to infer those vectors. As a limitation, skip-gram, and the previously proposed model, generates vector representations only for words that are present in corpus from which the model was trained.

To overcome such a restriction, fastText emerges as an alternative that allows the generation of words that are not present in the vocabulary of the initial corpus, since it considers the composition of the words in n-grams of letter in its training process [2]. Such optimization allows not only covering absent words, but also producing a better representation for the words present in the vocabulary.

4.2 Text Classifier

We analyzed the performance of a text classifier based on fastText, similarly to that presented by Joulin et al. [8] as shown in Fig. 2. The classifier applies linear regression on a normalized text vector, which is generated from the average of vectors' dimensions that compose the text, trained in a linearly decaying learning rate with stochastic gradient descent [8]. To identify the class, it uses a hierarchical softmax, which takes into consideration the hierarchy between TGs and their institutions.

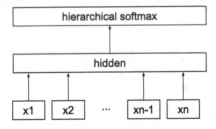

Fig. 2. Architecture of the text classifier, where the *hidden* layer represents the average of the input vectors x_i from fastText, and the output is produced by the *hierarchical softmax* layer.

4.3 Text Representation

A bug report is a structured document composed of both textual and categorical attributes. The fastText model, however, expects as input a text to train the classifier. In order to feed the model appropriately, we concatenated all attributes in a single text, to allow the model to learn a text embedding that represents the entire report. As a side-effect of this simplicity, the approach present some drawbacks, as the categorical attributes having potential syntactic and semantic mismatching when artificially added to textual attributes, and the algorithm not leveraging different degrees of importance of in each attribute. In the experiments section we explore the impact of those drawbacks in the results.

The textual attributes, i.e., *title*, *description* and *steps to reproduce*, are pre-processed using standard techniques: tokenization, stemming, and stop word removal.

5   Experiments

We evaluate our approach in a real world dataset from a global leader company in the mobile sector. The dataset consists of 410,631 bug reports collected from September 2020 to March 2021. We used only closed issues since those are associated to the TG that fixed it and serve as a gold standard. Table 3 lists the attributes used in this experiment.

The TGs has a hierarchical structure with different levels. It means a TG could have other TGs associated to it and so on. In this work, we are using the lower level TGs in the hierarchy to avoid the problem of re-assignment from a parent TG to a child TG, since it increases the number of classes to predict and directly affects the experiment accuracy.

We used a hold-out strategy to split the dataset into a train and test. The split takes into account both the TG distribution and the chronological order of the issues. Thus, the 90% oldest bug reports of each TG was used to train the classifier and the 10% remaining are used for test, as illustrated in Fig. 3. This approach aims to create a model that cover a large amount of TGs, since using just the chronological order of the reports may leave out the TGs that haven't solve newly bugs.

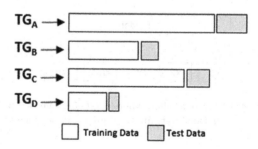

Fig. 3. Hold-out strategy implemented in T-REC [3]. The split is made for each TG where 90% of its oldest bug reports are used for training and 10% newer for test.

5.1 Model Training

The `fastText` classifier has a set of hyperparameters to tune its learning process, such as learning rate, epochs, etc. As finding the best set of hyperparameters is a non-trivial task, we used the autotune feature from the model to automatically optimize the hyperparameters that better fits our dataset.

To serve as a baseline, we selected the LC25F approach from Pahins et al. (2019) [3] since it presented one of best performance. In our context, LC25F is a method adapted for the bug triage problem that derives from the work of Sun et al. [15], whose primary goal is to identify duplicated bugs. It computes the similarity between a new bug report and the reports of each TG in the repository, returning then a top-K TGs with high similarities. LC25F is implemented using a linear combination of the report attributes weighted by its degree of importance. The similarity of the textual features are measured using an extension of BM25F, a well-know algorithm in information retrieval, whereas the similarities of the categorical attributes uses a simple comparison, i.e., 1 if they are equal, 0 otherwise.

The effectiveness of each method is measured by the Accuracy@K and Mean Reciprocal Rank (MRR), which are commonly used in information retrieval and recommendation systems to evaluate the quality of a ranked list. The Accuracy@K, depicted in Eq. 1, measures the fraction the relevant items (n_{hit}) (i.e. the TG that fixed the issue) that was successfully retrieved in the top-k list, regardless of its position, among all test cases (N).

$$Accuracy@K = \frac{n_{hit}}{N} \qquad (1)$$

MRR considers the position of the first relevant item, i.e., how close to the top is the target TG, and is computed as follow:

$$MRR(Q) = \frac{1}{|Q|} \sum_{i=1}^{|Q|} \frac{1}{index_i}, \qquad (2)$$

where Q represents the subset of bug reports in test set and $index_i$ is the position where the targeted TG was retrieved.

The experiments were executed on a Linux machine running CentOS 7 with 72-core CPU with 188GB of RAM memory. The `fastText`[1] version used was 0.9.2. As described in the previous section, LC25F is inspired by Sun et al. [15] that has a public implementation available in the web[2].

Considering our production setting, where our recommendation system returns a list of the 20 most relevant TGs, displaying 5 TGs per time, our experiments evaluates also the top-20 list, giving specially focus on the top-5 results as they are the first TGs seen by our users.

---

[1] Available at: https://github.com/facebookresearch/fastText/.
[2] Available at: https://www.comp.nus.edu.sg/~specmine/suncn/ase11/.

6   Results and Discussion

Table 2 shows the results of Accuracy@K, MRR and Runtime for `fastText` and LC25F. The difference between the results of the two models were assessed using a two-tailed *t-test* ($p < 0.05$). Regarding the use of both textual and categorical attributes simultaneously, both approaches presented better results when compared with their respective versions using only textual features. However, the difference between `fastText` and LC25F when using only textual features is significantly large.

When using both textual and categorical features, the `fastText`-based model performed better than LC25F in the first rank positions with relative improvements in Accuracy@1 and Accuracy@3 of more than 7% and 2% respectively. Nonetheless, the Accuracy@4 and Accuracy@5 show no statistical difference between the methods.

Table 3. Issues attributes to experiment

Type	Attributes
Textual	title, description, steps to reproduce
Categorical	module name, module detail, reporter department

The LC25F model tends to outperforms `fastText` when considering higher rankings as shown in Fig. 4. From the 6th to the 20th position, when it achieves an accuracy of 0.86, with `fastText` obtaining 0.85.

The `fastText` model also presented a better MRR with a relative improvement of 3% over LC25F which reinforces its capability to position the target TG at a higher rank in the recommendation list.

However, the main advantage of `fastText` over LC25F is regarding to the run time. From Table 2, we can see that `fastText` significantly reduces the time used to run the experiment from 5 h to 22 min. This result motivated us to replace the LC25F approach by the `fastText` on our production environment, since both methods have a similar accuracy.

The advantage we most miss from LC25F is its ability by design to learn from new examples while operating, whereas *fastText* demands the execution of its learning process from scratch to take advantage of new samples.

Contrary to Sarkar et al. (2019) [14], our experiments also shown that selecting a dataset composed of more recent bug report increases the performance, whose distinction in the results may be attributed to dataset properties. For instance, the level of stability of technical groups (their members) may be higher in those datasets assessed by Sarkar et al. (2019) compared to ours.

7 Summary

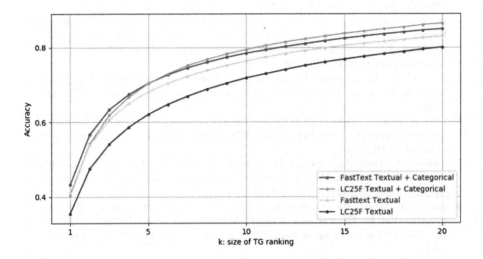

Fig. 4. Accuracy of FastText and LC25f

In this paper, we presented an analysis of two off-the-shelf methods for the problem of bug triage in a real-world scenario with a target set of hundreds of TG and more than 400,000 bug reports. The experiments suggested the `fastText` model can deliver better running performance with better or competitive accuracy compared with the baseline in all of the scenarios of evaluation.

As a future work, we plan to *(i)* investigate other strategies to explore to use the categorical attributes of a bug report, benefiting from their different degree of importance, *(ii)* assess the performance of the current approach when associated with textual representations from the *bidirectional encoder representations from transformers*, the so-called BERT language model[4], and *(iii)* analyze the use of hybrid models that also consider features from the source code.

References

1. Aktas, E.U., Yilmaz, C.: Automated issue assignment: results and insights from an industrial case. Empir. Softw. Eng. **25**(5), 3544–3589 (2020). https://doi.org/10.1007/s10664-020-09846-3
2. Bojanowski, P., Grave, E., Joulin, A., Mikolov, T.: Enriching word vectors with subword information. Trans. Assoc. Comput. Linguist. **5**, 135–146 (2017)
3. De Lara Pahins, C.A., D'Morison, F., Rocha, T.M., Almeida, L.M., Batista, A.F., Souza, D.F.: T-REC: towards accurate bug triage for technical groups. In: 2019 18th IEEE International Conference on Machine Learning and Applications (ICMLA), pp. 889–895 (2019). https://doi.org/10.1109/ICMLA.2019.00154

4. Devlin, J., Chang, M.W., Lee, K., Toutanova, K.: BERT: pre-training of deep bidirectional transformers for language understanding. In: Proceedings of the 2019 Conference of the North American Chapter of the Association for Computational Linguistics: Human Language Technologies, vol. 1 (Long and Short Papers), pp. 4171–4186. Association for Computational Linguistics, Minneapolis, Minnesota, June 2019. https://doi.org/10.18653/v1/N19-1423, https://www.aclweb.org/anthology/N19-1423

5. Etemadi, V., Bushehrian, O., Akbari, R., Robles, G.: A scheduling-driven approach to efficiently assign bug fixing tasks to developers. J. Syst. Softw. **178**, 110967 (2021)

6. Guo, S., et al.: Developer activity motivated bug triaging: via convolutional neural network. Neural Process. Lett. **51**(3), 2589–2606 (2020). https://doi.org/10.1007/s11063-020-10213-y

7. Jonsson, L., Borg, M., Broman, D., Sandahl, K., Eldh, S., Runeson, P.: Automated bug assignment: ensemble-based machine learning in large scale industrial contexts. Empir. Softw. Eng. **21**(4), 1533–1578 (2016)

8. Joulin, A., Grave, É., Bojanowski, P., Mikolov, T.: Bag of tricks for efficient text classification. In: Proceedings of the 15th Conference of the European Chapter of the Association for Computational Linguistics, vol. 2, Short Papers, pp. 427–431 (2017)

9. Lee, I., Shin, Y.J.: Machine learning for enterprises: applications, algorithm selection, and challenges. Bus. Horiz. **63**(2), 157–170 (2020)

10. Mikolov, T., Sutskever, I., Chen, K., Corrado, G., Dean, J.: Distributed representations of words and phrases and their compositionality. arXiv preprint arXiv:1310.4546 (2013)

11. Neeley, T.: Global teams that work. Harv. Bus. Rev. **93**(10), 74–81 (2015)

12. Nicolás, J., De Gea, J.M.C., Nicolas, B., Fernandez-Aleman, J.L., Toval, A.: On the risks and safeguards for requirements engineering in global software development: systematic literature review and quantitative assessment. IEEE Access **6**, 59628–59656 (2018)

13. Parviainen, P., Tihinen, M.: Knowledge-related challenges and solutions in GSD. Expert. Syst. **31**(3), 253–266 (2014)

14. Sarkar, A., Rigby, P.C., Bartalos, B.: Improving bug triaging with high confidence predictions at ericsson. In: 2019 IEEE International Conference on Software Maintenance and Evolution (ICSME). pp. 81–91 (2019). https://doi.org/10.1109/ICSME.2019.00018

15. Sun, C., Lo, D., Khoo, S.C., Jiang, J.: Towards more accurate retrieval of duplicate bug reports. In: 2011 26th IEEE/ACM International Conference on Automated Software Engineering (ASE 2011), pp. 253–262 (2011). https://doi.org/10.1109/ASE.2011.6100061

16. Tahir, H., Khan, S.U.R., Ali, S.S.: LCBPA: an enhanced deep neural network-oriented bug prioritization and assignment technique using content-based filtering. IEEE Access **9**, 92798–92814 (2021). https://doi.org/10.1109/ACCESS.2021.3093170

17. Turney, P.D., Pantel, P.: From frequency to meaning: vector space models of semantics. J. Artif. Intell. Res. **37**, 141–188 (2010)

18. Vitter, J.S.: Random sampling with a reservoir. ACM Trans. Math. Softw. **11**(1), 37–57 (1985)

19. Xia, X., Lo, D., Ding, Y., Al-Kofahi, J.M., Nguyen, T.N., Wang, X.: Improving automated bug triaging with specialized topic model. IEEE Trans. Software Eng. **43**(3), 272–297 (2017). https://doi.org/10.1109/TSE.2016.2576454

20. Yadav, A., Singh, S.K.: A novel and improved developer rank algorithm for bug assignment. Int. J. Intell. Syst. Technol. Appl. **19**(1), 78–101 (2020)
21. Zhang, W.: Efficient bug triage for industrial environments. In: 2020 IEEE International Conference on Software Maintenance and Evolution (ICSME), pp. 727–735 (2020). https://doi.org/10.1109/ICSME46990.2020.00082

Linguistically Enhanced *Text to Sign Gloss* Machine Translation

Santiago Egea Gómez[1]([✉]) [iD], Luis Chiruzzo[2] [iD], Euan McGill[1] [iD],
and Horacio Saggion[1] [iD]

[1] Universitat Pompeu Fabra, 08002 Barcelona, Spain
{santiago.egea,euan.mcgill,horacio.saggion}@upf.edu
[2] Universidad de la República, Uruguay, 11200 Montevideo, Uruguay
luischir@fing.edu.uy

Abstract. In spite of the recent advances in Machine Translation (MT) for spoken languages, translation between spoken and Sign Languages (SLs) or between Sign Languages remains a difficult problem. Here, we study how Neural Machine Translation (NMT) might overcome the communication barriers for the Deaf and Hard-of-Hearing (DHH) community. Namely, we approach the Text2Gloss translation task in which spoken text segments are translated to lexical sign representations. In this context, we leverage transformer-based models via (1) injecting linguistic features that can guide the learning process towards better translations; and (2) applying a Transfer Learning strategy to reuse the knowledge of a pre-trained model. To this aim, different aggregation strategies are compared and evaluated under Transfer Learning and random weight initialization conditions. The results of this research reveal that linguistic features can successfully contribute to achieve more accurate models; meanwhile, the Transfer Learning procedure applied conducted to substantial performance increases.

Keywords: Neural transformers · Linguistic features · Sign gloss machine translation · Sign language

1 Introduction

In the era of mass communication and wide uptake of digital technologies amongst the general public, there still exist barriers for many people where access to information is of concern, and this is particularly the case for the DHH community. Of the 466 million people worldwide with some kind of hearing loss[1], around 70 million communicate through Sign Languages (SLs)[2] - the preferred mode of communication among the DHH people [21]. Recently, the European Commission adopted the Strategy for the rights of persons with disabilities[3],

---

[1] https://www.who.int/news-room/fact-sheets/detail/deafness-and-hearing-loss.
[2] https://wfdeaf.org/our-work/.
[3] https://ec.europa.eu/social/main.jsp?catId=738&langId=en&pubId=8376.

P. Rosso et al. (Eds.): NLDB 2022, LNCS 13286, pp. 172–183, 2022.
https://doi.org/10.1007/978-3-031-08473-7_16

which indicates the need to provide SL interpretation to improve accessibility for the DHH community. There is a great opportunity for MT to bridge the gap between written/spoken languages and SLs. But, in spite of the recent advances in MT for spoken languages, translation between spoken and SLs or between SLs (SLT) remains a challenge.

In terms of data and resource availability, SLs are considered 'extremely low resource' languages [13], which implies a salient issue for MT applied to SL. The latest approaches to MT are based on neural networks, particularly transformer models [22, 24]. Transformer-based systems are data-hungry and computationally expensive, so their viability for SLT is yet to be fully established.

Unlike spoken languages, a linear stream of information in the oral-auditory modality, SLs exist in the gestural-visual modality consisting of often parallel manual and non-manual cues [14]. This modality difference poses an important challenge in building corpora. Writing systems capturing the exact pattern and timing of signs are extant [8], however these systems are not widely used to annotate SL corpora nor are they widely known by signers [9]. Instead, SL glosses are preferred as an intermediate representation between SL video data and text in a MT paradigm (e.g. [5,13,23]). Glosses, and the Text2Gloss (T2G) process, are used as a tool to represent a given sign as a lexeme - usually in the ambient language of the geographical area where a SL is native[4]. In spite of criticism towards gloss annotation [23], one advantage of glosses in lexical signs is their suitability as a text representation to feed into machine learning models. These glosses can be represented within embedding vectors that are fed into neural models where mappings between the input and output texts can be established.

In our previous work [7], we showed how word dependencies can boost T2G translation. Here, we extend the experiments considering a range of linguistic features and different ways of injecting them into transformer models. We also show that Transfer Learning (TL) can be successfully applied to this particular MT task, spoken German to German Sign Language (DGS) translation.

2   Related Work

Translation between spoken and sign languages is not new and it has been investigated from several angles including example-based [12], rule-based [2], and statistical-based MT [18]. Transformer-based NMT models have been shown to be successful in producing translations for a wide range of language pairs with state-of-the-art accuracy [10], including low resource spoken languages [22]. Perhaps the most notable is mBART [24], a widely used pretrained transformer architecture for NMT. A key benefit of these powerful models is their ability to be fine-tuned to a downstream task in NLP such as MT.

SLT as a subset of MT is, however, a more challenging area. The task is inherently multimodal, and has severely limited resources. While E2E translation is possible from text to sign [6,15], 'cascaded' systems involving intermediate steps

---

[4] For example, glosses in written English for American Sign Language.

appear to yield higher translation accuracy [5,25]. Therefore it is important for the moment to focus on improving these intermediate stages. Cascaded building blocks for SLT may involve continuous SL recognition as a computer vision task, SL generation (e.g. [1]) from glosses into SL through 3D avatars, and Text2Gloss or Gloss2Text to facilitate translation through a text-to-text mapping.

A wide range of resources exist across multiple SLs such as parallel corpora, video corpora and repositories of signs produced in isolation. One problem is that for comparatively widely spoken languages, the size of these corpora are markedly smaller [9]. Co-occurring issues include domain specificity [5,19] without examples of alternative semantic fields, little variation in signers both in diversity and positioning in 3D space [15] and a noise-free video background [25]. On top of cascading, breaking up SLT into a pipeline, there are further mitigation strategies to augment the training data available such as back-translation, previously avoided in SLT [25], or rule-based generation of glosses [13]. Alternatively, it is possible to augment the existing data with more information during training. This study follows the latter approach.

Sennrich and Haddow [20] introduced a 'Factored Transformer' model which inserts linguistic feature embeddings (lemmas, part-of-speech tags, lexical dependencies and morphological features) into the encoder of an attention-based NMT architecture. This schema was then used on a low-resource translation task English-Nepali [3] that improved performance on FLoRes[5] by 1.2 BLEU. Our recent work in Text2Gloss [7] explored the use of lexical dependencies in the model embeddings obtaining a peak improvement of 5.7 BLEU over a baseline.

Considering previous research, we hypothesize that linguistic features may boost model performances for T2G. We formulate three main research questions based on this prediction: (1) Which are the most informative features? (2) How do we inject them into transformer models? and (3) Can Transfer Learning provide performance increases when linguistic features are injected to the models? In order to shed light on these research questions, we propose a T2G system, analyse its performance, and discuss alternatives.

3   System Overview

The T2G translation system presented here is composed of three key components that Fig. 1 shows: (1) a *Text Processing* step to generate linguistic features to be injected to the model; (2) a *T2G Model* based on the mBart architecture [24]; and (3) a *Transfer Learning* process to get advantage of pretrained weights. We make the implementation of our system available in GitHub[6], along with an extended results analysis.

Considering the linguistic rules applied in the SL gloss production, we predict that linguistic features might play a relevant role in T2G translation task. Therefore, we use the available language resources to generate the linguistic features

---

[5] Facebook Low Resource benchmark.

[6] https://github.com/LaSTUS-TALN-UPF/Linguistically-Enhanced-Text2Gloss-MT.

described in the Sect. 3.1. These features are aligned with the subword tokens generated by the mBART tokenizer as is depicted in Fig. 1. Unfortunately, there are not equivalent resources for DGS, an important restriction for us in exploring Gloss2Text translation.

As mBART architecture is difficult to manage due to its very large number of parameters, we have designed a strategy to take advantage of TL while using a much simpler neural architecture. Namely, we employ a transformer with 3 multi-attention layers with 4 heads for both the encoder and decoder, and the internal and output dimensions are set to 1024 and 512 respectively. Regarding the embeddings, we use 512-length vectors in two separate tables: One for subword tokens and another for linguistic features. The word and linguistic features are aggregated using different strategies which are also a matter of study of this research (Sect. 3.2).

In order to exploit the knowledge acquired by mBART during its multilingual pre-training, we filter and align the original mBART embedding table keeping only the tokens appearing in our training corpus. Additionally, the linguistic embeddings are initialized by randomly selecting vectors from mBART embeddings. As there are not control tokens to represent SLs in mBART, we reuse the Dutch language one to represent DGS; since German and Dutch are closely related languages. To fit the mBART weights into our architecture model, slicing is applied so that the vector elements are adapted to our neural architecture size.

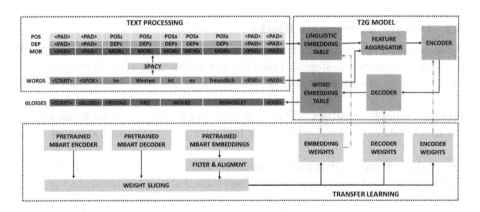

Fig. 1. An overview of the proposed system.

3.1 Linguistic Features

We labeled the input text with linguistic features using the de_core_news_sm model of the spaCy[7] library. This model is trained over the TIGER Korpus [4], a widely used German corpus partially annotated with POS, morphological information, and syntactic structure. The dependency labels used by spaCy are based

---

[7] https://spacy.io/.

on the TIGER Korpus format and differ from Universal Dependencies. The linguistic features calculated for the input text are: Part-of-Speech (**POS**, 16 unique labels), dependency labels from the parse tree (**DEP**, 38 unique labels), and morphological information (**MOR**).

The tagger incorporates different types of morphological information for each word, including person and tense for verbs, and case and gender for nouns. We generate a tag that combines the different feature-value pairs into a single morphological label. For example, the noun *Westen* in the example from Fig. 1 would have the **MOR** label `Case_Dat-Gender_Masc-Number_Sing`. However, there is a large number of possible combinations of these features and their values: in the training corpus we found around 400 combinations, most of them used only a few times. To reduce the sparsity of this information, we used the following heuristic when creating the tag:

- If the combination of feature-value pairs of a word belongs to the top 60 most frequent combinations, we use the serialized combination described before (this covers around 66% of the corpus).
- Otherwise, we use the **POS** tag. This covers cases in which the morphological analyzer returns an empty value (around 32% of the words), so the labels can at least discriminate by POS in those cases.

As we used the mBART SentencePiece tokenizer [11], each word in the input might be split into one or more subword tokens, so the corresponding linguistic feature labels are associated to each of the tokens a word is split into.

3.2   Feature Aggregation Blocks

We aggregated the word information and the linguistic features in each experiment using different strategies. The following aggregation rules were applied to each linguistic feature separately (ablation study) and to all three jointly.

Reduce Sum & Product . These are very simple rules that enable combining the input features without adding new learnable parameters in the model.

Learnable Sum & Product. Learnable weights are incorporated into the ReduceSum&Prod operations. Namely, one learnable vector is multiplied by each input embedding to strengthen or weaken its contribution in the resulting vector.

Concatenation Mapping (ConcatMap). The embeddings are concatenated and fed to a dense network that maps the vector to a dimension of 512. The weights of the mapping network are also learned during training.

Convolutional Block (ConvBlock). As words and linguistic features could conceal complex relation patterns, a CNN network is employed with the aim of mining these complex relationships. Firstly, the input is reshaped to (32,16), and it is fed to the following layers: CNN_1(kernel = (8,8), channels = 4)-CNN_2(kernel = (8,8), channels = 4). Finally, the generated vectors are flattened and fed to a mapper network to adapt the dimensions to the encoder input shape.

Table 1. Data partitions Information

	Samples	Words		Glosses	
		Total	Unique	Total	Unique
Train	7096	99081	2887	55247	1085
Dev	519	6820	951	3748	393
Test	642	7816	1001	4264	411

4 Methods and Material

4.1 Phoenix Dataset

The corpus employed in our experiments is the *RWTH-PHOENIX-2014-T* [5], a very well-known SL corpus that is publicly available[8], which includes images and transcriptions in German text and DGS glosses. The data was extracted and annotated from weather forecasting news in a public TV station. And, in spite of its semantic limited domain, it comprises a rich vocabulary of 1117 different signs produced by nine different signers, being quite popular in SLT research. We focus on text and gloss data in this paper. The dataset is split into *train (≈ 86%)*, *development (≈ 6%)* and *test (≈ 8%)* partitions with the data distribution presented in Table 1. The partitions were created to ensure they contain a variety of syntactic structures.

4.2 Training and Evaluation Settings

Regarding the training settings, we train all models on the *train* data for 500 epochs using a learning rate of $5e^-6$. The learning objective is the *Cross Entropy loss function* without any regularization term at loss level. We apply generation on *development* partition using Beam Decoding with 5 beams. The best epoch model is selected and the scores are confirmed on *test* data. These steps are repeated 5 times for all models and the means and standard deviations are reported to avoid misleading observations due to randomness during training.

4.3 Performance Metrics

To evaluate our models, SacreBLEU [17] with word tokenization is assumed as main metric in model selection. SacreBLEU consists of a standardized version of traditional BLEU, which uses input tokenization to obtain more comparable results. This metric analyzes different N-grams against reference segments and aggregates them for a robust evaluation. Furthermore, we analyze other performance metrics during the test phase to have a wider understanding of how linguistic features contribute to the T2G task. The selected metrics are: Sacre-BLEU with character-level tokenization, which is used in our previous work [7]

---

[8] https://www-i6.informatik.rwth-aachen.de/~koller/RWTH-PHOENIX-2014-T/.

and can be analyzed in a comparative manner. METEOR is also used, which evaluates the word alignments according to precision and recall using unigrams - giving recall higher importance to the metric computation.

5   Experimental Results

In this section we report and discuss the results obtained in our experiments involving the linguistic features (Sect. 3.1) and different feature aggregators (Sect. 3.2) under random initialization (RI) and Transfer Learning (TL) settings. First, we compare the aggregators under RI; then, TL is explored for the best aggregation rules; finally, we study individually the advantage of each linguistic feature. Afterwards the performances are analyzed on the *test* partition.

5.1   Comparison Amongst Aggregation Blocks

Here, we compare the different aggregation rules including a model (*OnlyWords*) as baseline, which only uses the word embedding table. Figure 2 presents the SacreBLEU scores obtained on the *development* partition during the whole training. As can be observed, the best aggregation strategy is *ConvBlock*, which outperforms *OnlyWords* at certain epochs. The highest SacreBLEU produced by *ConvBlock* is 17.59 after 305 epochs, overcoming the best *OnlyWords* (17.21 at 270 epochs). In the case of *ConcatMap*, the highest SacreBLEU happens at 220 epochs obtaining a score very similar to *OnlyWords* (17.13), but slightly lower. The rest of aggregation rule models perform worse compared to *OnlyWords*, with *LearnableProd* and *ReduceProd* as clearly the poorest aggregators. The reason why the aggregation rules using prod obtained the worst scores might be due to the scale in the produced embedding vectors.

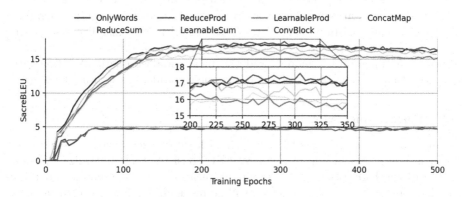

Fig. 2. SacreBLEU curves for the different aggregation blocks with random initialization.

As *ConvBlock*, *OnlyWords* and *ConcatMap* are the three best models, we compare them using TL and RI in the following section.

5.2   Transfer Learning vs Random Initialization

Figure 3 presents the SacreBLEU curves obtained for the three best models (selected from the previous experiment) when TL and RI is employed. The effect of TL is evident for all models, and the improvements respecting RI reach up to 5 sacreBLEU in certain cases. Again, the best model is produced by *ConvBlock* aggregation rule when TL is applied, achieving a SacreBLEU of 22.17 at 285 training epochs. The benefits of TL are also marked for *ConcatMap* and *OnlyWords*, obtaining SacreBLEUs of 21.70 and 21.41 respectively. These performance increases confirm that the TL strategy applied to our models allows them to take advantage of the pre-learned knowledge of mBART, but using a more manageable architecture. Also interestingly, *ConvBlock-TL* exhibits better performances than other aggregation strategies, which reveals that the CNNs are extracting patterns that enrich the embeddings input into the encoder.

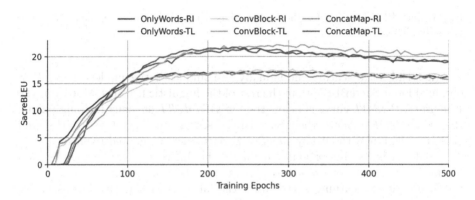

Fig. 3. SacreBLEU curves for the three best models with and without Transfer Learning.

5.3   Ablation Study: Comparison Amongst Linguistic Features

In this section, we assess the contributions of each linguistic feature for the translation task. To this end, we compare the SacreBLEU produced by different aggregation rules when each linguistic feature is individually injected. This analysis is performed anew with focus on the best models found during the previous experiments. Thus, we compare *ConcatMap-TL* and *ConvBlock-TL* using all (denoted by ALL) and individual features; and, additionally, we include the *OnlyWords-TL* as a baseline. The metric curves for these models are presented in Fig. 4. As it can be observed, the best models are generated using *ConvBlock* with *DEP* and *ALL* features. Also, the differences between these two models are not substantial. Therefore, *ConvBlock* extracts rich embedding vectors using only *DEP* and without needing to include *MOR* and *POS*.

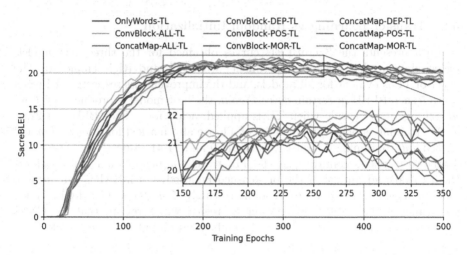

Fig. 4. SacreBLEU curves for the best models using all linguistic features and each one individually

Analyzing each feature individually, we find that the models using *POS* obtained lower SacreBLEU than the rest of the linguistic features. Moreover, the *ConvBlock-POS-TL* curve is below the *OnlyWords-TL* at many training points. Regarding *MOR* models, their SacreBLEU scores are very close to *DEP* and *ALL* models, but without any superior performances compared to them.

Finally, it is also important to highlight the differences between aggregation blocks. The behavior of *ConvBlock* differs from the *ConcatMap* in the fact that the former starts learning slower than the latter (which is clearly observable between 50–200 training epochs). On the contrary *ConvBlock* scores overcome the *ConcatMap* ones, showing more stability after 250 epochs.

5.4   Results on *test* data

To conclude our study, we analyze the scores over the *test* partition of the models that had best SacreBLEU on *development*. In this case, we include additional performance metrics that might reveal relevant behaviors about the models analyzed. From Table 2, we can observe that the improvements achieved by the TL strategy are also noticeable on the *test* data for all the aggregation rules and all performance metrics. Comparing *ConvBlock-ALL-TL* & *RI*, we find that SacreBLEU-Char increases up to more than 5 points in the case of *ConvBlock* and METEOR improves by around .052. These improvements are also evident for *ConcatMap* and *OnlyWords* models.

Contrary to the findings on *development*, the effect of using *ALL* features and each feature individually is not so notable in the case of *ConvBlock*. Using *ALL* features with *ConcatMap* result in increases of up to 1 point in SacreBLEU-Word. Meanwhile, similar results are seen in METEOR and SacreBLEU-Char.

Table 2. Performance metrics computed on *test*. We report average metric (and standard deviation) for 5 experiment iterations. SacreBLEU-Word & Char denote the different tokenization methods for this metric.

	SacreBLEU-Word↑	SacreBLEU-Char↑	METEOR↑
OnlyWords-RI	16.61 (.664)	52.70 (.664)	.409 (.005)
OnlyWords-TL	19.89 (.441)	56.01 (.783)	.454 (.005)
ConvBlock-ALL-RI	16.72 (.608)	52.63 (.805)	.406 (.005)
ConvBlock-ALL-TL	20.24 (.976)	57.30 (.365)	.458 (.005)
ConvBlock-DEP-TL	20.11 (.310)	<u>57.45</u> (.406)	.460 (.004)
ConvBlock-POS-TL	19.94 (.526)	56.75 (.390)	.456 (.004)
ConvBlock-MOR-TL	20.36 (.759)	<u>57.45</u> (.565)	<u>.461</u> (.005)
ConcatMap-ALL-RI	16.77 (.298)	51.79 (.521)	.408 (.003)
ConcatMap-ALL-TL	<u>20.57</u> (.737)	56.53 (.375)	.458 (.005)
ConcatMap-DEP-TL	19.56 (.760)	56.49 (.865)	.452 (.005)
ConcatMap-POS-TL	19.69 (.885)	56.82 (.746)	.453 (.006)
ConcatMap-MOR-TL	19.30 (.392)	56.20 (.702)	.450 (.005)

Globally, we can observe that *ConvBlock* produces better performance than other aggregation rules for all settings and metrics explored, with the exception of *ConcatMap-ALL-TL* in terms of SacreBLEU-Word. This result may be caused by the simple architecture tuning explored in this research. We posit that it might be possible to enhance the pattern mining with CNNs including more layers and regularization techniques. Finally, considering our previous research [7], we can observe a substantial improvement of around 4 points in SacreBLEU-Char and 0.6 in METEOR when CNNs and TL is applied.

6   Conclusions and Future Work

In this paper, we study the potential of injecting linguistic features into neural transformers for a T2G translation task. The experiments presented involve several types of linguistic features which are aggregated to the traditional subword embeddings according to different aggregation strategies. These strategies comprise of simple rules (such as ReduceSum & Prod) and more sophisticated aggregators able to mix the features while extracting hidden patterns (CNNs, Learnable Sum & Prod, and so on). Furthermore, we show that TL can robustly improve the performance of T2G models via applying a simple, but effective, filtering and slicing procedure.

According to our results, using CNNs or concatenating features produces the best results. Regarding the features to include in the models, we find interesting improvements when using all available linguistic features on *development* data, but this is not so clear for the *test* data. Finally, the most remarkable performance improvements are produced when TL is applied according to the method described in this paper, resulting in improvements on all metrics. For the sake of research reproducibility, we make our implementations available in GitHub[9].

The experimental results reported here leave room for interesting future research that may be materialized in the following research lines. (1) Approaching the translation task in the other direction (Gloss2Text), which requires the production of linguistic resources to annotate SLs, (2) Extending the experiments to other SLs and SL corpora, which could involve multilingual settings, and (3) Integrating multimodal features, such as manual and/or non-manual information, and visual features. For achieving (1), it will be necessary to create a tagger and a dependency parser for DSG, which would imply annotating many resources. This has been tried for other languages in the past (e.g. for Swedish Sign Language [16]), but so far existing corpora annotated in this way is very scarce, making this a very challenging problem.

Acknowledgements. This work has been conducted within the SignON project. SignON is a Horizon 2020 project, funded under the Horizon 2020 program ICT-57-2020 - "An empowering, inclusive, Next Generation Internet" with Grant Agreement number 101017255.

References

1. Almeida, I., Coheur, L., Candeias, S.: From European Portuguese to Portuguese sign language. In: 6th WS on Speech and Language Processing for Assistive Technologies. pp. 140–143. ACL, Dresden, Germany, September 2015. https://doi.org/10.18653/v1/W15-5124
2. Almeida, I., Coheur, L., Candeias, S.: Coupling natural language processing and animation synthesis in Portuguese sign language translation. In: 4th Workshop on Vision and Language, pp. 94–103, January 2015
3. Armengol-Estapé, J., Costa-jussà, M.R.: Semantic and syntactic information for neural machine translation. Mach. Transl. **35**(1), 3–17 (2021). https://doi.org/10.1007/s10590-021-09264-2
4. Brants, S., et al.: TIGER: linguistic interpretation of a German corpus. J. Lang. Comput. **2**, 597–620 (2004). https://doi.org/10.1007/s11168-004-7431-3
5. Camgoz, N., Hadfield, S., Koller, O., Ney, H., Bowden, R.: Neural sign language translation. In: CVPR 2018, pp. 7784–7793, March 2018. https://doi.org/10.1109/CVPR.2018.00812
6. Camgoz, N.C., Koller, O., Hadfield, S., Bowden, R.: Sign language transformers: joint end-to-end sign language recognition and translation. In: CVPR 2020, pp. 10020–10030 (2020). https://doi.org/10.1109/CVPR42600.2020.01004
7. Egea Gómez, S., McGill, E., Saggion, H.: Syntax-aware transformers for neural machine translation: the case of text to sign gloss translation. In: 14th Workshop on BUCC, pp. 18–27. INCOMA Ltd., Online, September 2021. https://aclanthology.org/2021.bucc-1.4
8. Hanke, T.: HamNoSys-representing sign language data in language resources and language processing contexts. In: LREC 2004, Workshop on RPSLs, pp. 1–6. Paris, France, May 2004

---

[9] https://github.com/LaSTUS-TALN-UPF/Linguistically-Enhanced-Text2Gloss-MT.

9. Jantunen, T., Rousi, R., Raino, P., Turunen, M., Valipoor, M., García, N.: Is there any hope for developing automated translation technology for sign languages?, pp. 61–73, March 2021. https://doi.org/10.31885/9789515150257.7

10. Jurafsky, D., Martin, J.H.: Speech and Language Processing (3rd Edition Draft) (2021). https://web.stanford.edu/jurafsky/slp3/

11. Kudo, T., Richardson, J.: SentencePiece: a simple and language independent sub-word tokenizer and detokenizer for neural text processing. In: EMNLP 2018, pp. 66–71. ACL, Brussels, Belgium, November 2018. https://doi.org/10.18653/v1/D18-2012

12. Morrissey, S., Way, A.: An example-based approach to translating sign language. In: 2nd Workshop on Example-Based MT, September 2005

13. Moryossef, A., Yin, K., Neubig, G., Goldberg, Y.: Data augmentation for sign language gloss translation (2021). https://arxiv.org/abs/2105.07476

14. Mukushev, M., Sabyrov, A., Imashev, A., Koishybay, K., Kimmelman, V., Sandygulova, A.: Evaluation of manual and non-manual components for sign language recognition. In: LREC 2020, pp. 6073–6078. ELRA, Marseille, France, May 2020. https://www.aclweb.org/anthology/2020.lrec-1.745

15. Nunnari, F., España-Bonet, C., Avramidis, E.: A data augmentation approach for sign-language-to-text translation in-the-wild. In: LDK 2021, Zaragoza, Spain. OpenAccess Series in Informatics (OASIcs), vol. 93. Dagstuhl Publishing, September 2021

16. Östling, R., Börstell, C., Gärdenfors, M., Wirén, M.: Universal dependencies for Swedish sign language. In: Proceedings of the 21st Nordic Conference on Computational Linguistics, pp. 303–308 (2017)

17. Post, M.: A call for clarity in reporting BLEU scores. In: 3rd Conference on MT, pp. 186–191. ACL, Belgium, Brussels, October 2018. https://doi.org/10.18653/v1/W18-6319

18. San-Segundo, R., et al.: Design, development and field evaluation of a Spanish into sign language translation system. Pattern Anal. Appl. **15**(2), 203–224 (2012)

19. San-Segundo, R., López, V., Martín, R., Sánchez, D., García, A.: Language resources for Spanish - Spanish sign language (LSE) translation. In: 4th Workshop on RPSLs, pp. 208–211 (2010). http://www-gth.die.upm.es/research/documentation/AG-096Lan-10.pdf

20. Sennrich, R., Haddow, B.: Linguistic input features improve neural machine translation. In: 1st Conference on MT, pp. 83–91. ACL, Berlin, Germany, August 2016. https://doi.org/10.18653/v1/W16-2209

21. Stoll, S., Camgoz, N.C., Hadfield, S., Bowden, R.: Text2Sign: towards sign language production using neural machine translation and generative adversarial networks. Int. J. Comput. Vision **128**(4), 891–908 (2019). https://doi.org/10.1007/s11263-019-01281-2

22. Xue, L., et al.: mT5: a massively multilingual pre-trained text-to-text transformer. In: NAACL 2021, pp. 483–498. ACL, Online, June 2021. https://doi.org/10.18653/v1/2021.naacl-main.41

23. Yin, K., Read, J.: Better sign language translation with STMC-transformer. In: COLING 2020, pp. 5975–5989, ICCL, Online, December 2020. https://doi.org/10.18653/v1/2020.coling-main.525

24. Liu, Y., et al.: Multilingual denoising pre-training for neural machine translation. CoRR, pp. 1–17 (2020). https://arxiv.org/abs/2001.08210

25. Zhang, X., Duh, K.: Approaching sign language gloss translation as a low-resource machine translation task. In: AT4SSL 2021, pp. 60–70. AMTA, Online, August 2021. https://aclanthology.org/2021.mtsummit-at4ssl.7

Preprocessing Requirements Documents for Automatic UML Modelling

Martijn B. J. Schouten$^{(\boxtimes)}$ ⓘ, Guus J. Ramackers ⓘ, and Suzan Verberne ⓘ

Leiden Institute of Advanced Computer Science, Niels Bohrweg 1, 2333 CA Leiden,
The Netherlands
m.b.j.schouten@umail.leidenuniv.nl,
{g.j.ramackers,s.verberne}@liacs.leidenuniv.nl

Abstract. Current approaches to natural language processing of requirements documents restrict their input to documents that are relevant to specific types of models only, such as domain- or process-focused models. Such input texts do not reflect real-world requirements documents. To address this issue, we propose a pipeline for preprocessing such requirements documents at the conceptual level, for subsequent automatic generation of class, activity, and use case models in the Unified Modelling Language (UML) downstream. Our pipeline consists of three steps. Firstly, we implement entity-based extractive summarization of the raw text to enable highlighting certain parts of the requirements that are of interest to the modelling goal. Secondly, we develop a rule-based bucketing method for selecting sentences into a range of 'buckets' for transformation into their corresponding UML models. Finally, to prove the effectiveness of supervised machine learning models on requirements texts, a sequence labelling model is applied to the text specific for class modelling to distinguish classes and attributes in the running text. In order to enable this step of our pipeline, we address the lack of available annotated data by labelling the widely used PURE requirements dataset on a word level by tagging classes and attributes within the texts. We validate our findings using this extended dataset.

Keywords: Unified Modelling Language (UML) · Natural Language Processing (NLP) · Machine Learning (ML) · Conceptual models · Model-driven architecture · Requirements engineering

1 Introduction

When engineering software systems, the main assumption is that the computational environment is predictable and fully specifiable. However, in the current world, systems are increasingly spread out over parts and layers built by many organizations, in different environments, and require cooperation from human operators. As a result, software engineering is increasingly confronted with uncertainty and complexity [10]. Because of that, deciding what to build, the process of defining software requirements, has become harder [4].

© The Author(s), under exclusive license to Springer Nature Switzerland AG 2022
P. Rosso et al. (Eds.): NLDB 2022, LNCS 13286, pp. 184–196, 2022.
https://doi.org/10.1007/978-3-031-08473-7_17

A good understanding of requirements is the basis of creating systems that satisfy the expectations of stakeholders. Early construction of a software-system architecture is helpful for the discovery of further requirements and constraints, feasibility and determining alternatives for implementation [19]. For this, stakeholder involvement is key. The lack of stakeholder involvement is the predominant reason for software projects to run into difficulties [21]. Therefore, achieving a higher level of stakeholder involvement has been a much-researched topic in requirements engineering (RE).

A definite solution to solidifying early requirements is not offered, nor does current research answer the problem of bridging the gap between stakeholders and system architects in the early stages of requirements engineering. But what if the solution does not lie with the stakeholders but with the process itself?

A new research area is focused on applying natural language processing (NLP) techniques to assist software requirements analysis. This field helps plan out software projects early on by generating architecture requirements models [24]. As requirements documents and domain descriptions are typically provided in natural language, structuring this knowledge can form the basis for the software development process. This early-stage modelling allows individual stakeholders to conceptualize their visions faster, and human error in communicating requirements can be dealt with immediately. With this approach, stakeholders can intervene in the development process at a stage where the detection of errors does not escalate exponentially in later stages of development.

Several methods have been proposed for generating UML models from requirements texts. However, most of these previous implementations rely on structured input texts, which are not representative of real-world requirements documents. In addition, real world-world requirements texts mix specifications for different kinds of UML models in the same document. Furthermore, distinctions between UML elements, for instance classes versus attributes in class modelling, are not explicitly identified.

In this work, we address these limitations by creating an interactive preprocessing pipeline for raw requirements texts that, with intervention of the human modeller, outputs structured and separated texts that can be used to generate UML models.

To aid downstream model generation, we suggest hints in the form of metadata alongside the output text of the pipeline. For now, this metadata is limited to suggestions on distinguishing classes and attributes, which is regarded as a longstanding research problem within automatic class model generation. However, with this approach we suggest an architecture to generate more metadata to target specific downstream NLP transformation modelling issues in the future.

In summary, the main research objective is to develop a pipeline system that is able to preprocess real-world requirements texts describing system requirements and process them into uniform class, use case and activity texts as input for downstream NLP to UML transformation. The complete pipeline, including the produced datasets, models and experiments are available on GitHub for reference. The repository can be found here: https://github.com/MeMartijn/text2uml.

The structure of this paper is as follows: we discuss an overview of related work on applying NLP techniques to UML modelling in Sect. 2 to set the general stage for the context of this research. In Sect. 3 we present the architecture of the developed pipeline, with a detailed explanation on the methods per step of the pipeline. In this section the reader can also find the used models and datasets. In Sect. 4, results of the pipeline are discussed. Finally, in Sect. 5, we discuss the practical implications of our work and suggest future research directions.

2   Related Work

Several previous research approaches have been made to assist UML modellers by applying NLP techniques to requirements texts. For **class modelling**, multiple approaches have been proposed to partly automate the process of creating class models. Using hard-coded rules based on Part-of-Speech (POS) tagging, the Linguistic assistant for Domain Analysis (LIDA) by Overmeyer et al. [20] identifies objects, their attributes and methods. The Graphic Object-Oriented Analysis Laboratory (GOOAL) developed by Perez-Gonzaled and Kalita [22] takes a similar rule-based approach, but regulates the requirements document before constructing a model. However, it can only handle simple problem domains and the texts still need to be structured before being able to be processed by the system.

Rule-based approaches are also taken by Azzouz et al. [2] that use over a thousand hand-written patterns, and Narawita and Vidanage [17] that extend a rule-based approach with Weka software for recognizing relationship types and multiplicity with their UML Generator. Contrasting previous approaches, Tang [25] combined parts of previous approaches to create a semi-automatic class modeller that supports extensive interactivity with the end-user for refining and finalizing diagrams, but similar problems are still apparent: because the tool uses a list of keywords to distinguish and link classes and attributes, the input text needs to be structured before being used.

The research field for automatic **activity- and use case modelling** is considerably less extensive, but have the same challenges as automatic class modelling. Iqbal and Bajwa [12] rely on the usage of natural language requirements in a formal structure in order to extract basic UML elements of an activity model. This approach is very similar to Nassar and Khamayseh [18], who specify clear guidelines for the requirements texts to follow before being able to generate activity models, and the method proposed by Maatuk and Abdelnabi [16], that requires input texts to follow a set of sixteen syntactic rules before facilitating UML element extraction for activity- and use case models.

For use case models, structuring raw text continues to be an apparent issue as well. An implementations by Deeptimahanti et al. [5] normalize incoming texts using NLP tools before automatically forming class- and use case and models. The approach by Elallaoui et al. [6] relies on user stories, which inherently provide a strict structure already. Finally, the method developed by Hamza and Hammad [11] involves an intricate preprocessing step, including spelling checking, and an approach is taken depending on found structures in the text that indicate whether the sentence is written in an active or passive voice.

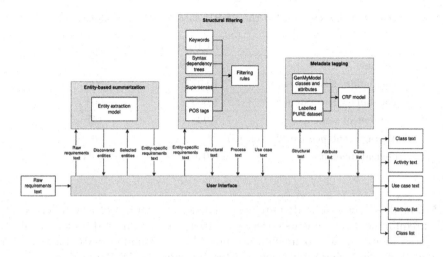

Fig. 1. Architecture pipeline for going from input to output.

To conclude, existing implementations for automatic generation of class-, activity- and use case models provide promising results, but share the same problem: the input text is limited to following a certain, predefined structure, and do not account for mixed model documents [24]. This underlines the need for a unified approach for processing raw, real-world requirements texts that can be used as a preprocessing step for (semi-)automatic UML modelling downstream.

3   Method

3.1   Architecture Overview

The three step pipeline architecture makes use of the following NLP techniques: i) entity-based summarization, ii) structural filtering, and iii) metadata tagging. These three steps are discussed in detail below. An overview of the complete pipeline is shown in Fig. 1.

For the implementation of our preprocessing modules, we make use of BookNLP, an NLP pipeline in Python 3 specifically developed for operations on long texts. BookNLP uses Spacy for POS tagging and dependency parsing. For the more complex tasks, it uses BERT models trained on different datasets, depending on the task at hand [1].

3.2   Datasets

PURE: A Dataset of Public Requirements Documents. Even though there is a lack of requirements texts with attached UML models, there are two relatively large datasets for standalone requirements texts and for standalone

Table 1. Characteristics of the PURE dataset and the validation set.

Metric	PURE (training set)	Validation
Tokens	187,649	2,722
Vocabulary size (tokens)	10,977	805
Vocabulary size (stems)	8,688	664
Number of sentences	7,928	147
Average sentence length (tokens)	24	18
Lexical diversity	0.046	0.244

UML models. The Public Requirements dataset is a dataset of 79 publicly available requirements documents covering a variety of domains and topics. A subset of these requirements documents are ported to a common XML format with the goal of facilitating replication of NLP experiments [7]. We made use of this subset in this project, resulting in 18 requirements texts being used for training. Details on amount of tokens, vocabulary and lexical diversity can be found in Table 1.

Validation Set. To test our approach on new data, we gathered a selection of 5 requirements documents which are currently being used as training material by a large American software company for their software consultants and architects. An overview of the metrics of this validation set and how it relates to the training set can be found in Table 1.

3.3 Entity-Based Summarization

The first step of the preprocessing pipeline is an entity-based extractive summarization step to extract sentences from requirements based on entities of interest using BookNLP. This step contains two substeps: presenting the modeller all discovered entities and allowing them to select entities of interest, and extract sentences that relate to the entities of interest.

We first extract all entities from the raw requirements texts using the entity annotation module of BookNLP, which has been trained on an annotated dataset of 968K tokens, combining public domain materials in LitBank with a dataset of approximately 500 contemporary books.

From all discovered entities, two categories of entities are excluded: Geopolitical entities (GPE) and Organizations (ORG), together with all pronouns. These categories are excluded because they often refer to named entities, which are typically not modelled in UML diagrams, leaving us with concepts that are more likely to refer to UML objects.

The entity extraction step often results in duplicate entities: for example, BookNLP classifies 'customer', 'each customer' and 'group of customers' as separate entities. To combine these into a set of unique entities, we rely on the

POS tags of the detected entities: we remove all words of the entity groups that are not a noun or adjective according to the POS tagging of Spacy and remove duplicates.

After performing these transformations, the user is presented with all the extracted entities and makes a selection of entities that the modeller wants to use in modelling downstream.

After this selection, the next substep is the filtering of relevant sentences based on the relevant entities. Only sentences that contain (references to) the selected entities of interest are returned to the user for further preprocessing in the pipeline. Thus, sentences that do not contain entities of interest directly, or have indirect links to the entities of interest via words such as "their" and "this" will be removed from the running text before continuing to the next step in the pipeline.

The benefit of the interactive, entity-based summarization step is two-fold: firstly, by extracting sentences we omit the processing of the whole document which often includes irrelevant parts such as tables of content, management summaries, reasons for development, appendices etc. that are not useful for modelling. Secondly, allowing the user to focus on specific parts of the software allows for compartmentalized and incremental development, where big software systems can be split into smaller parts.

3.4   Structural Filtering

The next step in the pipeline is forming three 'buckets' to put sentences in: one for class modelling, one for activity modelling and one for use case modelling. The output of these steps is therefore three texts that are concatenations of the sentences that belong in these buckets: a text for class modelling, a text for activity modelling and a text for use case modelling.

One sentence can appear in multiple buckets, as long as it conforms to the filtering rules that are defined for each of the buckets. These rules are based on four characteristics of the sentences, or a combination of multiple of characteristics: keywords, syntax dependencies, supersenses and POS tags. For syntactic dependency parsing we use word-level information of Spacy. Supersenses are a classification scheme for nouns and verbs that groups them based on semantic meaning of the words [14]. For supersense tagging we use the supersenses module from BookNLP, which was trained on SemCor. SemCor is a subset of the Brown Corpus (360K tokens) that is annotated with supersenses [23]. The combination of syntax dependencies and POS tags with supersenses allows us to create rules that both target syntactic and semantic structures within sentences.

The filtering rules for the class- and use case texts are based on this combination. Combinations are made based on manual observations of the requirements texts in the PURE dataset, which is introduced in Sect. 3.2. We manually labeled all sentences of this dataset with whether they had indicators for class- and use case modelling, gathered all sentences for class- and use case modelling, generated their characteristics, and created rules that were as abstract as possible in order to keep the rules as high-level as possible, not focusing on edge cases. This process resulted in 16 manually defined structural rules for class texts and 4 rules for use case texts. Contrasting this approach, the filtering rules for activity texts are based on keywords, extracted from previous research conducted by Friedrich et al. [9] and Ferreira [8] in the Business Process Model and Notation (BPMN) domain.

3.5   Metadata Tagging

The last step of the process takes as input the class text gathered from the previous step, and identifies and label classes and attributes that are present in the text. For this purpose, we use a supervised sequence labelling model, conditional random fields (CRF). As stated previously, the relatively limit availability of publicly available training data for requirements engineering is a limitation of this research field. By using a CRF model, we can classify elements in a running text with only a small amount of training data.

For creating our training data, we again made use of the PURE dataset. We analyzed the requirements texts in this dataset with the BookNLP modules and used coarse- and fine-grained POS tags, lemmas, dependency relations, supersense categories, entity numbers, entity types and ACE 2005 entity categories as features. In the running pipeline, these features used for predictions are by-products of the previous two steps of the pipeline, and therefore require no additional computing power. To boost performance of the model, we also added a class-attribute ratio as a feature to noun groups, as well as fastText word embeddings [3].

We manually added the target variable, the IOB tag indicating whether a word belongs to a group of classes, attributes, or does not belong to either, to the training data. As a result, we publish a new dataset that can be used for machine learning tasks for the identification of classes and attributes in requirements texts based on the PURE dataset. The dataset is available in the public GitHub repository linked in the Sect. 1.

There are several large repositories available of UML models to be used for research purposes. Through MAR, a search engine for models, we gathered a dataset of 352,216 XML files containing UML diagrams from GenMyModel, an online modelling tool [15]. These files make use of a shared UML namespace, making it relatively easy to extract classes and attributes by extracting elements with the xsi:type attribute uml:Class, giving one the class objects, and then searching for owned attributes within this object, which are the attributes of the object. After stripping the names of the extracted classes and attributes, this resulted in 344,981 unique classes and 455,730 unique attributes.

Because within this project we focus ourselves on the larger applications of UML, we apply some additional syntactic preprocessing steps to transform programmatic class- and attribute names. First, we remove function calls, getters and setters, dot-separated widgets and filenames, comma-separated attributes, HTML and XML tags, dollar signs at the start of strings, digits attached to the end of words and all notions of "my" before another word, left-over parentheses, dashes, square brackets, hashtags, stars and slashes. Then, we transform all

The Right-Way Rental Truck Company rents small moving trucks and trailers for local and one-way usage. We have 347 rental offices across the western United States. Our rental stock includes a total of 5,780 vehicles including various types of trucks and trailers. We need to implement a system to track our rental agreements and our vehicle assignments. Each rental office rents vehicles that they have in stock to customers ready to take possession of the vehicle. We don't take reservations, or speculate on when the customer will return rented vehicles. The central office oversees the vehicle distribution, and directs transfers of vehicles from one rental office to another. Each rental office has an office name like "Littleton Right-Way". Each office also has a unique three digit office number. We also keep each office's address. Each office is a home office for some of our vehicles, and each vehicle is based out of a single home office. Each vehicle has a vehicle id, state of registration, and a license plate registration number. We have five different types of vehicles: 36' trucks, 24' trucks, 10' trucks, 8' covered trailers, and 6' open trailers. Yes, we do have a vehicle type code. For all our vehicles, we need to track the last maintenance date, and expiration date of its registration. For our trucks, we need to know the current odometer reading, the gas tank capacity, and whether or not it has a working radio. For long moves, customers really prefer a radio. We log the current mileage just before we rent a truck, and then again when it is returned. Most of our rental agreements are for individual customers, but a rental agreement can either be for an individual or for a company. We do rent a small percentage of our trucks to companies. We assign each company an identifying company number and track the company's name and address. No, we don't need to worry about any additional information about a company. Our corporate sales group handles all that information separately. For each individual customer, we record the customer's name, home phone, address, and driver's license state, number, and expiration date. We like to keep track of all our customers. If a customer damaged a vehicle, abandoned it, or didn't fully pay the bill, then we tag the customer as a poor risk, and won't rent to that customer again. We only allow a single individual or company for a given rental agreement, and we write a separate rental agreement for each vehicle. Yes, we do have customers rent two or more vehicles at the same time. Each rental agreement is identified by the originating rental office number and a rental agreement number. We also need to track the rental date, the anticipated duration of the rental, the originating rental office, the drop-off rental office, the amount of the deposit paid, the quoted daily rental rate, and the quoted rate per mile. Of course for the trailers, there isn't a mileage charge. No, we don't need to automate the financial side of our business, just our rental agreement tracking and vehicle assignment functions.

Fig. 2. Applying the entity-based extractive summarization step on the validation text.

programmatic cases (snake case, camel case etc.) into space-separated text in order to reflect running texts as best as possible. Next, we replace abbreviations for implementation, reference, and the ampersand for their written-out version. Finally, we remove duplicate spaces and all entries that contain non-Latin characters.

Because the models are multi-lingual, the last cleaning step is to remove all non-English files out of the dataset. For this, we use fastText's language identification model, which allows for fast and reliable language identification which can recognize 176 languages [13].

The end result is a list of 908,946 classes, of which 180,429 are unique, and 1,232,355 attributes, of which 203,154 are unique. This list of classes and attributes is then used as a ratio that states how many times the word group has been used as an attribute and how many times as a class in the GenMy-Model dataset. This list of classes and attributes is then used as follows: we attach three values to a token if it belongs to a noun group. The first value indicates the total amount of times the noun group is observed in the GenMyModel dataset. The second and the third value give the absolute counts of times this noun group appears as a class and as an attribute, respectively. For example, the word 'address' appears 21,845 times as an attribute, and 1,287 times as a class. This results in a total amount of occurrences of 23,132.

4   Results

To evaluate the results of our pipeline, we run one text out of our validation set through the steps. Where possible, we provide quantitative results to accompany our qualitative example.

4.1   Entity-Based Summarization

The contents of the validation text is shown in Fig. 2. The named entity extraction model discovers the following entities in this text: *small truck trailer, rental*

Each rental office rents vehicles that they have in stock to customers ready to take possession of the vehicle. We don't take reservations or speculate on when the customer will return rented vehicles. The central office oversees the vehicle distribution and directs transfers of vehicles from one rental office to another. Each office is a home office for some of our vehicles, and each vehicle is based out of a single home office. Each vehicle has a vehicle id, state of registration, and a license plate registration number. For all our vehicles, we need to track the last maintenance date and expiration date of its registration. If a customer damaged a vehicle, abandoned it, or didn't fully pay the bill, then we tag the customer as a poor risk, and won't rent to that customer again.	We don't take reservations or speculate on when the customer will return rented vehicles. If a customer damaged a vehicle, abandoned it, or didn't fully pay the bill, then we tag the customer as a poor risk, and won't rent to that customer again.	We don't take reservations or speculate on when the customer will return rented vehicles. For long moves, customers really prefer a radio. If a customer damaged a vehicle, abandoned it, or didn't fully pay the bill, then we tag the customer as a poor risk, and won't rent to that customer again. Yes, we do have customers rent two or more vehicles at the same time.
(a) Class text.	(b) Activity text.	(c) Use case text.

Fig. 3. Applying the structural filtering step on the summarized text to create 3 'buckets'.

office, vehicle various type truck, customer, customer ready possession, vehicle, rented vehicle, central office, office, single home office, different type vehicle, truck, individual customer, individual, company, home, driver, single individual company, more vehicle, truck trailer and *open trailer*.

The results of selecting the entities *customer*, *vehicle* and *truck* for the entity-based summarization are also shown in Fig. 2. The selected text is displayed in green, the discarded text is not highlighted. Because of our efforts of grouping (semi-)duplicate entities together, we achieve good qualitative results on this step, allowing the user to effectively select parts of the system for further modelling, while keeping in mind the user experience by not presenting the complete list of detected entities in the text.

4.2 Structural Filtering

In Fig. 3, the filtered output texts of the first step of the pipeline are shown. The usage of a broad range of rules for the class text results in the longest text of the three (a). Due to the limitations of the use of keywords to find sentences related to processes, the activity text only consists of two sentences. Finally, our rules result in a use case text that contains sentences that always involve an actor in an active way, giving us a satisfactory result overall.

To provide a benchmark for future research, we have labelled all sentences in our validation set with for which type of modelling the sentence seems useful. The validation set contains 145 sentences, and each sentence can be labelled as useful for more than one type of modelling. Even though this is only a small collection, we show the classification result in Table 2. We achieve relatively high accuracy scores for activity- and use case filtering (87% an 76% respectively), but this is large due to the skewed nature of the validation set.

Table 2. Classification scores of the structural filtering step.

	Precision	Recall	F1-score	Support	Accuracy
Useful for class modelling	0.79	0.56	0.66	110	0.56
Not useful for class modelling	0.28	0.54	0.37	35	
Useful for activity modelling	0.60	0.41	0.49	22	0.87
Not useful for activity modelling	0.90	0.95	0.92	123	
Useful for use case modelling	0.38	0.44	0.41	27	0.76
Not useful for use case modelling	0.87	0.83	0.85	118	

Table 3. Classification scores for the CRF model of the final step of the pipeline.

	Default			With ratio			With embeddings			Everything combined		
	Precision	Recall	F1-score	Precision	Recall	F1-score	Precision	Recall	F1-score	Precision	Recall	F1-score
B-class	0.633	0.377	0.472	0.580	0.353	0.439	0.588	0.358	0.445	0.585	0.367	0.451
I-class	0.571	0.235	0.333	0.472	0.200	0.281	0.472	0.200	0.281	0.472	0.200	0.281
B-attr	0.824	0.300	0.440	0.764	0.300	0.431	0.741	0.307	0.434	0.816	0.286	0.423
I-attr	0.744	0.235	0.358	0.721	0.228	0.346	0.705	0.228	0.344	0.744	0.235	0.358

4.3   Metadata Tagging

Table 3 displays all gathered classification results of the trained CRF model on the validation set. The scores are displayed in four stages in order to approximate the influence of each group of features on the end result. For each training stage, we tuned the hyperparameters c1 and c2 using randomized search. The first stage entailed a minimal training setup: we trained the CRF model using our base features, which only included the base information for each token (POS tag, dependency relation, supersense, entity type, entity category, surrounding words and POS tags, etc.). In the second stage, we added information from the GenMyModel dataset: training was conducted on the base information in combination with the amount of occurrences of the token in the GenMyModel dataset, and how many of those occurrences were labelled as classes or attributes. The third stage combined the base information with fastText embeddings for each token. Finally, in the last stage, all of the additional features were combined.

By default, the training materials were sparse in terms of classes and attributes as compared to the validation materials. As a result, the related F1-scores are generally not very high, however, some interesting differences between the stages exist. One observation is that the stage that included information from the GenMyModel dataset performed significantly worse than the default. This again indicates the subtleties that arise with UML modelling: word-level information seems to have a negative influence on the model. Combining this with the results of the training stage that included word embeddings, which are still lower than the default training stage, indicate that context-level information is needed as opposed to word-level details for disambiguating aspects of class models in requirements texts.

5 Conclusion

In previous sections, this paper laid out a pipeline for preprocessing real-world requirements texts into structured texts for the purpose of generating class-, activity-, and use case models, including metadata for class modelling specifically. Our experimental results set a benchmark for future work, provide new training material, and provide a new direction of methods for the analysis of requirements texts, including the novel use of entity extraction to gather entities of interest for UML modelling. To conclude, this paper forms a basis to a more uniform approach on preprocessing requirements texts, with the goal of advancing research in this area.

Looking at the limitations of our research, future work is needed on automatically locating parts of requirements texts that are useful for systems design. We especially see opportunities in a more context-aware method of distinguishing classes and attributes from each other, but more research on the difference between classes and attributes on the word level is also welcomed. To conclude, the lack of datasets on this topic remains a limitation for future research. Even though considerable work went into creating labelled datasets to support this paper, independent validation of our data, or extension of this work into, for example, attributes and methods versus classes and subclasses would be a valuable addition to this research.

References

1. Bamman, D.: BookNLP, a natural language processing pipeline for books (2021). https://github.com/booknlp/booknlp
2. Ben Abdessalem Karaa, W., Ben Azzouz, Z., Singh, A., Dey, N., Ashour, A.S., Ben Ghazala, H.: Automatic builder of class diagram (ABCD): an application of UML generation from functional requirements. Softw. Pract. Exp. **46**(11), 1443–1458 (2016)
3. Bojanowski, P., Grave, E., Joulin, A., Mikolov, T.: Enriching word vectors with subword information. arXiv preprint arXiv:1607.04606 (2016)
4. Brackett, J.W.: Software requirements. Technical report, Carnegie-Mellon University Software Engineering Institute (1990)
5. Deeptimahanti, D.K., Sanyal, R.: Semi-automatic generation of UML models from natural language requirements. In: Proceedings of the 4th India Software Engineering Conference, pp. 165–174 (2011)
6. Elallaoui, M., Nafil, K., Touahni, R.: Automatic transformation of user stories into UML use case diagrams using NLP techniques. Procedia Comput. Sci. **130**, 42–49 (2018)
7. Ferrari, A., Spagnolo, G.O., Gnesi, S.: PURE: a dataset of public requirements documents. In: 2017 IEEE 25th International Requirements Engineering Conference (RE), pp. 502–505 (2017). https://doi.org/10.1109/RE.2017.29

8. Ferreira, R.C.B., Thom, L.H., Fantinato, M.: A semi-automatic approach to identify business process elements in natural language texts. In: ICEIS, no. 3, pp. 250–261 (2017)
9. Friedrich, F., Mendling, J., Puhlmann, F.: Process model generation from natural language text. In: Mouratidis, H., Rolland, C. (eds.) CAiSE 2011. LNCS, vol. 6741, pp. 482–496. Springer, Heidelberg (2011). https://doi.org/10.1007/978-3-642-21640-4_36
10. Garlan, D.: Software engineering in an uncertain world. In: Proceedings of the FSE/SDP Workshop on Future of Software Engineering Research, pp. 125–128 (2010)
11. Hamza, Z.A., Hammad, M.: Generating UML use case models from software requirements using natural language processing. In: 2019 8th International Conference on Modeling Simulation and Applied Optimization (ICMSAO), pp. 1–6. IEEE (2019)
12. Iqbal, U., Bajwa, I.S.: Generating UML activity diagram from SBVR rules. In: 2016 Sixth International Conference on Innovative Computing Technology (INTECH), pp. 216–219. IEEE (2016)
13. Joulin, A., Grave, E., Bojanowski, P., Douze, M., Jégou, H., Mikolov, T.: Fast-Text.zip: compressing text classification models. arXiv preprint arXiv:1612.03651 (2016)
14. Kipper, K., Korhonen, A., Ryant, N., Palmer, M.: Extending VerbNet with novel verb classes. In: LREC, pp. 1027–1032 (2006)
15. López, J.A.H., Cuadrado, J.S.: MAR: a structure-based search engine for models. In: Proceedings of the 23rd ACM/IEEE International Conference on Model Driven Engineering Languages and Systems, pp. 57–67 (2020)
16. Maatuk, A.M., Abdelnabi, E.A.: Generating UML use case and activity diagrams using NLP techniques and heuristics rules. In: International Conference on Data Science, E-Learning and Information Systems 2021, pp. 271–277 (2021)
17. Narawita, C.R., Vidanage, K.: UMl generator-use case and class diagram generation from text requirements. Int. J. Adv. ICT Emerg. Regions (ICTer) 10, 1 (2018). https://doi.org/10.4038/icter.v10i1.7182
18. Nassar, I.N., Khamayseh, F.T.: Constructing activity diagrams from Arabic user requirements using natural language processing tool. In: 2015 6th International Conference on Information and Communication Systems (ICICS), pp. 50–54. IEEE (2015)
19. Nuseibeh, B.: Weaving together requirements and architectures. Computer 34(3), 115–119 (2001)
20. Overmyer, S.P., Benoit, L., Owen, R.: Conceptual modeling through linguistic analysis using LIDA. In: Proceedings of the 23rd International Conference on Software Engineering, ICSE 2001, pp. 401–410. IEEE (2001)
21. Paetsch, F., Eberlein, A., Maurer, F.: Requirements engineering and agile software development. In: WET ICE 2003. Proceedings. Twelfth IEEE International Workshops on Enabling Technologies: Infrastructure for Collaborative Enterprises, pp. 308–313. IEEE (2003)
22. Perez-Gonzalez, H.G., Kalita, J.K.: GOOAL: a graphic object oriented analysis laboratory. In: Companion of the 17th Annual ACM SIGPLAN Conference on Object-Oriented Programming, Systems, Languages, and Applications, pp. 38–39 (2002)
23. Petrolito, T., Bond, F.: A survey of wordnet annotated corpora. In: Proceedings of the Seventh Global WordNet Conference, pp. 236–245 (2014)

24. Ramackers, G., Griffioen, P., Schouten, M., Chaudron, M.: From prose to proto-type: synthesising executable UML models from natural language. In: Proceedings of the 23rd ACM/IEEE International Conference on Model Driven Engineering Languages and Systems, pp. 380–389 (2021)
25. Tang, T.: From natural language to UML class models: an automated solution using NLP to assist requirements analysis. Master's thesis, Leiden University (2020)

A Methodology for Enabling NLP Capabilities on Edge and Low-Resource Devices

Andreas Goulas[1], Nikolaos Malamas[1,2(✉)], and Andreas L. Symeonidis[1]

[1] School of Electrical and Computer Engineering, AUTH, 54124 Thessaloniki, Greece
{nmalamas,symeonid}@ece.auth.gr
[2] Gnomon Informatis S.A., Antoni Tritsi 21, 57001 Thessaloniki, Greece
nmalamas@gnomon.com.gr

Abstract. Conversational assistants with increasing NLP capabilities are becoming commodity functionality for most new devices. However, the underlying language models responsible for language-related intelligence are typically characterized by a large number of parameters and high demand for memory and resources. This makes them a no-go for edge and low-resource devices, forcing them to be cloud-hosted, hence experiencing delays. To this end, we design a systematic language-agnostic methodology to develop powerful lightweight NLP models using knowledge distillation techniques, this way building models suitable for such low resource devices. We follow the steps of the proposed approach for the Greek language and build the first - to the best of our knowledge - lightweight Greek language model, which we make publicly available. We train and evaluate GloVe word embeddings in Greek and efficiently distill Greek-BERT into various BiLSTM models, without considerable loss in performance. Experiments indicate that knowledge distillation and data augmentation can improve the performance of simple BiLSTM models for two NLP tasks in Modern Greek, i.e., Topic Classification and Natural Language Inference, making them suitable candidates for low-resource devices.

Keywords: Natural language processing · Knowledge distillation · Word embeddings · Lightweight models

1 Introduction

In the last few years, we have witnessed significant growth in the area of smart conversational assistants, aspiring to change the way we receive information and control devices. To do so, significant advancements in the Natural Language Processing (NLP) field have taken place. The release of the Transformer architecture in [33] practically enabled the harnessing of NLP advantages, as many efficient Transformer-based models such as BERT [5] and GPT [26] have been introduced. Among others, these models work toward reducing the gap between human and

P. Rosso et al. (Eds.): NLDB 2022, LNCS 13286, pp. 197–208, 2022.
https://doi.org/10.1007/978-3-031-08473-7_18

robot understanding on various language tasks, such as Named Entity Recognition and Natural Language Inference, this way improving the overall behavior of smart assistants.

As discussed in [18], the state-of-practice for conversational assistants is a gradual migration of the services needed from cloud-based infrastructures to user devices, in order to improve user experience. However, a significant constraint comes with this particular approach as the above-mentioned NLP models are resource and time-intensive both training- and inference-wise, making them cumbersome and difficult to use on real-time responsive applications and interfaces. In addition, many studies argue that these NLP models are overparameterized and there is a redundancy of information among the parameters and the attention heads [13,27]. Hence, they argue that they can be efficiently represented by smaller models, either Transformer-based [9,28,30] or even simple RNNs, usually BiLSTMs [31,34], without any major loss in performance. Such systems are considered more appropriate choices in cases where time and resources matter.

Although various small models have been introduced, to the best of our knowledge no systematic methodology has been presented for developing light-weight models leveraging larger existing ones, especially for supporting not-so-widely-spoken languages. To this end, we describe the appropriate steps in this direction, and, without loss of generality, we implement this methodology for the Greek language. Particularly, we develop Greek GloVe embeddings [24] that we then use to distill Greek-BERT, a monolingual Greek version of the vanilla BERT model [5], into 1-layer and 2-layer BiLSTMs. We evaluate our models on two NLP tasks, i.e., Natural Language Inference (NLI) and Topic Classification (TC), and show that these lightweight models are more appropriate choices for low-resource or edge devices as their overall user experience performance (combination of inference time and language understanding) is significantly better. Finally, we contribute to the community by making all the developed models and embeddings publicly available.[1] The rest of the paper is organized as follows. Section 2 discusses the state-of-the-art in word representations and distillation approaches both in Greek and other languages. Section 3 presents the methodology followed, while Sect. 4 outlines the experiments conducted and the results achieved. Finally, Sect. 5 summarizes the work, draws conclusions, and discusses future research.

2   Related Work

2.1   Language Representations

Word embeddings are static vector representations of words in a multi-dimensional space, in which distances indicate word similarity. They first came into existence when word2vec was introduced [20], a method that leverages shallow neural networks that consider the context of each word to create their embeddings. An extension of word embeddings are FastText embeddings [2], which use a similar approach but split the input sentences into n-grams instead of words,

---

[1] https://github.com/AuthEceSoftEng/Greek-NLP-Distillation-Paper.

leading to faster and more robust results. Global Vectors (GloVe) embeddings [24] were also introduced, which offer word representations that leverage word co-occurrence to derive semantic relationships between them.

Bidirectional Encoder Representations from Transformers (BERT) [5] was among the first models that offered contextual embeddings, i.e., vector representations of words that can vary under different contexts. In addition, BERT can be fine-tuned for every NLP task achieving great results. Since then, many such models have been established like RoBERTa [16] and DeBERTa [6], aiming to further push the state-of-the-art. However, all these systems share the same primary issues related to their size, as reported in various studies [13,27]. Particularly, they are heavily overparameterized large models built on an excessive number of layers and attention heads; in fact, many of those may be discarded without significant performance loss. This is due to the fact that, in these models, multiple heads learn the same patterns, hence exhibiting a large degree of redundancy.

To this end, various studies have been performed aiming to decrease the size of these models. One simple approach is to train similar models, using fewer heads and parameters [32]. Another common path is to compress an existing model via quantization [29] or pruning [19]. Finally, another path is to use the large pre-trained models in order to extract knowledge during training. The latter is a process called knowledge distillation, which has shown promising results; this is where we focus our study on.

2.2   Distillation Approaches of BERT

Knowledge distillation, first proposed in [7], is the process of transferring knowledge from an already trained large or complex model called the *teacher* to another smaller model called the *student*. Specifically, the student is trained to match the probability distribution of the teacher's output layer, also known as *logits*, as these values tend to encapsulate more information than the original output labels. This process has been widely used to distill models like BERT into two types of models: Transformer-based models and RNNs.

Regarding the first category, DistilBERT [28] is a general-purpose distilled model, which has 40% fewer parameters compared to BERT, while it retains 97% of its performance on GLUE benchmark tasks. Another Transformer distillation approach was presented in [9], where BERT was distilled in a smaller Transformer model of 4 (or 6) layers, called TinyBERT. Specifically, this was accomplished in two steps, i.e., the general distillation, using the pre-trained BERT model, and the task-specific distillation process, using a fine-tuned BERT. Another such approach is Patient Knowledge Distillation (PKD) [30], proposed in two variations: PKD-Last and PKD-Skip. In PKD-Last, the student Transformer model learns the last k layers of the teacher model, while in PKD-Skip, the student model learns from one every k layers, skipping the intermediate ones. Using a 12-layer BERT-base model as the teacher, they reported better results in several GLUE tasks compared with BERT models of equal sizes.

Regarding RNN-based models, a 1-layer BiLSTM was trained in [34] using a fine-tuned BERT model as the teacher model, achieving similar results with

ELMo [25], while using 100 times fewer parameters. Furthermore, the knowledge from a pre-trained BERT model was transferred into a BiLSTM network by directly distilling the sentence representations from the teacher [34], creating a model that can be later fine-tuned for sentence-level downstream tasks.

2.3 Greek NLP

Considering the Greek language, many studies have been conducted with promising results, as discussed in [23]. Specifically, FastText [2] was initially developed to support 157 languages, one of which is Greek. In addition, a testing schema was developed in [22] to measure word analogy and word similarity, which is highly inspired by the approach used in word2vec. It was then used to compare the authors' own implementation of Greek word2vec models with the existing FastText model. Furthermore, in another study, the Continuous Bag-of-Skip-grams (CBOS) was proposed [15], a model that combines the two methods of word2vec and achieves better performance.

As for contextual word representations, there are only a few multilingual models that have been trained in Greek. Two such approaches are mBERT and XLM-R [3]. The former is the multilingual version of BERT [5] developed to support 104 languages. However, it is common knowledge that multilingual models suffer from the *curse of multilinguality* [3], i.e., the underlying vocabulary contains words from so many languages that the model learns only a few words from each one and tends to suffer in low-resource languages, such as Greek. XLM-R, on the other hand, was trained on a corpus of 100 languages and outperformed mBERT in several tasks, but still reported similar limitations, such as the trade-off between low-resource and high-resource languages and the curse of multilinguality. Apart from these two approaches, Greek-BERT [12] is to this day the state-of-the-art Greek model in various NLP tasks. It is based on the original BERT-base [5] using the same architecture and is trained on three Greek corpora, namely articles from Wikipedia, OSCAR [21] and the European Parliament Proceedings Parallel Corpus [11].

3 Methodology

In this section, we present an appropriate methodology to distil models into lightweight ones. As presented in Fig. 1, we first choose our teacher model and collect our corpora in order to develop word representations. We then train and evaluate various distilled models on NLP tasks, leveraging those embeddings. Finally, in cases where the task-specific datasets are rather small, we can optionally augment them using our embeddings and further assist our models.

3.1 Corpus Preprocessing and GloVe Embeddings Training

We collected our data from the same corpus that was used for the pre-training of Greek-BERT. This ensures that the comparison between the proposed models

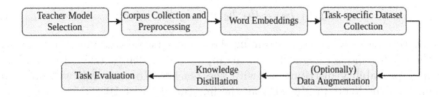

Fig. 1. Methodology pipeline.

and Greek-BERT is fair. We preprocessed our corpus as follows: we removed non-Unicode characters and non-readable Unicode characters, we performed lower-casing and removed word accent. Then, we tokenized the documents by splitting the texts into white spaces, in punctuation marks, and in non-ASCII characters.

We employed the original GloVe embeddings process to create our own static word representations leveraging this corpus. As earlier discussed, the GloVe model uses the statistics of word occurrences in large corpora in an unsupervised manner in order to identify words that are semantically related.

3.2   Distilled Models

As discussed earlier, our aim is to distill knowledge obtained from the existing Greek-BERT model to small BiLSTM networks. The first step towards this direction is to fine-tune the *teacher* model, i.e., Greek-BERT, in each studied task. To this end, we follow the fine-tuning process presented in [5]. We then develop the *student* models, 1-layer and 2-layer BiLSTM networks encompassing 3.6M and 9.9M parameters, respectively (the Greek-BERT model encompasses 110M parameters).

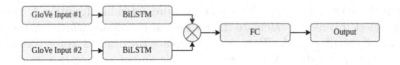

Fig. 2. Siamese model architecture for sentence-pair tasks. The two BiLSTM networks have shared weights.

These networks comprise an input embedding layer, 1 or 2 BiLSTM layers, and a 2-layer fully connected layer to serve as the classifier. Regarding sentence-pair tasks, we use a siamese architecture, where we share the weights between the two BiLSTM networks, one for each sentence. We, then, perform a concatenation-compare operation on the output hidden layers and feed the result in the classification layer, as shown in Fig. 2. This operation is presented in Eq. 1, where h_1 and h_2 are the outputs of the hidden layers of the two networks and the ∘ operator denotes element-wise multiplication. Finally, we add a dropout layer between the two layers of the classifier to avoid overfitting.

$$f(h_1, h_2) = [h_1; h_2; h_1 \circ h_2; |h_1 - h_2|] \tag{1}$$

Distillation is achieved by training the student model to mimic the behavior of the teacher model. Regardless of the input, the student is trained to produce similar probability distributions with the teacher. To this end, we train our models on the logits produced from the fine-tuned Greek-BERT for each given input. We examined two objective functions, specifically the cross-entropy and the mean square error between the probability distributions of the teacher model and of the student model, $T(x)$ and $S(x)$, respectively, as presented in Eqs. 2 and 3.

$$L_{CE} = -\sum T(x) \log S(x) \tag{2}$$

$$L_{MSE} = \frac{1}{N} \sum (T(x) - S(x))^2 \tag{3}$$

Finally, regarding the input data, we preprocess the sentences for the BiL-STM models in a particular manner. Specifically, we normalize each sentence, perform lower-casing and remove accent. We tokenize the sentences by employing spaCy [8] and we also add two special tokens, *pad* for padding the end of the sentence and *unk* for unknown words. We use GloVe embeddings to represent each token. The *unk* token is represented by the mean of the 100 rarest words of our model.

Data Augmentation. During training, it is possible that the size of the training set is not adequate to efficiently transfer knowledge from Greek-BERT to the student model. Thus, we perform a data augmentation step to generate a larger training set, in order to improve our distillation performance. Following the work in [9], we augment each sentence from the dataset by employing the developed GloVe embeddings. This process is presented in Algorithm 1. We iteratively select tokens and calculate their k nearest neighbors, which are the most semantically similar words. Then, we can replace the original words considering a probability p, creating N new sentences. We do not replace stop words, i.e., the most frequent words of a language such as *and* or *the*, in order to preserve the structure of the sentence. Since the word replacement process may alter the meaning of a sentence, hence its class, we leverage a fine-tuned Greek-BERT to label each new sentence to the most appropriate class.

4   Experiments

In the following section, an evaluation of the created embeddings and models is outlined.

Algorithm 1: Data augmentation algorithm for a single sentence.

Input   : x: Sequence of tokens, p: Replacement probability
N: Number of iterations, k: Number of candidate words
W: Word vectors
Output: D: Augmented dataset
$D \leftarrow \{x\}$;
for $n \leftarrow 1$ **to** N **do**
  $x_n \leftarrow x$;
  for $i \leftarrow 1$ **to** $\mathrm{len}(x)$ **do**
    if $x[i]$ *is not a stop-word* **then**
      $C \leftarrow \mathrm{kNN}(W, x[i], k)$;
      $p_i \sim \mathrm{Uniform}(0, 1)$;
      if $p_i \leq p$ **then**
        | $x_n[i] \leftarrow$ Sample random word from C;
  end
  $D \leftarrow D \cup \{x_n\}$
end

4.1   GloVe Evaluation

We developed word embeddings for the 400K most common words of our corpus using a dimension size of 300 and a co-occurrence window of size 15. We trained the model for 100 epochs with an initial learning rate of 0.05. To evaluate our embeddings, we employed the word analogy and word similarity datasets presented in [22]. Regarding the former, the dataset contains a total of 39,174 questions of semantic or syntactic analogies. One such example is the following: "a is to a^* as b is to b^*", where b^* is hidden and word embedding models try to predict it. After discarding examples that contained words unknown to our model, we used 35,697 of them (91% of the total dataset) and report our results in Table 1. Following other studies [14], we report the 3CosAdd and 3CosMul metrics, explained in Eqs. 4 and 5. As for the word similarity task, we measured the cosine similarity between 348 word pairs translated from the WordSim353 [1] set to Greek and report the Pearson correlation coefficient, the corresponding p-value, and the percentage of unknown words of each model in Table 2.

$$3CosAdd = \underset{b^* \epsilon V \backslash \{a, a^*, b\}}{\arg \max} \cos(b^*, a^* - a + b) \tag{4}$$

$$3CosMul = \underset{b^* \epsilon V \backslash \{a, a^*, b\}}{\arg \max} \frac{\cos(b^*, b) \cos(b^*, a^*)}{\cos(b^*, a) + \epsilon} \tag{5}$$

We compare our GloVe embeddings with word2vec and FastText embeddings as reported in [22]. We observe a comparable model performance with the other systems, confirming the quality of the developed embeddings, even with less than half the vocabulary size (e.g., word2vec has a 1M word vocabulary and it has been trained on 50 GB of text). In addition, we notice that the GloVe embeddings outperform FastText in the task of word similarity, which further strengthens our confidence in the soundness of the developed embeddings.

Table 1. Word analogy results.

Embeddings	Vocab	3CosAdd	3CosMul
GloVe	400K	52.37	53.57
word2vec	1M	52.66	55.10
FastText	2M	68.97	70.12

Table 2. Word similarity results.

Embeddings	Pearson	p-value	Unknown
GloVe	0.5822	1.3e−32	1.1%
word2vec	0.5879	4.4e−33	2.3%
FastText	0.5311	1.7e−25	4.9%

4.2 Tasks and Datasets

We assess our models on two major NLP tasks, i.e., Natural Language Inference and Topic Classification. Particularly, in the NLI task, given a *premise* sentence, a model has to decide whether a *hypothesis* sentence is true (entailment), undetermined (neutral) or false (contradiction). In our study, we use the Greek part of the XNLI dataset [4], which contains 340K sentence pairs for training, 2.5K for development, and 5K for testing. Regarding the Topic Classification task, we used the "Makedonia" newspaper corpus,[2] which contains 8,005 articles from a local Greek newspaper on various topics, such as sports, economy, etc. In order to eliminate imbalances, we only used articles from the seven topics with the most examples and split it into 70% training, 15% test, and 15% validation sets in a balanced manner. The number of total sentences of each topic is depicted in Table 3.

Table 3. Number of examples in each topic of the Makedonia dataset.

Sports	Reportage	Economy	Politics	World news	TV	Arts-culture
3,358	1,342	600	490	447	413	338

4.3 Distillation Evaluation

To fine-tune Greek-BERT, we trained the model for 3 epochs with the AdamW optimizer [17], a batch size of 32, a maximum sentence length of 128 and a dropout rate of 10%. We selected the best learning rate among $\{5e-05, 4e-05, 3e-05, 2e-05\}$ on the development set. Since the "Makedonia" dataset is rather small, we repeated the training process 10 times using different random seeds. We kept the model that performed best on the development set considering the macro F1-score and evaluated it on the test set. We report the results on the test sets in Table 4.

Regarding the BiLSTM networks, we first trained two models with 1 and 2 hidden layers directly on the training set. We selected 512 units for the hidden layers of the BiLSTMs and 256 for the hidden layer of the classifier. We employed the developed GloVe embeddings to represent the input sentences, which have 300 dimensions and 400K vocabulary size. We chose a batch size of 256, a maximum sentence length of 128, a dropout rate of 10% and the best learning rate

[2] https://inventory.clarin.gr/corpus/909.

among $\{5e-03, 1e-03, 5e-04, 3e-04, 2e-04\}$, using the Adam optimizer [10]. We used early stopping with a patience of 3 epochs. The BiLSTM models were also trained 10 times using different random seeds and the best-performing model was evaluated on the test set as reported in Table 4.

Next, we distilled the fine-tuned Greek-BERT models into the two BiLSTM models using the same hyperparameters as the above BiLSTM. We selected the best learning rate among $\{1e-03, 5e-04, 3e-04\}$. Finally, we augmented the "Makedonia" dataset using replacement probability $p = 0.4$, sampling from the $k = 15$ nearest words for $N = 30$ iterations resulting in 152,706 sentences. We did not augment the XNLI set as its training set is already large enough and we empirically noticed that data augmentation did not influence the performance of the model. The performance improvements are shown in Table 4, where the models are compared based on their macro F1-score.

The tests reported in Table 4 reveal that the approach we followed can improve a basic 1-layer BiLSTM model by 5.6% on TC and by 0.7% on NLI. Such a model is 29.4× times faster than Greek-BERT, while it retains 96% and 86.9% of the teacher macro F1 performance on those tasks. Regarding the 2-layer networks, knowledge distillation improves a basic BiLSTM by 4.6% on TC and by 0.8% on NLI, while the developed model is 10.7× times faster than Greek-BERT and holds 96.2% of the performance on TC and 88.4% on NLI. Furthermore, we also notice that this approach offers only a slight improvement for models trained on the XNLI corpus. This task requires a deeper understanding of the text, which cannot be modeled effectively by the BiLSTM networks resulting in a more significant performance drop compared with TC. Finally, the effectiveness of data augmentation is depicted. The proposed algorithm improves the 1-layer BiLSTM network by 2.7% and the 2-layer network by 1.7%. However, we empirically found that this process can not be utilized in more complex tasks, such as NLI.

Table 4. Macro F1-scores for the distilled models on test data.

	XNLI	Makedonia
1-layer BiLSTM	67.8	78.7
+ Knowledge Distillation	68.5	81.6
+ Data Augmentation	–	84.3
2-layer BiLSTM	68.9	79.9
+ Knowledge Distillation	69.7	82.8
+ Data Augmentation	–	84.5
Greek-BERT	78.8	87.8

We finally compared the inference time amongst Greek-BERT and the developed BiLSTMs. We estimated the number of examples each model can process on average per second on an NVIDIA RTX 2060 6 GB, without considering the data transfer or CPU time and we report the acceleration obtained when using smaller RNN models in Table 5.

Table 5. Model inference speed. We report the average GPU inference time per sample and the number of trainable parameters for each model.

	Parameters (M)	Speed (ms)	Acceleration
Greek-BERT	110	4.76	1×
1-layer BiLSTM	3.6	0.16	29.4×
2-layer BiLSTM	9.9	0.44	10.7×

5   Conclusion and Future Work

In this paper, we presented a systematic approach to creating lightweight models suitable for low-resource and edge systems, using knowledge distillation. We followed this methodology focusing on the Greek language and distilled Greek-BERT into BiLSTM networks of different architectures. Our results are promising in two popular NLP tasks, indicating the redundancy of parameters in large Transformer networks and, in our case, Greek-BERT. This comes in agreement with other studies associated with the English language. In addition, during this process, we introduced the Greek version of GloVe embeddings achieving interesting results. The inference speed was significantly improved using the lightweight models, while the loss of language understanding performance was minimal.

We focused our study on distilling knowledge directly from a task-specific larger model and, given the promising results, various future directions seem interesting. Another approach that could be explored is to distill a pre-trained Greek Transformer model to an RNN in a two-stage manner, i.e., pretraining and fine-tuning. Another path would be to assess Transformer-based models, such as DistilBERT or TinyBERT, for the Greek language. Finally, based on the results related to speed and computational performance, we plan to embed our developed lightweight models in various low-resource devices, such as Raspberry Pis or Jetson Nanos, this way boosting the responsiveness of conversational assistants hosted entirely on those devices, as discussed in [18].

Acknowledgements. This research has been co-financed by the European Regional Development Fund of the European Union and Greek national funds through the Operational Program Competitiveness, Entrepreneurship and Innovation, under the call RESEARCH - CREATE - INNOVATE (project code: T1EDK-02347).

References

1. Placing search in context: the concept revisited. ACM Trans. Inf. Syst. **20**(1), 116–131 (2002). https://doi.org/10.1145/503104.503110
2. Bojanowski, P., Grave, E., Joulin, A., Mikolov, T.: Enriching word vectors with subword information. Trans. ACL **5**, 135–146 (2017)
3. Conneau, A., et al.: Unsupervised cross-lingual representation learning at scale. In: Proceedings of the 58th Annual Meeting of the ACL, pp. 8440–8451. ACL, July 2020. https://doi.org/10.18653/v1/2020.acl-main.747

4. Conneau, A., et al.: XNLI: evaluating cross-lingual sentence representations. In: Proceedings of the 2018 Conference on Empirical Methods in Natural Language Processing, Brussels, Belgium, October–November 2018, pp. 2475–2485. ACL (2018). https://doi.org/10.18653/v1/D18-1269

5. Devlin, J., Chang, M.W., Lee, K., Toutanova, K.: BERT: pre-training of deep bidirectional transformers for language understanding. arXiv:1810.04805 (2019)

6. He, P., Liu, X., Gao, J., Chen, W.: DeBERTa: decoding-enhanced BERT with disentangled attention (2021)

7. Hinton, G., Vinyals, O., Dean, J.: Distilling the knowledge in a neural network. In: NIPS Deep Learning and Representation Learning Workshop (2015). http://arxiv.org/abs/1503.02531

8. Honnibal, M., Montani, I.: spaCy 2: natural language understanding with Bloom embeddings, convolutional neural networks and incremental parsing (2017)

9. Jiao, X., et al.: TinyBERT: distilling BERT for natural language understanding. In: Findings of the ACL: EMNLP 2020, pp. 4163–4174. ACL, November 2020. https://doi.org/10.18653/v1/2020.findings-emnlp.372

10. Kingma, D., Ba, J.: Adam: a method for stochastic optimization. In: International Conference on Learning Representations (2014)

11. Koehn, P.: Europarl: a parallel corpus for statistical machine translation (2005)

12. Koutsikakis, J., Chalkidis, I., Malakasiotis, P., Androutsopoulos, I.: GREEK-BERT: the Greeks visiting sesame street. In: 11th Hellenic Conference on Artificial Intelligence, SETN 2020, pp. 110–117. Association for Computing Machinery, New York (2020). https://doi.org/10.1145/3411408.3411440

13. Kovaleva, O., Romanov, A., Rogers, A., Rumshisky, A.: Revealing the dark secrets of BERT. In: Proceedings of the 2019 Conference on Empirical Methods in Natural Language Processing and the 9th International Joint Conference on Natural Language Processing (EMNLP-IJCNLP), Hong Kong, China, pp. 4365–4374. ACL, November 2019. https://doi.org/10.18653/v1/D19-1445

14. Levy, O., Goldberg, Y., Dagan, I.: Improving distributional similarity with lessons learned from word embeddings. Trans. ACL **3**, 211–225 (2015). https://doi.org/10.1162/tacl_a_00134

15. Lioudakis, M., Outsios, S., Vazirgiannis, M.: An ensemble method for producing word representations focusing on the Greek language. arXiv preprint arXiv:1904.04032 (2020)

16. Liu, Y., et al.: RoBERTa: a robustly optimized BERT pretraining approach (2019)

17. Loshchilov, I., Hutter, F.: Decoupled weight decay regularization. In: International Conference on Learning Representations (2019). https://openreview.net/forum?id=Bkg6RiCqY7

18. Malamas, N., Symeonidis, A.: Embedding rasa in edge devices: capabilities and limitations. Procedia Comput. Sci. **192**, 109–118 (2021). https://doi.org/10.1016/j.procs.2021.08.012

19. McCarley, J.S., Chakravarti, R., Sil, A.: Structured pruning of a BERT-based question answering model. arXiv: Computation and Language (2019)

20. Mikolov, T., Chen, K., Corrado, G., Dean, J.: Efficient estimation of word representations in vector space. In: Proceedings of Workshop at ICLR 2013 (2013)

21. Ortiz Suárez, P.J., Sagot, B., Romary, L.: Asynchronous pipelines for processing huge corpora on medium to low resource infrastructures. In: Proceedings of the Workshop on Challenges in the Management of Large Corpora (CMLC-7) 2019, Cardiff, Leibniz-Institut für Deutsche Sprache, Mannheim, 22nd July 2019, pp. 9–16 (2019). https://doi.org/10.14618/ids-pub-9021

22. Outsios, S., Karatsalos, C., Skianis, K., Vazirgiannis, M.: Evaluation of Greek word embeddings. arXiv preprint arXiv:1904.04032 (2019)
23. Papantoniou, K., Tzitzikas, Y.: NLP for the Greek language: a brief survey. In: 11th Hellenic Conference on Artificial Intelligence, SETN 2020, pp. 101–109. Association for Computing Machinery, New York (2020). https://doi.org/10.1145/3411408.3411410
24. Pennington, J., Socher, R., Manning, C.: GloVe: global vectors for word representation. In: Proceedings of the 2014 Conference on Empirical Methods in Natural Language Processing (EMNLP), Doha, Qatar, pp. 1532–1543. ACL, October 2014. https://doi.org/10.3115/v1/D14-1162
25. Peters, M.E., et al.: Deep contextualized word representations. In: Proceedings of the 2018 Conference of the North American Chapter of the ACL: Human Language Technologies, New Orleans, Louisiana, vol. 1, pp. 2227–2237. ACL, June 2018. https://doi.org/10.18653/v1/N18-1202
26. Radford, A., Narasimhan, K.: Improving language understanding by generative pre-training (2018)
27. Rogers, A., Kovaleva, O., Rumshisky, A.: A primer in BERTology: what we know about how BERT works. Trans. ACL 8, 842–866 (2020). https://doi.org/10.1162/tacl_a_00349
28. Sanh, V., Debut, L., Chaumond, J., Wolf, T.: DistilBERT, a distilled version of BERT: smaller, faster, cheaper and lighter. arXiv:1910.01108 (2019)
29. Shen, S., et al.: Q-BERT: Hessian based ultra low precision quantization of BERT (2019)
30. Sun, S., Cheng, Y., Gan, Z., Liu, J.: Patient knowledge distillation for BERT model compression. In: Proceedings of the 2019 EMNLP-IJCNLP, Hong Kong, China, pp. 4323–4332. ACL, November 2019. https://doi.org/10.18653/v1/D19-1441
31. Tang, R., Lu, Y., Liu, L., Mou, L., Vechtomova, O., Lin, J.J.: Distilling task-specific knowledge from BERT into simple neural networks. arXiv:1903.12136 (2019)
32. Turc, I., Chang, M., Lee, K., Toutanova, K.: Well-read students learn better: the impact of student initialization on knowledge distillation. CoRR arXiv:1908.08962 (2019)
33. Vaswani, A., et al.: Attention is all you need. In: Advances in Neural Information Processing Systems, vol. 30. Curran Associates, Inc. (2017). https://proceedings.neurips.cc/paper/2017/file/3f5ee243547dee91fbd053c1c4a845aa-Paper.pdf
34. Wu, B., et al.: Towards non-task-specific distillation of BERT via sentence representation approximation. In: Proceedings of the 1st Conference of the Asia-Pacific Chapter of the ACL and the 10th International Joint Conference on Natural Language Processing, Suzhou, China, pp. 70–79. ACL, December 2020. https://aclanthology.org/2020.aacl-main.9

RUTA:MED – Dual Workflow Medical Speech Transcription Pipeline and Editor

Arturs Znotins[1]([✉]), Roberts Dargis[1], Normunds Gruzitis[1], Guntis Barzdins[1], and Didzis Gosko[2]

[1] Institute of Mathematics and Computer Science (IMCS), University of Latvia, Raina bulvaris 29, Riga 1459, Latvia
{arturs.znotins,roberts.dargis,normunds.gruzitis}@lumii.lv
[2] Riga East University Hospital (REUH), Hipokrata iela 2, Riga 1079, Latvia

Abstract. In the medical domain various approaches are used to produce examination reports and other medical records. Depending on the language-specific technology support, the type of examination, the size of the hospital or clinic, and other aspects, the reporting workflow can range from completely manual to (semi-)automated. A manual workflow may completely depend on the doctor itself or may include a transcriptionist centre in the loop. In an automated workflow, the transcriptionist centre is typically replaced by an automatic speech recognition (ASR) system. While the latter approach is well suited for high resource languages where word error rate (WER) is as low as 5–10%, for less resourced languages a dual approach combining automated transcription with the support from a transcriptionist centre may be more suited. In this paper, we present a platform that supports both workflows simultaneously. The RUTA:MED platform currently includes an ASR pipeline for the less resourced Latvian language, and it is being deployed and tested at several hospitals and clinics in Latvia. The platform can be adopted for any other language, and it emphasizes that WER is only one of the performance indicators in case of medical transcription.

Keywords: Speech recognition · Medical transcription · Post-editing

1 Introduction

We present a software platform for automated transcription of medical dictations, developed by a leading Latvian language technology research group at IMCS in cooperation with the largest hospital in Latvia (REUH). Our initial focus was on digital imaging reports (computed tomography, magnetic resonance, etc.), but the scope has been extended to include other areas (histopathology, gastroenterology, etc.).

In Latvia, medical reports so far were produced completely manually. Several hospitals and clinics employ transcriptionist centres to assist the production of medical reports. Due to a constant growth of diagnostic and laboratory examinations, clinicians and patients often have to wait for the reports up to several

P. Rosso et al. (Eds.): NLDB 2022, LNCS 13286, pp. 209–214, 2022.
https://doi.org/10.1007/978-3-031-08473-7_19

days if they are not considered urgent. The manual transcription of a dictation takes about a day of the total waiting time, and the doctor must verify the final report. Services of transcriptionist centres are expensive, and smaller hospitals and clinics often cannot afford it. Thus, a more efficient approach and technology infrastructure is clearly needed to significantly reduce the dependency on transcriptionist centres. However, many doctors would prefer to keep transcriptionist centres (in a reduced capacity) as an option.

RUTA:MED[1] is a platform for automated medical transcription, which addresses these issues. It is not only a speech transcription pipeline consisting of an ASR system and automatic post-processing modules – it also provides an integrated editor (text-audio alignment) and supports both workflows: it greatly facilitates post-editing by the doctor him/her self, but it also allows to submit the dictation and its draft transcript to a transcriptionist centre any time.

RUTA:MED builds on our previous work on a general-domain speech transcription system for Latvian [5], which we have adapted and extended for the medical domain [1,2]. The platform is showcased with the less resourced Latvian language and the situation in Latvia regarding the usage of automatic speech recognition (ASR) and text processing technologies in the medical domain, however, the Latvian case is not unique. RUTA:MED can be adopted for other languages by replacing the language-specific ASR and text post-processing components. We argue that word error rate (WER) – the standard metric used to evaluate ASR systems – is only one of the performance indicators in case of medical transcription. The integrated editor and the dual workflow which involves a transcriptionist centre is relevant not only for less resourced languages but also in case of high resource languages (like English, French and German) to reduce the workload of doctors, especially in case of complex examinations.

The Latvian-specific resources and components of RUTA:MED are described in more detail by Dargis et al. [1] and Gruzitis et al. [2]. In this system demo paper, we focus on the whole platform and the dual workflow it supports. While the web-based UI and API of RUTA:MED, as well as its back-end components, are continuously being enhanced and extended, the platform is production-ready and is being used in a trial mode by several healthcare institutions in Latvia.

2   Related Work

Medical ASR products by Nuance, like PowerScribe One[2] for radiologists, are among the most widely used in case of high resource languages. Apart from ASR and text post-processing, they provide many other features and integration options. RUTA:MED has a comparatively narrow focus and is aimed at less resourced languages for which transcriptionist centres are still a relevant option.

Another well-known product – Trint[3] – represents a more general kind of speech-to-text transcription platforms. Like Trint, RUTA:MED editor provides

---

[1] https://med.ailab.lv/demo.

[2] https://nuance.com/healthcare/diagnostics-solutions/.

[3] https://trint.com.

interactive text and speech alignment which facilitates the post-editing process, while RUTA:MED supports the specialised dual workflow in addition to the specialised ASR and post-processing components.

As for the ASR and post-processing part, we were inspired by the development of the Estonian ASR for Radiology [3], since Estonian is a similar-size language having comparable amount of language resources available, but again – RUTA:MED adds the dual workflow and interactive editing support.

3   RUTA:MED Platform

RUTA:MED is a web application that integrates an ASR and post-processing pipeline with the help of a task queue for scalability (see Fig. 1). This allows for simple setup and integration with other web-based medical information systems.

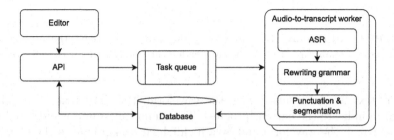

Fig. 1. Overall architecture of the RUTA:MED platform

3.1   Speech Recognition and Post-processing Pipeline

Before a transcription is available for post-editing, the submitted dictation goes through multiple processing stages. First, the audio is processed with an ASR system adapted to the medical domain. The Latvian language model is trained on 1.5 GB of plain-text, extracted from the REUH archive of medical reports. The pronunciation lexicon is automatically extracted from the same text corpus, manually extended with pronunciation of abbreviations, Latin terms, drug names, etc. Second, the automatic transcriptions are processed with a rewriting grammar to acquire concise reports, thus, minimise the post-editing work, and to interpret explicit and implicit voice commands. The grammar is implemented as a cascade of finite-state transducers using the OpenFST-based Thrax framework [4]. The final transcription post-processing step is punctuation restoration and text segmentation with a neural network model trained on the text corpus.

3.2   Integrated Editor

The key user-facing RUTA:MED element is the integrated audio-synchronized transcript editor (see Fig. 2). The core of this web-based open-source editor was developed in the H2020 project SELMA for the video subtitling purposes and is adapted in RUTA:MED for the post-editing of medical transcripts.

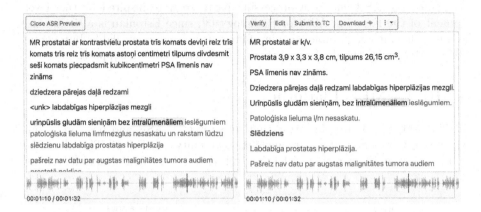

Fig. 2. RUTA:MED editor views: preview of the ASR output (left); the automatically post-processed transcript (right); the time-code synchronized cursor (highlighted)

The text is synchronised with the waveform. Both the text area and the waveform indicate the current progress. The audio timestamp is indicated by a vertical bar in the waveform and by a highlighted background in the text area. The user can click anywhere in the text to navigate in audio or click anywhere in waveform to highlight the corresponding word/segment.

The editor provides basic text formatting functions, such as bold, italic, underline, sub- and superscript, numbered and bullet lists. Structural formatting (predefined fields of the report) is recognized in the post-processing step. The final text can be copied to a medical information system or a Word document.

3.3   Dual Workflow

The RUTA:MED workflow is designed for two user scenarios that can be switched on the fly. In the primary scenario, we expect that in many cases when a report is fluently dictated and hence has resulted in an overall accurate and clean transcription the doctor who was so far used to the services of a transcriptionist centre will be motivated to use the RUTA:MED platform in a self-service manner, i.e., will prefer to do quick post-editing of the automatic transcription rather than wait for a transcriptionist centre to produce the report.

In the alternative scenario, we anticipate that a transcriptionist centre would still be preferred in the loop by many radiologists in case of more complicated examinations and therefore less fluent dictations. Nevertheless, transcriptionist centres will become more productive, since part of their workload will be overtaken by the self-service user scenario, as well as draft transcripts (generated by RUTA:MED) will be available to the operators for post-editing instead of transcribing whole reports manually from scratch.

Figure 3 depicts the dual RUTA:MED workflow which involves an optional transition of a report via an associated transcriptionist centre.

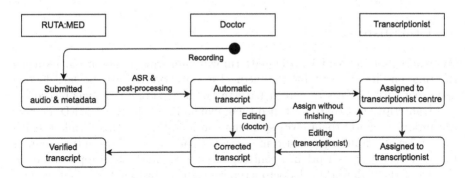

Fig. 3. State diagram of the RUTA:MED dual workflow

Although the RUTA:MED platform currently is not directly integrated with third-party medical information systems, the universal copy-paste integration which has already been exploited in the legacy workflows in Latvia and elsewhere can be used for the time being. Development of a widget and a browser plugin which could be used in combination with any other information system for convenient transfer of the final transcripts is in progress.

4   Initial Evaluation

Word error rate (WER) is the most commonly used metric for performance evaluation of ASR systems. Although WER is an excellent metric to compare the performance of different ASR systems, user experience is the most important criteria that shows how successful the platform actually is.

The user experience (UX) evaluation has to include two aspects – user interviews and feedback (qualitative analysis), and statistical key performance indicators (KPI). The RUTA:MED platform tracks three such KPIs:

- How many of the reports doctors decide to post-edit themselves instead of assigning them to a transcriptionist centre.
- How much time it takes to post-edit a report relatively to the duration of a dictation and the number of characters in the transcription.
- How many words and characters are changed in the final transcript compared to the automatic output of the ASR and post-processing pipeline.

The data collected is also an invaluable resource for further development and improvement. The post-edited texts add to the text corpus used for language modeling. It also helps to extend the lexicon by both reducing the out-of-vocabulary (OOV) rate and adding alternative pronunciations. The aggregated user edits also provide excellent insight in what needs to be improved in the rewriting grammar as well (e.g. by adding new or alternative voice commands or by extending the set of text shortening rules).

The evaluation phase of the project has just begun and the data is being collected, but the initial user feedback is very positive.

5   Conclusion

We expect that the RUTA:MED platform will improve patient care by reducing the time one has to wait for the medical examination report. So far, doctors operating with the less resourced Latvian language submitted their recordings to a transcriptionist centre or typed them manually. With RUTA:MED, doctors can produce reports themselves spending considerably less time, while keeping the service of a transcriptionist centre as a fall-back option. This in turn reduces the workload of transcriptionist centres, allowing to finish other reports sooner.

Due to the high workload, doctors typically are against anything that requires additional efforts. One of the biggest advantage of RUTA:MED is that its workflow is very simple and close to the current practice. The recording and submission workflow is very similar among hospitals and clinics. The RUTA:MED workflow allows doctors to simply delegate a transcription to an operator if postediting would be too time consuming at the moment. This is especially crucial for ASR systems with higher error rates.

Acknowledgements. This work was funded by ERDF (grant No. 1.1.1.1/18/A/153). Core development of the editor was done in the H2020 project SELMA (grant No. 957017).

References

1. Dargis, R., Gruzitis, N., Auzina, I., Stepanovs, K.: Creation of language resources for the development of a medical speech recognition system for Latvian. In: Human Language Technologies - The Baltic Perspective, Frontiers in Artificial Intelligence and Applications, vol. 328, pp. 135–141. IOS Press (2020)
2. Gruzitis, N., Dargis, R., Lasmanis, V.J., Garkaje, G., Gosko, D.: Adapting automatic speech recognition to the radiology domain for a less-resourced language: the case of Latvian. In: Nagar, A.K., Jat, D.S., Marín-Raventós, G., Mishra, D.K. (eds.) Intelligent Sustainable Systems. LNNS, vol. 333, pp. 267–276. Springer, Singapore (2022). https://doi.org/10.1007/978-981-16-6309-3_27
3. Paats, A., Alumäe, T., Meister, E., Fridolin, I.: Retrospective analysis of clinical performance of an Estonian speech recognition system for radiology: effects of different acoustic and language models. J. Digit. Imaging **31**(5), 615–621 (2018). https://doi.org/10.1007/s10278-018-0085-8
4. Tai, T., Skut, W., Sproat, R.: Thrax: an open source grammar compiler built on OpenFst. In: IEEE ASRU Workshop (2011)
5. Znotins, A., Polis, K., Dargis, R.: Media monitoring system for Latvian radio and TV broadcasts. In: Proceedings of the 16th Annual Conference of the International Speech Communication Association (INTERSPEECH), pp. 732–733 (2015)

A BERT-Based Model for Question Answering on Construction Incident Reports

Hebatallah A. Mohamed Hassan$^{(\boxtimes)}$ (ID), Elisa Marengo (ID), and Werner Nutt (ID)

Faculty of Computer Science, Free University of Bozen-Bolzano, Bolzano, Italy
{hebatallah.mohamed,elisa.marengo,werner.nutt}@unibz.it

Abstract. Construction sites are among the most hazardous workplaces. To reduce accidents, it is required to identify risky situations beforehand, and to describe which countermeasures to put in place. In this paper, we investigate possible techniques to support the identification of risky activities and potential hazards associated with those activities. More precisely, we propose a method for classifying injury narratives based on different attributes, such as *work activity*, *injury type*, and *injury severity*. We formulate our problem as a Question Answering (QA) task by fine-tuning BERT sentence-pair classification model, and we achieve state-of-the-art results on a dataset obtained from the Occupational Safety and Health Administration (OSHA). In addition, we propose a method for identifying potential hazardous items using a model-agnostic technique.

Keywords: Hazard identification · Question answering · BERT · Model-agnostic interpretability

1 Introduction

According to the latest fatal work injury rates reported by the International Labour Organization (ILO), construction sites are the most hazardous workplaces [14]. A standard method for identifying hazards in the production industries is the Job Hazard Analysis (JHA). It consists of identifying the work activity, identifying potential hazards related to those work activities, and proposing procedures to eliminate, reduce or control each of the hazards.

In this paper, we investigate possible techniques to support the identification of the risky activities and the identification of hazards related to those work activities. The idea is to leverage on existing data on past dangerous situations or on injury reports to extract such information. Injury reports produced by workers are typically unstructured or semi-structured free-text data, which traditionally relies on human oversight to extract actionable information. Most of the existing works formalize the task of automatic narrative classification as a standard text classification task which consists of two steps: *text feature extraction* and *classification*, with an underlying assumption that the entire text has

P. Rosso et al. (Eds.): NLDB 2022, LNCS 13286, pp. 215–223, 2022.
https://doi.org/10.1007/978-3-031-08473-7_20

an overall topic. However, injury reports in construction typically contain different topics or aspects, such as: *work activity, incident type, injury type,* and *injury severity.*

Inspired by the recent trend of formalizing different Natural Language Processing (NLP) problems as a Question Answering (QA) task [5,12], we transform the injury narrative classification into a sentence-pair classification task, where the input to the classification model consists of question and narrative pairs. The questions are formulated based on different aspects, such as *work activity, incident type, injury type,* or *injury severity.* The idea is that the incorporation of aspects forces the classification model to attend to the part of the narrative related to that aspect, and therefore enhances the classification performance. Moreover, we identify potential hazards by extracting the predictive words from the narratives that are most informative for *incident type* classification (e.g. narratives classified to 'fall' if 'scaffold' hazard presents), using the Local Interpretable Model-agnostic Explanations (LIME) technique.

2   Related Work

Several approaches have been proposed for extracting precursors from injury reports based on an entirely hand-written lexicon and set of rules [1,15,16]. Hand crafting of rules has the advantage of being accurate. However, the rule creation process is resource intensive, both in terms of time and human input.

A wide variety of classical machine learning techniques have been employed for classifying injury narratives. For example, [3] proposed an unsupervised approach using TF-IDF and K-Means to cluster injury narratives. [6] evaluated different supervised techniques, and found that SVM produces the best performance. The authors further presented an ensemble approach for construction injury narrative classification [18]. Similarly, [20] proposed an ensemble model to classify injury narratives, and a rule based chunker approach is explored to identify the common objects which cause the accidents. A significant drawback, however, of the TF-IDF is that it ignores the semantics of words.

Recently, there are few works that exploited deep learning techniques. For example, [2] utilised Convolutional Neural Networks (CNN) and Hierarchical Attention Networks (HAN) to classify injury narratives, where for each model, a method is proposed to identify (after training) the textual patterns that are the most predictive of each safety outcome. In [7,21], the word embedding of Bidirectional Encoder Representations from Transformers (BERT) base model is used to model accident narratives. However, to the best of our knowledge, fine-tuning BERT for QA has not been investigated for this task.

3   Dataset

The dataset[1] used in this study is collected from the Occupational Safety and Health Organization (OSHA) website.[2] It has been released by [17] to be used

---

[1] https://github.com/Tixierae/WECD/blob/master/classification_data_set.csv.

[2] https://www.osha.gov/pls/imis/accidentsearch.html.

as a benchmark for construction injury report classification. The dataset contains 5,845 injury cases, where each case is annotated with different information, including: (1) *identification number*, (2) *narrative*, (3) *cause/work activity* (the activity the worker was involved in before the accident), (4) *fatCause/incident type* (what is the accident, e.g., 'Fall'), (5) *injury type* (the injury nature, e.g. 'Fracture'), (6) *injury severity* (the worker has died, hospitalized, or non-hospitalized).

As shown in Table 1, a narrative is a short text that provides a complete description of the accident. It includes events that led to the accident and causal factors, such as *work activity* and *incident type*. It also states the outcome from the accident, such as *injury type* and *injury severity*. As a preprocessing step, we remove dates and special characters from the narratives using the NLTK[3] Python library. The average length of a narrative is 104 words after the preprocessing step.

Table 1. Sample accident report from OSHA dataset.

Narrative	'On April 9, 2013, Employee #1 was **installing vinyl sidings** on a single story residence. The employee was standing an A-frame ladder that was set on a plank of a scaffold. The scaffold moved causing to lose his balance. The employee **fell** from the ladder approximately 12-ft to the ground. Employee #1 was transported to an area hospital, where he was treated for an abdominal **fracture**. The employee remained **hospitalized**.'
Activity	'Exterior carpentry'
Incident type	'Fall'
Injury type	'Fracture'
Injury severity	'Hospitalized'

4   BERT for Question Answering

4.1   Methodology

Given an input narrative text $x = x_1, \ldots, x_L$, where L denotes the length of the text x. We need to classify x with a label $y \in Y$. Each label y is associated with a natural language description $q_y = q_{y1}, \ldots, q_{yM}$, where M denotes the length of the label description q_y.

We consider our task as a sentence-pair classification problem by generating a set of (NARRATIVE, ASPECT + LABEL DESCRIPTION) pairs, with new binary labels $\in \{yes, no\}$, indicating whether a label should be assigned to the narrative or not with respect to a given aspect. ASPECT + LABEL DESCRIPTION, we name it $\hat{q}_y$, represents the aspect concatenated with the ground truth label to form a question, such as "Is the *work activity* of the narrative *excavating*?" or "Is the *severity* of the narrative *hospitalized*?".

---

[3] http://www.nltk.org.

We fine-tune BERT sentence-pair model [4]. Thus, we concatenate the label description $\hat{q}_y$ with the narrative text x to generate $\{[CLS]; \hat{q}_y; [SEP]; x\}$, where [CLS] and [SEP] are special tokens. The concatenated sequence is fed to multi-layer transformers in BERT, from which we obtain the final hidden vector $\mathbb{C} \in \mathbb{R}^H$ corresponding to the first input token ([CLS]) as the aggregate representation. Then, we add a classification layer with weight matrix $W \in \mathbb{R}^{K \times H}$, where K is the number of labels (two in our case). We compute a standard classification loss by a softmax function $f = \text{softmax}\left(CW^{\mathrm{T}}\right)$. We then consider the label description that generates the highest probability for 'yes' when concatenated with the narrative, as the predicted label of that narrative.

4.2 Baselines

We use the following models as baselines:

- **FastText**: A word embedding model[4] that uses a character level n-gram, which makes it capable of generating embeddings for out-of-vocabulary words [8]. Once the embeddings are obtained, a max-pooling operation is applied, followed by a softmax function to derive label predictions.
- **Convolutional Neural Networks (CNN)**: A classic baseline for text classification [9]. It applies CNN based on FastText pre-trained word embedding.
- **Hierarchical Attention Networks (HAN)**: This method deals with the problem of classifying long documents by modeling attention at each level of the document structure, i.e. words and sentences [19]. This allows the model to first put attention on word encoder outputs, in a sentence, and then on the sentence encoder outputs to classify a document.
- **BERT-base**: We use the BERT-base model [4] and we follow the standard classification setup in BERT, in which the embedding is fed to a softmax layer to output the probability of a label being assigned to an instance.

4.3 Experimental Setup

We split the dataset into a training and a testing set of 80% and 20%, respectively. For HAN baseline, similar to [2], we set the maximum length of a sentence to 50 words, and the maximum number of sentences in a document to 14 sentences. While for CNN baseline, the hyperparameters are set as follows: filter size = 5; number of filters = 128, similar to [22]. For BERT-base and BERT-QA models, we use the pytorch-transformers[5] library, and the uncased version of the pre-trained BERT-Base[6] model. We fine-tune the models for 3 epochs to minimize the negative log-likelihood of predicting the correct labels of the narratives in the training set, using stochastic gradient descent with the Adam [10] optimizer, an initial learning rate of 3e−5 [13], and batch size of 6. Finally, we run our experiments on NVIDIA Tesla K80 GPU with 12 GB of RAM.

---

[4] https://github.com/amaiya/ktrain.

[5] https://github.com/huggingface/transformers.

[6] https://storage.googleapis.com/bert_models/2018_10_18/uncased_L-12_H-768_A-12.zip.

4.4   Results

In Table 2, we present the performance of our fine-tuned BERT model (BERT-QA) and the baseline models, in terms of macro-averaged precision, recall and F1-score. We observe substantial better performance of BERT-QA in general over the other models. More precisely, the QA strategy using BERT sentence-pair model outperforms the classical BERT classification model. It achieves a performance gain of +2.0% in terms of F1-score for classifying narratives based on *work activity*, +2.0% for *incident type*, +3.0% for *injury type* and +3.0% for *severity*. This means that the incorporation of aspects and label description gives the model the ability to attend to the relevant text in the narratives.

However, the classification based on *work activity* still suffers from poor performance in general, since there are many labels that represent activities which are practically very close to one another (e.g., excavating and trenching).

Table 2. Precision (Prec), recall (Rec) and F1 of the classification models.

Model		Activity	Incident type	Injury type	Severity
FastText	Prec	0.58	0.63	0.75	0.82
FastText	Rec	0.56	0.63	0.73	0.78
FastText	F1	0.56	0.63	0.74	0.80
CNN	Prec	0.62	0.77	0.76	0.89
CNN	Rec	0.54	0.75	0.73	0.79
CNN	F1	0.55	0.75	0.74	0.82
HAN	Prec	0.64	0.71	0.71	0.84
HAN	Rec	0.49	0.73	0.75	0.89
HAN	F1	0.50	0.71	0.72	0.86
BERT-base	Prec	0.62	0.83	0.79	0.90
BERT-base	Rec	0.61	0.82	0.78	0.86
BERT-base	F1	0.61	0.82	0.79	0.87
BERT-QA	Prec	**0.66**	**0.86**	**0.82**	**0.91**
BERT-QA	Rec	**0.63**	**0.82**	**0.79**	**0.91**
BERT-QA	F1	**0.63**	**0.84**	**0.81**	**0.91**

5   Model-Agnostic Interpretability for Identifying Hazards

In this section, we propose a method to automatically extract words related to potential hazards, based on the explanation of *incident type* classification, using the fine-tuned BERT model. More precisely, we automatically extract the parts of the narratives that influence the correct prediction of *incident type* using LIME [11]. LIME is a technique used to explain predictions of any complex or

Table 3. Examples of the extracted hazards per *incident type*

Fall			
Ladder	Rope	Scaffold	Sludge pond
Rung	Heart attack	Walkway	Elevator

Struck by falling object			
Falling tree	Hammer	Pipe fell	Tunnel fell
Falling wood	Load fell	Rods fell	Assembly broken

Struck by moving object			
Backhoe slid	Roller overturned	Vehicle	Securing pins
Compactor	Truck	Fall protection	Asphalt roller

Collapse of structure			
Bridge	Columns	Rot	Prefabricated wood
Not designed	Roof collapsed	Falling debris	Collapsed covering
Falling deck			

Electrocution			
Backhoe contacted	Power line	Wire contacted	Fuse
Unprotected conductor	Halogen	Transformer	High voltage

Fire/explosion			
Acetylene	Natural gas	Combustible liquid	Torch
Kettle pot	Unauthorized personnel		

Exposure to extreme temperatures			
Cold	Hot	Humid	Overheated
Steam	Sunlight		

Exposure to chemical substance			
Sulfide	Carbon	Methane	Monoxide
Kerosene	Gas	Bacterial	Hydrogen

non-linear classification model by approximating the underlying model by an interpretable linear model, learned on perturbations of the original instance (i.e. removing words), and then uses the weights of the linear model to determine feature importance scores. In other words, LIME ensures both interpretability and local fidelity by minimising how unfaithful is the local approximation of the surrogate model, g, to the complex classifier, f. The explanation, R, produced by LIME is obtained by the following equation:

$$\xi(x) = \operatorname*{argmin}_{g \in G} \mathcal{L}\left(f, g, \pi_x\right) + \Omega(g) \tag{1}$$

where x refers to the instance being explained, G denotes a class of potentially interpretable models, $L(f, g, \pi_x)$ is the fidelity function, measuring the reliability of the approximation provided by the interpretable model in the vicinity defined by π_x, and $\Omega(g)$, denotes the complexity of the interpretable model.

employee #1 was installing vinyl sidings on a single story residence. the employee was standing an a-frame ladder that was set on a plank of a scaffold. the scaffold moved causing employee #1 to lose his balance. the employee fell from the ladder approximately 12-ft to the ground. employee #1 was transported to an area hospital, where he was treated for an abdominal fracture. the employee remained hospitalized.

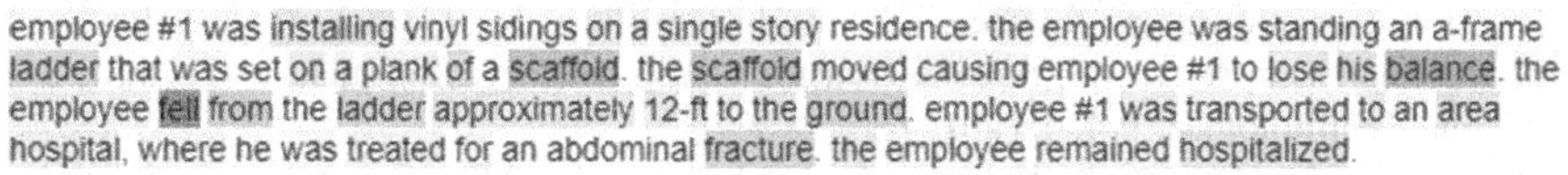

Fig. 1. Explanation of a narrative classified as 'Fall'.

Figure 1 shows an example of LIME visualization for a narrative that is correctly classified as 'Fall', where the most predictive words are 'fell', 'balance', 'scaffold', and 'ladder'. From this we can consider 'scaffold' and 'ladder' as hazardous items. Table 3 shows some examples for the hazards identified for each *incident type*.

Even though the proposed solution does not guarantee to retrieve all possible hazards from the narratives, since it is not simple or straightforward enough to determine the exact source of those accidents, it will help in identifying potential hazards which can then be validated by safety managers. After identifying the potential hazards, we could also produce useful insights about the association between work activities and hazards. For example, most of the injury narratives containing 'scaffold' are related to 'exterior carpentry' *work activity*. We can also get insights about the severity of the injuries when a certain hazard presents. For example, the *injury severity* is 'Hospitalized' and the *injury type* is 'Fracture' for most of the narratives that includes 'scaffold' and related to 'exterior carpentry'.

6   Conclusion

In this paper, we formalize the classification of construction injury narratives as a question answering task. We fine-tune BERT sentence-pair classification model, and we achieve state-of-the-art performance on OSHA dataset. Additionally, we present a method for automatically extracting hazardous items from text based on model-agnostic explanation technique. As a future work, we will expand the questions with synonyms in order to make them more descriptive. Additionally, in the context of a research project COCkPiT, we are developing a tool to assist project managers in scheduling the activities to be performed on-site. We will extend such a tool with a functionality able to highlights the risky activities.

References

1. Baker, H., Hallowell, M.R., Tixier, A.J.P.: AI-based prediction of independent construction safety outcomes from universal attributes. Autom. Constr. **118**, 103146 (2020)

2. Baker, H., Hallowell, M.R., Tixier, A.J.P.: Automatically learning construction injury precursors from text. Autom. Constr. **118**, 103145 (2020)
3. Chokor, A., Naganathan, H., Chong, W.K., El Asmar, M.: Analyzing Arizona OSHA injury reports using unsupervised machine learning. Procedia Eng. **145**, 1588–1593 (2016)
4. Devlin, J., Chang, M.W., Lee, K., Toutanova, K.: BERT: pre-training of deep bidirectional transformers for language understanding. In: Conference of the North American Chapter of the Association for Computational Linguistics: Human Language Technologies, vol. 1 (2019)
5. Gardner, M., Berant, J., Hajishirzi, H., Talmor, A., Min, S.: Question answering is a format; when is it useful? arXiv preprint arXiv:1909.11291 (2019)
6. Goh, Y.M., Ubeynarayana, C.: Construction accident narrative classification: an evaluation of text mining techniques. Accid. Anal. Prev. **108**, 122–130 (2017)
7. Goldberg, D.M.: Characterizing accident narratives with word embeddings: improving accuracy, richness, and generalizability. J. Safety Res. **80**, 441–455 (2022)
8. Joulin, A., Grave, E., Bojanowski, P., Mikolov, T.: Bag of tricks for efficient text classification. CoRR arXiv:1607.01759 (2016)
9. Kim, Y.: Convolutional neural networks for sentence classification. arXiv preprint arXiv:1408.5882 (2014)
10. Kingma, D.P., Ba, J.: Adam: a method for stochastic optimization. arXiv preprint arXiv:1412.6980 (2014)
11. Ribeiro, M.T., Singh, S., Guestrin, C.: "Why should I trust you?" Explaining the predictions of any classifier. In: Proceedings of the 22nd ACM SIGKDD International Conference on Knowledge Discovery and Data Mining, pp. 1135–1144 (2016)
12. Sun, C., Huang, L., Qiu, X.: Utilizing BERT for aspect-based sentiment analysis via constructing auxiliary sentence. arXiv preprint arXiv:1903.09588 (2019)
13. Sun, C., Qiu, X., Xu, Y., Huang, X.: How to fine-tune BERT for text classification? In: Sun, M., Huang, X., Ji, H., Liu, Z., Liu, Y. (eds.) CCL 2019. LNCS (LNAI), vol. 11856, pp. 194–206. Springer, Cham (2019). https://doi.org/10.1007/978-3-030-32381-3_16
14. Takala, J.: Burden of injury due to occupational exposures. In: Handbook of Disability. Work and Health, pp. 1–22. Springer, Cham (2019). https://doi.org/10.1007/978-3-319-75381-2_5-1
15. Tixier, A.J.P., Hallowell, M.R., Rajagopalan, B., Bowman, D.: Application of machine learning to construction injury prediction. Autom. Constr. **69**, 102–114 (2016)
16. Tixier, A.J.P., Hallowell, M.R., Rajagopalan, B., Bowman, D.: Automated content analysis for construction safety: a natural language processing system to extract precursors and outcomes from unstructured injury reports. Autom. Constr. **62**, 45–56 (2016)
17. Tixier, A.J.P., Vazirgiannis, M., Hallowell, M.R.: Word embeddings for the construction domain. CoRR arXiv:1610.09333 (2016)
18. Ubeynarayana, C., Goh, Y.: An ensemble approach for classification of accident narratives. In: Computing in Civil Engineering 2017, pp. 409–416 (2017)
19. Yang, Z., Yang, D., Dyer, C., He, X., Smola, A., Hovy, E.: Hierarchical attention networks for document classification. In: Proceedings of the 2016 Conference of the North American Chapter of the Association for Computational Linguistics: Human Language Technologies, pp. 1480–1489 (2016)

20. Zhang, F., Fleyeh, H., Wang, X., Lu, M.: Construction site accident analysis using text mining and natural language processing techniques. Autom. Constr. **99**, 238–248 (2019)
21. Zhang, J., Zi, L., Hou, Y., Deng, D., Jiang, W., Wang, M.: A C-BiLSTM approach to classify construction accident reports. Appl. Sci. **10**(17), 5754 (2020)
22. Zhong, B., Pan, X., Love, P.E., Ding, L., Fang, W.: Deep learning and network analysis: classifying and visualizing accident narratives in construction. Autom. Constr. **113**, 103089 (2020)

Argumentation

Predicting Argument Density from Multiple Annotations

Gil Rocha[1,3], Bernardo Leite[1,3], Luís Trigo[1,3(✉)], Henrique Lopes Cardoso[1,3], Rui Sousa-Silva[2,4], Paula Carvalho[5], Bruno Martins[5], and Miguel Won[5]

[1] Faculdade de Engenharia, Universidade do Porto, Porto, Portugal
{gil.rocha,bernardo.leite,ltrigo,hlc}@fe.up.pt
[2] Faculdade de Letras, Universidade do Porto, Porto, Portugal
rssilva@letras.up.pt
[3] Laboratório de Inteligência Artificial e Ciência de Computadores (LIACC), Porto, Portugal
[4] Centro de Linguística da Universidade do Porto (CLUP), Porto, Portugal
[5] INESC-ID, Lisboa, Portugal
pcc@inesc-id.pt, {bruno.g.martins,miguelwon}@tecnico.ulisboa.pt

Abstract. Annotating a corpus with argument structures is a complex task, and it is even more challenging when addressing text genres where argumentative discourse markers do not abound. We explore a corpus of opinion articles annotated by multiple annotators, providing diverse perspectives of the argumentative content therein. New annotation aggregation methods are explored, diverging from the traditional ones that try to minimize presumed errors from annotator disagreement. The impact of our methods is assessed for the task of argument density prediction, seen as an initial step in the argument mining pipeline. We evaluate and compare models trained for this regression task in different generated datasets, considering their prediction error and also from a ranking perspective. Results confirm the expectation that addressing argument density from a ranking perspective is more promising than looking at the problem as a mere regression task. We also show that probabilistic aggregation, which weighs tokens by considering all annotators, is a more interesting approach, achieving encouraging results as it accommodates different annotator perspectives. The code and models are publicly available at https://github.com/DARGMINTS/argument-density.

Keywords: Argument annotation · Perspectivist NLP · Argument density prediction · Argument mining

1 Introduction

An opinion article is a written piece, usually published in a newspaper, that reflects the author's opinion about a specific topic. Opinion articles often exhibit a free writing style that makes it harder to clearly identify the exposed arguments. In this paper, we explore a corpus of Portuguese opinion articles annotated with argument structures. In the annotation process, annotators were asked to detect Argument Discourse Units (ADUs) – premises or conclusions – at the token-level and connect them via argumentative relations, forming argument diagrams constrained to paragraph boundaries. A considerable

P. Rosso et al. (Eds.): NLDB 2022, LNCS 13286, pp. 227–239, 2022.
https://doi.org/10.1007/978-3-031-08473-7_21

variability in terms of annotated content is observed across paragraphs – ranging from no argumentative content to several arguments enclosed in a single paragraph. Given the complexity of full argument mining [21] in this text genre, a first task to address with this corpus is determining whether a given paragraph contains argumentative content. More specifically, we propose *argument density prediction*: determining the density of tokens in a paragraph that are argumentative (i.e., included in ADUs). We frame this task as a regression problem, where the density score can range from 0 (no argumentative content in the paragraph) to 1 (all paragraph tokens are included in ADUs). This task has a clear practical impact, as it can be used to guide the reader/system to the parts of the article that are more likely to contain argumentative content.

The process of collecting annotations from multiple annotators is necessary to study (dis)agreement between them, which is typically used to evaluate the complexity of a given annotation task and to assess the reliability of the annotation study. Inherent disagreement between annotators is expected and widely studied in the NLP community, especially for complex discourse analysis [22] and semantically-demanding interpretation tasks [20]. Identifying argumentative structures is one such task, often requiring refined interpretation and inference skills – difficult for both humans and machines [16,25]. Enforcing a single gold standard annotation in the presence of disagreement, a common practice in the NLP community, might obfuscate some valuable linguistic information [22] and the inherent subjectivity of some data instances [17]. A recent trend in the NLP community concerns adopting a *perspectivist* approach [3,4], which advocates the need to accommodate different perceptions from multiple annotators when generating gold standards for subjective phenomena. In this line, we focus on studying the impact that different annotation aggregation techniques have in the task of Argument Density (AD) prediction, in two different axes. First, we explore different strategies to aggregate annotations from different annotators. Second, we analyze to which extent selecting different subsets of annotators influences the performance of AD prediction models, and whether such insights are aligned with inter-annotator agreement. Finally, as a practical use-case, we analyse the problem from a ranking perspective, where AD predictions are used to rank paragraphs. Figure 1 reveals the workflow for both AD prediction and ranking tasks.

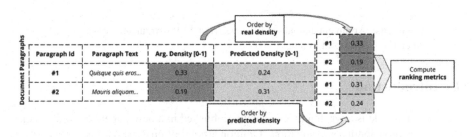

Fig. 1. Workflow for both AD prediction and ranking tasks.

2   Related Work

Argument mining aims to automatically identify, extract and classify argumentative content from text [14]. Given the complexity of the task of extracting structured arguments, the complete problem is typically framed as a pipeline of subtasks [21], namely: text segmentation, identification of ADUs, ADU type classification, relation identification, and relation type classification. The corpus explored in this work is composed of opinion articles. In this text genre, arguments might be spread throughout the document, with some paragraphs exhibiting a stronger argumentative content, while others being more of a descriptive nature and lacking explicit argumentative structures. Consequently, identifying the paragraphs that contain argumentative content is relevant in this genre of text. From the paragraphs signalled as containing argumentative content, further analysis can then be performed. Teufel *et al.* [30,31] have carried out a pioneering work to determine the zones of text that contain argumentative content. Specifically devised for scientific articles, they propose argumentative zoning as the task of classifying sentences by their rhetorical and argumentative role. They present an algorithm that classifies the content into a fixed set of fifteen categories (argumentative zones). Since then, a variety of approaches have been proposed to identify the portions of text that contain argumentative content, ranging from heavily engineered feature-based approaches [9,13,18,19,23,28] to deep neural networks [8,29,32]. Most of these approaches frame the problem as sentence classification task [13,18,19,23,28], while others perform a fine-grained analysis to identify the token-level boundaries of each argument component [8,9,32].

As a first attempt to explore the annotations in our corpus, we aim to address the task of detecting the presence of argumentative content at the paragraph-level. This simpler task is relevant when working with opinion articles, as it allows us to seek for the more argumentative parts within the article. We frame this problem as AD Prediction (further detailed in Sect. 3). The notion of argument density was introduced by Visser *et al.* [33] as a metric to compare corpora in terms of their argumentative richness. Argument density is calculated by normalising the number of annotated inference relations to the number of words in the corpus. The authors employ this metric to compare different monologic and dialogic corpora. Even though this could be a useful comparative metric, the authors raise some practical concerns regarding its meaning due to the variability of annotation guidelines employed in different corpora. These differences in annotation guidelines can change the notion of argument concepts and relations and, consequently, there is no guarantee that we are measuring comparable properties of the corpora. In our work, we reuse this notion of argument density, but the metric is obtained from the token-level annotations (to capture how much content in the paragraph was actually used in argument structures), instead of annotated inference relations, whose connection to the argumentative richness of a span of text is less clear. Furthermore, we consider that our formulation is closer to the first subtask that an argument mining system aims to address: the identification of zones of text that contain potential arguments [30,31]. Finally, we use this argument density metric consistently for all the datasets generated in this work and we do not use it to compare different corpora. Regarding the aggregation of annotations, previous works, including more nuanced ones [7,27], focus on the pursuit of aggregated annotations that minimize the impact of annotation errors – these errors are also seen by traditional approaches as natural in large crowdsourced annotated corpora.

A few works have addressed the similar genre of news editorials, which, together with opinion articles, typically follow a loose structure. In this textual genre, argumentative content often includes figures of speech such as metaphors, irony, or satire, which, together with a free writing style, makes it harder to clearly identify arguments in the text. In fact, the lack of explicit argument markers hinders the task of distinguishing between descriptive and argumentative content. Bal and Saint-Dizier [2] point out that the argumentation structure in such texts usually does not resemble the standard forms of rational thinking or reasoning, which complicates the annotation process. After observing that editorials lack a clear argumentative structure and frequently resort to enthymemes, Al-Khatib *et al.* [1] aim at mining argumentation strategies at a macro document level, as opposed to a finer granularity of analyzing individual arguments.

3 Argument Density Prediction

We frame the AD prediction task as a regression problem, with the goal of predicting the density of argumentative content in a given input sequence: a density of 1 means that all the tokens in the input sequence are included in ADUs; a density of 0 means that the input sequence does not contain any ADUs. A model trained to perform this task can be employed to signal the passages of an article that should be further analyzed in terms of argumentative structure. AD scores are derived from token-level annotations of argumentative content. In the corpus used for this task (further detailed in Sect. 4), each annotated argument – and consequently its ADUs – is constrained to paragraph-level boundaries. As such, we calculate AD for each paragraph as the number of annotated tokens divided by the total number of tokens in the paragraph.

More formally, let $T = \langle t_1, ..., t_m \rangle$ be a paragraph with m tokens t_i. Additionally, let T^* denote the tokens annotated as argumentative content, that is, $T^* = \langle T_1^*, ..., T_n^* \rangle$, subject to $n \leq m$, $\forall i : T_i^* \in T, \forall T_i^*, T_{i+1}^* : T_i$ occurs before T_{i+1} in T. The argument density for the paragraph is $\rho = |T^*|/m$. In this paper, we study different methods to aggregate the annotations provided by a set of expert annotators. We now detail how AD scores for each paragraph are determined using different aggregation techniques. Let T^k denote the set of tokens annotated by an annotator k, where $k \in K$ and K corresponds to our set of annotators. The Union set ($\mathcal{U}$) corresponds to the set of tokens that were annotated by at least one annotator k, i.e., $\mathcal{U} = \langle t_i : \bigvee t_i \in T^k, \forall k \in K, \forall i \in [1, m] \rangle$. Following union, argument density is given by $\rho(\mathcal{U}) = |\mathcal{U}|/m$. The Intersection set ($\mathcal{I}$) corresponds to the set of tokens that were annotated by all annotators. i.e., $\mathcal{I} = \langle t_i : \bigwedge t_i \in T^k, \forall k \in K, \forall i \in [1, m] \rangle$. Following intersection, argument density is given by $\rho(\mathcal{I}) = |\mathcal{I}|/m$. A more accommodating and diffused notion of AD consists of capturing the ratio of annotators that have annotated each token. To this end, we propose the Probabilistic set ($\mathcal{P}$). In this formulation, we attribute a weight w to each token in T, i.e., $\mathcal{P} = \langle w_i, \forall i \in [1, m] \rangle$, where w_i corresponds to the ratio of annotators that annotated t_i. Argumentative density is calculated as follows: $\rho(\mathcal{P}) = (\sum_i^m w_i)/m$.

For the sake of illustration, consider a paragraph with 20 tokens, where each annotator has annotated different spans: tokens [3-10], [3-12], [7-15], respectively. From these annotations, we get: a union span of [3-15], thus $\rho(\mathcal{U}) = 13/20 = 0.65$; an intersection span of [7-10], thus $\rho(\mathcal{I}) = 4/20 = 0.2$; and a probabilistic span containing tokens [7-10] in three annotations, tokens [3-6] and [11-12] in only two annotations, and tokens [13-15] in a single annotation, thus $\rho(\mathcal{P}) = (4 \times 3 + 6 \times 2 + 3 \times 1)/3/20 = 0.45$.

To further assess the capabilities of trained models to determine the AD of a given paragraph in each of the aforementioned setups, we also evaluate models from a ranking perspective. In this formulation, we aim to determine if a model can be employed to determine the relative argumentative density of a document's paragraphs. More formally, for an article with n paragraphs, each with an argumentative density score ρ_j, where $j \in [1, n]$, we aim to determine to what extent the predictions ρ'_j provided by the model can be used to rank the paragraphs in descending order of argumentative density, that is, how well an ordering $\succ_{\rho'}$ matches the gold ordering $\succ_{\rho}$. The gold standard ranking is obtained by arranging the paragraphs of a given article according to the argumentative density scores ρ_j obtained from the annotations (using one of the aggregation techniques detailed above). The predicted ranking is obtained from the predictions ρ'_j made by the model for each paragraph (no additional training is performed). In the case of ties, we rank the paragraphs in the order they appeared in the article (for both the gold standard and predicted rankings). To evaluate the ranking formulation, we employ widely used evaluation metrics in ranking problems, as detailed in Sect. 6.

4   Corpus and Annotations

The corpus consists of 373 opinion articles from a Portuguese newspaper[1], published between June 2014 and June 2019. Each article is annotated with paragraph-contained arguments and attack/support relations [24]. Articles were written by different authors, and have an almost uniform distribution regarding eight topics (Culture, Economy, Local, Politics, Sci-Tech, Society, Sports, and World). In this work, we focus only on annotated ADU spans (i.e., we disregard additional annotations, such as relations). We study Inter-Annotator Agreement (IAA) for the task of AD prediction at the paragraph-level. Based on prior analysis [24], we conclude that annotators present different annotation profiles while performing the annotation task, evidence that their prior distributions should be modeled independently. Each article was annotated by 3 of the 4 recruited annotators, with an even distribution of possible annotator trios. We determine IAA scores individually for each article and report the average score over the complete collection as described in Gate user guide [5].

By doing so, we acknowledge the diversity of the articles in the corpus, which results in different difficulty degrees in the annotation. As agreement metrics, we employ Krippendorff's α_U [11], which has been widely used to measure IAA. We use DKPro Agreement [15], a widely used and well-tested implementation of these metrics in different studies. We use the Ratio distance function, typically employed to measure the distance between ratio-scaled categories in a coding annotation setup, in which categories are numerical values whose difference and distance to a zero element can be measured [15]. We obtain an $\alpha_U = 0.39$, which corresponds to "Fair"

---

[1] https://www.publico.pt/.

agreement [11]. Additionally, we also analyze the IAA scores for each annotator trio. The averaged scores over the resulting collection of articles for each annotator trio are shown in Table 1. The presence of annotator D seems to lower the scores. However, the difference in scores is relatively low, indicating that there is no clear outlier annotator in this annotation study.

Table 1. Krippendorff's α_U for argument densities regarding annotator trios

	(A,B,C)	(A,B,D)	(A,C,D)	(B,C,D)	Mean
α_U	.43	.36	.38	.41	.39

To assess agreement in terms of the ranking formulation, we derive rankings of each article's paragraphs based on their AD scores and compare the rankings obtained from each annotator. The Spearman rank correlation (r_s) [10] is a pairwise metric that we use to assess raters' agreement in Table 2. The first half of the table shows that pair $\langle A, C \rangle$ has the best agreement score. In the second half of the table, we calculate the correlation mean of all pairs followed by each trio combination. The annotator that contributes with less agreement is D and the one with more contribution is C. These results suggest that the task of predicting a raw score for argument density can be challenging. However, when we frame it as a ranking problem we obtain higher IAA scores, which indicates that there is a significant agreement in the relative ranking of paragraphs in terms of argumentative density. Overall, the obtained IAA scores in these two formulations are aligned with IAA studies for similar tasks in terms of complexity [12,26]. This indicates that the exploration of machine learning models in these datasets is expected to be challenging.

Table 2. Spearman rank correlation coefficient for annotator pairs and pair combinations Spearman rank correlation coefficient for annotator pairs and pair combinations

	(A,B)	(A,C)	(A,D)	(B,C)	(B,D)	(C,D)	*Pairs mean*	(A,B,C)	(A,B,D)	(A,C,D)	(B,C,D)
r_s	.43	.52	.37	.48	.42	.40	.43	.48	.41	.43	.43

5   Experimental Setup

We first perform an analysis for the regression formulation, where the goal is to predict the AD ρ'_j of a given paragraph, and compare it to the density ρ_j obtained from the annotations. We then proceed to analyze results in the ranking formulation. Given a set of paragraphs in a document, ordered by the predicted density value, the goal is to verify how well the most argumentative paragraphs are covered by the ones with higher predicted density (a step towards comparing orderings $\succ_\rho$ and $\succ_{\rho'}$). For this purpose, we make use of two evaluation ranking metrics (Sect. 6).

Data Preparation. From the initial corpus, 15 datasets are generated (5 combinations of annotators × 3 aggregation techniques). The first annotator combination (*All*) includes density values when considering all annotators involved. In each of the other four variants, the density values are calculated for each annotator trio: $\langle A, B, C \rangle$, $\langle A, B, D \rangle$, $\langle A, C, D \rangle$ and $\langle B, C, D \rangle$. By doing this, we aim to study the impact of excluding certain annotators on the learning capability of the employed models. Additionally, as stated in Sect. 3, we are considering three aggregation sets: union $(\mathcal{U})$, intersection $(\mathcal{I})$ and probabilistic $(\mathcal{P})$. Figure 2 shows the distribution of paragraph densities, according to each aggregation technique. It should be noted that the intersection setup presents extremely unbalanced data (82% of paragraphs have 0.0 densities).

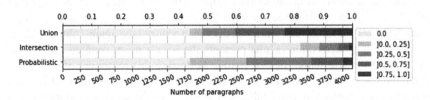

Fig. 2. Distribution of paragraph densities, according to each aggregation technique. Central tendency values are presented in Table 3 (MGT column).

Train/Validation/Test Splits. We carry out 10-fold cross-validation. In total, ten iterations are performed per dataset. For each iteration, we have an 8-1-1 split. The validation set is used to detect early stopping conditions. We would like to emphasize two major points: (1) Each iteration includes a different test set so that at the end of all iterations the whole dataset has been used for testing. More specifically, we aggregate all test set results from all iterations, thus obtaining overall results for the original dataset. This is particularly important since it allows an overall comparison between the different datasets. Have we used only part of each dataset for testing, the comparison would rely instead on different parts of the data, which would be undesirable. (2) In each aggregation technique, all sets (training, validation, and test) contain paragraphs with similar mean density – this is achieved by performing data binning.

Model Setup. We stress out the fact that our goal is not to obtain the best possible model for the predictive task, but rather to compare the results in different generated datasets, using a state-of-the-art model. Recent studies show that pre-trained multilingual language models obtain state-of-the-art results on a variety of downstream tasks and languages. Our approach consists of employing a fine-tuned language model for a specific task (regression) and language (Portuguese). We make use of the pre-trained multilingual BERT language model [6], to which we add a linear layer on top of the pooled output. The maximum token length is 512. We use mean squared error (MSE) as the loss function. The training process is done under a maximum of 8 epochs, using patience of 3. We use a batch size of 32, 50% dropout, and Adam optimizer with a learning rate of 2×10^{-5} (as suggested by Devlin *et al.* [6]).

Baseline. A simple baseline heuristic is one that always predicts the mean of the training set. Hence, we use the predictions of a baseline from scikit-learn dummy regressor as a way to compare them to the ones obtained using the BERT model.

6   Results

6.1   Density Prediction

The results for AD prediction are shown in Table 3. Overall, results improve when employing the BERT model – mean squared error is less than or equal when compared to the baseline heuristic. Improvements regarding baseline are more noticeable when using the union aggregation technique. On the other hand, the highest mean squared errors are obtained in this setting. This can be partially explained by the high standard deviation values observed in the union ground-truth density mean values (see column "MGT"). In contrast, the intersection aggregation technique reveals the lowest standard deviation values for its ground-truth density mean values (see again column "MGT"). The fact that the intersection results presents the lowest mean squared errors can be justified by the sparse nature of that setting. Following this reasoning, it makes sense that the intersection baseline presents values closer to those provided by BERT. When comparing "All" with each trio, "All" consistently yields results with reduced error for both intersection and probabilistic aggregation techniques. We validate this by applying the z-test between "All" and each trio. The results support this evidence given that the p-value is less than .05 for all[2] tests. Finally, the results are not aligned with IAA scores (Table 1). Previously $\langle A, C, D \rangle$ (without B) and $\langle A, B, D \rangle$ (without C) obtained the lowest IAA scores, meaning that both annotators B and C help to improve IAA. There is no clear trend on the contribution of each annotator to density prediction, and thus we cannot perceive a relation between AD prediction and IAA.

Table 3. Mean squared error results for AD prediction (lower is better), obtained from aggregating all test folds in the cross-validation process. "*bl*" stands for baseline and "*MGT*" stands for the mean ground-truth density values observed in each dataset.

	All			$\langle A, B, C \rangle$			$\langle A, B, D \rangle$			$\langle A, C, D \rangle$			$\langle B, C, D \rangle$		
	bl	Bert	MGT	bl	Bert	MGT	bl	Bert	MGT	bl	Bert	MGT	bl	Bert	MGT
$\mathcal{U}$	.14	.09	.37 ±.37	.12	.09	.31 ±.35	.13	.09	.33 ±.36	.12	.08	.29 ±.35	.13	.09	.34 ±.37
$\mathcal{I}$	.03	.02	.07 ±.17	.04	.04	.1 ±.21	.04	.03	.09 ±.2	.03	.03	.08 ±.19	.05	.04	.11 ±.22
$\mathcal{P}$	.06	.03	.2 ±.24	.06	.04	.2 ±.25	.06	.04	.21 ±.25	.06	.04	.18 ±.24	.07	.04	.22 ±.26

6.2   Paragraph Ranking

The goal of paragraph ranking evaluation is to validate whether the paragraphs with the highest predicted AD correspond to the paragraphs that actually have the highest argumentative density, according to the annotators. The ranking evaluation is done at the document level, and we make use of two distinct metrics. The normalized discounted

---

[2] This does not hold for the z-test "All" vs. $\langle A, C, D \rangle$ (probabilistic) where the p-value is 0.059, although it stays very close to a statistical significance.

cumulative gain $(NDCG)$[3] sums the true scores ranked in the order induced by the predicted scores, after applying a logarithmic discount. Then it divides by the best possible score (ideal discounted cumulative gain, obtained for a perfect ranking) to obtain a score between 0 and 1. Formally, $NDCG$ is computed as shown in Eq. 1, where DCG_p is the discounted cumulative gain accumulated at a particular rank position p, and rel_i is the graded relevance of the result at position i. $IDCG_p$ is the ideal discounted cumulative gain, where REL_p represents the list of relevant paragraphs (ordered by density) in the document up to position p. Using this metric, and taking into account that the median number of paragraphs per document is 10, we experimented with $k = \{1, 5\}$ (by only considering the highest 1 and 5 density scores in the ranking) and $k =$ "all" (by considering all density scores in the ranking).

$$NDCG = \frac{DCG_p}{IDCG_p} = \frac{\sum_{i=1}^{p} \frac{rel_i}{\log_2(i+1)}}{\sum_{i=1}^{|REL_p|} \frac{rel_i}{\log_2(i+1)}} \tag{1}$$

Additionally, we use the *Top-k Accuracy* evaluation metric, which computes how many of the k most argumentative paragraphs are among the k predicted as being the most argumentative ones. For this metric, we would obtain the maximum result for $k = all$, which however is not informative. It should be noted that here we consider a different number of documents for each k: more specifically, 373 and 323 documents for $k = 1$ and $k = 5$, respectively. The reason for this is to avoid documents with k or fewer paragraphs. For instance, it wouldn't be reasonable to assess *Top-5 Accuracy* for a document with 5 or fewer paragraphs, as the result will be the maximum.

NDCG. All *NDCG* results for paragraph ranking are shown in Table 4. Overall, BERT has an average percentage improvement of 48%, 90% and 61% for union, intersection and probabilistic aggregation techniques, correspondingly. Also, the results improve as the k-value increases (as expected). The best values are obtained with the union and probabilistic aggregation techniques. The intersection technique presents lower results. This can be explained by the extremely unbalanced nature of the data obtained using the intersection aggregation technique (Fig. 2). For $k =$ "All", scores are promising for both the union and probabilistic aggregation techniques. The observed drop in the scores from $k =$ "All" to $k = 5$ reveals that the task of predicting the most argumentative paragraphs is challenging. When comparing each trio for both union and probabilistic aggregation techniques, the lowest scores (although the differences are hundredths) are obtained with trio $\langle A, B, C \rangle$. Additionally, we conclude that there is no clear alignment between these results and the IAA analysis performed in Sect. 4. This seems to convey that divergent perspectives provide a wider spectrum of annotation possibilities.

---

[3] https://scikit-learn.org/stable/modules/generated/sklearn.metrics.ndcg_score.html.

Table 4. NDCG results for paragraph ranking (higher is better).

	k	All			$\langle A, B, C \rangle$			$\langle A, B, D \rangle$			$\langle A, C, D \rangle$			$\langle B, C, D \rangle$		
		1	5	all	1	5	all	1	5	all	1	5	all	1	5	all
$\mathcal{U}$	baseline	.45	.56	.75	.41	.54	.73	.42	.54	.73	.38	.52	.71	.43	.55	.74
		±.16	±.18	±.10	±.16	±.19	±.11	±.16	±.18	±.10	±.15	±.19	±.11	±.16	±.18	±.11
	BERT	.74	.81	.89	.66	.76	.86	.72	.80	.88	.71	.78	.87	.70	.79	.87
		±.29	±.16	±.09	±.34	±.18	±.12	±.29	±.15	±.09	±.32	±.17	±.11	±.32	±.17	±.11
$\mathcal{I}$	baseline	.16	.34	.48	.20	.39	.54	.19	.37	.52	.18	.36	.50	.21	.39	.55
		±.12	±.20	±.20	±.13	±.19	±.17	±.13	±.19	±.18	±.12	±.20	±.19	±.13	±.19	±.17
	BERT	.44	.61	.66	.47	.65	.71	.49	.65	.71	.47	.64	.69	.50	.66	.73
		±.45	±.29	±.31	±.43	±.29	±.25	±.44	±.30	±.27	±.45	±.33	±.29	±.43	±.29	±.25
$\mathcal{P}$	baseline	.37	.52	.71	.36	.51	.70	.36	.52	.70	.34	.49	.68	.37	.52	.70
		±.15	±.18	±.10	±.15	±.18	±.11	±.15	±.18	±.11	±.14	±.19	±.11	±.15	±.18	±.11
	BERT	.71	.81	.88	.65	.77	.86	.70	.79	.87	.70	.79	.87	.69	.79	.87
		±.32	±.15	±.09	±.34	±.18	±.12	±.33	±.16	±.11	±.33	±.17	±.11	±.33	±.17	±.11

Top-k Accuracy. The *Top-k Accuracy* results are shown in Table 5. BERT is able to improve over the baseline, except for the intersection aggregation technique. Following previous observations, we believe that this is due to the extremely unbalanced nature of the dataset obtained using this aggregation technique. When comparing "All" with each trio, there is no clear conclusion regarding the best aggregation technique, since their relative ranking scores are mixed. As k increases, there are significant improvements in the obtained results, as expected. It is worth noting that the $k = 1$ setup is very challenging, where the majority of results stay below 0.3. In contrast, $k = 5$ obtains satisfactory scores for both union and probabilistic techniques. While the best results are obtained with the probabilistic setup, these are close to the ones reported in union (similar to what we have observed for *NDCG*).

Table 5. Top-K accuracy results for paragraph ranking (higher is better).

	k	All		(A, B, C)		(A, B, D)		(A, C, D)		(B, C, D)	
		1	5	1	5	1	5	1	5	1	5
$\mathcal{U}$	baseline	.09±.28	.54±.26	.10±.31	.56±.26	.10±.29	.54±.27	.09±.29	.57±.26	.10±.29	.54±.26
	BERT	.21±.41	.69±.21	.22±.41	.67±.21	.19±.39	.70±.20	.25±.43	.70±.19	.21±.41	.69±.21
$\mathcal{I}$	baseline	.21±.41	.80±.20	.16±.37	.75±.22	.18±.38	.75±.23	.19±.39	.77±.22	.15±.36	.73±.23
	BERT	.29±.45	.59±.25	.28±.45	.63±.22	.31±.46	.62±.23	.30±.46	.61±.23	.29±.45	.63±.22
$\mathcal{P}$	baseline	.10±.30	.54±.27	.13±.33	.56±.26	.09±.29	.55±.27	.10±.31	.57±.27	.10±.30	.54±.27
	BERT	.33±.47	.72±.18	.28±.45	.70±.19	.33±.47	.71±.19	.35±.48	.72±.19	.32±.47	.70±.19

7 Discussion and Conclusions

In this study, we propose addressing the task of argument density prediction. We make use of a Portuguese corpus of opinion articles annotated with argument structures. Each article was annotated with ADUs at the paragraph level by at least three different annotators. The task of argument density prediction is formulated as a regression problem, where the density score ranges from 0 to 1. We used three different aggregation techniques for getting a consensus between annotators: Union ($\mathcal{U}$), Intersection ($\mathcal{I}$) and Probabilistic ($\mathcal{P}$). The first point that stands out is that regression scores are satisfactory but hard to interpret. The ranking formulation shows that the models learn to perform the task reasonably well. *NDCG* results reported for $k = all$ are very promising for both Union and Probabilistic aggregation techniques. The drop in scores for $k = 5$ shows that predicting the most argumentative paragraphs is a very challenging task. However, BERT performs relatively well in these cases. Overall, BERT improvements over the baseline heuristic are promising and demonstrate that the model can be useful in practical scenarios. However, we should not be extreme in restraining k.

Regarding aggregation techniques, the intersection is not appropriate due to the extremely unbalanced nature of the dataset. In what concerns annotator combinations, removing one annotator does not seem to bring any improvement, except for very specific setups. Despite the relatively modest IAA scores, aggregating the annotations of all annotators is a reasonable option, as it provides a representative view of the different perspectives [3,4] regarding the article analysis. IAA does not seem to indicate which annotators are more problematic – in the sense of adding noise to the aggregated data – to train the models; IAA should be seen as an indicator for the complexity of this annotation task in this text genre.

As future work, we intend to train the models directly in the ranking task and, in addition, explore other aggregation techniques, including more recent Bayesian and vector-based approaches.

Acknowledgements. This research is supported by project DARGMINTS (POCI/01/0145/ FEDER/031460), LIACC (FCT/UID/ CEC/0027/2020), INESC-ID (UIDB/50021/2020) and CLUP (UIDB/00022/2020), funded by Fundação para a Ciência e a Tecnologia (FCT). Gil Rocha is supported by a PhD studentship (SFRH/BD/140125/2018) from FCT. Bernardo Leite is supported by a PhD studentship (2021.05432.BD) from FCT.

References

1. Al-Khatib, K., Wachsmuth, H., Kiesel, J., Hagen, M., Stein, B.: A news editorial corpus for mining argumentation strategies. In: Proceedings of COLING 2016, Osaka, Japan, pp. 3433–3443 (2016)
2. Bal, B.K., Saint Dizier, P.: Towards building annotated resources for analyzing opinions and argumentation in news editorials. In: Proceedings 7th Language Resources and Evaluation Conference, ELRA, Valletta, Malta (2010)
3. Basile, V.: It's the end of the gold standard as we know it. In: Baldoni, M., Bandini, S. (eds.) AIxIA 2020. LNCS (LNAI), vol. 12414, pp. 441–453. Springer, Cham (2021). https://doi. org/10.1007/978-3-030-77091-4_26

4. Basile, V., et al.: We need to consider disagreement in evaluation. In: Proceedings 1st Workshop on Benchmarking: Past, Present and Future, pp. 15–21. ACL, Online (2021)

5. Cunningham, H., et al.: Developing Language Processing Components with GATE Version 8 (a User Guide), University of Sheffield Department of Computer Science (2014)

6. Devlin, J., Chang, M.W., Lee, K., Toutanova, K.: BERT: Pre-training of deep bidirectional transformers for language understanding. In: Proceedings 2019 NAACL, pp. 4171–4186. ACL, Minneapolis, Minnesota (2019)

7. Dumitrache, A., Inel, O., Aroyo, L., Timmermans, B., Welty, C.: Crowdtruth 2.0: Quality metrics for crowdsourcing with disagreement. arXiv preprint arXiv:1808.06080 (2018)

8. Eger, S., Daxenberger, J., Gurevych, I.: Neural end-to-end learning for computational argumentation mining. In: Proceedings 55th Annual Meeting of the ACL, pp. 11–22. ACL, Vancouver, Canada (2017)

9. Goudas, T., Louizos, C., Petasis, G., Karkaletsis, V.: Argument extraction from news, blogs, and social media. In: Likas, A., Blekas, K., Kalles, D. (eds.) Artificial Intelligence: Methods and Applications, pp. 287–299. Springer International Publishing, Cham (2014)

10. Krahmer, E., Theune, M. (eds.): EACL/ENLG -2009. LNCS (LNAI), vol. 5790. Springer, Heidelberg (2010). https://doi.org/10.1007/978-3-642-15573-4

11. Krippendorff, K.: Measuring the reliability of qualitative text analysis data. Qual. Quant. **38**, 787–800 (2004)

12. Lawrence, J., Reed, C.: Argument mining: a survey. Comput. Linguist. **45**(4), 765–818 (2019)

13. Levy, R., Bilu, Y., Hershcovich, D., Aharoni, E., Slonim, N.: Context dependent claim detection. In: Proceedings COLING 2014, pp. 1489–1500. ACL, Dublin, Ireland (2014)

14. Lippi, M., Torroni, P.: Argumentation mining: state of the art and emerging trends. ACM Trans. Int. Technol. **16**(2), 1–25 (2016)

15. Meyer, C.M., Mieskes, M., Stab, C., Gurevych, I.: DKPro agreement: An open-source Java library for measuring inter-rater agreement. In: Proceedings COLING 2014, pp. 105–109. ACL, Dublin, Ireland (2014)

16. Moens, M.F.: Argumentation mining: how can a machine acquire common sense and world knowledge? Argument Comput. **9**(1), 1–14 (2017)

17. Ovesdotter Alm, C.: Subjective natural language problems: motivations, applications, characterizations, and implications. In: Proceedings 49th Annual Meeting of the ACL, pp. 107–112. ACL, Portland, Oregon, USA (2011)

18. Palau, R.M., Moens, M.F.: Argumentation mining: the detection, classification and structure of arguments in text. In: Proceedings 12th International Conference on Artificial Intelligence and Law, p. 98–107. ACM, New York, NY, USA (2009)

19. Park, J., Cardie, C.: Identifying appropriate support for propositions in online user comments. In: Proceedings 1st Workshop on Argumentation Mining, pp. 29–38. ACL (2014)

20. Pavlick, E., Kwiatkowski, T.: Inherent disagreements in human textual inferences. Trans. Assoc. Comput. Linguist. **7**, 677–694 (2019)

21. Peldszus, A., Stede, M.: Joint prediction in MST-style discourse parsing for argumentation mining. In: Proceedings EMNLP, pp. 938–948. ACL, Lisbon, Portugal (2015)

22. Plank, B., Hovy, D., Søgaard, A.: Linguistically debatable or just plain wrong? In: Proceedings 52nd Annual Meeting of the ACL. pp. 507–511. ACL, Baltimore, Maryland (2014)

23. Rinott, R., Dankin, L., Alzate Perez, C., Khapra, M.M., Aharoni, E., Slonim, N.: Show me your evidence - an automatic method for context dependent evidence detection. In: Proceedings 2015 EMNLP, pp. 440–450. ACL, Lisbon, Portugal (2015)

24. Rocha, G., et al.: Annotating arguments in a corpus of opinion articles. In: Proceedings 13th Language Resources and Evaluation Conference, ELRA (2022)

25. Saint-Dizier, P.: Challenges of argument mining: Generating an argument synthesis based on the qualia structure. In: Proceedings 9th International Natural Language Generation Conference, pp. 79–83. ACL, Edinburgh, UK (2016)
26. Schaefer, R., Stede, M.: Argument mining on twitter: a survey. IT-Inf. Technol. **63**(1), 45–58 (2021)
27. Simpson, E.D., Gurevych, I.: A Bayesian approach for sequence tagging with crowds. In: Proceedings 2019 EMNLP and 9th IJCNLP, pp. 1093–1104. ACL, Hong Kong, China (2019)
28. Stab, C., Gurevych, I.: Identifying argumentative discourse structures in persuasive essays. In: Proceedings of the 2014 Conference on Empirical Methods in Natural Language Processing (EMNLP), pp. 46–56. Association for Computational Linguistics, Doha, Qatar (2014)
29. Stab, C., Miller, T., Schiller, B., Rai, P., Gurevych, I.: Cross-topic argument mining from heterogeneous sources. In: Proceedings 2018 EMNLP, pp. 3664–3674. ACL (2018)
30. Teufel, S.: Argumentative Zoning: Information Extraction from Scientific Text. Ph.D. thesis, University of Edinburgh (1999)
31. Teufel, S., Siddharthan, A., Batchelor, C.: Towards discipline-independent argumentative zoning: evidence from chemistry and computational linguistics. In: Proceedings 2009 EMNLP, pp. 1493–1502. ACL, USA (2009)
32. Trautmann, D., Daxenberger, J., Stab, C., Schütze, H., Gurevych, I.: Fine-grained argument unit recognition and classification. In: Proceedings of the AAAI Conference on AI, vol. 34, no. 05, pp. 9048–9056 (2020)
33. Visser, J., Konat, B., Duthie, R., Koszowy, M., Budzynska, K., Reed, C.: Argumentation in the 2016 US presidential elections: annotated corpora of television debates and social media reaction. Lang. Res. Eval. **54**(1), 123–154 (2019). https://doi.org/10.1007/s10579-019-09446-8

A Decade of Legal Argumentation Mining: Datasets and Approaches

Gechuan Zhang[1] , Paul Nulty[2] , and David Lillis[1(✉)]

[1] School of Computer Science, University College Dublin, Dublin, Ireland
gechuan.zhang@ucdconnect.ie, david.lillis@ucd.ie
[2] Department of Computer Science and Information Systems, Birkbeck,
University of London, London, UK
p.nulty@bbk.ac.uk

Abstract. The growing research field of argumentation mining (AM) in the past ten years has made it a popular topic in Natural Language Processing. However, there are still limited studies focusing on AM in the context of legal text (Legal AM), despite the fact that legal text analysis more generally has received much attention as an interdisciplinary field of traditional humanities and data science. The goal of this work is to provide a critical data-driven analysis of the current situation in Legal AM. After outlining the background of this topic, we explore the availability of annotated datasets and the mechanisms by which these are created. This includes a discussion of how arguments and their relationships can be modelled, as well as a number of different approaches to divide the overall Legal AM task into constituent sub-tasks. Finally we review the dominant approaches that have been applied to this task in the past decade, and outline some future directions for Legal AM research.

Keywords: Argumentation mining · Legal text · Text analysis

1 Introduction

Since Mochales and Moens presented their work on detecting arguments from legal texts in 2011, argumentation mining (AM), automatic detection of arguments and reasoning from texts [13], has become a popular research field. Meanwhile, attention in legal text processing has grown both in research and industry, leading to progress in new tasks such as legal topic classification [14], judicial decision prediction [4], and Legal AM [11]. Given that arguments are a core component of legal analysis, Legal AM has many important potential applications.

Although there are some works that describe the state-of-the-art of artificial intelligence (AI) and law [2], which have introduced AM, there is still a lack of a thorough review of Legal AM and its datasets or tools. Here, we present what is to our knowledge the first survey of Legal AM from a data-driven perspective. In particular, our work reviews this interdisciplinary field from two aspects: 1) corpus annotation, 2) argument extraction and relation prediction.

P. Rosso et al. (Eds.): NLDB 2022, LNCS 13286, pp. 240–252, 2022.
https://doi.org/10.1007/978-3-031-08473-7_22

The lack of suitable open-source corpora is still a challenge in Legal AM, and complex annotation schemes can make evaluation difficult. Most present Legal AM work focuses on detecting text arguments, since relation prediction is the remaining challenge. In the remainder, Sect. 2 provides the related background in computational argumentation as well as the models used to structure human language. Section 3 discusses the existing annotation schemes and corpus creation. Section 4 investigates practical methods and the implementation of argument extraction and relation prediction in legal text. Section 5 contains our conclusions and prospects for Legal AM in the future.

2   Related Work

2.1   Computational Argumentation

In order to detect text arguments automatically, computational argumentation that expresses human language into structured data is required. At present, there are two types of computational argumentation models: abstract argumentation models (aka. argumentation frameworks [6], AFs), and structural argumentation models [22,30], which individually focus on a macro (external) or a micro (internal) structure of argumentation. Abstract argumentation models treat each argument as the elementary unit without further details and emphasise relationships between arguments. To deal with the complex linguistic environment of legal texts, inner argumentation structure is required. As a result, structural argumentation models, including components within individual argument, are often used in Legal AM annotation scheme.

2.2   Structural Argumentation Model

Structural argumentation models assume a tentative proof of a given argument, then apply a set of rules on their substructures in order to formalise it and represent internal argument components and relations [9]. The logic-based definition of argument in structural argumentation models presents as a pair $< \phi, \alpha >$, where ϕ is a set of support formulae, and α is the consequent [1]. Here, we review two classic structural argumentation models.

- **Toulmin Model** [22] is a classic argumentation model that considers the inner structure of arguments. It has been used in debates, persuasive articles, and academic writing, long before being applied in NLP tasks. [22] designs a complete argument structure consisting of six components: *claim* (*conclusion*), *ground* (*data*), *warrant*, *support*, *qualifier*, *rebuttal*. The first three are the foundations which every argument starts with.
- **Walton Model** [30] proposes a simplified structure. [30] states an argument as a set of statements (propositions), made up of three components: a *conclusion*, a set of *premises*, and an *inference* from the premises to the conclusion. The model also includes higher-level bipolar relations between arguments: an argument can both be *supported* or *attacked* by other arguments.

3   Creating Annotated Legal Corpora

Like most interdisciplinary studies, the requirement of professional guidance increases the cost in time and labour when developing new AM corpora [10,18]. This situation leads to two urgent needs in Legal AM: first, legal text corpora with accurate manual annotation; second, basic standard protocols when creating annotations. This section reviews several important works that create legal argument annotation schemes and describe the annotation of various types of legal texts, including case laws [11,32], online comments on public rules [16], and judicial decisions [26]. The papers and corpora discussed in this work are listed in Table 1. Annotation details are concluded in Table 2. This work focuses on English texts. Legal texts in other languages [23] are also worth exploring in the future study of Legal AM.

Table 1. Papers on argumentation mining on legal text (ECHR = European Court of Human Rights, CDCP = Consumer Debt Collection Practices, VICP = Vaccine Injury Compensation Program, CanLII = Canadian Legal Information Institute, CA = corpus annotation, AD = argument and relation detection, doc = document, set = sentence, rec = record).

Authors	Abbr.	Source	Task	Corpus size
Mochales and Moens [13]	MM2011	ECHR	CA, AD	47 doc, 2,571 set
Teruel et al. [21]	TCCA2018		CA	7 doc
Poudyal et al. [18]	PSI2020		CA, AD	42 doc
Niculae et al. [15]	NPC2017	CDCP	CA, AD	731 rec, 3,800 set
Park and Cardie [17]	PC2018		CA	731 rec, 3,800 set
Galassi et al. [7]	GLT2021		AD	
Walker et al. [26]	WCDL2011	VICP	CA	30 doc
Grabmair et al. [8]	GACS2015		AD	
Walker et al. [27]	WHNY2017	BVA	CA	20doc, 5,674 set
Walker et al. [24]	WFPR2018		CA	30doc, 8,149 set
Walker et al. [28]	WPDL2019		CA, AD	50doc, 6,153 set
Westermann et al. [31]	WSWA2019		AD	
Walker et al. [29]	WSW2020		CA, AD	75 doc, 623 set
Xu et al. [32]	XSA2020	CanLII	CA, AD	683 doc, 30,374 set
Xu et al. [34]	XSA2021a		CA, AD	1,148 doc, 127,330 set
Xu et al. [33]	XSA2021b		CA, AD	2,098 doc, 226,576 set

[12] provided the initial study on computational argumentation in legal text. In MM2011, they produced a corpus including 47 English-language cases (judgments and decisions) from the HUDOC[1] open-source database of the European

---

[1] https://hudoc.echr.coe.int/eng.

Court of Human Rights (ECHR), a common resource for legal text processing research. MM2011 applied a sentence-level annotation scheme on ECHR files based on Walton's model. Segmented clauses were labelled as: *premise, conclusion* and *non-argumentative*. According to the distribution of clause-types in MM2011, there was an imbalance between premises and conclusions. [13] suggested one conclusion was often connected with multiple premises to build up a complete and stable argument in practical legal files. The annotation scheme in MM2011 had two further aspects. First, it considered the recurrent structure of sub-arguments in an argument. MM2011 concluded the argumentation into a tree structure where the leaves were arguments linked through argument relations, and all together supported a final conclusion. Second, the argument relations were annotated as rhetorical patterns. MM2011 explained that they did not judge the interaction between rhetorical and argument relations. The final IAA between four lawyers reached 0.75 of Cohen's κ [5].

Table 2. Legal text annotation result (LA = logic annotation of argumentation model, CA = character annotation of legal context, Cmp = component, Rel = relation, IR = inner relation, OR = outer relation, Bi = bipolar relation, IRA = implicit relation annotation, ERA = explicit relation annotation; a = argument, c = component, r = relation, s = summary, f = full text, cκ = Cohen's κ, α = Krippendorf's α, N/A = not applicable).

Paper	LA	CA	Cmp	Rel	IR	OR	Bi	IRA	ERA	IAA
MM2011	*	*	*	*	*	*	*		*	a 0.75 (cκ)
TCCA2018	*	*	*	*	*	*	*		*	a 0.77–0.84 (cκ)
										c 0.48–0.64 (cκ)
										r 0.85–1.00 (cκ)
PSI2020	*		*	*	*			*		a 0.80 (cκ)
NPC2017	*	*	*	*	*				*	c 0.65 (α)
PC2018	*	*	*	*	*				*	r 0.44 (α)
WCDL2011	*	*	*	*	*		*		*	N/A
WFPR2018	*	*	*	*	*		*		*	N/A
WPDL2019	*	*	*	*	*		*		*	N/A
WSW2020	*	*	*	*	*		*		*	N/A
XSA2020	*		*							c (s/f) 0.71/0.77 (cκ)
XSA2021a	*		*							c (s/f) 0.71/0.83 (cκ)
XSA2021b	*		*							c (s/f) 0.73/0.60 (cκ)

Although MM2011 did not open-source the data, another ECHR AM corpus was more recently released by PSI2020. PSI2020 used the same corpus annotation process as MM2011. Four annotators achieved Cohen's κ inter-annotator agreement (IAA) of 0.80. For each clause, PSI2020's annotation included: a unique identifier and a character offset for start and end. Clause types in PSI2020 was aligned with MM2011: *premise, conclusion,* and *non-argument.* The PSI2020 annotation scheme highlighted the overlap between arguments: some clauses may be both premises and conclusions for different arguments. PSI2020 stored two types of information for each argument: 1) a list of clauses annotated as premises, and 2) the unique conclusion clause of the argument. The conclusion clause in each argument was treated as the conclusion type, any clause in the premise list was a premise type, and a clause which does not appear in any argument was a non-argument type. Unlike MM2011, PSI2020 omitted relations between individual arguments. The support relations from premises to conclusions were not explicitly annotated with labels. Instead, PSI2020 stored whole arguments as items and implicitly presented the support relations among each argument.

TCCA2018 includes annotations of 7 ECHR judgments (28,000 words). Their annotation scheme merged both the Toulmin model and previous guidelines [20] into three types of argument components: *major claim, claim* and *premise.* In contrast to the premise/conclusion model in MM2011 and PSI2020, TCCA2018 treated the *major claim* as the highest level that can be *supported* or *attacked* by other arguments [20]. The bipolar relations between premises and claims also differ from the implicit support connections in PSI2020. Moreover, TCCA2018 conducted further classification on claims and premises: each (major-) claim was associated with its actor (ECHR, applicant, government), and premises were classified with sub-labels (Facts, Principles of Law and Case Law). TCCA2018 annotate both *support* and *attack* relations between argument components. In addition, TCCA2018 established two minor argument relations: *duplicate,* and *citation.* One of the seven judgements was annotated by all 4 annotators as training material (Cohen's $\kappa \geq 0.54$). TCCA2018 suggested IAA on argumentative/non-argumentative sentences was high (κ ranging between 0.77 and 0.84). The IAA dropped when annotating argument components, mainly due to disagreements of major claims.

Another widely used Legal AM corpus, Consumer Debt Collection[2] Practice (CDCP), is annotated by PC2018. The data consists of 731 user comments on Consumer Debt Collection Practices (CDCP) rules by the Consumer Financial Protection Bureau (CFPB). In order to structure the arguments, PC2018 uses a self-designed annotation scheme containing two parts: elementary units and support relations. The elementary units are sentences or clauses with different semantic types. Non-argumentative parts in comment texts (i.e., greetings, names) were removed when segmenting. To evaluate arguments, PC2018's annotations include two types of support relations: reason and evidence.

Apart from ECHR cases, the Research Laboratory for Law, Logic and Technology[3] (LLT Lab) from Hofstra University has annotated diverse samples of judicial decisions from U.S. courts. Their Vaccine/Injury Project (V/IP) used rule-based protocols, Default-Logic Framework (DLF) [25], to extract arguments

---

[2] http://www.regulationroom.org/.
[3] https://www.lltlab.org/.

in judicial decisions selected from the U.S. Court of Federal Claims. WCDL2011 modelled the fact-finding reasoning (a special argumentation in law) with DLF annotations. The annotation process (extracting the DLF structure from the judicial decision) is two-step. First, identifying sentences including argumentation information. Second, annotating sentences' inferential roles and support-levels in the rule-tree. WCDL2011 designed logical connectives [26] to represent argumentation relations between supporting reasons (premises) and conclusions. In addition, evidentiary propositions (premises and conclusions) have plausibility-values to measure the level of confidence in legal argumentation. The complexity of DLF made the manual annotation much harder. As a result, the final V/IP corpus in WCDL2011 contained sufficient semantic and logic information, which is represented in a rule-tree structure and stored in XML files.

The Veteran's Claim Dataset (or BVA) is another publicly available corpus annotated by the LLT Lab, using judicial-claim decisions from the Board of Veterans Appeals (BVA). WHNY2017 regarded legal argumentation the same as legal reasoning, and also modelled arguments with premise/conclusion model. The BVA decisions were annotated with semantic information of legal professional argumentation, including sentence roles and propositional connectives. These two groups of annotations matched the components and relations in broad argumentation model. The annotation scheme in WHNY2017 involved ten sentence reasoning roles and eight propositional connectives. The sentence types then acted as anchors when mining arguments (in WSWA2019). The propositional connectives represented argumentation relations from premises to conclusions. The argumentation relations have two properties: polarity and logical functionality. The polarity defines the support/oppose relation between the premises and the conclusion. The functionality measures the plausibility of an argument. The annotation work on BVA datasets continued for years; the initial corpus in WHNY2017 was only 20 documents (5,674 sentences), which was later enlarged to 30 documents (8,149 sentences) in WFPR2018. WPDL2019 expanded the dataset and analysed 50 judicial decisions. In the recent WSW2020, a second BVA dataset (25 decisions) has been annotated and published.

In a similar vein, the Intelligent Systems Program from University of Pittsburgh developed a series of corpora based on legal cases, which were sampled from the Canadian Legal Information Institute[4] (CanLII). They annotated argument structure as the *legal argument triples* (*IRC triples*): 1) *issue*, the legal question addressed in a legal case; 2) *conclusion*, the court's decision for the issue; 3) *reason*, sentences of why the court reached the conclusion. Based on the IRC annotation scheme, two annotators identified sentence-level argument components that form pairs of human-prepared summaries and full texts cases. They conduct annotations in two steps: first, annotating the case summaries in terms of IRC triples; second, annotating the corresponding sentences in full texts by mapping the annotations from summaries. This Legal AM dataset is still under development. From its initial version in XSA2020 with 574 legal case summaries and 109 full texts, the research group have enlarged the number of

---

[4] https://www.canlii.org/en/.

annotated documents to 574 full texts in XSA2021a. The latest CanLII corpus in XSA2021b contains 1049 annotated pairs of legal case summaries and full texts.

4   Practical Approaches for Legal Argumentation Mining

AM systems are generally organised as a two-stage pipeline: *argument extraction* and *relation prediction* [3]. Argument extraction, which typically contains sub-tasks, aims to identify arguments from input texts. Relation prediction focuses on the relations between (or within) identified arguments. Although identifying accurate argument boundaries is always a problem under discussion [19], AM annotations on legal text are usually at the sentence level, where a complete argument is a group of sentences or clauses with different logic functions.

After analysing the literature, we divide the Legal AM problem into the following sub-tasks: 1) argument information detection, 2) argument component classification, 3) argument relation prediction. Argument information detection and argument component classification together comprise argument extraction. Table 3 summarises the prominent papers in the field, under a number of headings. It includes a) the specific sub-tasks that each study attempted to solve, b) the particular technologies used for AM and c) the argument components that the reasoning was performed on, along with the specific types of relationship that could exist between argument components in the model that was used.

Table 3. Legal Text Annotation Schemes and Analysis Technologies (ID = Information Detection, CC = Component Classification, RP = Relation Prediction, emb = word embeddings, cr = classification rules, sm = statistical models, nn = neural networks.)

Paper	ID	CC	RP	emb	cr	sm	nn	Annotation
MM2011	*	*	*		*	*		**Component** Premise/Conclusion/Non-argumentative **Relation** Support/Against/Conclusion/Other/None
PSI2020	*	*	*	*			*	**Component** Premise/Conclusion/Non-argument
NPC2017		*	*	*		*	*	**Component** Fact/Testimony/Value/Policy/Reference
GLT2021		*	*	*			*	**Relation** Reason/Evidence
GACS2015		*				*		**Component**
WPDL2019		*				*		Reasoning roles (e.g., Evidence, Finding)
WSWA2019		*			*	*		**Relation**
WSW2020		*					*	Logical connectives (e.g., positive/negative)
XSA2020	*	*		*		*	*	**Component**
XSA2021a		*		*			*	Issue/Reason/Conclusion/Non-IRC
XSA2021b		*		*			*	

4.1 Argument Information Detection

Although arguments are considered as their major proportion, legal documents (e.g., case-laws) still have redundant parts without argument information. The first task in an AM system is to shrink the scope of argumentative content as well as filter out unrelated parts.

MM2011 considered this to be binary classification: whether a proposition (segmented clause) is argumentative or not. A number of statistical machine learning (ML) classifiers were used: Naïve Bayes (NB), Maximum Entropy (ME), and Support Vector Machine (SVM) with n-grams, Parts Of Speech (POS) tagging, hand-crafted features, etc. They received best results (accuracy = 0.80) through the ME model and the NB classifier. Likewise, PSI2020 began similarly, but using the transformer-based neural network RoBERTa rather than traditional ML models. They adapted the pre-trained network for contextual word embedding features. To understand the performance of ML techniques on the CanLII corpus, XSA2020 designed an experiment to classify IRC labelled sentences and non-IRC sentences using Random Forest (RF), Long Short-Term Memory (LSTM), Convolutional Neural Network (CNN) and FastText. They achieved best weighted F1 of 0.72 on summaries and 0.94 on full case texts.

4.2 Argument Component Classification

This refers to the classification of segmented sentences (clauses) as particular types of argument components. In some works, the input texts have previously been identified as argumentative, or already filtered during preprocessing. In other cases, this is merged with argument information detection by adding an extra label (i.e., "N/A") and formulating it as a multi-classification problem.

MM2011 handled this task as a second text classification problem following argument information detection. The best results (premise F1 = 0.68, conclusion F1 = 0.74) were achieved by using Context-Free Grammar (CFG) and statistical classifiers (ME classifier and SVM). To simplify their experiment process, PSI2020 presumed all argumentative clauses had previously been successfully detected. Considering that a clause may act as a premise in one argument and conclusion in another, they divided this task into two binary classifications. They then applied separate RoBERTa models with the F1 measure reported individually (premise F1 = 0.86, conclusion F1 = 0.63).

The LLT Lab have built a variety of AM systems on the V/IP and BVA datasets. Using AM as a base module, GACS2015 introduced a legal document retrieval architecture where ten cases from the annotated V/IP corpus were used to train a classifier to predict component annotations of all non-gold-standard documents. This used NB, Decision Tree (DT), and Logistic Regression (LR) models with TF-IDF feature-vectors of n-grams, sub-sentences, etc. Their LR model reached the best Micro F1 (0.24) and Macro F1 (0.31), and DT achieved the best accuracy (0.97). In the study of the BVA corpus, WPDL2019 used a qualitative methodology to analyse a small sample (530 sentences) and developed rule-based scripts for component classification. They compared the result with other ML algorithms (NB, LR, and SVM) trained and tested on a large dataset (5,800 sentences). Both LR and SVM reached an average accuracy of 0.86. WSWA2019 presented an explainable classifier using Boolean search rules to categorise segmented legal text as argument components. They developed an interactive environment to create Boolean rules for both annotation and classification. One motivation for using rule-based classifiers was that they are more explainable than ML models, and required less labelled data. They trained four benchmark ML models (RF, SVM, FastText, and SKOPE-rules), which performed better than human-generated rules. WSW2020 also studied component classification on the BVA corpus from a linguistic polarity perspective. They designed a five-layer neural network with two evaluation datasets, a train-test cross validation on 50 decisions and a test-only experiment on 25 decisions. In two experiments, they achieved accuracy of 0.89 and 0.88 respectively.

Among the research of argument component (IRC-triple) classification on the CanLII corpus, XSA2020 measured three types of techniques: traditional ML model (RF), deep neural networks (LSTM, CNN), and FastText with GloVe embeddings. Among all the models, CNN and RF achieved the highest scores on case summaries (weighted $F1 = 0.63$) and full text (weighted $F1 = 0.91$). XSA2021a continued the exploration of deep neural networks. They used LSTM, CNN, BERT, and model combinations. Instead of manually mapping the IRC annotations from case summaries to full texts, they investigated whether this process can be automatic. XSA2021b expanded the previous study, demonstrating that domain-specific pre-training corpora enhance BERT models' performance in Legal AM. They then merged BERT embeddings with a bidirectional LSTM (BiLSTM) network, and proved the position information enhancement on argument component classification. Although, compared to XSA2021a, the test scores decreased, XSA2021b suggested it was caused by lack of training data.

4.3 Argument Relation Prediction

Predicting argument relations is the most difficult part of the AM pipeline, aiming to discover relations between arguments and argument components. Since the argument relation annotations vary between corpora (see Sect. 3), in this task, we include the predictions of both inner relations which link between argument components and outer relations which link between arguments.

The final stage in MM2011 is to detect relations between full arguments, which requires the determination of the limits of individual arguments and relations with surrounding arguments. They studied argumentative parsing using rhetorical structure theory and POS tagging, then parsed the text by manually derived rules into their self-defined CFG. By parsing via this CFG, MM2011 reached an accuracy around 0.60 in detecting the complete argumentation structure. In contrast to MM2011, relation prediction in PSI2020 aimed to group argumentative clauses (components) into arguments where they are implicitly connected by relations. PSI2020 simplified this task as a sentence-pair classification problem to predict whether a pair of argumentative clauses belong to the same argument. This allows individual clauses to be recognised in multiple arguments. PSI2020 used a sliding window (size = 5) to generate the sentence pairs, and assumed that all the argumentative clauses have been identified successfully. The RoBERTa classifier reached an F1 of 0.51. PSI2020 explained an extra operation was still needed to arrange the identified pairs into arguments.

Since over 20% of the argument relations in CDCP do not suit the tree structure, NPC2017 transformed the pipeline into a document-level joint learning model, and represented the argumentation as factor graphs. They aimed to predict argument component types for sentences, and argument relations for sentence pairs. Several techniques (e.g., pre-defined rules, patterns in valid graph, etc.) were applied to constrain and train the model. To represent argument components and relations in the factor graph, various types of features (e.g., hand-crafted, contextual, lexical, etc.) were stored as variables. Using GloVe embeddings, NPC2017 built a linear structured SVM, and a BiLSTM network. The linear-SVM achieved the best results on component classification (F1 = 0.73) and relation prediction (F1 = 0.27). Inspired by NPC2017, GLT2021 designed a neural network with stacked modules, which jointly performed both component classification and relation prediction (also using GloVe embeddings). The neural network consisted of a residual network model, with an LSTM network, and an attention block. They tested a new prediction strategy, using multiple models ensemble voting. In this case, they improved component classification F1 score to 0.79 and relation prediction F1 score to 0.30.

5   Conclusion and Outlook

In reviewing the development of Legal AM in the past decade, our work presents a comprehensive survey from two aspects: annotated legal corpora, and practical AM implementations. As well as identifying and analysing the available annotated corpora, our work also reviews the performance of previous ML techniques on Legal AM. During our study, we detected several remaining challenges and prospects which require future work, as follows.

Many previous Legal AM studies relied on rule-based or statistical models. Although researchers have begun switching to neural networks, much remains to be explored, especially when applying advanced NLP approaches. Supervised learning used by neural networks requires substantial annotated data, and the balance between system performance and the expert labour required for annotation is always an issue. Pre-trained NLP models (e.g., BERT) have shown strong performance on downstream tasks with limited corpora, which is a promising approach for Legal AM [36,37].

Many annotation schemes are designed according to semantic rule and knowledge graph. At present, tools to visualise the retrieved argumentation details are still required. There is potential for NLP models and knowledge graphs to be merged together to enhance Legal AM and to present text information in a way that suits legal professionals better.

The pipeline structure remains the dominant design for Legal AM. Nevertheless, error propagation remains an unavoidable issue between tasks, whereby errors in earlier stages of the pipeline have a cascading effect on later stages. This is challenging for evaluation and for practical use. We suggest that other innovative methods and tools, like dependency parsing, multi-task learning, and graph neural networks, may replace the pipeline structure. These techniques have already achieved breakthroughs in general AM research [7,35].

References

1. Besnard, P., Hunter, A.: A logic-based theory of deductive arguments. Artif. Intell. **128**(1–2), 203–235 (2001)
2. Bibal, A., Lognoul, M., de Streel, A., Frénay, B.: Legal requirements on explainability in machine learning. Artif. Intell. Law **29**(2), 149–169 (2020). https://doi.org/10.1007/s10506-020-09270-4
3. Cabrio, E., Villata, S.: Five years of argument mining: a data-driven analysis. In: IJCAI, vol. 18, pp. 5427–5433 (2018)
4. Chalkidis, I., Androutsopoulos, I., Aletras, N.: Neural legal judgment prediction in English. In: Proceedings of the 57th Annual Meeting of the Association for Computational Linguistics, pp. 4317–4323 (2019)
5. Cohen, J.: A coefficient of agreement for nominal scales. Educ. Psychol. Measure. **20**(1), 37–46 (1960)
6. Dung, P.M.: On the acceptability of arguments and its fundamental role in non-monotonic reasoning, logic programming and n-person games. Artif. Intell. **77**(2), 321–357 (1995)
7. Galassi, A., Lippi, M., Torroni, P.: Multi-task attentive residual networks for argument mining. arXiv preprint arXiv:2102.12227 (2021)
8. Grabmair, M., et al.: Introducing LUIMA: an experiment in legal conceptual retrieval of vaccine injury decisions using a UIMA type system and tools. In: Proceedings of the 15th International Conference on Artificial Intelligence and Law, pp. 69–78 (2015)
9. Lippi, M., Torroni, P.: Argument mining: a machine learning perspective. In: Black, E., Modgil, S., Oren, N. (eds.) TAFA 2015. LNCS (LNAI), vol. 9524, pp. 163–176. Springer, Cham (2015). https://doi.org/10.1007/978-3-319-28460-6_10
10. Lippi, M., Torroni, P.: Argumentation mining: state of the art and emerging trends. ACM Trans. Internet Technol. (TOIT) **16**(2), 1–25 (2016)
11. Mochales, R., Ieven, A.: Creating an argumentation corpus: do theories apply to real arguments? A case study on the legal argumentation of the ECHR. In: Proceedings of the 12th International Conference on Artificial Intelligence and Law, pp. 21–30 (2009)
12. Mochales, R., Moens, M.F.: Study on the structure of argumentation in case law. In: Legal Knowledge and Information Systems, pp. 11–20. IOS Press (2008)
13. Mochales, R., Moens, M.F.: Argumentation mining. Artif. Intell. Law **19**(1), 1–22 (2011)
14. Nallapati, R., Manning, C.D.: Legal docket-entry classification: where machine learning stumbles. In: 2008 Conference on Empirical Methods in Natural Language Processing, p. 438 (2008)
15. Niculae, V., Park, J., Cardie, C.: Argument mining with structured SVMs and RNNs. In: Proceedings of the 55th Annual Meeting of the Association for Computational Linguistics (Volume 1: Long Papers), pp. 985–995 (2017)

16. Park, J., Blake, C., Cardie, C.: Toward machine-assisted participation in eRule-making: an argumentation model of evaluability. In: Proceedings of the 15th International Conference on Artificial Intelligence and Law, pp. 206–210 (2015)

17. Park, J., Cardie, C.: A corpus of eRulemaking user comments for measuring evaluability of arguments. In: Proceedings of the Eleventh International Conference on Language Resources and Evaluation (LREC 2018) (2018)

18. Poudyal, P., Šavelka, J., Ieven, A., Moens, M.F., Gonçalves, T., Quaresma, P.: ECHR: legal corpus for argument mining. In: Proceedings of the 7th Workshop on Argument Mining, pp. 67–75 (2020)

19. Savelka, J., Walker, V.R., Grabmair, M., Ashley, K.D.: Sentence boundary detection in adjudicatory decisions in the united states. Traitement automatique des langues **58**, 21 (2017)

20. Stab, C., Gurevych, I.: Annotating argument components and relations in persuasive essays. In: Proceedings of COLING 2014, the 25th International Conference on Computational Linguistics: Technical Papers, pp. 1501–1510 (2014)

21. Teruel, M., Cardellino, C., Cardellino, F., Alemany, L.A., Villata, S.: Legal text processing within the MIREL project. In: 1st Workshop on Language Resources and Technologies for the Legal Knowledge Graph, p. 42 (2018)

22. Toulmin, S.E.: The Uses of Argument. Cambridge University Press, Cambridge (2003)

23. Urchs, S., Mitrovic, J., Granitzer, M.: Design and implementation of German legal decision corpora. In: ICAART, vol. 2, pp. 515–521 (2021)

24. Walker, V., Foerster, D., Ponce, J.M., Rosen, M.: Evidence types, credibility factors, and patterns or soft rules for weighing conflicting evidence: argument mining in the context of legal rules governing evidence assessment. In: Proceedings of the 5th Workshop on Argument Mining, pp. 68–78 (2018)

25. Walker, V.R.: A default-logic paradigm for legal fact-finding. Jurimetrics **47**, 193 (2006)

26. Walker, V.R., Carie, N., DeWitt, C.C., Lesh, E.: A framework for the extraction and modeling of fact-finding reasoning from legal decisions: lessons from the vaccine/injury project corpus. Artif. Intell. Law **19**(4), 291–331 (2011)

27. Walker, V.R., Han, J.H., Ni, X., Yoseda, K.: Semantic types for computational legal reasoning: propositional connectives and sentence roles in the veterans' claims dataset. In: Proceedings of the 16th Edition of the International Conference on Artificial Intelligence and Law, pp. 217–226 (2017)

28. Walker, V.R., Pillaipakkamnatt, K., Davidson, A.M., Linares, M., Pesce, D.J.: Automatic classification of rhetorical roles for sentences: comparing rule-based scripts with machine learning. In: ASAIL@ ICAIL (2019)

29. Walker, V.R., Strong, S.R., Walker, V.E.: Automating the classification of finding sentences for linguistic polarity. In: ASAIL@ JURIX (2020)

30. Walton, D.: Argumentation theory: a very short introduction. In: Simari, G., Rahwan, I. (eds.) Argumentation in Artificial Intelligence, pp. 1–22. Springer, Boston (2009). https://doi.org/10.1007/978-0-387-98197-0_1

31. Westermann, H., Savelka, J., Walker, V.R., Ashley, K.D., Benyekhlef, K.: Computer-assisted creation of Boolean search rules for text classification in the legal domain. In: JURIX, pp. 123–132 (2019)

32. Xu, H., Šavelka, J., Ashley, K.D.: Using argument mining for legal text summarization. In: Legal Knowledge and Information Systems, pp. 184–193. IOS Press (2020)

33. Xu, H., Savelka, J., Ashley, K.D.: Accounting for sentence position and legal domain sentence embedding in learning to classify case sentences. In: Legal Knowledge and Information Systems, pp. 33–42. IOS Press (2021)
34. Xu, H., Savelka, J., Ashley, K.D.: Toward summarizing case decisions via extracting argument issues, reasons, and conclusions. In: Proceedings of the Eighteenth International Conference on Artificial Intelligence and Law, pp. 250–254 (2021)
35. Ye, Y., Teufel, S.: End-to-end argument mining as biaffine dependency parsing. In: Proceedings of the 16th Conference of the European Chapter of the Association for Computational Linguistics: Main Volume, pp. 669–678 (2021)
36. Zhang, G., Lillis, D., Nulty, P.: Can domain pre-training help interdisciplinary researchers from data annotation poverty? A case study of legal argument mining with BERT-based transformers. In: Proceedings of the Workshop on Natural Language Processing for Digital Humanities (NLP4DH), pp. 121–130. Association for Computational Linguistics (2021)
37. Zhang, G., Nulty, P., Lillis, D.: Enhancing legal argument mining with domain pre-training and neural networks. J. Data Mining Digit. Humanit. NLP4DH (2022). https://doi.org/10.46298/jdmdh.9147

Information Extraction and Linking

Information Extraction and Linking

A Text Structural Analysis Model for Address Extraction

Rishabh Kumar[(✉)], Kamal Jakhar, Hemant Tiwari, Naresh Purre,
Priyanshu Kumar, Jiban Prakash, and Vanraj Vala

Samsung R&D Institute, Bangalore, India
{rish.kumar,kamal.jakhar,h.tiwari,naresh.purre,
priyanshu.k,p.jiban,vanraj.vala}@samsung.com

Abstract. Textual data is being generated at an enormous pace in today's world. Analyzing this data to extract actionable information is one of the biggest challenges faced by researchers. In this paper we tackle the problem of extracting addresses from unstructured texts. Postal address denotes the unique geographical information of a place, person or an organization. Extracting this information automatically with high precision is helpful for public administration & services, location based service companies, geo-spatial mapping, delivery companies, recommendation systems for tourists, OCR based event creation etc. Address formats varies widely based on countries and regions. Even within a same region people can choose to adopt different formats and notations, hence extracting addresses from text becomes a challenging and interesting task in NLP research. In this paper we propose a text structural analysis model, consisting of a novel gazetteer assisted CNN architecture. It uses structural pattern detection capabilities of a CNN to empirically prove that for address extraction task structural analysis is more efficient than pure semantic approach. We further did an ablation study to find the importance of external knowledge for our architecture.

Keywords: Address extraction · Gazetteer Assisted CNN · Text structural analysis

1 Introduction

There is a huge amount of textual data being generated across web in the form of text messages, blogs, social media posts, articles etc. Extracting relevant information from these unstructured text sources can help in providing personalized services and value addition in numerous down stream tasks like suggestion, search and recommendation. However, due to the massive volume of such data it is impossible to analyze and extract information from it manually. With the growth of social media networks and messaging apps this textual data is growing at an even faster pace. Hence, it is important to develop techniques for analyzing and extracting information from the textual data automatically.

Automatically extracting postal address information using deep learning techniques can be helpful for public administration and services, location-based

© The Author(s), under exclusive license to Springer Nature Switzerland AG 2022
P. Rosso et al. (Eds.): NLDB 2022, LNCS 13286, pp. 255–266, 2022.
https://doi.org/10.1007/978-3-031-08473-7_23

services and e-commerce companies. There are many location based applications like geo-spatial mapping for easy navigation, search engine to find nearby facilities like restaurants, hospitals etc. Address extraction can also be used for recommendation and suggestions to tourists and potential travelers. In recent time, OCR is being used to provide various suggestions like event creation from invitation, saving business cards etc. Hence extracting entities like address from this data can result in providing more intelligent suggestions.

Researchers have tackled the problem of extracting Named Entities from texts and achieved good results for the task [8]. However, in these tasks the goal is to tag words that denote a place, more formally known as places of interests, rather than extracting complete street addresses. Other researches have tried to extract street addresses from unstructured text using only knowledge sources [14] or statistical approaches [15] or only deep learning techniques [11]. Some researchers have also focused on tagging different components like unit number, street name, province, postal code etc. of an already extracted address [1].

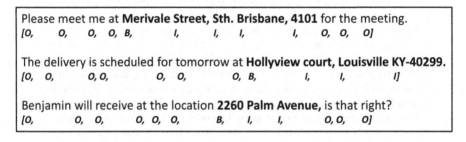

Fig. 1. Examples showing that in a sentence containing address information, the address part (bold) contains a high density of Uppercase letters (red), Punctuations (brown) and Numbers (blue). This shows that a structural analysis of a sentence can help to detect the presence of an address. Below each word is the label predicted by our model where 'B' denotes - starting of an address, 'I' - part of the address and 'O' - not an address. (Color figure online)

Even though no fixed format is followed while writing an address but they are usually characterized by a higher density of uppercase letters, special characters, punctuations and numbers. Figure 1 shows few examples from our training set highlighted to depict these characteristics. This provides us a motivation to explore ways for exploiting this property of addresses to extract them from unstructured texts. CNNs have proved their usefulness in detecting the presence of such patterns. They are effectively used in many NLP applications [19]. We also explore the effect of using external knowledge in the form of a gazetteer of famous places, states, cities and countries for address extraction. Although knowledge sources have been used previously for this purpose but using it as a feature for CNN model has not been tried before.

1.1 Our Contributions

The main contributions of our paper is as follows.

- We propose a novel Gazetteer Assisted CNN architecture (Gaze-CNN) for address extraction from unstructured text.
- We prove the effectiveness of CNNs to detect the patterns in a sentence at character level and word level for the task of address extraction.
- We show empirically that gazetteer assisted structural analysis by CNN is more suitable for address extraction than pure semantic analysis.
- We also did an ablation study to find the importance of external knowledge gazetteer in our architecture.

2 Related Work

We now showcase the previous works in the domain of entity extraction and the use of external knowledge sources and deep neural networks for the task of address extraction.

2.1 NER and Use of Gazetteer for Address Extraction

There have been various attempts to classify intent and extract the related entities. The very first dedicated study was in Sixth Message Understanding Conference (MUC-6) [7] as a part of Information Extraction subtask named "Named Entity Recognition and Classification (NERC)". However attempts to extract entities also date to as early as 1991 when Rau et al. [13] tried to extract company names using handcrafted rules and heuristics.

Subsequently the handcrafted features gave way to statistical methods of extraction e.g. usage of Hidden Markov Models [15], Conditional Random Fields [10] and Support Vector Machines [3] to extract the entities. However these methods required extensive empirical hand crafting of features to get the best possible performance from models. The need for feature engineering was reduced by emergence of deep learning in 2010s when Collobert et al. [5] present a CNN based architecture and showed improved state of the art performance at time. In 2015 Huang et al. [8] used Bi-LSTM to achieve state of the art performance. In 2019, xiaoya et al. [9] framed the NER problem as Machine Reading Comprehension Problem. However, all the above mentioned work focus on extracting specific places of interest from the text and not street addresses. Also, they don't take in to account the unique structural characteristics of entities similar to address before extraction.

There have also been efforts to use knowledge contexts for improving the entity recognition, Banerjee et al. [4] formulated the NER task as Knowledge Guided QA task and observed significant improvement in performance. Specifically for address extraction, Schmidt [14] suggested use of freely available knowledge to create patterns and gazetteers to improve accuracy. Paolo et al. [11] also used hybrid approach of NLP techniques with gazetteers.

2.2   Convolution Neural Networks in NLP

Convolution Neural Network are widely used in image processing algorithms due to their capability of detecting patterns effectively. However, CNN can also prove effective in understanding natural language and patterns in written text. As shown by [19], CNN are specially good for keyphrase extraction and question answer matching tasks. Vu et al. [16] also reports better performance of CNN for the task of relation extraction compared to other deep learning networks like RNN. The effectiveness of CNN over RNN based architectures for various NLP tasks is also verified by the authors of [2].

There is a need to continuously develop and improve methods which can take advantage of existing and novel approaches by combining them to deliver good results for the task of address extraction. In this paper, we combined the effectiveness of CNN to detect patterns and the power of gazetteer to provide external knowledge to create a novel gazetteer assisted CNN architecture for address extraction.

3   Methodology

In this section we formally define the task of address extraction as a sequence labeling problem. We also explain the details of Convolution Neural Networks and External Knowledge Sources in the form of Gazetteer. We then describe our proposed architecture in detail.

3.1   Problem Formulation

Given a sentence $S = [W_1, W_2...W_n]$ where W_i represents i^{th} word of the sentence, our task is to generate a sequence of output labels $L = [l_1, l_2...l_n]$ corresponding to each word of the input sentence where $l_i \in \{B, I, O\}$,

- **B** if the given word is the first word of the address.
- **I** if the given word is the part of the address.
- **O** if the given word is not the part of the address.

Figure 1 shows some sample input and output for the address extraction task, formulated as a sequence to sequence problem.

3.2   Convolution Neural Networks

Convolution layers are the foundation of CNNs, these layers are used to extract features from data. As shown in Fig. 2 this layer performs a dot product between two matrices, where one matrix is a set of learnable parameters known as kernels/filters, other matrix is a part of the input. The kernel matrix slides over the input matrix and produces feature maps, which emphasizes the important features and patterns. A CNN is able to capture spatial and temporal dependency of the input. We then use max pooling to extract dominant features from the

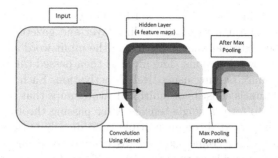

Fig. 2. Working of a convolution layer. Input values are convoluted using kernel to produce feature maps in each hidden layer. The dominant features are extracted using max pooling operation

feature map. Max pooling down samples the input along its spatial dimensions by taking the maximum value over an input window (of size defined by pool size) for each channel of the input. Just like images can be represented as an array of pixel values, we can represent the text as an array of vectors (each word mapped to a specific vector in a vector space composed of the entire vocabulary) that can be processed with the help of a CNN. Given a sequence of words $[W_1, W_2...W_n]$, each word is associated with an embedding vector of dimension 'D'. A 1-D convolution of width 'k' is the result of moving a sliding-window of size 'k' over the sentence, and applying the same convolution filter to each window in the sequence, i.e. a dot-product between the concatenation of the embedding vectors and a weight vector 'u' This is then often followed by a non-linear activation function.

3.3 Knowledge Gazetteer

External knowledge has proven its usefulness in many entity extraction tasks. Augmenting the feature vector using task specific knowledge helps the upstream models/algorithms to generalize better. External knowledge can be efficiently used as part of entity extraction pipeline using space and time efficient knowledge gazetteer as shown by Graf and Lemire [6]. For the task of address extraction we select the list of famous places, states, cities and countries (details mentioned in Sect. 4.2) to be the part of gazetteer. The gazetteer is not required to be an exhaustive list of all the possible places but rather a hint provided to the model for extraction of address. Input sentence is augmented using gazetteer knowledge before passing to the model.

3.4 Gaze-CNN: Gazetteer Assisted CNN Architecture

As shown in Fig. 3 the Gaze-CNN architecture consists of three channeled input. The first channel is formed by splitting the input sentence at character level. Each character is passed through a randomly initialized, trainable embedding layer.

Other two channels are formed using word level inputs. Each word of the input sentence is passed through word embedding layer and gazetteer augmentation. The gazetteer uses external knowledge to tag the input word as country, states, cities and other known locations. The input is then passed through convolution layer followed by max pooling using 'ReLU' activation. Each convolution layer from the three channels consists of multiple feature maps that are then flattened and concatenated to form a single tensor. After passing through another dense layer, the input is passed through multiple time distributed dense layers with 'ReLU' activation. These connected time distributed layers ensure the temporal dependency between words of the sentences and produce one output label out of B, I, O for each input word using softmax activation function. Thus gazetteer

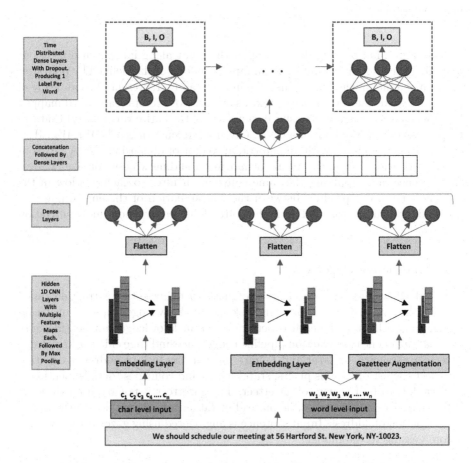

Fig. 3. Architecture of Gazetteer Assisted CNN model. The input sentence is passed into three channels namely character, word and gazetteer augmented input. After passing through multiple convolution and max pooling layers the output is flattened and concatenated. This tensor is passed through another dense layer followed by Time Distributed dense layers to produce one output label (B, I, O) per word.

assisted CNN architecture allows the model to recognize spatial and temporal dependency of the input sentences and learn pattern specific to addresses at both character and word level. The external knowledge helps the model to generalize on unknown data using tagging from the gazetteer. We used weighted categorical cross entropy loss function and adam optimizer to train our model. More details about hyper parameters and implementation can be found in Sect. 4.2

4   Experiments

In this section we describe the datasets used in our experiments for training and evaluation, the implementation details of our proposed model and the details of baselines and metrics used for evaluation of our model.

Table 1. Details of address dataset used

Type	Number of countries	Count of samples	Avg. words per sample	Avg. chars per sample
Training	6	31930	23	133
Validation	6	3548	22	145
Testing	8	8520	23	138

Table 2. Number of samples from each country in the dataset

Country	Training	Validation	Testing
Australia	5321	591	1065
Bangladesh	5325	596	1085
Canada	5348	630	1100
Singapore	5315	590	1050
United Kingdom	5321	591	1065
United States	5300	550	1020
India	–	–	1070
New Zealand	–	–	1065

4.1   Datasets

For the task of postal address extraction from unstructured texts there is a lack of good quality standard datasets. Hence, we created our own dataset, with the help of professional annotators for ground truth tagging, by merging address of multiple countries provided by Deepparse [18] and dialogue context for location provided by Google DSTC Schema Guided Dialogue [12]. Table 1 shows the count of samples and number of unique countries present in training, testing and validation split of the dataset. It also shows the average count of words and characters per sentence for each of the split.

Table 2 shows that we used addresses from 6 countries 'United States', 'Australia', 'United Kingdom', 'Canada', 'Bangladesh' & 'Singapore' to include multiple address formats from different regions of the world. For training and validation splits we have more than 31k and 3.5k samples respectively. In testing set of 8.5k samples we have also added the addresses from 'India' and 'New Zealand' along with previously mentioned countries to test the generalization capability of the model on new address formats. These addresses were inserted in the location related dialogues provided by google-dstc to finally generate conversational input sentences with address.

4.2   Implementation and Training Details

As mentioned in Sect. 3.1 we have formulated address extraction as a sequence to sequence labeling problem, where each word is assigned a label $l_i \in B, I, O$. Since, for any given sentence it will have much more non address words (label O) compared to address words (label B and I) the data is highly biased towards 'O' labels. To overcome this we have used weighted categorical cross entropy loss function with weights of B, I, O as 7, 1, 0.25 respectively. These weights were calculated based on the ratio of labels in training data. The embedding layer provides 100 dimensional embedding for both char and word level input. The Knowledge Gazetteer sourced from Geonames [17] consists of 251 countries, 1k popular locations, 50k states and cities sorted by population. The entire gazetteer was compressed to a size of just 102 KB using [6].

We used two 1-D Convolution Layers of kernel size 2 and 4 respectively, each containing 32 feature maps with 'ReLU' activation. The pool size of max pooling layer was 3. The dense layer after flattening and concatenation consisted of 256, 200 units respectively with 'ReLU' activation and the Time Distributed layer consists of dense layer with 128, 64 units with a dropout of 0.2. The final output was provided by softmax layer of size 3 denoting the scores of each of the three labels for each word. All the hyper parameters were selected based on performance over validation set using Grid Search.

The model was trained on a system with Intel core i7-6700HQ CPU and Nvidia 920MX GPU with 16 GB RAM. Training was performed for 10 epochs and took 1.5 h to complete using tensorflow v2.6.

4.3   Baselines and Metrics

To compare the gazetteer assisted CNN architecture with pure semantic based approaches we evaluated our model against the following baselines.

- **Word BiLstm:** Word level BiLstm model (WordBiLstm).
- **Character BiLstm:** Character level BiLstm model (CharBiLstm).
- **Word & Character BiLstm:** Concatenation of Word and Character level features followed by BiLstm layers (Word + Char BiLstm).

- **Word BiLstm with GloVe:** Word level BiLstm with contextual 200 dimensions GloVe embeddings (GloVeBiLstm).

We further compared different CNN architectures for our ablation study to determine the effect of using gazetteer on address extraction task.

- **Word CNN without Gazetteer:** Our proposed architecture without character level input and gazetteer augmentation (WordCnn).
- **Character CNN without Gazetteer:** Our proposed architecture without word level input and gazetteer augmentation (CharCnn).
- **Word & Character CNN without Gazetteer:** Our proposed architecture without gazetteer augmentation (Word + Char Cnn).

All the BiLstm based models used 4 hidden BiLstm layers of 256, 128, 128, 64 units and 'ReLU' activation with a recurrent dropout of 0.2, followed by 2 Time Distributed dense layer of 100, 50 units respectively. The output was predicted using softmax activation and weighted categorical cross entropy loss with weights same as mentioned in Sect. 4.2. To ensure fair comparison of the models we selected the architectures in such a way so as to keep the number of trainable parameters approximately similar in all the experiments. The hyper parameters for each experiment was selected using Grid Search.

We compare the performance of our model using precision, recall and f1 scores of the 'B' and 'I' tags. We also find the accuracy of the models for extracting address, by forming the predicted address by concatenating 'B' and 'I' tagged words.

5   Results

This section showcase the results of our experiments on the proposed architecture and compares it to the baselines mentioned in Sect. 4.3.

5.1   Performance of Gaze-CNN Model

Performance of Gaze-CNN model is evaluated on the dataset mentioned in Sect. 4.1. For each word of the input sentence we predict a label (B, I, O) indicating whether the word is starting of an address, part of the address or not an address. We present the precision, recall and f1 scores for B and I tags in Table 3. We also extracted the final address for the input by concatenating all the consecutive 'I' tagged words, which are present just after a 'B' tagged word (Fig. 1). The accuracy for this is shown in Table 4. From the two tables, we observe that the Gaze-Cnn model which is a combination of character level, word level and gazetteer extracted features outperforms all other models. It shows a precision of 0.96 for 'B' tags and 0.97 for 'I' tags. Further the recall for both 'B' and 'I' tag is 0.98, resulting in an F1 score of 0.969 and 0.974 respectively. The Gaze-Cnn model shows 92.4% accuracy for the final address extraction task.

Table 3. Precision, recall and F1 scores for B and I tags.

Model	B tag			I tag		
	Precision	Recall	F1	Precision	Recall	F1
Gaze-Cnn	**0.96**	**0.98**	**0.969**	**0.97**	0.98	**0.974**
WordCnn	0.89	0.92	0.904	0.85	0.93	0.888
CharCnn	0.91	0.92	0.914	0.91	0.96	0.934
Word+Char Cnn	0.93	0.94	0.934	0.94	0.95	0.944
WordBiLstm	0.92	0.97	0.944	0.89	0.92	0.904
CharBiLstm	0.84	0.85	0.844	0.88	0.91	0.894
Word+Char BiLstm	0.92	0.95	0.934	0.94	0.97	0.954
GloVeBiLstm	0.94	0.98	0.959	0.94	0.99	0.964

Table 4. Accuracy values for address extraction by concatenation of B and I tags

Model	Accuracy (%)
Gaze-Cnn	**92.4**
WordCnn	83.5
CharCnn	88.1
Word+Char Cnn	88.7
WordBiLstm	86.1
CharBiLstm	81.6
Word+Char BiLstm	86.5
GloVeBiLstm	90.3

5.2 Comparison with Other Architectures

From Tables 3 and 4 we observe that the Gaze-CNN model is better than all
the pure semantic as well as structural analysis without gazetteer, approaches in
terms of F1 score and accuracy. It shows a 2.1% increase in accuracy from the
next best model GloVeBiLstm, which uses GloVe embedding for contexual and
semantic relationships between words. Other CNN models like CharCnn also
outperforms BiLstm models like WordBiLstm and CharBiLstm. It is interesting
to note that for CNN models the character level model, performs better than
word level model by 4.6% whereas for BiLstm models the word level model
outperforms character level model by 4.5%. This shows that for CNN character
level features are more informative and for BiLstm, word level features hold
more value. Combining word and character level features is beneficial for both
the approaches with Word + Char Cnn and BiLstm showing 88.7% and 86.5%
accuracy respectively. The GloVe BiLstm model performs better than any other
bilstm model with 90.3% accuracy, 0.959 F1 score for B Tag and 0.964 F1 score
for I Tag. This shows the importance of contextual semantic embedding for

bilstm models. However, it still falls short in all the metrics when compared to our Gaze-CNN architecture.

5.3 Importance of Knowledge Gazetteer

The Gaze-CNN architecture uses external knowledge gazetteer to tag countries, states, cities and popular locations. This tagging of known words provides extra hint to the model while extracting address. This is verified by the 3.7% improvement in accuracy shown by Gaze-Cnn model over Word+Char Cnn. The gazetteer based model also shows better precision, recall and F1 scores for both B and I tags compared to other non gazetteer augmented models. It is because of this knowledge that the Gaze-Cnn outperforms GloVe BiLstm model whereas Word+Char Cnn fails to do so, thereby showcasing the effectiveness and power of knowledge gazetteer for address extraction task.

6 Conclusion and Future Work

In this paper, we presented a novel Text Structural Analysis Model which uses a Gazetteer Assisted CNN architecture (Gaze-CNN) for address extraction from unstructured texts. We formulated the problem of address extraction as a sequence to sequence labeling task and did extensive comparisons of our proposed architecture with multiple pure semantic based approaches. We showcased that our model outperforms other architectures thereby proving its effectiveness for this task. The importance of gazetteer was highlighted by our ablation study which showed that the same CNN architecture without augmentation from external knowledge is not at par in accuracy with the Gaze-CNN model. We also showcased the generalizing capabilities of our model by including addresses from different countries of the world and previously unseen formats in the testing set.

Future scope of the work include extending Gaze-CNN architecture for other entities that can utilize its pattern detection capabilities. We also aim to extend the approach for other languages. In addition, the Gaze-CNN model can be used for downstream tasks in NLP and recommendation systems.

References

1. Abid, N., ul Hasan, A., Shafait, F.: DeepParse: a trainable postal address parser. In: 2018 Digital Image Computing: Techniques and Applications (DICTA), pp. 1–8 (2018). https://doi.org/10.1109/DICTA.2018.8615844
2. Adel, H., Schütze, H.: Exploring different dimensions of attention for uncertainty detection. In: Proceedings of the 15th Conference of the Association for Computational Linguistics, pp. 22–34 (2017). https://aclanthology.org/E17-1003
3. Asahara, M., Matsumoto, Y.: Japanese named entity extraction with redundant morphological analysis. In: Proceedings of the 2003 Conference of the North American Chapter of the Association for Computational Linguistics on Human Language Technology, vol. 1, pp. 8–15 (2003). https://doi.org/10.3115/1073445.1073447

4. Banerjee, P., Pal, K.K., Devarakonda, M., Baral, C.: Biomedical named entity recognition via knowledge guidance and question answering. ACM Trans. Comput. Healthcare **2**(4) (2021). https://doi.org/10.1145/3465221

5. Collobert, R., Weston, J.: A unified architecture for natural language processing: deep neural networks with multitask learning. In: Proceedings of the 25th International Conference on Machine Learning, pp. 160–167. Association for Computing Machinery (2008). https://doi.org/10.1145/1390156.1390177

6. Graf, T.M., Lemire, D.: Xor filters: faster and smaller than bloom and cuckoo filters. CoRR (2019). http://arxiv.org/abs/1912.08258

7. Grishman, R., Sundheim, B.: Message understanding conference- 6: a brief history. In: COLING 1996 Volume 1: The 16th International Conference on Computational Linguistics (1996). https://aclanthology.org/C96-1079

8. Huang, Z., Xu, W., Yu, K.: Bidirectional LSTM-CRF models for sequence tagging. CoRR (2015). http://arxiv.org/abs/1508.01991

9. Li, X., Feng, J., Meng, Y., Han, Q., Wu, F., Li, J.: A unified MRC framework for named entity recognition. CoRR (2019). http://arxiv.org/abs/1910.11476

10. McCallum, A., Li, W.: Early results for named entity recognition with conditional random fields, feature induction and web-enhanced Lexicons. In: Proceedings of the Seventh Conference on Natural Language Learning at HLT-NAACL 2003, pp. 188–191 (2003). https://aclanthology.org/W03-0430

11. Nesi, P., Pantaleo, G., Tenti, M.: Ge(o)lo(cator): geographic information extraction from unstructured text data and web documents. In: 2014 9th International Workshop on Semantic and Social Media Adaptation and Personalization, pp. 60–65 (2014). https://doi.org/10.1109/SMAP.2014.27

12. Rastogi, A., Zang, X., Sunkara, S., Gupta, R., Khaitan, P.: Towards scalable multi-domain conversational agents: the schema-guided dialogue dataset. In: Proceedings of the AAAI Conference on Artificial Intelligence, vol. 34, pp. 8689–8696 (2020)

13. Rau, L.F.: Extracting company names from text. In: Proceedings the Seventh IEEE Conference on Artificial Intelligence Application. IEEE Computer Society (1991)

14. Schmidt, S., Manschitz, S., Rensing, C., Steinmetz, R.: Extraction of address data from unstructured text using free knowledge resources. In: Proceedings of the 13th International Conference on Knowledge Management and Knowledge Technologies (2013). https://doi.org/10.1145/2494188.2494193

15. Taghva, K., Coombs, J.S., Pereda, R., Nartker, T.A.: Address extraction using hidden Markov models. In: Document Recognition and Retrieval XII, vol. 5676, pp. 119–126. International Society for Optics and Photonics (2005)

16. Vu, N.T., Adel, H., Gupta, P., Schütze, H.: Combining recurrent and convolutional neural networks for relation classification. CoRR (2016). http://arxiv.org/abs/1605.07333

17. Wick, M.: Geonames. http://www.geonames.org/

18. Yassine, M., Beauchemin, D.: DeepParse: a state-of-the-art deep learning multinational addresses parser (2020). https://deepparse.org

19. Yin, W., Kann, K., Yu, M., Schütze, H.: Comparative study of CNN and RNN for natural language processing. CoRR (2017). http://arxiv.org/abs/1702.01923

Extracting Domain Terms from Data Model Elements
Task Overview in One Implementation

Esmé Manandise$^{(\boxtimes)}$ [iD]

Intuit Marine Way, 2632, Mountain View, CA 94043, USA
esme_manandise@intuit.com

Abstract. In the compliance domain of tax laws, a barrier to term extraction from *documents written in natural language* is getting a sizable training set of documents to train a well-grounded term-extraction model. To alleviate term-extraction *silence*, i.e. the outcome of the automated process missing legitimate term candidates, we extract terms from a string datatype that is written in a *quasi-natural* language. Domain software applications rely on structured content in XML documents for their processes. One type of XML data is the element; elements have names typically written in a *variant* of a natural language. Term extraction restores the element names to the detected natural language. These extracted expressions are either novel terms for our terminology or are flagged as synonymous expressions to existing terms. Increasing term coverage improves semantic parsing, query understanding and explanation generation. For a subset of XML documents of one tax-domain software application, we augment the existing terminology by 49%.

Keywords: Abjad · Digraphs · Data model element · Disemvowelment · Term extraction · Trigraphs · XML/XSD documents · XPaths

1 Introduction

Extracting automatically single-token and multi-token terms as the string units that denote the concepts and entities in a domain is a core task of knowledge modeling and natural language processing (NLP). Typically, terms are extracted from unstructured or semi-structured domain-relevant texts in machine-readable format.

Various automated approaches to term extraction from texts have been implemented with great results (for a survey [15]). However, co-occurrence/collocation statistical/probabilistic-based methods for promoting term candidates fail to extract terms that appear infrequently in domain corpora. For instance, in our domain, terminology *silence* can be particularly acute as there are many instances

P. Rosso et al. (Eds.): NLDB 2022, LNCS 13286, pp. 267–278, 2022.
https://doi.org/10.1007/978-3-031-08473-7_24

of terms each of which appears only once in the entire corpus[1] [12]. Extracting infrequently-occurring terms like *universal child care* or *mining exploration tax credit* is not only crucial to generate terminologies with adequate coverage [1] [6, 7, 11], but many tasks such as query understanding, semantic parsing and explanation generation rely on pre-extracted terms to represent utterance meaning accurately [13].

We explored extracting domain terms which, while infrequent in our raw textual corpus, are more frequently instantiated in our domain structured content.

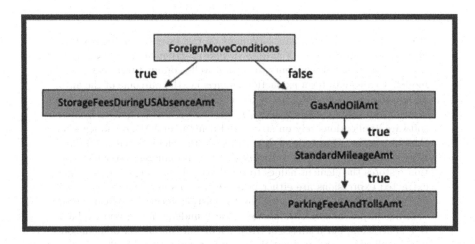

Fig. 1. Simple model graph for expression *ForeignMoveConditions*.

A necessary step in the generation of software code for applications is data modeling for the domain under focus. Data modeling is not only about formalizing and structuring the data as objects and relationships within specific domain application, but it also consists in specifying **explicitly and unambiguously**, in some language notation, the concepts, entities and relationships that define the domain (see Fig. 1). The smallest data unit is a data model element (**DME**).

DMEs require that they be named. Once named, they become the discrete meaningful expressions of the language defined manually by the domain-application experts and engineers. Together, they form the *vocabulary* of the domain model. Typically, they are units of domain meaning (single-token or multi-token terms), that *backend automated processes* manipulate.

In Fig. 1, we have a tax concept for moving outside of the United States (*ForeignMoveConditions*). While the edges signify the relational conditions that need satisfaction, the nodes (in blue) correspond to the related concepts. The node

---

[1] The corpus referenced here is the collection of tax forms and related instructions published in 2019 by the United States Internal Revenue Service (IRS) and the Canada Revenue Agency (CRA).

labels or DMEs, respectively, *StorageFeesDuringUSAbsenceAmt*, *GasAndOil-Amt*, *StandardMileageAmt*, and *ParkingFeesAndTollsAmt*, are domain terms.

At the most elementary level, the DME terms are encoded according to predefined naming and spelling conventions. In Fig. 1, they each present with *textbook* quality-easy to decompose and to understand by English-speaking individuals, and by automated extraction processes[2].

DMEs do not occur in isolation. Typically, DMEs are stored in documents in Extended Markup Language (XML) or XML Schema Definition (XSD) language. Elements and their defining content are delimited by logic and functional start- and end-tags (see Fig. 2 for single element named *DeductibleClergyMileageAmt*).

```
<xsd:element name="DeductibleClergyMileageAmt" type="USAmountType" minOccurs="0">
        <xsd:annotation>
            <xsd:documentation>
                <LineNumber>2A</LineNumber>
                <ELFFieldNumber>0040</ELFFieldNumber>
            </xsd:documentation>
        </xsd:annotation>
</xsd:element>
```

Fig. 2. DME with context in XSD format.

This paper describes **broadly** the motivation behind and an approach for extracting terms from a collection of data model elements. For our purpose, the data model elements are collected as XPaths expressions[3]. The implementation exploits established statistical and corpus-based techniques and libraries for measuring edit distance and similarities to extract the mappings between term candidates [2,12,13]. The combination of extracting terms from both DMEs and documents written in natural language is particularly suitable for software-application domains where training data is scarce and accuracy of interpretation is of high importance for automated processes that reference terms [13]. We provide background description for the task of generating automatically executable code from raw tax laws, which are *natively* rich in domain terms. The discussion references North American income-tax forms. In one experiment, we augment the existing terminology by 49% with new terms mined from DMEs.

---

[2] The spelling convention indicators are clearly detectable. Camel notation with uppercase letter signifies word boundaries for individual single-token term. For instance, *ParkingFeesAndTollsAmt* has 4 tokens and one abbreviation.

[3] Single DMEs are embedded in XML paths that provide local context like natural-language tokens in a phrase or utterance. For instance, *IRS1040/WagesSalaries AndTipsWorksheet/TotalWagesSalariesAndTips /TotalOtherNonEarned-Income*. The single DMEs are separated by forward slashes.

2 Mining DMEs for the Good of a NLP Pipeline

In a pilot project, we explored the feasibility of accelerating the generation of executable code by translating automatically tax laws written in English into executable code. Figure 3 shows a simple tax arithmetic calculation *'Enter the smallest of line 3, 4 or 5'* and its XML conversion[4].

```
Enter the smallest of line 3, 4 or 5
                |
                ▼
<Node name=
    "/Temporary/MinimumOfPrimaryTaxpayerAndTotalQualifieddExpensesOrLimitAmt">
  <Inputs>
    <Input>xxxx/xxxx//IRSxxxx/EarnedIncomeOfPrimaryTaxpayerAmt</Input>
    <Input>xxxx/xxxx//IRSxxxx/TotalQualifiedExpensesOrLimitAmt</Input>
  </Inputs>
  <Gist>
    <Minimum>
      <InputRoles>
        <Value>xxxx/xxxx//IRSxxxx/EarnedIncomeOf PrimaryTaxpayerAmt</Value>
        <Value>xxxx/xxxx//IRSxxxx/TotalQualifiedExpensesOrLimitAmt</Value>
      </InputRoles>
      <Configuration>
        <SkipToMinimumInput>xxxx/xxxx//IRSxxxx/TotalQualifiedExpensesOrLimitAmt,
                            xxxx/xxxx//IRSxxxx/PrimaryEarnedIncomeAmt
        </SkipToMinimumInput>
      </Configuration>
    </Minimum>
  </Gist>
</Node>
```

Fig. 3. Paired arithmetic calculation and XML conversion.

We designed a NLP pipeline that consists of various modules where the output of one process is input to another downstream component. The generation of XML executable code from raw tax laws is an end-to-end process with no-human in the loop (see Fig. 4).

After content extraction from PDF documents[5], logic-based semantic parsing [13,16] outputs bracketed expressions to represent utterances. The parsers use terms as atoms with which to build the bracketed semantic expressions. Terms can be either predicates and/or arguments depending on the syntactic and semantic function they play in the utterances (see Table. 1).

---

[4] XML has been anonymized and simplified.

[5] On 500 individual tax forms, content structuring from PDFs extracts with 95% accuracy.

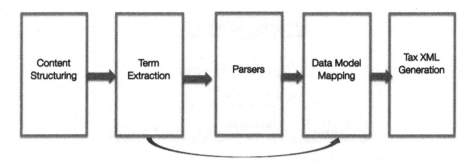

Fig. 4. NLP pipeline for conversion from raw tax laws to tax XML.

For instance, the second English utterance in Table 1 states that the smallest[6] amount of two amounts must be elected (*min operator.*) The first amount is a dollar constant amount; the second is the total amount of line 101 and line 104 for the tax concept of *employment income*[7].

Table 1. Tax form utterances and corresponding semantic parsing representations

No	Tax Form Utterances	Semantic Parsing
1	Enter the sum of exclusion of income from Puerto Rico and form 4563 line 15.	add(exclusion_of_income(puerto_rico),form(4563,line(15)))
2	Enter $1,195 or the total of your employment income you reported on lines 101 and 104 of your return, whichever is less.	min(1195, employment_income(add(line(101),line(104))))
3	Enter $75,300 if married filing jointly or qualifying widow(er)	ifte(or(eq(filing status(taxpayer),married_filing_jointly), eq(filing status(taxpayer),qualifying_widow(er))),75300)

3   Term Extraction

For term extraction[8], we use a combination of n-gram and word co-occurrence statistical analysis for noun-phrase identification plus validation rules to automatically check for the well-formedness of the multi-token candidates. On a corpus of 82.9k sentences from IRS income-tax forms and 187.6k sentences from associated instruction documents, we extract valid 13k terms. The terminology is used by the semantic parsing and the data-model mapping modules.

---

[6] The notion of smallest is conveyed by the relative clause at the end of the utterance *whichever is less.*

[7] We use underscores to bind together single tokens in a multi-token term.

[8] Publicly-available tax terminologies are relatively small in size (less than a thousand entries). Typically, they are published by government agencies, private outfits and international organizations like *Organisation for Economic Co-operation and Development.*

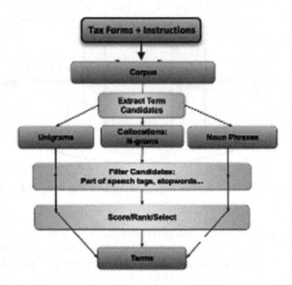

Fig. 5. Term extraction process.

3.1   *Silence* in Term Extraction

Semantic parsing must determine the dependencies between the individual tokens in an utterance. For parsing, multi-token terms are in fact *single* monolithic literal strings. The parser need not parse the individual tokens within the terms. However, when potential multi-token terms are missing from the terminology used for parsing, there are more tokens available to parse, which increases the chances of inaccurate parses [8,12,13].

Inaccurate parsing directly impacts the interpretation of utterances [4,10]. A downstream component will take the incoming input as truth of what needs further manipulation. As the original input moves down the pipeline, the transformation from one format into another can no longer affect the semantic dependencies already identified[9].

Consider the case of coordination scope. The expressions *married and retired* versus *tuition and fees*. The expression *married and retired* is not a term but a Boolean expression. For a correct interpretation, each member of the coordination must be separately verified, i.e. whether a taxpayer status is married and whether a taxpayer status is retired. If both are true, something specific to this state ensues, otherwise not. In contrast, *tuition and fees* describes a class of transactions[10] specific to tax educational-related forms and instructions. However, the originally out-of-vocabulary or silent term *tuition and fees* was interpreted by the pipeline as a Boolean operation requiring the independent verification of each coordinated member *tuition* and *fees*.

---

[9] This type of correction closer to XML generation would be costly corrective backtracking.

[10] In effect, it is a label for descriptive educational categories.

3.2 Closely-Related *Silent* (S) Examples

For parsing, multi-token terms are string singletons; their internal structure remains opaque. Most importantly, having multi-token terms enables semantic parsing to represent similar dependencies similarly and to do so independently of the internal complexity of multi-token terms.

Table 2. Utterances with terms and *Silent* terms

No	Term	Tax Form Utterances	Semantic Parsing
1	Yes	amount for an eligible dependant, claim $85.00	ifte(eligible_dependant,85.00)
2	S	amount for a qualified dependant, claim $85.00	ifte(dependant(qualified),85.00)
3	Yes	amount for a single parent's qualified dependant, claim $64.00	ifte(single_parent_qualified_dependant,64.00)
4	S	amount for a single parent's eligible dependant, claim $64.00	ifte(eligible dependant(single_parent),64.00)

In Table 2, utterances 1 and 2 differ by the tokens *eligible* and *qualified*. In 1, *eligible* is part of the term *eligible_dependant*. Utterance 3 contains one single four-token term *single_parent_qualified_dependant*; utterance 4 counts two separate two-token terms, namely, *single_parent* and *eligible_dependant*. In utterances 2 and 4 with silent terms, the parser parses *qualified* and *single_parent* as left modifiers to the head of the noun phrases.[11]

Intuitively, each of the 4 utterances should be of the form *ifte X, Y* where *X* is one multi-token term with no internal structure for the parser to consume [4].

This type of infelicitous discrepancy in predicate-argument or head-modifier alignments across syntactically- and/or semantically-similar utterances percolates to downstream components jeopardizing accuracy during the conversion to XML name elements, input elements, or value elements (see Fig. 3).

4 At Last: A Hypothesis and Data

In addition to named elements, XML and XSD documents contain human-made annotations in natural language. These annotations correspond to either terms, lexical definitions, paraphrases, or synonymous variants *not only* of the DMEs themselves, *but also* of the terms extracted from tax documents. Clearly, tax documents written for filing by humans do not need the depth of semantic granularity that automation requires. DMEs are defining features of tax concepts and entities, and as such are a resource of domain knowledge to be leveraged by parsing and other tasks.

---

[11] The modifiers are enclosed in parentheses.

4.1 Hypothesis

Given that the total number of single DMEs (40K) is more than three times the terminology resulting from term extraction from documents (13K), and given that DMEs denote domain concepts, entities and relations, we hypothesize that a subset of DMEs correspond to *silent* terms, i.e. terms that automatic term extraction missed because of data sparsity in out raw-text corpus.

4.2 Data

XSD Descriptions. In addition to the documents in PDF format written for human consumption, the IRS provides a schema, called *Modern eFiling* (MeF) [9], for tax-preparation software development. The MeF schema serves as seed canonical tax model for building tax preparation software strongly focusing on **tax compliance**. The description of MeF elements is stored in the element annotation inside the documentation for the element. Consider the simple example in (Fig. 6). The element *FirstNm* is fully spelled out in the description annotation as *First Name*.

XPaths. XPaths like ***Form1040/WagesAndSalariesAndTipsWorksheet/ TotalWagesAndSalariesAndTips/TotalOtherNonEarnedIncome*** specify the information to extract[12]. It is a language that is used for document queries and scraping the web. Node names in XML documents often consist of XPath names. In the example above, the XPath tells that the DME *TotalOtherNonEarnedIncome* can be figured out by using the worksheet for 'Wages, Salaries and Tips' (DME *WagesAndSalariesAndTipsWorksheet*) of tax form *IRS F1040*. In a query system, the queries in natural language can be mapped onto the text descriptions of XPaths in the XML documents.

One tax software application version counts some 400,000 XPaths in various functional categories (Table 3).

From Raw DME Extraction to English Translation. For our pilot experiment, we extracted randomly 100,000 XPaths from a collection of some 400,000. We then split each of the 100,000 XPaths (list 1) into individual phrases using the forward slash. This process resulted in more than 140,000 individual DMEs (list 2), counting duplicated DMEs. Finally, we selected randomly another 100,000 individual DMEs from list 2 (Table 4). Each DME was tokenized at word boundaries indicated by the uppercase in Camel notation. Each token was then looked up in our single- and multi-token terminologies. The tokens that were not found by this simple lookup were further automatically analyzed for consonant and vowel distributions, which reveal a high incidence of tokens as pure consonant clusters (digraph and trigraph sequences). Individual tokens with DMEs are often written as abjad, i.e. DME tokens are disemvoweled (Table 5).

---

[12] XPaths never use blank space to separate functional or semantic units.

```
<xsd:element name="FirstNm">
  <xsd:annotation>
    <xsd:documentation>
      <Description>First Name</Description>
    </xsd:documentation>
  </xsd:annotation>
</xsd:element>
```

Fig. 6. MeF element from XSD document.

Given the percentage of disemvoweled tokens in DMEs, we automatically disemvoweled each entry in the terminology (and single- and multi-tokens). Aided by an indexing scheme for fast lookup, each term is aligned with at least one abjad or quasi-abjad spelling. For instance, the DME token *taxable* is written in abjad like *txbl* or in quasi-abjad with an errant vowel as in *taxbl, txabl* or even *txble*. Of course, *taxable* appears fully-spelled out in some DMEs. Pure abjad expressions amount for 69% of the 73% of unknown terms (Table 5).

We rely heavily on the Damerau-Levenshtein distance as a string metric for measuring the edit distance between DMEs (Table 4), XSD descriptions (Fig. 6), and existing terminology terms. Combining the Damerau-Levenshtein algorithm and aligning terms together with corresponding terms in abjad in the terminology is **sufficient** to *reduce the original abjad percentage from 69% to 10% of remaining unknown abjad expressions.* The percentage of unknown non-abjad expressions are reduced from 31% to 8%.

Table 3. Types and total of XPaths

Categories	Elements as XPaths		
	Constants	Total	> 400,000
	Pure Data Model Elements		
	Errors		
	Temporary		

4.3 Evaluation Summary

For the evaluation, we conducted different types of tests. First, we collected 500 XSD descriptions (Fig. 6) from the XSD *Modern eFiling* corpus. Using various algorithms for edit distance, similarity and fuzzy string matching, we calculated how close the terms extracted from DMEs are from XSD description sub-strings or whole XSD descriptions. For a preset threshold, 87% of terms extracted from DMEs can be matched with confidence against descriptions.

Table 4. Compliant and non-compliant terms

No	Compliant DMEs	Non-Compliant DMEs
1	ChildTaxCreditWorksheet	AddnlDepreciation1969To1976Amt
2	CreditsSummary	CalculatedMonthlyPymtAmt
3	DependencySupportWorksheet	EnergyEfficHomeCrEIN
4	DependentCareEarnedIncomeWorksheet	EmplprovChildCareEIN
5	DepreciationAndAmortization	ForeignPersonSubjectToWthldAmt
6	EducationTuitionAndFeesSummary	FairMarketValueDayBfrExptrtAmt
7	EducatorExpensesWorksheet	HomeSoldToUnrltPrsnNoGainInd
8	LatePenaltiesInterestWorksheet	NonmrktblStockSecIssdFrgnCoGrp
8	MedicalExpenses	QlfyElecMotorVehCrAmtPP
10	MiscItemizedDeductionsWorksheet	SelfEmpldHealthInsDedAmt
11	StateAndLocalPropertyTaxRefund	SmllrReducedGainAddnlDeprecAmt

Table 5. Terminology lookup distribution for individual DMEs

					Terminology Terms	21%
DME Total	100,000	Term Matching	Known	27%	Acronyms	2%
					Abbreviations	4%
			Unknown	73%	Non-Abjad	31%
					Abjad	69%

In addition, we ran 2 end-to-end NLP pipeline tests on 250 income-tax forms, i.e. the first using the standard terminology only, and the second with the standard terminology augmented with terms extracted from DMEs. We focused on arithmetic operations which, in the tax domain, routinely use English terms for their operands (Table 2). With the English-translated DMEs added to the terminology, 31% new arithmetic operations completed automatically in the end-to-end run.

5   Related Work

There are few descriptions of implementations and research on methods for interpreting automatically tax laws and for generating executable code from them. However, in the last few years, interest has been growing. Discussions center on tax language, ontologies and logic from various perspectives [1,3,5–7,11,14,17]. However, to the best of our knowledge, there is **no publicly available** descriptions of **end-to-end frameworks** to translate tax laws (or a subset of such laws like tax calculations) **automatically into executable code.**

6   Conclusion

In this paper, we describe the motivation for extracting terms from DMEs in domain XPaths. To increase coverage, DME-based terms are pushed into our preexisting terminology. Increasing terminology coverage improves automatic conversion of tax laws written in natural language into executable code, in particular, tax calculations (Table 2).

Future exploration include exploring the feasibility of the approach on non-English-written XML documents. In addition, we would like to develop validation tooling to ensure consistency and lack of ambiguity in DME naming and spelling across a domain software application.

Acknowledgments. We thank R. Meike, C. de Peuter and three anonymous reviewers for helpful insight and comments.

References

1. An, Y.J., Wilson, N.: Tax knowledge adventure: ontologies that analyze corporate tax transactions. In: Proceedings of the 17th International Digital Government Research Conference on Digital Government Research (2016)
2. Baldwin, T.: Compositionality and multiword expressions: six of one, half a dozen of the other? In: Proceedings of the Workshop on Multiword Expressions: Identifying and Exploiting Underlying Properties, p. 1. Association for Computational Linguistics, Sydney, Australia (2006). https://aclanthology.org/W06-1201
3. Blank, J.D., Osofsky, L.: Simplexity: plain language and the tax law. 66 Emory L. J. **189** (2017)
4. Boguraev, B., Manandise, E., Segal, B.: The bare necessities: increasing lexical coverage for multi-word domain terms with less lexical data. In: Proceedings of the 11th Workshop on Multiword Expressions, pp. 60–64. Association for Computational Linguistics, Denver, Colorado (2015). https://doi.org/10.3115/v1/W15-0910, https://aclanthology.org/W15-0910
5. Cohen, S.B.: Words! words! words!: teaching the language of tax. Legal Scholarship Education (LSN) (Topic), EduRN (2005)
6. Curtotti, M., McCreath, E.C.: A Corpus of Australian contract language: description, profiling and analysis. In: ICAIL (2011)
7. Distinto, I., Guarino, N., Masolo, C.: A well-founded ontological framework for modeling personal income tax. In: ICAIL (2013)
8. Foufi, V., Nerima, L., Wehrli, É.: Parsing and MWE detection: fips at the PARSEME shared task. In: Proceedings of the 13th Workshop on Multiword Expressions (MWE 2017), pp. 54–59. Association for Computational Linguistics, Valencia, Spain (2017). https://doi.org/10.18653/v1/W17-1706, https://aclanthology.org/W17-1706
9. IRS: Modernized e-file status. http://www.irs.gov/e-file-providers/modernized-e-file-mef-status. Accessed 27 Feb 2022

10. Korkontzelos, I., Manandhar, S.: Can recognising multiword expressions improve shallow parsing? In: NAACL (2010)

11. Manandise, E.: Towards unlocking the narrative of the united states income tax forms. In: FNP (2019)

12. Manandise, E., de Peuter, C.: Mitigating silence in compliance terminology during parsing of utterances. In: FNP (2020)

13. Manandise, E., de Peuter, C., Mukherjee, S.: From tax compliance in natural language to executable calculations: combining lexical-grammar-based parsing and machine learning. In: FLAIRS Conference (2021)

14. Morris, J.: Rules as code: how technology may change the language in which legislation is written, and what it might mean for lawyers of tomorrow. In: TECHSHOW 2021, pp. 2–16, New York (2021)

15. Šajatović, A., Buljan, M., Šnajder, J., Dalbelo Bašić, B.: Evaluating automatic term extraction methods on individual documents. In: Proceedings of the Joint Workshop on Multiword Expressions and WordNet (MWE-WN 2019), pp. 149–154. Association for Computational Linguistics, Florence, Italy (2019). https://doi.org/10.18653/v1/W19-5118, https://aclanthology.org/W19-5118

16. Wang, Y., Berant, J., Liang, P.: Building a semantic parser overnight. In: Proceedings of the 53rd Annual Meeting of the Association for Computational Linguistics and the 7th International Joint Conference on Natural Language Processing (Volume 1: Long Papers), pp. 1332–1342. Association for Computational Linguistics, Beijing, China (2015). https://doi.org/10.3115/v1/P15-1129, https://aclanthology.org/P15-1129

17. Wong, M.W.: Rules as code - seven levels of digitisation. In: Research Collection, pp. 1–24. Research Collection School Of Law, Singapore (2020). https://ink.library.smu.edu.sg/sol_research/3093

Slot Filling for Extracting Reskilling and Upskilling Options from the Web

Albert Weichselbraun[1,2]([⊠]) [iD], Roger Waldvogel[1] [iD], Andreas Fraefel[1],
Alexander van Schie[1], and Philipp Kuntschik[1] [iD]

[1] University of Applied Sciences of the Grisons, 7000 Chur, Switzerland
{albert.weichselbraun,roger.waldvogel,andreas.fraefel,alexander.vanschie,
philipp.kuntschik}@fhgr.ch
[2] webLyzard Technology, 1090 Vienna, Austria

Abstract. Disturbances in the job market such as advances in science
and technology, crisis and increased competition have triggered a surge
in reskilling and upskilling programs. Information on suitable continuing
education options is distributed across many sites, rendering the search,
comparison and selection of useful programs a cumbersome task.

This paper, therefore, introduces a knowledge extraction system that
integrates reskilling and upskilling options into a single knowledge graph.
The system collects educational programs from 488 different providers and
uses context extraction for identifying and contextualizing relevant content. Afterwards, entity recognition and entity linking methods draw upon
a domain ontology to locate relevant entities such as skills, occupations and
topics. Finally, slot filling integrates entities based on their context into the
corresponding slots of the continuous education knowledge graph.

We also introduce a German gold standard that comprises 169 documents and over 3800 annotations for benchmarking the necessary content extraction, entity linking, entity recognition and slot filling tasks,
and provide an overview of the system's performance.

Keywords: Content extraction · Knowledge extraction · Knowledge
base population · Entity recognition · Entity classification · Entity
linking · Slot filling · Gold standard

1 Introduction

The automated extraction of structured knowledge from Web content for knowledge base population is a challenging task, since it requires combining content
extraction and context aware knowledge extraction. In the continuing education
domain, for example, Web pages promoting courses and degree programs often
contain information on learning outcomes and course prerequisites which use
entities of similar types (e.g., skills, degrees, etc.). Correctly interpreting these
entities requires contextual knowledge of the section in which they appear.

The presented research has been motivated by an industry project, which
aims at creating a knowledge graph of national and international educational

© The Author(s), under exclusive license to Springer Nature Switzerland AG 2022
P. Rosso et al. (Eds.): NLDB 2022, LNCS 13286, pp. 279–290, 2022.
https://doi.org/10.1007/978-3-031-08473-7_25

programs relevant to the Swiss reskilling and upskilling market. To improve the performance of knowledge extraction tasks, the industry partner contributed a comprehensive domain ontology which formalizes domain knowledge such as occupations, skills, topics and positions.

Once completed, the system will cover almost 100,000 educational programs spanning a heterogeneous set of sources such as academic programs, continuing education certificates, courses, seminars, and international online courses. The created knowledge graph will power a search platform and recommender system that will support users in locating suitable reskilling and upskilling programs.

The main contributions of this paper are: (i) the application of content extraction and knowledge extraction methods to a complex industry-driven setting that requires building a knowledge graph of educational offerings suitable for reskilling and upskilling; (ii) the introduction of methods capable of performing the required complex slot filling task on Web pages retrieved from numerous different education providers; (iii) the integration of background knowledge available in the industry partner's domain ontology with state-of-the-art content extraction and knowledge extraction methods; (iv) the creation of an infrastructure for assessing the overall task and subtask performance which can be used for benchmarking slot filling on educational content. This infrastructure comprises a German gold standard dataset that contains two partitions of 169 and 75 documents, and six evaluation tasks that consider content extraction, entity extraction, and slot filling.

2   Related Work

In recent years, industry-scale knowledge graphs such as the Google Knowledge Graph, Microsoft's Bing knowledge graph, and the knowledge graphs deployed by Facebook, eBay and IBM Watson have emerged [8]. Creating and maintaining such comprehensive knowledge graphs requires significant resources, which has further accelerated research in automated knowledge extraction methods.

Knowledge base population, for instance, applies knowledge extraction techniques to discover facts in unstructured textual resources to integrate them into a knowledge base or knowledge graph. DBpedia, for example, is constructed by extracting knowledge from Wikipedia Web pages and storing them in the form of (subject, predicate, object) triples [4]. Other approaches operate on more heterogeneous document collections, as reflected in the composition of evaluation datasets covering News articles [6], question answering [2], and even general Web documents [3].

Slot filling is a knowledge extraction technique that extracts information on predefined slots (e.g., a person's occupation, age, etc.). When applied to open-world scenarios, slot filling is very challenging, as demonstrated by the TAC 2017 Cold Start Slot Filling Task in which even the winning systems only obtained F-measures below 20% [5]. If applied to a single domain, considerably better scores are achieved, as demonstrated by Ritze et al. [10] who use slot filling for augmenting knowledge bases. Most state-of-the-art systems such as Coach [7],

RSZ [11] and LEONA [12] deploy deep learning to improve system performance, and transfer learning to allow adaptation to new domains.

The research introduced in this paper, in contrast, customizes slot filling to the target domain by combining deep learning with domain knowledge encoded in a skill and education ontology.

3   Method

The presented knowledge extraction system populates the continuing education knowledge graph by drawing upon a skill and education ontology to extract knowledge on educational offerings from websites published by educational institutions such as universities, schools, and course providers.

3.1   System Overview and Formalization

Figure 1 illustrates the developed knowledge extraction and knowledge base population process, which operates on Web pages from 488 different education providers.

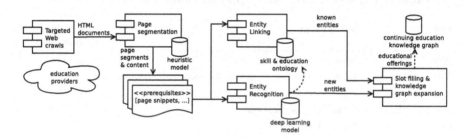

Fig. 1. Overview of the automatic knowledge base population process.

The system's knowledge graph population pipeline expands the continuing education knowledge graph by analyzing the Web pages doc_i of educational offerings i. A page segmentation and classification component extracts relevant page segments $seg_i^{type} \in doc_i$ with $type \in \{target\ group,\ prerequisite,\ learning\ objective,\ course\ content,\ certificates\ \&\ degree\}$ from these pages. Afterwards, entity linking identifies known entities e_{ij}^{known} such as skills and occupation within the segments and links them to the skill and education domain ontology. We complement entity linking with entity recognition which is capable of identifying entities e_{ij}^{new} that are not yet available in the domain ontology and, therefore, significantly improves the coverage of the entity extraction process.

Finally, the **slot filling component** fills for each educational offering i the slots outlined in Table 1 by contextualizing the extracted entities $e_{ij} = e_{ij}^{known} \cup e_{ij}^{new}$ with the information on the page segment seg_i^{type} from which they have

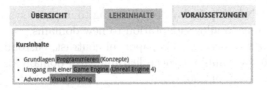

Fig. 2. Annotated example course description taken from sae.edu. Blue highlighting indicates identified entities, and the red border outlines the corresponding page segment. (Color figure online)

been extracted. New entities that have been discovered by the ER component are assigned unique identifiers that can be used for linking them to the domain ontology at a later stage.

In the real-world example shown in Fig. 2, the slot value with surface form "Programmierung" (`edu:prog`) extracted from the page segment "Lehrinhalte" (`edu:course_content`), for example, fills the course content slot, while the same entity extracted from the segment 'Voraussetzungen" (`edu:prerequisites`) would be considered a prerequisite for visiting the course.

Table 1. Target slot, valid entity types and cardinalities of course entities.

Slot	(entity) type	Cardinality (min, max)
School	School	(1, 1)
Target group	Topic, occupation, degree, education, industry, position	(0, *)
Prerequisite	Topic, skill, occupation, position, education	(0, *)
Learning objective	Topic, skill, occupation	(1, *)
Course content	Topic, skill	(1, *)
Certificates	Degree, education	(0, *)

After the completion of the slot filling process, the system integrates the information on each educational offering into the **knowledge graph** by forming the corresponding triples (e.g., `<https://sae.edu#c01> edu:content edu:prog.`).

3.2 Knowledge Extraction

Page Segmentation. Most websites structure educational offerings in sections, such as course prerequisites and learning objectives. Extracting the content from these sections and correctly labeling it allows contextualization of mined entities, which helps to distinguish slots such as prerequisites, learning outcomes and certificates.

The developed page segmentation system deploys the following three-step process for identifying page segments within the documents: (i) *Text segmentation* compares the document's HTML structure with the corresponding text representation generated by the Inscriptis content extraction framework [13]. Based on the HTML structure, the text is split into segments whenever separator elements $m = \{$*div, p, li, td, th, dt, dd, summary, legend, h1, h2, h3, h4, h5, h6*$\}$, which enclose a text and usually do not contain any other element m, occurs. (ii) *Titles and text clusters* are identified by combining HTML elements with a fallback heuristic which annotates non-standard titles based on their length (max. 3 words) and a task-specific list of commonly used title terms (e.g., 'prerequisite', 'content', and 'degree') obtained from the domain-ontology. After identifying the title element, it is used to determine the text cluster by merging all segments until the next title is reached. (iii) The final *cluster classification* step compares the title terms with word sequences from the skill & education ontology to determine the cluster type.

Entity Linking. The system uses a graph-based entity linking approach [14] that draws upon the project's skill and education database. We customized the component to differentiate between the project-specific entity types (i) education, (ii) function (i.e., occupation and position), (iii) skill and (iv) topic.

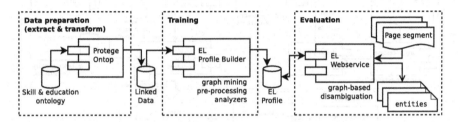

Fig. 3. Overview of the EL process: data preparation transforms the data into a Linked Data repository, training mines the data repository to create a serializable EL profile, and evaluation uses the profile to annotate new and unknown documents.

Figure 3 illustrates the utilization of the industry partner's skill and education ontology within the EL component. The ontology covers most areas relevant to the human resource sector by organizing domain knowledge into 42 tables which combine custom schemas with industry standards such as the *Standard Classification of Occupations*[1] and multiple industry directories. The given EL task utilizes tables covering classes, relations and instances on skills, educations, occupations, topics, industries and schools. The system's data preparation step deploys Protege Ontop[2], a framework that allows translating SPARQL into SQL queries, to transforms these relational data into a Linked Data repository.

The training step utilizes SPARQL queries to mine, pre-process, and classify relevant entities and context information from the created Linked Data repository. The EL Profile Builder further applies multiple pre-processors and analyzers to the query results which create artificial name variations such as plural,

---

[1] https://www.bls.gov/soc/.

[2] https://github.com/ontop/ontop.

possessive forms and abbreviations to maximize the EL profile's coverage, and determine whether the mined surface forms are unambiguous (e.g., "hedge fund manager"), ambiguous (e.g., "wolf of wallstreet") or provide additional context (e.g., "occupation"). The EL Profile Builder concludes the training by serializing an EL profile containing all information required for the EL process. The EL Web service deploys the profile in conjunction with a graph-based disambiguation algorithm [14] that identifies mentions of entities and links them to the ontology concepts.

Entity Recognition and Entity Classification serves as a fallback for entities that have not yet been included into the industry partner's skill and education ontology. Entity recognition not only provides an efficient mitigation strategy for identifying these missing entities, but also suggests concepts for inclusion into the skill & education ontology, which helps in improving its coverage over time.

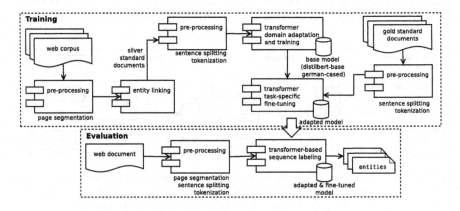

Fig. 4. Transformer model used for entity recognition and entity classification.

We model entity recognition and entity classification as a token classification problem, where a deep learning model takes a sequence of tokens (e.g., a sentence) and then provides labels for each of them. The entity classification component draws upon the *distilbert-base-german-cased* model provided by the popular transformers library [15], using the Adam solver with a learning rate of $5 \cdot 10^{-5}$, and a dropout of 0.1. Figure 4 outlines the model structure and the training process.

The domain adaptation step draws upon a domain corpus of 28,000 documents that has been enriched with silver standard annotations obtained from the previously described EL component. Afterwards, fine-tuning draws upon the gold standard documents to further improve the model's capabilities of capturing new entities and to generate the final model. During benchmarking, a five-fold cross evaluation procedure ensures that no training documents are used within the evaluation step.

4   Evaluation

4.1   Gold Standard

The CareerCoach 2022 gold standard is available for download in the NIF and JSON format[3], and draws upon documents from a corpus of over 99,000 education courses which have been retrieved from 488 different education providers. The project's industry partner classified 20 of these education providers "high priority", since they play a key role in the Swiss continuing education market. The list of high priority education providers contains ten academic institutions (universities and universities of applied sciences), five companies focusing on IT education certification, and the five largest education providers not fitting into any of these categories.

Gold Standard Partitions. The corpus contains two partitions. Partition (P1) supports the content extraction tasks and comprises 169 documents and gold standard annotations for page segments. Since the structure of HTML pages frequently differs even within educational offerings, this corpus contains up to five documents per website and also considers a higher total number of education providers. P1 has been created by sampling (i) five random documents per "high priority" education provider and (ii) one random document taken from a selection of 69 randomly selected standard priority education providers.

The second partition (P2) only contains 75 documents but also a significantly richer set of annotations that considers page segments, entities and slots. It, therefore, supports benchmarking knowledge extraction tasks such as entity extraction and slot filling on top of the content extraction task. Since these tasks draw upon the extracted and normalized content, a higher document variability within an education provider seems to be less beneficial, particularly when considering that creating this much richer set of annotations is also very time intensive.

Annotation Guidelines. The gold standard annotation process involved two researchers and two industry experts who also outlined guidelines specifying: (i) *relevant classes* for the page segment recognition and classification tasks, and information on how to identify them; and (ii) the *entities* supported by the entity extraction tasks and detailed instructions for identifying and distinguishing these entities. This has been particularly important for the 'topic' and 'skill' entity types, which provide valuable context information but are less intuitive to annotators. Entities are mapped to unique identifiers, and the entities of type 'occupation', 'degree', 'education', 'industry', 'school' and 'position' have also been linked to the corresponding *DBpedia, Wikidata* and *European Skill/Competences, qualifications and Occupations (ESCO)*[4] concepts.

---

[3] https://github.com/fhgr/careercoach2022.
[4] https://ec.europa.eu/esco/portal/download.

During the annotation process, the guidelines have been revisited and further optimized. We drew upon the introduced knowledge extraction pipeline to create candidate annotations that have then been manually corrected and improved by domain experts. In a final step, two additional domain experts from the industry partner manually validated the gold standard annotations based on 28 documents that comprised 1533 annotations, reported potential problems and triggered further improvements to the gold standard and annotation guidelines. At this point, the inter-rater-agreement between domain experts from the research institution and the industry experts for partition P2 has been 0.85 (Cohen's Kappa), and 0.88 (pairwise F1 score) [1] for annotated entities. Within the sample, the experts agreed on all page segment annotations, suggesting that the page partitioning task can be easily performed by humans based on the provided annotation guidelines. The substantial inter-rater-agreement also indicates that pre-annotating the corpus is unlikely to introduce any significant bias.

Gold Standard Properties. Table 2 provides basic statistics and summarizes information on the number of annotated classes, and annotations per document. The table also gives an impression on the differences to expect between education providers. For instance, there are documents that do not contain any relevant contents (i.e., no relevant page segment) as well as cases where page segments appear multiple times. The entity extraction and slot filling tasks are also confronted with a large variety of entities, ranging from 2 entities per document to a total of 235 entities identified in a single document.

Table 2. Corpus properties

	P1: Content extraction	P2: Entity extraction and slot filling
Number of documents	169	75
Number of education providers	89	55
Number of annotation classes	5	8
Min. annotations in document	0	2
Avg. annotations in document	3.4	43.9
Median annotations in document	3	30
Max. annotations in document	17	235

4.2 Evaluation Tasks

The evaluation draws upon the gold standard and supports benchmarking the following six tasks performed by the introduced knowledge extraction system:

Content Extraction. Content extraction identifies and classifies text segments relevant for the slot filling tasks. We distinguish between

1. *T1: page segment recognition* - identifies page segments within HTML pages doc and extracts the text strings $seg_i^j \in doc_i$ from these segments.
2. *T2: page segment classification* - assigns each extracted text segment seg_i^j to a class *type* $\in$ {*target group, prerequisite, learning objective, course content, certificates & degree*}.

We evaluate the page segment recognition task (T1) by comparing the tokens in the extracted page segments $t_i \in seg_i^j$ with the tokens in the gold standard segments $t_g \in s_g^j$. The evaluation of the page segment classification also requires that the types of the gold standard page segment t_g^{type} and of the extracted segment t_g^{type} match.

Entity Extraction. The entity extraction tasks aim at identifying mentions of entities of type $tp_i \in T_i$ within the extracted page segments. The corpus contains annotations of the following entity types: 'skill', 'occupation', 'topic', 'position', 'school', 'industry', 'education', 'degree'.

1. *T3: entity recognition* - locates mentions m_i of entities within text segments.
2. *T4: entity classification* - assigns each mention m_i to the corresponding entity type $tp_i \in T_i$.
3. *T5: entity linking* - links mentions m_i to the appropriate entity e_i in the knowledge graph KG. Entities that are not yet available in the knowledge graph are handled as NIL entities (i.e., they are assigned a temporary identifier that is unique for all mentions which refer to the same entity).

We distinguish between two evaluation settings: strict and relaxed. In the strict settings, mentions m_i identified by the entity recognition component for task T3 are considered true positives (TP), if they are identical to a gold standard mention m_g. The entity classification task (T4) also requires that both entities have been assigned to the same entity type tp_i, and the linking task (T5) requires linking the mention to the correct knowledge base entity e_i.

The *relaxed setting* eases these conditions by also considering mentions that overlap a gold standard mention as correct.

Entities that do not appear in the gold standard are considered false positives (FP), and false negatives (FN) refer to gold standard entities which have been missed by the entity extraction task.

Slot Filling. The slot filling task (T6) combines all the tasks above. The page segment recognition (T1) identifies page segments. Afterwards, the page segment classification (T2) assigns them to the corresponding segment cluster, and entity recognition (T3), entity classification (T4) and entity linking (T5) are performed. Finally, we assign the extracted entities e_i, which have been contextualized based on the classification of the page segment in which they have been identified, to the corresponding slot.

4.3   Experiments and Discussion

Table 3 summarizes the results of a five-fold cross evaluation on the CareerCoach 2022 gold standard. For the entity linking and slot filling task, the evaluation also distinguishes between the strict and the relaxed setting.

Table 3. Slot filling and per component evaluation results.

Component	P	R	F1
T1: page segment recognition	0.82	0.84	0.83
T2: page segment classification	0.82	0.84	0.83
T3: entity recognition	0.82	0.66	0.73
T4: entity classification	0.78	0.63	0.70
T5: entity linking (strict)	0.67	0.80	0.73
T5: entity linking (relaxed)	0.67	0.82	0.74
T6: slot filling (strict)	0.48	0.60	0.54
T6: slot filling (relaxed)	0.50	0.62	0.55

A comparison of the page segment recognition and page segment classification performance reveals the same scores for both tasks. This confirms that the developed simple segment classification heuristic has been very effective and has classified all page segments correctly.

The results indicate that both entity recognition and entity classification have been optimized towards a higher precision, to spare domain experts, which need to confirm new entity types in the production process. Entity linking, in contrast, has been optimized towards recall, as outlined in the evaluation results.

The evaluation of the overall slot filling process only considers correctly assigned slots (i.e., course, slot and slot value are correct) as true positives. All other values are considered false positives, and missing values as false negatives. The F1 score of the slot filling process indicates that the system is not yet suitable for fully automated knowledge population, but rather enables a semi-automated process that significantly improves throughput when compared to the prior deployed manual approaches.

4.4   Automatic Knowledge Graph Population

Running the presented system on 55 course descriptions (one per unique education provider) from the gold standard, extends the knowledge base by 453 unique statements (Fig. 5). Most of these statements (222) describe the course content, followed by target groups (90), learning objectives (61), course prerequisites (51) and certificates (29). In addition, 511 slot values have been marked as "related" since the system hasn't been able to unequivocally resolve their slot, due to shortcomings in the page partitioning process. This result indicates, that further improving the page partitioning process will be key towards enhancing the system's recall.

```
<https://sae.edu#c01>  edu:prerequisite      edu:matura, edu:student;
                       edu:course_content    edu:Design, edu:Podcasting;
                       skos:related          edu:Web_Design, edu:Publishing.
```

Fig. 5. Snippet of six RDF triples that have been integrated into the knowledge graph.

5   Outlook and Conclusions

Performing slot filling tasks on third-party websites is a challenging task, requiring content extraction and knowledge extraction methods to work in concert.

This paper introduces a slot filling system that mines education provider websites for a wide range of educational offerings such as academic programs, continuing education programs, courses, seminars and online courses. Integrating background knowledge from a proprietary ontology allows the application of graph-based entity linking methods for the identification of known entities, which are complemented by entity recognition to mitigate coverage issues within the ontology. The slot filling component contextualizes entities to distinguish between ambiguous slots such as *prerequisites* versus *learning outcomes*, and afterwards integrates them into a continuing education knowledge graph.

An evaluation framework comprising six evaluation tasks and a publicly available German gold standard allows benchmarking the content extraction and knowledge extraction methods utilized within the slot filling system. The framework did not only yield information on the components' performance, but also guided the system development by providing rapid feedback on the impact of changes and improvements. In addition, it offers a reliable benchmark to third-party researchers interested in the described slot filling task.

Future work will focus on: (i) improving the slot filling performance by enhancing page segmentation, increasing the coverage of the proprietary knowledge graph used for entity linking, and fine-tuning the entity recognition component. Given the importance of the created benchmarking framework for the research and development process, we plan on (ii) further increasing its size and coverage; and (iii) integrating the gold standard with explainable benchmarking frameworks such as Orbis [9] to make it more accessible to third-party researchers.

Acknowledgments. The research presented in this paper has been conducted within the CareerCoach project (www.fhgr.ch/CareerCoach) which is funded by Innosuisse.

References

1. Brandsen, A., Verberne, S., Wansleeben, M., Lambers, K.: Creating a dataset for named entity recognition in the archaeology domain. In: Proceedings of the 12th Language Resources and Evaluation Conference, Marseille, France, pp. 4573–4577, May 2020

2. Dubey, M., Banerjee, D., Abdelkawi, A., Lehmann, J.: LC-QuAD 2.0: a large dataset for complex question answering over Wikidata and DBpedia. In: Ghidini, C., et al. (eds.) ISWC 2019. LNCS, vol. 11779, pp. 69–78. Springer, Cham (2019). https://doi.org/10.1007/978-3-030-30796-7_5

3. Glass, M., Gliozzo, A.: A dataset for web-scale knowledge base population. In: Gangemi, A., et al. (eds.) ESWC 2018. LNCS, vol. 10843, pp. 256–271. Springer, Cham (2018). https://doi.org/10.1007/978-3-319-93417-4_17

4. Lehmann, J., et al.: DBpedia – a large-scale, multilingual knowledge base extracted from Wikipedia. Semant. Web 6(2), 167–195 (2015)

5. Lim, S., Kwon, S., Lee, S., Choi, J.: UNIST SAIL system for TAC 2017 cold start slot filling. In: TAC (2017)

6. Lin, X., Chen, L.: Canonicalization of open knowledge bases with side information from the source text. In: 2019 IEEE 35th International Conference on Data Engineering (ICDE), pp. 950–961, April 2019

7. Liu, Z., Winata, G.I., Xu, P., Fung, P.: Coach: a coarse-to-fine approach for cross-domain slot filling. In: Proceedings of the 58th Annual Meeting of the Association for Computational Linguistics, pp. 19–25. Online, July 2020

8. Noy, N., Gao, Y., Jain, A., Narayanan, A., Patterson, A., Taylor, J.: Industry-scale knowledge graphs: lessons and challenges. Commun. ACM 62(8), 36–43 (2019)

9. Odoni, F., Brasoveanu, A.M., Kuntschik, P., Weichselbraun, A.: Introducing orbis: an extendable evaluation pipeline for named entity linking drill-down analysis. In: 82nd Annual Meeting of the Association for Information Science (ASIS&T 2019), Melbourne, Australia, vol. 56, pp. 468–471 (2019)

10. Ritze, D., Lehmberg, O., Oulabi, Y., Bizer, C.: Profiling the potential of web tables for augmenting cross-domain knowledge bases. In: Proceedings of the 25th International Conference on World Wide Web, WWW 2016, Montréal, Canada, pp. 251–261 (2016)

11. Shah, D., Gupta, R., Fayazi, A., Hakkani-Tur, D.: Robust zero-shot cross-domain slot filling with example values. In: Proceedings of the 57th Annual Meeting of the Association for Computational Linguistics, Florence, Italy, pp. 5484–5490, July 2019

12. Siddique, A., Jamour, F., Hristidis, V.: Linguistically-enriched and context-awarezero-shot slot filling. In: Proceedings of the Web Conference 2021, WWW 2021, New York, NY, USA, pp. 3279–3290 (2021)

13. Weichselbraun, A.: Inscriptis - a Python-based HTML to text conversion library optimized for knowledge extraction from the Web. J. Open Source Softw. 6(66), 3557 (2021)

14. Weichselbraun, A., Kuntschik, P., Brasoveanu, A.M.P.: Mining and leveraging background knowledge for improving named entity linking. In: 8th International Conference on Web Intelligence, Mining and Semantics (WIMS 2018), Novi Sad, Serbia, June 2018

15. Wolf, T., et al.: Transformers: state-of-the-art natural language processing. In: Proceedings of the 2020 Conference on Empirical Methods in Natural Language Processing: System Demonstrations, pp. 38–45. Online, October 2020

Better Exploiting BERT for Few-Shot Event Detection

Aboubacar Tuo$^{(\boxtimes)}$ ⓘ, Romaric Besançon ⓘ, Olivier Ferret ⓘ,
and Julien Tourille ⓘ

Université Paris-Saclay, CEA, List, 91120 Palaiseau, France
{aboubacar.tuo,romaric.besancon,olivier.ferret,julien.tourille}@cea.fr

Abstract. Recent approaches for event detection rely on deep supervised learning, which requires large annotated corpora. Few-shot learning
approaches, such as the meta-learning paradigm, can be used to address
this issue. We focus in this paper on the use of prototypical networks with
a BERT encoder for event detection. More specifically, we optimize the
use of the information contained in the different layers of a pre-trained
BERT model and show that simple strategies for combining BERT layers
can outperform the current state-of-the-art for this task.

Keywords: Few-shot event detection · Meta-learning · BERT

1 Introduction

Event extraction aims to automatically extract structured information about
events from text. It can be compared to filling a form with entities, each field of this
form corresponding to an argument of the event. Earlier methods for event extraction were based on handcrafted rules [1]. These methods were gradually replaced
by machine learning algorithms with the development of statistical learning and
neural networks in recent years. In this context, [16] proposes a structured prediction model based on numerous lexico-syntactic features, [20] uses convolutional
networks to exploit contextual information, [19] defines models based on recurrent networks, and [18,21], and [31] exploit graph convolution models to capture
syntactic dependencies between different parts of sentences.

While the objective of event extraction is to identify all arguments connected
to a particular event, datasets since ACE 2005 [30] have introduced the concept
of *event trigger*, designating the word or group of words that indicate as clearly
as possible the presence of an event in a sentence. The intention is to define a
lexical anchor to help in the search for arguments. We focus in this paper on the
detection and the classification of those triggers according to a restricted set of
predefined types, a task generally called *Event Detection* or *Trigger Detection*.

Supervised learning methods are costly since they require large corpora that
are manually annotated. Hence, a current challenge is to investigate methods

This publication was made possible by the use of the FactoryIA supercomputer, financially supported by the Île-de-France Regional Council.

P. Rosso et al. (Eds.): NLDB 2022, LNCS 13286, pp. 291–298, 2022.
https://doi.org/10.1007/978-3-031-08473-7_26

that reduce the development cost of these systems. In this context, we investigate Few-Shot Learning (FSL) for trigger detection.

Few Shot Event Detection (FSED) has been recently the focus of several studies with various configurations: generalization of models to new types of events using keyword lists [2,14], data enrichment with external resources [7], Zero-Shot Learning with the use of class descriptions or external resources [33], and FSL [3,4,26]. Other studies have also focused on Few-Shot Event Classification, which restricts FSED to assigning an event type to a candidate trigger already identified in a sentence [6,13,15].

In this paper, our contribution focuses on a better exploitation of the BERT language model representations for FSED, more specifically by studying the importance of these different representations and by evaluating different ways to associate them.

2   Method

2.1   Problem Formulation

We cast FSED as a sequence labeling task [23], using the IOB format (*Inside Outside Beginning*), which can be addressed as a multi-class classification task.

Recent studies in FSL use meta-learning, which is often defined as *learning to learn*. The main idea behind meta-learning is to train models on several tasks, each with a limited number of instances, so that the learned model can quickly perform similar tasks on new data. The methods that have emerged in recent years for solving FSL tasks with the help of meta-learning fall into three main categories: model-based methods [25,32], optimization-based algorithms [10,22,24], and metric-based methods [27–29]. Among the latter, we adopted prototypical networks [27] in our study, similarly to most works about FSED.

We adopt the standard N-way, K-shot episodic formulation, as described in [29]. An episode $\mathcal{E}$ is composed of a *support set* and an associated *query set*. During each episode, the model is defined by relying on a subset $\mathcal{S}$ of the available labeled data, the support set, which contains N types of events and K annotated instances per type (K being generally small, e.g. 1, 5, or 10):

$$\mathcal{S} = \{(x_1^1, t_1^1, y^1), \ldots, (x_k^1, t_k^1, y^1), \ldots, (x_1^N, t_1^N, y^N), \ldots, (x_k^N, t_k^N, y^N)\}$$

where $x_i^n = \{w_1, \ldots, w_L\}$ is a sequence of tokens of length L containing a trigger of type n, t_i^n, the position of the trigger, and y^n, the corresponding sequence of labels. The training in this context is done by updating the weights of the model based on the prediction on the instances of the query set, which has the same structure as the support set.

2.2   Model Architecture

We use a Prototypical Network model with episodic learning to combine meta-learning and FSL. An overview of our model, composed of three modules, is presented in Fig. 1.

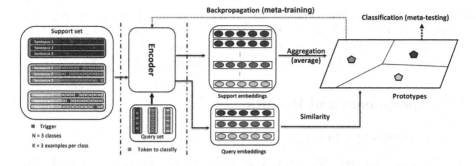

Fig. 1. Our few-shot event detection model based on prototypical networks.

Encoder Module. Given a sentence $x = \{w_1, \ldots, w_L\}$ of length L, the objective of this module is to construct a representation e_i of each word $w_i \in x$ in a d-dimensional space. Importantly, during the episodic learning phase, only the encoder part of the model is actually updated. We use the BERT [8] language model as our encoder, with $H_i = [h_i^1, h_i^2, \ldots, h_i^{12}]$, its representations for the word w_i and $h_i^j \in \mathbb{R}^d$. The main objective of our work is to study different options for selecting and combining the 12 layers of BERT to obtain more relevant token representations for the event detection task. More precisely:

- **Average**: embedding e_i of the word w_i = average of the representations of m consecutive layers. $e_i = \frac{1}{m} \sum_{k=1}^{m} h_i^k$ or $e_i = \frac{1}{m} \sum_{k=12-m+1}^{12} h_i^k$ depending on whether the layers are aggregated from the first or the last layer.
- **Max-pool**: max-pooling on each dimension p for m consecutive layers. The p-th element of the embedding e_i is given by: $(e_i)_p = \max((h_i^1)_p, \ldots, (h_i^m)_p)$
- **Concat**: concatenation of m consecutive BERT layers $e_i = [h_i^1 \,||\, h_i^2 \,||\, \ldots \,||\, h_i^m]$ or $e_i = [h_i^{12} \,||\, h_i^{11} \,||\, \ldots \,||\, h_i^{12-m+1}]$
- **Weighted**: linear combination of the 12 BERT layers. $e_i = \sum_{k=12}^{12} \alpha^k h_i^k$, where the α^k are randomly initialized and learned.
- **ATT**: linear combination of BERT layers for each dimension using an attention mechanism. The objective is to identify the most important layers for each dimension. The p-th element of e_i is given by $(e_i)_p = \sum_{k=1}^{12} \alpha^k (h_i^k)_p$ where the α^k are learnt from a linear combination of the 12 layers and a softmax normalization.

Prototypical Module. The objective of this module is to build a prototype for each class and then, to classify new examples according to their similarity to these prototypes. We take the average of the examples in the support set as prototypes for each class, as proposed by [27]. Since we are using the IOB format, we build a prototype for classes B and I, as well as for class O (the *null* class for all event types), which refers to words that are not triggers of any event. Hence, we obtain $2N + 1$ prototypes for an episode composed of N types.

Classification Module. This module classifies the words of a query sequence according to their similarity to the prototypes. The probability of a given word to belong to a particular class is computed according to its similarity to the class' prototype. The model is trained using the cross-entropy loss.

3   Experiments and Results

3.1   Experimental Setup

Evaluation Dataset. We experiment on the FewEvent corpus [6] for FSED. This corpus is composed of 70,852 event mentions divided into 100 types. We use the same split as [4] for comparison purposes. This split includes 80 types in the training set, 10 types in the test set, and the remaining 10 types in the validation set.

Model Parameters. We use the BERT-base pre-trained model as our encoder. To evaluate the impact of our modifications of this encoder, we rely on two models presented in [4]: **Proto-dot**, a prototypical model based on the dot product for its similarity function, which is our baseline model, and **PA-CRF**, an improvement of the previous model using CRFs (*Conditional Random Field*) [12] to estimate the transition probabilities between different IOB labels as proposed by [11]. The PA-CRF model is the main contribution of [4] and is, to our knowledge, the best performing model for FSED. We take as input 128-word sentences (with padding if needed) and train the model with a learning rate of 10^{-5}.

Evaluation. To test our model, we construct $3,000$ episodes $\mathcal{E}^i \triangleq \{\mathcal{S}^i, \mathcal{Q}^i\}$ with N types of events randomly sampled for each episode. We then select K examples per class in the support set and one example per class in the query set. The examples in the support set are used to build prototypes and the examples in the query set are classified based on their similarity to these prototypes. We consider an event trigger to be correct if its type and position in the sentence are correctly predicted, as in previous work about event detection [4,5,17].

3.2   Results and Discussion

We compute the micro F1-score to evaluate the performance and report the means and standard deviations over 5 runs in Table 1 with different values of N and K. For the encoders **Average**, **Concat**, and **Max-pool**, we only consider the last 4 layers (as suggested in [8]) for the results reported in Table 1. We compare our model to our implementation of [4], which gives the best current performance on the same task (**BERT** line in Table 1) and report the results provided in their article (**BERT[Cong]** line in Table 1).

Whatever the model used (Proto-dot or PA-CRF), all the encoder improvements, except the **Concat** configuration for the 10 ways condition of PA-CRF, significantly improve the performance compared to the classical BERT encoder. Thus, a better exploitation of the information of the BERT model leads to

Table 1. Results: mean and standard deviation of the micro F1-score over 5 trials. **bold**, the best performance on average; underlined, the second best. * denotes the best statistically significant model compared to the second best using the significance test of [9].

Model	Encoder	5 ways 5 shots	5 ways 10 shots	10 ways 5 shots	10 ways 10 shots
Proto-dot	BERT [Cong]	58.82±(0.88)	61.01±(0.23)	55.01±(1.62)	58.78±(0.88)
	BERT	61.22±(0.90)	60.84±(1.58)	58.14±(1.69)	59.85±(2.01)
	Average	64.34±(1.94)	65.37±(0.66)	61.85±(2.05)	63.93±(1.08)
	Max-pool	64.10±(1.78)	65.80±(0.91)	61.15±(1.51)	63.37±(1.03)
	Concat	61.99±(0.46)	61.94±(0.97)	57.47±(0.65)	59.02±(1.39)
	Weighted	65.62±(1.55)	**67.15±(0.88)***	**62.63±(1.18)***	**65.22±(0.98)***
	ATT	**65.64±(0.90)**	65.63±(0.46)	62.22±(0.52)	64.23±(0.99)
PA-CRF	BERT [Cong]	62.25±(1.42)	64.45±(0.49)	58.48±(0.68)	61.54±(0.89)
	BERT	63.63±(2.01)	63.66±(1.54)	62.11±(1.58)	62.47±(1.29)
	Average	65.09±(0.40)	66.70±(0.45)	62.32±(1.51)	65.38±(1.71)
	Max-pool	63.95±(1.99)	66.94±(1.20)	61.74±(1.95)	64.77±(1.84)
	Concat	64.30±(1.99)	64.31±(1.80)	62.01±(1.28)	61.88±(1.05)
	Weighted	**66.26±(1.16)***	**66.97±(0.95)***	**63.90±(1.23)***	**67.21±(1.27)***
	ATT	63.65±(1.35)	66.40±(1.03)	62.41±(1.73)	64.32±(1.64)

outperform the improvements brought by the more sophisticated model of [4], representing the current state of the art.

Among all the tested strategies, those allowing the model to learn the weights of the linear combination of BERT's layers generally yield better results, with the **Weighted** strategy proving to be the best in almost all configurations.

Finally, the fact that the gains observed for the Proto-dot model are also found for the PA-CRF model, which is a more elaborate version of the Proto-dot model, shows that the proposed improvements are complementary to those that can be made to the other modules (prototypical and classification modules).

Influence of the Episodic Formulation N Ways k Shots. We observe logically that the task is more difficult when the number of types (N) increases and that the results are improved with a larger number of annotated examples (K). Furthermore, we assess the robustness of the evaluation protocol by experimenting with different numbers of evaluation episodes for the encoder **Average** (between 500 and 5,000). The score variation between our different runs remains within a range of ±0.5 points.

Layer Analysis. We perform experiments to determine the influence of the number of layers selected for the encoders **Average**, **Concat**, and **Max-pool**, which do not have the capability to perform this selection on their own, contrary to **Weighted** and **ATT**. We report in Fig. 2 the results obtained by these three models for the *5 ways 5 shots* task, taking into account n successive layers starting from the first layer (Fig. 2a) or the last one (Fig. 2b).

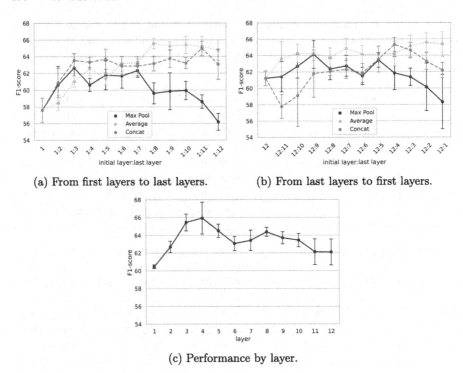

(a) From first layers to last layers.   (b) From last layers to first layers.

(c) Performance by layer.

Fig. 2. Figures (a) and (b) present the influence of the number of layers selected for the encoders **Average**, **Concat**, and **Max-pool** on the performance of the model. Figure (c) presents the performance of the model for only one single layer.

We observe that the encoder **Average** is more stable than the other two and that its performance tends to increase steadily with the number of layers. Its best results are also competitive with the **Weighted** strategy, which shows that taking into account all the layers is beneficial, even with a very simple strategy such as averaging. We can also observe that the other strategies do not exploit all the information. This is particularly noticeable for **Max-pool**, which probably tends to increasingly smooth out the outstanding dimensions as the number of layers increases. Concerning **Concat**, it seems that the strategy creates large layered representations that are probably not very informative for the model.

In this context, Figs. 2a and 2b also show that the combination of the last layers seems more interesting than the combination of the first ones. This observation may reflect the intrinsic presence of more useful information for the task in these layers, or simply be explained by a more important influence of the learning linked to the task at their level because of their closeness to the model output. Finally, Fig. 2c reports the limiting case of considering only one layer, with, from first to last layers, a strong increase of results until layer 4, which reaches a performance comparable to **Average** but with a larger variance, and then, a soft decrease.

4   Conclusions and Perspectives

In this article, we have studied different ways to better exploit the information contained in the BERT pre-trained model for the task of detecting events from a few examples. We have shown that the improvements brought by our proposals outperform the state-of-the-art results on this task. We plan to pursue the improvement of the encoder by studying other representation models and by enriching these representations with external knowledge or lists of examples of triggers. Furthermore, we will study how the improvements of the encoder can be combined with improvements of the prototypical and classification modules.

References

1. Ahn, D.: The stages of event extraction. In: Workshop on Annotating and Reasoning about Time and Events, Sydney, Australia, pp. 1–8 (2006)
2. Bronstein, O., Dagan, I., Li, Q., Ji, H., Frank, A.: Seed-based event trigger labeling: how far can event descriptions get us? In: ACL-IJCNLP, pp. 372–376 (2015)
3. Chen, J., Lin, H., Han, X., Sun, L.: Honey or poison? Solving the trigger curse in few-shot event detection via causal intervention. arXiv:2109.05747 (2021)
4. Cong, X., Cui, S., Yu, B., Liu, T., Yubin, W., Wang, B.: Few-shot event detection with prototypical amortized conditional random field. In: Findings of ACL-IJCNLP, pp. 28–40 (2021)
5. Cui, S., Yu, B., Liu, T., Zhang, Z., Wang, X., Shi, J.: Edge-enhanced graph convolution networks for event detection with syntactic relation. In: Findings of EMNLP, pp. 2329–2339 (2020)
6. Deng, S., Zhang, N., Kang, J., Zhang, Y., Zhang, W., Chen, H.: Meta-learning with dynamic-memory-based prototypical network for few-shot event detection. In: WSDM, Houston, TX, USA, pp. 151–159 (2020)
7. Deng, S., et al.: OntoED: low-resource event detection with ontology embedding. In: ACL-IJCNLP, pp. 2828–2839 (2021)
8. Devlin, J., Chang, M.W., Lee, K., Toutanova, K.: BERT: pre-training of deep bidirectional transformers for language understanding. In: NAACL-HLT, pp. 4171–4186 (2019)
9. Dror, R., Shlomov, S., Reichart, R.: Deep dominance - how to properly compare deep neural models. In: ACL, pp. 2773–2785 (2019)
10. Finn, C., Abbeel, P., Levine, S.: Model-agnostic meta-learning for fast adaptation of deep networks. arXiv:1703.03400 [cs] (2017)
11. Hou, Y., et al.: Few-shot slot tagging with collapsed dependency transfer and label-enhanced task-adaptive projection network. In: ACL, pp. 1381–1393 (2020)
12. Lafferty, J.D., McCallum, A., Pereira, F.C.N.: Conditional random fields: probabilistic models for segmenting and labeling sequence data. In: ICML, pp. 282–289 (2001)
13. Lai, V., Dernoncourt, F., Nguyen, T.H.: Learning prototype representations across few-shot tasks for event detection. In: EMNLP, pp. 5270–5277 (2021)
14. Lai, V.D., Nguyen, T.: Extending event detection to new types with learning from keywords. In: W-NUT 2019, Hong Kong, China, pp. 243–248 (2019)
15. Lai, V.D., Nguyen, T.H., Dernoncourt, F.: Extensively matching for few-shot learning event detection. In: Workshop NUSE, pp. 38–45 (2020)

16. Li, Q., Ji, H., Huang, L.: Joint event extraction via structured prediction with global features. In: ACL, Sofia, Bulgaria, pp. 73–82, August 2013
17. Liu, S., Cheng, R., Yu, X., Cheng, X.: Exploiting contextual information via dynamic memory network for event detection. In: EMNLP, pp. 1030–1035 (2018)
18. Liu, X., Luo, Z., Huang, H.: Jointly multiple events extraction via attention-based graph information aggregation. In: EMNLP, pp. 1247–1256 (2018)
19. Nguyen, T.H., Cho, K., Grishman, R.: Joint event extraction via recurrent neural networks. In: NAACL-HLT, San Diego, California, pp. 300–309 (2016)
20. Nguyen, T.H., Grishman, R.: Event detection and domain adaptation with convolutional neural networks. In: ACL-IJCNLP, Beijing, China, pp. 365–371 (2015)
21. Nguyen, T.H., Grishman, R.: Graph convolutional networks with argument-aware pooling for event detection. In: AAAI (2018)
22. Nichol, A., Achiam, J., Schulman, J.: On first-order meta-learning algorithms. arXiv:1803.02999 (2018)
23. Ramshaw, L., Marcus, M.: Text chunking using transformation-based learning. In: Workshop on Very Large Corpora (1995)
24. Ravi, S., Larochelle, H.: Optimization as a model for few-shot learning. In: ICLR (2017)
25. Santoro, A., Bartunov, S., Botvinick, M., Wierstra, D., Lillicrap, T.: Meta-learning with memory-augmented neural networks. In: ICML, pp. 1842–1850 (2016)
26. Shen, S., Wu, T., Qi, G., Li, Y.F., Haffari, G., Bi, S.: Adaptive knowledge-enhanced Bayesian meta-learning for few-shot event detection. In: Findings of ACL-IJCNLP, pp. 2417–2429 (2021)
27. Snell, J., Swersky, K., Zemel, R.: Prototypical networks for few-shot learning. In: Advances in Neural Information Processing Systems, vol. 30 (2017)
28. Sung, F., Yang, Y., Zhang, L., Xiang, T., Torr, P.H.S., Hospedales, T.M.: Learning to compare: relation network for few-shot learning. In: 2018 IEEE/CVF Conference on Computer Vision and Pattern Recognition, pp. 1199–1208 (2018)
29. Vinyals, O., Blundell, C., Lillicrap, T., Kavukcuoglu, k., Wierstra, D.: Matching networks for one shot learning. In: NeurIPS, vol. 29 (2016)
30. Walker, C., Strassel, S., Medero, J., Maeda, K.: ACE 2005 Multilingual Training Corpus (2006)
31. Yan, H., Jin, X., Meng, X., Guo, J., Cheng, X.: Event detection with multi-order graph convolution and aggregated attention. In: EMNLP-IJCNLP, pp. 5766–5770 (2019)
32. Yan, W., Yap, J., Mori, G.: Multi-task transfer methods to improve one-shot learning for multimedia event detection. In: BMVC, pp. 37.1–37.13 (2015)
33. Zhang, H., Wang, H., Roth, D.: Zero-shot label-aware event trigger and argument classification. In: Findings of ACL-IJCNLP, pp. 1331–1340 (2021)

Named Entity Recognition for Partially Annotated Datasets

Michael Strobl[1]([✉]), Amine Trabelsi[2], and Osmar Zaïane[1]

[1] University of Alberta, Edmonton, Canada
{mstrobl,zaiane}@ualberta.ca
[2] Lakehead University, Thunder Bay, Canada
atrabels@lakeheadu.ca

Abstract. The most common Named Entity Recognizers are usually sequence taggers trained on fully annotated corpora, i.e. the class of all words for all entities is known. Partially annotated corpora, i.e. some but not all entities of some types are annotated, are too noisy for training sequence taggers since the same entity may be annotated one time with its true type but not another time, misleading the tagger. Therefore, we are comparing three training strategies for partially annotated datasets and an approach to derive new datasets for new classes of entities from Wikipedia without time-consuming manual data annotation. In order to properly verify that our data acquisition and training approaches are plausible, we manually annotated test datasets for two new classes, namely food and drugs.

Keywords: Named entity recognition · Partially annotated datasets

1 Introduction

Named Entity Recognition (NER) is one of the most popular tasks in NLP. The goal for NER is to classify each token in a sequence according to a scheme and a set of classes. The set of classes a model can recognize is dependent on the dataset it is trained on, e.g. *Person, Organization, Location* and *Miscellaneous* for the popular CoNLL 2003 NER dataset [6]. Typically a sequence tagging model (e.g. [3]) is used to achieve this task, which takes a sentence of tokens as input and outputs a sequence of classes.

In order to train such a model, high-quality manually annotated data is necessary with each entity in the dataset assigned its correct class. Datasets with partial annotations, mainly without all entities being annotated, are noisy and lead to worse model performance. This is due to the fact that entities in the dataset, which are not annotated as such, are automatically considered as belonging to the *Outside* class, i.e. tokens not belonging to an entity. Therefore, the model is trained not to recognize these, even though it should, leading to a model which may be tempted to ignore a certain number of entities.

© The Author(s), under exclusive license to Springer Nature Switzerland AG 2022
P. Rosso et al. (Eds.): NLDB 2022, LNCS 13286, pp. 299–306, 2022.
https://doi.org/10.1007/978-3-031-08473-7_27

However, partially annotated data is often easier to come by, e.g. through using hyperlinks from Wikipedia[1] as entities. This is especially useful if classes other than the ones seen in common NER datasets are of interest. Furthermore, intuitively, why should it be necessary to annotate every single entity in a dataset to make a model learn this task? Humans are perfectly able to recognize mentions of an entity consistently after having it "classified" once. Consider the following sentence with partial links for animals from Wikipedia[2]:

> "Stauffer's animal crackers include bear, bison, camel, **cow**, **cat**, **donkey**, elephant, hippopotamus, horse, lion, **mountain goat**, rhinoceros, and tiger."

This sentence originally contains four links to animals, while the other nine animals are not linked. Wikipedia often contains partially annotated sentences due to a Wikipedia policy discouraging editors either from linking the same article more than once or linking popular articles all together since they would not provide any new information to the reader. However, if the goal is to train a model, which is capable of recognizing the class "Animal", being able to use such data without manual annotations would simplify the task significantly.

Therefore, this paper aims to describe how it is possible to train commonly used models for NER on partially annotated datasets for new classes, without a significant manual effort for data annotation.

These are our main contributions:

- Describing a procedure on how we can create partially annotated datasets for new classes derived from Wikipedia categories semi-automatically.
- Providing and comparing training strategies for NER models on partially annotated datasets.
- Releasing two manually annotated dataset of 500 sentences each for the classes *Food* and *Drugs* in order to test how generalizable our data extraction techniques are.

The remainder of this paper is outlined as follows: Sect. 2 shows some related work on how the problem of training models on partially annotated datasets has been approached before. We propose our method for data extraction from Wikipedia and model training strategies in Sect. 3. The experimental evaluation can be found in Sect. 4 with a conclusion in Sect. 5.

Datasets and code are publicly available.[3] A more detailed version of this paper is also available [7].

2   Related Work

Jie et al. [2] proposed an approach to train a BiLSTM-CRF model on partially annotated datasets. Their iterative approach tried to find the most

---

[1] https://www.wikipedia.org/.

[2] https://en.wikipedia.org/wiki/Animal_cracker.

[3] https://github.com/mjstrobl/NER_for_partially_annotated_data.git.

likely labelling sequence that is compatible with the existing partial annotation sequence, i.e. the model is supposed to learn to assign the highest weight to the most likely (ideally correct) labelling sequence.

The CoNLL 2003 dataset for English was used (among other datasets) for the evaluation. 50% of the labelled entities were removed for testing their model. The best model achieved a 1.4% F1-score reduction on CoNLL 2003 (compared to the same model architecture trained on the complete dataset without any entities removed). Only fully annotated (yet artificially perturbed) datasets were considered for the evaluation.

A different approach was proposed by Mayhew et al. [5] for training BiLSTM-CRF models on existing datasets for a variety of languages, e.g. the CoNLL 2003 dataset. They used an iterative approach in order to learn a weight between 0.0 and 1.0 for each token, depending on whether the corresponding prediction should add to the loss. Whenever a span of tokens representing an entity is considered as non-entity, the weight should be close to 0.0, and in case of a proper entity annotation, the weight should be 1.0. The dataset was artificially perturbed to reduce precision as well as recall. Therefore, instead of trying to label the training sequence correctly, they tried to figure out which tokens are of class *Outside* with high confidence (weight = 1.0) and which ones are probably entities (weight = 0.0) that should not add to the loss. Their best model still suffered from an F1-score reduction of 5.7% and in the same experiments the models from [2] had an 8% reduction. Note that the dataset also contained random spans of tokens added as entities, which was not tested by [2]. Although, it is not known which mistakes can be attributed to lowering recall or precision in the training dataset.

In addition, both aforementioned model architectures seem to be outdated as models based on the Transformer architecture [9], specifically the pre-trained BERT model [1], achieve a significantly higher F1-score than BiLSTM-CRF models when trained on unperturbed datasets, e.g. see [1] compared to the popular LSTM-based approach from [3], which was specifically developed for NER. Both models are not tested on new datasets with new entity classes.

3   Method

This section proposes our approach to create partially annotated NER datasets from Wikipedia for new classes and strategies to train models on these datasets without sacrificing prediction performance on entities from existing classes.

3.1   Data Creation

When creating datasets for new classes for NER there are two problems to solve:

1. Where can we get text data from? Entities of the class of interest maybe less abundant than common classes. If simply random sentences, e.g. from the web, are included, the fraction of useful token spans maybe quite low.

302   M. Strobl et al.

2. How can we annotate relevant token spans? Manual data annotation is a time-consuming task, even if done partially, which should be avoided.

Wikipedia as a whole can be considered as a partially annotated dataset. Hyperlinks in articles correspond to entities and the hierarchical category system can be considered as a class hierarchy, which can be used to classify entities. Therefore, we only need to know which categories are relevant for the class of interest in order to extract a set of articles to create a partially annotated dataset.

Our iterative procedure to extract a set of categories from the Wikipedia category hierarchy is based on Breadth-first-search. We start at a base-category, e.g. "Category:Food and Drink"[4] for the class *Food*. At each iteration, a sub-category and 10 corresponding articles are presented to the user, who has to make a decision whether to keep it. If it is kept, all sub-categories (if available) are added to the queue. Ultimately, all categories the user wants to keep including all articles in these categories are considered for the class of interest, and text from Wikipedia can be extracted. In our experience it seems to be possible to finish it within 1 to 2 h, at least for our test classes.

Since the training corpus for the new class C should be somewhat difficult for a model to be trained on, it is also necessary to consider articles, which share aliases with articles in C (many entity mentions can refer to entities of different types). This can be done with an alias dictionary derived from Wikipedia hyperlinks. We used the parser from [8] including their alias dictionary in order to extract sentences from Wikipedia, which contain hyperlinks of articles in C (annotated as entities of class C) or hyperlinks of other articles that share aliases with those in C (annotated as non-entities). This results in a partially annotated corpus of sentences mentioning entities and non-entities of class C.

In addition, the alias dictionary is used to annotate potential entities with an unknown type since, as we pointed out, not all entities are annotated in Wikipedia. Depending on the model, these entities would be excluded from training since the type is unknown. This is applied to all datasets used for training, e.g. CoNLL 2003 may contain entities of type *Food*, which can be found and potentially excluded this way. Since an NER model should be trained on this kind of dataset as well as other datasets, such as CoNLL 2003, the CoreNLP NER [4] is used to find all other entities of type *Person, Location, Organization* and *Miscellaneous*. These additional entities are also considered as non-entities.

3.2 Model Training Strategies

When partially annotated data is introduced, the main goals for model training are:

1. Classification accuracy for entities of existing classes should not suffer from the introduction of new data. We still rely on the CoNLL 2003 dataset.

---

[4] https://en.wikipedia.org/wiki/Category:Food_and_drink.

2. Similarly, a new entity class is introduced through partially annotated data and predictions by a model trained on such data should still be of high quality.

In the following, we propose multiple strategies for NER with partially annotated data with an evaluation in Sect. 4.

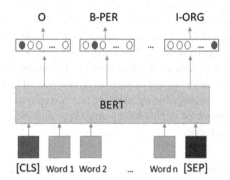

Fig. 1. BERT embeddings are used as input for the final classification layer.

Softmax Model. The model described here is used as starting point for all subsequent models. We are using the NER model proposed in [1], which was published with the ubiquitous BERT model and shown in Fig. 1. An output layer with a softmax activation is used for token classification. The Categorical Cross-Entropy is used as loss function.

This loss function is not capable of taking advantage of non-entities as well as entities of unknown type in the training dataset. Therefore, these entities are considered to belong to the *Outside* class for this model.

Softmax (Weighted). If a span of tokens was annotated as non-entity or an entity of unknown type, it is probably detrimental for the model to simply classify it as *Outside*. Therefore, through adjusting the loss function to ignore these tokens when training, we do not harm the model. A weight w is added for each token with $w = 0$ for non-entity tokens and tokens of unknown type, the model should not be trained on, and $w = 1$ for all other tokens.

Sigmoid (Weighted). So far, the problem of taking advantage of the fact that some spans of tokens are known to be entities not belonging to the new class C, but unknown which is the true class, has not been solved yet. In order to do so, our model can be slightly adapted through using a weighted multiclass multi-label approach with a sigmoid activation for each class in the output layer, using a binary cross-entropy loss. Therefore, each class for each token can be weighted separately, in contrast with Softmax (weighted). This model is able to specifically learn that an entity is not part of a particular class and is able to take advantage of all available information in the partially annotated datasets.

4 Evaluation

4.1 Datasets Derived from Wikipedia

We created two datasets, for the classes *Food* and *Drugs*, referring to the Wikipedia categories "Food and Drink"[5] and "Drugs",[6] respectively. Table 1 shows statistics about these datasets. *Positive Entities*[7] refer to the number of entities of the corresponding new class, detected through matching the set of class-related articles and hyperlinks in Wikipedia. *Non-Entities*[8] denote entities that are linked to other articles in Wikipedia. *Excluded Entities*[9] are entities that could potentially refer to an entity of the type of interest, e.g. through matching an alias of a corresponding article, but a hyperlink is missing. *Entities* correspond to the number of entities for each type and *Sentence* to the number of sentences in each dataset.

Table 1. Statistics for datasets for the types Food and Drugs.

Entity type	Pos. entities	Non-entities	Excl. entities	Entities	Sentences
Food	246,292	139,825	293,926	17,164	283,635
Drugs	93,439	16,772	65,350	27,863	82,498

A part of the sentences were left out for manual annotation, resulting in datasets with 280,000 and 80,000 sentences for *Food* and *Drugs*, respectively. 500 of each of these sets of sentences were manually annotated by an annotator familiar with the task. These datasets are referred to as *Food* and *Drugs gold* in the following. We used a Train-Dev-Test split: 80%-10%-10% with corresponding Wikipedia and CoNLL datasets merged.

4.2 CoNLL + Wikipedia

Table 2 shows the performance of the trained models for the classes *Food* and *Drugs*. The results for CoNLL test can be seen as a sanity check whether the newly added data is too noisy and the output layer and loss function may or may not be able to compensate for this. In order to compare, *Softmax (CoNLL)* denotes a model, which was trained on CoNLL only, without any new Wikipedia-based datasets and entity classes.

---

[5] https://en.wikipedia.org/wiki/Category:Food_and_drink.
[6] https://en.wikipedia.org/wiki/Category:Drugs.
[7] All three models can be trained on these.
[8] Only *Sigmoid (weighted)* can properly use these, excluded from training for *Softmax (weighted)*, considered as *Outside* for the *Softmax* model.
[9] Excluded from training for the *weighted* models, *Outside* for the *Softmax* model.

Table 2. Results for new datasets. Best F1-score for each dataset in bold.

Food	CoNLL test			Food test			Food gold		
Model	P	R	F1	P	R	F1	P	R	F1
Softmax (CoNLL)	0.90	0.92	**0.91**	–	–	–	–	–	–
Softmax	0.89	0.86	0.88	0.79	0.82	0.80	0.73	0.42	0.53
Softmax (weighted)	0.90	0.90	0.90	0.93	0.95	**0.94**	0.52	0.70	0.59
Sigmoid (weighted)	0.89	0.88	0.88	0.93	0.93	0.93	0.66	0.65	**0.65**
Baseline	–	–	–	–	–	–	0.28	0.51	0.36
Drugs	CoNLL test			Drugs test			Drugs gold		
Softmax	0.90	0.90	0.90	0.88	0.91	0.89	0.75	0.65	**0.69**
Softmax (weighted)	0.91	0.90	**0.91**	0.98	0.97	**0.97**	0.58	0.80	0.67
Sigmoid (weighted)	0.89	0.90	0.89	0.95	0.96	0.96	0.62	0.74	0.67
Baseline	–	–	–	–	–	–	0.28	0.44	0.34

All three approaches are able to produce reasonable results for CoNLL. Our experience was that the new datasets did not contain many entities of class *Person, Location, Organization* or *Miscellaneous*. Therefore, it is not surprising that these datasets did not add too much noise harming the ability of the model to still recognize the original entity classes.

Results for *Food/Drugs test* show the ability of the model to adapt to presumably noisy data. The *weighted* approaches clearly outperform the *Softmax* approach. This shows the necessity of at least excluding mentions that are known to be ambiguous from training. The *Sigmoid (weighted)* approach does not seem to add any benefit in this setting. The dictionary-based *Baseline* approach performs poorly in both cases.

The results on the *Food gold* dataset are slightly more diverse. The *Sigmoid (weighted)* approach returned the best results with almost balanced *Precision* and *Recall*. Both, *Softmax* and *Softmax(weighted)* result in a much larger gap. *Softmax* on the one hand produces a high *Precision* and low *Recall*, indicating that it is capable of recognizing very few entities relatively consistently. *Softmax (weighted)* on the other hand produces a high *Recall* and low *Precision*. When compared to the balanced result of the *Sigmoid (weighted)* approach, it seems that this model is not able to recognize non-food-entities as *Outside* properly.

The distinction between *Softmax (weighted)* and *Sigmoid (weighted)* is less clear for the dataset *Drugs gold*. We assume that drug names in general are less ambiguous and therefore less non-entities are found (in fact only ≈10% of all found entities from Wikipedia in the *Drugs*-dataset are non-entities, compared to ≈20% for the *Food*-dataset). In addition, we noticed that, during manual annotation, this dataset is less noisy than the *Food* dataset. The *Softmax* model is even able to outperform the other approaches at least on the *Drugs gold* dataset, while still under-performing on *Drugs test*.

5   Conclusion

We proposed an approach to extract partially annotated datasets for Named Entity Recognition semi-automatically from Wikipedia. In addition, three model architectures, based on the commonly used BERT model, differing only in the activation function of the output layer as well as the loss function, were compared. Two of the tested models, introducing simple changes to the base model, show promising results when trained on partially annotated Wikipedia-based data and tested on similar data as well as on a small amount of manually annotated data for the classes *Food* and *Drugs*. Performance on the CoNLL 2003 NER dataset is not harmed significantly through adding data for the tested new entity classes. Dictionary-based approaches can be outperformed by a large margin.

References

1. Devlin, J., Chang, M.W., Lee, K., Toutanova, K.: Bert: pre-training of deep bidirectional transformers for language understanding. In: Conference of the North American Chapter of the Association for Computational Linguistics: Human Language Technologies, vol. 1, pp. 4171–4186 (2019)
2. Jie, Z., Xie, P., Lu, W., Ding, R., Li, L.: Better modeling of incomplete annotations for named entity recognition. In: Conference of the North American Chapter of the Association for Computational Linguistics: Human Language Technologies, vol. 1, pp. 729–734 (2019)
3. Lample, G., Ballesteros, M., Subramanian, S., Kawakami, K., Dyer, C.: Neural architectures for named entity recognition. In: Proceedings of the 2016 Conference of the North American Chapter of the Association for Computational Linguistics: Human Language Technologies, San Diego, California, pp. 260–270. Association for Computational Linguistics, June 2016. https://doi.org/10.18653/v1/N16-1030
4. Manning, C.D., Surdeanu, M., Bauer, J., Finkel, J., Bethard, S.J., McClosky, D.: The Stanford CoreNLP natural language processing toolkit. In: Association for Computational Linguistics (ACL) System Demonstrations, pp. 55–60 (2014)
5. Mayhew, S., Chaturvedi, S., Tsai, C.T., Roth, D.: Named entity recognition with partially annotated training data. In: Proceedings of the 23rd Conference on Computational Natural Language Learning (CoNLL), pp. 645–655 (2019)
6. Sang, E.T.K., De Meulder, F.: Introduction to the CoNLL-2003 shared task: language-independent named entity recognition. In: Proceedings of the Seventh Conference on Natural Language Learning at HLT-NAACL 2003, pp. 142–147 (2003)
7. Strobl, M., Trabelsi, A., Zaiane, O.: Named entity recognition for partially annotated datasets. arXiv:2204.09081 (2022)
8. Strobl, M., Trabelsi, A., Zaïane, O.R.: WEXEA: Wikipedia exhaustive entity annotation. In: Proceedings of The 12th Language Resources and Evaluation Conference, pp. 1951–1958 (2020)
9. Vaswani, A., et al.: Attention is all you need. In: Advances in Neural Information Processing Systems, vol. 30 (2017)

Automatic Mapping of Quranic Ontologies Using RML and Cellfie Plugin

Ibtisam Khalaf Alshammari[1,2](✉) ⓘ, Eric Atwell[1] ⓘ,
and Mohammad Ammar Alsalka[1] ⓘ

[1] University of Leeds, Leeds, UK
{ml18ikfa,e.s.atwell,m.a.alsalka}@leeds.ac.uk
[2] University of Hafr Al-Batin, Hafr Al-Batin 39524, Kingdom of Saudi Arabia
ikalshammari@uhb.edu.sa

Abstract. The text of the Qur'an has been analysed, segmented and annotated by linguists and religious scholars, using a range of representations and formats, Quranic resources in different scopes and formats can be difficult to link due to their complexity. Qur'an segmentation and annotation can be represented in a heterogeneous structure (e.g., CSV, JSON, and XML). However, there is the lack of a standardised mapping formalisation for the data. For this reason, this study's motivation is to link morphological segmentation tags and syntactic analyses, in Arabic and Buckwalter forms, to the Hakkoum ontology to enable further clarification of the Qur'an. For achieving this aim, the paper combines two mapping methods: the RDF (resources description framework) mapping language, which is an R2RML extension (the W3C level necessary when mapping relational databases into RDF), and Cellfie plugin, which is a part of the Protégé system. The proposed approach provides the possibility to automatically map and merge the heterogeneous data sources into an RDF data model. Also, the integrated ontology is evaluated by a SPARQL query using an Apache Jena Fuseki server. This experiment was conducted in all the Qur'an chapters and verses, containing all the words and segments of the entire Qur'an corpus.

Keywords: Classical Islamic text · Heterogeneous data · Ontology mapping · Ontology integration · RML · Cellfie plugin

1 Introduction

Islamic knowledge has naturally always been an interest of Muslims and has been a growing interest of non-Muslims, especially knowledge of the Holy Qur'an. This is because the Qur'an is the primary sacred text in Islam and the Muslim belief that it is an essential source of information, wisdom, and law. Indeed, due to its unique style and metaphorical nature, the Holy Qur'an requires special consideration when it comes to search and information retrieval concerns. The Holy Qur'an text is written in Classical Arabic text and it is divided into 30 divisions (أَجزاء), 114 chapters (سُور), and subdivided into 6236 verses (آيات).

P. Rosso et al. (Eds.): NLDB 2022, LNCS 13286, pp. 307–314, 2022.
https://doi.org/10.1007/978-3-031-08473-7_28

Many studies have been conducted to accomplish keyword searches with the Holy Qur'an, based on developing Quranic resources and ontologies. The fundamental issues with these works are that the ontologies are incomplete, cover different scopes, and represented in various formats, such as CSV, JSON, and XML files.

The benefit of building a Qur'an ontology-based knowledge base lies in the power of ontologies to enable exploration of semantic relations among concepts. Subsequently, Our hypothesis was that integrating the available resources would enrich an ontology that covers as many of the Quranic concepts as possible. Thus, in this paper, we describe an experiment that combines two ontology mapping methods: the resource description framework (RDF) mapping language and Cellfie plugin to extract, map and integrate the selected resources.

The following section provides insight into the Hakkoum ontology and Qac-Segment dataset. In Sect. 3, the related work is discussed. Section 4 illustrates how the framework can be applied for ontology mapping and integration. Section 5 presents the results obtained from the experiment and visualises the first chapter of the Qur'an, as an example. In the final section, we conclude by summarising our work and describing the outlook for further work.

2   Existing Qur'an Resources

A number of studies aimed to enrich Quranic resources and ontologies. Some ontologies covered most of the Quranic topics as [8], while others focused on specific concepts such as [13] covered the prayer topic (الصلاة), and [15] covered Umrah pilgrims concept. In this section, Hakkoum ontology and QacSegment corpus are presented in order to be mapped and merged using the proposed framework in Fig. 1.

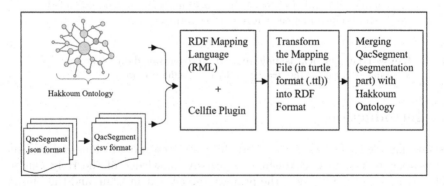

Fig. 1. The proposed framework

2.1 Hakkoum Ontology

Hakkoum ontology, Qur'an Ontology[1], was constructed by Aimad Hakkoum [8]. Hakkoum ontology has been chosen for extension because it includes key annotation datasets of the Holy Qur'an. This ontology was created using Protégé editor with an aim to represent the Quranic concepts and their relationships. Hakkoum resource has more than one million triples, its size is 123 939 KB.

The Hakkoum ontology links the Quranic text from Tanzil project. Tanzil project provides Qur'an metadata, Qur'an plain Arabic, Uthmani, and English translation texts. It encompasses Qur'an descriptions from the books Tafsir Al-Jalalayn and Al-Muyasser. Furthermore, Hakkoum resource contains the topics discussed in the Holy Qur'an from the index of a widely-cited Qur'an commentary, Tafsir Ibn Kathir, captured and encoded in the Qurany project [1]. The Hakkoum ontology also has the most significant Quranic annotations in the QurAna dataset [14]. However, the morphological segmentation tags and syntactic annotation of each word, in the Arabic and Buckwalter[2] forms, are not included in the Hakkoum ontology.

QacSegment Dataset. QacSegment.json[3] is a JSON encoding of the Quanic Arabic Corpus annotated data-set [4,5] developed by Sharaf and Atwell [14]. This corpus covers the prefix features, roots, lemma, and morphological analysis for each word of the Holy Qur'an. This resource is including the morphological segmentation tags of each Quranic word, which is our interest. Moreover, the syntactic annotation is included that focuses on the dependency grammar to showcase the functional relations between Quranic words. For instance, ["GEN"] is attributed to the last part of a preposition phrase.

3 Related Work

3.1 Ontology

According to Gruber, *"An ontology is an explicit specification of a conceptualization"* [7, p. 199]. Ontology is defined as structuring and representing knowledge explicitly in a machine-readable format that may be integrated into computer-based applications and systems. As a result, the number of researchers studying ontologies for developing Qur'an knowledge bases has increased significantly. The importance of the morphological annotation is demonstrated in [2]. Morphology analysis and a dependency treebank are two popular techniques that can contribute to various natural language processing (NLP) applications such as a knowledge base.

---

[1] Qur'an ontology Data can be downloaded via: http://Quranontology.com/.

[2] This is a computer-readable orthographic transliteration technique that uses ASCII characters to represent Arabic text for non-Arabic academics.

[3] It is can be accessed via: http://textminingthequran.com/.

Ontology Mapping. It is called ontology integration or ontology alignment and is the consideration of the semantic correspondences between similar concepts from various ontologies. Ontology mapping plays a crucial role in data interoperability in the semantic web [10]. Ontology mapping aims to unify multiple ontologies within a particular domain [16].

RDF Mapping Language. The Consortium for the World Wide Web created the RDF mapping language (RML) to exhibit particular rules for mapping from various data structures and serialisations, such as tables in the form of comma-separated values (CSV), JavaScript object notation (JSON), and extensible markup language (XML) files to the RDF data model [12]. RML is a suggestion that extends the R2RML recommendation to include diverse data sources [11].

RML is used to map heterogeneous and hierarchical data sources into RDF. [3] provided examples to generate data from two different formats, such as XML and JSON files. To conclude, they evaluated their experiment against various criteria and then stated that RML provided an optimal solution as it was semantically richer and better interlinked than alternatives.

Cellfie is a Protégé plugin that automatically imports and maps spreadsheets to ontologies in OWL (the abbreviation for the web ontology language). It can be used by setting transformation rules to convert spreadsheets into OWL formats. For example, in [6] the Cellfie plugins were used to import data related to COVID-19 from the Indian province of Karnataka. They explained that each row was transformed into a patient class individual, with the values such as patient case and age.

4   Methodology

4.1   Data Preparation

This section describes the vital stage of our work in the initial preparation of the data. The Hakkoum ontology was reviewed and evaluated manually, and we noticed the following limitations:

First, the Hakkoum ontology was built based on Qur'an metadata resource, and the Qur'an metadata has three types of chapter names: Arabic, English, and transliterated, i.e. Arabic words written with English alphabet. However, Hakkoum does not distinguish between transliterated and English names because the ontology has 47 chapter names in English, and 67 chapter names in transliterated words. For example, the chapter "The Opening" (سورة الفاتحة) is represented in the Hakkoum ontology as the English form "The Opening," While the chapter "The Women" (سورة النساء) is expressed in the transliterated word "An-Nisaa." Therefore, we modified the transliterated names manually using Protégé and changed them to English names.

Second, the Hakkoum ontology covers many areas related to Qur'an verses and words, such as displaying the text in simple and Uthmany style, showing the Ayah numbers for each chapter, dividing each verse into words, indicating the pronoun reference of each term, and showing the word's lemma and root. However, it does not have morphological segmentation tags and syntactic features. Hence, we contribute by linking the QacSegment resource with the morphological segmentation layer and syntactic analyses to clarify the Qur'an text further.

Before conducting our experiment, the QacSegment dataset was downloaded and prepared for the second phase by converting the JSON file to CSV file by importing the CSV and JSON Python libraries. Then, building a conceptual model for the CSV file and extract the keys represented in our ontology such as classes and data properties. We manually created only the class names and data properties to be able to automatically extract their data, the individuals.

RDF Mapping Language. The RDF mapping language (RML) is used to express bespoke mapping rules from the CSV file to the RDF data model. The first step was to map the Hakkoum classes and CSV columns. For instance, in our CSV file, the "SurahId" column was mapped to the "Chapter" class. The same process was applied to the other Hakkoum classes and the CSV columns. The segmentation class was then created and linked with the "Word" concept in the Hakkoum ontology. Although the RML mapped the CSV file instances, it did not connect the Arabic words because the Arabic language is not supported in RML. Finally, the mapped file was saved in the terse RDF triple language (or "turtle") format (.ttl).

Cellfie Plugin. The purpose of using the Cellfie tool is to extract the Arabic text by customising specific rules because the RML does not support the Arabic language. The initial step was to convert the CSV file into an Excel file as the Cellfie plugin can handle the Excel format.

Then, SDM-RDFizer is used to transform the turtle file into RDF. SDM-RDFizer is a mapping rule interpreter to transform unstructured data into RDF. The obtained result, N-triple, will be uploaded to the Protégé editor and then converted to OWL format to be uploaded again. Finally, we can import the Hakkoum ontology to finalise our experiment.

5 Results

The integrated ontology is mapped and linked the chosen resources properly. Then, the first chapter "Al-Fateeha" of the integrated ontology is visualised (see Fig. 4). We display the first chapter because the image for all the Qur'an chapters is large. Table 1 shows a comparison of Hakkoum and the integrated ontologies. We can notice that the size of the integrated ontology is increased by 131 88 KB, from 123 939 to 137 127 KB.

5.1 Apache Jena Fuseki

This can be defined as a SPARQL server that can run as an operating system service. This stage of our experiment evaluates the resulting ontology to check the classes and triples. Figure 2 shows the Arabic and Buckwalter segmentation's SPARQL queries, and Fig. 3 illustrates their results. The purpose of using Apache Jena Fuseki is that Protégé editor cannot create a SPARQL query for a large RDF triples. Protege is widely used for research on small example ontologies. However, it does not scale up to very large data-sets.

Analysis. The Protégé editor did not work very well and crashed during some attempts; we tried to increase the maximum memory allocation pool for a Java virtual machine (JVM) through running a batch file to improve its performance.

Furthermore, the process was time consuming when we linked the Arabic concepts with the Cellfie plugin. Also, during development, another issue had arisen: a SPARQL query cannot work through Protégé; we, therefore, used Apache Jena Fuseki because it had good performance and could process the SPARQL query.

Table 1. Comparing the integrated ontology to Hakkoum ontology

Matrices	Hakkoum ontology	Integrated ontology
Axiom	1 282 191	2 471 467
Class count	46	47
Individual count	110 939	239 158
Data property count	23	29

```
PREFIX rdf: <http://www.w3.org/1999/02/22-rdf-syntax-ns#>
PREFIX owl: <http://www.w3.org/2002/07/owl#>
PREFIX rdfs: <http://www.w3.org/2000/01/rdf-schemas#>
PREFIX universityOfLeeds:<http://www.qurankb.org/universityOfLeeds/>
SELECT ?Word ?Segmentation
WHERE {   ?Word universityOfLeeds:hasArabicSegment ?Segmentation
} LIMIT 5000
```

(a)

```
PREFIX rdf: <http://www.w3.org/1999/02/22-rdf-syntax-ns#>
PREFIX owl: <http://www.w3.org/2002/07/owl#>
PREFIX rdfs: <http://www.w3.org/2000/01/rdf-schemas#>
PREFIX universityOfLeeds:<http://www.qurankb.org/universityOfLeeds/>
SELECT ?Word ?Segmentation
WHERE{ ?Word universityOfLeeds:hasBuckwalterSegment ?Segmentation
} LIMIT 5000
```

(b)

Fig. 2. SPARQL query to generate (a) Arabic and (b) Buckwalter segment

universityOfLeeds:quran1-1-1-Seg1	"بِ"
universityOfLeeds:quran1-1-1-Seg2	"سْمِ"
universityOfLeeds:quran1-1-2-Seg1	"ٱللَّهِ"

(a)

universityOfLeeds:quran1-1-1-Seg1	"bi"
universityOfLeeds:quran1-1-1-Seg2	"somi"
universityOfLeeds:quran1-1-2-Seg1	"{ll~ahi"

(b)

Fig. 3. Segmentation results in (a) Arabic and (b) Buckwalter of SPARQL queries

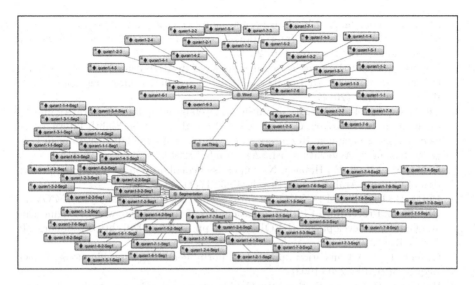

Fig. 4. Integrated ontology visualisation for the first chapter

6 Conclusion and Future Work

The contribution of this paper is the development of a framework of ontology mapping techniques applied to the linguistic and religious annotations of the Quran corpus: RML and Cellfie plugin with the tool interpreter, SDM-RDFizer. Although we faced difficulties with the RML method because it does not support the Arabic language, it merged the proposed ontologies. In addition, the Apache Jena Fuseki SPARQL server was used to handle the very large knowledge base. The findings of this study were sufficient because the morphological annotations and syntactic analyses were linked to all the Qur'an chapters, verses, and words in the Hakkoum ontology.

For future work, we intend to continue working on the same process with the remaining Quranic resource content. We can contribute to mapping the transliterated names from the Qur'an metadata resource. Furthermore, we plan to map the Quranic ontology with Hadith in order to build a comprehensive knowledge base of the most important Islamic concepts.

Acknowledgements. Ibtisam Alshammari would like to express her deepest gratitude to Saudi Arabia Cultural Bureau (SACB) in London, United Kingdom, as well as University of Leeds, and University of Hafr Al-Batin.

References

1. Abbas, N.H.: Qur'an 'Search for a Concept' tool and website. Unpublished Dissertation. University of Leeds (2009)

2. Ayed, R., Chouigui, A., Elayeb, B.: A new morphological annotation tool for Arabic texts. In: IEEE/ACS 15th International Conference on Computer Systems and Applications (AICCSA), pp. 1–6 (2018)

3. Dimou, A., et al.: Mapping hierarchical sources into RDF using the RML mapping language. In: IEEE International Conference on Semantic Computing, pp. 151–158. IEEE, New York (2014)

4. Dukes, K., Atwell, E.: LAMP: a multimodal web platform for collaborative linguistic analysis. In: Calzolari, C. et al. (eds.) Proceedings of the Eighth International Conference on Language Resources and Evaluation (LREC 2012). European Language Resources Association (ELRA), Istanbul (2012)

5. Dukes, K., Atwell, E., Habash, N.: Supervised collaboration for syntactic annotation of Quranic Arabic. Lang. Res. Eval. J. **47**(1), 33–62 (2013)

6. Dutta, B., DeBellis, M.: CODO: an ontology for collection and analysis of COVID-19 data. In: Proceeding of 12th International Conference on Knowledge Engineering and Ontology Development (KEOD), vol. 2, pp. 76–85 (2020). https://doi.org/10.5220/0010112500760085

7. Gruber, T.R.: A translation approach to portable ontology specifications. Knowl. Acquis. **5**(2), 199–220 (1993)

8. Hakkoum, A., Raghay, S.: Semantic Q&A system on the Qur'an. Arab. J. Sci. Eng. (2016). https://doi.org/10.1007/s13369-016-2251-y

9. Ma, C., Molnár, B.: Use of ontology learning in information system integration: a literature survey. In: Sitek, P., Pietranik, M., Krótkiewicz, M., Srinilta, C. (eds.) ACIIDS 2020. CCIS, vol. 1178, pp. 342–353. Springer, Singapore (2020). https://doi.org/10.1007/978-981-15-3380-8_30

10. Mao, M.: Ontology mapping: an information retrieval and interactive activation network based approach. In: Aberer, K., et al. (eds.) ASWC/ISWC -2007. LNCS, vol. 4825, pp. 931–935. Springer, Heidelberg (2007). https://doi.org/10.1007/978-3-540-76298-0_72

11. Meester, B.D., Heyvaert, P., Verborgh, R., Dimou, A.: Mapping languages analysis of comparative characteristics. In: Knowledge Graph Building and Large Scale RDF Analytics. CEUR Workshop Proceedings, vol. 2489 (2019)

12. RDF Mapping Language (RML). https://rml.io/specs/rml/. Accessed 13 Dec 2021

13. Saad, S., Salim, N., Zainal, H.: Towards context-sensitive domain of Islamic knowledge ontology extraction. Int. J. Infonomics (IJI) **3**(1), 197–206 (2010)

14. Sharaf, A.-B., Atwell, E.: QurAna: corpus of the Qur'an annotated with pronominal anaphora. In: Calzolari, C. et al. (eds.) Proceedings of the Eighth International Conference on Language Resources and Evaluation (LREC 2012), pp. 130–137. European Language Resources Association (ELRA), Istanbul (2012)

15. Sharef, N.M., Murad, M.A.A., Mustapha, A., Shishehchi, S.: Semantic question answering of Umra pilgrims to enable self-guided education. In: 13th International Conference on Intelligent Systems Design and Applications (ISDA 2013), pp. 141–146, Kuala Lumpur (2013)

16. Zaeri, A., Nematbakhsh, M.: A semantic search algorithm for ontology matching. Semant. Web J., 254 (2015)

Improving Relation Classification Using Relation Hierarchy

Akshay Parekh[(✉)] [iD], Ashish Anand, and Amit Awekar

Indian Institute of Technology Guwahati, Guwahati, India
{akshayparakh,anand.ashish,awekar}@iitg.ac.in

Abstract. The relation classification (RC) task classifies a relation present between two target entities in a given context. It is an important task of information extraction and plays a significant role in several NLP applications. Most of the existing studies consider relation classes as a flat list of classes and thus ignore hierarchical relation between classes. This study explores the application of relation hierarchy in improving relation classification performance. In particular, we focus on the following two applications of relation hierarchy: (i) detecting noisy instances; and (ii) modifying the cross-entropy (CE) loss function. We use TACRED, the most widely used RC dataset for this purpose. We build a taxonomical relation hierarchy over the relation classes of TACRED and use it for filtering and relabeling ambiguous or noisy instances of TACRED. For better optimization, we also introduce hierarchical-distance scaled cross-entropy loss (HCE Loss), using the shortest-path distance between ground truth and predicted label for scaling cross-entropy loss. Our extensive empirical analyses indicate that relation hierarchy-inspired filtering, relabeling, and the HCE loss help in improving the relation classification.

Keywords: Information extraction · Relation classification · Relation hierarchy

1 Introduction

Relation classification (RC) plays a significant role in several NLP tasks, including automatic knowledge base completion [7], information retrieval [14], and question answering [3]. The goal of RC is to classify the relation mention between a pair of real-world entities in a given sentence with an appropriate relation label. These relation labels can be arranged into a taxonomical relation hierarchy (TRH). A TRH can play a significant role in all applications of RC. Parekh et al. [8] have created a TRH using multiple KBs. However, the idea of utilizing relations between relation labels or TRH for RC remains largely unexplored.

This study focuses on a few potential applications of a TRH using TACRED [15], the most widely used large-scale RC dataset. A few studies [1,11] have shown that TACRED is noisy and contains several incorrectly annotated relation

© The Author(s), under exclusive license to Springer Nature Switzerland AG 2022
P. Rosso et al. (Eds.): NLDB 2022, LNCS 13286, pp. 315–322, 2022.
https://doi.org/10.1007/978-3-031-08473-7_29

labels. This study focuses on two questions: (i) Can TRH assist in identifying noisy instances? (ii) Can the cross-entropy (CE) loss function be modified to use TRH to improve classifier performance?

To achieve these objectives, we create a TRH of TACRED relation labels using the template followed in [8]. This TRH is further used to analyze the noisy nature of TACRED [1,11] and to define a novel scaled cross-entropy (CE) loss, referred to as *Hierarchical distance scaled CE (HCE)* loss.

Our analysis of TACRED data instances indicates the following issues: (i) the existence of instances where object entity types do not align with the annotated relation labels, (ii) certain labels have very few training instances, and (iii) there are few relations with overlapping relation boundaries. We introduce filtering and relabeling heuristics using the TRH to take care of the three issues. The filtering heuristic allows instances with ambiguous subject-object entity types to be eliminated from the TACRED. Relabeling heuristic relabel instances to coarser relation labels using the TRH to address the second and third issues. On the resulting dataset, *TACRED-FR*, all baseline models performed better.

Finally, we have used TRH to define HCE, a scaled cross-entropy loss. The primary objective here is to penalize more if the distance between the ground truth and the prediction in the relation hierarchy is high. The empirical results show that models perform better with the proposed HCE loss. Further analysis of the results of models using HCE loss shows that the number of misclassifications, where the distance between predicted and ground-truth labels was high, is reduced significantly.

Primary contributions of the work can be summarized as follows:

- Using relation hierarchy based filtering and relabeling to target RC dataset challenges such as, incorrect object entity type sentence detection, long-tail distribution, and overlapping relation label boundary.
- Using hierarchical distance to scale cross-entropy loss for better optimisation.

2   Related Works

Wang et al. [13] was the first to propose an SVM-based model for hierarchical relation extraction on the ACE 2004 dataset. Later, a few studies [5,12] have target hierarchical relation extraction on distantly supervised 2010 NYT dataset [10]. Chen et al. [2] proposed a bi-directional LSTM network along with a loss function using a hierarchy of relations adopted from Wikidata. Although these studies have shown improvement, consideration of a shallow hierarchy specific to a dataset and their respective method is the major bottleneck for generalization.

Recently, Parekh et al. [8] introduced a TRH by organizing more than 600 relations between *Person, Organization,* and *Location*, collected from Wikipedia infoboxes, DBpedia, and Wikidata. Although the method of generating TRH and the generated TRH itself is very generic, they did not provide any experiments on the use-case of the generated TRH. In this work, we derive a similar TRH for TACRED. We have used it to further improve the performance of baseline models by working on the caveats of TACRED. Furthermore, we have proposed a scaling loss function using this TRH for better model optimization.

3   Application of Relation Hierarchy: Case Study on TACRED

This section first discusses the creation of TRH on TACRED relation labels and then discusses some of the potential use cases of this TRH for RC.

TACRED is a sentence-level dataset where each instance contains a sentence and a pair of entities. One entity represents the *subject entity* and the other represents the *object entity*. Each instance is labeled with one of the 41 relation labels (positive label) or *no_relation* (negative label). The TACRED dataset has a total of seventeen entity types. Subject entity types for all relations in TACRED are either *PERSON* or *ORGANIZATION* and object entity types can be mapped to one of the four coarse types, namely, *PERSON*, *ORGANIZATION*, *LOCATION*, and *MISC*.

Following [8], we create eight relation buckets based on the two subject and four object entity types. Relations in each bucket are manually arranged following *is-a relation*. We have also introduced a few new relations in the hierarchy to better represent the taxonomic relationship between the relations. For example, we have introduced a new relation *PER:LOCATION_OF_BIRTH*. This relation is the parent node for the following relations: *PER:CITY_OF_BIRTH*, *PER:COUNTRY_OF_BIRTH* and *PER:STATE_OR_PROVINCE_OF_BIRTH*. In all, we introduce a total of seventeen new relations corresponding to non-leaf nodes in the hierarchy. All relations from the original TACRED dataset are mapped to the leaf nodes in the TRH.

3.1   Filtering Ambiguous Instances

A relation is defined between a pair of entities hence, the domain and range of a relation are defined over entity types. Certain relations can be defined with multiple subject and object entity types. For example, relation *PARENT* can exist between two *PERSON*s as well as between two *ORGANIZATION*s. Thus, some relations can have multiple entity types for subject and object entities. Moreover, in one of the recent works, [9], authors have observed that the RC models rely heavily on entity type information. Therefore, the RC model needs to consider unambiguous combinations of subject and object entity types for a given relation. However, some instances in the TACRED dataset do not follow this rule. There are instances in the training datasets with *COUNTRY* and *LOCATION* as object entity types for the relation *ORG : SUBSIDIARIES*. A country or location cannot be a subsidiary of an organization. This indicates an annotation error.

On examining positive instances from the TACRED training dataset, we found that all the positive instances can be divided into 69 distinct relation triples *(subj_ent_type, relation, obj_ent_type)*. Out of these 69 distinct triples, there are 11 triples for 6 relations consisting of ambiguous object entity types. Corresponding instances or data points are likely to be noisy and, hence, should be eliminated while training and testing the RC models. We eliminated 164 sentences from the TACRED dataset following this approach.

3.2 Fine to Coarse Re-labeling

TACRED has an inequitable distribution of instances in training data. Each of the top three relations in TACRED has more than 2000 instances, while the bottom five have less than 100 instances. This shows the long-tail distribution in relation to labels. Another challenge with RC datasets is the identification of class boundaries between certain relation labels due to overlapping contexts. When one such relation is also part of the long-tail distribution, then learning about such relation labels gets even more difficult.

To tackle the problems mentioned above, we leverage relation between relations from the TRH. We merge the finer relations from TRH into coarser relations. For example, relations *CITY_OF_BIRTH*, *COUNTRY_OF_BIRTH*, and *STATE_OR_PROVINCE_OF_BIRTH* are fine-grained with these issues. Thus instances of all the three relations are merged into the corresponding parent relation *LOCATION_OF_BIRTH*. Although this decreases the granularity, it helps in increasing the number of instances for a similar relation concept, thus helping the models learn relation boundaries efficiently.

3.3 Hierarchical Scaled Cross-Entropy Loss

Cross-Entropy Loss estimates the negative log-likelihood of a class label t_i under a categorical distribution y (Eq. (1)).

$$J = -\sum_{i=1}^{n_r} t_i log(y_i) \tag{1}$$

Here, n_r is number of relation labels. CE loss does provide a good estimate of how far the model is off in predicting the correct label. However, Ghosh et al. [4] have shown that the cross-entropy loss function is not robust for multi-class classification with noisy labels.

Considering the class labels can be arranged in a label hierarchy, in this work, we introduce hierarchical distance scaled cross-entropy (HCE) loss. We modify the CE loss function by scaling it with the shortest path distance between the ground-truth and predicted label in the relation hierarchy $d_{y^*,\hat{y}}$ as follows.

$$J^* = d_{y^*,\hat{y}} * J \tag{2}$$

where, J is cross-entropy loss, y^* is the ground-truth and $\hat{y}$ is the predicted relation label. This modification ensures that when the distance between the ground-truth and predicted label is high in the hierarchical tree, it is penalized higher compared to when the distance is smaller.

4 Experiment Setup

4.1 Experimental Setup and Baseline Models

We have used PALSTM [15], SpanBERT [6], BERT and RoBERTA [16] in our experiments. All the models are trained on TACRED using the hyper-parameters reported in the respective contributions.

Table 1. Evaluation results of dataset relabeling followed by filtering on TACRED following 4 baseline models.

Model	Metric	TACRED	
		Original	TACRED-FR
PALSTM [15]	Precision	66.5	68.1
	Recall	65.7	65.7
	F1	66.1	66.9
SpanBERT [6]	Precision	66.4	70.7
	Recall	66.1	65.5
	F1	66.3	68
BERT [16]	Precision	71.1	73.1
	Recall	71.4	71.4
	F1	71.2	72.2
RoBERTA [16]	Precision	75.4	75.2
	Recall	73.1	74.5
	F1	74.2	74.9

We evaluate the performance of the proposed HCE loss function, considering the CE loss as the baseline. We have fine-tuned the hyper-parameters of the SOTA model SpanBERT for this set of experiments. With relevant fine-tuning, similar results can be obtained for other models as well.

Since *NO_RELATION* is not part of the relation set, there must be an appropriate penalty associated with it. Based on our experiments, we penalize the model with twice the maximum distance if a label is a relation and prediction is *NO_RELATION* and 1.75 times the maximum distance for the reverse misclassification.

4.2 Evaluation Metric

We consider macro-averaged precision (P), recall (R), and F1-Score (F1) for all our experiments. We also consider positive accuracy, i.e. how efficient a model is in correctly classifying positive relations for evaluation. This is equivalent to a macro-averaged recall.

All the above-mentioned evaluation metrics efficiently provide overall information on how well the model is performing. However, they fail to provide any information on the severity of errors while evaluating the RC models. Hence, we propose *prediction at distance d* to measure the performance of the model with fine-grained details.

Prediction at distance d shows the fine-grained analysis of model errors. For each test data instance, we have a ground truth annotation label (AL) from the dataset and the model's prediction as to the predicted label (PL). The shortest distance path between AL and PL in TRH is computed. This distance is referred to as a prediction at distance d. The greater the distance between PL and AL, the greater the severity of a model prediction error.

Table 2. SpanBERT performance for challenging relations group on TACRED and TACRED-FR

Relation	#Test instances	TACRED prediction	TACRED-FR prediction
PER:FAMILY	306	140	221
PER:LOCATION_OF_BIRTH	18	5	6
PER:LOCATION_OF_DEATH	51	8	16
PER:LOCATIONS_OF_RESIDENCES	418	219	217

5   Results and Discussion

5.1   Model Performance on TACRED and Variants

Effects of Filtering and Relabeling. The main motivation behind filtering and relabeling instances with their coarser labels is to reduce the noise from the dataset and to mitigate the effects of relation labels with fewer instances sharing context with other relation labels. Relation labels with very few instances often get classified with the other relation labels having overlapping or very similar contexts. Combining relation labels with similar information helps the model learn better. Table 1 shows the performance of the model when trained and evaluated on the new dataset TACRED-FR. It can be observed that all the models show significant performance improvement.

Alt et al. [1] have discussed in their work that TACRED relations under the bucket *per-loc* and *per-per* are adversely affecting the model performance. After relabeling those instances with their coarser relation labels, except for *PER:LOCATIONS_OF_RESIDENCES* relation, we have observed performance improvement in all the coarser relations (Table 2).

5.2   Performance of Proposed Loss Function on TACRED

To better understand the learning with HCE loss, we tracked the F1-score and accuracy of positive instances on the validation set during the training (Fig. 1). Even though the model that uses HCE loss is relatively slow to converge, the model gets better at predicting the positive instances (Fig. 1b). This shows that scaling with the shortest distance between prediction and ground truth helps the model learn better.

One of the main objectives behind scaling the CE loss using RH was to reduce the number of predictions at larger distances. For example, instances with AL belonging to *per* relation bucket getting PL from *org* relation bucket. And, it is evident from *Prediction at distance d* results from Table 3 that our proposed heuristic is very close to the objective.

Table 3 presents the performance of the SpanBERT model using the proposed loss and baseline CE loss functions. The model using HCE loss shows an improvement of 2.8% over the baseline. On further analyzing the predictions made by the model, we observe the following:

Table 3. Test Performance of different methods on TACRED and TACRED-FR dataset using SOTA model SpanBERT. All the results are based on our implementation of original code provided by the author.

Dataset	Methods	P	R	F1	Prediction at distance d = x								
					d = 0	d = 2	d = 3	d = 4	d = 5	d = 6	d = 7	d = 8	d = 16
TACRED	CE loss	66.4	66.1	66.3	2199	53	28	18	43	36	39	5	904
	HCE loss	68.9	69.2	69.1	2302	89	25	29	3	0	0	0	877
TACRED-FR	CE loss	70.7	65.5	68	2171	31	0	3	30	25	32	6	1015
	HCE loss	68.4	68.2	68.3	2259	24	0	0	21	9	31	0	969

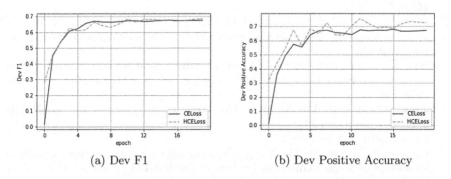

(a) Dev F1   (b) Dev Positive Accuracy

Fig. 1. Dev set performance at different epoch for SpanBERT model.

- significant reduction of misclassification to *NO_RELATION*. The usage of HCE loss helped several instances to be predicted as one of the positive relation class.
- significant reduction in misclassification of instances of relation classes with overlapping context. For example, *ORG:COUNTRY_OF_HEADQUARTERS* was being predicted for some instances for which the ground-truth relation label was *PER:COUNTRIES_OF_RESIDENCES*. However, with HCE loss, such misclassification got reduced.

6   Conclusion and Future Work

This paper builds upon the impact of taxonomical relation hierarchy on the large-scale relation classification task. It shows that using the heuristics utilizing TRH, some of the noisy instances can be easily filtered and relabeled. Furthermore, this work shows that the use of scaled CE loss using the TRH can further improve the performance of the models. All the above impacts have been shown on the most commonly used large-scale relation classification dataset, TACRED. This work can be further extended by using the TRH for data augmentation by leveraging triples from knowledge bases.

References

1. Alt, C., Gabryszak, A., Hennig, L.: TACRED revisited: a thorough evaluation of the TACRED relation extraction task. In: Proceedings of the 58th Annual Meeting of the ACL, pp. 1558–1569 (2020)
2. Chen, J., Liu, L., Xu, J., Hui, B.: Hierarchical relation extraction based on bidirectional long short-term memory networks. In: Proceedings of the 2019 International Conference on Data Mining and Machine Learning, pp. 110–113 (2019)
3. Cui, W., Xiao, Y., Wang, H., Song, Y., Hwang, S., Wang, W.: KBQA: Learning question answering over QA corpora and knowledge bases. Proc. VLDB Endowm. **10**(5), 565 (2017)
4. Ghosh, A., Kumar, H., Sastry, P.: Robust loss functions under label noise for deep neural networks. In: Proceedings of the AAAI Conference on Artificial Intelligence, vol. 31 (2017)
5. Han, X., Yu, P., Liu, Z., Sun, M., Li, P.: Hierarchical relation extraction with coarse-to-fine grained attention. In: Proceedings of the EMNLP 2018, pp. 2236–2245 (2018)
6. Joshi, M., Chen, D., Liu, Y., Weld, D.S., Zettlemoyer, L., Levy, O.: SpanBERT: improving pre-training by representing and predicting spans. Trans. Assoc. Comput. Linguist. **8**, 64–77 (2020)
7. Lin, Y., Liu, Z., Sun, M., Liu, Y., Zhu, X.: Learning entity and relation embeddings for knowledge graph completion. In: Twenty-Ninth AAAI Conference on Artificial Intelligence (2015)
8. Parekh, A., Anand, A., Awekar, A.: Taxonomical hierarchy of canonicalized relations from multiple knowledge bases. In: Proceedings of the 7th ACM IKDD CoDS and 25th COMAD, pp. 200–203 (2020)
9. Peng, H., et al.: Learning from context or names? an empirical study on neural relation extraction. In: Proceedings of the EMNLP 2020, pp. 3661–3672 (2020)
10. Riedel, S., Yao, L., McCallum, A.: Modeling relations and their mentions without labeled text. In: Joint European Conference on Machine Learning and Knowledge Discovery in Databases, pp. 148–163 (2010)
11. Stoica, G., Platanios, E.A., Poczos, B.: Re-tacred: addressing shortcomings of the tacred dataset. In: Proceedings of the AAAI Conference on Artificial Intelligence, vol. 35, pp. 13843–13850 (2021)
12. Takanobu, R., Zhang, T., Liu, J., Huang, M.: A hierarchical framework for relation extraction with reinforcement learning. In: Proceedings of the AAAI Conference on Artificial Intelligence, vol. 33, pp. 7072–7079 (2019)
13. Wang, T., Li, Y., Bontcheva, K., Cunningham, H., Wang, J.: Automatic extraction of hierarchical relations from text. In: European Semantic Web Conference, pp. 215–229 (2006)
14. Xiong, C., Power, R., Callan, J.: Explicit semantic ranking for academic search via knowledge graph embedding. In: Proceedings of the 26th International Conference on World Wide Web, pp. 1271–1279 (2017)
15. Zhang, Y., Zhong, V., Chen, D., Angeli, G., Manning, C.D.: Position-aware attention and supervised data improve slot filling. In: Proceedings of the EMNLP 2017, pp. 35–45 (2017)
16. Zhou, W., Chen, M.: An improved baseline for sentence-level relation extraction. arXiv preprint arXiv:2102.01373 (2021)

A Framework for False Negative Detection in NER/NEL

Maria Quijada⬤, Maria Vivó⬤, Álvaro Abella-Bascarán[(✉)]⬤,
Paula Chocrón⬤, and Gabriel de Maeztu

IOMED Medical Solutions SL, Barcelona, Spain
alvaro.abella@iomed.es, alvaro.abella@iomed.health
https://iomed.health

Abstract. Finding the false negatives of a NER/NEL system is fundamental to improve it, and is usually done by manual annotation of texts.
However, in an environment with a huge volume of unannotated texts
(e.g. a hospital) and a low frequency of positives (e.g. a mention of a
particular disease in the clinical notes) the task becomes very inefficient.
This paper presents a framework to tackle this problem: given an existing NER/NEL system, we propose a technique consisting of using text
similarity search to rank texts by probability of containing false negatives of a given concept, using as a query those texts where the existing
NER/NEL system has found positives of this concept. We formulate text
similarity as a function of shared medical entities between texts, and we
re-purpose an existing public dataset (CodiEsp) to propose an evaluation
strategy.

Keywords: Natural language processing · NLP · Clinical NLP · False
negatives · Document representation · Text similarity search · Named
Entity Recognition · NER · Named Entity Linking · NEL

1 Introduction

Natural language processing has attracted a great deal of attention in recent
times in the clinical domain. The reason behind this interest is that textual
data (consisting of clinical notes containing patients' medical history, diagnoses,
medications, etc.) is a highly abundant resource in the clinical setting, greatly
exceeding structured data. One of the most frequent applications of NLP methods in clinical research consists in finding instances of a certain medical concept
(a specific disease, treatment, etc.) in a huge corpus of clinical notes (e.g. in a
whole hospital). This task usually consists of two parts: Named Entity Recognition (NER, recognizing the entity in text and associating a category such as
'disease', 'finding', 'substance', etc.) and Named Entity Linking (NEL). In this

---

M. Quijada and M. Vivó—Contibuted equally.
Á Abella-Bascarán and P. Chocrón—Contributed equally.

P. Rosso et al. (Eds.): NLDB 2022, LNCS 13286, pp. 323–330, 2022.
https://doi.org/10.1007/978-3-031-08473-7_30

context, NEL means assigning to each entity a code which specifies the meaning of the entity under some medical terminology (for example, the ICD10-CM terminology for diagnoses and ICD10-PCS for procedures). These two tasks are the basis for many use cases of clinical NLP, such as recruiting patients for clinical studies, finding underdiagnosed patients, pharmacovigilance, etc.

A myriad of techniques and algorithms have been explored in the clinical domain to perform the task of finding medical entities (NER) and linking them to specific codes (NEL), from simple gazetteers to complex architectures including transformers. These methods are classically evaluated using the notions of *True Positives* (TP, entities found by the system which are correct), *False Positives* (FP, predicted entities that are incorrect), and False Negatives (FN, entities that were not found). Independently from the algorithm at hand, the staggering amount of clinical texts in a hospital (often in the order of tens of millions), together with the few occurrences of certain medical entities (frequently in the order of hundreds) poses one main challenge for any NER/NEL system: in order to improve such system (via retraining or addition of new vocabulary) it is essential to retrieve FNs; however, due to the low frequency of positives this is extremely hard, making the task intractable via traditional manual annotation of a random sample of texts.

Automatically finding FNs would be the holy grail in almost any Machine Learning scenario, where the standard procedure is using human labour to annotate data in a costly and time consuming manner. In our case we propose an intermediate setting, where instead of automatically finding FN entities, we automatize the search of notes with a high probability of containing them. Then, human annotators can review these notes to find the actual FN entities. This can be done by gathering notes which contain positives found by our NER/NEL system, and using them to search for similar notes where our NER/NEL system has not found any positive. By doing this we reformulate the problem in a way which is easily solved with existing technology, since finding similar documents is an extensively researched NLP task. Here, the most common approach is a two-step method: create a mathematical representation of the documents where texts with similar meaning have similar vector representations, and compute the similarity distance between them.

As summary, this paper presents a framework to tackle the problem of finding FNs in a NER/NEL task conducted over a large, unannotated corpus. We propose a technique consisting of employing a text similarity search to rank texts by probability of containing FNs of a given medical concept, using as a query those texts where our existing NER/NEL system has found positives. We formulate text similarity as a function of shared medical entities between texts, and we re-purpose an existing public dataset (CodiEsp) to propose an evaluation strategy.

2   Technical Background

One of the most used techniques to represent documents in a mathematical form is *Term Frequency - Inverse Document Frequency* (TF-IDF) due to its simplicity and robustness [1,11,19]. This technique has been improved by applying different dimension reduction techniques such as singular value decomposition (SVD) [9,10]. On the other hand, documents can be represented making use of Word Embeddings learned with shallow neural networks. Word Embeddings, as Word2Vec, are vector representations capable of capturing syntactic and semantic relationships between words [12,15]. Several attempts have been made to combine these word vector representations to obtain a document representation: from a simple averaging of the word vectors to sophisticated architectures (CNN, RNNs, etc.) [6,8]. A third methodology to obtain document embedding is the usage of transformers such as BERT [4], although without fine-tuning these sometimes exhibit poor performance for semantic similarity search [13], and in our case are too slow to be considered a viable option.

Some advanced weighted averagings of the word vectors have been proposed, such as the *Inverse Document Frequency* (IDF) term, assigning vector importance according to their global occurrence or considering as well the local frequency (*Delta, SIF*) [2,18]. Authors have also used PCA with these weightings to get rid of shared information, removing the projections of the average vectors on the first singular vector (*SIF*) [2,7,18]. These methods improve the performance of textual similarity by about 10% to 30% [2,20].

As for the similarity distances, they can be divided into two groups: those that measure the lexical distance between document vectors and those that measure the semantic distance [5]. The latter, as in Word2Vec, appeals to us as a better scenario in which we are not only treating words as discrete symbols, but are introducing their semantics into the similarity search. Nevertheless, semantic distances, as the *Word Mover's Distance* [21], are more computationally expensive than length distances (e.g. cosine similarity, euclidean distance or Levenshtein distance) and according to previous research not introduce a significant improvement on the performance of document similarity search [17]. Cosine similarity is often the chosen approach, specially when using TF-IDF, since it is an angular distance which better tolerates sparsity [3].

3   Dataset

The corpus used to conduct the experimentation for our FN-retrieval system was CodiEsp (Clinical Case Coding in Spanish Shared Task) [16]. This set of clinical documents contains annotations over diagnostics and procedures. The CodiEsp corpus consists of 1000 clinical case studies selected manually by a practicing physician and a clinical documentalist, with an average of 396.2 words per document. These documents are in Spanish and have 18,483 annotated ICD10 codes that cover a variety of medical topics. The codes can be classified in two groups: diagnostics codes (ICD10-CM) and procedures codes (ICD10-PCS). CodiESP was devised for evaluation of clinical NER/NEL tasks, and therefore represents a ground truth of the medical entities found in clinical notes (circumscribed to diagnoses and procedures). Since the dataset is small and fully annotated, we can expect that all diseases and procedures have been annotated.

We are not using CodiEsp for evaluation of a NER/NEL system. Instead, we are using it to evaluate methodologies for finding FNs based on a sample of positives and a text similarity search. In order to do this, we re-purpose the dataset to evaluate text similarity tasks, where the text similarity between two texts is a function of the medical entities shared between those texts.

The rationale behind using CodiEsp is having a dataset the most similar to our target documents, but publicly available so that other researchers can further experiment or develop on this approach. Our target documents are clinical narratives written in Spanish, similar to the ones found in CodiEsp, but with the main difference that CodiEsp notes are in general better written, containing no orthographic mistakes or misspellings, and having more elaborate sentences. The entities annotated in CodiEsp are procedures and diseases, which are two of the categories of entities we often deal with, which also makes the dataset attractive to simulate our final use case. The coding scheme is different, since CodiEsp uses ICD-10 and we rely mostly on SNOMED; although we expect the granularity of the ontology to affect the results, we do not consider this an impediment to generalize the results to our use case: the granularity of ICD-10 is higher than that of SNOMED for conditions and procedures, which makes our final task potentially easier to tackle than the CodiEsp case.

4   A Text Similarity-Based Framework to Retrieve False Negatives

In order to find clinical notes that are most likely to contain a target entity, we present a FN-retrieval framework consisting of three phases:

1. **Note representation:** the first stage consists in learning a low-dimensional representation of clinical notes that allocates similar notes nearby in a vector space. Since our goal is to find notes with similar medical concepts, we should make sure that similarity correlates with shared medical concepts.
2. **Query construction:** in the second stage, given a target medical concept (e.g. the disease 'psoriasis' with its specific ICD10-CM code), and a set of notes were our NER/NEL system found this entity, we want to find clinical notes where this system didn't find 'psoriasis', but which have a high probability of containing this concept. To do this we construct what we call the 'query vector': an average of the vector representations of a set of clinical notes which contain positive cases.
3. **Document ranking:** once the query vector is built, we use it to compute document distances with the rest of the corpus. The lower the distance of a note is to the query vector, the higher the probability is of containing the target medical concept.

These three stages are in themselves areas of research and can be tackled in many different ways. A critical problem, however, is how to evaluate their performance for the downstream task of finding false negatives. In Sect. 4.1 we present an evaluation framework that uses the CodiEsp corpus described before, and in Sect. 4.2 we discuss the different types of note representation methodologies that we explored.

4.1 Evaluation Framework

In this section we present our evaluation framework which re-purposes the CodiEsp corpus. As explained above, this corpus contains notes with annotated procedures and diagnoses, where each of these entities has an associated ICD10 code representing the medical concept. In our case we have discarded codes with a frequency of less than 50 occurrences.

Once we have chosen a note representation strategy, a method for query construction, and a system for document ranking, the evaluation strategy works as follows:

1. Given a total of M codes, for each of the codes Ci where $i \in [1, M]$, we select a subset Pi of notes which contain at least one entity with this code (here P is for 'positive') . In a real scenario for our framework, these would be the notes where our NER/NEL system has found positives for this code. If there is a total of Ni notes with code Ci, then there are $Mi = Ni - Pi$ notes which fall outside this selected subset, and which in the real scenario would be those notes containing positive cases which our system has missed. In other words, notes which do not fall into our selected subset represent notes containing FNs of our NER/NEL system.
2. For each code Ci, we use the subset of Pi notes to build a query vector (let's call this the 'query subset'). Each of the other notes in the corpus (the other Mi notes with code Ci, plus all the notes without the code) is assigned a text similarity distance with respect to this query vector. A threshold T can be used to choose which notes are considered positives (those whose distance to the query vector falls below T, and therefore they more probably contain the code) and negatives (those whose distance to the query vector exceeds T, and therefore less probably contain the code). Since we know the ground truth, we can compute the True Positive Rate and False Positive Rate for different thresholds, and calculate the Area Under the Curve (AUC), which will serve as our evaluation metric.
3. Once we have the AUC for each code, we can summarize them into a single metric via the average of AUC scores, or via the calculation of a confidence interval.

4.2 Clinical Note Representation

For the representation of clinical notes we have leveraged two types of algorithms, based on the co-occurrence matrix and on the distributional hypothesis. We must acknowledge that this is an area of extensive research and that more complex methods could be used, such as encoder-decoder architectures based on CNNs, LSTMs or transformers. However, we have chosen simple methods with a very low computational cost, which can be easily used with a corpus of hundreds of thousands or millions of texts.

As a representative of the co-occurrence approach, TF-IDF has been selected and implemented on the corpus, resulting on a huge sparse matrix. To make the approach scalable, this matrix has been factorized using Truncated Singular Value Decomposition (SVD). The first 150 components have been selected as a final vector representation of documents. The resulting matrix directly encodes the document vector and no further transformations are required.

As a method representative of the distributional hypothesis, we have used Word2Vec [14] word embeddings as the means of creating document representations. IOMED's Word2Vec model was used, which was trained on a private clinical corpus with more than 7 billion tokens, using 100 dimensions and a maximum vocabulary size of one million terms. In order to obtain a representative document representation, a Smooth Inverse Frequency (SIF) ponderation strategy is implemented, based on the approach in [2]. Word embeddings are weighted and added for all documents, and then PCA is performed to subtract the projection of the document vector to the first principal component.

5   Results

Results for the note representation algorithms on CodiEsp corpus are depicted in Table 1, showing the lower (LCI) and higher (HCI) limit of the 95% confidence interval of AUCs. We see how 'simpler' methodologies yield top performances in this case. TF-IDF with SVD is the best performing model, as well as the lighter model and the second fastest (being TF-IDF the fastest).

The dimensionality reduction performed over TF-IDF yields very similar results, which was expected and desirable, since the goal here was to increase scalability through smaller vectors, and not to improve performance.

With respect to Word2Vec, we expected it to better capture the semantics of the text. We must take into account, however, that it has been used through a simple approach of averaging of vectors (or weighting + averaging), ignoring word order and document structure as with any other Bag of Words (BOW) method. This is also the case of TF-IDF, but the amount of information captured by TF-IDF vectors might be even larger due to the much higher dimensionality. Since the final document vector obtained from Word2Vec representations has a much smaller dimensionality, there is a risk of losing too much information depending on the method employed to aggregate word vectors. We believe that more sophisticated methods which take into account word order, such as encoder-decoder architerctures based on CNNs, LSTMs or transformers, might yield better results.

The improvement of Word2Vec when using SIF was very significant and this is probably due to down-weighting high frequency words which would otherwise introduce too much noise into the final document vectors.

Table 1. Performance of vectorization techniques on CodiEsp corpus for codes with over 50 occurrences.

Lower (LCI) and higher (HCI) limit of the 95% confidence interval of AUCs		
Vectorizer	AUC - LCI	AUC - HCI
TF-IDF	0.796	0.847
TF-IDF SVD	**0.803**	**0.855**
Word2Vec	0.555	0.620
Word2Vec SIF	0.748	0.798

6   Conclusions and Future Work

We have shown that the task of finding NER/NEL FNs can be partially automated by a framework which uses text similarity search, employing notes containing positives as a query. Also, we have devised a strategy to evaluate this framework in the clinical domain, using the CodiEsp dataset, and we have used this evaluating strategy to compare four different methods of document vectorization and search.

The approach we describe only requires a NER/NEL dataset, regardless of language, domain or coding scheme, and therefore is not constrained to CodiEsp. The only requirement would be being able to prepare a note representation method for the target domain (which can be as simple as computing a TF-IDF or training a Word2Vec). This would allow to test the efficacy of this approach for finding NER/NEL FNs in new domains, languages or coding schemes, prior to employing it for the actual task of retrieving FNs to improve a NER/NEL system.

As a future work we will show the effectiveness of this framework on a real clinical dataset, using it to retrieve FNs of a specific clinical concept for which a very low amount of positives was found. More sophisticated strategies for producing document vectors in a scalable way will also be explored.

References

1. Alodadi, M., Janeja, V.P.: Similarity in patient support forums using TF-IDF and cosine similarity metrics. In: 2015 International Conference on Healthcare Informatics, pp. 521–522 (2015). https://doi.org/10.1109/ICHI.2015.99
2. Arora, S., Liang, Y., Ma, T.: A simple but tough-to-beat baseline for sentence embeddings. In: ICLR (2017)
3. Aryal, S., Ting, K.M., Washio, T., Haffari, G.: A new simple and effective measure for bag-of-word inter-document similarity measurement. arXiv preprint arXiv:1902.03402 (2019)
4. Devlin, J., Chang, M., Lee, K., Toutanova, K.: BERT: pre-training of deep bidirectional transformers for language understanding. CoRR abs/1810.04805 (2018). http://arxiv.org/abs/1810.04805

5. Farouk, M.: Measuring sentences similarity: a survey. CoRR abs/1910.03940 (2019). http://arxiv.org/abs/1910.03940

6. Gao, M., Li, T., Huang, P.: Text classification research based on improved Word2vec and CNN. In: Liu, X., et al. (eds.) ICSOC 2018. LNCS, vol. 11434, pp. 126–135. Springer, Cham (2019). https://doi.org/10.1007/978-3-030-17642-6_11

7. Gupta, V., Saw, A., Nokhiz, P., Netrapalli, P., Rai, P., Talukdar, P.P.: P-SIF: document embeddings using partition averaging. CoRR abs/2005.09069 (2020). https://arxiv.org/abs/2005.09069

8. Jang, B., Kim, M., Harerimana, G., Kang, S.U., Kim, J.W.: Bi-LSTM model to increase accuracy in text classification: combining Word2vec CNN and attention mechanism. Appl. Sci. **10**(17) (2020). https://doi.org/10.3390/app10175841, https://www.mdpi.com/2076-3417/10/17/5841

9. Kadhim, A.I., Cheah, Y.N., Ahamed, N.H.: Text document preprocessing and dimension reduction techniques for text document clustering. In: 2014 4th International Conference on Artificial Intelligence with Applications in Engineering and Technology, pp. 69–73 (2014). https://doi.org/10.1109/ICAIET.2014.21

10. Kadhim, A.I., Cheah, Y.N., Hieder, I.A., Ali, R.A.: Improving TF-IDF with Singular Value Decomposition (SVD) for feature extraction on Twitter (2017)

11. Lahitani, A.R., Permanasari, A.E., Setiawan, N.A.: Cosine similarity to determine similarity measure: study case in online essay assessment. In: 2016 4th International Conference on Cyber and IT Service Management, pp. 1–6 (2016). https://doi.org/10.1109/CITSM.2016.7577578

12. Le, Q.V., Mikolov, T.: Distributed representations of sentences and documents. In: International Conference on Machine Learning (2014)

13. Li, B., Zhou, H., He, J., Wang, M., Yang, Y., Li, L.: On the sentence embeddings from pre-trained language models. CoRR abs/2011.05864 (2020). https://arxiv.org/abs/2011.05864

14. Mikolov, T., Chen, K., Corrado, G.S., Dean, J.: Efficient estimation of word representations in vector space. In: ICLR (2013)

15. Mikolov, T., Sutskever, I., Chen, K., Corrado, G., Dean, J.: Distributed representations of words and phrases and their compositionality. CoRR abs/1310.4546 (2013), http://arxiv.org/abs/1310.4546

16. Miranda-Escalada, A., Gonzalez-Agirre, A., Armengol-Estapé, J., Krallinger, M.: Overview of automatic clinical coding: annotations, guidelines, and solutions for non-English clinical cases at codiesp track of CLEF eHealth 2020. In: Working Notes of Conference and Labs of the Evaluation (CLEF) Forum. CEUR Workshop Proceedings (2020)

17. Sato, R., Yamada, M., Kashima, H.: Re-evaluating word mover's distance. CoRR abs/2105.14403 (2021). https://arxiv.org/abs/2105.14403

18. Schmidt, C.W.: Improving a TF-IDF weighted document vector embedding. CoRR abs/1902.09875 (2019). http://arxiv.org/abs/1902.09875

19. Tata, S., Patel, J.M.: Estimating the selectivity of TF-IDF based cosine similarity predicates. ACM SIGMOD Rec. **36**(2), 7–12 (2007)

20. Wieting, J., Bansal, M., Gimpel, K., Livescu, K.: Towards universal paraphrastic sentence embeddings. CoRR abs/1511.08198 (2016)

21. Wu, L., et al.: Word mover's embedding: from Word2Vec to document embedding. CoRR abs/1811.01713 (2018). http://arxiv.org/abs/1811.01713

User Profiling

Zero and Few-Shot Learning for Author Profiling

Mara Chinea-Rios[iD], Thomas Müller[iD], Gretel Liz De la Peña Sarracén[iD], Francisco Rangel[iD], and Marc Franco-Salvador[(✉)][iD]

Symanto Research, Valencia, Spain
{mara.chinea,thomas.muller,gretel.delapena,francisco.rangel,
marc.franco}@symanto.com
http://www.symanto.com

Abstract. Author profiling classifies author characteristics by analyzing how language is shared among people. In this work, we study that task from a low-resource viewpoint: using little or no training data. We explore different zero and few-shot models based on entailment and evaluate our systems on several profiling tasks in Spanish and English. In addition, we study the effect of both the entailment hypothesis and the size of the few-shot training sample. We find that entailment-based models outperform supervised text classifiers based on roberta-XLM and that we can reach 80% of the accuracy of previous approaches using less than 50% of the training data on average.

Keywords: Author profiling · Zero-shot text classification · Few-shot text classification · Entailment

1 Introduction

Author profiling [27] aims to identify the characteristics or traits of an author by analyzing its sociolect, i.e., how language is shared among people. It is used to determine traits such as age, gender, personality, or language variety. The popularity of this task has increased notably in the last years.[1] Since 2013, the *Uncovering Plagiarism Authorship and Social Software Misuse*[2] (PAN) Lab at CLEF conference organized annual shared tasks focused on different traits, e.g. age, gender, language variety, bots, or hate speech and fake news spreaders.

Data annotation for author profiling is a challenging task. Aspects such as the economic and temporal cost, the psychological and linguistic expertise needed by the annotator, and the congenital subjectivity involved in the annotation task, make it difficult to obtain large amounts of high quality data [2,33]. Furthermore, with few exceptions for some tasks (e.g. PAN), most of the research has been conducted on English corpora, while other languages are under-resourced.

---

[1] According to https://app.dimensions.ai/, the term "Author profiling" tripled its frequency in research publications in the last ten years.

[2] https://pan.webis.de/.

P. Rosso et al. (Eds.): NLDB 2022, LNCS 13286, pp. 333–344, 2022.
https://doi.org/10.1007/978-3-031-08473-7_31

Few-shot (FS) learning aims to train classifiers with little training data. The extreme case, zero-shot (ZS) learning [6,15], does not use any labeled data. This is usually achieved by representing the labels of the task in a textual form, which can either be the name of the label or a concise textual description. One popular approach [12,34,36,37] is based on textual entailment. That task, a.k.a. Natural Language Inference (NLI) [3,8], aims to predict whether a textual premise implies a textual hypothesis in a logical sense, e.g. *Emma loves cats* implies that *Emma likes cats*. The entailment approach for text classification uses the input text as the premise, and the text representing the label as the hypothesis. An NLI model is then applied to each premise-hypothesis pair, and the entailment probability is used to get the best matching label.

Our contributions are as follows: (i) We study author profiling from a low-resourced viewpoint and explore different zero and few-shot models based on textual entailment. This is, to the best of our knowledge, the first attempt to use zero and few-shot learning for author profiling. (ii) We study the identification of age, gender, hate speech spreaders, fake news spreaders, bots, and depression, in English and Spanish. (iii) We analyze the effect of the entailment hypothesis and the size of the few-shot training sample on the system's performance. (iv) Our novel *author instance selection* method allows to identify the most relevant texts of each author. Our experiments show that on average we can reach 80% of the accuracy of the top PAN systems using less than 50% of the training data.

2 Zero and Few-shot Author Profiling Approach

In this section, we give details zero and few-shot text classification based on textual entailment and describe how we apply it to author profiling.

2.1 Zero and Few-shot Text Classification

We follow the so called entailment approach [12,34,36,37] to zero-shot text classification. The approach relies on the capabilities of neural language models such as BERT [9] trained on large NLI datasets such as Stanford NLI [3]. These models are trained to predict whether a hypothesis text follows from a premise text. The entailment approach consists of using the input text of a classification problem as the premise. A hypothesis in textual form is then defined for each label. The model is applied to each text-hypothesis pair and the label with the highest entailment probability is chosen as the predicted class.

To use this approach in a few-shot setup, we need to create a training set. We follow the related work [34] and generate the examples in the following manner: Given an text instance and its reference label, we create an instance of class *entailed* using the premise of the hypothesis of the reference label. For every other label hypothesis, we create an instance of class *contradicted*.

The neural models used for entailment classification are usually based on cross attention which means that both inputs (premise and hypothesis) are encoded jointly and their tokens can attend to each other. However, recent work

[7,18] has shown that Siamese networks can also work well if pre-trained on NLI data. A Siamese network encodes premise and hypotheses into a high dimensional vector space and uses a similarity function such as the dot-product to find the hypothesis that best matches the input text. These model can also be used in a few-shot set up. Here we follow the common approach [18] of using the so called *batch softmax* [13]: $\mathcal{J} = -\frac{1}{B} \sum_{i=1}^{B} \left[S(x_i, y_i) - \log \sum_{j=1}^{B} \exp S(x_i, y_j) \right]$, where B is the batch size and $S(x, y) = f(x) \cdot f(y)$ the similarity between input x and label text y under the current model f. All other elements of the batch are used as *in-batch negatives*. We construct the batches so that every batch contains exactly one example of each label.

2.2 Author Profiling

Author profiling represents each author as a collection of texts. The objective is to assign each author to a label of a given set. As the transformer models we employ in this study are large and scale quadratically with the input length we process each text as a separate instance. Following the literature [10], we determine an author's class y in function of the probabilities of classification of its texts: $y = \text{argmax}_{c \in C} \sum_{i=1}^{n} P(c \mid t_i)$, where C is the total number of classes and $[t_1, ..., t_n]$ is the list of texts of that specific author.

Typically, the labeled texts of an author are random and might thus not be representative of the author's label. Especially, when separating the texts into individual training instances, this might produce noisy or misleading instances. In this work, we propose an *instance selection* method to mitigate this effect. Given the texts T, it returns the set of texts $T' = \{t_1, ..., t_m\}$ where each text t_i is the closest to the ith centroid $d_i \in D$. The cluster set D results of applying the Agglomerative Clustering method with cosine distance to the texts in T. Following other work[3], we use scikit-learn [21] and a distance threshold of 1.5 to get a dynamic number of clusters depending on the author and its information.

3 Related Work

Early *Author Profiling* attempts focused on blogs and formal text [1,14] based on Pennebaker's [22] theory, which connects the use of the language with the personality traits of the authors. With the rise of social media, researchers proposed methodologies to profile the authors of posts where the language is more informal [5]. Since then, several approaches have been explored. For instance, based on second order representation which relates documents and user profiles [17], the Emograph graph-based approach enriched with topics and emotions [24], or the LDSE [26], commonly used as a baseline at PAN. Recently, the research has focused on the identification of bots and users who spread harmful information (e.g. fake news and hate speech). In addition, there has been work to leverage the impact of personality traits and emotions to discriminate between classes [11].

---

[3] https://tinyurl.com/st-agg-cluster.

Table 1. Dataset overview. train and test show the number of users for each class. The depression categories are minimal (--), mild (-), moderate (+) and severe (++).

Task	Language	Train	Test
Gender [29]	EN	female:1427, male:1453	female:1200, male:1200
	ES	female:1681, male:1679	female:1400, male:1400
Age [28]	EN	18-24:58, 25-34:60, 35-49:22, 50+:12	18-24:56, 25-34:58, 35-49:20, 50+:8
	ES	18-24:22, 25-34:46, 35-49:22, 50+:10	18-24:18, 25-34:44, 35-49:18, 50+:8
Hate speech [30]	EN	hate:100, not-hate:100	hate:50, not-hate:50
	ES	hate:100, not-hate:100	hate:50, not-hate:50
Bots [25]	EN	bot:2060, human:2060	bot:1320, human:1320
	ES	bot:1500, human:1500	bot:900, human:900
Fake news [23]	EN	spreader:150,not-spreader:150	spreader:100, not-spreader:100
	ES	spreader:150, not-spreader:150	spreader:100, not-spreader:100
Depression [20]	EN	--:14, -:27, +:27, ++:22	--:6, -:34, +:27, ++:13

Zero and Few-shot Text Classification has been explored in different manners. Semantic similarity methods use the explicit meaning of the label names to compute the similarity with the input text [31]. Prompt-based methods [32] use natural language generation models, such as GPT-3 [4], to get the most likely label to be associated with the input text. In this work, we use entailment methods [12,36]. Recently, Siamese Networks have been found to give similar accuracy while being much faster [18].

4 Experimental Setup

4.1 Dataset

We conduct a comprehensive study in 2 languages (English and Spanish) and 7 author profiling tasks: demographics (gender, age), hate-speech spreaders, bot detection, fake news spreaders, and depression level. We use datasets from the PAN and *early risk prediction on the internet* (eRisk) [20] shared tasks. Table 1 gives details on the datasets.

4.2 Entailment Models for Zero and Few Shot

In our experiments, we use pretrained models hosted on Hugging Face [35]. Based on our prototyping experimentation, for the Cross Attention (CA) models, we use a *BART large* [19] model[4] for English and a *XLM roberta-large*[16] model[5] for Spanish. Following [18], for the Siamese Networks (SN) model, we use *paraphrase-multilingual-mpnet-base-v2*[6], a sentence transformer model [31], for English and Spanish. All models have been trained on NLI data. The SN models has additionally been trained on paraphrase data.

---

[4] https://tinyurl.com/bart-large-snli-mnli.
[5] https://tinyurl.com/xlm-roberta-large-xnli-anli.
[6] https://tinyurl.com/paraphrase-multilingual-mpnet.

4.3   Baseline and Compared Approaches

- *Best performing system* (winner): We show the test results of the system that ranked first at each shared task overview paper. The reference to those specific systems can be found in the Appendix (Sect. 7).
- *Sentence-Transformers with logistic regression* (ST-lr): We use the scikit-learn logistic regression classifier [21] on top of the embeddings of the Sentence Transformer model used for the Siamese Network experiments.
- *Character n-grams with logistic regression* (user-char-lr): We use [1..5] character n-grams with a TF-IDF weighting calculated using all texts. Note that $n - grams$ and logistic regression are predominant among the best systems in the different PAN shared tasks [23, 25].
- *XLM-RoBERTa* (xlm-roberta): Model based on the pre-trained *XLM roberta-base* [16]. Trained for 2 epochs, batch size of 32, and learning rate of 2e-4.
- *Low-Dimensionality Statistical Embedding* (LDSE): This method [26] represents texts based on the probability distribution of the occurrence of their terms in the different classes. Key of LDSE is to weight the probability of a term to belong to each class. Note that this is one of the best ranked baselines at different PAN editions.

4.4   Methodology and Parameters

We conduct our validation experiments using 5-fold cross-validation. We report the mean and standard deviation among folds. Using this scheme we fine-tune the few-shot models in terms of users per label ($n \in [8, 16, 32]$), best entailment hypothesis, learning rate, and user instance selection method. Following the literature [18], SN uses a batch size equal to the number of labels and trains for 10 epochs. CA uses a batch size of 8 and trains for 10 epochs.

We compare our author Instance Selection (IS) method (Sect. 2.2) with two baseline methods that respectively select 1 and 50 random instances from the author text list (Ra_1 and Ra_{50}). We use the *paraphrase-multilingual-mpnet-base-v2* model to obtain the instance embeddings required by IS. The resulting tuned CA learning rates are 1e-8 and 1-e6 for Ra_x and IS, respectively. For SN they are 2e-5 and 2e-6.

We use macro F1-score (F_1) as our main evaluation metric and accuracy ($Acc.$) to compare with the official shared task results.

4.5   Hypotheses of the Entailment Models

We compared 68 different hypotheses for the CA and SN entailment models. We included the *identity hypothesis*: represent the label using its raw string label. Table 2 shows the best performing hypothesis for each task and model. We use those for the rest of the evaluation. See the Appendix (Sect. 7) for a complete list with results of all the hypotheses explored in our experiments.

Table 2. Best performing entailment hypotheses. #{EN,ES} indicates the number of explored hypotheses per language.

Task	model	English #EN	Per-class hypothesis list	Spanish #ES	Per-class hypothesis list
Gender	CA	8	I'm a {female, male}	4	*identity hypothesis*
	SN	8	My name is {Ashley, Robert}	4	Soy {una mujer, un hombre}
Age	CA	6	*identity hypothesis*	5	La edad de esta persona es {entre 18 y 24, entre 25 y 34, entre 35 y 49, más de 50} años
	SN	6	I am {a teenager, a young adult, an adult, middle-aged}	5	*identity hypothesis*
Hate speech	CA	8	This text expresses prejudice and hate speech; This text does not contain hate speech	6	Este texto expresa odio o prejuicios; Este texto es moderado, respetuoso, cortés y civilizado
	SN	8	This text contains prejudice and hate speech directed at particular groups; This text does not contain hate speech	6	Odio esto; Soy respetuoso
Bots	CA	7	This is a text from a machine; This is a text from a person	6	*identity hypothesis*
	SN	7	*identity hypothesis*	6	Soy un bot; Soy un usuario
Fake news	CA	8	This author spreads fake news; This author is a normal user	6	Este autor publica noticias falsas; Este autor es un usuario normal
	SN	8	*identity hypothesis*	6	Este usuario propaga noticias falsas; Este usuario no propaga noticias falsas
Depression	CA	4	The risk of depression of this user is {minimal, mild, moderate, severe}		
	SN	4	*identity hypothesis*		

5 Results and Analysis

In this section, we analyze the results of the Siamese networks (SN) and the Cross-Attention (CA) models among different author profiling tasks in English and Spanish. We compare the performance in function of the number of training users (n), author instance selection method (Inst. sel.), and total training size (s). The few-shot results of user-char-lr can be found in the Appendix (Sect. 7).

Table 3 shows the English validation results. Regarding the zero-shot setting ($n = 0$), SN outperforms CA in Age and Bots. However, it obtains lower numbers in tasks such as Gender and Hate Speech. Regarding the few-shot setting ($n > 0$), the Ra_{50} author instance selection method outperforms Ra_1 in combination with SN. Interestingly, the contrary happens for CA, where Ra_{50} is only superior in Bots. Comparing Ra_x and IS, with SN both obtain similar results in four tasks and the later exceeds in two. For the CA model, IS is superior in three tasks and similar in the rest. IS uses much less training data (s) than Ra_{50} in all cases and thus reduces training time and cost. Looking at the overall English few-shot results, SN outperforms CA in four tasks (Age, Hate Speech, Fake News and Depression) and is out-performed in two (Gender and Bots). However, there exist overlaps between some confidence intervals, suggesting a low significance. SN gives more stable results across tasks. Finally, there is a general trend of more

Table 3. English Validation results of the CA and SN models. n shows the number of training users and s the total training size. Top results are highlighted with **bold**.

	n	Inst. Sel.	Gender		Age		Hate speech		Bots		Fake news		Depression	
			s	F_1	s	F_1	s	F_1	s	F_1	s	F_1	s	F_1
Cross-Attention (CA)	0	-	0	$74.7_{1.5}$	0	$27.6_{2.6}$	0	$\mathbf{71.0_{2.8}}$	0	$42.4_{1.2}$	0	$63.8_{3.7}$	0	$24.1_{2.3}$
	8	Ra_1	16	$74.9_{1.5}$	32	$27.4_{3.0}$	16	$68.8_{4.4}$	16	$74.4_{11.5}$	16	$62.3_{5.2}$	29	$27.6_{1.9}$
		Ra_{50}	800	$73.2_{2.7}$	1057	$14.9_{4.0}$	800	$45.9_{6.9}$	800	$86.3_{1.4}$	800	$57.7_{8.3}$	$1,3k$	$20.5_{6.5}$
		IS	257	$67.5_{4.3}$	361	$34.6_{3.3}$	348	$60.1_{7.2}$	191	$87.6_{1.4}$	203	$54.8_{3.1}$	$1,9k$	$23.6_{10.9}$
	16	Ra_1	32	$74.9_{1.5}$	46	$27.4_{2.4}$	32	$66.1_{3.8}$	32	$79.2_{6.2}$	32	$62.6_{4.1}$	45	$\mathbf{27.8_{2.0}}$
		Ra_{50}	$1,6k$	$67.7_{5.3}$	$2,3k$	$12.5_{0.6}$	$1,6k$	$45.5_{5.0}$	$1,6k$	$87.1_{0.4}$	$1,6k$	$55.9_{8.5}$	$2,2k$	$13.6_{6.4}$
		IS	501	$71.3_{3.6}$	611	$37.1_{6.1}$	697	$59.6_{6.0}$	385	$88.5_{1.2}$	432	$62.3_{4.9}$	$2,9k$	$21.4_{6.7}$
	32	Ra_1	64	$74.8_{1.5}$	78	$27.2_{2.3}$	64	$65.9_{5.5}$	64	$86.3_{3.3}$	64	$65.9_{5.5}$	-	-
		Ra_{50}	$3,2k$	$69.2_{4.1}$	$3,9k$	$12.5_{0.6}$	$3,2k$	$56.2_{10.3}$	$3,2k$	$88.8_{1.3}$	$3,2k$	$48.4_{2.8}$	-	-
		IS	$1,0k$	$75.5_{3.4}$	$1,0k$	$\mathbf{41.7_{3.4}}$	$1,4k$	$56.0_{6.5}$	756	$89.7_{1.2}$	880	$61.3_{4.5}$	-	-
	48	Ra_1	96	$74.8_{1.2}$	-	-	96	$62.2_{8.1}$	96	$89.9_{1.2}$	96	$65.5_{3.5}$	-	-
		Ra_{50}	$4,8k$	$72.5_{1.9}$	-	-	$4,8k$	$56.1_{10.3}$	$4,8k$	$90.5_{0.9}$	$4,8k$	$50.0_{4.5}$	-	-
		IS	1517	$75.0_{2.6}$	-	-	2059	$66.4_{11.0}$	1132	$90.4_{1.4}$	1320	$\mathbf{65.8_{5.3}}$	-	-
	64	Ra_1	128	$74.5_{1.2}$	-	-	128	$59.0_{10.5}$	128	$90.7_{1.2}$	128	$65.3_{3.3}$	-	-
		Ra_{50}	$6,4k$	$74.8_{2.2}$	-	-	$6,4k$	$62.9_{14.3}$	$6,4k$	$90.1_{2.1}$	$6,4k$	$53.0_{2.6}$	-	-
		IS	$2,0k$	$75.6_{2.7}$	-	-	$2,2$	$59.5_{8.7}$	$1,5k$	$90.4_{1.4}$	$1,8k$	$61.2_{4.1}$	-	-
	128	Ra_1	256	$74.9_{0.8}$	-	-	-	-	256	$90.4_{2.0}$	-	-	-	-
		Ra_{50}	$12,8k$	$74.3_{1.6}$	-	-	-	-	$12,8k$	$92.3_{1.9}$	-	-	-	-
		IS	$4,0k$	$76.4_{1.7}$	-	-	-	-	$3,0k$	$92.1_{1.6}$	-	-	-	-
	256	Ra_1	512	$75.6_{1.3}$	-	-	-	-	512	$91.3_{0.8}$	-	-	-	-
		Ra_{50}	$25,6k$	$73.9_{0.9}$	-	-	-	-	$25,6k$	$95.8_{1.3}$	-	-	-	-
		IS	$8,0k$	$\mathbf{79.0_{1.2}}$	-	-	-	-	$6,0k$	$94.5_{1.4}$	-	-	-	-
	512	Ra_1	$1,0k$	$70.9_{1.3}$	-	-	-	-	$1,0k$	$93.0_{1.1}$	-	-	-	-
		Ra_{50}	$51,2k$	$74.3_{0.6}$	-	-	-	-	$51,2k$	$\mathbf{97.9_{0.6}}$	-	-	-	-
		IS	$16,0k$	$77.5_{2.3}$	-	-	-	-	$11,9k$	$97.0_{0.6}$	-	-	-	-
Siamese Network (SN)	0	-	0	$38.1_{3.5}$	0	$37.4_{6.6}$	0	$46.3_{12.4}$	0	$62.2_{1.4}$	0	$51.8_{2.4}$	0	$21.9_{5.2}$
	8	Ra_1	16	$55.1_{8.7}$	32	$39.6_{10.9}$	16	$41.7_{6.1}$	16	$50.4_{10.1}$	16	$58.8_{7.9}$	29	$26.3_{5.5}$
		Ra_{50}	800	$63.1_{6.4}$	1057	$50.5_{7.1}$	800	$62.6_{7.8}$	800	$84.5_{1.3}$	800	$55.8_{5.6}$	$1,4k$	$29.2_{3.5}$
		IS	257	$65.2_{4.8}$	361	$51.7_{7.5}$	348	$60.9_{3.7}$	191	$86.1_{1.8}$	203	$54.0_{5.5}$	$1,9k$	$\mathbf{32.7_{7.2}}$
	16	Ra_1	32	$59.4_{3.2}$	46	$39.6_{7.1}$	32	$47.1_{7.1}$	32	$73.3_{8.9}$	32	$59.5_{3.0}$	45	$23.7_{5.5}$
		Ra_{50}	$1,6k$	$68.2_{4.1}$	$2,3k$	$55.4_{4.2}$	$1,6k$	$55.4_{5.7}$	$1,6k$	$84.7_{2.8}$	$1,6k$	$58.2_{7.4}$	$2,2k$	$25.1_{7.1}$
		IS	501	$69.3_{3.6}$	611	$50.9_{4.2}$	697	$60.7_{9.4}$	385	$86.9_{1.8}$	432	$61.7_{7.4}$	$2,9k$	$28.8_{4.8}$
	32	Ra_1	64	$59.6_{5.9}$	78	$38.5_{7.1}$	64	$49.0_{4.9}$	64	$84.5_{1.8}$	64	$60.4_{3.8}$	-	-
		Ra_{50}	$3,2k$	$71.6_{2.3}$	$3,9k$	$\mathbf{52.9_{7.4}}$	$3,2k$	$58.8_{5.2}$	$3,2k$	$87.1_{4.1}$	$3,2k$	$65.2_{5.7}$	-	-
		IS	$1,0k$	$71.4_{2.7}$	$1,0k$	$51.4_{8.0}$	$1,4k$	$60.4_{5.3}$	756	$88.6_{1.6}$	880	$62.6_{5.5}$	-	-
	48	Ra_1	96	$65.6_{3.8}$	-	-	96	$57.9_{7.2}$	96	$86.5_{2.9}$	96	$63.3_{3.3}$	-	-
		Ra_{50}	$4,8k$	$73.1_{1.6}$	-	-	$4,8k$	$65.5_{4.9}$	$4,8k$	$89.6_{1.4}$	$4,8k$	$65.5_{4.9}$	-	-
		IS	$1,5k$	$72.6_{2.4}$	-	-	$2,0k$	$67.8_{4.1}$	$1,1k$	$90.1_{1.7}$	$1,3k$	$\mathbf{68.4_{5.8}}$	-	-
	64	Ra_1	128	$66.5_{4.2}$	-	-	128	$56.3_{9.5}$	128	$88.2_{1.5}$	128	$56.3_{9.5}$	-	-
		Ra_{50}	$6,4k$	$74.1_{2.1}$	-	-	$6,4k$	$68.7_{6.0}$	$6,4k$	$89.6_{1.5}$	6400	$63.9_{4.5}$	-	-
		IS	$2,0k$	$74.4_{2.6}$	-	-	$2,2k$	$\mathbf{68.4_{5.9}}$	$1,5k$	$89.8_{1.5}$	$1,8k$	$63.0_{6.2}$	-	-
	128	Ra_1	256	$67.8_{2.3}$	-	-	-	-	256	$89.8_{1.9}$	-	-	-	-
		Ra_{50}	$12,8k$	$75.8_{0.7}$	-	-	-	-	$12,8k$	$92.4_{1.7}$	-	-	-	-
		IS	$4,0k$	$75.3_{0.6}$	-	-	-	-	$3,0k$	$92.5_{1.7}$	-	-	-	-
	256	Ra_1	512	$70.3_{1.9}$	-	-	-	-	512	$91.2_{1.6}$	-	-	-	-
		Ra_{50}	$25,6k$	$77.1_{1.5}$	-	-	-	-	$25,6k$	$95.4_{1.7}$	-	-	-	-
		IS	$8,0k$	$76.4_{1.4}$	-	-	-	-	$6,0k$	$94.5_{2.2}$	-	-	-	-
	512	Ra_1	$1,0k$	$73.9_{1.9}$	-	-	-	-	$1,0k$	$93.4_{1.7}$	-	-	-	-
		Ra_{50}	$51,2k$	$77.1_{1.7}$	-	-	-	-	$51,2k$	$\mathbf{97.8_{0.9}}$	-	-	-	-
		IS	$15,9k$	$\mathbf{77.1_{2.0}}$	-	-	-	-	$11,8k$	$96.9_{1.1}$	-	-	-	-

Table 4. Spanish Validation results of the CA and SN models. n shows the number of training users and s the total training size. Top results are highlighted with **bold**.

	n	Inst. Sel.	Gender		Age		Hate speech		Bots		Fake news	
			s	F_1	s	F_1	s	F_1	s	F_1	s	F_1
Cross Attention (CA)	0	-	0	$68.1_{2.6}$	0	$\mathbf{27.1_{4.3}}$	0	$60.5_{9.0}$	0	$36.1_{1.2}$	0	$36.3_{3.5}$
	8	Ra_1	16	$61.9_{11.3}$	26	$14.0_{2.3}$	16	$61.9_{11.3}$	16	$68.0_{4.1}$	16	$35.1_{2.5}$
		Ra_{50}	800	$61.3_{2.1}$	$1,2k$	$12.8_{0.4}$	800	$64.2_{7.5}$	800	$72.6_{5.3}$	800	$34.5_{2.6}$
		IS	204	$64.0_{7.3}$	248	$24.1_{7.8}$	272	$63.2_{14.4}$	160	$77.0_{4.4}$	168	$66.0_{7.5}$
	16	Ra_1	32	$67.7_{2.4}$	40	$14.0_{2.3}$	32	$61.1_{10.7}$	32	$72.1_{2.1}$	32	$35.1_{2.5}$
		Ra_{50}	$1,6k$	$56.8_{13.1}$	$1.9k$	$12.8_{0.4}$	$1,6k$	$69.6_{7.3}$	$1,6k$	$79.2_{4.8}$	$1,6k$	$45.3_{9.5}$
		IS	401	$65.6_{3.8}$	474	$18.4_{8.1}$	542	$68.9_{7.7}$	326	$82.0_{2.9}$	334	$70.9_{4.5}$
	32	Ra_1	64	$67.6_{2.1}$	-	-	64	$62.8_{12.1}$	64	$74.9_{4.0}$	64	$35.3_{2.5}$
		Ra_{50}	$3,2k$	$59.9_{15.0}$	-	-	$3,2k$	$59.6_{7.9}$	$3,2k$	$82.9_{2.8}$	$3,2k$	$63.5_{4.5}$
		IS	807	$69.5_{1.6}$	-	-	$1,9k$	$75.8_{2.0}$	630	$84.7_{1.8}$	673	$73.6_{2.1}$
	48	Ra_1	96	$67.3_{2.2}$	-	-	96	$63.7_{11.0}$	96	$77.4_{2.4}$	96	$35.3_{2.5}$
		Ra_{50}	$4,8k$	$61.2_{15.6}$	-	-	$4,8k$	$50.5_{6.8}$	$4,8k$	$84.8_{4.2}$	$4,8k$	$65.2_{4.9}$
		IS	$1,2k$	$69.1_{2.2}$	-	-	$1,6k$	$74.9_{5.0}$	954	$85.1_{3.9}$	$1.0k$	$\mathbf{77.5_{3.3}}$
	64	Ra_1	128	$67.1_{2.0}$	-	-	128	$62.3_{9.5}$	128	$78.4_{2.5}$	128	$34.8_{2.6}$
		Ra_{50}	$6,4k$	$61.4_{15.7}$	-	-	$6,4k$	$49.1_{4.7}$	$6,4k$	$86.1_{2.5}$	$6,4k$	$67.4_{3.9}$
		IS	$1,6k$	$69.5_{2.6}$	-	-	$2,2k$	$\mathbf{77.1_{2.0}}$	$1,3k$	$86.0_{2.2}$	$1,3k$	$75.0_{2.2}$
	128	Ra_1	256	$65.8_{2.2}$	-	-	-	-	256	$83.1_{2.0}$	-	-
		Ra_{50}	$12,8k$	$55.0_{17.8}$	-	-	-	-	$12,8k$	$91.4_{1.7}$	-	-
		IS	$3,3k$	$72.1_{2.0}$	-	-	-	-	$2,6k$	$89.9_{1.8}$	-	-
	256	Ra_1	512	$63.4_{1.4}$	-	-	-	-	512	$87.1_{1.9}$	-	-
		Ra_{50}	$25,6k$	$68.1_{2.6}$	-	-	-	-	$25,6k$	$95.3_{1.4}$	-	-
		IS	$5,2k$	$70.4_{3.0}$	-	-	-	-	$5,1k$	$92.5_{1.5}$	-	-
	512	Ra_1	$1,0k$	$61.5_{1.9}$	-	-	-	-	$1,0k$	$89.0_{1.2}$	-	-
		Ra_{50}	$51,2k$	$68.1_{2.6}$	-	-	-	-	$51,2k$	$\mathbf{97.4_{1.7}}$	-	-
		IS	$13,0k$	$\mathbf{72.5_{2.0}}$	-	-	-	-	$10,3k$	$94.9_{1.7}$	-	-
Siamese Network (SN)	0	-	0	$33.6_{1.3}$	0	$31.8_{3.6}$	0	$36.9_{3.9}$	0	$50.1_{1.6}$	0	$51.5_{6.7}$
	8	Ra_1	16	$50.1_{7.1}$	26	$31.8_{5.0}$	16	$54.4_{16.6}$	16	$68.8_{12.1}$	16	$64.0_{8.2}$
		Ra_{50}	800	$60.2_{6.7}$	$1,2k$	$51.0_{12.6}$	800	$70.3_{10.0}$	800	$76.4_{3.6}$	800	$71.7_{8.0}$
		IS	204	$62.0_{6.9}$	248	$44.4_{12.0}$	272	$71.0_{12.5}$	160	$80.2_{4.9}$	168	$70.5_{5.0}$
	16	Ra_1	32	$60.7_{4.3}$	40	$30.7_{9.6}$	32	$63.8_{8.2}$	32	$76.8_{7.7}$	32	$65.7_{6.6}$
		Ra_{50}	$1,6k$	$61.7_{2.2}$	$2,0k$	$\mathbf{53.0_{10.2}}$	$1,6k$	$71.0_{7.0}$	$1,6k$	$78.3_{6.3}$	$1,6k$	$74.3_{3.7}$
		IS	401	$63.9_{1.7}$	474	$49.6_{12.7}$	542	$75.5_{4.6}$	326	$82.6_{3.8}$	334	$73.9_{2.4}$
	32	Ra_1	64	$64.1_{2.7}$	-	-	64	$68.8_{7.5}$	64	$82.1_{1.4}$	64	$71.3_{7.1}$
		Ra_{50}	$3,2k$	$66.7_{2.7}$	-	-	$3,2k$	$74.9_{3.6}$	$3,2k$	$74.9_{3.6}$	$3,2k$	$74.9_{3.6}$
		IS	807	$67.1_{1.6}$	-	-	$1,9k$	$78.1_{4.6}$	630	$85.3_{3.5}$	673	$75.0_{2.6}$
	48	Ra_1	96	$64.9_{2.8}$	-	-	96	$68.8_{11.0}$	96	$83.2_{1.2}$	96	$72.0_{6.5}$
		Ra_{50}	$4,8k$	$66.2_{1.5}$	-	-	$4,8k$	$74.4_{5.1}$	$4,8k$	$82.5_{4.3}$	$4,8k$	$77.5_{3.1}$
		IS	$1,2k$	$66.9_{2.1}$	-	-	$1,6k$	$\mathbf{78.6_{4.2}}$	954	$87.0_{1.4}$	$1.0k$	$77.0_{4.6}$
	64	Ra_1	128	$65.5_{2.6}$	-	-	128	$72.4_{7.0}$	128	$84.0_{1.7}$	128	$74.4_{3.9}$
		Ra_{50}	$6,4k$	$68.1_{1.5}$	-	-	$6,4k$	$76.1_{5.1}$	$6,4k$	$84.4_{2.5}$	$6,4k$	$\mathbf{78.6_{3.1}}$
		IS	$1,6k$	$67.7_{1.8}$	-	-	$2,2k$	$78.5_{5.2}$	$1,3k$	$87.7_{1.6}$	$1,3k$	$77.7_{4.0}$
	128	Ra_1	256	$65.4_{2.9}$	-	-	-	-	256	$87.2_{2.2}$	-	-
		Ra_{50}	$12,8k$	$68.7_{1.5}$	-	-	-	-	$12,8k$	$89.8_{1.2}$	-	-
		IS	$3,3k$	$69.1_{1.8}$	-	-	-	-	$2,6k$	$90.5_{1.4}$	-	-
	256	Ra_1	512	$66.6_{2.2}$	-	-	-	-	512	$89.3_{1.9}$	-	-
		Ra_{50}	$25,6k$	$69.4_{1.2}$	-	-	-	-	$25,6k$	$95.4_{1.7}$	-	-
		IS	$5,2k$	$69.6_{1.8}$	-	-	-	-	$5,1k$	$92.9_{1.4}$	-	-
	512	Ra_1	$1,0k$	$66.0_{2.6}$	-	-	-	-	$1,0k$	$91.7_{1.2}$	-	-
		Ra_{50}	$51,2k$	$\mathbf{70.7_{2.2}}$	-	-	-	-	$51,2k$	$\mathbf{96.5_{1.1}}$	-	-
		IS	$13,0k$	$70.0_{1.8}$	-	-	-	-	$10,3k$	$95.2_{0.8}$	-	-

Table 5. Test set results of CA and SN compared to several baseline and reference approaches. n shows the number of training users. Per-block top results without confidence interval overlaps are highlighted with **bold**.

English dataset results

System	n	Gender Acc.	F_1	Age Acc.	F_1	Hate speech Acc.	F_1	Bots Acc.	F_1	Fake news Acc.	F_1	Depression Acc.	F_1
winner	all	**82.3**	-	83.8	-	**74.0**	-	**96.0**	-	**75.0**	-	41.3	-
ST-lr	all	76.0	76.0	72.1	47.4	64.0	63.8	90.2	90.2	68.0	67.8	28.0	20.2
xlm-roberta	all	53.2	39.5	73.1	41.9	52.6	39.0	86.6	86.3	57.4	47.4	33.8	21.3
user-char-lr	all	79.2	79.2	73.9	45.0	62.4	62.1	91.2	91.2	70.5	70.4	35.2	24.0
LDSE	all	74.7	74.7	**85.2**	**76.5**	70.0	70.0	90.6	90.5	74.5	74.5	**45.0**	**38.2**
CA	0	**75.3**	**75.2**	63.4	35.1	70.0	69.9	52.3	38.4	64.0	63.9	36.2	25.5
SN	0	38.0	37.6	38.7	29.7	45.0	44.1	**62.5**	**62.5**	60.0	56.3	17.5	15.9
CA	all	**76.1**	**76.0**	65.9	36.6	**63.4**	**63.3**	**88.2**	**88.0**	59.3	56.2	**34.2**	19.4
SN	all	76.0	76.0	**78.3**	**61.5**	60.4	60.2	86.0	85.8	**65.7**	**65.6**	32.1	**22.9**
CA	best	**77.3**	**77.3**	72.3	44.6	**70.0**	**69.9**	**87.8**	**87.7**	62.6	61.7	**33.5**	24.7
SN	best	76.3	76.3	**72.4**	**61.2**	62.2	62.1	87.4	87.2	**65.5**	**65.1**	29.8	**25.7**

Spanish dataset results

System	n	Gender Acc.	F_1	Age Acc.	F_1	Hate speech Acc.	F_1	Bots Acc.	F_1	Fake news Acc.	F_1		
winner	all	**83.2**	-	**79.6**	-	**85.0**	-	**93.3**	-	**82.0**	-		
ST-lr	all	70.3	70.3	62.7	48.7	80.8	80.6	87.3	87.3	76.5	76.5		
xlm-roberta	all	53.8	42.2	50.0	16.7	75.6	75.2	86.2	86.1	71.4	67.9		
user-char-lr	all	77.8	77.8	69.5	56.5	80.0	79.9	92.5	92.5	75.6	75.4		
LDSE	all	71.9	71.9	78.4	64.9	82.0	82.0	83.7	83.7	79.0	78.9		
CA	0	**68.3**	**68.2**	21.6	16.4	**79.0**	**78.6**	**50.1**	33.6	**51.0**	36.3		
SN	0	38.1	33.9	**48.6**	**32.6**	49.0	34.5	41.5	**38.4**	49.5	**44.3**		
CA	all	**71.7**	**71.7**	66.4	51.1	76.6	76.4	**87.1**	**87.0**	78.3	78.0		
SN	all	71.0	71.0	**66.8**	**51.6**	**77.4**	**77.1**	83.6	83.2	77.8	77.6		
CA	best	**73.7**	**73.4**	40.9	27.8	80.0	79.8	**88.3**	**88.2**	74.7	74.4		
SN	best	72.7	72.5	**66.8**	**56.0**	**80.8**	**80.7**	86.5	86.4	**76.3**	**76.2**		

training users giving better results. Nevertheless, as proved by our *IS* method the information used from those users matters.

Table 4 shows the Spanish validation results. Regarding the zero-shot setting, similarly to English, SN outperforms CA in Age and Bots. In Addition, it also improves in Fake News. Looking at the few-shot setting, the results also show a clear improvement trend while increasing the number of training users. This is more clear for SN, improving from the beginning ($n = 8$), than for CA, which sometimes requires additional training users and failed at improving the Age zero-shot results. Regarding the author instance selection method, in general, *IS* in combination with CA outperforms random selection on most datasets. For SN, we find similar results for Ra_{50} and *IS*, while *IS* uses 75% less training instances. This highlights again its capability to select the most relevant training instances. Looking at the overall Spanish few-shot results, SN outperforms in three tasks

(Age, Hate Speech and Fake News) and CA in two (Gender and Bots). However, both models offer a similar performance; with the exception of Age, where CA failed to converge. This, together with the English results, leave SN as the most stable across tasks and languages.

The few-shot experiments with the test sets use the best configurations obtained at our validation phase, i.e., the number of training users ($n =$ best) and author instance selection method for each language and task. Table 5 compares the test set results of CA and SN with several baselines and reference approaches (see Sect. 4.3). Note that the baselines use all the available training data ($n =$ all) and that we show both the SN and CA zero and few-shot results.[7] As you can see, the zero-shot models outperform xlm-roberta in English. CA also does it for Spanish. Comparing them against other approaches, including the shared task top systems (*winner*), we find encouraging results: the zero-shot models ranked third at some tasks, e.g. EN CA Hate Speech, EN CA Gender, and EN CA Depression. This is remarkable considering that those models did not use any training data, and shows their potential for low-resource author profiling. Note that few shot (*best*) worked similarly or better than the CA and SN models trained with all the train set (*all*). Interestingly, LDSE, a popular profiling baseline, ranks first for Depression.[8]

As expected, few-shot out-performs zero-shot in most tasks with few exceptions for CA: EN Hate Speech, EN Fake News, and EN Depression. Similar to the validation experiments, as CA failed to converge for some tasks, SN offers higher stability. Finally, the comparison of the few-shot models with the rest of approaches shows it is ranking third for some tasks and languages: EN CA Gender, EN CA Hate Speech, ES CA Bots, ES SN Fake News. In comparison with *winner* the FSL models reach 80% of the accuracy of the winner system in 90% of the cases and 90% in 50% of the cases. They do so using less than 50% of the training data. This shows that FSL often yields competitive systems with less individual tuning and less annotation effort.

6   Conclusions

In this work, we studied author profiling from a low-resource perspective: with little or no training data. We addressed the task using zero and few-shot text classification. We studied the identification of age, gender, hate speech spreaders, fake news spreaders, bots, and depression. In addition, we analyzed the effect of the entailment hypothesis and the size of the few-shot training sample on the system's performance. We evaluated corpora both in Spanish and English. On the comparison of Cross Attention and Siamese networks, we find that the former performs better in the zero-shot scenario while the latter gives more stable few-shot results across the evaluated tasks and languages. We find that entailment-based models out-perform supervised text classifiers based on roberta-XLM and

---

[7] The standard deviation results of Table 5 are omitted due to space. However, this does not affect our analysis. Omitted values can be found in Appendix (Sect. 7).

[8] The accuracy of the eRisk SOTA system corresponds to the DCHR metric used in the shared task.

that we can reach 80% of the state-of-the-art accuracy using less than 50% of the training data on average. This highlights their potential for low-resource author profiling scenarios.

Acknowledgments. The authors gratefully acknowledge the support of the Pro^2 Haters - Proactive Profiling of Hate Speech Spreaders (CDTi IDI-20210776), XAI-DisInfodemics: eXplainable AI for disinformation and conspiracy detection during info-demics (MICIN PLEC2021-007681), and DETEMP - Early Detection of Depression Detection in Social Media (IVACE IMINOD/2021/72) R&D grants.

7   Appendix

The repository at https://tinyurl.com/ZSandFS-author-profiling contains experimental details and results.

References

1. Argamon, S., Koppel, M., Fine, J., et al.: Gender, genre, and writing style in formal written texts. In: TEXT, pp. 321–346 (2003)
2. Bobicev, V., Sokolova, M.: Inter-annotator agreement in sentiment analysis: machine learning perspective. In: RANLP, pp. 97–102 (2017)
3. Bowman, S.R., Angeli, G., Potts, C., et al.: A large annotated corpus for learning natural language inference. In: EMNLP, pp. 632–642 (2015)
4. Brown, T.B., Mann, B., Ryder, N., et al.: Language models are few-shot learners. In: Advances in NIPS, pp. 1877–1901 (2020)
5. Burger, J.D., Henderson, J., Kim, G., et al.: Discriminating gender on Twitter. In: EMNLP, pp. 1301–1309 (2011)
6. Chang, M.W., Ratinov, L.A., Roth, D., et al.: Importance of semantic representation: dataless classification. In: AAAI, pp. 830–835 (2008)
7. Chu, Z., Stratos, K., Gimpel, K.: Unsupervised label refinement improves dataless text classification. arXiv (2020)
8. Dagan, I., Glickman, O., Magnini, B.: The Pascal recognising textual entailment challenge. In: Machine Learning Challenges Workshop, pp. 177–190 (2006)
9. Devlin, J., Chang, M.W., Lee, K., et al.: BERT: pre-training of deep bidirectional transformers for language understanding. In: NAACL-HLT, pp. 4171–4186 (2019)
10. Franco-Salvador, M., Rangel, F., Rosso, P., et al.: Language variety identification using distributed representations of words and documents. In: CLEF, pp. 28–40 (2015)
11. Ghanem, B., Rosso, P., Rangel, F.: An emotional analysis of false information in social media and news articles. ACM Trans. Internet Technol. **20**, 1–18 (2020)
12. Halder, K., Akbik, A., Krapac, J., et al.: Task-aware representation of sentences for generic text classification. In: COLING, pp. 3202–3213 (2020)
13. Henderson, M.L., Al-Rfou, R., Strope, B., et al.: Efficient natural language response suggestion for smart reply. arXiv (2017)
14. Koppel, M., Argamon, S., Shimoni, A.R.: Automatically categorizing written texts by author gender. Linguist. Comput. **17**, 401–412 (2004)
15. Larochelle, H., Erhan, D., Bengio, Y.: Zero-data learning of new tasks. In: National Conference on Artificial Intelligence, pp. 646–651 (2008)

16. Liu, Y., Ott, M., Goyal, N., et al.: Roberta: a robustly optimized BERT pretraining approach. arXiv (2019)
17. Lopez-Monroy, A.P., Montes-Y-Gomez, M., Escalante, H.J., et al.: INAOE's participation at PAN'13: author profiling task. In: CLEF (2013)
18. Müller, T., Pérez-Torró, G., Franco-Salvador, M.: Few-shot learning with siamese networks and label tuning. In: ACL (2022, to appear)
19. Nie, Y., Williams, A., Dinan, E., et al.: Adversarial NLI: a new benchmark for natural language understanding. arXiv (2019)
20. Parapar, J., Martín-Rodilla, P., Losada, D.E., et al.: Overview of eRisk at CLEF 2021: early risk prediction on the Internet. In: CLEF (2021)
21. Pedregosa, F., Varoquaux, G., Gramfort, A., et al.: Scikit-learn: machine learning in Python. J. Mach. Learn. Res. **12**, 2825–2830 (2011)
22. Pennebaker, J.W., Mehl, M.R., Niederhoffer, K.G.: Psychological aspects of natural language use: our words, our selves. Ann. Rev. Psychol. **54**, 547–577 (2003)
23. Rangel, F., Giachanou, A., Ghanem, B.H.H., et al.: Overview of the 8th author profiling task at pan 2020: profiling fake news spreaders on Twitter. In: CEUR, pp. 1–18 (2020)
24. Rangel, F., Rosso, P.: On the impact of emotions on author profiling. Inf. Process. Manag. **52**, 73–92 (2016)
25. Rangel, F., Rosso, P.: Overview of the 7th author profiling task at pan 2019: bots and gender profiling in Twitter. In: CEUR, pp. 1–36 (2019)
26. Rangel, F., Rosso, P., Franco-Salvador, M.: A low dimensionality representation for language variety identification. In: CICLING, pp. 156–169 (2016)
27. Rangel, F., Rosso, P., Koppel, M., et al.: Overview of the author profiling task at pan 2013. In: CLEF, pp. 352–365 (2013)
28. Rangel, F., Rosso, P., Potthast, M., et al.: Overview of the 3rd author profiling task at pan 2015. In: CLEF (2015)
29. Rangel, F., Rosso, P., Potthast, M., et al.: Overview of the 5th author profiling task at pan 2017: gender and language variety identification in Twitter. In: CLEF, pp. 1613–0073 (2017)
30. Rangel, F., Sarracén, G., Chulvi, B., et al.: Profiling hate speech spreaders on Twitter task at pan 2021. In: CLEF (2021)
31. Reimers, N., Gurevych, I.: Sentence-BERT: sentence embeddings using Siamese Bert-networks. In: EMNLP (2019)
32. Schick, T., Schütze, H.: Exploiting cloze-questions for few-shot text classification and natural language inference. In: EACL, pp. 255–269 (2021)
33. Troiano, E., Padó, S., Klinger, R.: Emotion ratings: how intensity, annotation confidence and agreements are entangled. In: Workshop on Computational Approaches to Subjectivity, Sentiment and Social Media Analysis, pp. 40–49 (2021)
34. Wang, S., Fang, H., Khabsa, M., et al.: Entailment as few-shot learner. arXiv (2021)
35. Wolf, T., Debut, L., Sanh, V., et al.: Transformers: state-of-the-art natural language processing. In: EMNLP (2020)
36. Yin, W., Hay, J., Roth, D.: Benchmarking zero-shot text classification: datasets, evaluation and entailment approach. In: EMNLP, pp. 3914–3923 (2019)
37. Yin, W., Rajani, N.F., Radev, D., et al.: Universal natural language processing with limited annotations: try few-shot textual entailment as a start. In: EMNLP, pp. 8229–8239 (2020)

Profiling Fake News Spreaders on Twitter: A Clickbait and Linguistic Feature Based Scheme

Raksha Agarwal$^{(\boxtimes)}$, Sharut Gupta , and Niladri Chatterjee

Indian Institute of Technology Delhi, Delhi 110016, India
{raksha.agarwal,sharut.gupta.mt617,niladri}@maths.iitd.ac.in

Abstract. Easy accessibility to various kinds of information causes huge misuse of social media platforms in modern times. Fake news spreaders are making use of these platforms to exploit the gullibility of common people to satisfy their own purpose. As a consequence, identification of Fake News spreaders is of prime consideration. The present paper focuses on automatic identification of Fake News Spreaders using Machine Learning based techniques. Different linguistic, personalized, stylistic features and word embeddings have been extracted form a large collection of tweet data to train the model. The dataset used for the model is taken from PAN@CLEF Profiling Fake News Spreaders on Twitter competition. The above features along with the clickbait feature have been found to achieve the best accuracy of 77% with XGBoost classifier. This outperforms the state of the art deep learning technique, viz. FakeBERT, as well as several other deep learning-based methods available in literature.

Keywords: Author profiling · Clickbait · Fake news spreader · Twitter

1 Introduction

Social media platforms, such as Facebook, Twitter, Instagram, have significantly changed the way information is accessed and consumed by the people. On one hand, it facilitates easy dialogue and widespread reachability paving way for positive societal changes through online social revolutions. On the other hand, it has given birth to a multi-million dollar industry of scammers scrounging the online space for naive internet users. Dissemination of distorted facts and figures, more commonly known as Fake News, is being used to taint the social, political and economical ecosystem. According to Vosoughi et al. [20], Fake News spreads faster than the truth. Since the onset of COVID-19, false messages on a range of issues, such as fake diagnosis and treatment, false notifications and lockdown guidelines among others have flooded the social media. This calls for development of digital gate-keeping protocols aimed at blocking misinformation.

R. Agarwal and S. Gupta—Equal Contribution.

P. Rosso et al. (Eds.): NLDB 2022, LNCS 13286, pp. 345–357, 2022.
https://doi.org/10.1007/978-3-031-08473-7_32

According to Hopp et al. [8] certain groups of people are disproportionately responsible for sharing misleading information on the internet. Thus, in order to curb the spread of harmful Fake News and to ensure cybersecurity, it is important to identify and weed out Fake News Spreaders from the online diaspora [16].

Algorithmic detection of Fake News in social media involves prediction of veracity of each individual post using expert domain knowledge and using manual labour at times, posing serious scalability issues. In order to stem the tide of Fake News, we consider identification of users behaving as super-spreaders of misinformation as an important step. This is achieved using latent textual analysis of individual posts of the user and transmission behaviour of these posts.

In the present work, binary classification is performed to identify Fake News Spreaders among a set of 300 Twitter users. This is done by analyzing 100 tweets of a user, and extracting their statistical and linguistic features. The average clickbait score of the tweets of a user is also utilised in the proposed approach.

The paper is organised as follows. Some previous works related to Fake News Spreader detection is discussed in Sect. 2. The method proposed in the present work is discussed in Sect. 3. Section 4 discusses the results obtained using the proposed approach, and provides a detailed analysis of the feature space considered. The paper is concluded in Sect. 5.

2   Related Work

Shu et al. [18] characterized user profiles based on features related to profile, content and network of the user. Giachanou et al. [6] trained a CNN model on a hybrid feature space consisting of word embeddings with features representing users' personality traits and linguistic patterns, to discriminate between Fake News Spreaders and Fact-Checkers. Ghanem et al. [5] extracted a set of features comprising emotion, morality, sentiment, style and GloVe[1] embeddings from the timelines of news Twitter accounts by treating posts as chunks.

Detection of Fake News Spreaders via network analysis has been performed by Rath et al. [15]. A Graph Neural Network model was trained based on the community health assessment model. The system was trained to identify nodes of a social network graph which were likely to be Fake News Spreaders without analyzing the text of the user's posts.

Since the above-mentioned works did not release the data used in their study, a major contribution for the task of Author profiling for Fake News Spreader detection was the release of a collection of labelled Twitter profiles, also known as PAN@CLEF dataset [14]. The dataset was a part of PAN shared task and contained user profiles consisting of tweets in English and Spanish. The present work is restricted to user profiles tweeting in English only. Rangel et al. [14] provides a detailed description of various models that have been proposed by different groups. Some of the best performing models on the blind test set of PAN@CLEF English dataset has been discussed below.

The best performing model by Buda et al. [3] used a stacking ensemble of five different Machine Learning (ML) models for predicting whether a Twitter

---

[1] https://nlp.stanford.edu/projects/glove/.

user is a Fake News Spreader. The models were trained on a feature space consisting of n-grams and statistical features corresponding to the tweets of the user. The system achieved accuracy of 0.75 for English Tweets of the CLEF dataset. Shashirekha et al. [17] obtained 0.735 accuracy using an ensemble approach based on majority voting of the three classifiers built on a feature space comprising of TF-IDF, n-gram, and Doc2Vec. Pizarro [12] also achieved 0.735 accuracy using an SVM classifier trained with character and word n-grams.

Fenandez et al. [10] showed that traditional ML methods performed better than deep learning architectures (e.g. RNN, LSTM) for detection of Fake News Spreaders. The feature space comprised GloVe and Word2Vec word embeddings. Their system achieved 0.735 accuracy for English Tweets of the CLEF dataset.

In the work of Baruah et al. [2], tweets of a user are represented by Max-pooling 1024-dimensional BERT embeddings of individual tweets of the user. The system achieved an accuracy of 0.69 on the English dataset of PAN@CLEF. One can observe that although different approaches have been employed, none of them could achieve an accuracy score greater than 0.75.

Post competition Cervaro et al. [4] reported experiments which considers both text-related and image-related features. Image features were extracted from the tweets using unmasked (raw) version of the PAN@CLEF dataset which is not available publicly. Their system achieved an accuracy of 0.775 using a combination of the baselines trained on n-grams plus an XGBoost model fed with personality scores and VGG16-Inception vectors.

Vogel et al. [19] reported an accuracy of 0.78 on the English dataset of PAN@CLEF using an ensemble of SVM and Logistic Regression. However, the accuracy was not reported on the standard PAN@CLEF test dataset.

3   The Proposed Method

This section describes the proposed method, dataset and the extracted features. The dataset from PAN@CLEF Profiling Fake News Spreaders on Twitter [14] competition is used in the present work. The training corpus consists of tweets from 300 anonymised Twitter user accounts. For each user, 100 past tweets are available. Each user is given a binary label: 0 for True and 1 for Fake. Moreover, URL links are replaced by '#URL#', retweeted tweet is indicated by '#RT#', hashtag mentions are replaced by '#HASHTAG#'. The dataset is balanced with each of the labels having exactly 150 twitter account users identified as spreaders of Fake News. An excerpt of the dataset is presented in Table 1.

For the purpose of training the dataset is split into 70:30 ratio for the training and validation sets. Final performance is reported on the hidden test set, provided by the organizers of the PAN@CLEF challenge on special request. The test set contains tweet data for 200 user profiles.

3.1   Preprocessing and Feature Extraction

Feature Engineering: Raw tweets might contain spurious and unwanted features which may result in inefficient training and low-performing models. Hence,

Table 1. An excerpt from the data of PAN@CLEF 2020 Challenge for English News Tweets on Fake News Spreader Detection

True tweets	Fake tweets
RT #USER#: People don't think La Liga players try to kick Messi? Did you miss the CL final when peak Vidic	Isn't It A 'Climate Crisis'? Liz Warren Hides Behind Staffers After She Steps Out Of A Private Jet (Video)... #URL#
Let me break it down! advances are usually paid to an artist, songwriter, producer, against their future earnings! It can	Pro-Abortion Pete Asked By Pro-Life Democrat If Her Views Are Still Acceptable By The Party. Here's ...#URL#

it becomes imperative to get rid of these unnecessary features and utilize only those which truly affect the labels. In order to choose the correct set of features, the distribution of key tokens were analyzed. Apart from analyzing the occurrences of these placeholders, context features, personality features and stylistic features were also analyzed as described below.

- User feature count: This maintained the count of user stylistic features, such as URLs, hashtags, re-tweets and other user mentions.
- Named Entity Recognition (NER): This maintains a count of three major categories of named entities - name of persons, organizations and locations. In this study, NER is implemented using NLTK (Natural Language Toolkit)[2] and SpaCy[3] library of python.
- Sentiment Analysis: This involves classifying texts or parts of texts into a predefined sentiment. Python's SpaCy and TextBlob[4] libraries have been used to classify each tweet as positive, negative or neutral.
- Statistical stylistic features: Other statistical features describing the tweet of each author were also calculated. For each user the length of his/her tweets in terms of number of words and number of characters have been computed. In the proposed system the maximum, minimum and the range (i.e. maximum -minimum) have also been considered as features.

The key observations from values corresponding to the extracted variables presented in Table 2 can be summarised as follows. Fake News Spreaders tend to:

- Use fewer number of hashtags (#HASHTAG#)
- Utilize more URL links (#URL#)
- Have fewer re-tweets compared to the true authors (#RT#).
- Have higher number of user mentions (#USER#)
- Use remarkably less number of emojis
- Have lower maximum length of tweet when measured vis-a-vis word count.
- Use more tweets which carry negative or neutral in sentiment.
- Utilize more uppercase characters
- Mention names of locations less often

---

[2] https://www.nltk.org.
[3] https://spacy.io.
[4] https://textblob.readthedocs.io/en/dev/.

Table 2. An excerpt from the English data of PAN@CLEF 2020

Features	True	Fake
No. of #HASHTAG#	6005	4415
No. of #URLS#	16220	16874
No. of #RT#	2326	1098
No. of #USER#	16220	16874
NER Person	5814	7499
NER Org	6311	6936
NER Loc	204	184

Features	True	Fake
Positive sentiment	6175	5464
Negative sentiment	1970	2475
Neutral sentiment	6855	7061
Emojis	471	144
Uppercase characters	113357	128767
Uppercase words	8664	8273

Preprocessing: It is important for improving the performance of any text classification model [7]. The data was preprocessed using the following pipeline:

- Multiple white spaces were normalized to single space.
- After extracting case information, the entire text was changed to lower case.
- Placeholders for URLS, Hashtags, Re-tweets etc. were left intact.
- Emoticons in the text were replaced with the placeholder #EMOJI#.
- Majority of the irrelevant signs and non-alphanumeric symbols (except #) like punctuations, brackets etc. were removed.
- Stop words were removed using Python's NLTK library.

Embeddings and Vectorization: Apart from the above handcrafted features, experiments were also conducted with two different embeddings described below.

1. Term Frequency-Inverse Document Frequency (TF-IDF): This vectorization technique is used to weigh down the common words and give more importance to less frequent words. Python's scikit-learn[5] library is used for this task. Hyperparameter tuning is performed by varying the number of n-grams, sublinear term frequency and minimum document frequency.
2. Global Vectors for Word Representation (GloVe): This vectorization technique highlights word-word co-occurences to extract meaning. Since the dataset used contains tweets, we used GloVe [11] pre-trained on two billion tweets[6] and experimented with varying dimensions[7] of the embeddings.

Clickbait Feature. Clickbait refers to a certain kind of web content designed to attract attention of the readers, and lure them into clicking an accompanying link. Typically, it is a sensationalized headline appealing to the emotions and curiosity of the reader. Clickbait on social media is on the rise in recent years, and is being used deliberately by publishers to spread false news. Intuitively, a

---

[5] https://scikit-learn.org/.

[6] glove-twitter-50.

[7] {25, 50, 100, 200}, best performance obtained with 50.

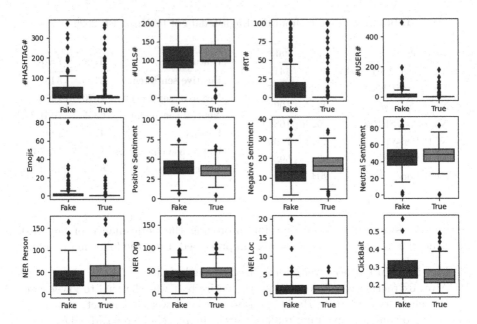

Fig. 1. Boxplot for handcrafted features and clickbait score for each class

Fake News tends to have high sensationalism or tendency to be a clickbait. To target important stylistic features of the Fake Tweet authors, a model has been developed to rate the degree of clickbaitiness of a tweet.

Dataset: Webis Clickbait Corpus [13][8] 2017 has been used for training the clickbait model. It consists of Twitter posts from 27 major US news publishers. Each post is rated on a 4-point scale - not click baiting (0.0), slightly click baiting (0.33), considerably click baiting (0.66), heavily click baiting (1.0).

Training: For training a clickbait classifier, FullNetPost model [1] Clickbait Detection Challenge[9] has been used. It is trained using AdaDelta optimizer, mean squared error loss and early stopping with patience of seven epochs. FullNetPost consists of a Bidirectional GRU with 128 units and a Dropout layer (D) with dropout probability 0.2. The train features are sequentially passed through D followed by a Bidirectional GRU. The output from the GRU is concatenated with the output of D, which serves as an input to the final dense layer with a sigmoid activation function. This model is trained to get the *clickbait score* for each tweet of the Fake News detection PAN@CLEF 2021 dataset. The individual tweet score is averaged for all the 100 tweets corresponding to a distinct user, to get the clickbait score of the use. Boxplots for different handcrafted features and clickbait scores are presented in Fig. 1.

---

[8] https://webis.de/events/clickbait-challenge/.
[9] https://github.com/clickbait-challenge/blobfish.

Emotional Quotient. A reader's comprehension often depends upon his/her understanding of the emotional intent of the focused words present in the text. In order to analyse the emotional quotient of a Fake News author, the emotion associated with each word of the tweets written by a user is calculated using NRC[10] emotion dictionary. It categorizes each token into ten different types of emotions namely, fear, anger, anticipation, trust, surprise, positive, negative, sadness, disgust and joy. Corresponding to each word in a given tweet, a set of probable emotions (none, one or more) is extracted and count of each of these emotions is incremented by one. As a result, iterating through all the words in a tweet can be represented by a dictionary containing the emotions as keys and counts of each emotion as the corresponding value. This process is repeated for all the tweets associated with a user. Finally, each count value in the resultant dictionary is then normalized with the total count of words which had at least one emotion attached with them. This 10×1 vector per author has been used as an emotional quotient feature along with the other handcrafted features.

3.2 Machine Learning Models and Training

To train the model on embeddings extracted from the text corpus, we experimented with Random Forests (RF), Support Vector Machines (SVM), XGBoost Classifiers (XGB), Logistic Regression (LR) and Light Gradient Boosting Machine Classifier (LGBM). Extensive hyperparameter tuning was carried out using grid search performed in the training phase. All tested parameters and their values are summarized in Table 3. The systems are evaluated using Macro Average Precision, Macro Average Recall and Accuracy.

3.3 Deep Learning Based Technique

In order to compare the proposed framework against the state of the art approaches, a BERT-based approach called FakeBERT [9] has been trained. FakeBERT architecture is a combination of baseline BERT model and three parallel blocks of one dimensional CNNs. It utilizes the automatic feature extraction performed by the CNN model. All the 100 tweets corresponding to a user are concatenated and tokenized, resulting in text IDs, attention masks and Token IDs. These outputs are used as inputs to the pre-trained BERT model followed by a Dropout layer (dropout probability $= 0.3$) and a linear layer with 768 units.

4   Results and Analysis

Training on TF-IDF Embeddings: Performance of different machine learning algorithms on the extracted TF-IDF vectors from the given corpus have been analyzed. Model hyperparameters are tuned on the validation dataset and final performance is reported on the test set. As observed from Table 4a, LGBM

---

[10] https://pypi.org/project/NRCLex/.

Table 3. Hyperparameters tuned using grid search for different ML models

Model	Hyperparameter	Values	Optimal value
RF	Criterion	{Gini, Entropy}	Entropy
	Number of trees	{10, 50, 100, 200, 300}	300
SVM	Regularization	{1, 10, 100, 500, 1000}	100
	Kernel	{RBF, Linear, Poly}	Linear
	Degree	{1, 2, 3, 4, 5, 6, 10}	1
XGB	Min. child weight	{1, 2, 5, 10}	2
	Learning Rate (ETA)	{0.02, 0.05, 0.1, 0.2, 0.3}	0.02
	Max. Depth	{3, 4, 5, 6, 10}	6
	Subsample	{0.5, 0.6, 0.8, 1.0}	0.6
	Col. Sample (tree)	{0.6, 0.7, 0.8, 0.9, 1.0}	0.6
	Col. Sample (level)	{0.6, 0.8, 1.0}	0.8
LR	Penalty	{L1, L2, Elasticnet}	L1
	Regularization	{0.1, 1, 10, 100, 500}	100
	Warm start	{True, False}	True
	L1 Ratio	{0.1, 0.2, 0.5, 0.8, 1}	0.1
LGBM	Learning Rate	{0.005, 0.01}	0.01
	Num. of estimators	{8, 16, 24}	24
	Boosting type	{gbdt, dart}	dart
	Col. Sample (tree)	{0.64, 0.65, 0.66}	0.64
	Subsample	{0.7, 0.75}	0.7
	L1 regularization (α)	{1, 1.2}	1.2
	L2 regularization (λ)	{1, 1.2, 1.4}	1.4

has the highest performance with an accuracy of 76%. SVM, XGBoost and LR also exhibit competitive performances with 74% accuracy. TF-IDF vectors with maximum n-gram value of 2 yields the best performance. The optimal hyperparameters for the different models are given in Table 3.

Training on GloVe Embeddings: GloVe embeddings extracted from the dataset were also tested with the different machine learning algorithms mentioned in Sect. 3.2. From the results in Table 4b, it can be observed that mean embeddings yields better results over sum embeddings. However, the performance with GloVe is poorer than with TF-IDF.

Training on Handcrafted Features: Performance of all further experiments are reported only for XGBoost, since the other classifiers resulted in poorer performance. The values of all the three measures, namely Precision, Recall, and Accuracy, before and after hyperparameter tuning are 0.66 and 0.68, respectively. The performance of this model is lower than that using TF-IDF vectorization.

Table 4. Performance of standalone machine learning models on the test set in terms of Precision(P), Recall(R), and Accuracy(Acc)

(a) Using TF-IDF vectors

Model	P	R	Acc
RF	0.71	0.71	0.71
SVM	0.74	0.74	0.74
XGB	0.74	0.73	0.73
LR	0.74	0.72	0.73
LGBM	**0.76**	**0.76**	**0.76**

(b) Using 50-dimensional GloVe vectors

Model	Mean embedding			Sum embedding		
	P	R	Acc	P	R	Acc
RF	0.68	0.68	0.67	0.66	0.66	0.65
SVM	0.64	0.64	0.63	0.63	0.62	0.62
XGB	0.64	0.64	0.63	0.63	0.62	0.62
LR	0.67	0.67	0.66	0.68	0.68	0.67
LGBM	0.65	0.65	0.65	0.64	0.64	0.64

Table 5. Best Performance on different combinations of the extracted features with XGBoost classifier

	Handcrafted	TF-IDF	GloVe	ClickBait	Precision	Recall	Accuracy
1	Yes	No	No	No	0.68	0.68	0.68
2	No	Yes	No	No	0.74	0.73	0.73
3	No	No	Yes	No	0.64	0.64	0.63
4	Yes	Yes	No	No	0.74	0.73	0.73
5	Yes	No	Yes	No	0.71	0.71	0.71
6	Tes	No	No	Yes	0.69	0.69	0.69
7	No	Yes	No	Yes	**0.77**	**0.77**	**0.77**
8	No	No	Yes	Yes	0.69	0.69	0.69
9	No	Yes	Yes	Yes	0.76	0.76	0.76
10	Yes	Yes	No	Yes	0.74	0.73	0.73
11	Yes	Yes	Yes	No	0.76	0.76	0.76
12	Yes	Yes	Yes	Yes	0.75	0.74	0.74

Feature Union: In order to improve the performance, the handcrafted features are concatenated with TF-IDF and GloVe embeddings. It can be observed from Rows 2, 4 and 5 of Table 5 that after feature union, the model performs at par with the standalone model trained simply on the TF-IDF embedding.

Clickbait and Feature Union with TF-IDF Embeddings: Clickbait score (Sect. 3.1) is concatenated with the handcrafted features, then with the TF-IDF embeddings and finally with the feature union of handcrafted and TF-IDF embeddings. It can be inferred from Table 5 that using clickbait feature along with handcrafted features (Row 6) gives a boost to the model trained solely on the handcrafted features (Row 1). On the contrary, inclusion of clickbait feature with the feature union of TF-IDF and handcrafted features (Row 4, Row 10) does not affect the model's performance. When the model is trained with just the clickbait feature and TF-IDF, using a minimum term occurrence frequency

Table 6. Best Performance on different combinations of the extracted features

	Handcrafted	TF-IDF	ClickBait	Emotion	Precision	Recall	Accuracy
1	No	No	No	Yes	0.62	0.62	0.62
2	No	No	Yes	Yes	0.64	0.64	0.64
3	No	Yes	No	Yes	0.75	0.74	0.74
4	Yes	No	No	Yes	0.70	0.70	0.70
5	No	Yes	Yes	Yes	**0.75**	**0.75**	**0.75**
6	Yes	No	Yes	Yes	0.70	0.70	0.70
7	Yes	Yes	No	Yes	**0.75**	**0.75**	**0.75**
8	Yes	Yes	Yes	Yes	0.71	0.72	0.72

of 4 to construct the TF-IDF, the model achieves an accuracy of 77% (Row 7) on the test set. This indicates the importance of clickbait feature and its capability to encode the most important information from the dataset. Using this set of hyperparameters, the feature space is of dimension 19,500 with one dimension corresponding to clickbait feature and rest representing the vocabulary size.

Clickbait and Feature Union with GloVe Embeddings: A similar study has been conducted with GloVe embeddings and feature concatenation. The results of this approach can be found in Table 5. It maybe noted that GloVe embeddings are able to perform well only when concatenated with the clickbait feature, TF-IDF embeddings and the handcrafted features (Row 12). On the contrary, the TF-IDF embeddings produces better performance utilizing the clickbait feature (Row 7), and not the handcrafted features. Furthermore, using TF-IDF with clickbait is preferred over feature concatenation of GloVe, clickbait and TF-IDF embeddings due to smaller size of feature space

Emotional Quotient and Feature Union: Similar to the above combinations, different extracted features are concatenated with the features indicating the emotional quotient. Results of these experiments are listed in Table 6. It can be seen that feature union of emotional quotient with clickbait and TF-IDF embeddings (Row 5) gives a performance accuracy of 75%. This performance is still lower than the performance of feature concatenation of clickbait and TF-IDF embeddings. To summarise, although emotional quotient results in a performance close to the highest performance, but it is slightly lower.

Comparison with Deep Learning Based Approach. Here the performance with FakeBERT is being reported. The inbuilt BERT Tokenizer with truncation to the maximum length of 512 tokens has been used. A Binary Cross Entropy Loss (BCE Loss) has been used as the loss criterion and a learning rate of $2e^{-5}$ with ADAM optimizer. Further, the ADAM algorithm with weight decay for all layer's except the Layer Norm and Bias associated with the each layer has been implemented. The training is supplemented using a linear scheduler with warm start of 10 steps. Considering the size of datasets, a batch size of 8 for training and 4 for validation is chosen. The model is trained for 20 epochs after which the validation performance starts to decrease. Maximum test accuracy of 69.5% was achieved on the test set even after rigorous fine-tuning over the hyper-parameters in the model. This is significantly lower than the accuracy achieved by XGBoost trained on ClickBait and TF-IDF features i.e. 77%. A possible explanation is that with the latter, the model is trained only on a set of relevant features. However, using FakeBERT, the model may give higher weights to lesser important features, which might have lead to overfitting.

5   Conclusion and Future Work

In this work a novel technique with clickbait score has been studied for identification of Fake News Spreaders using the PAN@CLEF 2020 dataset for Profiling Fake News Spreaders on Twitter challenge. Rigorous experiments were conducted with GloVe and TF-IDF word embeddings, and additional features, such as the emotional quotient, clickbait, stylistic and linguistic features. The best results were obtained using feature concatenation of clickbait score along with word embeddings generated using TF-IDF. The proposed method with TF-IDF and Clikbait feature achieved an accuracy of 77% on the English corpus beating the best performance of this challenge by Buda et al. [3]. The performance is only slightly lower than 77.5% of Cervero et al. [4] which uses an additional image based feature extraction scheme using a complex deep neural network. It may be observed that in comparison with the complexity of the additional image based features, the gain in performance is significantly less. The proposed system performs at par with it in spite of a much simpler feature space.

It was further observed that XGBoost model with the proposed feature space outperforms FakeBERT architecture as well as other deep learning-based techniques [2,10] discussed in Sect. 2. The present work shows the importance of clickbait feature as a substitute for the entire collection of stylistic user features. Further, since not all the tweets corresponding to a Fake News Spreader might be fake, we plan to explore a feature utilizing the Fake News score for each tweet.

Additional set of experiments with respect to concatenation of handcrafted features with FakeBERT may also be performed in future. The efficacy of the proposed approach may be studied on the PAN@CLEF Spanish Twitter dataset subject to availability of a Spanish clickbait detection dataset. Further, we plan to explore personality traits that is expected to provide additional information useful for improving the robustness of the model.

Acknowledgements. Raksha Agarwal acknowledges Council of Scientific and Industrial Research, India for supporting the research under Grant no: SPM-06/086(0267)/2018-EMR-I. The authors thank Prof. Paulo Rosso and Francisco Manuel Rangel Pardo for providing access to the PAN@CLEF dataset.

References

1. Arendt, D., Shaw, Z., Shrestha, P., Ayton, E., Glenski, M., Volkova, S.: CrossCheck: rapid, reproducible, and interpretable model evaluation. In: Proceedings of the 2nd Workshop on Data Science with Human in the Loop: Language Advances, Online, June 2021, pp. 79–85. Association for Computational Linguistics (2021)
2. Baruah, A., Das, K., Barbhuiya, F., Dey, K.: Automatic detection of fake news spreaders using BERT. In: CLEF 2020 Labs and Workshops, Notebook Papers, September 2020, pp. 1–6. CEUR-WS.org (2020)
3. Buda, J., Bolonyai, F.: An Ensemble model using n-grams and statistical features to identify fake news spreaders on Twitter. In: CLEF 2020 Labs and Workshops, Notebook Papers, September 2020, pp. 1–11. CEUR-WS.org (2020)
4. Cervero, R., Rosso, P., Pasi, G.: Profiling fake news spreaders: personality and visual information matter. In: Métais, E., Meziane, F., Horacek, H., Kapetanios, E. (eds.) NLDB 2021. LNCS, vol. 12801, pp. 355–363. Springer, Cham (2021). https://doi.org/10.1007/978-3-030-80599-9_31
5. Ghanem, B., Ponzetto, S.P., Rosso, P.: FacTweet: profiling fake news Twitter accounts. In: Espinosa-Anke, L., Martín-Vide, C., Spasić, I. (eds.) SLSP 2020. LNCS (LNAI), vol. 12379, pp. 35–45. Springer, Cham (2020). https://doi.org/10.1007/978-3-030-59430-5_3
6. Giachanou, A., Ríssola, E.A., Ghanem, B., Crestani, F., Rosso, P.: The role of personality and linguistic patterns in discriminating between fake news spreaders and fact checkers. In: Métais, E., Meziane, F., Horacek, H., Cimiano, P. (eds.) NLDB 2020. LNCS, vol. 12089, pp. 181–192. Springer, Cham (2020). https://doi.org/10.1007/978-3-030-51310-8_17
7. HaCohen-Kerner, Y., Miller, D., Yigal, Y.: The influence of preprocessing on text classification using a bag-of-words representation. PLoS ONE 15(5), 1–22 (2020)
8. Hopp, T., Ferrucci, P., Vargo, C.J.: Why do people share ideologically extreme, false, and misleading content on social media? A self-report and trace data-based analysis of countermedia content dissemination on Facebook and Twitter. Hum. Commun. Res. 46(4), 357–384 (2020)
9. Kaliyar, R.K., Goswami, A., Narang, P.: FakeBERT: fake news detection in social media with a BERT-based deep learning approach. Multimedia Tools Appl. 80(8), 11765–11788 (2021). https://doi.org/10.1007/s11042-020-10183-2
10. López Fernández, J., López Ramírez, J.: Approaches to the profiling fake news spreaders on Twitter task in English and Spanish. In: CLEF 2020 Labs and Workshops, Notebook Papers, September 2020, pp. 1–9. CEUR-WS.org (2020)
11. Pennington, J., Socher, R., Manning, C.D.: Glove: global vectors for word representation. In: Proceedings of the 2014 Conference on Empirical Methods in Natural Language Processing (EMNLP), pp. 1532–1543 (2014)
12. Pizarro, J.: Profiling bots and fake news spreaders at PAN'19 and PAN'20 : bots and gender profiling 2019, profiling fake news spreaders on Twitter 2020. In: 2020 IEEE 7th International Conference on Data Science and Advanced Analytics (DSAA), pp. 626–630 (2020)
13. Potthast, M., Köpsel, S., Stein, B., Hagen, M.: Clickbait detection. In: Ferro, N., et al. (eds.) ECIR 2016. LNCS, vol. 9626, pp. 810–817. Springer, Cham (2016). https://doi.org/10.1007/978-3-319-30671-1_72
14. Rangel, F., Giachanou, A., Ghanem, B., Rosso, P.: Overview of the 8th author profiling task at PAN 2020: profiling fake news spreaders on Twitter. In: CLEF 2020 Labs and Workshops, Notebook Papers, September 2020, pp. 1–18. CEUR-WS.org (2020)

15. Rath, B., Salecha, A., Srivastava, J.: Detecting fake news spreaders in social networks using inductive representation learning. preprint arXiv:2011.10817 (2020)
16. Rosso, P.: Profiling bots, fake news spreaders and haters. In: Proceedings of the Workshop on Resources and Techniques for User and Author Profiling in Abusive Language, Marseille, p. 1. European Language Resources Association (2020)
17. Shashirekha, H., Anusha, M.D., Prakash, N.: Ensemble model for profiling fake news spreaders on Twitter. In: CLEF 2020 Labs and Workshops, Notebook Papers, September 2020, pp. 1–9. CEUR-WS.org (2020)
18. Shu, K., Wang, S., Liu, H.: Understanding user profiles on social media for fake news detection. In: IEEE Conference on Multimedia Information Processing and Retrieval (MIPR), pp. 430–435. IEEE (2018)
19. Vogel, I., Meghana, M.: Detecting fake news spreaders on Twitter from a multilingual perspective. In: IEEE 7th International Conference on Data Science and Advanced Analytics (DSAA), pp. 599–606 (2020)
20. Vosoughi, S., Roy, D., Aral, S.: The spread of true and false news online. Science 359(6380), 1146–1151 (2018)

Detecting Early Signs of Depression in the Conversational Domain: The Role of Transfer Learning in Low-Resource Scenarios

Petr Lorenc[1(✉)], Ana-Sabina Uban[2,3], Paolo Rosso[2], and Jan Šedivý[4]

[1] Faculty of Electrical Engineering, Czech Technical University in Prague, Prague, Czechia
`lorenpe2@fel.cvut.cz`
[2] PRHLT Research Center, Universitat Politècnica de València, Valencia, Spain
`auban@fmi.unibuc.ro, prosso@dsic.upv.es`
[3] Faculty of Mathematics and Computer Science, University of Bucharest, Bucharest, Romania
[4] CIIRC, Czech Technical University, Prague, Czechia
`jan.sedivy@cvut.cz`

Abstract. The high prevalence of depression in society has given rise to the need for new digital tools to assist in its early detection. To this end, existing research has mainly focused on detecting depression in the domain of social media, where there is a sufficient amount of data. However, with the rise of conversational agents like Siri or Alexa, the conversational domain is becoming more critical. Unfortunately, there is a lack of data in the conversational domain. We perform a study focusing on domain adaptation from social media to the conversational domain. Our approach mainly exploits the linguistic information preserved in the vector representation of text. We describe transfer learning techniques to classify users who suffer from early signs of depression with high recall. We achieve state-of-the-art results on a commonly used conversational dataset, and we highlight how the method can easily be used in conversational agents. We publicly release all source code (https://github.com/petrLorenc/mental-health)

Keywords: Depression detection · Conversational domain · Transfer learning

1 Introduction

The World Health Organization[1] estimates that over 300 million people suffer from depression. However, there are approximately only 70 mental health professionals available for every 100,000 people in high-income nations, and this number can drop to 2 for every 100,000 in low-income countries [14]. It leads to

---

[1] https://apps.who.int/iris/handle/10665/254610.

© The Author(s), under exclusive license to Springer Nature Switzerland AG 2022
P. Rosso et al. (Eds.): NLDB 2022, LNCS 13286, pp. 358–369, 2022.
https://doi.org/10.1007/978-3-031-08473-7_33

a high percentage of the world population suffering from depression, and only a tiny fraction has access to psychiatric care to detect early signs of any mental illness, including depression. On the other hand, almost everyone has access to smartphones [28], and with the rise of conversational agents like Siri or Alexa [24], people are getting used to communicating with their smartphones or smart speakers on daily basis [10]. This evolution of conversational agents allows for building mental health applications, like the virtual therapists TalkToPoppy![2]. It brings new challenges to recognize early signs of mental illnesses such as depression immediately during the conversation.

Unfortunately, there is a scarcity of conversational data usable for the detection of early signs of depression. The lack of these data is due to several problems. Authors of such datasets need to collect a representative sample of data to balance positive and especially negative examples [3], and typically cross-reference data with medical records, but this process can raise ethical issues. Some of these problems are mitigated in social media, such as Reddit or Twitter. On social media platforms, we usually get access to vast amounts of self-labeled data [16]. In addition, self-stated diagnoses remove some overheads of annotating data but increase the false-positive noise. Therefore, based on the data scarcity, we focus on sequential transfer learning [23] which helps mainly in the target domain with limited data and it is based on transferring knowledge from a related domain with a sufficient amount of data,.

As shown in [2], there are several indicative symptoms of depression like a loss of interest in everyday activities, feelings of worthlessness, and also a change in the use of language [17,33]. Because the change in language use can be detected, there are several lexicon-based approaches [19,21] to extracting semantic features from text. These approaches suffer from a limited size of vocabulary and require human annotation. This paper investigates sentence embeddings [4,7] and whether they can capture these changes in the use of language without the need for a time-consuming design of lexicons. Furthermore, recent works focus on attention mechanisms [34], showing promising results in the social media [29]. We propose a novel model that combines attention mechanisms with sentence embeddings.

Our contributions can be summarized as follows:

1. We evaluate the usage of sentence embeddings to detect change in the use of language for the detection of early signs of depression and its possible combination with attention mechanisms;
2. We explore sequential transfer learning from social media to the conversational domain;
3. We achieve state-of-the-art results on retrieving indications of early signs of depression in the conversational domain;

The rest of the paper is organized as follows. Section 3 introduces the used data, methodology for transfer learning, and our novel model. Section 4 introduces the experimental setting and Sect. 5 shows the results and proposes possible usage.

---

[2] https://www.talktopoppy.com/.

2   Related Work

Previous works on textual depression detection were mainly focused on detecting early signs of depression in the social media domain [5,16,32,35], in contrast to the conversational domain, which has received rarer attention [11].

2.1   Early Sign of Depression Detection

Datasets - The most remarkable conversational dataset related to virtual mental health applications is The Distress Analysis Interview Corpus (DAIC) [11]. As for datasets focusing on online forums and social networks, there is a sufficient number of them. The eRisk dataset [16], RSDD dataset [35] or the dataset introduced by [32] are extracted from Reddit. Additionally, there is the CLPsych 2015 Shared Task [5] focusing on depression and PTSD on Twitter.

Depression Detection in the Conversational Domain - Several works [8, 17,33] have focused on the DAIC-WOZ dataset [11]. In [17], the authors used the Hierarchical Attention Model [34] with a low-level representation of words based on word vector representation—GloVe [22] embeddings. They used word embeddings together with different types of the Hierarchical Attention Model to obtain a high-level representation of participant texts. Similarly, [33] uses Hierarchical Attention Model with a combination of lexical features like LIWC [21], NRC Emotion Lexicon (Emolex) [19], and many others. In contrast to [17, 33], we perform an extensive study of transfer learning techniques, and similarly to [8], we find that proper hyperparameters are critical for training the model.

Depression Detection in Social Media - The primary studies focusing on depression detection in the social media domain are also based on lexicon-based features, as well as word embeddings [29]. Similarly to [17,33], [29] uses the Hierarchical Attention Model with additional features. Nevertheless, in [13], it is shown that simpler models with additional emotional and linguistic features can achieve comparable results. Because of that, we include a simple baseline model, such as Logistic regression [20].

2.2   Transfer Learning

Transfer learning is used to improve a learner from one domain by transferring information from a related domain [31]. It has been shown that if the two domains are related, transfer learning can potentially improve the results of the target learner [26]. Furthermore, it was shown by [26] that transfer learning can improve the performance in anxiety and depression classification. They examine the performance of deep language models for pre-training the model. Similarly, he authors of [1] demonstrate usefulness of transfer learning for depression detection from social media postings, applied to the eRisk [16] dataset. In [30], the authors show that transfer learning can be effective for improving prediction performance for disorders where little annotated data is available. They explore different transfer learning strategies for both cross-disorder (across disorders) and cross-platform transfer (across different social media platforms).

3   Methodology

In the following section, we introduce the datasets and metrics. We also discuss our novel chunk-based model.

3.1   Data

To study detection of depression, we set The Distress Analysis Interview Corpus as our target dataset. Source dataset was eRisk data which is labeled for early signs of depression, where for each user with depression there are possibly texts posted before the diagnosis or the onset of the disease. Additionally, we use General Psychotherapy Corpus, leaving other datasets for future research. All datasets contain two categories of participant, depressed (positive) and non-depressed (negative). Each participant is linked with a sequence of sentences. The data statistics for all mentioned datasets, can be seen in Table 1 and the description of these datasets follows.

The Distress Analysis Interview Corpus - Wizard-of-Oz (DAIC-WOZ) is part of a larger corpus, the Distress Analysis Interview Corpus (DAIC) [11]. These interviews were collected as part of a more significant effort to create a conversational agent that interviews people and identifies verbal and non-verbal indicators of mental illness [6]. Original data collected include audio and video recordings and extensive questionnaire responses. DAIC-WOZ includes the Wizard-of-Oz interviews, conducted by a virtual interviewer called Ellie, controlled by a human therapist in another room. The data have been transcribed and annotated for various verbal and non-verbal features.

The eRisk dataset [16] consists of data for the Early Detection of Signs of Depression Task presented at CLEF (specifically 2017[3]). The texts were extracted from the social media platform Reddit, and it uses the format described in [16].

Additionally, we apply our models to the General Psychotherapy Corpus (GPC) collected by the "Alexander Street Press"[4] (ASP). This dataset contains over 4,000 transcribed therapy sessions, covering various clinical approaches and mental health issues. The data collection was compiled according to [33] and we chose only transcripts related to depression. It results in 147 sessions. Additionally, we randomly chose 201 sessions annotated with mental illnesses different than depression in order to use them as a control group.

3.2   Metrics

As suggested by [17,33], we used the Unweighted Average Recall (UAR) between the ground-truth and the predicted labels associated with each participant (see Eq. 1). As shown in [33], the UAR metric is also suitable when the label distribution of the dataset is unbalanced. Additionally, we measure Unweighted Average

---

[3] https://clef2017.clef-initiative.eu/.

[4] Can be found at https://alexanderstreet.com/.

Table 1. Data statistics. *A* stands for all data. *P* stands for utterances of participant.

Dataset		# dialogues	# utterances	Vocabulary	Labels 0/1	Train/Valid/Test
DAIC-WOZ	A	189	20,857	8,272	133/56	107/35/47
DAIC-WOZ	P	189	10,505	8,263	133/56	107/35/47
eRisk	A	1304	811,586	322,634	214/1090	387/97/820
GPC	A	348	54,588	54,844	201/147	208/70/70
GPC	P	348	26,860	45,205	201/147	208/70/70

Precision (UAP), same as UAR but recall is substituted by precision and macro F1 score (macro-F1) for completeness.

$$UAR = \frac{Recall_0 + Recall_1}{2} = \frac{\frac{TP_0}{TP_0+FN_0} + \frac{TP_1}{TP_1+FN_1}}{2} \tag{1}$$

where TP_0, FP_0, FN_0 are true positives, false positives and false negatives for non-depressed participants, respectively. TP_1, FP_1, FN_1 represent true positives, false positives and false negatives for depressed participants, respectively.

3.3   Chunk-Based Classification

Since natural conversation is an infinite sequence of utterances, our proposed Chunk-based model works based on a sliding window as shown in Fig. 1. We classify each chunk of the conversation with a binary label, then we sum up all the obtained classifications (zeros for chunks corresponding to non-depressed participants and ones for depressed participants). Then we divide the sum by the number of chunks to normalize for different conversation lengths. To obtain a prediction for an entire conversation, we use a threshold on the ratio between positive and negative labels. More concretely, the conversation C_i is created during an iterative process of conversation. Then, each conversation C is composed of a set of utterances U, where each utterance u_i is composed of one or more sentences S, as shown in Eq. 2.

$$C_i = \{U_i\} = \{u_1, u_2, ..., u_n\} = \{\{S_1\}, \{S_2\}, ...\{S_n\}\} \tag{2}$$

Further, in order to allow for the iterative evaluation of the conversation in a real-time setting, we performed classification using a sliding window at the chunk level. Each chunk X_i is labeled according to the label y of the conversation C_i from which the chunk is derived. These chunks are overlapping, as shown in Fig. 1. All chunks of the same length (shown for the length of three in Eq. 3) have same label y_i derived from label y_i of conversation C_i.

$$X_1 = (u_1, u_2, u_3)$$
$$X_2 = (u_2, u_3, u_4)$$
$$...$$
$$X_N = (u_{N-2}, u_{N-1}, u_N)$$

(3)

Firstly, we train the model M to classify each chunk of the conversation $M(X_n)$ into a binary label y. After training, we classify all N chunks obtained in the validation set data and perform the search for the best threshold T_{best} for distinguishing conversations of depressed participants from non-depressed ones. The best value of the threshold T_{best} is based on the accuracy over the whole validation set. The expression describing a classification f for a conversation C is shown in Eq. 4.

$$f(C) = f(\{X_1, X_2, ..., X_N\}) = \begin{cases} \text{depressed} & \frac{\sum_N z(X_n,0)}{\sum_N z(X_n,1)} > T_{\text{best}} \\ \\ \text{non-depressed} & \frac{\sum_N z(X_n,0)}{\sum_N z(X_n,1)} <= T_{\text{best}} \end{cases} \quad (4)$$

where

$$z(X_n, i) = \begin{cases} 1 & M(X_n) = i \\ 0 & \text{otherwise} \end{cases} \quad (5)$$

Obviously, a smaller chunk size allows us to make more precise predictions gradually as new participant utterances occur. However, a smaller chunk size leads to loss of context information for particular classification.

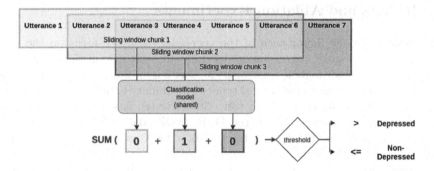

Fig. 1. The conversation is divided into sliding window chunks. Each chunk is classified independently from the others. The positive/negative labels ratio is used to determine the best threshold.

4 Experimental Setting

This section highlights the setting of the suggested models and discusses their usability. We measure the performance of our model over the DAIC-WOZ dataset. First setting was without transfer learning. Then we measure the influence of transfer learning as a way to improve the performance of our model on the DAIC-WOZ dataset using the eRisk and GPC datasets as source domains.

In our experiments, we use recurrent neural networks as model M for each chunk, concretely Long Short Term Memory (LSTM) [12] which is commonly used for sequence labeling in the conversational domain [24]. As input to the LSTM model, we included multi-head self-attention Transformer architecture [7,25] and Deep Average Architecture [4]. Specifically, the input to the model M consists of sentence embeddings obtained from the pooled output of the fine-tuned BERT [25] (sBERT), the output of the Universal Sentence Encoder - Deep Average Network [4] (DAN), or the output of the Universal Sentence Encoder - Transformer based [4] (USE$_5$). Additionally, as in [17,29,33], we evaluate an attention mechanism. We use two settings, the Hierarchical Attention Network (HAN) based on the GloVe embedding as in [29] and pure attention based on a dot-product of the hidden states of LSTM and learned attention weights.

We follow the evaluation process described in [17]. However, in contrast to [17,33], we perform Bayesian hyperparameter optimization [27]. The reported results are with the best performing setting of hyperparameters.

We follow the common setup of transfer learning using the fine-tuning approach in a cross-domain setting [26]. More specifically, we train the model on source domain data until convergence. The learning rate is then reduced in order to avoid catastrophic forgetting [18]. Then, the training continues in the target domain. The decrease of the learning rate also reduces the overwriting of useful pretrained information and maximizes positive transfer. The weights of sentence embedding model are frozen.

5   Results and Ablation Experiments

To demonstrate the importance of the vocabulary size, we focus on the performance of the logistic regression model using different sizes of the vocabulary. Therefore, we include logistic regression [20] over bag-of-words vectors [36] as the baseline model. We extracted several types of vocabulary based on the utterances of participants in the DAIC-WOZ (**3k** - 3000 words), based on the utterances of participants and therapists in the DAIC-WOZ (**6k** - 6000 words), as well as based on posts in the eRisk dataset (**20k** - 20000 words). The best results were achieved with the logistic regression and the *3k* vocabulary consisting of 3000 most used words based only on the participants' utterances - UAR (0.583), UAP (0.603) and macro-F1 (0.593), in contrast to UAR (0.579), UAP (0.561) and macro-F1 (0.570) for the *6k* vocabulary or UAR (0.583), UAP (0.580) and macro-F1 (0.581) for the *20k* vocabulary. We infer that a more extensive vocabulary probably introduces additional noise for the classification model. We use the best performing vocabulary for the rest of the experiments when working with logistic regression.

To confirm the difference between the vocabulary of depressed and non-depressed patients, we then examine the weights W_x learned by the logistic regression model. We look at the most significant logistic regression weights in absolute value, both positive and negative, and map the weights to the vocabulary words. The results indicate that words like environment (-7.5), open-minded (-6.3), or accomplish (-4.7) correspond with a non-depressed patient. In contrast, insignificant (5.36), television (5.66), or pollution ($+6.1$) relate to a depressed patient. It confirms results reported in [17,33], showing the difference between the depressed and non-depressed groups in terms of the use of language, more specifically, at the level of word usage.

Finally, we test the performance of the classification models proposed in Sect. 3.3. Our results, shown in Table 2, show the high performance of transfer learning approach. We achieve a new state-of-the-art result, specifically using the chunk-based model based on bidirectional LSTM over sentence embedding. The input to the models was based on the Universal Sentence Encoder - Transformer (USE_5).

The transfer learning achieved a notable outcome on data from the domain of social media. We also assume that this was caused by the implicit ability of sentence embedding to capture different language characteristics [15]. We discuss these results in more depth in Sect. 5. According to our results, attention is not beneficial for chunk-based classification. We assume it is caused by the sliding window chunk-based classification, where the attention mechanism is not fully utilized.

Table 2. Results - **LR** stands for Logistic Regression, **HAN** - Hierarchical Attention Model, **Chunk-biLSTM** - our Chunk-based model based on bidirectional LSTM, **DAN** - sentence embeddings based on Deep Average Network, USE_5 - sentence embeddings based on Transformer trained by [4], **sBERT** - sentence embeddings based on Transformer trained by [25], **att** stands for the attention mechanism.

Model	Unweighted average recall		
HCAN [17]	0.54		
HLGAN [17]	0.60		
HAN [33]	0.54		
HAN + L [33]	**0.72**		
	DAIC-WOZ	eRisk/GPC without fine-tuning	eRisk/GPC with fine-tuning
LR + unigrams 3k	0.553	0.559/0.547	0.613./0.553
HAN + GloVe	0.541	0.511/0.535	0.529/0.613
Chunk-biLSTM + DAN	0.595	0.559/0.470	0.625/0.541
Chunk-biLSTM + DAN + att	**0.666**	0.630/0.333	0.676/0.494
Chunk-biLSTM + USE_5	0.660	**0.651**/0.440	**0.803/0.690**
Chunk-biLSTM + USE_5 + att	0.529	0.541/**0.589**	0.613/0.595
Chunk-biLSTM + sBERT	0.440	0.505/0.523	0.613/0.541
Chunk-biLSTM + sBERT + att	0.442	0.5/0.523	0.636/0.577

Also, we present various ablation experiments to provide some interpretations of our findings.

Are Sentence Embeddings Able to Encode Information Present in Lexicon-Based Features? We are interested in verifying whether lexicon-based features are helpful to our classifiers or if the sentence embeddings already encode the information provided by the lexicons. To test this assumption, we performed another experiment using the best-performing architecture, where we added linguistic characteristics (emotions and LIWC) as input features along with sentence embeddings. Results, shown in Table 3, indicate that there is no improvement in using linguistic characteristics. Therefore, we conclude that the sentence embeddings already include linguistic characteristics needed for detection.

Table 3. Results - **Chunk-biLSTM** - our Chunk-based model based on bidirectional LSTM, USE_5 - sentence embeddings based on Transformer trained by [4], **feat** stands for additional features.

	DAIC-WOZ	eRisk/GPC without fine-tuning	eRisk/GPC with fine-tuning
Chunk-biLSTM + USE_5	**0.660**	**0.651**/0.440	**0.803**/0.690
Chunk-biLSTM + USE_5 + feat	0.565	0.541/0.410	0.597/0.511

Is the Size of the Source Domain Dataset More Critical than Domain Relatedness? Results in Table 2 show that transfer learning can help with improving the classification performance on the conversational dataset. At the same time, we find a surprising result showing that using GPC as the source domain underperforms the setting in which eRisk data is used as the source domain, even though GPC is a more similar type of data to our target dataset (they are both conversational datasets). We assume, that the smaller data size can cause poor performance when using the GPC dataset: to test this hypothesis, we evaluate a smaller version of eRisk (eRisk small). With 66,516 utterances and 388/96/820 participants. The new smaller dataset is closer to the GPC dataset in respect to size. Results, in Table 4, suggest that the size of the source domain dataset is as much important as domain closeness.

Table 4. Results - **Chunk-biLSTM** - our Chunk-based model based on bidirectional LSTM. The double horizontal line divides the table with results on **eRisk** (above) and results on **eRisk-small** (below).

	DAIC-WOZ	without fine-tuning	with fine-tuning
Chunk-biLSTM + USE_5	**0.660**	**0.651**	**0.803**
Chunk-biLSTM + USE_5	**0.660**	0.642	0.690

5.1 Usage

Because our approach is based on sliding window chunks, we are able to perform a real-time evaluation of the conversation as soon as the number of utterances reaches the size of the sliding window chunk. Our experiments are performed with 50 as the chunk size. This allows for including the classification model as another part of the Natural Language Understanding (NLU) unit commonly used in conversational agents [9, 24]. As opposed to other models proposed in literature such as [17, 29, 33], our suggested model is independent of external lexical features, such as lexicon-based features, and therefore it can be run in parallel with other NLU units.

6 Conclusion and Future Work

In this paper, we addressed the problem of detecting early signs of depression in the conversational domain. We achieve state-of-the-art results on the DAIC-WOZ dataset using transfer learning from the social media domain. The proposed model was based on a sequence of chunk classification and uses a recurrent neural network with sentence embedding as input features. Additionally, we show that the attention mechanism is not beneficial for our chunk-based model. We show that transfer learning helps improve the performance in a domain with a lack of data utilizing data from a related domain. Additionally, we demonstrate that the size of the source dataset is as important as the domain relatedness between the source and the target. We also suggest a possible usage of our model as a tool for therapists, who may retrieve early signs of depression from a broad range of conversational systems.

6.1 Ethical Concern

This paper showed a possible usage of automatic techniques for detecting early signs of depression. Unfortunately, false positive and false negative cases can cause tremendous damage when used in the conversational agent. We claim that if our model or proposed techniques are used in real-life scenarios, they has to be supervised by a qualified therapist. Also, as we have shown, domain adaptation plays a crucial role too. Our approach, even if quite general, has to be carefully adapted to a specific domain. We also suggest not relying on the classification system only, but using it as another source of information for a qualified therapist. With this setting, we can minimize possible harm and allow the therapist to speed up their work.

Acknowledgments. The research work of Petr Lorenc and Jan Šedivý was partially supported by the Grant Agency of the Czech Technical University in Prague, grant (SGS22/082/OHK3/1T/37). The research work of Paolo Rosso was partially funded by the Generalitat Valenciana under DeepPattern (PROMETEO/2019/121). The work of Ana Sabina Uban was carried out at the PRHLT Research Center during her postdoc internship. Her work was also partially funded by a grant from Innovation Norway, project "Virtual simulated platform for automated coaching-testing", Ref No 2021/331382.

References

1. Abed-Esfahani, P., et al.: Transfer learning for depression: early detection and severity prediction from social media postings. In: CLEF (Working Notes), vol. 1, pp. 1–6 (2019)
2. American Psychiatric Association: Diagnostic and statistical manual of mental disorders, 5th edn. Autor, Washington, DC (2013)
3. Batista, G., Prati, R., Monard, M.C.: A study of the behavior of several methods for balancing machine learning training data. In: SIGKDD Explorations, vol. 6, pp. 20–29 (2004)
4. Cer, D.M., et al.: Universal sentence encoder. arXiv (2018)
5. Coppersmith, G., Dredze, M., Harman, C., Hollingshead, K., Mitchell, M.: CLPsych 2015 shared task: Depression and PTSD on Twitter. In: Proceedings of the 2nd CLPsych, Denver, Colorado, 5 June 2015, pp. 31–39. ACL (2015)
6. DeVault, D., et al.: Verbal indicators of psychological distress in interactive dialogue with a virtual human. In: SIGDIAL 2013 Conference, pp. 193–202. Association for Computational Linguistics (2013)
7. Devlin, J., Chang, M.W., Lee, K., Toutanova, K.: Bert: pre-training of deep bidirectional transformers for language understanding. In: NAACL (2019)
8. Dinkel, H., Wu, M., Yu, K.: Text-based depression detection: what triggers an alert. arXiv (2019)
9. Finch, S.E., et al.: Emora: an inquisitive social chatbot who cares for you. In: Alexa Prize Proceedings, vol. 3 (2020)
10. Gabriel, R., et al.: Further advances in open domain dialog systems in the third Alexa prize socialbot grand challenge. In: Alexa Prize Proceedings, vol. 3 (2020)
11. Gratch, J., et al.: The distress analysis interview corpus of human and computer interviews. In: LREC 2014, pp. 3123–3128 (2014)
12. Hochreiter, S., Schmidhuber, J.: Long short-term memory. Neural Comput. **9**, 1735–80 (1997)
13. Islam, M.R., Kabir, A., Ahmed, A., Kamal, A., Wang, H., Ulhaq, A.: Depression detection from social network data using machine learning techniques. In: Health Information Science and Systems, vol. 6, p. 8 (2018)
14. Lee, M., Ackermans, S., van As, N., Chang, H., Lucas, E., IJsselsteijn, W.: Caring for Vincent: a chatbot for self-compassion. In: Proceedings of the 2019 CHI Conference on Human Factors in Computing Systems (2019)
15. Liu, N.F., Gardner, M., Belinkov, Y., Peters, M.E., Smith, N.A.: Linguistic knowledge and transferability of contextual representations. In: NAACL-HLT (2019)
16. Losada, D.E., Crestani, F.: A test collection for research on depression and language use. In: Conference Labs of the Evaluation Forum (2016)
17. Mallol-Ragolta, A., Zhao, Z., Stappen, L., Cummins, N., Schuller, B.: A hierarchical attention network-based approach for depression detection from transcribed clinical interviews. In: Interspeech, pp. 221–225 (2019)
18. McCloskey, M., Cohen, N.J.: Catastrophic interference in connectionist networks: the sequential learning problem. In: Psychology of Learning and Motivation, vol. 24, pp. 109–165 (1989)
19. Mohammad, S., Turney, P.: Crowdsourcing a word-emotion association lexicon. In: Computational Intelligence, vol. 29 (2013)
20. Peng, J., Lee, K., Ingersoll, G.: An introduction to logistic regression analysis and reporting. J. Educ. Res. **96**, 3–14 (2002)

21. Pennebaker, J.W., Francis, M.E., Booth, R.J.: Linguistic Inquiry and Word Count, vol. 71. Lawrence Erlbaum Associates (2001)

22. Pennington, J., Socher, R., Manning, C.: Glove: global vectors for word representation. In: EMNLP, vol. 14, pp. 1532–1543 (2014)

23. Phang, J., Févry, T., Bowman, S.R.: Sentence encoders on stilts: supplementary training on intermediate labeled-data tasks. arXiv (2018)

24. Pichl, J., Marek, P., Konrád, J., Lorenc, P., Ta, V.D., Sedivý, J.: Alquist 3.0: Alexa prize bot using conversational knowledge graph. In: Alexa Prize Proceedings, vol. 3 (2020)

25. Reimers, N., Gurevych, I.: Sentence-BERT: sentence embeddings using siamese BERT-networks. In: Association for Computational Linguistics (EMNLP), November 2019 (2019). https://arxiv.org/abs/1908.10084

26. Rutowski, T., Shriberg, E., Harati, A., Lu, Y., Chlebek, P., Oliveira, R.: Depression and anxiety prediction using deep language models and transfer learning. In: 7th BESC, vol. 1, pp. 1–6 (2020)

27. Snoek, J., Larochelle, H., Adams, R.P.: Practical Bayesian optimization of machine learning algorithms. In: Advances in Neural Information Processing Systems, vol. 25. Curran Associates, Inc. (2012)

28. Tsetsi, E., Rains, S.: Smartphone internet access and use: extending the digital divide and usage gap. Mob. Media Commun. 5, 239–255 (2017)

29. Uban, A.S., Chulvi, B., Rosso, P.: An emotion and cognitive based analysis of mental health disorders from social media data. Fut. Gener. Comput. Syst. 124, 480–494 (2021)

30. Uban, A.S., Chulvi, B., Rosso, P.: Multi-aspect transfer learning for detecting low resource mental disorders on social media. In: Proceedings of the 13th Language Resources and Evaluation Conference (2022, to appear)

31. Weiss, K.R., Khoshgoftaar, T., Wang, D.: A survey of transfer learning. J. Big Data 3, 1–40 (2016)

32. Wolohan, J., Hiraga, M., Mukherjee, A., Sayyed, Z.A., Millard, M.: Detecting linguistic traces of depression in topic-restricted text: attending to self-stigmatized depression with NLP. In: Language Cognition and Computational Models, Santa Fe, New Mexico, USA, August 2018, pp. 11–21. ACL (2018)

33. Xezonaki, D., Paraskevopoulos, G., Potamianos, A., Narayanan, S.: Affective conditioning on hierarchical attention networks applied to depression detection from transcribed clinical interviews. In: Interspeech, pp. 4556–4560. ISCA (2020)

34. Yang, Z., Yang, D., Dyer, C., He, X., Smola, A., Hovy, E.: Hierarchical attention networks for document classification. In: Proceedings of the 2016 (NAACL-HLT), pp. 1480–1489 (2016)

35. Yates, A., Cohan, A., Goharian, N.: Depression and self-harm risk assessment in online forums. In: EMNLP, Copenhagen, Denmark, September 2017, pp. 2968–2978. ACL (2017)

36. Zhang, Y., Jin, R., Zhou, Z.H.: Understanding bag-of-words model: a statistical framework. Int. J. Mach. Learn. Cybern. 1, 43–52 (2010)

Detecting Vaccine Skepticism on Twitter Using Heterogeneous Information Networks

Tim Kreutz$^{(\boxtimes)}$ ⓘ and Walter Daelemans ⓘ

CLiPS - Computational Linguistics Group, University of Antwerp, Antwerp, Belgium
{tim.kreutz,walter.daelemans}@uantwerpen.be
https://www.uantwerpen.be/en/research-groups/clips/

Abstract. Identifying social media users who are skeptical of the COVID-19 vaccine is an important step in understanding and refuting negative stance taking on vaccines. While previous work on Twitter data places individual messages or whole communities as their focus, this paper aims to detect stance at the user level. We develop a system that classifies Dutch Twitter users, incorporating not only the texts that users produce, but also their actions in the form of following and retweeting. These heterogeneous data are modelled in a graph structure. Graph Convolutional Networks are trained to learn whether user nodes belong to the skeptical or non-skeptical group. Results show that all types of information are used by the model, and that especially user biographies, follows and retweets improve the predictions. On a test set of unseen users, performance declines somewhat, which is expected considering these users tweeted less and had fewer connections in the graph on average. To consider multiple degrees of vaccine skepticism, the test set was annotated with more fine-grained labels and the model was repurposed to do multiclass classification. While the model trained on binary labels was unsuited for this additional task, heterogeneous information networks were found useful to both accurately model and visualize complex user behaviors.

Keywords: Vaccination · Stance detection · Social media · Twitter · Graph Convolutional Networks

1 Introduction

The vaccine roll out during the COVID-19 pandemic has posed numerous diplomatic and societal challenges for governments around the world. Now that vaccines are available in most countries, significant parts of the world population remain unvaccinated not for logistical reasons but because of vaccine skepticism.

Vaccine skepticism is defined as a delayed acceptance of the COVID-19 vaccine, or the outright refusal to take a vaccine despite its availability [7]. Willingness to get vaccinated has become a polarizing issue and its contention has increasingly moved to online spaces. Social media in particular, are used to share not only

P. Rosso et al. (Eds.): NLDB 2022, LNCS 13286, pp. 370–381, 2022.
https://doi.org/10.1007/978-3-031-08473-7_34

personal opinions, but information from family, friends, health professionals, local governments and a mixture of accurate and questionable news outlets.

A 2020 study found that vaccine hesitancy is more prevalent amongst people who list the internet as one of their main sources of medical information [4]. The proliferation of questionable information, ranging from misleading news to conspiracy theories about the ongoing pandemic, has lead to a social media *infodemic* [7]. Especially in times when skepticism of government measures can cause difficulties in overcoming a crisis, it is important to identify and understand the users who believe such misinformation.

This paper sets out to identify Dutch speaking Twitter users who are skeptical of vaccination against COVID-19. We choose Twitter as a platform because its user profiles as well as most user interactions are publicly available. We target Dutch speaking users because the group of anti vaccination users is still marginal compared to the United States [11], making it feasible to scale our tool to give a complete picture of anti vaccination groups in the two countries.

Our aim is to reflect the dynamic nature of the vaccine skeptics both in their behaviors and communications by acknowledging that degrees of skepticism exist. We therefore implement a heterogeneous information network which models a user's actions as well as their language. Users actively decide who to follow or retweet, and tweet out in support or opposition of ideas. All of this information is relevant to positioning users relative to each other and identifying their group membership.

1.1 Contributions of This Work

The aim of this work is to identify users who are skeptical of vaccines on Dutch speaking Twitter. We specifically answer the following three questions:

1. Which behaviors convey vaccine skepticism on Twitter?
2. Can we improve detection of skeptical users by using a combination of linguistic and network features in a heterogeneous information network?
3. Can a model trained for making the binary distinction between skeptical and non-skeptical users be reused to identify degrees of skepticism?

Our contribution is to develop an accurate model which takes into account network features and linguistic cues for classifying Twitter users as skeptical of vaccines or not. The model output warrants further research into the spectrum of skepticism, which can range from hesitant users who simply ask questions about the vaccines to anti-vaccination users who actively spread conspiracy theories amongst their followers.

The next section will discuss related research to contextualize this work. We explain how we constructed our corpus and how it is fit into the mold of a heterogeneous information network in the methodology section. We first develop a model to make binary distinctions between users who are skeptical of vaccination and those who are not. The model output is evaluated in terms of its discriminative accuracy and performance outside the initial dataset on unseen users.

We then discuss our findings with an error analysis and consider how the binary model could be used to target more specific groups of users on the spectrum of vaccine skepticism.

2   Background

Detecting stance on Twitter has been frequently organized as a shared task on a wide range of polarizing topics, including vaccination. The last iteration of the stance detection tasks at IberLEF [1] provides meta-information of messages and users to incorporate social features in the submitted systems. These features could however not be used to connect users and messages in a network of data to exploit graph edges in that way.

This work fits a larger context of research done to improve understanding of negative opinions about vaccines online. The Vaccine Confidence project (VCP)[1] for instance, has monitored concerns over vaccines in media reports since 2012 to show where and when specific concerns arise. Most notably, it tracked opinions about vaccination for the influenza A(H1N1) virus outbreak in 2009, for the human papillomavirus (HPV) and for coronavirus SARS-CoV-2.

Previous work on Twitter data has cast detection of vaccine skepticism as a text categorization problem. [6] collected 6,000 tweets about HPV to better understand the low vaccination coverage in the U.S. Their setup used SVMs with basic n-gram features to determine whether a tweet was positive, negative or neutral about vaccination for HPV.

[9] translated this approach for the context of COVID-19 in the Netherlands with the goal of identifying tweets with a negative stance towards vaccination. The study finds that identifying such tweets is a non-trivial problem, due to the many motivations for adopting a negative stance and the relative scarcity of the negative class, especially when compared to a larger community of anti vaccination users in the U.S. context.

Vaccine skepticism can alternatively be cast as a social phenomenon which exhibits itself in complex user interactions, rather than in the broadcasting of a static opinion. [13] focus more on network dynamics when tracking sentiments about the H1N1 vaccine on Twitter. Negative sentiment is observed to be more contagious than positive sentiment, but a larger opinionated neighborhood inhibits this contagion. The results in [13] suggest that vaccine skeptic content is mostly circulated in small groups of homophilic Twitter users.

This is further underlined by a recent report by the Center for Countering Digital Hate (CCDH) entitled The Disinformation Dozen [5]. In the report a massive stream of anti vaccination misinformation on Facebook and Twitter is shown to originate from only twelve influencers.

Beyond just describing network features, [2] aim to discover such clusters on Twitter with several existing community detection algorithms. They find negative sentiments to persist in groups of few users that are not well connected.

---

[1] https://www.vaccineconfidence.org/.

In a preliminary geographical analysis, these negative networks seem to operate mostly in U.S. territories. Although the setup is useful for identifying several key ,drivers of vaccine skepticism on Twitter, it misses those users that are simply hesitant about vaccination.

We primarily differ from previous setups by framing vaccine skepticism as a social problem at the level of the user. Although identifying skepticism on a document level can help detect skeptical users, it ignores other public user information. Especially on Twitter, where messages are short and lacking of context, using all available information albeit tweets, public user profiles or interactions with others, is important to develop an accurate model. Conversely, algorithms classifying subgraphs, such as in community detection, do identify drivers of vaccine skepticism using network features, but will be less useful for finding hesitant users, who would more likely operate in the periphery of such communities.

The current work is situated at the interface of text categorization and network analysis by employing recent graph based methods which work both with content as well as network features. Methodologically, our work is closest to [3] who classify a tweet on the basis of its content, the content of previous tweets by the same user, and a user representation based on the reply network of the tweet. Adding the network representation lead to substantial improvements in the accuracy of a logistic regression classification model.

3   Methods

Twitter allows diverse interactions between users, all giving different signals about the social relationships between them. Our methodology is derived from this social nature of the data, modelling the interactions between users as faithfully and completely as possible.

Network graphs are suitable for modelling many real-world data, social networks among them [14]. Starting from the straightforward and homogeneous network of followers, we increase complexity of the graph representation by introducing encoded user biographies and tweets. As such, we end up with a heterogeneous information network which inherently stores network features and contains linguistic features at the node level; User behavior is modelled as actions (*"who do users follow?"*) and words (*"what do users write?"*).

We choose Graph Convolutional Networks (GCNs) to do node prediction for the unlabeled samples. GCNs are a Convolutional Neural Networks (CNN) implementation operating directly on graph-structured data [8]. GCNs learn a function of signals and features on a graph by optimizing cross-entropy loss on labelled samples. An unlabelled node is passed signals from nearby nodes, using the learnt weights to predict its class.

The GCN algorithm scales linearly for graphs with huge numbers of nodes and edges, and accurately learns node representations from both graph structure and neighboring node features. With only a very limited number of nodes annotated (<10%), GCNs significantly outperformed other graph-based algorithms on a range of graph-learning tasks, node prediction among them [8].

Relational Graph Convolution Networks (RGCNs) [14] are a necessary extension of the GCN approach to operate on graphs with multiple types of nodes and edges, or heterogeneous graphs. Node representations are created by merging signals from different edge types. To return to the case of a social network: an unlabeled user node is passed the features from its own authored tweets, tweets it has retweeted, and from users in its social network.

We describe the corpus of Twitter data below. The experiments were designed to first learn prototypical distinctions between users who are skeptical of COVID-19 vaccinations and others who frequently tweet about vaccination. We then expand the data to show how our prototypical model can be applied to unseen users. In an additional task, we aim to repurpose the outputs of the binary model to identify multiple degrees of skepticism. As such, it could identify users who position themselves on the edge of radicalization, being themselves hesitant of COVID-19 vaccination and in search of answers.

3.1   Data

The training data is taken from a snapshot of Dutch tweets from January 2020 to June 2021. A filter was applied based on a regex that was designed to retrieve mentions of vaccines and relevant pharmaceutical companies. In the chosen period, we found 660,415 users having at one point tweeted about these topics. To make annotating an initial set of users feasible, we further limited the group to those users who posted an original tweet about the relevant topics at least once in each of the 18 months included in the dataset; The 3,565 users that were found this way can easily be inspected by hand to assign accurate labels, and are guaranteed to actively have taken a stance on COVID-19 vaccination.

Annotation Task. An annotation task was set up to assign labels to the 3,565 users. A single annotator was shown the biographic text from a user's Twitter profile as well as three randomly chosen tweets about vaccines from their timeline. If the annotator saw clear evidence of vaccine skepticism either in the biography or in the written tweets a SKEP label was assigned. If the biography and initial three tweets did not give clear indication of a stance either way, three more tweets could be shown. Eventually, if no clear signs of skepticism were found in any of the tweets, the user is assigned to the non-skeptical group by default.

The result is a dataset with 1,781 skeptical users, and 1,784 non-skeptical users. We first extract a list of followers for each user, and model a homogeneous graph with users as nodes and follows as edges. An extract from the network of training data is shown in Fig. 1a.

Biographies. We then implemented encoded user biographies as node features. Most users (84%) in the annotated data added a biography to their profile. The short texts were encoded using Sentence-BERT [12], a state-of-the-art language model for sentence encoding. The specific model (all-mpnet-base-v2) was picked for its accuracy in diverse use cases, as well as its relative speed which becomes important when encoding a large number of tweets in later steps.

Tweets. The final graph representations implement tweet nodes. Users connect to tweet in one of two ways: either by having written a tweet, or by having retweeted a tweet. Tweet nodes carry their Sentence-BERT encodings as feature values. Convolutions by the GCN over edges are performed separately for each edge type, making the graph in Fig. 1b truly heterogeneous. We follow the same iterative increasing of complexity in the graph in the results section to see how the heterogeneous information contributes to user node classification.

Table 1. Differences between the data used to train a prototypical model of learning vaccine skepticism and the test data consisted of unseen users. The test users are generally less active (writes and retweet edges) and less connected (follow edges). More fine-grained labels were assigned to the test group to evaluate the suitability of the prototypical model for detecting degrees of skepticism.

Training data		Test data	
Skeptical	1,781	Anti	627
		Hesitant	297
Other	1,784	Unknown	220
		Pro	404
Total	3,565	Total	1,548

(a) Labels

	Training data	Test data
Users	3,565	1,548
Tweets	530,935	111,177
Follows	353,074	34,384
Writes	530,935	111,177
Retweets	303,523	23,338

(b) Network information

Unseen Users. The pre-filtering that was applied when selecting users for training may restrict how well the model generalizes to unseen users. We selected 1,548 Twitter users randomly, placing only the restriction that they have at one point tweeted about vaccination, as test data to evaluate whether the model will generalize to users that may show less evidence of skepticism simply because they are less active and well-connected in the network.

The test set received more fine-grained labels to better reflect different degrees of skepticism. We took definitions from [10] and divided vaccine skepticism into two classes: anti vaccination and hesitant. The non-skeptical users were divided into pro vaccination users and unknown users. The differences between the data used for training the model and the test data is described in Table 1.

To translate to a multiclass setting, we take the softmax output of the binary model and subtract the probability for the positive class (SKEP) from the negative. The resulting predictions form a distribution ranging from -1 to 1. The model, being unaware of prior class distribution over unseen users, heuristically creates buckets of samples per quantile, corresponding to their respective labels: ANTI, HES, UNK, and PRO.

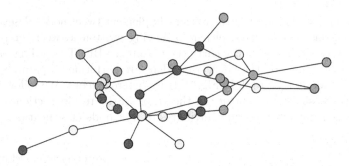

(a) Extract from the homogeneous graph with user nodes and following as edges. The complete graph consists of 5,113 user nodes with 387,557 follow edges between them.

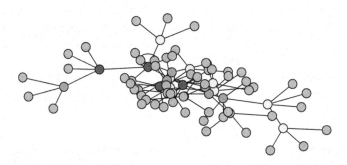

(b) Extract from the heterogeneous graph with user and tweet nodes. The complete graph consists of 5,113 users, 642,112 tweets, 387,557 follow edges, 642,112 write edges and 326,861 retweet edges.

Fig. 1. Steps of increasing complexity in a network modelling Twitter users central to discussions about vaccines.

4   Results

The Graph Convolutional Networks were trained with default parameters from the implementation in [8]: one hidden layer, .01 learning rate, 50% dropout for 200 epochs. Signals passed from different relation types in the heterogeneous setting were grouped by summing, then reduced by taking the mean of the different signals like the standard implementation in [14].

4.1   Graph Performance

Increasing the graph complexity does not necessarily instill more useful information in the network. Tweets about topics other than COVID-19 vaccinations may introduce noise while retweeting other users may not always signal support for their message. Table 2 shows the performance of individual graph implementations on a validation set. We vary the percentage of supervised nodes that propagate information elsewhere in the network to see the effect of training size. The size of the validation set inversely consists of the remaining unsupervised user nodes.

The first graph implementation is featureless (see Fig. 1a), meaning GCNs rely only on network information to induce node embeddings. Much improvement can be made by using encoded biographies as user features (#2). This result is especially impressive considering nearly 16% of users in the training data and validation data does not have a biography in their profile.

The network structure in graph #3 is further enriched by incorporating retweets. Users that did not previously share any formal ties, can convey similarity by retweeting the same tweet. Finally, encoded tweet features and write edges to propagate them are implemented in graph #4 (Fig. 1b).

Increasing the training size had a positive effect for the graph implementations with more (types of) edges and nodes. This is somewhat expected as diversity of examples increases with network complexity. However, the effect was surprisingly small. GCNs that trained only on 20% of the available annotations (713 users), performed nearly as well as those trained in four times as much training samples. In fact, the featureless implementation performed better when using only few samples.

4.2   Test Results

The results on test users drop off somewhat since the method by which they were selected differs from the users in the training and validation data. Whereas the latter group tweeted about vaccination more actively and is well-connected in the network, as partly reflected in the network information in Table 1b, the test setting simulates plugging any unseen Twitter profile into the network and asking our classifier about their stance on vaccination. Not only could the GCNs have fewer information to work with, the very label may be more doubtful as the user may not take a firm stance one way or the other.

Table 2. Node prediction accuracy on validation data. Improvements were made by iteratively increasing the complexity of the graph representation, first adding user features (biographies), retweet relationships, tweet features and write edges. There was a limited effect of training size, affirming that GCNs work well even with very limited supervision.

Graph	Features	Edges	20%	40%	60%	80%
#1	–	F	**.647**	.624	.643	.615
#2	U	F	.803	.793	.793	**.808**
#3	U	F + R	.861	.860	.868	**.871**
#4	U + T	F + W + R	.862	.871	.874	**.879**

U = User features, T = Tweet features,
F = Follow edges, R = Retweet edges, W = Write edges

Still, the graph implementation that used both user and tweets features, follow, write and retweet edges, trained on all available training data, was able to assign a correct binary label to unseen users in **74.1%** of cases.

Degrees of Skepticism. The confusion matrix in Fig. 2 shows the types of errors made by the classifier in the binary setting, resulting in the accuracy mentioned above, as well as in the setting with a multi class distinction. As expected, anti vaccination and pro vaccination sentiments, representing the extremes of the scale, are easier to predict, while vaccine hesitancy is predicted correctly as skeptical in only 62% of cases.

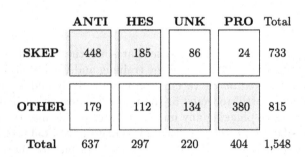

	ANTI	**HES**	**UNK**	**PRO**	Total
SKEP	448	185	86	24	733
OTHER	179	112	134	380	815
Total	637	297	220	404	1,548

Fig. 2. Confusion matrix comparing binary output from the first model to the true fine-grained labels, representing degrees of skepticism in the test data.

Note again that the model is not trained to do these multiclass predictions, as annotating sufficient data for training with such subtle distinctions becomes prohibitively time consuming. However, model confidence may serve as a proxy for identifying vaccine hesitancy, a heuristic based on how annotators themselves have trouble assigning labels to this group.

Table 3 shows the results of the softmax discretization heuristic. Again, the ANTI and PRO class are more accurately predicted than the HES and UNK users. We hypothesize that the binary model could recall more HES users, giving it purpose as a prefiltering model for further annotation or silver-labelling of a dataset. However, this did not turn out to be the case. Further development would be needed to employ the GCNs in this multiclass setting.

Table 3. Detailed results for each class in the multiclass setup. Discretizing softmax to multiple degrees of vaccine skepticism did not yield good results for the more subtle groups of hesitant users, and users who were labelled as unknown.

Class	P	R	F
ANTI	0.643	0.397	0.491
HES	0.222	0.290	0.251
UNK	0.142	0.250	0.181
PRO	0.509	0.488	0.499
AVG	0.388	0.373	0.368

5   Conclusion

In this paper we explored the ways in which Twitter users may show vaccine skepticism: through linking up with other users, by spreading their message, by communicating their stance in a self authored biographic text or by tweeting about vaccines.

Our main contributions stem from approaching the task of detecting vaccine skepticism as a problem at the user level. Abstracting away from individual documents allows connecting diverse types of information and outperforming the models who draw information only from text. Heterogenous graph representations are ideal for modelling both social action and linguistic features, and a new vein of neural graph-based models learn weights accurately and rapidly on these graphs, even with millions of nodes.

This heterogeneous information was modelled on a dataset of Dutch speaking Twitter users who tweet relatively often about vaccines. We trained Graph Convolutional Networks for predicting node labels, incrementally feeding it more types of edges, nodes and features.

The most complex graph, which incorporates user and tweet nodes and connects them through follow, write and retweet edges performed best on the validation data. The effect of training size was limited, showing that GCNs trained on few training samples are able to generalize well.

Each edge thus contributed to a better model. Biographies notably contained a lot of information directly and indirectly indicative of skepticism, shown in a huge leap in performance. Linking users to tweet they had retweeted was also very beneficial to the model, while write edges yielded limited improvement since they contributed only one edge.

In the test setting we implanted unseen users in the network that have at one point tweeted about vaccination in our data set. Results for this group were lower, although still impressive at 74.1% accuracy considering these nodes provided less context.

Unfortunately, the prototypical model could not be repurposed for detecting degrees of skepticism. The GCNs showed more confidence in predicting anti vaccination and pro vaccination users, but using these confidence scores to identify the group of hesitant users proved non-trivial. Future research could therefore focus on tuning a model specifically towards identifying hesitancy in vaccine stance.

Developing graph-based deep learning models is another useful avenue for future work. Especially in the case of complex user behaviors, which are often discretized on social media, GCNs show they can exploit network and node features in a complementary way. To encourage new work and the reproducibility of the current work, our code and the data representations are available from our repositories[2] upon request.

References

1. Agerri, R., Centeno, R., Espinosa, M., de Landa, J.F., Rodrigo, A.: VaxxStance@IberLEF 2021: overview of the task on going beyond text in cross-lingual stance detection. Procesamiento del Lenguaje Natural **67**, 173–181 (2021)
2. Bello-Orgaz, G., Hernandez-Castro, J., Camacho, D.: Detecting discussion communities on vaccination in Twitter. Futur. Gener. Comput. Syst. **66**, 125–136 (2017)
3. Béres, F., Csoma, R., Michaletzky, T.V., Benczúr, A.A.: Vaccine skepticism detection by network embedding. arXiv preprint arXiv:2110.13619 (2021)
4. Charron, J., Gautier, A., Jestin, C.: Influence of information sources on vaccine hesitancy and practices. Médecine et Maladies Infectieuses **50**(8), 727–733 (2020). https://doi.org/10.1016/j.medmal.2020.01.010. https://www.sciencedirect.com/science/article/pii/S0399077X20300457
5. Centre for Countering Digital Hate: The disinformation dozen: why platforms must act on twelve leading online anti-vaxxers. Counterhate.com (2021)
6. Du, J., Xu, J., Song, H., Liu, X., Tao, C.: Optimization on machine learning based approaches for sentiment analysis on HPV vaccines related tweets. J. Biomed. Semant. **8**(1), 1–7 (2017)
7. Hughes, B., et al.: Development of a codebook of online anti-vaccination rhetoric to manage COVID-19 vaccine misinformation. medRxiv (2021). https://doi.org/10.1101/2021.03.23.21253727. https://www.medrxiv.org/content/early/2021/03/26/2021.03.23.21253727
8. Kipf, T.N., Welling, M.: Semi-supervised classification with graph convolutional networks. arXiv preprint arXiv:1609.02907 (2016)
9. Kunneman, F., Lambooij, M., Wong, A., Van Den Bosch, A., Mollema, L.: Monitoring stance towards vaccination in Twitter messages. BMC Med. Inform. Decis. Mak. **20**(1), 1–14 (2020)
10. Larson, H.J., Broniatowski, D.A.: Volatility of vaccine confidence. Science **371**(6536), 1289–1289 (2021). https://doi.org/10.1126/science.abi6488. https://science.sciencemag.org/content/371/6536/1289

---

[2] https://github.com/clips/vaccine_skepticism.

11. Mitra, T., Counts, S., Pennebaker, J.W.: Understanding anti-vaccination attitudes in social media. In: International Conference on Web and Social Media (ICWSM), May 2016. AAAI (2016). https://www.microsoft.com/en-us/research/publication/understanding-anti-vaccination-attitudes-in-social-media/

12. Reimers, N., Gurevych, I.: Making monolingual sentence embeddings multilingual using knowledge distillation. In: Proceedings of the 2020 Conference on Empirical Methods in Natural Language Processing, November 2020. Association for Computational Linguistics (2020). https://arxiv.org/abs/2004.09813

13. Salathé, M., Vu, D.Q., Khandelwal, S., Hunter, D.R.: The dynamics of health behavior sentiments on a large online social network. EPJ Data Sci. $2(1)$, 1–12 (2013). https://doi.org/10.1140/epjds16

14. Schlichtkrull, M., Kipf, T.N., Bloem, P., van den Berg, R., Titov, I., Welling, M.: Modeling relational data with graph convolutional networks. In: Gangemi, A., et al. (eds.) ESWC 2018. LNCS, vol. 10843, pp. 593–607. Springer, Cham (2018). https://doi.org/10.1007/978-3-319-93417-4_38

Using Language Models for Classifying the Party Affiliation of Political Texts

Tu My Doan[(✉)] [iD], Benjamin Kille [iD], and Jon Atle Gulla [iD]

Norwegian University of Science and Technology, Trondheim, Norway
{tu.m.doan,benjamin.u.kille,jon.atle.gulla}@ntnu.no

Abstract. We analyze the use of language models for political text classification. Political texts become increasingly available and language models have succeeded in various natural language processing tasks. We apply two baselines and different language models to data from the UK, Germany, and Norway. Observed accuracy shows language models improving on the performance of the baselines by up to 10.35% (Norwegian), 12.95% (German), and 6.39% (English).

Keywords: Party affiliation classification · Political text representation · Language models

1 Introduction

Neural Language Models (LMs)—large neural networks capturing patterns in extensive corpora of written language—have changed our abilities for automatically processing natural language. Abilities include text translation [8], code completion [15], and conversational agents [12]. There is, however, limited exploration of the use of LMs for political texts. These texts become increasingly available as organizations such as the European Union demand transparency.[1] Consequently, member states have adopted measures to facilitate access to political information. Many parliaments regularly publish their proceedings digitally. Citizens can read about the views and opinions of their representatives.

With the available data sources, we ask whether LMs can capture the inherent structure of political speech? We consider data from a set of nations and explore whether LMs can identify the speakers' party affiliation. More demanding use cases, such as identifying viewpoints, demand a large collection of annotated texts, which are lacking. Concretely, we formulate two research questions:

RQ_1 Do language models identify the party affiliation of political texts *more accurately* than a Naïve Bayes classifier?
RQ_2 Does language models' accuracy vary with different languages?

---

[1] The Treaty of the European Union states that "Every citizen shall have the right to participate in the democratic life of the Union. Decisions shall be taken as openly and as closely as possible to the citizen." (see http://data.europa.eu/eli/treaty/teu_2016/art_10/oj).

P. Rosso et al. (Eds.): NLDB 2022, LNCS 13286, pp. 382–393, 2022.
https://doi.org/10.1007/978-3-031-08473-7_35

The remainder is structured as follow: Sect. 2 reviews related work. Section 3 outlines the data sets used for evaluation. Section 5 introduces the baselines and language models. Section 6 illustrates the results. Section 7 concludes.

2   Related Work

Classifying party affiliations takes a corpus of party-related texts and evaluates different predictors. Research on party classification has frequently used texts from the United States leading to a binary classification problem. For instance, Bei et al. [17] explore the use of Naïve Bayes (NB) and Support Vector Machines (SVM) on Congressional data. Dahllöf [4] uses SVMs to classify speeches of Swedish politicians. Wong et al. [16] focuses on identifying political leaning or voting preferences of Twitter users with data from the 2012 US. presidential election. The authors model the task as convex minimization. Rao and Spasojevic [10] use Recurrent Neural Networks (RNN) and word embeddings to detect political leaning of social media users. Again, the task was formed as binary classification (Democratic/Republican). Biessmann et al. [3] explore bag-of-word representation to predict whether texts come from government or opposition members. Høyland et al. [6] classify speeches in a multi-class setting with SVM. Baly et al. [2] use language models to classify news articles into left, center, and right. Kummervold et al. [7] fine-tuned a classifier on a balanced dataset of Norwegian Parliamentary speeches for party affiliation detection using Transformers and NB-BERT language model. Cases with a multi-party democracy represent a harder challenge than the binary classification into Democrat or Republican. We explore the use of language models for three such multi-class problems in the UK, Germany, and Norway.

3   Data

We consider three datasets of different languages (Norwegian, German, and English). First, we pre-process the data. Table 1 shows the datasets' composition. We split the data into training, validation, and test set (see Table 2).

3.1   Norwegian Parliamentary Speech Corpus (NPSC)

The Norwegian Language Bank at the National Library of Norway developed the NPSC [13] data set consisting of transcribed meeting recordings and speakers' meta data from 2017 and 2018. The recordings amount to 140 h of running speech, 65k sentences, and 1.2M words. We focus exclusively on the text data (speeches and metadata). As the average speech is 137 words long, we filtered out speeches with fewer than 150 words. To reduce the imbalance in this dataset, we decided to remove parties with less than 100 speeches. This resulted into a new dataset of total 3091 speeches of seven parties.

Table 1. Distribution of political speeches per party. We removed parties with fewer than 100 speeches of at least 150 words. ID refers to the party label. N refers to the initial number of speeches. M refers to the final number of speeches. Further, we show the proportion of speeches retained (% ret), and their distribution over all parties (% prop).

ID	Party	N	M	% ret	% prop
	Norwegian Parliamentary Speech Corpus (NPSC)				
–	Arbeidernes ungdomsfylking *(Workers' Youth)*	3	-	-	0.0
0	Arbeiderpartiet *(Norwegian Labour)*	2637	571	21.7	18.5
1	Fremskrittspartiet *(Progress Party)*	1444	632	43.8	20.4
2	Høyre *(Right Party)*	3216	977	30.4	31.6
3	Kristelig Folkeparti *(Christian Democrats)*	425	142	33.4	4.6
–	Miljøpartiet De Grønne *(Green Party)*	75	-	-	0.0
–	Rødt *(Red Party)*	30	-	-	0.0
4	SV - Sosialistisk Venstreparti *(Socialists)*	464	224	48.3	7.2
5	Senterpartiet *(Center Party)*	1090	351	32.2	11.4
6	Venstre *(Liberal Party)*	338	194	57.4	6.3
	Sum	9722	3091	31.8	100.0
	German Parliamentary Speech Corpus (GPSC)				
0	AFD *(Alternative for Germany)*	4437	2950	66.5	3.4
1	Bündnis 90/Die Grünen *(Green Party)*	23 975	13 789	57.5	15.9
2	CDU / CSU *(Christian Democrats)*	41 252	26 520	64.3	30.6
3	DIE LINKE *(Left Party)*	16 776	10 362	61.8	12.0
4	Fraktionslos *(without party affiliation)*	876	496	56.6	0.6
5	FDP *(Liberal Party)*	17 062	10 998	64.5	12.7
6	PDS *(Party of Democratic Socialism)*	1739	1066	61.3	1.2
7	SPD *(Social Democrates)*	29 497	20 396	69.1	23.6
–	not found	75	-	0.0	0.0
	Sum	135 689	86 577	63.8	100.0
	UK Parliamentary Debates Corpus (ParlVote)				
–	Alliance	13	-	-	0.0
0	Conservative	13 530	7915	58.5	41.4
1	Dup	578	269	46.5	1.4
–	Green	116	-	-	0.0
2	Independent	229	127	55.5	0.1
–	Independent-conservative	5	-	-	0.0
–	Independent-ulster-unionist	9	-	-	0.0
3	Labour	13 195	7557	57.3	39.5
4	Labourco-operative	784	426	54.3	2.2
5	Liberal-democrat	2864	1773	61.9	9.3
6	Plaid-cymru	338	167	49.4	0.9
–	Respect	6	-	-	0.0
7	Scottish-national-party	1436	756	52.6	4.0
8	Social-democratic-and-labour-party	189	128	67.7	0.7
–	Ukip	14	-	-	0.0
–	Uup	155	-	-	0.0
	Sum	33 461	19 118	57.1	99.5

3.2   German Parliamentary Speech Corpus (GPSC)

We use the data set created by Richter et al. [11] capturing the German parliament's speeches between 1949 and present. To establish a fair comparison, we extracted speeches from 2000 and later. The speeches contain some noise. First, the texts contained meeting minutes' page numbers. We removed both obtain a better textual representation of the actual speech. We obtained a total of 135 689 speeches. We applied the pre-processing pipeline and retained speeches with at least 150 words of parties with at least 100 such speeches. The dataset has 86 577 speeches of eight parties.

3.3   UK Parliamentary Debates Corpus (ParlVote)

Abercrombie and Batista-Navarro [1] collected transcribed parliament records[2] between 7 May 1997 and 5 November 2019. The dataset[3] contains 34 010 speeches with information about debate ID, motion, title, and speakers' metadata (ID, name, political party, and votes). There are two versions: *ParlVote_full* (34 010 speeches) and *ParlVote_concat* (33 461 speeches of 1995 debates). We work with the latter—pre-processed subset of data used for down-streaming task (sentiment analysis), and consider only speeches, and party. Applying same strategy as with NPSC and GPSC, the final dataset has 19 118 speeches of nine parties.

Table 2. Summary of the split datasets for running experiments.

Dataset	Total items	Train	Validate	Test	# Parties
NPSC	3091	2318	193	580	7
GPSC	86 577	64 932	5411	16 234	8
ParlVote	19 118	14 338	1195	3585	9

4   Methods

We consider three types of classifiers. First, we discuss the baselines. Second, we introduce a selection of language models. Finally, we explore how these language models can be fine-tuned for the task at hand.

4.1   Baselines

We need baselines to assess the added value of LMs. We consider two baselines.

Majority Class represents a trivial choice. The baseline predicts the same label for all instances in the test set corresponding to the majority class in

---

[2] https://www.theyworkforyou.com/.

[3] https://data.mendeley.com/datasets/czjfwgs9tm/2.

the training corpus. Consequently, the Majority Class baseline helps us to see whether the other approaches learn non-trivial pattern.

Naïve Bayes (NB) represents a more competitive baseline for comparison with the LMs. Naïve Bayes has been found to be a viable baseline for 'traditional' natural language processing tasks [17]. We use a TF-IDF representation and build a classifier with the auto generated vocabulary from `sklearn`[4].

4.2   Language Models

For Neural Nets (NN), we fine-tune classification models[5] for the task. We selected models that are either multi-lingual or based on texts of the needed language (English, German, Norwegian). We fine-tune the models for the classification task with the training data. Models are trained on NVIDIA A100 40 GB and 80 GB GPU. For finding hyperparameters for Transformer models, we explore with number of epoch max to 15, learning rates $\in$ {1e-5, 1e-4, 1e-3, 2e-5, 2e-4, 3e-5, 4e-5, 4e-4, 5e-5}, batch size $\in$ {32, 64} and max sequence length 512 for BERT and GPT-2 language model. Best hyperparamaters are chosen based on the accuracy on validation set. Table 3 shows selected training hyperparameters for fine-tuning models.

BERT. Introduced by Devlin et al. [5], BERT has been successfully achieving state of the art results for many NLP tasks such as question answering, text generation, and sentence classification. BERT is the contextual embeddings transformer-based model which is pre-trained on a huge corpus using two tasks: masked language model and next sentence prediction. The authors use Word-Piece tokenization and a 30 000 token vocabulary. There are two standard configurations: $BERT_{BASE}$ and $BERT_{LARGE}$. In the scope of this work, we use variations of BERT for different languages.

- *bert-base-multilingual-cased* [5][6]—a multilingual Transformer model for 104 languages. We use this language model for all three languages in our experiments.
- *nb-bert-base* [7][7]—A Norwegian transformer language model owned by the National Library of Norway.
- *bert-base-german-cased*[8]—a German BERT model developed by deepset.ai team in 2019.

---

[4] We use the `MultinomialNB` classifier, remove stopwords (Norwegian/German/English), use n-grams from 1 to 4. We determine the best hyperparameter configuration with grid search over maximum number of features {$30k, 50k, 100k$} and the learning rate $\alpha \in$ {$0.01, 0.1, 0.5, 1.0$}. For the NPSC data, we use 30 000 features and $\alpha = 0.01$. For the GPSC data, we use 100 000 features and $\alpha = 0.1$. For the ParlVote data, we use 100 000 features and $\alpha = 0.01$.
[5] https://huggingface.co.
[6] https://github.com/google-research/bert.
[7] https://github.com/NBAiLab/notram.
[8] https://huggingface.co/bert-base-german-cased.

Table 3. Fine-tuning hyperparameters for transformer models using validation set. #EP refers to number of trained epochs. #BS refers to batch size and LR denotes learning rate.

Dataset	Model name	#EP	#BS	LR
NPSC	TM-mbert	11	64	5×10^{-5}
	TM-nb-bert-base	13	64	5×10^{-5}
	TM-norwai-gpt2	11	32	1×10^{-4}
	TM-nb-bert-base-weighted	15	32	4×10^{-5}
	TM-nb-bert-custom-lm	10	32	5×10^{-5}
	TM-nb-bert-weighted-custom-lm	8	32	4×10^{-5}
GPSC	TM-mbert	5	64	3×10^{-5}
	TM-bert-base-german-cased	5	64	3×10^{-5}
	TM-german-gpt2	1	32	2×10^{-4}
	TM-bert-base-german-cased-weighted	9	32	4×10^{-5}
	TM-bert-base-german-cased-custom-lm	4	32	4×10^{-5}
	TM-bert-base-german-cased-weighted-custom-lm	13	64	5×10^{-5}
ParlVote	TM-mbert	3	32	4×10^{-5}
	TM-bert-base-cased	4	64	3×10^{-5}
	TM-english-gpt2	8	32	2×10^{-4}
	TM-mbert-weighted	13	64	2×10^{-5}
	TM-mbert-custom-lm	3	32	3×10^{-5}
	TM-mbert-weighted-custom-lm	12	32	4×10^{-5}

- *bert-base-cased* [5][9]—A pretrained model on English language using a masked language modeling (MLM) objective.

GPT-2. is a large language model by Radford et al. [9] which is built on transformer decoder block. GPT-2 is trained on WebText dataset in the self-supervised way. The model has achieved state of the art results on many NLP task and is the key importance to the success of zero-shot task transfer. GPT-2 uses Byte-Level BPE tokenizer with extended vocabulary size to 50 257. There are various sizes for GPT-2 whereas the largest has 1542M parameters and 117M parameters for the smallest.

- *norwai-gpt2*[10] - A Norwegian pretrained transformer model which is in the process of training by NorwAI.
- *german-gpt2*[11] – a language model for German owned by Bayerische Staatsbibliothek (Bavarian State Library).

---

[9] https://huggingface.co/bert-base-cased.
[10] https://www.ntnu.edu/norwai/new-language-models-in-norwai.
[11] https://huggingface.co/dbmdz/german-gpt2.

– *english-gpt-2*[12] [9] – a transformer model pretrained on a very large corpus of English data in a self-supervised fashion.

4.3   Models Refinement

We apply various strategies to the original transformer fine-tuning models to improve the accuracy of the classifiers. We pick the model with the highest accuracy in each corpus for refining. First, to deal with the imbalanced data, we calculate class weight where classes with more data have less weights than their counterparts. Second, we continue training the LM on the within-task training data. Finally, we combine both methods to check the effect on the accuracy. Table 5 shows results for all refined models.

Balancing Training Data with Class Weights: All datasets that we consider are highly imbalanced thus providing a bigger challenge for us. We can expect that the models overfit for the majority classes while performing poorly for the minority classes. To tackle the issue, we estimate class weights[13] for unbalanced data and integrate that into *CrossEntropyLoss*. Similar grid search and fine-tuning strategy are done.

Training Language Model on Custom Dataset: To improve the transformer models, we follow the strategy from Sun et al. [14] by training LMs using within-task training data. We use all speech data in the training set, split them into proportion of 0.9 and 0.1 respectively for training and validating language model. To find the best training hypeparameters for language models, we do grid search for batch size $\in$ {32, 64}, block size $\in$ {128, 256}, learning rate $\in$ {1e-5, 1e-4, 2e-5, 3e-5, 4e-5, 5e-5}, and maximum 10 000 training steps on small subset of data. Then, best parameters are used to train the language model with early stopping (see Table 4). Best checkpoint is selected based on evaluation loss. Later the transformer uses this language model for fine-tuning classifier.

5   Experiments

To answer our research questions, we define *accuracy* as our evaluation criterion. In other words, we measure the accuracy of both baselines, language models, and fine-tuned language models on all three datasets. Therein, we present the texts of the test set to all classifiers and check whether their predictions match the actual party-affiliations. We fine-tune the best-performing language model either with weighting, customization, or both. We do not distinguish between members of the governing parties and opposition members. Subsequently, we can compare the accuracy for the models and languages. The data, methods, and evaluation protocols are publicly available.[14]

---

[12] https://huggingface.co/gpt2.
[13] https://scikit-learn.org/stable/modules/generated/sklearn.utils.class_weight.
  compute_class_weight.html.
[14] https://github.com/doantumy/LM_for_Party_Affiliation_Classification.

Table 4. Parameters for training language models on within-task training data including max training steps (TS), batch size (BS), block size (BLS), and learning rate (LR)

Model name	Base model	Dataset	Parameters			
			TS	BS	BLS	LR
nb-bert-base-custom-ds	nb-bert-base	NLSP	$4k$	32	128	2×10^{-5}
bert-base-german-cased-custom-lm	bert-base-german-cased	GPSC	$100k$	64	256	1×10^{-4}
mbert-custom-ds	mbert	ParlVote	$13k$	64	256	1×10^{-4}

6   Results

Table 5 outlines the classifiers' overall performance on the three data sets. The trivial *Majority Class* baseline achieves the lowest accuracy. The Naïve Bayes classifier predicts the correct party for texts in about 12 to 13 in 20 cases. We observe that the language models outperform the Naïve Bayes classifier by up to 10.35% (Norwegian), 12.95% (German), and 6.39% (UK). Thus, we can conclude that overall language models predict the party affiliation of political texts more accurately than the 'traditional' Naïve Bayes classifier. Still, class-specific performance varies among approaches. For all data sets we observe some classes that challenge all approaches. For instance, the class 6 in the German data set sees the lowest performance by all methods. Note, the *Majority Class* baseline performs perfectly for one class while failing all others.

Figure 1a shows the distribution of the difference in class-specific accuracy between the language models and the Naïve Bayes baseline. The horizontal line at 0 highlights the point where baseline and language model perform identically. Much of the distribution is to the right of the line indicating that the language models perform better than the baseline in most cases. In particular, the German data reveals a large proportion of cases beyond 50%.

The difference in performance for *TM-mbert* shows the performance across language barriers. The accuracy varies marginally between 67.64% (German) and 71.58% (English). The superior performance in English could be the results of a majority of the training corpus being written in English.

Figure 1 shows the class-specific difference in performance of the best performing language model (*TM-nb-bert-weighted-custom-lm*) and the Naïve Bayes baseline for the Norwegian data set (other figures omitted due to space limitations). The cells show the difference in cases between the LM and the baseline. The rows correspond to predicted classes, whereas the columns represent the actual values. The cells are color-coded for better visualization. The language model performs slightly worse on the majority class with label 2. Conversely, the language model assigns labels more accurately for all other classes.

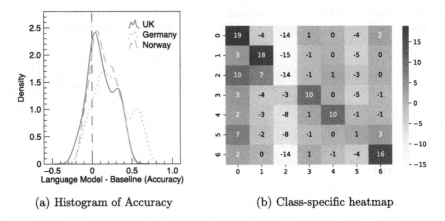

(a) Histogram of Accuracy   (b) Class-specific heatmap

Fig. 1. The left shows the performance differences between the language models and the Naïve Bayes baseline. The horizontal line at 0 highlights the point where baseline and language model perform identically. The right-hand side shows a heatmap of class-specific differences in accuracy between *TM-nb-bert-weighted-custom-lm* and the *Naïve Bayes* classifier.

Table 5. Results overview. For each data set and method, we show the overall accuracy, the best class-specific performance, as well as the worst class-specific performance. There are three groups of models per data set. First group shows the baselines. Second group represents classifiers with different language models. Third group denotes the refinement classifiers.

Dataset	Method	Accuracy	Best class	Label	Worst class	Label
NPSC	Majority Class (baseline)	31.55	100.00	(2)	0.00	(not 2)
	NB (baseline)	62.93	86.89	(2)	13.51	(6)
	TM-mbert	68.79	84.70	(2)	21.43	(4)
	TM-nb-bert-base	68.97	78.99	(1)	37.84	(6)
	TM-norwai-gpt2	66.03	75.41	(2)	42.86	(4)
	TM-nb-bert-base-weighted	69.14	76.47	(1)	51.35	(6)
	TM-nb-bert-custom-lm	72.24	86.89	(2)	43.24	(6)
	TM-nb-bert-weighted-custom-lm	**73.28**	87.40	(1)	50.00	(4)
GPSC	Majority Class (baseline)	30.64	100.00	(2)	0.00	(not 2)
	NB (baseline)	61.70	88.10	(2)	1.00	(6)
	TM-mbert	67.64	81.98	(2)	51.26	(6)
	TM-bert-base-german-cased	72.26	85.08	(2)	49.75	(6)
	TM-german-gpt2	70.64	86.53	(2)	54.27	(6)
	TM-bert-base-german-cased-weighted	71.35	81.05	(0)	53.77	(6)
	TM-bert-based-german-cased-custom-lm	73.60	82.59	(2)	34.67	(6)
	TM-bert-based-german-cased-weighted-custom-lm	**74.65**	82.13	(0)	57.29	(6)
ParlVote	Majority Class (baseline)	41.39	100.00	(0)	0.00	(not 0)
	NB (baseline)	66.72	81.81	(0)	0.00	(4)
	TM-mbert	71.58	81.93	(3)	0.00	(2)
	TM-bert-base-cased	71.24	83.96	(0)	0.00	(4, 8)
	TM-english-gpt2	66.47	81.47	(0)	6.25	(4)
	TM-mbert-weighted	56.80	60.20	(3)	17.50	(4)
	TM-mbert-custom-lm	**73.11**	87.94	(0)	3.75	(4)
	TM-mbert-weighted-custom-lm	73.02	84.23	(0)	12.50	(4, 8)

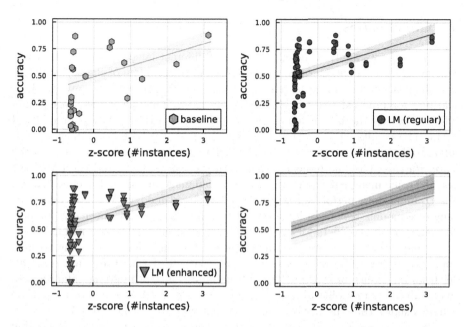

Fig. 2. Effect of the number of training instances and type of model on classification accuracy. For each of the model types (baseline, regular and enhanced language model), a figure shows the relation between the number of training instances (z-score) and the accuracy.

The performances seem consistent for all three languages. In all three data sets, a language model achieves the best performance with accuracy between 73.11 to 74.65%. The Naïve Bayes baseline achieves less accurate score in the range 61.70 to 66.72%. The *mbert* model represents a special case due to its multi-lingual character. We applied it to all three scenarios. We observed the best performance for the English data (71.58%) followed by the Norwegian (68.79%) and the German (67.64%) data. Language-specific models achieved higher accuracy for Norwegian (*TM-nb-bert-weighted-custom-lm* with 73.28%) and German (*TM-bert-base-german-case-weighted-custom-lm* with 74.65%).

Figure 2 shows the relation between the number of training instances and the model type with the classification accuracy. We computed the z-score of the number of training examples such that we can compare texts across lingual barriers. The plots show the data points, a linear regression, and the compatibility region. The subplot on the bottom right compares the three types of models. We observe that all types of models perform better for classes with more training instances. This confirms findings for Swedish by Dahllöf [4]. The enhance language models, which were tuned with the training samples, perform best. The regular language models still perform better than the baseline. The classes with few training examples show a high level of variance independent of the model type. Consequently, we can deduce that having more training examples represents a valuable asset for political text classification.

7 Conclusions

In conclusion, we analyze the effectiveness of different language models for three languages (Norwegian, German, and English) in the problem of classifying political affiliation of authors. Research on the use of artificial intelligence and machine learning for political texts is still relatively fresh. This work encourages more efforts towards the use of language models and related resources for political texts. The results show us that language models give better accuracy in classifying all three languages (RQ_1). The difference in accuracy compared to the *majority class* baseline indicates that both the Naïve Bayes and the LMs have learned some meaningful patterns. Further, language models with refinement on the training data performed better than unrefined models. We have seen that language models benefit of large sets of training examples. Conversely, the performance of all classifiers for classes with few training instances remained poor. This suggests that having a domain-specific language model is going to help improve the results of the task. The fact that all of the three data sets suffer from imbalance problem has raised the importance of building balanced and decent datasets for political research. The variance of *TM-mbert* across language barriers shows that the performance does not vary drastically (RQ_2).

As next steps, we will annotate a large corpus of political texts. Repeating the experiments with these additional resources ought to reveal whether more and better training data or more sophisticated, deep models promise better results. Besides, we plan to extend the experiment to further languages to verify that given a language model, the performance for party affiliation classification benefits. We will pay particular attention to languages which are under-resources such as Swedish, Danish, Finnish, Dutch, or Hungarian. Furthermore, we will carefully investigate errors made by the classifiers to better understand their deficiencies. With sufficient training data, we plan to create a LM specific to political speech. The data used for our experiments are publicly available. We hope that other researchers will join our efforts and replicate our experiment.

Acknowledgements. This work is done as part of the Trondheim Analytica project and funded under Digital Transformation program at Norwegian University of Science and Technology (NTNU), 7034 Trondheim, Norway.

References

1. Abercrombie, G., Batista-Navarro, R.: ParlVote: a Corpus for sentiment analysis of political debates. In: Proceedings of the 12th Language Resources and Evaluation Conference. pp. 5073–5078. European Language Resources Association (2020). https://aclanthology.org/2020.lrec-1.624
2. Baly, R., Da San Martino, G., Glass, J., Nakov, P.: We can detect your bias: predicting the political ideology of news articles. In: Proceedings of the 2020 Conference on Empirical Methods in Natural Language Processing (EMNLP), pp. 4982–4991 (2020). https://doi.org/10.18653/v1/2020.emnlp-main.404
3. Biessmann, F., Lehmann, P., Kirsch, D., Schelter, S.: Predicting political party affiliation from text. PolText **14**, 14 (2016)

4. Dahllöf, M.: Automatic prediction of gender, political affiliation, and age in Swedish politicians from the wording of their speeches—a comparative study of classifiability. Liter. Linguist. Comput. **27**(2), 139–153 (2012). https://doi.org/10.1093/llc/fqs010

5. Devlin, J., Chang, M.W., Lee, K., Toutanova, K.: BERT: pre-training of deep bidirectional transformers for language understanding. arXiv preprint arXiv:1810.04805 (2018). https://doi.org/10.18653/v1/N19-1423

6. Høyland, B., Godbout, J.F., Lapponi, E., Velldal, E.: Predicting party affiliations from European parliament debates. In: Proceedings of the ACL 2014 Workshop on Language Technologies and Computational Social Science, pp. 56–60 (2014)

7. Kummervold, P.E., De la Rosa, J., Wetjen, F., Brygfjeld, S.A.: Operationalizing a national digital library: the case for a Norwegian transformer model. In: Proceedings of the 23rd Nordic Conference on Computational Linguistics (NoDaLiDa), pp. 20–29 (2021). https://aclanthology.org/2021.nodalida-main.3

8. Luong, M.T., Kayser, M., Manning, C.D.: Deep neural language models for machine translation. In: Proceedings of the 19th Conference on Computational Natural Language Learning, pp. 305–309 (2015). https://doi.org/10.18653/v1/K15-1031

9. Radford, A., et al.: Language models are unsupervised multitask learners. OpenAI blog **1**(8), 9 (2019)

10. Rao, A., Spasojevic, N.: Actionable and political text classification using word embeddings and LSTM. arXiv preprint arXiv:1607.02501 (2016)

11. Richter, F., et al.: Open Discourse (2020). https://doi.org/10.7910/DVN/FIKIBO

12. Serban, I., Sordoni, A., Bengio, Y., Courville, A., Pineau, J.: Building end-to-end dialogue systems using generative hierarchical neural network models. In: Proceedings of the AAAI Conference on Artificial Intelligence, vol. 30 (2016)

13. Solberg, P.E., Ortiz, P.: The Norwegian parliamentary speech corpus. arXiv preprint arXiv:2201.10881 (2022)

14. Sun, C., Qiu, X., Xu, Y., Huang, X.: How to fine-tune BERT for text classification? In: Sun, M., Huang, X., Ji, H., Liu, Z., Liu, Y. (eds.) CCL 2019. LNCS (LNAI), vol. 11856, pp. 194–206. Springer, Cham (2019). https://doi.org/10.1007/978-3-030-32381-3_16

15. Wang, W., Shen, S., Li, G., Jin, Z.: Towards full-line code completion with neural language models. arXiv preprint arXiv:2009.08603 (2020)

16. Wong, F.M.F., Tan, C.W., Sen, S., Chiang, M.: Quantifying political leaning from tweets, retweets, and retweeters. IEEE Trans. Knowl. Data Eng. **28**(8), 2158–2172 (2016)

17. Yu, B., Kaufmann, S., Diermeier, D.: Classifying party affiliation from political speech. J. Inf. Technol. Polit. **5**, 33–48 (2008). https://doi.org/10.1080/19331680802149608

Investigating Topic-Agnostic Features for Authorship Tasks in Spanish Political Speeches

Silvia Corbara[1(✉)], Berta Chulvi Ferriols[2,3], Paolo Rosso[2],
and Alejandro Moreo[4]

[1] Scuola Normale Superiore, Pisa, Italy
`silvia.corbara@sns.it`
[2] Universitat Politècnica de València, Valencia, Spain
`berta.chulvi@upv.es, prosso@dsic.upv.es`
[3] Universitat de València, Valencia, Spain
[4] CNR, Istituto di Scienza e Tecnologie dell'Informazione, Pisa, Italy
`alejandro.moreo@isti.cnr.it`

Abstract. Authorship Identification is the branch of authorship analysis concerned with uncovering the author of a written document. Methods devised for Authorship Identification typically employ *stylometry* (the analysis of unconscious traits that authors exhibit while writing), and are expected not to make inferences grounded on the *topics* the authors usually write about (as reflected in their past production). In this paper, we present a series of experiments evaluating the use of feature sets based on rhythmic and psycholinguistic patterns for Authorship Verification and Attribution in Spanish political language, via different approaches of text distortion used to actively mask the underlying topic. We feed these feature sets to a SVM learner, and show that they lead to results that are comparable to those obtained by the BETO transformer when the latter is trained on the original text, i.e., when potentially learning from topical information.

Keywords: Authorship identification · Text distortion · Political speech

1 Introduction

In the authorship analysis field, Authorship Identification (AId) investigates the true identity of the author of a written document, and it is of special interest in cases when the author is unknown or debated. Two of the main sub-tasks of AId are Authorship Attribution (AA) and Authorship Verification (AV): in the former, given a document d and a set of candidate authors $\{A_1, \ldots, A_m\}$, the goal is to identify the real author of d among the set of candidates; instead, AV can be defined as a binary problem, in which the goal is to infer whether A (the only candidate) is the real author of d or not. While tackling these classification

P. Rosso et al. (Eds.): NLDB 2022, LNCS 13286, pp. 394–402, 2022.
https://doi.org/10.1007/978-3-031-08473-7_36

problems, researchers devise methods able to distinguish among the different styles of the authors of interest, often relying on supervised machine learning.

In this article, we evaluate the employment of rhythmic- and psycholinguistic-based features for AV and AA in Spanish. Concretely, we propose to generate new distorted versions of the original text extracting (i) the syllabic stress (i.e., strings of *stressed* and *unstressed* syllables), and (ii) the psycholinguistic categories of the words (as given by the LIWC dictionary – see Sect. 3.2). The resulting representations are topic-agnostic strings from which we extract n-grams features. We combine the resulting features with other feature sets that are by now consolidated in the AId field. In order to assess the different effect of our proposed feature sets on the performance, we carry out experiments of *ablation* (in which we remove one feature set from the whole at a time) and experiments of *addition* (in which we test the contribution of one single feature set at a time). Our results seem to indicate that our topic-agnostic features bring to bear enough authorial information as to perform comparably with BETO, the Spanish equivalent to the popular BERT transformer, trained on the original (hence topic-aware) text. The code of the project can be found at: https://github.com/silvia-cor/Topic-agnostic_ParlaMintES.

2   Related Work

The annual PAN shared tasks [1] offer a very good overview of the most recent trends in AId. In the survey by Stamatatos [9], the features that are most commonly used in AId studies are discussed; however, it is also noted that features such as word and character n-grams might prompt methods to base their inferences on topic-related patterns rather than on stylometric patterns. In fact, an authorship classifier (even a seemingly good one) might end up unintentionally performing topic identification if domain-dependent features are used [2]. In order to avoid this, researchers might limit their scope to features that are clearly topic-agnostic, such as function words or syntactic features [6], or might actively mask topical content via a text distortion approach [10]. As already mentioned in Sect. 1, in this project we experiment with features capturing the rhythmic and the psycholinguistic traits of the texts, employing a text distortion technique based on syllabic stress or LIWC categories.

The idea of employing rhythmic, or prosodic, features in the authorship field is not a new one. Their most natural use is in studies focused on poetry; nevertheless, they have also been employed in authorship analysis of prose texts. In particular, some researches have studied the application of accent, or stress, for AId problems in English [8]. In the work by Corbara et al. [4], the documents are encoded in sequences of long and short syllables, from which the relevant features are extracted and used for AA in Latin prose texts, with promising results. We aim to investigate the applicability of this idea to Spanish, a language derived from Latin: we thus exploit the concept of *stress*, which gained relevance over the concept of *syllabic quantity* in Romance languages.

Linguistic Inquiry and Word Count (LIWC) [7] is a famous software application for text analysis: its core is composed of a word dictionary where each entry is associated with one or more categories that are related to grammar, emotions, or various cognitive processes and psychological concepts. Nowadays it is a popular tool for the study of the psychological aspect of textual documents, usually by employing the relative frequency of each LIWC category. In the AId field, it has been used for the characterization of a "psychological profile" or a "mental profile mapping" for AA and AV studies [3]. It has also been profitably used for the analysis of speeches regarding the Spanish political debate [5].

3   Experimental Setting

3.1   Dataset: ParlaMint

For our experiments, we employ the Spanish repository of the *Linguistically annotated multilingual comparable corpora of parliamentary debates ParlaMint.ana 2.1*[1] by the digital infrastructure CLARIN, which contains the annotated transcriptions of many sessions of various European Parliaments. Because of their declamatory nature, between the written text and the discourse, these speeches seem particularly suited for an investigation on rhythm and psycholinguistic traits. Apart from lowercasing the text, we did not apply any further pre-processing steps.

In order to have a balanced dataset, we select the parties with more than 500 speeches and assign them to the Left or Right wing: PSOE, PSC-PSOE and UP to the former, and PP, PP-Foro and Vox to the latter. We then select for each wing the 5 authors with most speeches in the dataset. We see that the author in this subset with the lowest number of samples (Calvo Poyato) has 142 samples in total; while taking all her samples, we randomly select 142 samples for each other author. We finally end up with 10 authors and 1,420 samples in total. We show the total number of words for each speaker in Fig. 1.

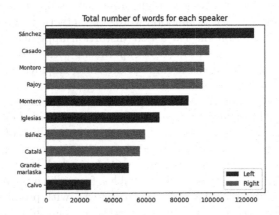

Fig. 1. Total number of words for each speaker

---

[1] https://www.clarin.si/repository/xmlui/handle/11356/1431.

3.2   Feature Extraction: BaseFeatures and Text Encodings

Our focus in this research is to evaluate the employment of rhythm- and psycho-linguistic-based features for AId tasks. To this aim, we explore various combinations including other topic-agnostic feature sets commonly used in literature.

As a starting point, we employ a feature set comprised of features routinely used in the AId field, including the relative frequencies of: function words (using the list provided by the NLTK library[2]), word lengths, and sentence lengths. We set the range of word (sentence) lengths to $[1, n]$, where n is the longest word (sentence) appearing at least 5 times in the training set. We call this feature set BASEFEATURES. We also employ a text distortion approach, where we replace each word in the document with the respective Part-of-Speech tag (we exploit the POS annotation already available in the ParlaMint dataset); from the encoded text, we then extract the word n-grams in the range $[1, 3]$ and compute the TfIdf weights, which we use as features. We call this feature set POS.

We follow a similar approach to extract the rhythm of the discourse, i.e., we convert the document into a sequence of stressed and unstressed syllables, using the output of the RANTANPLAN library;[3] from this encoding, we extract the character n-grams in the range $[1, 7]$ and compute the TfIdf weights as features. We call this feature set STRESS.

Similarly, in order to encode the psycholinguistic dimension of the document, we employ the LIWC dictionary.[4] We define three macro-categories from a subset of the LIWC category tags, representing (i) grammatical information, (ii) cognitive processes or actions, and (iii) feelings and emotions.[5] For each macro-category, we perform a separate text distortion by replacing each word with the corresponding LIWC category tag. Formally, LIWC can be seen as a map $m : w \rightarrow C$, where w is a word token and $C \subset \mathcal{C}$ is a subset of psycholinguistic categories $\mathcal{C}$. Given a macro-category $M \subset \mathcal{C}$, we replace each word w in a document by the categories $m(w) \cap M$. If $|m(w) \cap M| > 1$, then a new token is created which consists of a concatenation of the category names (following a consistent ordering). If $m(w) \cap M = \emptyset$, then w is replaced with the 'w' symbol. (Note that some entries in LIWC have the suffix truncated and replaced with an asterisk '*', e.g., *president**; the asterisk is treated as a wildcard in the mapping function, and in case more than one matches are possible, the one with the

---

[2] https://www.nltk.org/.

[3] https://github.com/linhd-postdata/rantanplan.

[4] We employ the Spanish version of the dictionary, which is based on LIWC2007.

[5] We use following categories for each macro-categoy: (i) Yo, Nosotro, TuUtd, ElElla, VosUtds, Ellos, Pasado, Present, Futuro, Subjuntiv, Negacio, Cuantif, Numeros, verbYo, verbTu, verbNos, verbVos, verbosEL, ver-bELLOS, formal, informal; (ii) MecCog, Insight, Causa, Discrep, Tentat, Certeza, Inhib, Incl, Excl, Percept, Ver, Oir, Sentir, NoFluen, Relleno, Ingerir, Relativ, Movim; (iii) Maldec, Afect, EmoPos, EmoNeg, Ansiedad, Enfado, Triste, Asentir, Placer. We avoid employing categories that would repeat information already captured by the POS tags, or topic-related categories such as Dinero or Familia.

longest common prefix is returned.) We show an example of the encodings we are using in Table 1. From a single encoding, we extract the word n-grams in the range $[1, 3]$ and compute the TfIdf weights, which we use as features. We call this feature sets LIWC_GRAM, LIWC_COG, and LIWC_FEELS, respectively.

3.3   Experimental Protocol

We perform experiments in two settings: Authorship Verification (AV) for each author (where each test sample is labelled as belonging to that class/author, or not) and Authorship Attribution (AA) (where each sample is labelled as belonging to one of the 10 classes/authors). We assess the usefulness of the different feature sets by evaluating the performance of a classifier trained using them. In particular, we use 90% of the whole dataset to train the classifier, and evaluate its performance on the remaining 10% test set (the split is done randomly in a stratified way). As evaluation measure, for the AV task we use the well-known F_1 function, and for the AA task we use the *macro-averaged* F_1 (hereafter: F_1^M) and *micro-averaged* F_1 (hereafter: F_1^μ) variants.

Table 1. Example of the encodings employed in the project. (Note there is not a one-to-one correspondence between syllables and stresses since the RANTANPLAN library caters for linguistic phenomenons across word boundaries, such as synalepha.)

Original text:	Gracias	.	No	hay	que	restituir lo	que	no	ha		existido .
POS:	NOUN	PUNCT	ADV	AUX	SCONJ	VERB	PRON	PRON	ADV	AUX	VERB PUNCT
LIWC_GRAM:	w		NEGACIO PRESENT w		w	ELELLA w		NEGACIO PRESENTVERBOSEL w			
LIWC_COG:	w		w	w	MECCOG w		w	MECCOG w		w	w
LIWC_FEELS:	AFECTEMOPOS		w	w	w	w	w	w	w	w	w
STRESS:	+ - + - - + - - + - + -										
English translation:	Thank you. There is no need to return what has not existed.										

We employ a Support Vector Machine (SVM) as learner[6], using the implementation of the SVC module from the `scikit-learn` package.[7] We perform the optimisation of various hyper-parameters: the parameter C, which sets the trade-off between the training error and the margin (we explore the range of values $[0.001, 0.01, 0.1, 1, 10, 100, 1000]$), the kernel function (we explore the following possibilities: *linear, poly, rbf, sigmoid*), and whether the classes weights should be balanced or not. The optimization is computed in a grid-search fashion, via 5-fold cross-validation on the training set. The selected model is then retrained on the whole training set and used for predictions on the test set.

---

[6] We also performed preliminary experiments with other learners: SVM showed a remarkably better performance than Random Forest, while no significant differences were noticed between SVM and Logistic Regression.

[7] https://scikit-learn.org/stable/modules/generated/sklearn.svm.SVC.html.

Finally, we also compare the results obtained with the aforementioned features with the results obtained by a method trained on the original text (hence, potentially mining topic-related patterns). To this aim, we employ the pre-trained transformer named 'BETO-cased', from the Huggingface library,[8] with the learning rate set to 10^{-6} and the other hyper-parameters set as default. We fine-tune the model for 50 epochs on the training set.

4   Results

We show the results of the AV experiments for each author in Table 2. In the first batch of results, we show the performance of the features sets in the experiments "by addition", using the BASEFEATURES set as a baseline; in the second batch of results, we report the experiments "by ablation", subtracting each feature set to the combination of all the feature sets we are exploring (named ALL). These results are obtained using a SVM learner. Finally, we report the results obtained using the BETO transformer. Even though BETO obtains better results in 6 out of 10 cases, the fact that our proposed model obtains a comparable performance, without the aid of topic-related information, is highly promising. It is also interesting that we observe markedly different results depending on the author considered, both regarding the highest F_1 value and, more importantly, which feature combinations achieve the highest performance. In fact, some feature sets seem to work very well for certain authors, while being detrimental for others (e.g., the LIWC_FEELS set, while being counterproductive in the case of Rajoy and Montero, greatly helps the evaluation in the case of Sánchez and Montoro). We hypothesize the demographic or political group each single author belongs to might be responsible for some of the differences in the results we have observed; we leave these considerations for future work. Nevertheless, the combination of many feature sets seems to usually lead to better performance.

We show the results of the AA experiments in Table 3. We proceed in the same way as for the report of the AV experiments (Table 2). In these experiments, the ALL features combination employing the SVM learner obtained the best results, even outperforming BETO. Moreover, every feature set causes a drop in the performance if taken out from the ALL combination. However, in the experiments by addition, the individual feature set appears to have little impact, especially in the case of STRESS and LIWC_FEELS.

We perform a non-parametric McNemar's paired test of statistical significance between the results obtained using our best SVM configuration and the results obtained using BETO, for each of the authorship tasks. The test is carried out by converting the predictions of the two methods into binary values, where 1 stands for a correct prediction and 0 stands for a wrong prediction. The test indicates the differences in performance are not statistically significant at a confidence level of 95% in most cases (the only exception being the AV experiment for Calvo). This brings further evidence that the (topic-agnostic) features

---

[8] https://huggingface.co/dccuchile/bert-base-spanish-wwm-cased. This model obtained better results than the 'uncased' version in preliminary experiments.

we propose in this work yield comparable results to a transformer trained on the original (topic-aware) text.

5   Government vs Opposition

In a final experiment, we test if the AV classification performance behaves differently depending on whether the speaker's speeches come from a period when their political party was part of the government, or instead was part as the opposition. To do this, we employ the speeches by the current Spanish Prime Minister, Pedro Sánchez Pérez-Castejón, who in the present dataset has 70 speeches dating back when he was in the opposition and 72 speeches since he has been in the government, hence making a rather balanced comparison. We thus perform the same AV experiment for the author as in Table 2, but only considering his speeches while he was either in the government or in the opposition as positive samples. The results are reported in Table 4.

Understandably, given the smaller number of positive samples, the general performance declines, except for the feature set + POS and for the BETO classifier, both when considering only the opposition speeches. More generally, it seems to be slightly easier to classify the author when they are in the opposition, probably because the role allows and demands a more personal and sharp language. Nevertheless, the generally small differences might denote a communication that remains largely stable regardless of the political position. In future work, we plan to better understand the possible relations between the differences in rhetorical style and the variance in performance we have observed in the + POS and BETO methods.

Table 2. Results for AV (divided in left-wing and right-wing speakers). The best result for the SVM methods is in bold, while the best result in general is in italic; the same format applies for the other tables as well.

Method	Sánchez	Iglesias	Montero	GMarlaska	Calvo	Method	Rajoy	Catalá	Báñez	Casado	Montoro
BaseFeatures	0.444	0.606	0.526	0.556	0.478	BaseFeatures	0.545	0.571	0.846	0.529	0.357
+ POS	0.571	**0.667**	0.667	**0.783**	0.429	+ POS	0.640	0.706	0.889	0.643	0.514
+ STRESS	0.261	0.538	0.571	0.581	**0.488**	+ STRESS	0.533	0.483	0.774	0.500	0.387
+ LIWC_GRAM	0.133	0.453	0.452	0.474	0.450	+ LIWC_GRAM	0.636	0.296	0.786	0.455	0.480
+ LIWC_COG	0.250	0.296	0.500	0.533	0.439	+ LIWC_COG	0.526	0.273	0.786	0.421	0.381
+ LIWC_FEELS	0.467	0.500	0.444	0.462	0.311	+ LIWC_FEELS	0.519	0.500	0.720	0.414	0.516
ALL	*0.692*	0.571	0.625	0.636	0.444	ALL	0.714	0.647	0.923	**0.720**	0.595
- BaseFeatures	0.636	0.538	0.417	0.545	0.429	- BaseFeatures	0.714	0.621	0.846	0.720	0.667
- POS	0.667	0.457	0.500	0.643	0.474	- POS	0.581	0.629	0.720	0.667	0.552
- STRESS	0.636	0.606	0.667	0.600	0.485	- STRESS	0.667	0.688	*0.963*	0.692	*0.647*
- LIWC_GRAM	0.640	0.529	0.667	0.600	0.387	- LIWC_GRAM	0.583	**0.727**	0.880	0.667	0.556
- LIWC_COG	0.560	0.500	0.625	0.571	0.452	- LIWC_COG	0.741	0.667	0.833	0.600	0.579
- LIWC_FEELS	0.316	0.645	**0.690**	0.645	0.483	- LIWC_FEELS	*0.828*	0.647	0.923	0.667	0.564
BETO_base_cased	0.286	*0.741*	*0.741*	*0.800*	*0.667*	BETO_base_cased	0.800	*0.889*	0.839	*0.889*	0.615

Table 3. Results for AA

Method	F_1^M	F_1^μ
BaseFeatures	0.584	0.585
+ POS	0.653	0.655
+ STRESS	0.521	0.528
+ LIWC_GRAM	0.558	0.563
+ LIWC_COG	0.610	0.620
+ LIWC_FEELS	0.500	0.500
ALL	*0.718*	*0.718*
- BaseFeatures	0.648	0.648
- POS	0.625	0.634
- STRESS	0.676	0.676
- LIWC_GRAM	0.668	0.669
- LIWC_COG	0.665	0.662
- LIWC_FEELS	0.685	0.683
BETO_base_cased	0.683	0.697

Table 4. Results for Government vs Opposition

Method	Government	Opposition
BaseFeatures	0.308	0.286
+ POS	0.250	**0.615**
+ STRESS	0.308	0.316
+ LIWC_GRAM	0.381	0.200
+ LIWC_COG	0.296	0.333
+ LIWC_FEELS	0.188	0.296
ALL	0.250	0.400
- BaseFeatures	0.000	0.222
- POS	0.250	0.154
- STRESS	0.250	0.182
- LIWC_GRAM	0.250	0.333
- LIWC_COG	*0.444*	0.400
- LIWC_FEELS	0.250	0.250
BETO_base_cased	0.222	*0.727*

6 Conclusion and Future Work

In this research, we investigate the extent to which rhythmic and psycholinguistic features sets, obtained via a text distortion approach, are useful for AId in Spanish language, tackling both AV and AA tasks using a dataset of political speeches. We show that such features perform comparably to a BETO transformer fine-tuned with the non-distorted texts (hence potentially learning from topic-related information). Moreover, we see that the combinations of different topic-agnostic feature sets are in general fruitful, although the effect of the single feature set changes considerably depending on the specific author.

In future work, we are interested in analysing the different performances obtained in our experiments, and in further studying a possible explanation for the variance in the results. Moreover, we are aware of the present limitations of the LIWC-based representation, since we currently do not attempt to disambiguate the polysemous words. Refining this aspect, while also developing an effective feature selection strategy, might improve the overall classification results.

Acknowledgment. The work by Silvia Corbara has been carried out during her visit at the Universitat Politècnica de València and has been supported by the AI4MEDIA project, funded by the European Commission (Grant 951911) under the H2020 Programme ICT-48-2020.

The research work by Paolo Rosso was partially funded by the Generalitat Valenciana under DeepPattern (PROMETEO/2019/121).

References

1. Bevendorff, J., et al.: Overview of PAN 2021: authorship verification, profiling hate speech spreaders on twitter, and style change detection. In: Candan, K.S., et al. (eds.) Experimental IR Meets Multilinguality, Multimodality, and Interaction: 12th International Conference of the CLEF Association, CLEF 2021, Virtual Event, September 21–24, 2021, Proceedings, pp. 419–431. Springer, Cham (2021). https://doi.org/10.1007/978-3-030-85251-1_26
2. Bischoff, S., et al.: The importance of suppressing domain style in authorship analysis. arXiv:2005.14714 (2020)
3. Boyd, R.L.: Mental profile mapping: a psychological single-candidate authorship attribution method. PLoS ONE **13**(7), e0200588 (2018)
4. Corbara, S., Moreo, A., Sebastiani, F.: Syllabic quantity patterns as rhythmic features for Latin authorship attribution. arXiv arXiv:2110.14203 (2021)
5. Fernández-Cabana, M., Rúas-Araújo, J., Alves-Pérez, M.T.: Psicología, lenguaje y comunicación: Análisis con la herramienta LIWC de los discursos y tweets de los candidatos a las elecciones gallegas. Anuario de Psicología **44**(2), 169–184 (2014)
6. Halvani, O., Graner, L., Regev, R.: TAVeer: an interpretable topic-agnostic authorship verification method. In: Proceedings of the 15th International Conference on Availability, Reliability and Security, ARES 2020, pp. 1–10 (2020)
7. Pennebaker, J.W., Boyd, R.L., Jordan, K., Blackburn, K.: The development and psychometric properties of LIWC2015. Technical report (2015)
8. Plecháč, P.: Relative contributions of Shakespeare and Fletcher in Henry VIII: an analysis based on most frequent words and most frequent rhythmic patterns. Digit. Sch. Humanit. **36**(2), 430–438 (2021)
9. Stamatatos, E.: A survey of modern authorship attribution methods. J. Am. Soc. Inform. Sci. Technol. **60**(3), 538–556 (2009)
10. Stamatatos, E.: Masking topic-related information to enhance authorship attribution. J. Am. Soc. Inf. Sci. **69**(3), 461–473 (2018)

Evaluating Gender Bias in Film Dialogue

Lesley Istead[1] , Andreea Pocol[2]([✉]) , and Sherman Siu[1,2]

[1] Carleton University, Ottawa, CA, Canada
LesleyIstead@cunet.carleton.ca
[2] University of Waterloo, Waterloo, CA, Canada
{apocol,ssiu}@uwaterloo.ca

Abstract. In this paper, we estimate gender bias in movies by evaluating the use of 'gendered language,' or utterances pertaining to a particular gender, such as *he, she, mother*, and *father*. We compute the bias over a corpus of over 40 thousand movie subtitle files and explore changes in bias by release year, genre, country of origin, MPAA rating, IMDb scores, and box office records. Our analysis indicates a prevalent male bias, with more than 75% of recent films exhibiting this bias. However, we observed that this bias has been decreasing over the last fifteen years. We also note that the disparity in box office sales between films with male and female bias has been closing.

Keywords: Sentiment analysis · Gender bias · Text processing

1 Introduction

The gender gap or gender bias in film has been an important topic of discussion over the last 15 years, and more recently, the entertainment industry. Gender bias has been found in every aspect of film, including salary, screen time, dialogue, award nominations, crew. Previous work, further detailed in Sect. 2, found that only 33% of leading roles are female, only 12% of films exhibit a female bias, and the majority of interactions are between male characters. Research indicates that the gap is closing, especially within certain genres, but parity has not been achieved yet and may not be for some time.

In this paper, we explore the use of gendered language in a corpus of 40 thousand movie English subtitle files. We count the number of male and female gendered words, e.g., pronouns, "actress," "actor," for each film, and compute a gender bias as a ratio of male to female words. We consider a male bias to be a ratio greater than 1.02, and any ratio within 2% of 1 to be neutral. We compare this bias against genre, IMDb (Internet Movie Database) rating, country of origin, MPAA (Motion Picture Association of America) rating, and box office sales—when available—for films produced in $[1960, 2020)$. Using gendered language to estimate gender bias has several advantages over previous approaches. First, it is a simple technique that requires no training, allowing it to scale easily to large datasets. Second, gendered language can be used to identify character gender, and it captures the gender(s) that are central to the film's plot, which

P. Rosso et al. (Eds.): NLDB 2022, LNCS 13286, pp. 403–410, 2022.
https://doi.org/10.1007/978-3-031-08473-7_37

is useful in estimating gender bias. For example, consider the 2013 Disney film *Frozen*. The plot of this film revolves around two sisters, Anna and Elsa, who are also the lead characters. In previous work, it was found that the film contains a slight male bias, as 60% of spoken lines are delivered by male characters [1]. However, our analysis indicates that 60% of the gendered words used are female, indicating that female characters are more often the subject of discussion than male characters (even if they have fewer lines), and hence, the plot likely revolves around one or more female characters. In addition to estimating gender bias using gendered language, we also explore the sentiment with which these gendered words are used.

2   Previous Work

Gender bias has been explored in film through various means. The Bechdel, or Bechdel-Wallace, test states that a film represents women fairly if [3]: there are at least two women, the women talk to each other, and the subject of conversation is not about a man. However, this test does not measure bias, and surprisingly many films with strong male biases pass this test. For example, the 1979 film *Alien* passes the Bechdel test, even though, of the nine principle characters, only two are female. A yearly report on gender bias in film production by Lauzen reports that bias is decreasing [8,9]. They note that only 42% of on-screen speaking roles are female and less than 35% of behind-the-scenes positions are held by women.

Scripts and film dialogue have also been analyzed to identify gender bias. Kagan *et al.* [6] construct a social network to identify the gender of characters, their relationships or connectivity, predict Bechdel test results, and evaluate gender representation in three-character interactions. Named entity extraction is used to discover the character names, which are then matched to spoken lines before construction the social network with using graph centrality and PageRank. The method was applied to 15 thousand subtitles from 15 thousand films and found that romance films had the highest percent of female characters in three-character interactions and war films had the lowest. Overall, the percentage of films with female characters in such interactions has increased since 1950 for most genres. Similar to Lauzon's observations, they found that lead roles were twice as likely to be male than female. However, they noted that the gap is decreasing and more films are passing the Bechdel test than in the past.

Anderson and Daniels analyzed 2000 screenplays by matching lines to the gender of the character [1]. The gender bias is then calculated as the ratio of lines spoken by male and female actors. They found that male characters, in 75% of studied films, deliver over 60% of dialogue. The remaining 25% of films had either parity, or a female bias. This bias in male-delivered dialogue persists across genre, but is stronger in action films. Schofield and Mehr explore gender-distinguishing features in film dialogue by evaluating 617 film scripts [11]. Similar to Kagan et al., they discovered a significant gender bias with only 33% of characters being women and the majority of character interactions being between men.

Similar studies have been conducted with various other media forms, concluding that bias is pervasive in media [4,5,10]. It is also observed that bias in the corpora used to trained NLP (natural language processing) systems results in bias in generated text [2].

Existing methods for evaluating gender bias in film dialogue tend to be either complex, or manual in nature. The evaluation is often limited and does not consider country of origin. Our proposed method is both simple and fast. It captures the high-level gender bias of the plot, and considers genre, country of origin, along with other metrics not previously studied.

3 Experiment Setup

Our dialogue data was provided by OpenSubtitles, a community-sourced website for film and television subtitles. From the dataset, we extracted only those subtitles belonging to films; no television shows are included in this study. We only chose subtitles provided by, at minimum, bronze-ranked members as a measure of quality, similar to [12]. Finally, we chose films released between 1960 and 2019 inclusive. We chose not to include films released during the global pandemic (2020–2022) as measures of IMDb rating and box office sales may differ from films released outside of the pandemic. Films were cross-referenced using the Open Movie Database (OMDb), which provides IMDb ratings, MPAA ratings, box office sales, release year, awards, and other metrics. In total, 41 thousand films were used in this study, 25% of which were produced in the USA.

We estimate gender bias by computing the ratio of male-to-female gendered words within each film's subtitle file. Dialogue is not wasteful; it tells the audience something about the character speaking, another character in the film, or information relevant to the plot. Gendered words in dialogue are used in other methods to predict individual character gender. Thus, we believe that gendered words in dialogue play an important role in the overall gender bias of the film as a whole. First, we constructed separate lists of male, female, and neutral gendered words used to refer to characters, similar to [5]. Each of these lists contain approximately 100 words such as pronouns, gendered familial titles and affectionate terms, noble titles, and gendered workplace labels such as "policeman" and "policewoman." Since gendered words and titles may end or start with other gendered terms, such as "policeman" and "boyfriend," we used several regular expressions to catch them. Our method proceeds as follows. For each subtitle file: remove film name, timestamps, and extraneous information; remove apostrophe endings from each word/token. Next, we count the occurrences of female, male, and neutral words. Finally, compute the film bias as $maleCount/femaleCount$. Note that our method, while simple, is also fast. Per script, the runtime is $O(kn)$, where n is the number of words in the subtitle file, and k is the total number of words used for comparison (the total number of male, female, and neutral words along with the number of unique regular expressions). In our experiments, $k < 200$, hence we achieve a runtime of $O(n)$. The space complexity of our method is $O(1)$, as for each script we keep 3 counters: the number of male words, the number of female words, and the number of neutral words. Our method runs once-per-script; we do not run separate training and classification passes. This is faster than the training time for the most common machine learning methods [7].

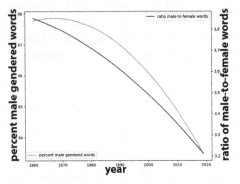

Fig. 1. The overall average percent (red) of male-gendered words by year – *male/(male + female)* – and the overall average ratio (blue) of male-to-female gendered words by year: *male/female* (Color figure online)

We compared our overall results against those from several other methods. Of the 40,391 films used in this experiment, 78.8% of films had a male bias. This is very similar to those of Anderson et al. [1], who indicated that 75.7% of films had a male bias based on a count of male-to-female cast. For 2018 and 2019, we computed the percentage of male-gendered words in dialogue to be 63%. Similarly, Lauzon reported that 58% of on-screen dialogue was spoken by male characters [9]. This is because men talk to other men, and women talking to other women are usually speaking about men [3,6]. Similar to [6,9,11], we also note in Fig. 1 that gender bias has been decreasing with time. Thus, our method of estimating gender bias is comparable to other techniques.

4   Results

We compute gender bias as a ratio of male-to-female gendered words (male/female), and group films according to year, genre, rating, IMDb score, and country. Note that films produced by multiple countries will appear in each country's statistics. We observed that bias has decreased over the last 10 years in all top-producing countries except Belgium, France, Japan, South Korea, and the UK, as seen in Fig. 3c. Looking at all films in our dataset that have a recorded box office sales value in the OMDb dataset, we computed the average box office by year for films with male and female bias. We note that while films with male bias, on average, earn more that films with female bias, the gap between the two is closing, as shown in Fig. 2.

We also looked at gender bias by genre, as shown in Fig. 3a. Over 90% of films in the western, war, action, adventure, history, and sports genres show a male bias. Adult genre films have the lowest bias at 58%. Surprisingly, 75% of romance films have a male bias. However, we attribute that to many romance films revolving around the subject of a male paramour. Another surprise was that 71% of horror films had a male bias, the second lowest in our study. This could be attributed to many horror films having a central female character/survivor. For example, *A Quiet Place*, *Alien*, and *Us*, all feature prominent, strong female characters in lead roles.

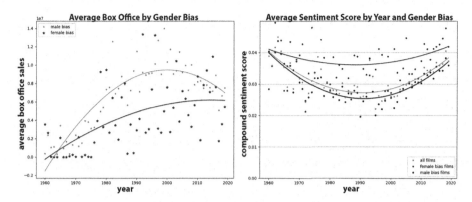

Fig. 2. Gender bias, box office, and sentiment

We further explored gender bias by MPAA rating, as shown in Fig. 3a. Agreeing with our discovery that adult genre films had the lowest male bias on average, we found that NC-17 and X rated films also had a lower male bias than films with less restrictive ratings.

Next, we break down our results by the three top-producing countries of films with English subtitles: USA, France, and the UK. Figure 4 illustrates the number of films with male and female bias by year, along with the average IMDb rating—with 10 being the highest rating representing the most liked films—by year, for films with male and female bias. Note that ratings are trending downwards, with male bias films having a higher rating on average than films with a female bias.

In addition to computing gender bias via gendered word counts, we were also curious about the context in which these gendered words are used. The sentiment of the sentences where gendered words are used tells us the perception of that person. For example, "I hate her," uses a female-gendered pronoun and expresses strong negative sentiment. Using NLTK (Natural Language Toolkit), we parsed the dialogue into sentences. For each of the films in our dataset, we computed the overall compound sentiment as a score from $[-1, 1]$. Negative scores reflect negative sentiments such as anger and fear. Positive scores reflect positive sentiments such as joy and excitement. We also computed the average sentiment of sentences containing male-gendered words, and female-gendered words. We note that in the last 20 years, male-gendered individuals were spoken of more positively than female-gendered individuals. We also computed the average sentiment surrounding male and female gendered words for each film by genre, as shown in Fig. 3b. Note that the coloured bars represent the average sentiment surrounding male-gendered words, while the overlapping grey bars represent the average sentiment around female-gendered words. The sentiment of male words in action films is more positive than the sentiment surrounding female words. In horror films, female words are surrounded with more negativity than male words. We also note that female words in adventure films are more positive than male words in adventure films. We compared the overall average sentiment of

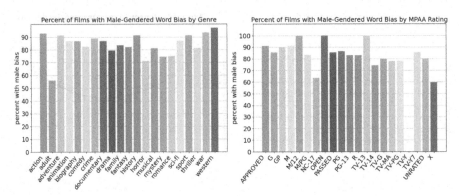

(a) Percent of films with male bias by genre (left), MPAA rating (right).

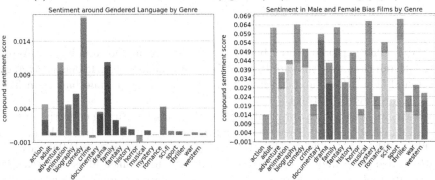

(b) Sentiment surrounding male (gray), and female (colour) language (left). Sentiment of films with male (gray) and female (colour) bias (right).

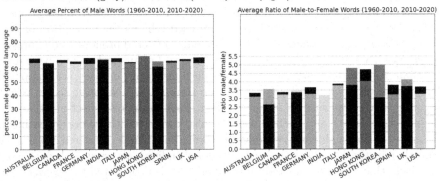

(c) Bias in various countries by years 1960-2010 (black), and 2010-2020 (colour).

Fig. 3. Bias by genre, year, and country of origin

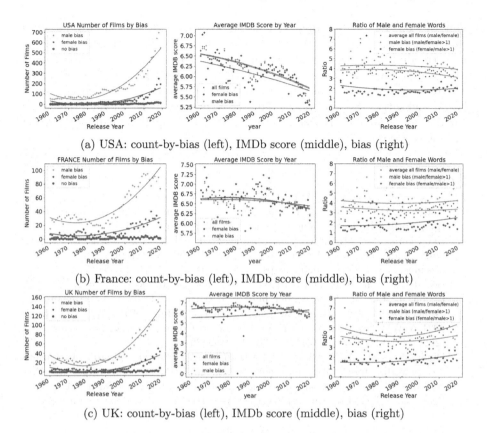

(a) USA: count-by-bias (left), IMDb score (middle), bias (right)

(b) France: count-by-bias (left), IMDb score (middle), bias (right)

(c) UK: count-by-bias (left), IMDb score (middle), bias (right)

Fig. 4. Bias in USA, France and UK from 1960 to 2019

films with a male bias to those films with a female bias. We observed that the average sentiment of films with a female bias are more positive than films with a male bias, as shown in Fig. 2. When broken down by genre, we observe that this trend of female bias films expressing more positive sentiment than negative carries across all genres, as seen in Fig. 3b. For countries producing at least 500 films between 1960 and 2019 inclusive, we observe a decrease in the percent of films with a male bias except in South Korea over the last 10 years, as shown in Fig. 3c.

5   Conclusion and Future Work

We explored gender bias in film through the use of gendered words in a corpus of 41 thousand film subtitle files. We found, as many others have, that a male bias exists in film dialogue. We further explored this bias across genre, IMDb rating, MPAA rating, box office sales, and country of origin and found that while a bias exists, the gap between male-bias and female-bias films is closing. We noted that the gap in IMDb rating, as well as box office sales, is closing for films with male and female bias. We also found that the overall sentiment in film has been trending upwards since 1990, but female characters were discussed more negatively than male characters. Furthermore, this sentiment varies by genre. The difference in sentiment for male and female characters is much greater in horror and action than in comedy, family, or romance films. We note that while our dataset is large, it is lacking many films from rapidly expanding markets such as Nigeria.

References

1. Anderson, H., Daniels, M.: The largest analysis of film dialogue by gender, Ever-Han, April 2016. https://pudding.cool/2017/03/film-dialogue/
2. Babaeianjelodar, M., Lorenz, S., Gordon, J., Matthews, J., Freitag, E.: Quantifying gender bias in different corpora, pp. 752–759. Association for Computing Machinery, New York (2020). https://doi.org/10.1145/3366424.3383559
3. Bechdel, A.: The Rule. Dykes to Watch Out For. Firebrand Books, Ithaca (1985)
4. Dacon, J., Liu, H.: Does gender matter in the news? Detecting and examining gender bias in news articles. In: Companion Proceedings of the Web Conference 2021, WWW 2021, pp. 385–392. Association for Computing Machinery, New York (2021). https://doi.org/10.1145/3442442.3452325
5. Dinan, E., Fan, A., Williams, A., Urbanek, J., Kiela, D., Weston, J.: Queens are powerful too: mitigating gender bias in dialogue generation. In: Proceedings of the 2020 Conference on Empirical Methods in Natural Language Processing (EMNLP), pp. 8173–8188. Association for Computational Linguistics, November 2020. https://doi.org/10.18653/v1/2020.emnlp-main.656, https://www.aclweb.org/anthology/2020.emnlp-main.656
6. Kagan, D., Chesney, T., Fire, M.: Using data science to understand the film industry's gender gap. Palgrave Commun. 6(1), 1–16 (2020). https://doi.org/10.1057/s41599-020-0436-1, https://ideas.repec.org/a/pal/palcom/v6y2020i1d10.1057_s41599-020-0436-1.html
7. Kumar, P.: Computational complexity of ml models (2019). https://medium.com/analytics-vidhya/time-complexity-of-ml-models-4ec39fad2770
8. Lauzen, M.M.: Boxed in 2018–2019: women on screen and behind the scenes in television (2020)
9. Lauzen, M.M.: Boxed in 2019–2020: women on screen and behind the scenes in television (2020)
10. Liu, H., Wang, W., Wang, Y., Liu, H., Liu, Z., Tang, J.: Mitigating gender bias for neural dialogue generation with adversarial learning (2020)
11. Schofield, A., Mehr, L.: Gender-distinguishing features in film dialogue. In: Gender-Distinguishing Features in Film Dialogue, pp. 32–39 (2016). https://doi.org/10.18653/v1/W16-0204
12. Vecchio, M.D., Kharlamov, A., Parry, G., Pogrebna, G.: Improving productivity in Hollywood with data science: using emotional arcs of movies to drive product and service innovation in entertainment industries. J. Oper. Res. Soc. 72(5), 1110–1137 (2021). https://doi.org/10.1080/01605682.2019.1705194

Semantics

The Case of Imperfect Negation Cues: A Two-Step Approach for Automatic Negation Scope Resolution

Daan de Jong and Ayoub Bagheri[(✉)] [iD]

Department of Methodology and Statistics, Utrecht University, Utrecht, The Netherlands
{d.dejong,a.bagheri}@uu.nl

Abstract. Negation is a complex grammatical phenomenon that has received considerable attention in the biomedical natural language processing domain. While neural network-based methods are the state-of-the-art in negation scope resolution, they often use the unrealistic assumption that negation cue information is completely accurate. Even if this assumption holds, there remains a dependency on engineered features from state-of-the-art machine learning methods. To tackle this issue, in this study, we adopted a two-step negation resolving approach to assess whether a neural network-based model, here a bidirectional long short-term memory, can be a an alternative for cue detection. Furthermore, we investigate how inaccurate cue predictions would affect the scope resolution performance. We ran various experiments on the open access Bio-Scope corpus. Experimental results suggest that word embeddings alone can detect cues reasonably well, but there still exist better alternatives for this task. As expected, scope resolution performance suffers from imperfect cue information, but remains acceptable on the Abstracts subcorpus. We also found that the scope resolution performance is most robust against inaccurate information for models with a recurrent layer only, compared to extensions with a conditional random field layer and extensions with a post-processing algorithm. We advocate for more research into the application of automated deep learning on the effect of imperfect information on scope resolution.

Keywords: Negation cue detection · Negation scope resolution · Bi-directional long short-term memory · LSTM · Conditional random field

1 Introduction

Negations play an important role in the semantic representation of biomedical text, because they reverse the truth value of propositions [1]. Therefore, correct negation handling is a crucial step whenever the goal is to derive factual knowledge from biomedical text. There are two distinguish ways to approach negations in medical text: negation detection and negation resolving. Negation detection is a form of assertion identification, in this case, determining whether a certain statement is true or false, or whether a medical condition is absent or present [2–7]. Negation resolving shifts the focus towards the token level by approaching the problem as a sequence labeling task [8]. This task is typically divided into two sub-tasks: (1) detecting the negation *cue*, a word expressing negation and (2) resolving its *scope*, the elements of the text affected by it. A cue can

P. Rosso et al. (Eds.): NLDB 2022, LNCS 13286, pp. 413–424, 2022.
https://doi.org/10.1007/978-3-031-08473-7_38

also be a morpheme ("*im*possible") or a group of words ("not at all"). As an example, in the following sentence the cue is underlined and its scope is enclosed by square brackets:

"I am sure that [neither
apples nor bananas are blue]."

Several studies adopted neural network-based approaches to resolve negations [10, 12,16]. This approach is shown to be highly promising, but most methods solely focus on scope resolution, relying on gold cue annotations. As Read et al. [9] point out: "It is difficult to compare system performance on sub-tasks, as each component will be affected by the performance of the previous." This comparison will not be easier when the performance on a sub-task is not affected by the performance of the previous component.

The main advantage of deep learning methods is their independence of manually created features, in contrast to other methods. However, by aiming at scope resolution only, they indirectly still use these features, or assume 100% accurate cues. For complete automatic negation resolving, a neural network model should detect the cue by itself. This raises two questions:

1. How does a neural network-based model perform on the cue detection task?
2. How does a neural network-based model perform on the scope resolution task with imperfect cue information?

This study addresses these questions by applying a Bi-directional Long Short-Term Memory (BiLSTM) model [10] to both stages of the negation resolving task. A BiLSTM model has proven to be good in various NLP tasks, yet not a very complex architecture. We develop the proposed model and their improvements on the BioScope Abstracts and Full Papers subcorpora [11].

As a secondary aim, the current study explores different methods to ensure continuous scope predictions. Since the BioScope corpus only contains continuous scopes, the Percentage Correct Scopes will likely increase after applying such a method. We compare a post-processing algorithm [8] with a Conditional Random Field (CRF) layer [12], in our experiments.

2 Task Modeling

Let a sentence be represented by a token sequence $\mathbf{t} = (t_1\, t_2\, \cdots\, t_n)$. Following Khandelwal and Sawant [14], we use the following labeling scheme for the cue detection task: For $k = 1, \ldots, n$, token t_k is labeled

- **C** if it is annotated as a single word cue or a discontinuous multiword cue
- **MC** if it is part of a continuous multiword cue
- **NC** if it is not annotated as a cue

The scope label of token t_k is

- **O** if it is outside of the negation cue scope
- **B** if it is inside the negation scope, *before* the first cue token

Table 1. Example of a token sequence and its cue and scope labels.

Tokens	It	Had	No	Effect	On	IL-10	Secretion	.
Cue labels	NC	NC	C	NC	NC	NC	NC	NC
Scope labels	O	O	C	A	A	A	A	O

- **C** if it is the first cue token in the scope
- **A** if it is inside the negation scope, *after* the first cue token

For each sentence, Task 1 is to predict its cue sequence: $\mathbf{c} = \{\mathbf{NC}, \mathbf{C}, \mathbf{MC}\}^n$, given its token sequence $\mathbf{t}$ and Task 2 is to subsequently predict the scope sequence: $\mathbf{s} = \{\mathbf{O}, \mathbf{B}, \mathbf{C}, \mathbf{A}\}^n$, given $\mathbf{t}$ and $\mathbf{c}$. Table 1 shows an example for the token sequence $\mathbf{t}$ with gold cue and scope labels for a given sentence: "It had [**no** effect on IL-10 secretion]."

2.1 Performance Measures

To measure performance, we evaluate whether the tokens are correctly predicted as cue or non-cue (Task 1) and as outside or inside the scope (Task 2). At the token level, both tasks are evaluated by precision, recall and F1 measures.

At the scope level, we report the percentage of exact cue matches (PECM) over the number of negation sentences for Task 1. All cue tokens in the sentences have to be correctly labeled to count as an exact match. For Task 2, we adopt the Percentage of Correct Scopes (PCS) as a measure of performance, the percentage of gold negation scopes that completely match. To evaluate the effectiveness of a 'smoothing' method, we compute the Percentage of Continuous Predictions (PCP) over all scope predictions.[1]

3   Model Architecture

In this section, we describe the proposed model architectures for Task 1 and Task 2. Both tasks are performed by a neural network consisting of an embedding layer, a BiL-STM layer and a softmax layer (Fig. 1). For Task 1, we define a baseline model with an embedding layer and a softmax. For both tasks, we add a model where the softmax layer is replaced by a CRF layer to obtain a joint prediction for the token sequence.

3.1   Word Embeddings for Cue Detection

The token sequence $\mathbf{t} = (t_1 \cdots t_n)$ is the only input for the cue detection models. Let $E^{d \times v}$ be an embedding matrix, where d is the embedding dimension and v is the vocabulary size. Then, each token in $\mathbf{t} = (t_1 \cdots t_n)$ is represented by a pre-trained

---

[1] Let the left and right boundary of a scope be defined as $k_L = \min \{k | s_k \in \{\mathbf{B}, \mathbf{C}, \mathbf{A}\}\}$ and $k_R = \max \{k | s_k \in \{\mathbf{B}, \mathbf{C}, \mathbf{A}\}\}$, respectively. We define a scope to be continuous if $t_k = 1$ for all $k_L < k < k_R$, and discontinuous otherwise.

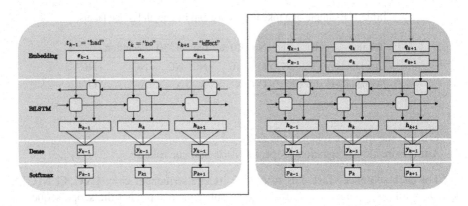

Fig. 1. Schematic representation of the BiLSTM model for cue detection (left) and scope resolution (right), for the example sentence "It had no effect on IL-10 secretion." at $k = 3$.

BioWordVec [18] embedding $\mathbf{e} \in \mathbb{R}^d$ corresponding to its vocabulary index. These embeddings were trained by the Fasttext subword embedding model with a context window size of 20 [19] on the MIMIC-III corpus [20]. This model is able to include domain-specific subword information into its vector representations. Out-of-vocabulary (OOV) tokens were represented by a d-dimensional zero vector.

Word embeddings may represent features that are already informative enough for the cue detection task. Therefore, we define a baseline model where the embeddings are directly passed to a 3-unit dense layer with weights $W_s^{3 \times d}$ and bias $\mathbf{b}_s \in \mathbb{R}^3$. The output vector

$$\mathbf{y}_k = W_s \mathbf{e}_k + \mathbf{b}_s = (y_k^{NC}, y_k^C, y_k^{MC})$$

contains to the 'confidence' scores of tagging token k as a non-cue, cue or multiword cue, respectively. These scores are used to obtain the final prediction label $p_k = \mathrm{softmax}(\mathbf{y}_k)$, where the softmax function $\mathbb{R}^3 \to \{\mathbf{NC}, \mathbf{C}, \mathbf{MC}\}$ is given by

$$\mathbf{y} \mapsto \left\{ \frac{e^{y^{NC}}}{Z}, \frac{e^{y^C}}{Z}, \frac{e^{y^{MC}}}{Z} \right\}, \quad Z = \sum_{y \in \mathbf{y}} e^y.$$

3.2 BiLSTM for Cue Detection

In the BiLSTM model, the token embeddings $(\mathbf{e}_1 \cdots \mathbf{e}_n)$ are passed to a BiLSTM layer [21] with $2U$ units, U in the forward direction and U in the backward direction. We represent an LSTM layer as a sequence of n identical cells. A cell at token k is described by the following set of equations corresponding to its input gate $\mathbf{i}_k$, forget gate $\mathbf{f}_k$, output gate $\mathbf{o}_k$, candidate memory state $\tilde{\gamma}_k$, memory state γ_k and hidden state $\mathbf{h}_k$, respectively:

$$\mathbf{i}_k = \sigma\big(W_e^{(i)}\mathbf{e}_k + W_h^{(i)}\mathbf{h}_{k-1} + \mathbf{b}^{(i)}\big),$$

$$\mathbf{f}_k = \sigma\big(W_e^{(f)}\mathbf{e}_k + W_h^{(f)}\mathbf{h}_{k-1} + \mathbf{b}^{(f)}\big),$$

$$\mathbf{o}_k = \sigma\big(W_e^{(o)}\mathbf{e}_k + W_h^{(o)}\mathbf{h}_{k-1} + \mathbf{b}^{(o)}\big),$$

$$\tilde{\gamma}_k = \tanh\big(W_e^{(\tilde{\gamma})}\mathbf{e}_k + W_h^{(\tilde{\gamma})}\mathbf{h}_{k-1} + \mathbf{b}^{(\tilde{\gamma})}\big),$$

$$\gamma_k = \mathbf{f}_k \odot \gamma_{k-1} + \mathbf{i}_k \odot \tilde{\gamma}_k,$$

$$\mathbf{h}_k = \mathbf{o}_k \odot \tanh(\gamma_k),$$

where $W_e^{U \times d}$ denote the weight matrices for the token embeddings, $W_h^{U \times U}$ denotes the recurrent weight matrix, $\mathbf{b} \in \mathbb{R}^u$ is a bias vector, $\odot$ denotes the Hadamard product, σ denotes the sigmoid function[2] and tanh denotes the hyperbolic tangent function.[3] The hidden state of the forward layer and backward layer are concatenated to yield a representation $\overleftrightarrow{\mathbf{h}}_k = (\overrightarrow{\mathbf{h}}_k; \overleftarrow{\mathbf{h}}_k) \in \mathbb{R}^{2u}$ for token k. For each token, the output $\overleftrightarrow{\mathbf{h}}_k$ of the BiLSTM layer is fed into a 3-unit softmax layer with weights $W_s^{3 \times 2U}$ and bias $\mathbf{b}_s \in \mathbb{R}^3$, as defined in the baseline model.

3.3 Adding a Conditional Random Field Layer

Although the context around token t is captured by the LSTM cell, the model will still assume independence between the token predictions when it maximizes a likelihood function. Alternatively, we can replace the softmax layer of the cue detection models by a Conditional Random Field (CRF) layer [22] to create a dependency between the predictions of adjacent tokens. This allows the model to learn that a single cue token is surrounded by non-cue tokens, and that a multiword cue token is always followed by a next one.

Let $Y = (\mathbf{y}_1 \cdots \mathbf{y}_n)$ be the $3 \times n$ matrix of model predicted scores

$$\begin{pmatrix} y_1^{NC} & y_2^{NC} & \cdots & y_n^{NC} \\ y_1^{C} & y_2^{C} & \cdots & y_n^{C} \\ y_1^{MC} & y_2^{MC} & \cdots & y_n^{MC} \end{pmatrix}.$$

Consider all possible label sequences enclosed by start/end labels $\mathcal{P} = \{\text{start}\} \times \{\text{NC}, \text{C}, \text{MC}\}^n \times \{\text{end}\}$. Let $\mathbf{p}^* \in \mathcal{P}$ and let $T \in \mathbb{R}^{5 \times 5}$ be a matrix of transition scores, such that score $T_{i,j}$ corresponds to moving from the i-th to the j-th label in the set $\{\text{NC}, \text{C}, \text{MC}, \text{start}, \text{end}\}$. Then, a linear CRF yields a joint prediction for a token sequence $\mathbf{t}$ by attaching it a global score

$$S(\mathbf{t}, \mathbf{c}, \mathbf{p}^*) = \sum_{k=1}^{n} Y_{p_k^*, k} + \sum_{k=0}^{n} T_{p_k^*, p_{k+1}^*}.$$

The model predicts the label sequence with the maximum score among all possible label sequences:

$$\mathbf{p} = _{\mathbf{p}^* \in \mathcal{P}} S(\mathbf{t}, \mathbf{c}, \mathbf{p}^*)$$

---

[2] The function $\mathbb{R} \to (0, 1)$ given by $x \mapsto 1/(1 + e^{-x})$.

[3] The function $\mathbb{R} \to (-1, 1)$ given by $x \mapsto (e^x - e^{-x})/(e^x + e^{-x})$.

3.4 BiLSTM for Scope Resolution

The scope resolution model accepts as input the token sequence $\mathbf{t}$ and a cue vector $(c_1 \cdots c_n) \in \{0,1\}^n$, where $c_k = 0$ if the (gold or predicted) cue label of token k is NC and $c_k = 1$ otherwise. The embedding layer yields a cue embedding $\mathbf{q} \in \{1\}^d$ if $c_k = 1$ and $\mathbf{q} \in \{0\}^d$ if $c_k = 0$. For the token input, we use the same embedding matrix $E^{v \times d}$ as in the previous model.

The token and cue embeddings are passed to a BiLSTM layer with $2U$ units. An LSTM layer is well-suited for the scope resolution, since it can capture long term dependencies between a cue token and a scope token. The bidirectionality accounts for the fact that a scope token can be located to the left and the right of a cue token. The hidden state of the forward layer and backward layer are concatenated to yield a representation $\overleftrightarrow{\mathbf{h}}_k = (\overrightarrow{\mathbf{h}}_k; \overleftarrow{\mathbf{h}}_k) \in \mathbb{R}^{2u}$ for token k.

For each token, the output $\overleftrightarrow{\mathbf{h}}_k$ of the BiLSTM layer is fed into a 4-unit dense layer with weights $W_s^{2 \times 2U}$ and bias $\mathbf{b}_s \in \mathbb{R}^2$. The output vector

$$\mathbf{y}_k = W_s \overleftrightarrow{\mathbf{h}}_k + \mathbf{b}_s = (y_k^O, y_k^B, y_k^C, y_k^A)$$

contains to the 'confidence' scores of the possible scope labels. These scores are used to obtain the final prediction label $p_k = \mathrm{softmax}(\mathbf{y}_k)$.

3.5 BiLSTM + CRF for Scope Resolution

A BiLSTM + CRF model is also used for the scope resolution task. The model might learn that certain sequences are impossible, for example, that a $\mathbf{B}$ will never follow a $\mathbf{C}$. Moreover, we expect that the model will yield more continuous scope predictions.

3.6 Model Training

The objective of the models is to maximize the likelihood $\mathcal{L}(\Theta)$ of the correct predictions $\mathbf{p}$ compared to the gold labels $\mathbf{g} = (g_1 \cdots g_n)$, with Θ the set of trainable model parameters and $\mathbf{X}$ the inputs of the model. For the BiLSTM models, this likelihood is

$$\mathcal{L}(\Theta) = \prod_{k=1}^{n} \left(p_k(\Theta, \mathbf{X}) \right)^{g_t} \left(1 - p_k(\Theta, \mathbf{X}) \right)^{1-g_t},$$

for the BiLSTM-CRF models, this likelihood is

$$\mathcal{L}(\Theta) = \frac{e^{S(\mathbf{X}, \mathbf{p})}}{\sum_{\mathbf{p}^* \in \mathcal{P}} e^{S(\mathbf{X}, \mathbf{p}^*)}}.$$

Hyperparameters. The models were compiled and fitted with the Keras functional API for TensorFlow 2.3.1 in Python 3.7.6. Based on validation results, we selected the Adam optimizer with an initial learning rate 0.001 with step decay to find optimal values for Θ. Scope resolution models were trained on 30 epochs with a batch size of 32. The cue detection models were trained with early stopping, since the model showed large overfitting on 30 epochs. For the architecture hyperparameters, we selected embedding dimension $d = 200$ and number of units in the LSTM-layer $U = 200$. Embeddings were not updated during training, except for the cue detection baseline model.

Table 2. Descriptive statistics of the subcorpora.

	Statistic	Abstracts	Full papers
Total	Documents	1,273	9
	Sentences	11,994	2,469
	Negation instances	14.3%	15.2%
	Tokens	317,317	69,367
	OOV	0.1%	1.4%
Sentence length n	$n \leq 25$	53.5%	50.6%
	$25 < n \leq 50$	43.2%	42.7%
	$50 < n \leq 75$	3.0%	5.6%
	$75 < n$	0.3%	1.1%
Scope length S	$S \leq 10$	69.9%	72.0%
	$10 < S \leq 30$	24.2%	22.1%
	$30 < S$	58.7%	58.7%
	Avg. S/n	0.33	0.30
Scope bounds	Avg. k_L	16.4	16.2
	Avg. k_R	23.1	22.8
	Avg. k_L/n	0.51	0.47
	Avg. k_R/n	0.76	0.70
	Scope starts with cue	85.5%	78.7%

Note: OOV = Out Of Vocabulary tokens, that is, not appearing in the BioWordVec pre-trained embeddings. Avg. = average.

3.7 Post-processing

In Task 2, we apply a post-processing algorithm on the predictions of the BiLSTM model to obtain continuous scope predictions [8]. We first ensure that the cue tokens are labeled as a scope token. In case of a discontinuous negation cue, the tokens between the cue tokens are also labeled as a scope token. The algorithm locates the continuous prediction 'block' containing the cue token and decides whether to connect separated blocks around it, based on their lengths and the gap length between them.

4 Experiments

4.1 Corpus

The current study made use of the Abstracts and Full papers subcorpora from the open access BioScope corpus [11]. Together, these subcorpora contain 14,462 sentences. For each sentence, the negation cue and its scope are annotated such that the negation cue is as small as possible, the negation scope is as wide as possible and the negation cue is always part of the scope. Resulting from this strategy, every negation cue has a scope and all scopes are continuous.

One sentence contained two negation instances. We represented this sentence twice, each such copy corresponded to a different negation instance. This resulted in 2,094 (14.48%) negation instances. A description of the subcorpora is provided in Table 2.

Tokenization. Biomedical text data poses additional challenges to the problem of tokenization [24]. DNA sequences, chemical substances and mathematical formula's appear frequently in this domain, but are not easily captured by simple tokenizers. Examples are "E2F-1/DP1" and "CD4(+)". In the current pipeline, the standard NLTK-tokenizer was used [25], in accordance with the tokenizer used by the BioWordVec model. This resulted in a vocabulary of 17,800 tokens, with each token present in both subcorpora. Tokenized sentences were truncated (23 sentences) or post-padded to match a length of 100 tokens.

5 Results and Discussion

5.1 Task 1 Performance

The results indicate that BiLSTM-based models can detect negation cues reasonably well in the Abstracts corpus, but perform poorly on the Full Papers corpus. The difference is not surprising, since we know from previous studies that most models perform worse on the Full Papers corpus. In Table 3, we report the performance of the proposed methods compared to the current state-of-the-art machine learning and neural network methods. It is clear that the models underperform on both corpora by a large margin.

The most surprising result is that none of the models perform remarkably better than the baseline model of non-trainable word embeddings. Adding a BiLSTM layer even leads to worse performance: The precision and recall measures indicate that less tokens are labeled as a cue with a BiLSTM layer, reducing the false positives, but increasing the false negatives. Apparently, the BiLSTM layer cannot capture more syntactical information needed for cue detection than already present in the embeddings. The embeddings do not benefit from a CRF layer either. It is only with a BiLSTM-CRF combination that the overall performance improves by predicting more non-cue labels for tokens that are indeed not a cue token. Among the currently proposed models, we conclude that the BiLSTM + CRF model is the best for the Abstracts corpus.

In contrast, training the embeddings does lead to a better performance on the Full Papers corpus. Here, the performance measures are more conclusive. The F1 measure is halved after adding a BiLSTM layer to the embeddings, and adding a CRF leads to no predicted cue labels at all. We therefore use the trained embeddings model to obtain the cue predictions for the Full Papers corpus.

5.2 Task 2 Performance

Overall, it is clear that the models suffer from imperfect cue information. The F1 on the scope resolution task can decrease up to 9% on the Abstracts corpus and 18% on the Full Papers corpus, when moving from gold to predicted information, see Table 4. The BiLSTM model seems to be the most robust against this effect. The transition scores

Table 3. Performance of the cue detection models.

BioScope abstracts				
Method	P	R	F1	PECM
Baseline	80.59	87.81	84.05	76.95
Emb. train (E)	79.87	89.61	84.46	74.22
E + BiLSTM	84.87	82.44	83.64	78.52
E + CRF	82.62	83.51	83.07	76.95
E + BiLSTM + CRF	83.22	87.10	85.11	80.86
Metalearner [15]	**100**	**98.75**	**99.37**	**98.68**
NegBERT [14]	NR	NR	95.65	NR
BioScope full papers				
Method	P	R	F1	PECM
Baseline	64.18	62.32	63.24	47.46
Emb. train (E)	60.23	76.81	67.52	49.15
E + BiLSTM	58.33	20.28	30.11	18.64
E + CRF	NaN	0	NaN	0
E + BiLSTM + CRF	60.53	66.67	63.45	45.76
Metalearner [15]	**100**	**95.72**	**96.08**	**92.15**
NegBERT [14]	NR	NR	90.23	NR

Note: PECM = Percentage Exact Cue Matches.

of a CRF layer might make the model more receptive to cue inputs. When the model is presented a false positive cue, the transition score from an **O**-label to a **C** makes it easier to predict a false positive **C**. It is also clear why the post-processing algorithm performs worse with imperfect cue information, as it guarantees that all false positive cues will receive a false positive scope label. This is confirmed by the sharp drop in precision (14%) and the small drop in recall (4%), see Table 5.

As a secondary aim, we investigated the effect of the CRF layer and the post-processing algorithm on the Percentage of Correct Scopes. In all cases, we see that the post-processing algorithm yields the highest PCS. However, this comes at the cost of a lower F1 measure at the token level when the model receives predicted cue inputs. Another disadvantage of this approach is that is not easily transferable to genres where the annotation style is different. For example, discontinuous scopes are quite common in the Conan Doyle corpus [13].

The results indicate that the BiLSTM + CRF model often resolves more scopes completely than the BiLSTM model. This could be partly explained by the increase in continuous predictions, as earlier suggested by Fancellu et al. [12]. However, on the Full Papers corpus with predicted inputs, the CRF-based model yields a lower PCS. The precision and recall measures indicate that the BiLSTM + CRF model predicts more positive cue labels, which may result in scopes that are too wide. We also see that there remains a substantive percentage of discontinuous predictions. This may be solved by higher-order CRF layers, that is, including transitions of label k to label $k + 2$.

Table 4. F1 scores on the scope resolution task with Gold versus Predicted cue inputs.

Abstracts, Cue detection F1 = 85.11

Method	Gold input	Predicted input	Difference
BiLSTM	90.25	83.90	**6.35**
BiLSTM + CRF	91.58	84.43	7.15
BiLSTM + post	90.17	80.87	9.30

Full papers, Cue detection F1 = 67.52

Method	Gold input	Predicted input	Difference
BiLSTM	72.80	56.98	**15.82**
BiLSTM + CRF	76.10	59.19	16.91
BiLSTM + post	73.29	54.79	18.50

Table 5. Performance of the scope resolution model on the Abstracts corpus.

BioScope abstracts

Cues	Method	P	R	F1	PCS	PCP
Gold	BiLSTM	89.80	90.70	90.25	68.34	87.89
	BiLSTM + CRF	91.07	**92.10**	91.58	70.31	92.19
	BiLSTM + post	90.43	89.92	90.17	72.66	100
	Metalearner [15]	90.68	90.68	90.67	73.36	100
	RecurCRFs* [17]	**94.9**	90.1	93.6	**92.3**	–
	NegBERT [14]	NR	NR	**95.68**	NR	NR
Pred	BiLSTM	**81.83**	86.08	83.90	58.59	83.07
	BiLSTM + CRF	81.29	**87.82**	**84.43**	58.98	87.40
	BiLSTM + post	76.40	85.90	80.87	60.55	100
	Metalearner [15]	81.76	83.45	82.60	**66.07**	100

BioScope full papers

Cues	Method	P	R	F1	PCS	PCP
Gold	BiLSTM	94.21	59.31	72.80	28.81	88.14
	BiLSTM + CRF	80.87	71.86	76.10	32.20	89.83
	BiLSTM + post	**94.86**	59.72	73.29	32.20	100
	Metalearner [15]	84.47	**84.95**	84.71	**50.26**	100
	NegBERT [14]	NR	NR	**87.35**	NR	NR
Pred	BiLSTM	67.69	49.19	56.98	18.64	56.92
	BiLSTM + CRF	57.55	60.93	59.19	16.95	63.08
	BiLSTM + post	49.92	60.73	54.79	22.03	100
	Metalearner [15]	**72.21**	**69.72**	**70.94**	**41.00**	100

Note: PCS = Percentage Correct Scopes, PCP = Percentage Continuous scope Predictions. *These results were reported for the complete BioScope corpus.

6   Conclusion and Future Work

The current study adopted a neural network-based approach to both sub-tasks of negation resolving: cue detection and scope resolution. In this way, the task would be completely independent of hand-crafted features, and would more realistically demonstrate the performance on the scope detection task. The study showed that the applicability of the BiLSTM approach does not extend to cue detection: isolated word embeddings are just as effective. These embeddings could capture features that are informative for cue detection, but they need more 'flexible' contextual information to distinguish negative or neutral use of a potential cue token within a given sentence.

The scope resolution performance of a BiLSTM + CRF-based method with inaccurate cue labels is hopeful. The model still outperforms most early methods, and performs on par with some recent methods. It would be interesting to assess the robustness of other neural network-based models against imperfect cue inputs, possibly with different levels and forms of cue accuracy. Additionally, this robustness could be integrated in the approach. For example, we could capture the prediction uncertainty of the cue inputs by feeding the probabilities instead of the labels to the scope resolution model.

References

1. Agirre, E., Bos, J., Diab, M., Manandhar, S., Marton, Y., Yuret, D.: * SEM 2012: The First Joint Conference on Lexical and Computational Semantics-Volume 1: Proceedings of the Main Conference and the Shared Task, and Volume 2: Proceedings of the Sixth International Workshop on Semantic Evaluation (SemEval 2012) (2012)
2. Mutalik, P.G., Deshpande, A., Nadkarni, P.M.: Use of general-purpose negation detection to augment concept indexing of medical documents: a quantitative study using the UMLS. J. Am. Med. Inform. Assoc. **8**(6), 598–609 (2001)
3. Chapman, W.W., Bridewell, W., Hanbury, P., Cooper, G.F., Buchanan, B.G.: A simple algorithm for identifying negated findings and diseases in discharge summaries. J. Biomed. Inform. **34**(5), 301–310 (2001)
4. Huang, Y., Lowe, H.J.: A novel hybrid approach to automated negation detection in clinical radiology reports. J. Am. Med. Inform. Assoc. **14**(3), 304–311 (2007)
5. Peng, Y., Wang, X., Lu, L., Bagheri, M., Summers, R., Lu, Z.: NegBio: a high-performance tool for negation and uncertainty detection in radiology reports. In: AMIA Summits on Translational Science Proceedings, p. 188 (2018)
6. Chen, L.: Attention-based deep learning system for negation and assertion detection in clinical notes. Int. J. Artif. Intell. Appl. (IJAIA) **10**(1) (2019)
7. Sykes, D., et al.: Comparison of rule-based and neural network models for negation detection in radiology reports. Nat. Lang. Eng. **27**(2), 203–224 (2021)
8. Morante, R., Liekens, A., Daelemans, W.: Learning the scope of negation in biomedical texts. In: Proceedings of the 2008 Conference on Empirical Methods in Natural Language Processing, pp. 715–724, October 2008
9. Read, J., Velldal, E., Øvrelid, L., Oepen, S.: UiO1: constituent-based discriminative ranking for negation resolution. In: * SEM 2012: The First Joint Conference on Lexical and Computational Semantics-Volume 1: Proceedings of the Main Conference and the Shared Task, and Volume 2: Proceedings of the Sixth International Workshop on Semantic Evaluation (SemEval 2012), pp. 310–318 (2012)

10. Fancellu, F., Lopez, A., Webber, B.: Neural networks for negation scope detection. In: Proceedings of the 54th Annual Meeting of the Association for Computational Linguistics, pp. 495–504, August 2016

11. Vincze, V., Szarvas, G., Farkas, R., Móra, G., Csirik, J.: The BioScope corpus: biomedical texts annotated for uncertainty, negation and their scopes. BMC Bioinform. **9**(11), 1–9 (2008)

12. Fancellu, F., Lopez, A., Webber, B., He, H.: Detecting negation scope is easy, except when it isn't. In: Proceedings of the 15th Conference of the European Chapter of the Association for Computational Linguistics: Volume 2, Short Papers, pp. 58–63, April 2017

13. Morante, R., Daelemans, W.: ConanDoyle-neg: annotation of negation in Conan Doyle stories. In: Proceedings of the Eighth International Conference on Language Resources and Evaluation, Istanbul, pp. 1563–1568, May 2012

14. Khandelwal, A., Sawant, S.: NegBERT: a transfer learning approach for negation detection and scope resolution. arXiv preprint arXiv:1911.04211 (2019)

15. Morante, R., Daelemans, W.: A metalearning approach to processing the scope of negation. In: Proceedings of the Thirteenth Conference on Computational Natural Language Learning (CoNLL 2009), pp. 21–29, June 2009

16. Lazib, L., Qin, B., Zhao, Y., Zhang, W., Liu, T.: A syntactic path-based hybrid neural network for negation scope detection. Front. Comp. Sci. **14**(1), 84–94 (2018). https://doi.org/10.1007/s11704-018-7368-6

17. Fei, H., Ren, Y., Ji, D.: Negation and speculation scope detection using recursive neural conditional random fields. Neurocomputing **374**, 22–29 (2020)

18. Chen, Q., Peng, Y., Lu, Z.: BioSentVec: creating sentence embeddings for biomedical texts. In: 2019 IEEE International Conference on Healthcare Informatics (ICHI), pp. 1–5. IEEE, June 2019

19. Bojanowski, P., Grave, E., Joulin, A., Mikolov, T.: Enriching word vectors with subword information. Trans. Assoc. Comput. Linguist. **5**, 135–146 (2017)

20. Johnson, A.E., et al.: MIMIC-III, a freely accessible critical care database. Sci. Data **3**(1), 1–9 (2016)

21. Graves, A., Schmidhuber, J.: Framewise phoneme classification with bidirectional LSTM and other neural network architectures. Neural Netw. **18**(5–6), 602–610 (2005)

22. Lafferty, J., McCallum, A., Pereira, F.C.: Conditional random fields: probabilistic models for segmenting and labeling sequence data (2001)

23. Abadi, M., et al.: TensorFlow: large-scale machine learning on heterogeneous distributed systems. arXiv preprint arXiv:1603.04467 (2016)

24. Díaz, N.P.C., Lóspez, M.J.M.: An analysis of biomedical tokenization: problems and strategies. In: Proceedings of the Sixth International Workshop on Health Text Mining and Information Analysis, pp. 40–49, September 2015

25. Loper, E., Bird, S.: NLTK: the natural language toolkit. arXiv preprint cs/0205028 (2002)

26. Peters, M.E., et al.: Deep contextualized word representations. arXiv 2018. arXiv preprint arXiv:1802.05365, December 2018

27. Banjade, R., Rus, V.: DT-Neg: tutorial dialogues annotated for negation scope and focus in context. In: Proceedings of the Tenth International Conference on Language Resources and Evaluation (LREC 2016), pp. 3768–3771, May 2016

28. Wang, T., Chen, P., Amaral, K., Qiang, J.: An experimental study of LSTM encoder-decoder model for text simplification. arXiv preprint arXiv:1609.03663 (2016)

Automatically Computing Connotative Shifts of Lexical Items

Valerio Basile[1]([✉]) [ID], Tommaso Caselli[3] [ID], Anna Koufakou[2] [ID],
and Viviana Patti[1] [ID]

[1] University of Turin, Torino, Italy
{valerio.basile,viviana.patti}@unito.it
[2] Florida Gulf Coast University, Fort Myers, FL, USA
akoufakou@fgcu.edu
[3] University of Groningen, Groningen, Netherlands
t.caselli@rug.nl

Abstract. Connotation is a dimension of lexical meaning at the semantic-pragmatic interface. Connotations can be used to express point of views, perspectives, and implied emotional associations. Variations in connotations of the same lexical item can occur at different level of analysis: from individuals, to community of speech, specific domains, and even time. In this paper, we present a simple yet effective method to assign connotative values to selected target items and to quantify connotation shifts. We test our method via a set of experiments using different social media data (Reddit and Twitter) and languages (English and Italian). While we kept the connotative axis (i.e., the polarity associated to a lexical item) fixed, we investigated connotation shifts along two dimensions: the first target shifts across communities of speech and domain while the second targets shifts in time. Our results indicate the validity of the proposed method and its potential application for the identification of connotation shifts and application to automatically induce specific connotation lexica.

Keywords: Connotative shift · Word embeddings · Social media

1 Introduction

Modelling the variations in meaning of lexical items plays a key role for the development of successful Natural Language Processing (NLP) systems. When discussing variation in meanings, we have to disentangle two different levels: the first is variation in **denotation**, while the second is variation in **connotation**. Changes in the denotation of a lexical item are changes at a purely semantic level where the same surface forms (i.e., *signifier*) can be used to refer to different entities or concepts (i.e., *significants*). Polysemy is a way in which denotative variations take place. On the contrary, changes in the connotation of lexical items are more complex as they represent an access point to the semantic-pragmatic interface of lexical items. Connotations are associated with lexical items: they

P. Rosso et al. (Eds.): NLDB 2022, LNCS 13286, pp. 425–436, 2022.
https://doi.org/10.1007/978-3-031-08473-7_39

represent subtle, implied, and emotional associations that extend and augment the denotative dimension(s) [1,5,11,18].

Recently, innovative methods to capture and model variations in meaning of lexical items have been developed and applied successfully in various NLP tasks. We refer to the large volume of work related to the development of word embedding representations [4,22,25], with a particular emphasis on contextual embedding methods such as ELMo [26] or BERT [8]. However, all of these models mainly capture variations in denotation but tend to conflate the connotative dimension in their representations [35]. This is also a direct consequence of the way these models are generated: the use of massive amount of textual data, more or less curated and of varying quality, combined with the adoption of a distributional approach to model the meaning of lexical items [15], clearly highlights variations and differences in meaning of a lexical item related to its context of occurrence. In other words, these models factor out any aspect associated with the connotative dimension.

A further aspect that is understudied when it comes to connotation is its variability according to the community of speakers [7,16,31]. The same lexical items can assume different connotation values according to who is using them. As exemplified by [13], the word *soft* can assume different connotation values when used within a discussion community of toys versus one dedicated to sport.

While some attempts focused on the development of domain- or community-specific lexical resources to make explicit connotation values of various lexical items, in this paper, we take a different route: we propose a new method to measure the difference of connotative values across communities of users from a large social media platform such as Reddit, and across time on Twitter. Our primary goal is not to induce a connotative rich lexicon but rather to measure whether and to what extent lexical items shift in their connotative values.

Our contributions can be summarised as follows: i) we introduce a simple unsupervised algorithm to automatically assign a connotative score to lexical items along an arbitrary connotative axis; ii) we present a method to assess the connotative shift of lexical items across the diastratic and the diachronic dimensions; iii) we report a set of experiments validating our method using sentiment polarity as a proxy to assess overall connotations of lexical items.

2   Related Work

The denotative and connotative dimensions of meaning are part of a long-standing philosophical debate that can be traced back to Frege [35]. Connotations are best described as the variations with which an object, a concept, or an event is referred to using different natural language expressions that, while preserving its denotation, have an impact on the perceptions of the receivers. For instance, the use of an adjective such as "vintage" to describe a piece of furniture not only expresses the fact that the furniture is old, but it also highlights that it is regarded as a fashionable item, and thus as something positive. The opposite effect is achieved if an adjective such as "decrepit" is used. Differences in connotations do not limit to the lexical dimension, but they can affect syntactic constructions. Previous work in psycholinguistics has shown that when reporting events involving violence, the linguistics backgrounding of the agents (e.g. by means of passive constructions) diminishes their perceived responsibility and potentially trigger victim's blaming effects [3, 12, 17, 21, 36].

As for NLP, a distinction has to be made between polarity and connotation. While the former targets the identification of lexical items that either directly or indirectly express a sentiment, the latter is broader and it investigates lexical items that evoke or are associated with the polarity of a sentiment or other dimensions [11]. Previous work on connotations in NLP has focused on subtle nuances in the use of language, ranging from good/bad effects of verbs [6], evoked emotions and sentiments [10, 19, 20, 23], pejorativity detection [9], to detailed psycho-sociological properties of words [32]. Other works have focused on connotation aspects of verbs, especially on the agent and theme roles of transitive verbs by collecting crowdsourced judgements to further train models to assign connotation frames [28, 29].

A further bulk of work has attempted to develop connotation lexicons in an unsupervised way. Early contributions have investigated the automatic assignment of connotation values either associated with predicates or in conjunctions with word senses using graph structures [11, 18]. More recently, an investigation on disentangling the connotative and denotative dimensions in pretrained word embeddings was presented [35], using the representations of political ideology as a proxy for connotations. Finally, a new approach to automatically generate a connotation lexicon for English was proposed [1] using a distant supervision approach. They address six fine-grained connotative axes (polarity, social value, politeness, impact, factuality, and emotional association) for nouns and adjectives. Their learning model is based on a BiLSTM with scaled dot-product attention [34] and makes use of ConceptNet embeddings [30] to initialise the network. Their evaluation shows that the automatically induced lexicon aligns with human judgements on the connotative axes and that the associated connotative embeddings are useful in a downstream task such as stance detection.

Although more focused on developing a sentiment lexicon rather than a connotative one, the work by [14] is particularly relevant. The authors present a method based on domain-specific word embedding representations used in conjunction with a label propagation framework to induce domain-specific polarity lexicons starting from a small set of seed words. Their approach is closely related to the method we present, however, we differ with respect to the following points: i) we target connotation values rather than merely sentiment values; although we are focusing on polarity, we can extend our method to more connotative axes; ii) our main goal is to measure the direction and extent of connotation shifts of lexical items across communities and time rather than inducing a polarity lexicon; and iii) our method is different since the connotative shifts are measured by comparing pairs of custom word embeddings to a hyperplane representing the targeted connotation axis, obtained by training on a minimal number of seed words.

3   Method

We propose a fully automated and unsupervised method to compute the connotative shift of words across domains and/or time based on training ad-hoc word embedding models.

The method makes use of four inputs:

1. **Target words**: the words for which we calculate the connotative shift;
2. **Seed words**: two sets of words assumed to lie at both extremes of the spectrum with respect to the connotative axis we aim to analyze;
3. A **domain** corpus: a collection of texts representing a specific language variety [27] and topic, more generally called "domain";
4. A **general** corpus of text with no specific domain.

The first step of the method is to train an embedding model for each target word using the concatenation of the domain and general corpora. Before computing the embeddings, the target word is modified to better represent the corpus where it occurs. Specifically, a random selection of two third of the occurrences of the target word in the domain corpus is labeled with a _DOM appendix, and similarly random selection of two third of the occurrences of the target word in the general corpus is labeled with a _GEN appendix. Therefore, the final corpus will contain three versions of the target word, roughly in the same amount of occurrences: word, word_DOM, and word_GEN.

The two corpora with the modified target words are merged and used to train a 100-dimensional *word2vec* skip-gram embedding model [22][1]. Given the input of the target word, the resulting embeddings will therefore contain three distinct representations of the target word, two domain-specific and one domain-agnostic, in the same proportion.

For the next step, we retrieve the vectors representing the seed words from the word embedding model, both from the positive and the negative end of the spectrum. This bi-partite set of vectors is used to train a Support Vector Machine (SVM) model, where the labels are the positions of the respective word in the connotative axis. We employ a cosine kernel for the SVM training because we are interested in measuring the angular distance between word embeddings, disregarding their magnitude which is influenced by the frequency of the words. The result of the SVM training is a *Connotative Hyperplane* which, by definition of the SVM model, is constructed to maximize the distance of each vector on both of its sides from the hyperplane itself.

After the training, we measure the distance of the vectors representing each target word from the hyperplane, in terms of cosine distance. This step produces two different scores for each target word, which could be negative or positive numbers depending on which side of the hyperplane the vectors are located. Moreover, the absolute value of the angular distance between a word vector and the hyperplane is an indication of the strength of the classification according

---

[1] We used the default hyperparameters of the Python Gensim implementation of word2vec: https://radimrehurek.com/gensim/models/word2vec.html.

to the SVM. Finally, we compute the connotative shift of a target word as the difference between the distances of the two domain-specific versions of that word. Figure 1 illustrates the whole process.

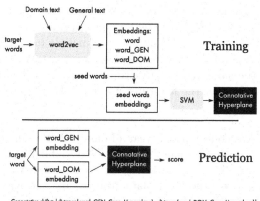

Fig. 1. Diagram od the Connotative Hyperplane algorithm.

As an example, in one experiment the word *price* in its general use is classified as carrying a positive connotation (as proxied by sentiment polarity) by the SVM, and the cosine distance of its corresponding vector representation in a word embedding space from the Connotative Hyperplane is 0.28. The vector representing the same word used in a forum of political discussion is instead classified as negative on the same connotative axis, with a distance of -0.02^2. Therefore, for the word *price*, a shift of magnitude 0.3 is measured towards the negative polarity in the context of politics.

4   Evaluation

To better assess the validity and versatility of the Connotative Hyperplane method, we run two sets of experiments both focused on the connotative axis of polarity, that is, whether and to what extent a word in context expresses a positive vs. negative sentiment. In both cases, we worked with social media data. However, the first set of experiments is run on English and focuses on connotative shifts across different communities represented as domains (Sect. 4.1). On the other hand, the second experiment is run on Italian and focuses on connotative shifts over time (Sect. 4.2).

---

[2] The negative and positive signs could be switched without loss of information, as the correspondence between the extremes of the connotative axis and the direction of the Connotative Hyperplane is purely conventional.

4.1 Connotative Shifts Across Domains

In this set of experiments, we test our method by computing the shift along the polarity axis across different communities of users of a social media platform in English. As seeds, we selected the top 1,000 words from the *NRC Valence, Arousal, and Dominance* lexicon [24] according to their valence score, for the positive polarity, and the bottom 1,000 words from the same list for the negative polarity. Examples of seed words from this set include *love*, *happy*, or *enjoyable* (positive), *horrifying*, *murderer*, or *nightmare* (negative). We ran each evaluation experiment with the same dataset five times and then calculated the mean of the connotation shifts over the five runs, as well as their standard deviation.

Reddit Datasets. We collected one year (January 2021–January 2022) of data from four Reddit forums: a general domain (AskReddit) and three specialised domains (Gaming, Politics, and Soccer). In each forum, we collected all comments on any post. To collect the data from reddit, we wrote a script using PRAW (Python Reddit API Wrapper[3]). We removed any comment shorter than ten characters. We then pre-processed all comments in each dataset using spaCy[4] sentencizer, markdown[5] and BeautifulSoup.[6]

The datasets with the resulting number of messages and of unique tokens are shown in Table 1. Due to the size of the forums and the nature of their posts and comments, the dataset vary in size. We were able to collect more than a million comments for the general domain (AskReddit), Gaming, and Politics, and almost 800k for the Soccer domain. While AskReddit may have its own lexical biases, we treat is as a domain-neutral forum because of its sheer size and it being a part of Reddit, as opposed to collecting text from other sources.

Table 1. The datasets we collected from four reddit forums: number of messages (comments on posts) and number of unique tokens after pre-processing.

Subreddit	Messages	Unique tokens
AskReddit	1,039,914	2,453,279
Gaming	1,034,323	2,464,742
Politics	1,042,210	2,553,004
Soccer	797,068	1,508,848

First Qualitative Evaluation: Common Words. As target words for the first experiment, we selected 20 words trying to avoid domain-specific terms. In order

---

[3] https://praw.readthedocs.io/en/stable.

[4] https://spacy.io/.

[5] https://pypi.org/project/Markdown/.

[6] https://pypi.org/project/beautifulsoup4/.

to do so, we computed the relative frequency of each word in each of the collected domains separately. We then computed the harmonic mean of the relative frequencies per word, and selected the top 20 words (ranked by harmonic mean). The rationale for using this approach is that the harmonic mean is lower if the word is infrequent in even just one subdomain, while it is higher only when the word is relatively frequent in all domains at the same time. The resulting list of target word is: *f*ck, money, man, world, bad, guy, high, play, pay, god, kids, school, kill, black, power, price, blue, free*. We ran the algorithm on this set of target words and textual data from pairs of subdomains: AskReddit vs. Soccer, AskReddit vs. Politics, and AskReddit vs. Gaming, therefore measuring their connotative shift.

Figure 2 shows the results of the experiment. The results are based on averages of five runs, with the standard deviation ranging from 0.011 and 0.095 depending on the target word. While the interpretation of the results needs to be contextualized carefully, a few strong signals can be observed. The word *kill* strongly shift towards the positive connotation in the soccer domain, likely due to the metaphorical use of the verb (e.g., as in "killing it on the field"). Similarly, *play* shifts negatively in politics. At a higher level of analysis, words related to economics (pay, price, money) consistently shifts towards the negative end in the politics domain. In the gaming domain, the average magnitude of the shifts is smaller, indicating that the selected words are less subject to connotative change.

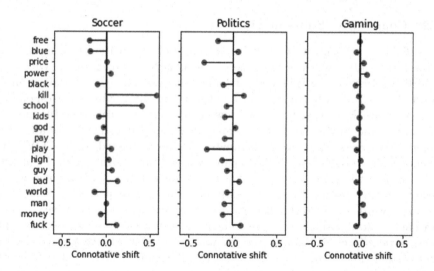

Fig. 2. Positive and negative polarity shift of common words across domains.

Second Qualitative Evaluation: Gender Words. For this experiment, we used a different set of target words, while keeping the rest of the parameters the same as for the previous experiment. With the aim of analyzing the connotative shift of words with a clear denotation, rather than uniformly common words, we selected as target words a small set of gender-related words: *male, boy, he, man, female, girl, she, and woman.*

The results depicted in Fig. 3, show an unfortunate yet clear trend. The majority of woman-related words exhibit a shift towards the negative connotation in both the soccer and politics domain, while for the man-related words the trend is neutral or reversed. The gaming community, instead, is showing less shift overall, and a slightly inverse trend with respect to the gender. The results are based on averages of five runs, with the standard deviation ranging from 0.004 and 0.084 depending on the target word.

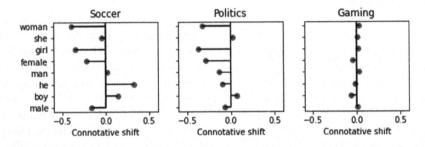

Fig. 3. Positive and negative polarity shift of gender words across domains.

4.2 Connotative Shifts in Time

As a final experiment, we tested the capability of our method to compute the connotative shift of words across time, i.e., in a diachronic perspective. We downloaded a selection of TWITA [2], a large-scale, domain-agnostic collection of tweets in the Italian language, and divided it into three subsets corresponding to three years. More specifically, we downloaded all the tweets from the months of March, June, September, and December of 2019, 2020, and 2021, for a total of about 17M tweets. We focused the analysis on terms related to the COVID-19 pandemic. Note that the COVID-19 pandemic hit Italy roughly at the beginning of 2020, and therefore we expected a strong connotative shift of some words related to this historical event. Consistently with this hypothesis, we selected as target words the following list: *positivo* [positive, *negativo* [negative], *vaccini* [vaccines], *letti* [beds], *governo* [government], *autocertificatione* [self-declaration], *mascherina* [(face) mask], *distanza* [distance]. As seed words, we selected the top and bottom 1,000 words from MAL [33], the Morphologically-inflected Affective Lexicon of Italian words associated with a sentiment polarity score. We preprocessed the data by stripping hashtags, users' mention and URLs. We then ran the Connotative Hyperplane method on the target words in order to compute two connotative shifts in sentiment polarity for each word, namely from 2019 to 2020 and from 2020 to 2021.

Figure 4 shows the results of this experiment. The words *positivo* and *negativo*, both carrying a strongly self-evident polarized connotation before the

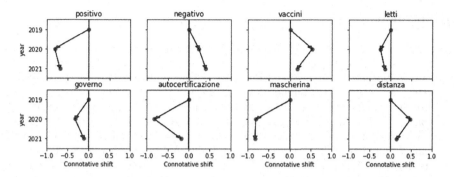

Fig. 4. Positive and negative polarity shift of Italian COVID-related words across years 2019–2021.

advent of the pandemic, essentially inverted their polarity with the COVID-19 pandemic, with the effects for *positivo* being particularly accentuated. An interesting pattern emerged for *vaccini*, where the word became associated with a more positive polarity in 2020, at the beginning of the pandemic, but then shifted back towards the negative end in 2021, possibly correlated to the rise of national and global anti-vax movements. The opposite trend is shown for *autocertificazione*, the term for a paper document that Italian citizens were mandated to carry during the lockdowns in 2020 (shifting towards negative polarity), subsequently replaced by digital forms of tracking in 2021 (returning to its more neutral connotation).

5   Conclusions and Future Work

In this paper, we propose an unsupervised method for assigning connotative values along any arbitrary axes and measuring connotation shifts of lexical items across dimensions. Starting from a list of seed words that proxy values of a targeted connotative axis (e.g., heavily loaded polarity words), our algorithm first generates a word embedding model for the seed words and subsequently trains an SVM on the basis of these embeddings. The SVM hyperplane is then used to classify a list of pre-selected *target* words from corpora containing diastratic or diachronic dimensions. In this way, each target word receives a connotation score that is further used to assess its connotation shift.

Future work includes further experimentation with additional word embedding models (e.g., contextual embeddings), and the automatic adaptation of affective lexicons to a domain, evaluating the resulting lexicons in a task such as sentiment analysis.

References

1. Allaway, E., McKeown, K.: A unified feature representation for lexical connotations. In: Proceedings of the 16th Conference of the European Chapter of the Association for Computational Linguistics: Main Volume, April 2021, pp. 2145–2163. Association for Computational Linguistics (2021). Online. https://doi.org/10.18653/v1/2021.eacl-main.184. https://aclanthology.org/2021.eacl-main.184

2. Basile, V., Lai, M., Sanguinetti, M.: Long-term social media data collection at the University of Turin. In: Proceedings of the 5th Italian Conference on Computational Linguistics, CLiC-it 2018, Torino, Italy, 10–12 December 2018 (2018)

3. Bohner, G.: Writing about rape: use of the passive voice and other distancing text features as an expression of perceived responsibility of the victim. Br. J. Soc. Psychol. 40(4), 515–529 (2001)

4. Bojanowski, P., Grave, E., Joulin, A., Mikolov, T.: Enriching word vectors with subword information. Trans. Assoc. Comput. Linguist. 5, 135–146 (2017). https://doi.org/10.1162/tacl_a_00051. https://aclanthology.org/Q17-1010

5. Carpuat, M.: Connotation in translation. In: Proceedings of the 6th Workshop on Computational Approaches to Subjectivity, Sentiment and Social Media Analysis, pp. 9–15 (2015)

6. Choi, Y., Wiebe, J.: +/-EffectWordNet: sense-level lexicon acquisition for opinion inference. In: Proceedings of the 2014 Conference on Empirical Methods in Natural Language Processing (EMNLP), Doha, Qatar, October 2014, pp. 1181–1191. Association for Computational Linguistics (2014). https://doi.org/10.3115/v1/D14-1125. https://aclanthology.org/D14-1125

7. Del Tredici, M., Fernández, R.: The road to success: assessing the fate of linguistic innovations in online communities. In: Proceedings of the 27th International Conference on Computational Linguistics, Santa Fe, New Mexico, USA, August 2018, pp. 1591–1603. Association for Computational Linguistics (2018). https://aclanthology.org/C18-1135

8. Devlin, J., Chang, M.W., Lee, K., Toutanova, K.: BERT: pre-training of deep bidirectional transformers for language understanding. In: Proceedings of the 2019 Conference of the North American Chapter of the Association for Computational Linguistics: Human Language Technologies, Volume 1 (Long and Short Papers), Minneapolis, Minnesota, June 2019, pp. 4171–4186. Association for Computational Linguistics (2019). https://doi.org/10.18653/v1/N19-1423. https://aclanthology.org/N19-1423

9. Dinu, L.P., Iordache, I.B., Uban, A.S., Zampieri, M.: A computational exploration of pejorative language in social media. In: Findings of the Association for Computational Linguistics, EMNLP 2021, Punta Cana, Dominican Republic, November 2021, pp. 3493–3498. Association for Computational Linguistics (2021). https://doi.org/10.18653/v1/2021.findings-emnlp.296. https://aclanthology.org/2021.findings-emnlp.296

10. Esuli, A., Sebastiani, F.: SENTIWORDNET: a publicly available lexical resource for opinion mining. In: Proceedings of the 5th International Conference on Language Resources and Evaluation, LREC 2006 (2006)

11. Feng, S., Bose, R., Choi, Y.: Learning general connotation of words using graph-based algorithms. In: Proceedings of the 2011 Conference on Empirical Methods in Natural Language Processing, pp. 1092–1103 (2011)

12. Gray, K., Wegner, D.M.: Moral typecasting: divergent perceptions of moral agents and moral patients. J. Pers. Soc. Psychol. 96, 505–520 (2009)

13. Hamilton, W.L., Clark, K., Leskovec, J., Jurafsky, D.: Inducing domain-specific sentiment lexicons from unlabeled corpora. In: Proceedings of the Conference on Empirical Methods in Natural Language Processing, vol. 2016, p. 595. NIH Public Access (2016)

14. Hamilton, W.L., Clark, K., Leskovec, J., Jurafsky, D.: Inducing domain-specific sentiment lexicons from unlabeled corpora. In: Proceedings of the 2016 Conference on Empirical Methods in Natural Language Processing, Austin, Texas, November 2016, pp. 595–605. Association for Computational Linguistics (2016). https://doi. org/10.18653/v1/D16-1057. https://aclanthology.org/D16-1057

15. Harris, Z.S.: Distributional structure. Word **10**(2–3), 146–162 (1954)

16. Hovy, D.: Demographic factors improve classification performance. In: Proceedings of the 53rd Annual Meeting of the Association for Computational Linguistics and the 7th International Joint Conference on Natural Language Processing (Volume 1: Long Papers), Beijing, China, July 2015, pp. 752–762. Association for Computational Linguistics (2015). https://doi.org/10.3115/v1/P15-1073. https:// aclanthology.org/P15-1073

17. Huttenlocher, J., Eisenberg, K., Strauss, S.: Comprehension: relation between perceived actor and logical subject. J. Verbal Learn. Verbal Behav. **7**, 527–530 (1968)

18. Kang, J.S., Feng, S., Akoglu, L., Choi, Y.: ConnotationWordNet: learning connotation over the word+sense network. In: Proceedings of the 52nd Annual Meeting of the Association for Computational Linguistics (Volume 1: Long Papers), pp. 1544–1554 (2014)

19. Kiritchenko, S., Mohammad, S.M.: Capturing reliable fine-grained sentiment associations by crowdsourcing and best-worst scaling. In: Proceedings of the 2016 Conference of the North American Chapter of the Association for Computational Linguistics: Human Language Technologies, San Diego, California, June 2016, pp. 811–817. Association for Computational Linguistics (2016). https://doi.org/10.18653/ v1/N16-1095. https://aclanthology.org/N16-1095

20. Klinger, R., De Clercq, O., Mohammad, S., Balahur, A.: IEST: WASSA-2018 implicit emotions shared task. In: Proceedings of the 9th Workshop on Computational Approaches to Subjectivity, Sentiment and Social Media Analysis, Brussels, Belgium, October 2018, pp. 31–42. Association for Computational Linguistics (2018). https://doi.org/10.18653/v1/W18-6206. https://aclanthology.org/ W18-6206

21. Meluzzi, C., Pinelli, E., Valvason, E., Zanchi, C.: Responsibility attribution in gender-based domestic violence: a study bridging corpus-assisted discourse analysis and readers' perception. J. Pragmat. **185**, 73–92 (2021). https://doi.org/10.1016/ j.pragma.2021.07.023

22. Mikolov, T., Sutskever, I., Chen, K., Corrado, G.S., Dean, J.: Distributed representations of words and phrases and their compositionality. In: Advances in Neural Information Processing Systems, pp. 3111–3119 (2013)

23. Mohammad, S., Kiritchenko, S.: Understanding emotions: a dataset of tweets to study interactions between affect categories. In: Proceedings of the 11th International Conference on Language Resources and Evaluation, LREC 2018, Miyazaki, Japan, May 2018. European Language Resources Association (ELRA) (2018). https://aclanthology.org/L18-1030

24. Mohammad, S.M.: Obtaining reliable human ratings of valence, arousal, and dominance for 20,000 English words. In: Proceedings of the Annual Conference of the Association for Computational Linguistics (ACL), Melbourne, Australia (2018)

25. Pennington, J., Socher, R., Manning, C.: GloVe: global vectors for word representation. In: Proceedings of the 2014 Conference on Empirical Methods in Natural Language Processing (EMNLP), Doha, Qatar, October 2014, pp. 1532–1543. Association for Computational Linguistics (2014). https://doi.org/10.3115/v1/D14-1162. https://aclanthology.org/D14-1162

26. Peters, M.E., et al.: Deep contextualized word representations. In: Proceedings of the 2018 Conference of the North American Chapter of the Association for Computational Linguistics: Human Language Technologies, Volume 1 (Long Papers), New Orleans, Louisiana, June 2018, pp. 2227–2237. Association for Computational Linguistics (2018). https://doi.org/10.18653/v1/N18-1202. https://aclanthology.org/N18-1202

27. Ramponi, A., Plank, B.: Neural unsupervised domain adaptation in NLP–a survey. In: Proceedings of the 28th International Conference on Computational Linguistics, Barcelona, Spain (Online), December 2020, pp. 6838–6855. International Committee on Computational Linguistics (2020). https://doi.org/10.18653/v1/2020.coling-main.603. https://aclanthology.org/2020.coling-main.603

28. Rashkin, H., Singh, S., Choi, Y.: Connotation frames: a data-driven investigation. In: Proceedings of the 54th Annual Meeting of the Association for Computational Linguistics (Volume 1: Long Papers), Berlin, Germany, August 2016, pp. 311–321. Association for Computational Linguistics (2016). https://doi.org/10.18653/v1/P16-1030. https://aclanthology.org/P16-1030

29. Sap, M., Prasettio, M.C., Holtzman, A., Rashkin, H., Choi, Y.: Connotation frames of power and agency in modern films. In: Proceedings of the 2017 Conference on Empirical Methods in Natural Language Processing, Copenhagen, Denmark, September 2017, pp. 2329–2334. Association for Computational Linguistics (2017). https://doi.org/10.18653/v1/D17-1247. https://aclanthology.org/D17-1247

30. Speer, R., Chin, J., Havasi, C.: ConceptNet 5.5: an open multilingual graph of general knowledge. In: 31st AAAI Conference on Artificial Intelligence (2017)

31. Taboada, M., Brooke, J., Tofiloski, M., Voll, K., Stede, M.: Lexicon-based methods for sentiment analysis. Comput. Linguist. $37(2)$, 267–307 (2011)

32. Tausczik, Y.R., Pennebaker, J.W.: The psychological meaning of words: LIWC and computerized text analysis methods. J. Lang. Soc. Psychol. $29(1)$, 24–54 (2010)

33. Vassallo, M., Gabrieli, G., Basile, V., Bosco, C.: The Tenuousness of lemmatization in lexicon-based sentiment analysis. In: Bernardi, R., Navigli, R., Semeraro, G. (eds.) Proceedings of the 6th Italian Conference on Computational Linguistics. CEUR Workshop Proceedings, Bari, Italy, 13–15 November 2019, vol. 2481. CEUR-WS.org (2019)

34. Vaswani, A., et al.: Attention is all you need. In: Advances in Neural Information Processing Systems, vol. 30 (2017)

35. Webson, A., Chen, Z., Eickhoff, C., Pavlick, E.: Are "undocumented workers" the same as "illegal aliens"? Disentangling denotation and connotation in vector spaces. In: Proceedings of the 2020 Conference on Empirical Methods in Natural Language Processing (EMNLP), Online, November 2020, pp. 4090–4105. Association for Computational Linguistics (2020). https://doi.org/10.18653/v1/2020.emnlp-main.335. https://aclanthology.org/2020.emnlp-main.335

36. Zhou, K., Smith, A., Lee, L.: Assessing cognitive linguistic influences in the assignment of blame. In: Proceedings of the 9th International Workshop on Natural Language Processing for Social Media, Online, June 2021, pp. 61–69. Association for Computational Linguistics (2021). https://doi.org/10.18653/v1/2021.socialnlp-1.5. https://aclanthology.org/2021.socialnlp-1.5

Studying the Role of Named Entities for Content Preservation in Text Style Transfer

Nikolay Babakov[1(✉)], David Dale[1], Varvara Logacheva[1], Irina Krotova[2], and Alexander Panchenko[1]

[1] Skolkovo Institute of Science and Technology, Moscow, Russia
{n.babakov,d.dale,a.panchenko}@skoltech.ru
[2] Mobile TeleSystems (MTS), Moscow, Russia

Abstract. Text style transfer techniques are gaining popularity in Natural Language Processing, finding various applications such as text detoxification, sentiment, or formality transfer. However, the majority of the existing approaches were tested on such domains as online communications on public platforms, music, or entertainment yet none of them were applied to the domains which are typical for task-oriented production systems, such as personal plans arrangements (e.g. booking of flights or reserving a table in a restaurant). We fill this gap by studying formality transfer in this domain.

We noted that, the texts in this domain are full of named entities, which are very important for keeping the original sense of the text. Indeed, if for example, someone communicates destination city of a flight is must not be altered. Thus, we concentrate on the role of named entities in content preservation for formality text style transfer.

We collect a new dataset for the evaluation of content similarity measures in text style transfer. It is taken from a corpus of task-oriented dialogues and contains many important entities related to realistic requests that make this dataset particularly useful for testing style transfer models before using them in production. Besides, we perform an error analysis of a pre-trained formality transfer model and introduce a simple technique to use information about named entities to enhance the performance of baseline content similarity measures used in text style transfer.

Keywords: Text style transfer · Content preservation · Named entities

1 Introduction

Text style transfer (**TST**) systems are designed to change the style of the original text to alternative one, such as more informal [25], more positive [17], or even more Shakespearean [11]. Such systems have gained significant popularity in the NLP within the last few years. They could be applied to many purposes: from diversifying responses of dialogue agents to creating artificial personalities.

More formally, TST system is a function $\alpha : S \times S \times D \rightarrow D$ that, given a source style s^{src}, a target style s^{dst}, and an input text d^{src}, produces an output text d^{dst} such that:

© The Author(s), under exclusive license to Springer Nature Switzerland AG 2022
P. Rosso et al. (Eds.): NLDB 2022, LNCS 13286, pp. 437–448, 2022.
https://doi.org/10.1007/978-3-031-08473-7_40

- The style of the text changes from the source style s^{src} to the target style s^{dst} : $\sigma(d^{src}) \neq \sigma(d^{dst})$, $\sigma(d^{dst}) = s^{dst}$;
- The content of the source text is saved in the target text as much as required for the task: $\delta(d^{src}, d^{dst}) \geq t^{\delta}$;
- The fluency of the target text achieves the required level: $\psi(d^{dst}) \geq t^{\psi}$,

where t^{δ} and t^{ψ} are task-specific thresholds for the content preservation (δ) and fluency (ψ) functions.

To measure if the content of the source text d^{src} is preserved in the target text d^{dst} a **content similarity measure** is used. This is a specific similarity measure sim which quantifies semantic relatedness of d^{src} and d^{dst} : $sim(d^{src}, d^{dst})$. The measure sim yields high score for the pairs with similar content and low score for ones with different content.

In the majority of recent TST papers [5,24,27] BLEU [21] is still the main way to evaluate the content similarity. More recent approaches as cosine similarity calculation between averaged word vectors [20], BLEURT [28] (which is a BERT [7] fine-tuned for semantic similarity evaluation task in cross-encoder manner on synthetic data) [14] and BERTScore [30] (F1-score over BERT-embeddings between tokens from initial and target sentences) [15] are also gaining popularity.

To the best of our knowledge, none of the newly proposed TST techniques have been tested in the domain of the personal plan. We consider the step towards such a domain in TST research valuable because it makes its application in the real world even more likely. One of the main distinguishing properties of this domain is a large number of named entities (**NE**). NEs are real-world objects, such as a person, location, organization, etc. Indeed, when a client wants to order a taxi or book a flight, and a dialogue agent's reply is modified to, for example, a more informal style to make a conversation more natural, it is crucial to keep all significant details of the client's request, as a destination of a taxi ride or a name of the departure airport.

We assume that if a NE is lost during TST, then some important parts of the original content are lost. For example, in [19] authors exploited a similar assumption and used the information about NEs and some other categories of words to improve measures like BLEU or METEOR [1] for question answering task. Thus, we dedicate our work to studying the role of named entities and other linguistic objects in the process of TST and, in particular, in content similarity scoring.

The contributions of our paper are as follows:

- We create and release[1] the first benchmark dataset for evaluating content similarity measures in style transfer in the task-oriented dialogue domain (Sect. 2);
- We perform an error analysis of a SOTA pre-trained text style transfer system in terms of content preservation (Sect. 3);
- We perform an error analysis of SOTA content similarity measures used in text style transfer (Sect. 4);

---

[1] https://github.com/skoltech-nlp/SGDD-TST.

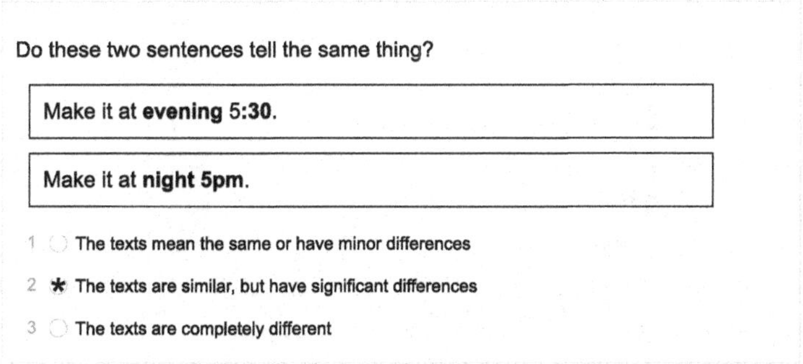

Do these two sentences tell the same thing?

Make it at **evening 5:30**.

Make it at **night 5pm**.

1 ◌ The texts mean the same or have minor differences

2 ✶ The texts are similar, but have significant differences

3 ◌ The texts are completely different

Fig. 1. The interface of the content similarity crowdsourcing task.

– We introduce a simple technique for enriching the content similarity measures with information about named entities, which increases the quality of strong baseline measures used in text style transfer (Sect. 5).

2   Dataset Collection

In this section, we describe the process of collection of SGDD-TST (Schema-Guided Dialogue Dataset for Text Style Transfer) – a dataset for evaluating the quality of content similarity measures for text style transfer in the domain of the personal plans. We use a pre-trained formality transfer model to create style transfer paraphrases from the task-oriented dialogue dataset. The obtained sentence pairs are then annotated with similarity labels by crowd workers.

2.1   Generation of Parallel Texts

One of the core contributions of our work is the new TST dataset annotated with content similarity labels. The topics of most of the existing TST formality datasets [3,13,29] are mostly related to common discussion of entertainment or family affairs [25], so it could be more useful to calculate content similarity for TST applied to real-world tasks, such as booking hotels or purchasing tickets.

The initial data for the dataset was collected from SGDD (Schema-Guided Dialogue Dataset) [26]. This dataset consists of 16,142 task-oriented dialogues, which are naturally full of NEs related to real-life tasks (booking of hotels, flights, restaurants). If a NE is lost or corrupted during TST the overall sense of the initial sentence is most probably lost as well. This makes the style transferred pairs particularly interesting for the task of content preservation control.

As far as SGDD is not originally related to TST, we use a base T5 model [23][2] fine-tuned for 3 epochs with learning rate $1e^{-5}$ with Adam optimizer on parallel GYAFC formality dataset [25] to generate style transferred paraphrases.

---

[2] https://huggingface.co/ceshine/t5-paraphrase-paws-msrp-opinosis.

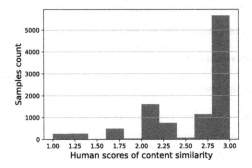

Fig. 2. Distribution of averaged human similarity score between original phrase and the phrase generated with the TST model. In most cases, the content in the text rewritten with the model is not lost.

2.2 Annotation Setup

The crowdsourcing report is performed according to recommendations by [4], where the authors propose a standardized way to open-source the details of collected TST datasets.

We need to choose the scale to evaluate the semantic similarity. For example in [29] 5 labels were used, but the final agreement by Krippendorf's alpha [12] coefficient is rather low: 0.34. Thus we use only three labels. An example of a crowdsourcing task interface can be found in Fig. 1.

The annotation is performed with the Yandex.Toloka[3] platform. To prepare the workers we use training tasks (with pre-defined answers and explanations) and control tasks (with pre-defined answers and without explanations). Workers are admitted to the real tasks after solving training and control tasks with acceptable grades. These tasks are also merged with the real ones. If the workers fail to pass them, they are banned and all their annotations are discarded.

2.3 Dataset Statistics

The final size of the dataset is 10,287 text pairs. The final similarity score for each pair was obtained by simply averaging the votes, where 1 point stands for "The texts are completely different", 2 stands for "The texts are similar but have significant differences", and 3 stands for "The texts mean the same or have minor differences". The distribution of the scores in the collected dataset can be found in Fig. 2. Some samples from the dataset are shown in Table 1.

The dataset was annotated by 1,214 workers (3 to 6 workers per sample). Krippendorf's alpha agreement score is 0.64. The average task annotation time is 15.7 s. The average percentage of right answers to control and training tasks merged with real tasks is 0.65.

There are similar datasets with human annotation about content similarity collected for different TST tasks: detoxification (Tox600 [6]), sentiment transfer

---

[3] https://toloka.yandex.com.

Table 1. Samples from the collected SGDD-TST dataset. Columns from third to fifth indicate the number of votes for one of the answers to the crowdsourcing task: #Different - "The texts are completely different", #Similar - "The texts are similar, but have significant difference", and #Same - "The texts mean the same or have minor difference". **Sim** shows the averaged human scores.

Original text	Generated text	#Different	#Similar	#Same	Sim
Where are you planning to leave from?	Where are you from and where is your plane?	3	0	0	1
I will depart from Vancouver	i'll go to Vancouver and get out of there	2	0	1	1.66
I have found 3 restaurants for you, one of which is called Locanda Positano which is located in Lafayette	I have found three restaurants for you, one is called Locanda Positano	0	3	0	2
I need a roundtrip flight departing from LAX please on any airline	I need a roundtrip flight departing from Los Angeles, please	0	1	2	2.66
Yes, I'd like to book the tickets	yes i wanna book the tickets	0	0	3	3

Table 2. Comparison of our SGDD-TST dataset with other TST datasets.

Name	xformal-FoST	Yam. GYAFC	STRAP. GYAFC	Tox600	Yam. Yelp	SGDD-TST
Size	2,458	6,000	684	600	2,000	10,287
Task	Formality transfer			Detoxification	Sentiment transfer	Task oriented formality transfer
Domain	Online communication about recreational topics				Service review	Personal plans

(Yam.Yelp [29]), and formality transfer (xformal-FoST [3], STRAP [13], and Yam.GYAFC [29]). To the best of our knowledge, our dataset is the biggest TST dataset with human annotations of content similarity (see Table 2). Moreover, while the existing formality transfer datasets are based on GYAFC [25] collected by formal rewrites of phrases from Yahoo Answers L6 corpus,[4] our dataset is the first one based on task-oriented dialogues, which allows making another step towards applying TST, in particular formality transfer, to real-world tasks.

3 Error Analysis of the Pre-trained Text Style Transfer System

In this section, we try to understand what kind of errors occur when a large TST model pre-trained on parallel data generates a new utterance that is considered different from the initial one by most human annotators.

---

[4] https://webscope.sandbox.yahoo.com/?guccounter=1.

3.1 Experimental Setting

We annotate 400 random pairs from the collected dataset which are annotated as not semantically equal by crowd workers. We use the following categories for annotation, which in most cases are mutually exclusive :

- **Named entities** We check whether the loss or corruption of NEs yields the content loss. In SGDD NEs are mostly related to time, places, and other objects used in different kinds of services;
- **Lost parts of speech** We check whether loss or corruption of some specific parts of speech (POS) not related to NEs affect the content of generated sentence;
- **Corrupted sentence type** We check whether the original sentence is related to one sentence type (declarative, imperative, interrogative, and exclamatory) and the newly generated one becomes related to another one.

3.2 Results

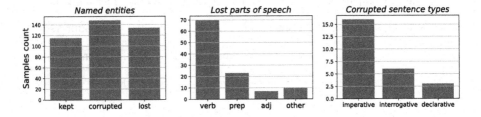

Fig. 3. Statistics of different reasons of content loss in TST.

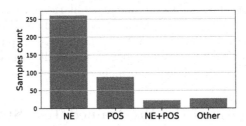

Fig. 4. Frequency of the reasons for the change of content between original and generated sentences: named entities (NE), parts of speech (POS), named entities with parts of speech (NE+POS), and other reasons (Other).

We show main results of the analysis in Figs. 3 and 4. Loss or corruption of NEs is present in the vast majority of cases when the content is lost. Moreover, the loss of significant verbs or prepositions or skipping several words which change the type of sentence (e.g. from imperative to declarative) could also change the final sense of the original utterance and spoil a client's experience with a dialogue agent. See Table 3 for examples.

Table 3. Examples of different reasons for changed content in the generated text.

Original text	Generated text	Lost or corrupted NEs	Lost or corrupted POS	Corrupted sentence type
I will arrive next Thursday and **depart** on the 14th of March	I will arrive on the 14th of March next Thursday	Kept	Verb	Not corrupted
In Paris on the 1st **until** Saturday this week	In Paris on the first Saturday of this week	Kept	Preposition	Not corrupted
I am looking for a **unisex** salon in SFO	I am looking for a **non-isex** salon in San Francisco	Kept	Adjective	Not corrupted
Hello, I need a bus to Sacramento **from Fresno** on the 5th of March	Hello, I need a bus to Sacramento on the 5th of March	Lost	Kept	Not corrupted
Move one thousand **two hundred** and forty dollars	move one thousand and forty bucks	Corrupted	Kept	Not corrupted
Can you please confirm that you need 3 rooms for the reservation on March 1st?	you need 3 rooms for the reservation on march 1st	Kept	Kept	Interrogative

4 Error Analysis of Content Similarity Measures

In this section, we analyze the failures of SOTA text similarity measures.

4.1 Content Similarity Measures Used in Our Study

We use both commonly used and recently proposed SOTA content similarity measures based on different calculation logic:

- Word and character ngrams-based (**ngram**): BLEU, METEOR [1], ROUGE based on unigrams/bigrams/trigrams/longest common sequence (ROUGE-1/2/3/L) [16], chrf [22];
- Averaged word vectors similarity (**vect-sim**): Word2vec [18], Fasttext [2];
- Large pre-trained models (**pre-trained**): BERTScore (modifications based on DeBERTa [9], RoBERTa [31] and BERT [7]), BLEURT[5].

4.2 Experimental Setting

We produce two rankings of sentences : a ranking based on their automatic scores and another one based on the manual scores, then sort the sentences by the absolute difference between their automatic and manual ranks, so the sentences scored worse with automatic measures are at the top of the list. We manually annotate the top 35 samples for a subset of the measures described in Sect. 4.1 based on various calculation logic. The annotation setup is similar to the Sect. 3.1.

---

[5] https://huggingface.co/Elron/bleurt-large-512.

4.3   Results

We plot the results of manual annotation in Fig. 5. The loss or corruption of NEs take a significant part in the failure of all measures. The loss of POS also takes part in the content loss, however, it looks much less significant. We don't report sentence type change here because this kind of change is almost absent in the analyzed samples. We also report the statistics of whether the measures scored a definite pair higher or lower than humans (to check this we apply a linear transformation to both automatic measures and human judgments so that their values are distributed between 0 and 1). In most cases of poor performance, measures assign higher scores than human annotators.

The examples of different types of content loss are shown in Table 3. In the most cases of worst measures performance, the original and generated sentences look almost the same but loss or corruption of NEs or POS play a significant role in the general meaning of the original sentence, which can be properly captured by human annotators and is hard to be captured with automatic measures.

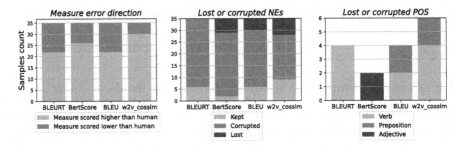

Fig. 5. Errors statistics of the analyzed measures. BertScore/DeBERTa is referred as BertScore here.

5   Named Entities Based Content Similarity Measure

In this section, we show how to use NEs for improving SOTA similarity measures.

5.1   Baseline Named Entities Based Approach

Our findings in Sects. 3 and 4 show that NEs play a significant role in the content loss, thus we try to improve existing measures with NE-based signals. To make the results of this analysis more generalizable we use the simple open-sourced Spacy NER-tagger to extract entities from the collected dataset. These entities are processed with lemmatization and then used to calculate the Jaccard index [10] over the intersection between entities from original and generated sentences. This score is used as a baseline NE-based content similarity measure. We use Spearman Rank Correlation Coefficient between human judgments and automatic scores to check the quality of content similarity measures.

Table 4. Spearman correlation of automatic content similarity measures with human content similarity scores with and without using auxiliary NE-based measure on the collected SGDD-TST dataset.

Similarity measure	Measure type	without NE	with NE	Improvement
BLEURT	pre-trained	0.56	0.56	0.00
BertScore/DeBERTa	pre-trained	0.47	0.45	−0.02
BertScore/RoBERTa	pre-trained	0.39	0.37	−0.02
BLEU	ngram	0.35	0.38	+0.03
ROUGE-1	ngram	0.29	0.36	+0.07
BertScore/BERT	pre-trained	0.28	0.36	+0.08
ROUGE-L	ngram	0.27	0.35	+0.08
chrf	ngram	0.27	0.30	+0.03
w2v_cossim	vect-sim	0.22	0.33	+0.11
fasttext_cossim	vect-sim	0.22	0.32	+0.10
ROUGE-2	ngram	0.15	0.22	+0.07
METEOR	ngram	0.10	0.25	+0.15
ROUGE-3	ngram	0.09	0.14	+0.05

5.2 Merging Named Entities Based Measure with Other Measures

The baseline NE-based measure has a low Spearman correlation with human scores - 0.06, so we use it as an auxiliary signal by merging two signals using the following formula: $M_{weigted} = M_{strong} \times (1 - p) + M_{NE} \times p$ where p is a percentage of NE tokens within all tokens in both texts, M_{strong} is an initial measure and M_{NE} is a NE-based signal. The intuition behind the formula is that the NE-based auxiliary signal is useful in the proportion equal to the proportion of NEs tokens in the text. Thus, the score of the main measure is not changed if there are no NEs in the text, and at the same time, the more NEs are in the text the more significantly the NE-based signal will affect the main score. We apply such merging to all measures presented in Sect. 4.1.

5.3 Results

The results of the proposed approach are in Table 4. All baseline measures (BLEU, ROUGE, METEOR) and some recent approaches (e.g. similarity between averaged embeddings) gain significant improvement from using this kind of auxiliary signal (the significance is measured with Williams test [8]). The most probable reason for this is that neither ngram-based measures nor vectors similarity-based measures process the information about the specific role of the NEs. However, the most modern trained measures like BLEURT and BertScore do not get any improvement from this approach. These approaches are based on large pre-trained models, so it is very likely that during training the models learned the concept of NEs and additional information can be not useful or in some cases even decrease the performance. Even though the research performed in Sect. 4 shows that the failures of top-performing measures are mostly related to loss or corruption of NEs, it seems that such a straightforward approach to enriching these measures with NE-related signal is not effective.

6   Conclusion

In this work, we collect the dataset for content similarity evaluation in text style transfer for the task-oriented dialogue domain. During the manual analysis of the collected dataset, we show that named entities play important role in the problem of content loss during text style transfer.

We show that such baseline content similarity measures as BLEU, METEOR, and ROUGE and even more recent approaches like cosine similarity between word2vec or fasttext embeddings fail to track perturbations of such entities, thus enriching these measures with named entities-based signal significantly improves their correlation with human judgments. At the same time, with the most recent approaches such as BLEURT or BERTScore, this kind of enrichment does not yield any improvement, and the correlations of these measures with human judgments are much higher than that of baseline approaches.

However, even the top-performing measures are still far from perfect in terms of the absolute value of correlation with human labels. Thus, the collected dataset with annotated human judgments about content similarity could foster future research supporting the development of novel similarity measures.

Acknowledgements. This work was supported by MTS-Skoltech laboratory on AI.

References

1. Banerjee, S., Lavie, A.: METEOR: An automatic metric for MT evaluation with improved correlation with human judgments. In: Proceedings of the ACL Workshop, Ann Arbor, Michigan, pp. 65–72. Association for Computational Linguistics (2005)
2. Bojanowski, P., Grave, E., Joulin, A., Mikolov, T.: Enriching word vectors with subword information. Trans. Assoc. for Comput. Linguist **5**, 135–146 (2017)
3. Briakou, E., Agrawal, S., Tetreault, J., Carpuat, M.: Evaluating the evaluation metrics for style transfer: a case study in multilingual formality transfer. In: Proceedings of the 2021 Conference on Empirical Methods in Natural Language Processing, pp. 1321–1336. Association for Computational Linguistics, Online and Punta Cana (2021)
4. Briakou, E., Agrawal, S., Zhang, K., Tetreault, J., Carpuat, M.: A review of human evaluation for style transfer. In: Proceedings of the 1st Workshop on Natural Language Generation, Evaluation, and Metrics, GEM 2021, pp. 58–67. Association for Computational Linguistics (2021)

5. Cao, Y., Shui, R., Pan, L., Kan, M.Y., Liu, Z., Chua, T.S.: Expertise style transfer: a new task towards better communication between experts and laymen. In:
   Proceedings of the 58th Annual Meeting of the Association for Computational
   Linguistics, pp. 1061–1071. Association for Computational Linguistics (2020)
6. Dementieva, D., et al.: Crowdsourcing of parallel corpora: the case of style transfer
   for detoxification. In: Proceedings of the 2nd Crowd Science Workshop: Trust,
   Ethics, and Excellence in Crowdsourced Data Management at Scale co-located
   with 47th International Conference on Very Large Data Bases, VLDB 2021. CEUR
   Workshop Proceedings, Copenhagen, Denmark, pp. 35-49 (2021). https://vldb.
   org/2021/
7. Devlin, J., Chang, M.W., Lee, K., Toutanova, K.: BERT: Pre-training of deep
   bidirectional transformers for language understanding. In: Proceedings of the 2019
   Conference of the North American Chapter of the Association for Computational
   Linguistics: Human Language Technologies, Minneapolis, Minnesota, Vol. 1 (Long
   and Short Papers), pp. 4171–4186. Association for Computational Linguistics
   (2019)
8. Graham, Y., Baldwin, T.: Testing for significance of increased correlation with
   human judgment. In: Proceedings of the 2014 Conference on Empirical Methods
   in Natural Language Processing, EMNLP, Doha, Qatar, pp. 172–176. Association
   for Computational Linguistics(2014)
9. He, P., Liu, X., Gao, J., Chen, W.: Deberta: Decoding-enhanced bert with disentangled attention. In: International Conference on Learning Representations (2021)
10. Jaccard, P.: Etude de la distribution florale dans une portion des alpes et du jura.
    Bull. Soc. Vaud. Sci. Nat. **37**, 547–579 (1901)
11. Jhamtani, H., Gangal, V., Hovy, E., Nyberg, E.: Shakespearizing modern language
    using copy-enriched sequence to sequence models. In: Proceedings of the Workshop
    on Stylistic Variation, Copenhagen, Denmark, pp. 10–19. Association for Compu-
    tational Linguistics (2017)
12. Krippendorff, K.: Content analysis: an introduction to its methodolog (1980)
13. Krishna, K., Wieting, J., Iyyer, M.: Reformulating unsupervised style transfer as
    paraphrase generation. In: Proceedings of the 2020 Conference on Empirical Meth-
    ods in Natural Language Processing, EMNLP, pp. 737–762. Association for Com-
    putational Linguistics (2020)
14. Lai, H., Toral, A., Nissim, M.: Thank you BART! rewarding pre-trained models
    improves formality style transfer. In: Proceedings of the 59th Annual Meeting of
    the Association for Computational Linguistics and the 11th International Joint
    Conference on Natural Language Processing, vol. 2 (Short Papers). pp. 484–494.
    Association for Computational Linguistics (2021)
15. Lee, D., Tian, Z., Xue, L., Zhang, N.L.: Enhancing content preservation in text style
    transfer using reverse attention and conditional layer normalization. In: Proceed-
    ings of the 59th Annual Meeting of the Association for Computational Linguistics
    and the 11th International Joint Conference on Natural Language Processing, vol.
    1 (Long Papers), pp. 93–102. Association for Computational Linguistics (2021)
16. Lin, C.Y.: Rouge: A package for automatic evaluation of summaries. In: Text Sum-
    marization Branches Out, pp. 74–81 (2004)
17. Luo, F., et al.: Towards fine-grained text sentiment transfer. In: Proceedings of the
    57th Annual Meeting of the Association for Computational Linguistics, Florence,
    Italy, pp. 2013–2022. Association for Computational Linguistics (2019)
18. Mikolov, T., Grave, E., Bojanowski, P., Puhrsch, C., Joulin, A.: Advances in pre-
    training distributed word representations (2017). arXiv preprint, arXiv:1712.09405

19. Nema, P., Khapra, M.M.: Towards a better metric for evaluating question generation systems. In: Proceedings of the 2018 Conference on Empirical Methods in Natural Language Processing, Brussels, Belgium, pp. 3950–3959. Association for Computational Linguistics (2018)

20. Pang, R.Y., Gimpel, K.: Unsupervised evaluation metrics and learning criteria for non-parallel textual transfer. In: Proceedings of the 3rd Workshop on Neural Generation and Translation, Hong Kong, pp. 138–147. Association for Computational Linguistics (2019)

21. Papineni, K., Roukos, S., Ward, T., Zhu, W.J.: Bleu: a method for automatic evaluation of machine translation. In: Proceedings of the 40th annual meeting of the Association for Computational Linguistics, pp. 311–318 (2002)

22. Popović, M.: chrF: character n-gram F-score for automatic MT evaluation. In: Proceedings of the Tenth Workshop on Statistical Machine Translation, Lisbon, Portugal, pp. 392–395. Association for Computational Linguistics (2015)

23. Raffel, C., et al.: Exploring the limits of transfer learning with a unified text-to-text transformer. J. Mach. Learn. Res. **21**, 140:1–140:67 (2020)

24. Rane, C., Dias, G., Lechervy, A., Ekbal, A.: Improving neural text style transfer by introducing loss function sequentiality. In: Diaz, F., Shah, C., Suel, T., Castells, P., Jones, R., Sakai, T. (eds.) SIGIR 2021: The 44th International ACM SIGIR Conference on Research and Development in Information Retrieval, Virtual Event, Canada, pp. 2197–2201, 11–15 July 2021. ACM (2021)

25. Rao, S., Tetreault, J.: Dear sir or madam, may I introduce the GYAFC dataset: Corpus, benchmarks and metrics for formality style transfer. In: Proceedings of the 2018 Conference of the North American Chapter of the Association for Computational Linguistics: Human Language Technologies, New Orleans, Louisiana, vol. 1 (Long Papers), pp. 129–140. Association for Computational Linguistics (2018)

26. Rastogi, A., Zang, X., Sunkara, S., Gupta, R., Khaitan, P.: Towards scalable multi-domain conversational agents: The schema-guided dialogue dataset. In: Proceedings of the AAAI Conference on Artificial Intelligence, vol. 34, pp. 8689–8696 (2020)

27. Riley, P., Constant, N., Guo, M., Kumar, G., Uthus, D., Parekh, Z.: TextSETTR: few-shot text style extraction and tunable targeted restyling. In: Proceedings of the 59th Annual Meeting of the Association for Computational Linguistics and the 11th International Joint Conference on Natural Language Processing, vol. 1 Long Papers, pp. 3786–3800. Association for Computational Linguistics (2021)

28. Sellam, T., Das, D., Parikh, A.: BLEURT: learning robust metrics for text generation. In: Proceedings of the 58th Annual Meeting of the Association for Computational Linguistics, pp. 7881–7892. Association for Computational Linguistics, Online (2020)

29. Yamshchikov, I.P., Shibaev, V., Khlebnikov, N., Tikhonov, A.: Style-transfer and paraphrase: Looking for a sensible semantic similarity metric. In: Proceedings of the AAAI Conference on Artificial Intelligence, vol. 35(16), pp. 14213–14220 (2021)

30. Zhang, T., Kishore, V., Wu, F., Weinberger, K.Q., Artzi, Y.: Bertscore: evaluating text generation with bert (2019). arXiv preprint arXiv:1904.09675

31. Zhuang, L., Wayne, L., Ya, S., Jun, Z.: A robustly optimized BERT pre-training approach with post-training. In: Proceedings of the 20th Chinese National Conference on Computational Linguistics. pp. 1218–1227. Chinese Information Processing Society of China, Huhhot, China (2021)

A BERT-Based Approach for Multilingual Discourse Connective Detection

Thomas Chapados Muermans and Leila Kosseim[✉]

Computational Linguistics at Concordia (CLaC) Laboratory,
Department of Computer Science and Software Engineering,
Concordia University, Montréal, QC, Canada
thomas.chapadosmuermans@mail.concordia.ca, leila.kosseim@concordia.ca

Abstract. In this paper, we report on our experiments towards multilingual discourse connective (or DC) identification and show how language specific BERT models seem to be sufficient even with little task-specific training data. While some languages have large corpora with human annotated DCs, most languages are low in such resources. Hence, relying solely on discourse annotated corpora to train a DC identification system for low resourced languages is insufficient. To address this issue, we developed a model based on pretrained BERT and fine-tuned it with discourse annotated data of varying sizes. To measure the effect of larger training data, we induced synthetic training corpora with DC annotations using word-aligned parallel corpora. We evaluated our models on 3 languages: English, Turkish and Mandarin Chinese in the context of the recent DISRPT 2021 Task 2 shared task. Results show that the F-measure achieved by the standard BERT model (92.49%, 93.97%, 87.42% for English, Turkish and Chinese) is hard to improve upon even with larger task specific training corpora

Keywords: Discourse analysis · Multilingual discourse connective identification · Corpus creation

1 Introduction

Identifying discourse connectives (or DCs), such as "but" or "if", is fundamental to discourse analysis, which itself is useful to improve many downstream NLP tasks such as text generation, dialog systems and summarization, where understanding how textual elements are related to each other is crucial. Several datasets and formalisms have been proposed to study different aspects of computational discourse analysis, such as the Penn Discourse Treebank (PDTB) [15], Segmented Discourse Representation Theory (SDRT) [1] and Rhetorical Structure Theory (RST) [12]. For the task of DC identification, the PDTB is the most widely used resources, as it annotates lexical elements as DCs, whether they are explicit or not.

© The Author(s), under exclusive license to Springer Nature Switzerland AG 2022
P. Rosso et al. (Eds.): NLDB 2022, LNCS 13286, pp. 449–460, 2022.
https://doi.org/10.1007/978-3-031-08473-7_41

The recent 2019 and 2021 DISRPT shared tasks[1] aimed at the identification of multilingual DCs in three languages: English, Turkish and Chinese. In general most participating systems achieved higher performance for English than for Turkish and Chinese, whose discourse annotated training data are much smaller. In order to address this issue, this paper investigates methods to improve DC annotation of low resource languages. In particular, we developed a BERT based model DC annotation and fine-tuned it with synthetic corpora of discourse connective annotations developed using parallel corpora. Results show that the F-measure achieved by the standard BERT model (92.49%, 93.97%, 87.42%) is hard to improve upon even with larger task specific training corpora.

2 Related Work

The Penn Discourse Treebank (PDTB) [15] is the largest English corpus manually curated with discourse annotations. These annotations fall into two categories: explicit and non-explicit relations. The former are expressed linguistically by well-defined lexical elements called discourse connectives or DCs (e.g., "but", "since"); while the latter signal the relation by other means such as an alternative lexicalization to a DC (i.e. an *AltLex*) or an entity-relation (i.e. an *EntRel*). Due to its relatively straightforward annotations formalism, the PDTB framework has been adopted for the creation of similar corpora in many languages, notably Chinese (CDTB) [24] and Turkish (TDB) [22,23]. However, manually creating such high quality corpora is time consuming and expensive, hence very few languages have such data sets.

The earliest attempt at identifying DCs automatically using the PDTB dates back to [14] who used extracted features from gold-standard Penn Treebank parses and a maximum entropy classifier and obtained an F-measure of 94.19. Later, [7] showed that a simple logistic regression model could achieve better results without relying on gold-standard parse trees, but using only lexical features and part-of-speech tags. More recent approaches use neural methods which are more flexible for multilingual settings. In particular [13] employed multilingual BERT and bi-directional LSTMs and achieved F-measures of 88.60, 69.85, 79.32 in English, Turkish and Chinese respectively. These results seem to correlate with the size of the training set of 44k, 24k and 2k respectively. The most recent attempt for the detection of DCs, [4], used transformer models in addition to many handcrafted input features and a conditional random field as a final classifier instead of a linear output layer. This model achieved the best performance at DISRPT 2021 with an F-measure of 92.02%, 94.11%, 87.52% for English, Turkish and Chinese respectively; leading to a significant improvement in the state of the art in all three languages.

---

[1] https://sites.google.com/georgetown.edu/disrpt2021/home.

Corpus augmentation has been shown to improve many NLP tasks where anno-tated data sets are scarce. In particular, annotation projection has shown its useful-ness for many tasks, such as part-of-speech tagging [20], word sense disambigua-tion [2], dependency parsing [17] and discourse relations identification [9]. Since they are semantic and rhetoric in nature, it is often assumed that discourse anno-tations can be projected from one language to another through word alignment. In particular, [8] created a PDTB styled discourse corpus for French, by project-ing discourse annotation from English (the PDTB) to French and using statistical word-alignment to identify unsupported annotations that should not be projected. The resulting corpus improved the performance of their French DC parser by 15%. Given the success of annotation projection for discourse analysis, we investigated its use to create synthetic corpora for DC annotation in Turkish and Chinese.

3 Methodology

Our work was done using the data sets of the 2021 DISRPT Task 2 *discourse connective identification across languages*[2] shared task. The task aimed at iden-tifying DCs in three languages: English, Turkish and Chinese. For example, given the sentence:

(1) <u>In addition</u>, of course, some of the Japanese investments involved outright purchase of small U.S. firms.

Systems had to tag DCs using one of three tags: `B-Conn` (beginning of a DC), `I-Conn` (inside a DC) and `None` (not a DC). For example, the expected output for sentence (1) is shown in Fig. 1.

In	addition	,	of	course	,	some
B-Conn	I-Conn	None	None	None	None	None
of	the	Japanese	investments	involved	outright	purchase
None	None	None	None	None	None	None
of	small	U.S.	firms	.		
None	None	None	None	None		

Fig. 1. Expected output of the 2021 DISRPT Task 2 for the sentence *In addition, of course, some of the Japanese investments involved outright purchase of small U.S. firms.*

3.1 The DISRPT-2021 Dataset

To train systems, the DISRPT organizers provided three PDTB styled annotated corpora: the English PDTB [15], the Turkish Discourse Treebank (TDB) [22, 23]

---

[2] https://sites.google.com/georgetown.edu/disrpt2021/home.

Table 1. Statistics of the training and test data.

Corpus	Language	# of train sentences	% tok B-Conn + I-Conn	# of test sentences
PDTB	English	44,563	2.671	2,364
TDB	Turkish	24,960	1.900	3,289
CDTB	Chinese	2,049	2.249	404
ZHO-AG	Chinese	21,934	4.645	–
ZHO-PJ	Chinese	2,848	2.312	–
TUR-AG	Turkish	27,827	1.254	–
TUR-PJ	Turkish	4,468	4.191	–

PDTB, TDB, and CDTB were provided by the organisers of DISRPT 2021; while ZHO-AG, ZHO-PJ, TUR-AG, and TUR-PJ were created by our methods (see Sect. 3.3)

and the Chinese Discourse Treebank (CDTB) [24]. Table 1 shows statistics of these corpora. As Table 1 shows, the PDTB is the largest with approximately 44k training instances, far exceeding the number of training instances available for Chinese ($\approx$2k) and Turkish ($\approx$25k). Overall, in all 3 corpora the percentage of B-Conn and I-Conn labels is around 2% as most words are labelled as None.

3.2 The Base BERT DC Detection Model

To perform multilingual DC annotation, we developed a basic BERT DC annotation model using Pytorch and Huggingface [19]. The Huggingface tokenizer is used on the input sentences to produce sequences of word pieces, which are then fed to the model. As shown in Fig. 2, the model is composed of a language specific BERT embedding [3], which can be found on Huggingface [19] (bert-base-cased for English, bert-base-chinese for Chinese, dbmdz/bert-baseturkishcased for Turkish). The output is then fed to a dropout unit which is then fed to a linear layer that produces a score for each of the 3 labels (B-Conn, I-Conn, and None) based on the BERT embeddings only. These scores are then fed to a conditional random field (CRF) which produces the most likely final tags for each word given the whole sentence.

We trained one model for each language for a maximum of 40 epochs using early stopping with a patience of 20 epochs on each corpora given by the organizers (see Sect. 3.1). This led to F-measures of 92.49, 93.97, 87.42 on the tests sets for English, Turkish and Chinese respectively[3]. The lower performance on Chinese seemed to be directly attributable to the lower number of training instances (see Table 1), hence we attempted to increase the training corpus for Chinese by creating synthetic annotated corpus. We did the same for Turkish to see if the increased data would provide any benefit to this task.

---

[3] Using the official DISRPT 2021 scorer available at https://github.com/disrpt/sharedtask2021.

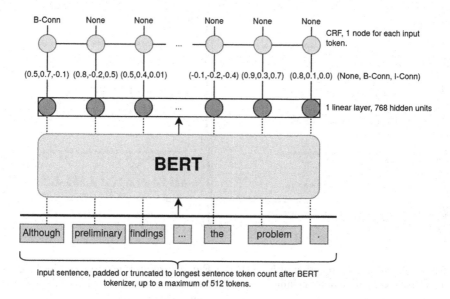

Fig. 2. Model overview of the BERT-base DC annotation model for English

3.3 Synthetic Corpora

To create the synthetic corpora annotated with DCs for Chinese and Turkish, we used two methods based on annotation projection and agreement on English-Chinese and English-Turkish parallel. To do so we first generated a list of English, Turkish and Chinese DCs from the provided PDTB, TDB, and CDTB respectively (see Sect. 3.1). This resulted in a list of 1160 English, 279 Turkish, and 195 Chinese connectives. The English connectives include the 100 DCs from the list of PDTB [15] plus 1060 AltLex that were labeled as DCs in the DISRPT training corpus.

Mandarin Chinese Synthetic Corpus. For Chinese, we used the Tsinghua alignment evaluation set version 2 [10,11], which contains 40,716 manually word aligned sentences. The Chinese and English sentences were already tokenized; and word alignment was already provided. We began by training our BERT based DC identification model (see Sect. 3.2) on the PDTB and CDTB corpora, then used it to identify DCs on both sides of the Tsinghua parallel corpus. Then, we created two synthetic datasets: one based on annotation projection, favoring recall; and one based on annotation agreement, favoring precision. As shown in Fig. 3, the projection method is applied when the annotation model has identified a DC in a source language sentence, but the target language model did not identify a DC in the aligned words. In that case, the DC annotation is projected onto the aligned words in the target language. On the other hand, the agreement method favors precision by comparing the annotated parallel sentences and retaining them in the synthetic corpus only if the annotations of the aligned

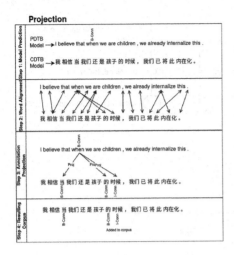
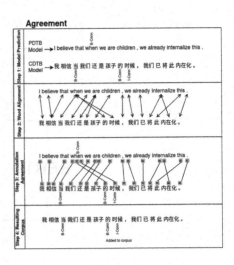

Fig. 3. Annotation projection of English discourse connectives onto a Chinese sentence.

Fig. 4. Annotation agreement of English discourse connectives with a Chinese discourse connectives.

words match; this is shown in Fig. 4. Finally, in both methods, in order to create corpora with a similar `B-Conn/I-Conn/None` balance as the DISRPT corpora, we dropped:

1. all sentences that contain no potential DC – i.e. no word in the sentence is part of the language specific list of DCs (see Sect. 3.3), and
2. 50% of the sentences with at least one potential DC marked as non discourse usage – i.e. at least one word in the sentence is part of the language specific list of DCs but is labeled as `None`.

As shown in Table 1, the two resulting corpora (ZHO-AG and ZHO-PJ) contain 21,943 and 2,848 sentences respectively. ZHO-PJ contains the same ratio of `B-Conn` + `I-Conn` as the CDTB ($\approx$2%); but the ZHO-AG contains $\approx$4%.

Turkish. The Turkish synthetic corpus is based on the seTimes [16] English-Turkish parallel corpus, which contains 207,677 aligned sentences. As the corpus was not word aligned, we tokenized it using Spacy [5] to split the words and punctuation. We then used SimAlign [6] to generate the word alignments with probabilities for each sentence. SimAlign can provide different alignment outputs based on three different algorithms: itermax, argmax and match. Based on the results of [6], itermax seems to perform better than the other methods; hence, we used the itermax alignments. In order to ensure that we have high quality alignment, we kept only the sentences with an average word alignment probability above 85%. Then, we proceeded the same way as we did for Chinese (see Sect. 3.3). As shown in Table 1, this produced a corpus of 27,827 sentences for the agreement method (TUR-AG), effectively doubling the original corpus, and 4,468 sentences for the projection method (TUR-PJ).

4   Evaluation of the Base BERT Model

We evaluated the base BERT DC annotator (see Sect. 3.2) by training it with and without the new synthetic data for Turkish and Chinese, and testing it with the DISRPT 2021 test set (see Table 1) and the official DISRPT evaluation script. Table 2 shows the performance of each model for Turkish, and Table 3 shows the performance for Mandarin Chinese.

Table 2. Performance of the base Turkish BERT model (`dbmdz/bertbaseturkish-cased`) on the TDB test set.

ID	Training set	Test set	Precision	Recall	F-measure
1	TDB	TDB	92.81 (±1.07)	95.17 (±0.77)	**93.97** (±0.34)
2	TUR-AG	TDB	87.62 (±2.32)	88.14 (±0.95)	87.86 (±0.71)
3	TUR-PJ	TDB	33.95 (±3.39)	52.10 (±4.18)	40.94 (±2.13)
4	TUR-AG + TUR-PJ	TDB	70.59 (±0.91)	86.85 (±1.21)	77.87 (±0.53)
5	TDB + TUR-AG	TDB	91.80 (±1.27)	94.53 (±2.75)	93.12 (±0.69)
6	TDB + TUR-PJ	TDB	89.90 (±1.17)	94.54 (±0.72)	92.16 (±0.34)
7	TDB + TUR-AG + TUR-PJ	TDB	90.97 (±0.68)	93.80 (±0.30)	92.37 (±0.49)

Table 3. Performance of the base Chinese BERT model (`bert-base-chinese`) on the CDTB test set.

ID	Training set	Test set	Precision	Recall	F-measure
1	CDTB	CDTB	88.78 (±1.60)	86.11 (±0.49)	**87.42** (±0.95)
2	ZHO-AG	CDTB	88.25 (±0.27)	85.90 (±0.85)	87.06 (±0.57)
3	ZHO-PJ	CDTB	62.34 (±4.62)	55.98 (±4.45)	58.86 (±2.97)
4	ZHO-AG + ZHO-PJ	CDTB	85.90 (±0.60)	85.26 (±0.85)	85.58 (±0.59)
5	CDTB + ZHO-AG	CDTB	89.16 (±1.03)	85.15 (±0.49)	87.10 (±0.46)
6	CDTB + ZHO-PJ	CDTB	87.52 (±0.50)	83.87 (±1.22)	85.65 (±0.51)
7	CDTB + ZHO-AG + ZHO-PJ	CDTB	88.15 (±0.85)	85.79 (±1.48)	86.95 (±1.03)

As shown in Tables 2 and 3, the best models are the ones trained only on the original TDB and CDTB datasets (rows 1). Using the synthetic datasets, on their own (rows 2–4) or in combination with TDB or CDTB (rows 5–7) only seems to decrease the performance of the BERT model. The projection method (rows 3) seems to lead to significantly lower results for both languages (F-measure of 40.94 for Turkish, and 58.86 for Chinese). This is in line with the fact that annotation projection maximizes recall, hence the resulting corpora may contain more noise. The agreement method (rows 2) optimises precision and leads to a lower decrease in performance. The observed performance for the model trained with on the ZHO-AG (row 2) (87.06%) had a difference of only 0.36% to the model trained on CDTB (row 1) (87.42%) alone which suggests that this dataset is of high quality and could easily be improved by human curation. While the F-measure with TUR-AG (row 2) (87.86%) had a difference of 6.11% with TDB (93.97), we believe this that this decrease in performance is due to error accumulation in the tokenization and word alignment steps (see Sect. 3.3). Further investigation would be required to verify the dataset.

For English we experimented with both the base and the large cased BERT embeddings [3]. As Table 4 shows, the performance of BERT-large did not lead to a significant increase in performance compared to BERT-base (93.12 versus 92.49), but did require more computational resources.

Table 4. Performance of base English BERT model on the PDTB test set – `bert-basecased` versus `bertlargecased`.

Model	Training set	Test set	Precision	Recall	F-measure
`bert-base-cased`	PDTB	PDTB	92.69 (±1.16)	92.31 (±0.41)	**92.49** (±0.77)
`bert-large-cased`	PDTB	PDTB	93.46 (±0.95)	92.79 (±0.69)	93.12 (±0.49)

5   Additional Experiments

In order to better understand the behavior of the model, we performed additional experiments with different configurations.

5.1   Multilingual BERT Embeddings

We attempted to use a multilingual model to use cross-lingual training. For this experiment we used multilingual BERT [3] embeddings, which are pre-trained on 104 different languages including English, Turkish and Chinese. To do so, we used two configurations. In the first configuration, we trained the model with all of the training data from the PDTB, TDB and CDTB (all data). In the second configuration, because the PDTB and TDB contain more training instances than the CTDB, we extracted a subset of the PDTB and TDB to balance the three corpora. The subsets we created are composed of 5% of the original PDTB and 10% of the original TDB, which were than used with the full CTDB to train a balanced model (balanced data).

Table 5 shows the results obtained using both settings: all data and balanced data, on the test sets of the PDTB, the TDB and the CDTB, when the model is trained on the PDTB, the TDB and the CTDB training sets simultaneously. As Table 5 shows, the multilingual BERT consistently under-performed when compared to the models pre-trained on the pertinent language, even when accounting for the differences in the corpora size. This in line with the findings of [18] who showed that multilingual BERT was not sufficient to outperform a BERT model pre-trained only on the language of study on a variety of NLP tasks such as POS tagging, named entity recognition, dependency parsing, and text classification.

Table 5. Performance of the multilingual BERT model (`bertbasemultilingualcased`) while training on all languages simultaneously.

Training set	Test set	All data (M-BERT)			Balanced data (M-BERT)		
		Precision	Recall	F-measure	Precision	Recall	F-measure
PDTB + TDB + CDTB	PDTB	91.53 (±0.78)	92.64 (±0.33)	92.08 (±0.25)	88.06 (±1.12)	88.31 (±0.64)	88.18 (±0.76)
PDTB + TDB + CDTB	TDB	89.29 (±1.60)	93.05 (±0.62)	91.12 (±0.82)	84.24 (±1.53)	88.17 (±1.31)	86.16 (±1.21)
PDTB + TDB + CDTB	CDTB	84.25 (±2.30)	85.19 (±1.76)	84.71 (±1.81)	85.05 (±1.39)	86.28 (±1.05)	85.65 (±0.93)

5.2 Linguistic Features

We investigated the use of additional linguistic information to see how the base BERT model would react. In particular, we added handcrafted features such as gold-standard universal part-of-speech tags, language-specific part-of-speech tag and universal dependency relations (provided in the DISRPT data set). These features only lowered the performance on the test set.

5.3 Bidirectional LSTM

Finally, we tried to pass the BERT output into 2 bidirectional LSTM layers instead of a CRF. Again, this either degraded the performance or took more epochs to get to a similar performance as using a CRF.

5.4 Comparison with the State-of-the-Art

Given that the base-BERT model could not be improved upon, we compared it to the state-of-the-art models. Table 6 shows the results of our base BERT model using the official scorer and datasets of the DISRPT-2021 shared task, while Table 7 shows the performance of the participating systems. As Table 6 shows, our base BERT model performs as well as, if not better than the top performing model, DiscoDisco [4], for all three languages; while being significantly simpler in terms of linguistic and computational resources. The DiscoDisco approach used a collection of handcrafted features including 3 sentence embeddings (2 trainable/fine-tuned, and 1 static), a variety of grammatical and textual features (UPOS, XPOS, universal dependency relations, head distance, sentence type, and sentence length), and also a representation of the context via neighboring sentences. On the other hand, our model is less resource-intensive as it consists of only a language specific BERT-base + CRF and only uses the current sentence as context. This seems to show that the language specific BERT-base model contains sufficient information to accomplish this task, and feeding the model with additional information is redundant and only increases its complexity without significant performance gain.

Table 6. Performance of our base BERT models (`bert-base-cased` for PDTB, `dbmdz/bert-base-turkish-cased` for PDTB and `bert-base-chinese` for CDTB) with the official DISRPT 2021 Task 2 scorer.

Test set	Our model base BERT		
	P	R	F1
PDTB	92.69	92.31	**92.49**
TDB	92.81	95.17	**93.97**
CDTB	88.78	86.11	**87.42**
Macro average	91.43	91.20	91.29
Micro average	92.49	93.45	92.96

Table 7. Performance of the participating systems with the official DISRPT 2021 Task 2 scorer, taken from [21].

Test set	Participating system											
	TMVM			DiscoDisco			disCut			SegFormers		
	P	R	F1	P	R	F1	P	R	F1	P	R	F1
PDTB	85.98	65.54	74.38	92.32	91.15	**92.02**	93.32	88.67	90.94	89.73	92.61	91.15
TDB	80.00	24.14	37.10	93.71	94.53	**94.11**	90.55	86.93	88.70	90.42	91.17	90.79
CDTB	30.00	0.96	1.86	89.19	85.95	**87.52**	84.43	66.03	74.10	85.05	87.50	86.26
Macro average	65.33	30.21	37.78	91.74	90.54	91.22	89.43	80.54	84.58	88.40	90.43	89.40
Micro average	79.00	38.75	49.30	92.87	92.64	92.85	91.22	86.22	88.60	89.79	91.49	90.63

6   Conclusion and Future Work

This paper has described our experiments to improve a BERT-base model for discourse connective annotation in a multilingual setting. We described two methods to induce discourse annotated corpora and proposed a simple BERT-base model that is capable of achieving similar results to the best performing model at the DISRPT 2021 task 2. Our experiments with additional data, different models architectures and different input features, suggest that language specific BERT models with a CRF output and small amount of data is all that is needed to achieve a strong performance on the task of multilingual discourse connective identification.

Future work is required to evaluate the quality of the synthetic datasets created and the inclusion of additional information such as the POS tags, dependency relations, and the type of discourse relation being signaled; this would make these datasets useful for other natural language processing tasks.

The synthetic corpora are publicly available at https://github.com/CLaC-Lab.

Acknowledgment. The authors would like to thank the anonymous reviewers for their valuable comments on an earlier version of this paper. This work was financially supported by the Natural Sciences and Engineering Research Council of Canada (NSERC).

References

1. Asher, N., Lascarides, A.: Logics of Conversation. Cambridge University Press, Cambridge (2003)
2. Bentivogli, L., Pianta, E.: Exploiting parallel texts in the creation of multilingual semantically annotated resources: the MultiSemCor Corpus. Nat. Lang. Eng. **11**(3), 247–261 (2005)
3. Devlin, J., Chang, M., Lee, K., Toutanova, K.: BERT: pre-training of deep bidirectional transformers for language understanding. CoRR abs/1810.04805 (2018). http://arxiv.org/abs/1810.04805
4. Gessler, L., Behzad, S., Liu, Y.J., Peng, S., Zhu, Y., Zeldes, A.: Discodisco at the DISRPT2021 shared task: a system for discourse segmentation, classification, and connective detection. CoRR abs/2109.09777 (2021). https://arxiv.org/abs/2109.09777
5. Honnibal, M., Montani, I., Van Landeghem, S., Boyd, A.: spaCy: Industrial-strength Natural Language Processing in Python (2020). https://spacy.io/
6. Jalili Sabet, M., Dufter, P., Yvon, F., Schütze, H.: SimAlign: high quality word alignments without parallel training data using static and contextualized embeddings. In: Proceedings of the 2020 Conference on Empirical Methods in Natural Language Processing, (EMNLP 2020), Punta Cana, Dominican Republic, pp. 1627–1643, November 2020. https://www.aclweb.org/anthology/2020.findings-emnlp.147
7. Johannsen, A., Søgaard, A.: Disambiguating explicit discourse connectives without oracles. In: Proceedings of the Sixth International Joint Conference on Natural Language Processing, (IJCNLP 2013), Nagoya, Japan, pp. 997–1001, October 2013. https://aclanthology.org/I13-1134
8. Laali, M.: Inducing discourse resources using annotation projection, Ph.D. thesis, Concordia University, November 2017. https://spectrum.library.concordia.ca/983791/
9. Laali, M., Kosseim, L.: Improving discourse relation projection to build discourse annotated corpora. In: Proceedings of the International Conference Recent Advances in Natural Language Processing, (RANLP 2017), Varna, Bulgaria, pp. 407–416, September 2017. https://doi.org/10.26615/978-954-452-049-6_0_54
10. Liu, Y., Liu, Q., Lin, S.: Log-linear models for word alignment. In: Proceedings of the 43rd Annual Meeting of the Association for Computational Linguistics (ACL 2005), Ann Arbor, Michigan, pp. 459–466, June 2005. https://doi.org/10.3115/1219840.1219897. https://aclanthology.org/P05-1057
11. Liu, Y., Sun, M.: Contrastive unsupervised word alignment with non-local features. In: Proceedings of the Twenty-Ninth Association for the Advancement of Artificial Intelligence Conference on Artificial Intelligence (AAAI 2015), pp. 2295–2301 (2015). http://arxiv.org/abs/1410.2082
12. Mann, W.C., Thompson, S.A.: Rhetorical structure theory: a framework for the analysis of texts. IPrA Papers Pragmatics **1**, 79–105 (1987)
13. Muller, P., Braud, C., Morey, M.: ToNy: contextual embeddings for accurate multilingual discourse segmentation of full documents. In: Proceedings of the Workshop on Discourse Relation Parsing and Treebanking 2019, Minneapolis, MN, pp. 115–124, June 2019. https://doi.org/10.18653/v1/W19-2715. https://aclanthology.org/W19-2715

14. Pitler, E., Nenkova, A.: Using syntax to disambiguate explicit discourse connectives in text. In: Proceedings of the Association for Computational Linguistics and International Joint Conference on Natural Language Processing (ACL-IJCNLP 2009), Suntec, Singapore, pp. 13–16, August 2009. https://aclanthology.org/P09-2004

15. Prasad, R., et al.: The Penn discourse TreeBank 2.0. In: Proceedings of the Sixth International Conference on Language Resources and Evaluation (LREC 2008), Marrakech, Morocco, pp. 2961–2968, May 2008. http://www.lrec-conf.org/proceedings/lrec2008/pdf/754_paper.pdf

16. Tiedemann, J.: Parallel data, tools and interfaces in opus. In: Chair, N.C.C., et al. (eds.) Proceedings of the Eight International Conference on Language Resources and Evaluation (LREC 2012), Istanbul, Turkey, pp. 2214–2218, May 2012. http://www.lrec-conf.org/proceedings/lrec2012/pdf/463_Paper.pdf

17. Tiedemann, J.: Improving the cross-lingual projection of syntactic dependencies. In: Proceedings of the 20th Nordic Conference of Computational Linguistics (NODALIDA 2015), Vilnius, Lithuania, pp. 191–199, May 2015. https://aclanthology.org/W15-1824

18. Virtanen, A., et al.: Multilingual is not enough: BERT for Finnish. CoRR abs/1912.07076 (2019). http://arxiv.org/abs/1912.07076

19. Wolf, T., et al.: Huggingface's transformers: state-of-the-art natural language processing. CoRR abs/1910.03771 (2019). http://arxiv.org/abs/1910.03771

20. Yarowsky, D., Ngai, G., Wicentowski, R.: Inducing multilingual text analysis tools via robust projection across aligned corpora. In: Proceedings of the First International Conference on Human Language Technology Research (HLT 2001), San Diego, California, pp. 1–8, March 2001. https://aclanthology.org/H01-1035

21. Zeldes, A., Liu, J.: DISRPT 2021 task 2 results (2021). https://sites.google.com/georgetown.edu/disrpt2021/results#h.gb445xshqmt7.   https://sites.google.com/georgetown.edu/disrpt2021/results

22. Zeyrek, D., Kurfalı, M.: TDB 1.1: extensions on Turkish discourse bank. In: Proceedings of the 11th Linguistic Annotation Workshop, Valencia, Spain, pp. 76–81, April 2017. https://doi.org/10.18653/v1/W17-0809. https://aclanthology.org/W17-0809

23. Zeyrek, D., Kurfalı, M.: An assessment of explicit inter- and intra-sentential discourse connectives in Turkish discourse bank. In: Proceedings of the Eleventh International Conference on Language Resources and Evaluation (LREC 2018), Miyazaki, Japan, pp. 4023–4029, May 2018. https://aclanthology.org/L18-1634

24. Zhou, L., Gao, W., Li, B., Wei, Z., Wong, K.F.: Cross-lingual identification of Ambiguous discourse Connectives for resource-poor Language. In: Proceedings of the 24th International Conference on Computational Linguistics: Technical Papers (COLING 2012), Mumbai, pp. 1409–1418, December 2012. https://aclanthology.org/C12-2138

Using Meaning Instead of Words to Track Topics

Judicael Poumay$^{(\boxtimes)}$ and Ashwin Ittoo

ULiege/HEC Liege, Rue Louvrex 14, 4000 Liege, Belgium
{judicael.poumay,ashwin.ittoo}@uliege.be

Abstract. The ability to monitor the evolution of topics over time is extremely valuable for businesses. Currently, all existing topic tracking methods use lexical information by matching word usage. However, no studies has ever experimented with the use of semantic information for tracking topics. Hence, we explore a novel semantic-based method using word embeddings. Our results show that a semantic-based approach to topic tracking is on par with the lexical approach but makes different mistakes. This suggest that both methods may complement each other.

Keywords: Topic tracking · Lexical · Semantic · Topic models

1 Introduction

Buried within the voluminous amounts of texts available online are meaningful insights, which could help in supporting business decision-making activities. Topic modelling methods extracts latent topic in a corpus [4,10] and can be used to discover these insights. Examples of applications include fraud detection [11], understanding employee and customer satisfaction [7,8]. Extracted topics can be tracked over time to understand their evolution or discover emerging one. Hence, we focus on this task of topic tracking in which the goal is to link instances of the same topic that have been extracted at different time periods.

Several methods for tracking topics have been proposed in the past [3,6,9,12, 13]. These methods use measures such as the JS divergence [9,12,13] or online topic models [3,6] which rely on lexical information to track topic across time.

However, no studies has ever experimented with using semantic information to track topics over time. Intuitively, semantic based approaches could be promising as they do not rely on simple surface form and can capture concepts such as synonymy. For example, given a topic about "AI", across time we could observe that the term "Machine Learning" has become more popular than "AI". However, a lexical approach to topic tracking would not be able to handle such lexical drift and to relate those words over time. Conversely, such lexical variation would have been captured by a semantic approach. Moreover, topic-word distributions are unstable across multiple runs [1], i.e. the resulting top words of a topic tend to change significantly. This entails that the lexical information

P. Rosso et al. (Eds.): NLDB 2022, LNCS 13286, pp. 461–468, 2022.
https://doi.org/10.1007/978-3-031-08473-7_42

we rely upon to track topics is also unstable even if the overall semantic of the topic remains the same. Thus, a semantic-based approach may be more robust.

Hence, our work aims at investigating on the use of semantic information for topic tracking and its comparison against lexical information. Therefore, as our main contribution, we propose a novel semantic topic tracking method known as Semantic Divergence (SD) based on word embeddings. As an ancillary contribution, we study the challenges of topic tracking in the context of hierarchical topic modelling.

2   Background and Related Work

2.1   Topic Modelling

LDA [4] is the first traditional topic model. At the core of LDA is a Bayesian generative model with two Dirichlet distributions, respectively for the document-topic distributions and for the topic-word distributions. These distributions are learnt and optimized via an inference procedure which enables topics to be extracted. The main weakness of LDA is that it requires the user to specify a predefined number of topics to be extracted.

More complex topic models have been proposed since LDA. In particular, HTMOT [10] was proposed to simultaneously model topic hierarchy and temporality. Specifically, HTMOT produces a topic tree in which the depth and the number of sub-topic for each branch is defined dynamically during training. Additionally, HTMOT models the temporality of topics enabling the extraction of topics that are lexically close but temporally distinct.

2.2   Topic Tracking

Topic tracking is the task of monitoring the evolution of topics through time. It was initially defined in a pilot study [2] in 1998 as the continuous automatic classification of a stream of news stories into known or new topics.

Currently, two general framework compete for topic tracking. The first stream is that of online topic models which incorporate new data incrementally [3,6]. In [3], the authors propose Online-LDA, a version of LDA able to update itself with new documents without having to access to previously processed documents. In practice, Online-LDA assumes that time is divided in slices and at each slice an LDA model is trained using the previous slice as prior. They were able to show that their system can find emerging topics by artificially injecting new topic into the news stream. They performed their experiments on the NIPS and Reuters-21578 datasets. Similarly in [6], the authors propose a model that can dynamically decide the right number of topics in an online fashion. They performed their experiments on the 20 Newsgroup and the TDT-2 datasets.

The second stream is concerned with linking topics extracted independently at different time periods [9,12,13]. In [13], the authors use about 30,000 abstracts of papers in various journals from 2000 to 2015. They then applied LDA to each year independently and linked topics using the Jensen-Shannon Divergence (JS) to measure their similarity [5]. In [12] the authors applied a similar method on news articles. However, they differ in that while [13] simply links topics together, [12] clusters them. This means that once two topic have been linked they form a cluster and subsequent topics will be compared to the whole cluster and not just the preceding topic. Finally in [9], the authors also proposed a tracking method using the JS divergence applied to scientific papers. However, they do not constraint linkage to a one-to-one mapping which allows for the fusion and splitting of topics. All of the aforementioned paper evaluated their topic tracking method using a qualitative analysis that demonstrated the performance of their technique.

We based our work on that second stream because it allows for better parallelization as time slices are processed independently.

3   Methodology

In this section, we will present our methodology for topic tracking. We will start by describing our corpus and topic extraction method. Next, we will define our SD measure. Finally, we will present the topic tracking algorithm.

3.1   Topic Extraction

To perform our experiments, we crawled 10k articles from the Digital Trends[1] archives from 2019 to 2020. This news website is mainly focused on technological news with topics such as hardware, space exploration and COVID-19. For all articles, we extracted the text, title, category and timestamp. We pre-possessed the corpus according to HTMOT [10].

To extract topics hierarchies (see Fig. 1), we used the HTMOT topic model [10]. The extracted topics are represented by a list of words and a list of entities.

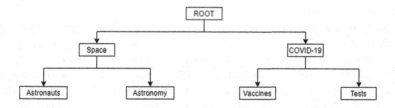

Fig. 1. Example of a topic hierarchy

We follow HTMOT [10] and only focus on the first and second level of topic extracted. Specifically, the authors observe that deeper topics becomes more esoteric making them harder to understand by annotators representing a general audience. Consequently, this makes it difficult to assess the correctness of tracked topics at deeper levels of the topic tree.

---

[1] https://www.digitaltrends.com/.

3.2   Proposed Semantic Divergence Measure

We will now describe our novel topic tracking method, which departs from the JS divergence traditionally applied in previous studies. We name our method "Semantic divergence" or SD. It uses word embeddings to measure the distance between topics. Each topic will be assigned an embedding as the sum of the embeddings of the top words in that topic weighted by their probability. Then, the distance between two topics is computed as the cosine distance of their respective embedding. We will use FastText as the word embedding. FastText helps with rare and out of vocabulary words. This is essential considering our pre-processing step includes lemmatization which may produce incorrectly spelled words. Hence the embedding of a topic is defined as follows:

$$emb(t) = \sum_{(w,p)\in t} p * FastText(w) \tag{1}$$

And the Semantic Divergence between two topics is defined as:

$$SD(t_1, t_2) = cosine(emb(t_1), emb(t_2)) \tag{2}$$

where w is a word in a topic t and p is the probability of that word.

3.3   Topic Tracking Algorithm

Finally, to track topics across time we applied HTMOT on our corpus. For each year (2019 and 2020), we obtained a corresponding topic tree. Then, we computed the distance between every topics across both years using either JS or SD. To do this we used the top 100 words and top 15 entities to represent each topic. Subsequently, we ranked order all computed pairs of topics and then iteratively selected the most similar pairs (lowest SD or JS score) such that each topic is paired only once. Finally, we used a pre-defined threshold to remove pairs with a poor score.

Note that our approach does not take into account structural information. Indeed, tracking topics in the context of hierarchical topic modelling presents another interesting challenge: there exist many possible resulting trees that are equally correct. In one run, we may extract the topic of space whose sub-topics can be grouped into space exploration and astronomy. Conversely, in another run, we may extract space exploration and astronomy as separate topics with their own sub-topics. Hence, it is difficult to leverage the structural information contained in the topic trees to track topics as it cannot be expected to respect a specific conceptual taxonomy.

4   Results: JS vs SD

In this section, we will discuss how our semantic based method compares with respect to the traditional lexical based method.

First, we studied the overlap between the two methods, i.e. the number of pairs extracted by both. We discovered that, 111 pairs were extracted with JS with a threshold of <0.4, while 121 pairs were extracted with SD with a threshold of <0.1. These threshold were set through empirical observation but may depend on the dataset used. These 111–121 pairs can be grouped into three categories (see Fig. 2). 72 pairs were the same between the two methods (60–65% of the total pairs). For example, topics such as space and video games were easily paired across both years by both methods. This already indicates that our SD method is able to pair topic across time with performance similar to JS. This leaves 39–49 pairs that are different across the two methods (35–40% of the total pairs) which we can evaluate. Out of those different pairs, we notice that in most cases one method (e.g. SD) would track/link a topic pair across both years, while the other method (e.g. JS) did not as the best possible pair was above the threshold. We are then left with 10 different pairs that can themselves be paired according to which 2019 or 2020 topic they share (see Fig. 2).

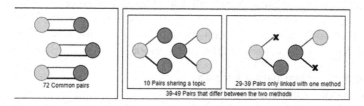

Fig. 2. The pairs extracted by both methods can be grouped into three categories. The circle represent topics and their color represent years (2019 blue; 2020 yellow). The link color represent the method used (JS red; SD green). The three categories are: 1) The pairs extracted by both methods (72). 2) The pairs that differ but share a topic (10) E.g. JS extracted the pair 4-D while SD extracted 4-E. 3) The pairs of topics that were only linked with one method (29–39). (Color figure online)

To compare the performance of the two tracking methods, we decided to use a survey comparing these 10 pairs of topics extracted by both JS and SD. Precisely, for each question, given an initial topic, annotators were shown the JS and SD pairing and asked which is better. Additionally, we also asked annotators to provide a confidence score on a scale from 1 to 5. In total, we received 38 answers coming from a small online community focused on answering surveys.[2] The survey can be found on github.[3]

Looking at the survey results (Table 1), it can be seen that SD slightly outperforms JS with 54% of annotators preferring the former to the latter. Moreover, we also note that the annotators were confident in their evaluation, with an average confidence score of 3.3. Interestingly, there is a lot of variability in the answers. Some topics were clearly better paired with one method or the other (Q3 and Q5) while for others, it wasn't as clear (Q1, Q2 and Q4).

---

[2] https://www.reddit.com/r/SampleSize/.
[3] https://github.com/JudicaelPoumay/TopicTrackingPaper.

Table 1. The "chose JS" column corresponds to the % of annotators that chose the JS pair as the best pair.

Questions	Chose JS	Confidence level
Q1	57.9% (22)	3.2
Q2	36.8% (14)	2.6
Q3	78.9% (30)	3.7
Q4	34.2% (13)	3.5
Q5	21.1% (8)	3.5
Average	46%	3.3

For example, Fig. 3 corresponds to Q1. It shows how a 2019 topic has been paired with 2020 topics using JS and SD. First, we can notice that the distance recorded between the pairs is close to the threshold for both methods. Specifically, 0.29 for the JS pair and 0.09 for the SD pair (threshold = 0.4 for JS and 0.1 for SD). This makes sense as good pairs (pairs with low JS/SD values) are extracted by both methods. Second, the 2019 topic is about social media data security. Whereas the chosen 2020 topic is about:

- Social media when paired with JS.
- Data security when paired with SD.

Hence, both pairing seems suitable, which could explain the indecisiveness of annotators. Specifically, 16 of them decided the SD pairing was better whereas 22 of them decided the JS pairing was better. Their confidence level for this question was 3.2 out of 5.

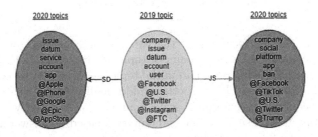

Fig. 3. A first example of different pairing between SD and JS on the same 2019 topic.

Similarly, Fig. 4 corresponds to Q5 and shows how another 2019 topic has been paired based on the two methods. Here, the 2019 topic is about web security. Whereas the chosen 2020 topic is about:

- Data security when paired with JS.
- Web security topic when paired with SD.

Moreover, the topic chosen by SD is a sub-topic of the topic chosen by JS which demonstrates the difficulty in topic tracking in a hierarchical setting. Indeed, it can be difficult to differentiate a topic from its sub-topic, especially if that sub-topic dominates the others as parent topics are the sum of their sub-topics. In this case, annotators agreed more and 30 out of 38 decided the SD pair was better. Their confidence level for this question was 3.5 out of 5.

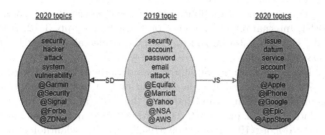

Fig. 4. A second example of different pairing between SD and JS on the same 2019 topic.

Hence, we argue that JS and SD are two fundamentally different approaches and that both have their advantages. JS is lexically driven and may work best for linking topics which tend to have a stable and precise vocabulary such as in legal documents. On the other hand, SD is driven by semantics and may be more appropriate for linking topics that have a greater lexical variability. Greater lexical variability may be the result of lexical drift over time as terms change in popularity or informal texts which do not use a standard vocabulary such as tweets. Hence, we believe that SD not only competes but complements JS for topic tracking.

5   Conclusion

In this paper, we presented a novel semantic-based topic tracking method (SD). We showed that its performance was comparable to that of the state of the art method (JS), which is lexically-based. This validates our hypothesis that semantic information is valuable for tracking topics.

Moreover, we have discussed the challenges associated with tracking topics in a topic hierarchy. First, topics and their sub-topic can be difficult to differentiate, which makes topic tracking more challenging. Second, deeper topics are more esoteric and consequently it is harder to assess the quality of their tracking. Finally, topic hierarchy may have many equally correct arrangements which makes it difficult to leverage structural information for topic tracking.

We believe that our work would benefit future studies investigating hybrid methods for topic tracking, such as by integrating lexical and semantic information.

References

1. Agrawal, A., Fu, W., Menzies, T.: What is wrong with topic modeling? And how to fix it using search-based software engineering. Inf. Softw. Technol. **98**, 74–88 (2018)
2. Allan, J., Carbonell, J.G., Doddington, G., Yamron, J., Yang, Y.: Topic detection and tracking pilot study final report (1998)
3. AlSumait, L., Barbará, D., Domeniconi, C.: On-line LDA: adaptive topic models for mining text streams with applications to topic detection and tracking. In: 2008 Eighth IEEE International Conference on Data Mining, pp. 3–12. IEEE (2008)
4. Blei, D.M., Ng, A.Y., Jordan, M.I.: Latent dirichlet allocation. J. Mach. Learn. Res. **3**, 993–1022 (2003)
5. Dagan, I., Lee, L., Pereira, F.: Similarity-based methods for word sense disambiguation. In: 35th Annual Meeting of the Association for Computational Linguistics and 8th Conference of the European Chapter of the Association for Computational Linguistics, Madrid, Spain, pp. 56–63. Association for Computational Linguistics, July 1997. https://doi.org/10.3115/976909.979625, https://aclanthology.org/P97-1008
6. Fan, W., Guo, Z., Bouguila, N., Hou, W.: Clustering-based online news topic detection and tracking through hierarchical Bayesian nonparametric models. In: Proceedings of the 44th International ACM SIGIR Conference on Research and Development in Information Retrieval, pp. 2126–2130 (2021)
7. Ibrahim, N.F., Wang, X.: A text analytics approach for online retailing service improvement: evidence from Twitter. Decis. Support Syst. **121**, 37–50 (2019).https://doi.org/10.1016/j.dss.2019.03.002, https://www.sciencedirect.com/science/article/pii/S0167923619300405
8. Jung, Y., Suh, Y.: Mining the voice of employees: a text mining approach to identifying and analyzing job satisfaction factors from online employee reviews. Decis. Support Syst. **123**, 113074 (2019)
9. Liu, H., Chen, Z., Tang, J., Zhou, Y., Liu, S.: Mapping the technology evolution path: a novel model for dynamic topic detection and tracking. Scientometrics **125**(3), 2043–2090 (2020). https://doi.org/10.1007/s11192-020-03700-5
10. Poumay, J., Ittoo, A.: HTMOT: hierarchical topic modelling over time. arXiv:2112.03104 (2021)
11. Wang, Y., Xu, W.: Leveraging deep learning with LDA-based text analytics to detect automobile insurance fraud. Decis. Support Syst. **105**, 87–95 (2018). https://doi.org/10.1016/j.dss.2017.11.001
12. Xu, G., Meng, Y., Chen, Z., Qiu, X., Wang, C., Yao, H.: Research on topic detection and tracking for online news texts. IEEE Access **7**, 58407–58418 (2019)
13. Zhu, M., Zhang, X., Wang, H.: A LDA based model for topic evolution: evidence from information science journals. In: Proceedings of the 2016 International Conference on Modeling, Simulation and Optimization Technologies and Applications (MSOTA 2016), pp. 49–54 (2016)

Sentence Alignment of Bilingual Survey Texts Applying a Metadata-Aware Strategy

Danielly Sorato[1]([⊠]) [iD] and Diana Zavala-Rojas[1,2] [iD]

[1] Research and Expertise Centre for Survey Methodology,
Universitat Pompeu Fabra, Barcelona, Spain
{danielly.sorato,diana.zavala}@upf.edu
[2] European Social Survey ERIC, London, UK

Abstract. Sentence alignment is a crucial task in the process of building parallel corpora. Off-the-shelf tools for sentence alignment generally perform well to this end. However in certain cases, depending on factors such as the sentence structure and the amount of contextual information, the sentence alignment task can be challenging and require further resources that may be difficult to find, such as domain-specific bilingual dictionaries. Although investing in creating additional linguistic resources is frequently the chosen option in these circumstances, leveraging extra-linguistic information such as sentence-level metadata can be an easier alternative to narrow the alignment search space. This paper presents a method designed for the alignment of bilingual survey questionnaires' texts, which leverages sentence-level metadata annotations. We build eight gold standards in four distinct languages to measure our sentence aligner performance, namely Catalan, French, Portuguese, and Spanish.

Keywords: Sentence alignment · Survey translation · Metadata

1 Introduction

A parallel corpus comprises a set of source texts and their translations into another language, i.e. the target text. In this context, source and target sentences can be linked through linguistic properties, such as equivalence of meaning.

The correspondence between source and target sentences is an important resource for a myriad of areas, such as machine translation [3,5,6,9], information retrieval [4,8], among others. Particularly, when such corpora comprise large amounts of data, computational methods for sentence alignment are of uttermost importance, since manual alignment becomes unfeasible.

Although widely used sentence alignment tools (e.g., Hunalign) perform well in most cases, depending on factors such as the sentence structure and the amount of contextual information, the alignment task can be hampered. Furthermore, it can be difficult to find domain-specific bilingual resources for some

© The Author(s), under exclusive license to Springer Nature Switzerland AG 2022
P. Rosso et al. (Eds.): NLDB 2022, LNCS 13286, pp. 469–476, 2022.
https://doi.org/10.1007/978-3-031-08473-7_43

language pairs, e.g. English-Catalan, which further hinders the application of alignment methods that require such linguistic resources. Therefore, in certain cases, an easier approach could be leveraging extra-linguistic sentence-level metadata to narrow down the alignment search space.

This paper presents a method for the alignment of bilingual survey texts, with the main features of the texts being domain-specific, extremely short in most cases, and having extra-linguistic metadata at the sentence level. This method of text alignment was implemented in the Multilingual Corpus of Survey Questionnaires (MCSQ) [12], which comprises survey items from large international survey projects, namely, the European Social Survey (ESS), the European Values Study (EVS), the Survey of Health Ageing and Retirement in Europe (SHARE), and the WageIndicator Survey (WIS).

We built eight gold standards in four different languages, namely Catalan, French, Portuguese, and Spanish, to compare the alignments derived from our alignment strategy with the ones resulting from LF Aligner, a wrapper that runs on top of the widely used aligner Hunalign [11]. Our results show that our metadata-aware alignment strategy achieved equal or better performance, without the need for additional linguistic resources such as model training or bilingual dictionaries.

2   Data

The Multilingual Corpus of Survey Questionnaires (MCSQ) is the first publicly available corpus of survey questionnaires. In its third version, the MCSQ contains approximately 766.000 sentences and more than 4 million tokens, comprising 306 distinct questionnaires designed in the source (British) English language and their translations into Catalan, Czech, French, German, Norwegian, Portuguese, Spanish, and Russian, adding to 29 country-language combinations (e.g., Switzerland-French).

All questionnaires in the MCSQ are composed of *survey items*. A survey item is a request for an answer with a set of answer options, and may include additional textual elements guiding interviewers and clarifying the information that should be understood and provided by respondents. The corpus and all its metadata are freely available both in the CLARINO repository [12] and the MCSQ query interface [10].

2.1   Metadata

The MCSQ contains rich metadata that facilitates finding and navigating amongst survey items. There are four variables that are relevant for the alignment method described in this work, namely, questionnaire module, survey item name, item type, and item value. The questions of the survey questionnaires are divided by thematic modules, e.g. "A - Media; social trust", "B - Politics". Therefore, filtering questions by the *questionnaire module* is useful to ensure that only questions of a same given module are being considered for alignment.

Likewise, the survey items within modules have unique names, e.g. "A1", "A3a", "A3b", that can be used to align survey items that have the same name.

The *item type* is a variable that indicates the role that a given sentence plays within a survey item. A sentence can assume one of 4 roles: introduction, instruction, request, or response. Finally, the *item value* links a given response category, or answer, to a numerical value. Examples of survey items and the aforementioned metadata are depicted in Fig. 1.

module	item_type	item_name	item_value	text
A - Media; social trust	INSTRUCTION	A1		CARD 1
A - Media; social trust	REQUEST	A1		On an average weekday, how much time, in total, do you spend watching television?
A - Media; social trust	INSTRUCTION	A1		Please use this card to answer.
A - Media; social trust	RESPONSE	A1	0	No time at all
A - Media; social trust	RESPONSE	A1	1	Less than ½ hour
A - Media; social trust	RESPONSE	A1	2	½ hour to 1 hour
A - Media; social trust	RESPONSE	A1	3	More than 1 hour, up to1½ hours
A - Media; social trust	RESPONSE	A1	4	More than 1½ hours, up to 2 hours
A - Media; social trust	RESPONSE	A1	5	More than 2 hours, up to 2½ hours
A - Media; social trust	RESPONSE	A1	6	More than 2½ hours, up to 3 hours
A - Media; social trust	RESPONSE	A1	7	More than 3 hours
A - Media; social trust	RESPONSE	A1	888	Don't know
A - Media; social trust	RESPONSE	A1	777	Refusal

Fig. 1. Example of a survey item and its item type annotations.

2.2 Gold Standard

We manually build sentence alignment gold standards for English questionnaires and its translations to 4 different languages to test the performance of our alignment strategy. In total, we built 8 gold standards using ESS questionnaires from rounds 7 and 8 comprising a total of 17, 567 alignments, from which 4673, 3755, 4444, and 4695 correspond to the Catalan, French, Portuguese, and Spanish languages, respectively. Overall, the length of the sentences contained in the questionnaires is quite small, with averages ranging between 26 to 33 characters.

Country-specific modules and responses, e.g. about religion denominations and education degrees, were removed from the gold standard, since they do not have corresponding English source versions. We also perform this same filtering for the questionnaires used as input for our baseline, the LF Aligner.

3 Method

Our alignment strategy, referred to as the *MCSQ aligner* in the remaining of this work, is centered on the very simple idea of leveraging extra-linguistic metadata to reduce the number of alignment candidates both within the questionnaire and the survey item. The pseudo-code for our alignment strategy is described in Algorithm 1[1].

---

[1] *preprocess()* is a generic preprocessing function that removes punctuation and tokenizes words in the sentences. *heuristic()* refers to a generic length-based heuristic to decide the best alignment candidates. *merge()* is a function that merges two sets of responses based on the values associated with each response.

Firstly, we filter the survey items by module and item name, so that only survey items within the same module and with the same item name are considered for alignment. Subsequently, we filter the sentences that have the same item type within a given survey item, that is, requests are aligned with requests, instructions with instructions, and so on. Then, we apply a straightforward length-based heuristic to define the alignment pairs, based on the idea that the length of a sentence is highly correlated with the length of its translation [1,2,7]. For the results hereby presented, we naively divided the number of words in the target sentence by the number of words in the source sentence, and select ratios that are closer to 1.

```
Input: Source and target questionnaires
Output: Sentence-aligned questionnaires
Function Align(sourceQuestionnaire, targetQuestionnaire):
    sourceModules = get_unique(sourceQuestionnaire);
    targetModules = get_unique(targetQuestionnaire);
    intersectingModules = sourceModules.intersection(targetModules);
    for module in intersectingModules :
        sourceItemNames = get_unique(sourceQuestionnaire[module]);
        targetItemNames = get_unique(targetQuestionnaire[module]);
        intersectingItemNames =
          sourceItemNames.intersection(targetItemNames);
        for itemName in intersectingItemNames :
            sourceItem = sourceQuestionnaire[item_name];
            targetItem = targetQuestionnaire[item_name];
            sourceItem = preprocess(sourceItem);
            targetItem = preprocess(targetItem);
            for itemType in ["introduction","instruction","request"] :
                sourceType = sourceItem[itemType] == itemType;
                targetType = targetItem[itemType] == itemType;
                segmentsAligned = heuristic(sourceType, targetType);
                save_alignments()
            endfor
            targetResponse = targetItem[itemType] == "response";
            sourceResponse = sourceItem[itemType] == "response";
            responseAligned = sourceResponse.merge(targetResponse, on =
              itemValue);
            save_alignments()
        endfor
    endfor
End Function
```

Algorithm 1: Pseudo-code of the MCSQ Aligner strategy.

Other than the basis alignment shown in the aforementioned pseudo-code, an additional condition is tested for sentences of the instruction type. For instance, a very common type of instruction in the questionnaire is one that instructs the interviewer to show an auxiliary card for the respondent to answer a given survey item. An example of this scenario is illustrated in Fig. 2, where the instruction "CARD 12" is aligned with its translation to Catalan "MOSTRAR TARGETA 12". In such scenarios, where there are more than two instructions within a given survey item, we additionally use a regular expression pattern to check for digits in the sentence. We use this as additional information to find the alignment pairs for instructions, which tend to be really short sentences, since the presence of digits in other instructions segments other than this "show card" instruction is very uncommon.

INTRODUCTION	B19	In politics people sometimes talk of "left" and "right".	En política a vegades es parla d'esquerra i de dreta.
INSTRUCTION	B19	ASK ALL	A TOTHOM
INSTRUCTION	B19	CARD 12	MOSTRAR TARGETA 12
REQUEST	B19	Using this card, where would you place yourself on this scale, where 0 means the left and 10 means the right?	Utilitzant aquesta targeta, on es col·locaria vostè en aquesta escala?
REQUEST	B19		El 0 vol dir "esquerra" i el 10 "dreta".
RESPONSE	B19	Left	ESQUERRA
RESPONSE	B19	Right	DRETA
RESPONSE	B19	Don't know	No ho sap
RESPONSE	B19	Refusal	No contesta

Fig. 2. Example of an aligned survey item containing "show card" instructions.

3.1 Metrics

To measure the performance of the MCSQ and LF aligners, we apply the precision and recall metrics described in Eqs. 1 and 2. Given a set of parallel sentences S, there is a number C of correct alignments between them. After the sentence alignment task is performed with a given aligner, T_S and C_S represents the number of total and correct alignments found by such aligner, respectively.

$$Precision = C_S/T_S \tag{1}$$

$$Recall = C_S/C \tag{2}$$

3.2 Baseline

We compare the alignments resulting from the MCSQ Aligner against the ones obtained by the LF Aligner. The LF Aligner is a wrapper around the Hunalign, which is a $C++$ implementation of the length-based Church-Gale algorithm [2]. Differently from the MCSQ Aligner, the LF Aligner uses a rich multilingual dictionary covering 832 combinations of 32 major languages, including all EU official languages. Such dictionaries are built based on the Wiktionary[2] and the Eurovoc glossary[3].

---

[2] https://www.wiktionary.org/.
[3] https://op.europa.eu/s/vU6q.

4 Results

We evaluate the MCSQ and LF aligners precision and recall using eight manually constructed gold standards in Catalan, French, Portuguese, and Spanish languages. As depicted in Table 1, the MCSQ Aligner achieved better or equal performance as the LF Aligner in most cases.

The two aligners achieved overall satisfactory performance in the benchmarks, except for the LF Aligner in the ESS round 7 Catalan questionnaire. For both the LF and the MCSQ Aligner, the highest performance was achieved with the English-French language pair. The MCSQ Aligner strategy has achieved better performance stability across languages, which is expected since it does not use language dependent resources.

Table 1. Precision and recall achieved by MCSQ and LF aligners per gold standard.

ESS round	Language	Alignment method	Precision	Recall
Round 7	Catalan (Spain)	MCSQ aligner	**0.93**	**0.93**
Round 7	Catalan (Spain)	LF aligner	0.67	0.60
Round 8	Catalan (Spain)	MCSQ aligner	0.92	0.91
Round 8	Catalan (Spain)	LF aligner	0.92	0.91
Round 7	Spanish (Spain)	MCSQ aligner	**0.91**	**0.91**
Round 7	Spanish (Spain)	LF aligner	0.90	0.90
Round 8	Spanish (Spain)	MCSQ aligner	0.92	0.91
Round 8	Spanish (Spain)	LF aligner	**0.93**	**0.92**
Round 7	Portuguese (Portugal)	MCSQ aligner	**0.93**	**0.93**
Round 7	Portuguese (Portugal)	LF aligner	0.88	0.89
Round 8	Portuguese (Portugal)	MCSQ aligner	0.94	**0.93**
Round 8	Portuguese (Portugal)	LF aligner	0.94	0.92
Round 7	French (Belgium)	MCSQ aligner	0.95	**0.94**
Round 7	French (Belgium)	LF aligner	0.95	0.93
Round 8	French (Belgium)	MCSQ aligner	0.96	0.95
Round 8	French (Belgium)	LF aligner	0.96	0.95

We further investigate how the length of the source and target sentences impacts the alignment errors. Most errors performed by the LF Aligner, especially in the Catalan, Portuguese, and Spanish benchmarks, are cases in which source or target sentences were assigned to an empty correspondence (1-0 alignment) or sentences with medium to large length, whereas the errors of the MCSQ Aligner are concentrated in small to medium length sentences.

By manually observing alignment errors, we verify that in the case of the MCSQ Aligner there is a prevalence of alignment errors were caused by the presence of many sentences of the same item type (e.g. instructions) and length within a given survey item. To circumvent this problem, it would be necessary to change our naive alignment cost computation based on sentence ratios.

As for the LF Aligner, we found that the instances of errors concerning large sentences were mostly caused by segmentation errors. Even though we provided the input questionnaires for the LF Aligner already correctly sentence segmented, we find that the it had difficulties, for instance with the Catalan symbol "·", thus re-segmenting the sentences such as "Utilitzant aquesta targeta, on es col·locaria vostè en aquesta escala?" ("Using this card, where would you place yourself on this scale") as if the "·" was a period.

Moreover, probably due to difficulties to dealing with the short sentences and the format of the text, the LF Aligner ignored the correct file segmentation provided in the input file, augmenting the sentence. For instance, a portion of the survey item that appears correctly aligned in Fig. 3 was incorrectly segmented by the LF Aligner as "Segueixi utilitzant la mateixa targeta. hauria de permetre que moltes vinguin a viure aquí", which then lead to other subsequent errors.

STILL CARD 15	CONTINUAR MOSTRANT TARGETA 15
How about people of a different race or ethnic group from most country people?	I què diria de les que són d'una raça o grup ètnic diferent al de la majoria dels espanyols?
Still use this card.	Segueixi utilitzant la mateixa targeta.
	Espanya...
Allow many to come and live here	hauria de permetre que moltes vinguin a viure aquí
Allow some	hauria de permetre que n'hi vinguin unes quantes
Allow a few	hauria de permetre que n'hi vinguin unes poques
Allow none	no hauria de permetre que n'hi vingui cap
Don't know	No ho sap
Refusal	No contesta

Fig. 3. Example of survey item that prompted segmenting errors in LF Aligner.

We cite the following limitations to this work: if the sentence-level metadata is incorrectly attributed, the error then propagates to the alignments. Furthermore, although this scenario is not very frequent in our corpus, cases where the instructions in the source and target survey items do not correspond to each other will result in incorrect alignments. The Fig. 4 depicts an example of this scenario, where the Catalan "show card" instruction does not have a correspondence with the source ones and vice-versa.

INSTRUCTION	C14	Can be asked as a country-specific question.	
INSTRUCTION	C14	To be recoded into the ESS coding frame below	
INSTRUCTION	C14		MOSTRAR TARGETA "23bRELIGIÓ"
REQUEST	C14	Which one?	De quina?

Fig. 4. Example of source and target instructions that do not correspond.

5   Conclusion

In this work, we presented our sentence alignment strategy, which leverages extra-linguistic metadata to narrow down the alignment candidates. We compared the alignments resulting from our method with the ones achieved by a widely used alignment tool, the LF Aligner, using eight gold standards in Catalan, French, Portuguese, and Spanish. The results show that, in most cases, our alignment strategy achieved better or equal precision and recall as the LF Aligner, without needing additional linguistic resources.

As future work, to improve our approach independent of linguistic resources, one option would be computing our alignment cost differently, such as using an implementation of the Gale-Church algorithm. In this sense, it would be possible to also further refine the granularity of certain item types, for instance subdividing the instructions type into instructions for the interviewer and instructions for the respondent. On the other hand, if we were to invest in linguistic resources, the options include integrating multilingual dictionaries, domain-specific bilingual lexicons, cross-lingual word or sentence embeddings, among others.

Acknowledgements. This work was developed in the SSHOC project, an EU Horizon 2020 Research and Innovation Programme (2014–2020) under Grant Agreement No. 823782. We thank Elsa Peris for her support to build the gold standards.

References

1. Brown, P.F., Lai, J.C., Mercer, R.L.: Aligning sentences in parallel corpora. In: 29th Annual Meeting of the Association for Computational Linguistics, pp. 169–176 (1991)
2. Gale, W.A., Church, K.W., et al.: A program for aligning sentences in bilingual corpora. Comput. Linguist. **19**(1), 75–102 (1994)
3. Luo, S., Ying, H., Yu, S.: Sentence alignment with parallel documents helps biomedical machine translation. arXiv preprint arXiv:2104.08588 (2021)
4. Niyogi, M., Ghosh, K., Bhattacharya, A.: Learning multilingual embeddings for cross-lingual information retrieval in the presence of topically aligned corpora. arXiv preprint arXiv:1804.04475 (2018)
5. Philip, J., Siripragada, S., Namboodiri, V.P., Jawahar, C.: Revisiting low resource status of Indian languages in machine translation. In: 8th ACM IKDD CODS and 26th COMAD, pp. 178–187 (2021)
6. Ramesh, S.H., Sankaranarayanan, K.P.: Neural machine translation for low resource languages using bilingual lexicon induced from comparable corpora. arXiv preprint arXiv:1806.09652 (2018)
7. Santos, A.: A survey on parallel corpora alignment. In: Proceedings of MI-Star, pp. 117–128 (2011)
8. Sharma, V., Mittal, N.: Refined stop-words and morphological variants solutions applied to Hindi-English cross-lingual information retrieval. J. Intell. Fuzzy Syst. **36**(3), 2219–2227 (2019)
9. Shi, X., Huang, H., Jian, P., Tang, Y.K.: Improving neural machine translation with sentence alignment learning. Neurocomputing **420**, 15–26 (2021)
10. Sorato, D., Zavala-Rojas, D.: The multilingual corpus of survey questionnaires query interface. In: Proceedings of the 5th Joint SIGHUM Workshop on Computational Linguistics for Cultural Heritage, Social Sciences, Humanities and Literature, pp. 43–48 (2021)
11. Varga, D., Halácsy, P., Kornai, A., Nagy, V., Németh, L., Trón, V.: Parallel corpora for medium density languages. In: Amsterdam Studies in the Theory and History of Linguistic Science Series, vol. 4 pp. 292, 247 (2007)
12. Zavala Rojas, D., Sorato, D., Hareide, L., Hofland, K.: [MCSQ]: the multilingual corpus of survey questionnaires (2021)

Language Resources and Evaluation

Turning Machine Translation Metrics into Confidence Measures

Ángel Navarro Martínez[(✉)] and Francisco Casacuberta Nolla

Research Center of Pattern Recognition and Human Language Technology,
Universitat Politècnica de València, 46022 Valencia, Spain
{annamar8,fcn}@prhlt.upv.es

Abstract. The Interactive Machine Translation (IMT) systems produce translations combining the knowledge of professional translators with the generation speed of the Machine Translation (MT) models. Both interact with the finality of generating error-free translations. The main goal of research in the IMT field is to reduce the effort that the professional translators have to perform during the IMT session. There are very different techniques to reduce this effort, from changing the display used to perform the corrections to changing the feedback signal that the user sends to the MT model. This article propose a method to reduce the effort performed by applying Confidence Measures (CMs) that give us a score for each translation and only let the user translate those that obtained a low score. We have trained for Recurrent Neural Network (RNN) models to approximate the scores from four of the most used metrics in MT: Bleu, Meteor, Chr-F, and Ter. We have simulated the user interaction with an Interactive-Predictive Neural Machine Translation (IPNMT) system to study the effort reduction that we can obtain while getting high-quality translations from the system. We have tested different thresholds values to consider that a translation has a low score, which gives us a transition between a convention IPNMT system where the system has to correct all the translations to an unsupervised MT system. The results showed that this method obtains very good translations – 70 points of Bleu – and reduces the human effort by 60%.

Keywords: Confidence measures · Interactive Machine Translation · Quality estimation

1 Introduction

Nowadays, research on the Machine Translation (MT) field can not produce perfect translations, although we are very near to asses human parity in many tasks [26]. To assure error-free translations, we have to require professional translators to perform a post-edit once the system has generated them or use Interactive Machine Translation (IMT) environments where the translator cooperates with the MT models to generate perfect translations. In Interactive-Predictive Neural Machine Translation (IPNMT) systems [7], the user only has to correct the first

© The Author(s), under exclusive license to Springer Nature Switzerland AG 2022
P. Rosso et al. (Eds.): NLDB 2022, LNCS 13286, pp. 479–489, 2022.
https://doi.org/10.1007/978-3-031-08473-7_44

error that he finds in the translation, then the system generates a new translation that has the user correction incorporated. This process is repeated until the user validates the complete translation. Usually, after each user correction, the system also fixes some following errors, speeding up the work and reducing the total number of words that the user has to correct compared to post-edit. There are domains where we do not require perfect translations, and Confidence Measures (CMs) [8,24] become very helpful.

CMs at the word level estimate the correctness of the words from the translations without accessing the ground truth. The system compares this score with a threshold value that is set to classify the words between correct and incorrect depending on whether their correctness score is lower or higher than the threshold set. Once the words are classified, the system follows the IPNMT procedure, where the user only has to correct the first error from the translation with the main difference that he only has to check the words classified as incorrect. As the total number of words that the user has to check decreases, it also makes the human effort required to correct all the sentences. If CMs were perfect, we could assure error-free translations with their application, but as they make mistakes, we have to suppose a drop in quality with the effort reduction.

Researchers have designed different techniques to calculate CMs, but not all are adequate for the IPNMT systems. Some of them use a large number of features or use the N-best translations for their calculation. These methods require complex computations and could interrupt the interaction process between the user and the MT model if they need more than 0.1 s to perform their calculations. In our case, we use a Recurrent Neural Network (RNN) that directly outputs the correctness estimation.

In our work, we have used the CMs method at the sentence level. Instead of giving an estimation score of each word of the translation, we calculate the score of the whole sentence. With this method, the system directly validates all the translations with a score higher than the threshold set, so the user only has to correct those classified as incorrect. As we want to test the usefulness of our CMs models at the sentence level, we will not apply them when the user corrects the incorrect translations. All the effort reduction will proceed from the sentences that are classified as correct, and the user has saved to correct.

2   Related Work

Confidence Estimation appeared first in the Speech Recognition (SR) field [29] to give a correctness score of the words that the system generates from the audio input. Slowly, researchers introduced this method to the MT field with the Statistical Machine Translation (SMT) models using target language features, translation tables, and word posterior probabilities [5,27]. With the apparition of the Neural Machine Translation (NMT) models, researchers introduced new techniques to estimate the correctness of the words that extracted helpful information from the NMT models or that train specific models that output the confidence score [12,13].

CMs have been implemented into IPNMT systems with different objectives in the last years [6]. The workbench CasMaCat [1] integrated different IMT techniques to reduce the human effort during the translation sessions. CasMaCat does not use CMs to reduce the number of words the user checks. In this case, the system painted the words with different colors according to the score obtained, giving the user a visual representation of the possible incorrect words. González et al. (2010) [9, 10] firstly implemented them on an Interactive-Predictive Statistical Machine Translation (IPSMT) system at the word level, using a statistical model similar to the IBM Model 1 to provide the estimations. Using also statistical models to calculate the confidence estimation, Navarro et al. (2021) [16] implemented the CMs into the IPNMT systems. With the improvement in the MT models from the last years, from SMT to NMT, the CMs have improved their classification accuracy, getting higher reductions on the human effort.

Inside the MT field, CMs are not only used in IMT systems. In other tasks having an estimation of the correctness of the words or translations that do not require a ground truth is also very useful, like ranking translations or generating new corpora by changing the worst words. For this reason, while the MT and CMs fields have improved in the last years, different CMs frameworks have appeared to implement confidence estimations quickly to different systems. Specia et al. (2013) [23] started with the framework Quest, a quality estimation framework that, among others, included 17 features that were summarized as the best in the literature. With the apparition of the neural models in the CM field, the frameworks OpenKiwi and DeepQuest appeared [12,13], which in addition to using statistical methods for the evaluation, also implemented neural models that output the score. These frameworks work at a word and sentence level, and DeepQuest is the first that also allows document-level quality estimations.

3   Sentence Confidence Measures

In a conventional IPNMT system, the human translator and the MT model collaborate to generate perfect translations. The user searches and fixes the first error from the translation, and with that information, the MT model generates a new translation that the user will correct again if it presents some error. Once the user has interactively translated all the source sentences, the output is an error-free set of translations. We propose an alternative where the user does not correct all the translations. In this scenario, the user only has to correct those translations that the system interprets as incorrect, according to some quality criterion. We propose to use CMs to perform the quality criterion for the first translation that the MT models generate for each source sentence.

This approach supposes a modification of the conventional IPNMT paradigm. The MT model generates an initial translation for each source sentence from the corpus. We process these initial translations with the CMs to obtain a correctness estimation that we will use to classify the translation between correct and incorrect. To perform this classification, we set a threshold value, and all the translations that obtain a score higher than it will be classified as correct, and the system outputs them as the final translation. On the other side, the translations classified as incorrect will be sent to the user to follow the conventional IPNMT paradigm with them until obtaining perfect translations.

As the system outputs all the sentences that are classified as correct without any user revision, this approach supposes a slight loss in quality. In fact, if we set the threshold to 0, the system classifies all the initial translations as correct, behaving as a fully automatic NMT system. On the contrary, if we set the threshold to 1, all the initial translations are classified as incorrect, and the system behaves as a conventional IPNMT system. So this method is valid for these cases where a small loss in translation can be tolerated for the sake of reducing the human effort.

We compute the sentence CMs by combining the scores given a word CM. We have trained four RNN models to provide a confidence estimation of each word based on four of the most common quality metrics in the MT field: Bleu, Meteor, Chr-F, and Ter [3,18,20,22]. These metrics provide a quality score of the whole sentence using the ground truth translation as a reference. In order to obtain the training dataset for our models, we had to split the metric scores between the words of the translations using the reward shaping method [2]. This method was initially used to overcome the shortcoming of the sparsity of rewards, helping to distribute a reward between intermediate steps. Given the source sentence $x_1^J = x_1, ..., x_J$, and the translation $y_1^I = y_1, ..., y_I$, the intermediate reward for the word at position i is denoted as $r_i(y_i, x_1^J)$ and is calculated as follows:

$$r_i(y_i, x_1^J) = R(y_1^i, x_1^J) - R(y_1^{i-1}, x_1^J) \tag{1}$$

where $R(y_1^i, x_1^J)$ is defined as the metric score of the partial translation y_1^i with respect to the source sentence x_1^J. Note that to use the method reward shaping, the next equation has to be fulfilled:

$$R(y_1^I, x_1^J) = \sum_{i=1}^{I} r_i(y_1^i, x_1^J) \tag{2}$$

Because some of the metrics used have a length penalization, in these cases, partial translations do not fulfill Eq. 2. For this reason, during the reward shaping in the metrics that had a length penalization, we added a special token to give all the partial translations the same length and fulfill the previous equation. To obtain the confidence value of word y_i, $c_\phi(y_i)$, is given by

$$c_\phi(y_i) = C(x_1^J, y_1^{i-1}, y_i; \phi) \tag{3}$$

where ϕ are the model parameters, and $C(x_1^J, y_1^{i-1}, y_i; \phi)$ is the model function with parameters ϕ, that receives the source sentence x_1^J, the previous words from the translation y_1^{i-1}, and the current translation word y_i to generate the confidence value for the current translation word. We used these different elements as input because they are the same that our NMT model uses to generate the translation, so we do not have to perform extra calculations to obtain the input elements and speed up the process.

From this word confidence measure equation, we perform a geometric mean of the confidence scores of all the words from the initial translation to calculate the sentence CM. This process is represented as follows:

$$c_M(y_1^I; \phi) = \sqrt[I]{\prod_{i=1}^{I} c_\phi(y_i)} \tag{4}$$

After computing the sentence CM of a translation, we classify it as correct or incorrect. To determine in which class each sentence should be, we use a threshold value that has to be set before the IPNMT session starts. If the sentence CM is lower than the threshold, the sentence is classified as incorrect, and the user will fix it, and if it is higher or equal to the threshold, the translation is classified as correct and output directly. This means that if the threshold is 1, all the translations are revised and corrected by the user, and if the threshold is 0, the system saves them without correction.

4   Experimental Setup

4.1   System Evaluation

MT evaluation is a difficult task, as each sentence has multiple translations that could be valid, but we only use one or a small set of translations as a reference to perform the quality evaluation. By extension, this is a problem that we encounter when we test our method in an IPNMT system. Although one translation has a high confidence estimation, it will decrease the quality score if it is not the same as the one used as a reference. As we want to test the human effort that we can reduce with our method while obtaining the higher quality possible, this will have repercussions on the quality scores.

We have used the metric Word Stroke Ratio (WSR) [25] to measure human effort in our experiments. WSR is computed as the total number of word strokes performed during the IPNMT session, normalized by the total number of words. In this context, we define a word stroke as the complete action of correcting one word, but it does not consider the cost of reading the new suffix provided by the system. As the user does not have to correct those translations classified as incorrect, the WSR will decrease as the number of sentences classified as correct increases.

To test the quality of the translations generated in the IPNMT session, we used the metric BiLingual Evaluation Understudy (Bleu) [18]. Bleu is computed as a geometric mean of the precision of n-grams multiplied by a factor to penalize short sentences. As we simulate the user interaction with the system, each one of the translations that are classified as incorrect provides an error-free translation after the simulated user corrects them using the reference. In this case, the Bleu score will decrease as the number of sentences classified as correct increases because the user will revise fewer translations.

4.2 Corpora

We have performed our experiments in the Spanish-English (Es-En) pair of languages from the corpus EU [4], for which we have described his statistics in Table 1. EU is a corpus extracted from the Bulletin of the European Union, which exists in all official languages and is publicly available on the internet. We have cleaned, lower-cased, and tokenized the corpus using the scripts included in the toolkit Moses [15]. Finally, once we had the corpus tokenized, we have applied the subword subdivision method Byte Pair Encoding (BPE) [21] with a maximum value of 32000 merges to generate the subwords.

Table 1. Statistics of the Spanish-English (Es-En) pair of languages of the EU corpus. K and M represents thousands and millions, respectively.

		Es-En	
Training	Sentences	214K	
	Average length	27	24
	Running words	6M	5M
	Vocabulary	84K	69K
Development	Sentences	400	
	Average length	29	25
	Running words	12K	10K
Test	Sentences	800	
	Average length	28	25
	Running words	23K	20K

4.3 Model Architecture

To train our neural models for the MT and the CM systems, we have used the open-source toolkit NMT-Keras [19]. We used the RNN architecture; as in this case, the decoding speed of the models is essential not to break the interaction between the user and the MT model. All the systems used the learning algorithm Adam [14], with a learning rate of 0.0002. We clipped the L_2 norm of the gradient to five, set the batch size to 50, and the beam size to six. The RNN models used an encoder-decoder architecture with an attention model [28] and LSTM cells [11]. We used a dimension of 512 for the encoder, decoder, attention model, and word embeddings. We only used a single hidden layer for the encoder and decoder.

The CMs models share the same architecture and parameters as the MT models. The main difference between them is that we have added a ReLu output layer of dimension one to the CM models to provide the confidence estimation of the last word sent by input.

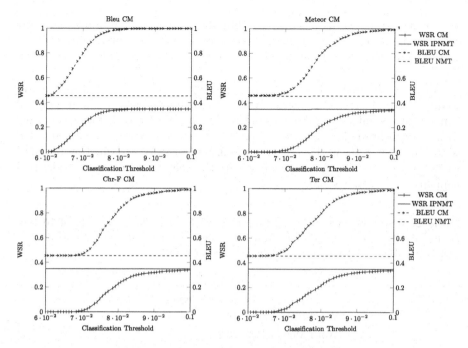

Fig. 1. Bleu translation and WSR scores across the range of thresholds between 0.06 and 0.1. The horizontal line *BLEU NMT* is the quality baseline from a conventional machine translation system. The horizontal line *WSR IPNMT* is the effort baseline from a conventional interactive-predictive machine translation system.

4.4 Results

To study the applicability of our method, we have studied how much human effort we can reduce while obtaining high-quality translations. We realized an experiment across the threshold range, from 0 to 1, where we simulated an IPNMT translation session with sentence CMs. We annotated the human effort in terms of WSR and the translation quality in terms of Bleu. With this information, we can display a graphic that shows the human effort performed and the quality of the translations generated for each threshold value. The perfect scenario of this experiment would be to obtain some threshold value where the quality decreases the fewest possible points while the human effort has been reduced to a bare minimum.

Figure 1 shows the WSR and Bleu scores for the threshold values used between 0.06 and 0.1. We have selected this range of values because, in this case, the transition between the behavior of an unsupervised NMT system to a conventional IPNMT system happens there. For thresholds lowers than 0.06, the systems classify all the translations as correct, and for thresholds higher than 0.1, they are classified as incorrect. This outcome is a consequence of using word CMs based on the intermediate steps of the MT metrics scores. As we split the sentence reward between all the words of the translation, the CM models learn to give the wrong words a score of 0, but the correct ones obtain a low score between this range. As we compute the sentence CM as a geometric mean of all the scores from a translation, the final estimation value is also between this range.

All the CMs models have obtained equivalent results; although each model seems to start the transition between the two behaviors from a different point, it happens at a similar ratio. In a perfect world, the WSR would start to decrease with a high threshold value, while the Bleu almost maintains identical. That is not our case. Still, we have to pay attention to the WSR reduction obtained while the system still generates high-quality translations, which we consider that happens at a 70 Bleu score.

Table 2. WSR reduction obtained from CMs with a translation quality of 70 Bleu points. Word Bleu, Word Meteor, Word Ter, and Word Chr-F from Navarro et al. (2022) [17]. Bleu, Meteor, Ter, and Chr-F from our results.

CM	WSR red. 70 Bleu points
Word Bleu [17]	48%
Word Meteor [17]	23%
Word Ter [17]	20%
Word Chr-F [17]	17%
Bleu	55%
Meteor	58%
Ter	57%
Chr-F	56%

Table 2 displays the WSR reduction that each CM has obtained in the threshold value where the quality of the translation gets a Bleu score of 70 points. As expected, because their transition along the threshold range was very similar, all the CM models obtained a similar WSR reduction, about 57%. We have compared the WSR reduction of our sentence CMs with previous work that used the CMs at the word level [17]. In their case, the behavior between the four CMs models was more different, as there is a clear differentiation in one of them. The Bleu CM obtained a 48% WSR reduction at the word level, a low score comparing with our results. Looking at this table, we can conclude that the CM models tested work better at the sentence level, obtaining higher WSR reductions.

5   Conclusions and Future Work

In this paper, we have proposed four different sentence CMs for IPNMT systems. We have implemented and tested them in an IPNMT environment, studying the WSR reduction and translation quality throughout all the possible threshold values. Because the quality of the translations decreases with the effort reduction, we have compared all of them in the threshold value where each one obtained a translation quality of 70 Bleu points. The four CM models have obtained a WSR reduction near the 60%. With this method, we have obtained high-quality translations while reducing more than half the human effort.

We have compared the results obtained in this project with a previous one that used these CMs at a word level. In their case, the maximum effort reduction obtained while getting high-quality translations was 48%. As we used the same CMs models to calculate our confidence estimations, we can conclude that CMs obtain better results at the sentence level. One possible cause for this is that at the word level, as the user only can check the words classified as incorrect if a previous one is misclassified can affect the translation process of the model and ends up getting a low-quality translation. In this case, working at the sentence level, misclassified translations do not affect the next ones, so the error is not propagated as in the other case.

In the project, we have only compared the translations with one reference, so it is very difficult for the translations classified as correct to obtain a perfect quality score. In the future, we want to work with a group of translators that evaluate the translations generated to see in which threshold value they think that the system starts to generate low-quality translations. We expect this threshold value to be lower than the one we set in our experiments, so the WSR reduction could be considered even higher.

Acknowledgements. This work received funds from the Comunitat Valenciana under project EU-FEDER (*IDIFEDER*/2018/025), Generalitat Valenciana under project ALMAMATER (*PrometeoII*/2014/030), Ministerio de Ciencia e Investigación/Agencia Estatal de Investigacion /10.13039/501100011033/and "FEDER Una manera de hacer Europa" under project MIRANDA-DocTIUM (RTI2018-095645-B-C22), and Universitat Politècnica de València under the program (PAID-01-21).

References

1. Alabau, V., et al.: CASMACAT: an open source workbench for advanced computer aided translation. Prague Bull. Math. Linguist. **100**(1), 101–112 (2013)
2. Bahdanau, D., et al.: An actor-critic algorithm for sequence prediction. arXiv preprint arXiv:1607.07086 (2016)
3. Banerjee, S., Lavie, A.: METEOR: an automatic metric for MT evaluation with improved correlation with human judgments. In: Proceedings of the Association for Computational Linguistics Workshop on Intrinsic and Extrinsic Evaluation Measures for Machine Translation and/or Summarization, Ann Arbor, Michigan, pp. 65–72. ACL, June 2005. https://aclanthology.org/W05-0909
4. Barrachina, S., et al.: Statistical approaches to computer-assisted translation. Comput. Linguist. **35**(1), 3–28 (2009). https://aclanthology.org/J09-1002
5. Blatz, J., et al.: Confidence estimation for machine translation. In: COLING 2004: Proceedings of the 20th International Conference on Computational Linguistics, pp. 315–321. COLING, Geneva, August 2004. https://aclanthology.org/C04-1046

6. Domingo, M., Peris, Á., Casacuberta, F.: Segment-based interactive-predictive machine translation. Mach. Transl. **31**(4), 163–185 (2018). https://doi.org/10. 1007/s10590-017-9213-3

7. Foster, G., Isabelle, P., Plamondon, P.: Target-text mediated interactive machine translation. Mach. Transl. **12**(1), 175–194 (1997)

8. González-Rubio, J., Ortíz-Martínez, D., Casacuberta, F.: Balancing user effort and translation error in interactive machine translation via confidence measures. In: Proceedings of the Association for Computational Linguistics 2010 Conference Short Papers, Uppsala, Sweden, pp. 173–177. ACL, July 2010. https://www. aclweb.org/anthology/P10-2032

9. González-Rubio, J., Ortíz-Martínez, D., Casacuberta, F.: On the use of confidence measures within an interactive-predictive machine translation system. In: Proceedings of the 14th Annual conference of the European Association for Machine Translation. EAMT, Saint Raphaël, May 2010. https://aclanthology.org/2010.eamt-1.18

10. Granell, E., Romero, V., Martínez-Hinarejos, C.D.: Study of the influence of lexicon and language restrictions on computer assisted transcription of historical manuscripts. Neurocomputing **390**, 12–27 (2020)

11. Hochreiter, S., Schmidhuber, J.: Long short-term memory. Neural Comput. **9**(8), 1735–1780 (1997)

12. Ive, J., Blain, F., Specia, L.: DeepQuest: a framework for neural-based quality estimation. In: Proceedings of the 27th International Conference on Computational Linguistics, Santa Fe, New Mexico, USA, pp. 3146–3157. ACL, August 2018. https://aclanthology.org/C18-1266

13. Kepler, F., Trénous, J., Treviso, M., Vera, M., Martins, A.F.T.: OpenKiwi: an open source framework for quality estimation. In: Proceedings of the 57th Annual Meeting of the Association for Computational Linguistics: System Demonstrations, Florence, Italy, pp. 117–122. ACL, July 2019. https://aclanthology.org/P19-3020

14. Kingma, D.P., Ba, J.: Adam: a method for stochastic optimization. arXiv preprint arXiv:1412.6980 (2017)

15. Koehn, P., et al.: Moses: open source toolkit for statistical machine translation. In: Proceedings of the 45th Annual Meeting of the Association for Computational Linguistics Companion Volume Proceedings of the Demo and Poster Sessions, Prague, Czech Republic, pp. 177–180. ACL, June 2007. https://www.aclweb.org/ anthology/P07-2045

16. Navarro, Á., Casacuberta, F.: Confidence measures for interactive neural machine translation. In: Proceedings of the IberSPEECH 2021, pp. 195–199. IberSPEECH (2021)

17. Navarro, Á., Casacuberta, F.: Neural models for measuring confidence on interactive machine translation systems. Appl. Sci. **12**(3), 1100 (2022)

18. Papineni, K., Roukos, S., Ward, T., Zhu, W.J.: BLEU: a method for automatic evaluation of machine translation. In: Proceedings of the 40th Annual Meeting of the Association for Computational Linguistics, Philadelphia, Pennsylvania, USA, pp. 311–318. ACL, July 2002. https://aclanthology.org/P02-1040

19. Peris, Á., Casacuberta, F.: NMT-Keras: a very flexible toolkit with a focus on interactive NMT and online learning. Prague Bull. Math. Linguist. **111**, 113–124, October 2018. https://ufal.mff.cuni.cz/pbml/111/art-peris-casacuberta.pdf

20. Popović, M.: chrF: character n-gram F-score for automatic MT evaluation. In: Proceedings of the Tenth Workshop on Statistical Machine Translation, Lisbon, Portugal, pp. 392–395. ACL, September 2015. https://aclanthology.org/W15-3049

21. Sennrich, R., Haddow, B., Birch, A.: Neural machine translation of rare words with subword units. In: Proceedings of the 54th Annual Meeting of the Association for Computational Linguistics (Volume 1: Long Papers), Berlin, Germany, pp. 1715–1725. ACL, August 2016. https://www.aclweb.org/anthology/P16-1162

22. Snover, M., Dorr, B., Schwartz, R., Micciulla, L., Makhoul, J.: A study of translation edit rate with targeted human annotation. In: Proceedings of the 7th Conference of the Association for Machine Translation in the Americas: Technical Papers, pp. 223–231. AMTA, Cambridge, Massachusetts, August 2006. https://aclanthology.org/2006.amta-papers.25

23. Specia, L., Shah, K., De Souza, J.G., Cohn, T.: QuEst-a translation quality estimation framework. In: Proceedings of the 51st Annual Meeting of the Association for Computational Linguistics: System Demonstrations, Sofia, Bulgaria, pp. 79–84. ACL, August 2013. https://aclanthology.org/P13-4014

24. Specia, L., Turchi, M., Cancedda, N., Cristianini, N., Dymetman, M.: Estimating the sentence-level quality of machine translation systems. In: Proceedings of the 13th Annual conference of the European Association for Machine Translation, vol. 9, pp. 28–35. EAMT (2009)

25. Tomás, J., Casacuberta, F.: Statistical phrase-based models for interactive computer-assisted translation. In: Proceedings of the COLING/ACL 2006 Main Conference Poster Sessions, Sydney, Australia, pp. 835–841. ACL, July 2006. https://aclanthology.org/P06-2107

26. Toral, A.: Reassessing claims of human parity and super-human performance in machine translation at WMT 2019. In: Proceedings of the 22nd Annual Conference of the European Association for Machine Translation, Lisboa, Portugal, pp. 185–194. EAMT, November 2020. https://aclanthology.org/2020.eamt-1.20

27. Ueffing, N., Macherey, K., Ney, H.: Confidence measures for statistical machine translation. In: Proceedings of Machine Translation Summit IX: Papers, MTSummit, New Orleans, USA, September 2003. https://aclanthology.org/2003.mtsummit-papers.52

28. Vaswani, A., et al.: Attention is all you need. arXiv preprint arXiv:1706.03762 (2017)

29. Wessel, F., Schluter, R., Macherey, K., Ney, H.: Confidence measures for large vocabulary continuous speech recognition. IEEE Trans. Speech Audio Process. 9(3), 288–298 (2001)

A Comparison of Transformer-Based Language Models on NLP Benchmarks

Candida Maria Greco, Andrea Tagarelli[(✉)], and Ester Zumpano

DIMES, University of Calabria, Rende (CS), Italy
{candida.greco,tagarelli,zumpano}@dimes.unical.it

Abstract. Since the advent of BERT, Transformer-based language models (TLMs) have shown outstanding effectiveness in several NLP tasks. In this paper, we aim at bringing order to the landscape of TLMs and their performance on important benchmarks for NLP. Our analysis sheds light on the advantages that some TLMs take over the others, but also unveils issues in making a complete and fair comparison in some situations.

Keywords: BERTology · Deep learning · Benchmarks

1 Introduction

Given the variety and complexity of NLP problems, benchmarks have long played a central role in NLP research, as they are the reference point to assess performance and make comparison of different solutions to NLP tasks. By analyzing the models also w.r.t. human level performance, benchmarks can be used to spot fundamental issues in the models, thus triggering the need for creating enhanced benchmarks or devising improvements in the existing models.

In the last few years, deep pre-trained language models based on the Transformer paradigm, such as BERT, have emerged showing outstanding effectiveness in several NLP tasks. Their ability to learn a contextual language understanding model allows for capturing language semantics and non-linear relationships between terms, including subtle and complex lexical patterns such as the sequential structure and long-term dependencies, thus obtaining comprehensive local and global feature representations of a text, without the need for feature engineering.

With such premises of groundbreaking technology, a plethora of models have indeed been developed at a surprisingly high rate, and this growth is expected to hold in the near future. This implies a difficulty in keeping pace with the overwhelming number of Transformer-based models for NLP.

Our motivation for this work stems from the above observations, and is supported by a lack in the literature of an extensive comparative analysis of most *Transformer-based language models* (TLMs) over the landscape of NLP benchmarks. Here we aim to contribute filling this gap in a twofold way: we consider a selection of different types of benchmarks for NLP, according to the interest they attracted as evaluation contexts for the most relevant as well as recently developed English TLMs, spanning the years 2019–2021; by comparing and analyzing the TLM performances on the NLP benchmarks, we shed light on the advantages that some methods take over the competitors, but also we unveil difficulties for a complete and fair comparison in some situations.

In the remainder of the paper, we first briefly overview main TLMs, then we discuss the NLP benchmarks considered in this study. Next, we provide our analysis of the comparison of TLMs on the NLP benchmarks, followed by a discussion on main findings, limitations and further perspectives.

2   Background on Transformer-Based Language Models

BERT [6] is regarded as the first TLM to represent a breakthrough in natural language understanding. It consists of a stack of Transformer encoder layers and its key advantages include the bidirectional unsupervised pre-training and the unified architecture across different tasks. The bidirectionality is obtained through the Masked Language Modeling (MLM) task, whose goal is to predict masked input words from unlabeled text by conjointly conditioning on left and right context-words. BERT also uses a Next Sentence Prediction (NSP) task, which is to determine if a sequence is subsequent to another.

RoBERTa [21] is based on BERT with substantial changes such as a much longer pre-training, with more training data, and the removal of the NSP task. AlBERT [16] improves upon the memory consumption of BERT while increasing the training speed, by leveraging on factorized embedding parameterization, which decomposes word embeddings in smaller matrices, and cross-layer parameter sharing across layers; moreover, AlBERT replaces the NSP task with Sentence-Order Prediction (SOP). DistilBERT [30] is a smaller version of BERT obtained through knowledge distillation. SpanBERT [12] masks adjacent random spans of text instead of single tokens like BERT does, and its training objective is to predict each token of the span by using only the observed tokens at the span boundaries. S-BERT resp. S-RoBERTa [29] are a modified version of BERT resp. RoBERTa specifically designed for semantic textual similarity, and use two Siamese and triplet networks to obtain semantically-expressive fixed-sized sentence embeddings. DeBERTa [10] introduces two novel techniques: the disentangled attention mechanism, which separates content and relative position encodings in two vectors, and enhanced mask decoder, which allows the model to consider relative position in all layers and absolute position when masked words need to be decoded.

GPT2 [26] is based on multi-layer Transformer decoders. Like its predecessor GPT, the core idea is to eliminate the task-specific model and directly use the pre-trained model for downstream tasks. GPT3 [3] has many more parameters than GPT2 (175B parameters), improving task-agnostic performance. T5 [27] is a unified approach that handles all the language problems as a text-to-text problem. The architecture, unsupervised objective, pre-training datasets, transfer learning approaches and scaling choices are the result of empirical investigations of the authors on many NLP approaches.

ELECTRA [4] uses a discriminative approach in the pre-training phase, whose task is to replace random tokens with plausible generated tokens so that the model has to discriminate real tokens from credible but fake tokens.

BART [17] consists of a bidirectional encoder, following BERT, and a left-to-right auto-regressive decoder, following GPT. It is pre-trained by first corrupting input text and then training the model to get back the original document. A key aspect is the noising flexibility, i.e., it allows to arbitrary choose any type of document corruption, including changing its length.

In DPR [13], two BERT encoders are combined to deal with open-domain question-answering. LongFormer [2] is a modified Transformer designed to handle long text sequences, combining local and global attention in order to reduce the standard self-attention operations. A variant of Longformer, Longformer-Encoder-Decoder (LED), simplifies the long sequences handling for sequence-to-sequence tasks such as summarization and translation. Like Longformer, Big-Bird [39] reduces the computational and memory cost of attention operations combining random attention, local attention and global attention. It is pretrained using the MLM objective starting from a RoBERTa checkpoint.

ERNIE [43] utilizes knowledge graphs to extract knowledge information with MLM and NSP tasks as the pre-training objectives, while a new pre-training objective is proposed to combine textual and knowledge features. ERNIE 3.0 [33] is a unified multi-paradigm pre-training framework that, through collaborative pre-training among multi-task paradigms, can handle both understanding and generation tasks with few-shot learning or fine-tuning.

LUKE [36] obtains contextualized representations of words and entities, treated as independent tokens. Self-attention mechanism in LUKE computes attention scores discriminating the types of tokens (words or entities). The pre-training objective is to mask random words and entities of an entity-annotated corpus.

XLNet [37] is a permutation language model that exploits the benefits of autoregressive models and denoising autoencoding models. It does not rely on masking approaches like BERT, but it permutes the factorization order of the context so that the model is forced to predict the target with a randomly ordered context. XLNet introduces a new self-attention mechanism called two-stream self-attention, where one stream is for content and the other is for the query. Prophetnet [25] uses a novel objective to encourage a model considering multiple future tokens instead of focusing on one token at a time. Moreover, it uses the n-stream self-attention mechanism, an extension of the two-stream self-attention proposed in XLNet to predict next n tokens simultaneously.

In Pegasus [41], the pre-training task is similar to extractive summarization, as relevant sentences are corrupted or removed and the aim is to regenerate them as a single sequence given the remainder of the sentences.

3   Benchmarks and Tasks

We organize our overview of benchmarks into six categories: question answering (QA), relation extraction (RE), document classification (DC), abstractive summarization (AS), semantic text similarity (STS), and multi-task benchmarks.

Question Answering. QA concerns automatically answering natural language questions, where answers can either be selected or generated, in a closed- or open-domain, and might rely on knowledge bases and automated reasoning.

One of the most popular QA benchmarks is SQuAD [28], which includes 100k crowdsourced questions on Wikipedia articles. Given a question and a Wikipedia passage, the task is to extract the answer span in the passage. There are two versions of the benchmark: SQuAD v1.1, where questions have always an answer in the corresponding passage, and SQuAD v2.0, which admits unanswerable questions. NewsQA [34] consists of 119k crowdsourced questions on a set of 10k CNN news articles. Given a question and an article, the task is to extract the answer span from the article. The span length is arbitrary and some questions are unanswerable. In SearchQA [8], 140k question-answer pairs are crawled from the J! Archive and augmented through web page snippets from Google. HotpotQA [38] involves multi-hop reasoning on 113k Wikipedia-based question-answer pairs, and a competing model is required to output also the supporting facts used to derive the answer.

Natural Questions (NQ) [14] contains about 300k examples of real questions issued to the Google search engine; given a question and a Wikipedia page, it is required to return a long answer and a short answer. SWAG [6,40] contains 113k sentence-pair completion examples; the goal is to choose the most credible prosecution of a sentence, given four possible choices. RACE [15] consists of 100k questions and 28k passages, created by human experts; given a question and a passage, the task is to choose the correct answer among four possible candidates. In Wikihop [35], multi-hop reading comprehension of Wikipedia articles is needed to answer multiple-choice questions.

Relation Extraction. RE requires the detection and classification of semantic relationships from a text. A major reference for RE is TACRED [42], which includes 100k examples for supervised Knowledge Base Population (KBP) relation extraction.[1] Given a sentence, the task is to predict the relation between two spans within the sentence, i.e., the subject and the object, by choosing from the TAC KBP relation types or no relation otherwise [12].

Document Classification. DC is to classify documents into one or more categories. Exemplary benchmarks in this context are IMDB for sentiment classification of movie reviews,[2] and Yelp datasets for users' star prediction (Yelp-5) and review polarity (Yelp-2).

Abstractive Summarization. AS is the task of generating a concise summary of a given text, based only on the reading comprehension of the model and using words from its own vocabulary. CNN/DM [11,22,31] is one of the representative datasets for AS, which consists of almost 300k examples of news articles from CNN and Daily Mail websites, paired with multi-sentence summaries. Unlike CNN/DM, where summaries tend to be similar to the article sentences, XSum [23], created from BBC articles, is highly abstractive and focuses

---

[1] https://tac.nist.gov/2015/KBP/.

[2] http://nlpprogress.com/english/sentiment_analysis.html.

on the *extreme summarization* task, i.e., to generate a single-sentence summary. Arxiv [5] builds on 215K scientific articles from the homonymous repository, where the abstracts of the papers are used as gold summaries. Analogously, the abstracts of patents are used as gold summaries in BigPatent [32], which includes 1.3 million of U.S. patents retrieved from the Google Patents Public Datasets.

Semantic Textual Similarity. STS is to determine semantic similarity relations between texts. An important benchmark for STS is STS-2016 [1], where the similarity degree of any two sentences is assigned a real-valued score ranging between 0 (semantic independence) and 5 (semantic equivalence).

Multitask Benchmarks. The well-known GLUE is a collection of nine NLU tasks having different domain, difficulty level, and data size. The tasks comprise both single-sentence and sentence-pair input modes and cover linguistic acceptability (CoLA), sentiment classification (SST-2), paraphrase identification (MRPC, QQP), sentence similarity (STS-B) and inference tasks (MNLI, QNLI, RTE, WNLI). SuperGLUE is a GLUE-styled benchmark with additional challenging tasks on question answering (BoolQ, COPA, MultiRC, ReCoRD), coreference resolution (WSC), word sense disambiguation (WiC), and natural language inference (CB, RTE). Both benchmarks assess a model by averaging its scores over the various tasks. While GLUE benchmarks concern natural language understanding tasks, the more recent GLGE [19] focuses on 8 generative tasks, covering abstractive summarization, answer-aware question generation, conversational question answering, and personalizing dialogue, each with three difficulty levels (i.e., easy, medium, hard).

4   Analysis

We present here our analysis of TLMs on the NLP benchmarks. To retrieve the performance scores, we referred to the original works of each TLM, with the complementary support of publicly available benchmark leaderboards (Table 1) that we accessed on February-March 2022.

Comparison of the Language Models on the Benchmarks. We begin with getting an overview of the popularity of the benchmarks in terms of TLMs involved. As shown in Table 2, we notice a higher participation in QA benchmarks and GLUE benchmarks, which is not surprising as they have been active for longer than other benchmarks; nonetheless, more recent benchmarks, such as GLGE, have been attracting attention from more advanced TLMs. In Fig. 1, we report the % scores of the top-3 TLM performers, also with the addition of BERT when available, for selected benchmarks.

In GLUE, the best TLM is ERNIE, which is also ranked 3rd in absolute position par with a combination of DeBERTa with CLEVER fine-tuning according to the current leaderboard. While BERT was the first TLM to advance GLUE state-of-the-art, ERNIE, DeBERTa and T5 have now pushed the benchmark to

Table 1. NLP benchmarks and corresponding leaderboards

Benchmarks	Leaderboards
GLUE	https://gluebenchmark.com/leaderboard
SuperGLUE	https://super.gluebenchmark.com/leaderboard
SQuAD v1.1	https://paperswithcode.com/sota/question-answering-on-squad11-dev
SQuAD v2.0	https://rajpurkar.github.io/SQuAD-explorer/
SWAG	https://leaderboard.allenai.org/swag/submissions/public
RACE	https://paperswithcode.com/sota/reading-comprehension-on-race
GLGE	https://microsoft.github.io/glge/
Yelp-2	https://paperswithcode.com/sota/text-classification-on-yelp-2
Yelp-5	https://paperswithcode.com/sota/text-classification-on-yelp-5
IMDB	https://paperswithcode.com/sota/text-classification-on-imdb
	https://paperswithcode.com/sota/sentiment-analysis-on-imdb
TACRED	https://paperswithcode.com/sota/relation-extraction-on-tacred
Wikihop	https://paperswithcode.com/sota/question-answering-on-wikihop
HotpotQA	https://hotpotqa.github.io/
NQ	https://ai.google.com/research/NaturalQuestions/leaderboard
STS-2016	https://paperswithcode.com/sota/semantic-textual-similarity-on-sts16
CNN/DM	https://paperswithcode.com/sota/abstractive-text-summarization-on-cnn-daily
XSum	https://paperswithcode.com/sota/text-summarization-on-x-sum
Arxiv	https://paperswithcode.com/sota/text-summarization-on-arxiv
BigPatent	https://paperswithcode.com/sota/text-summarization-on-bigpatent

Table 2. NLP benchmarks and involved TLMs

Benchmarks	Methods
Question-answering	
SQuAD v1.1	BERT, LUKE, SpanBERT, RoBERTa, DeBERTa, DistilBERT, AlBERT, T5, ELECTRA, BART, DPR
SQuAD v2.0	BERT, SpanBERT, RoBERTa, DeBERTa, AlBERT, ELECTRA, GPT-3, XLNet
NewsQA	BERT, SpanBERT, RoBERTa, AlBERT, BART
SearchQA	BERT, SpanBERT
HotpotQA	BERT, SpanBERT, RoBERTa, DPR, Longformer, BigBird
NQ	BERT, SpanBERT, RoBERTa, DPR, Longformer, BigBird, GPT-3
Wikihop	Longformer, BigBird
SWAG	BERT, RoBERTa, DeBERTa, AlBERT, T5, BART, BigBird, XLNet, Prophetnet
RACE	BERT, RoBERTa, DeBERTa, AlBERT, GPT-3, XLNet
Relation extraction	
TACRED	BERT, SpanBERT, ERNIE, LUKE
Document classification	
IMDB	BERT, RoBERTa, DistilBERT, Longformer, BigBird, XLNet
Yelp	Bigbird, RoBERTa, BERT, XLNet
Semantic textual similarity	
STS-2016	S-BERT, S-RoBERTA, BERT
Abstractive summarization	
CNN/DM	BART, T5, GPT-2, Pegasus, ProphetNet
XSUM	BART, Pegasus, BigBird
Arxiv	LED, Pegasus, BigBird
BigPatent	Pegasus, BigBird
Multitask	
GLUE	BERT, SpanBERT, RoBERTa, DeBERTa, DistilBERT, AlBERT, T5, ELECTRA, BART, BigBird, ERNIE
SuperGLUE	BERT, RoBERTa, DeBERTa, AlBERT, T5, ERNIE, GPT-3
GLGE	ProphetNet, BART

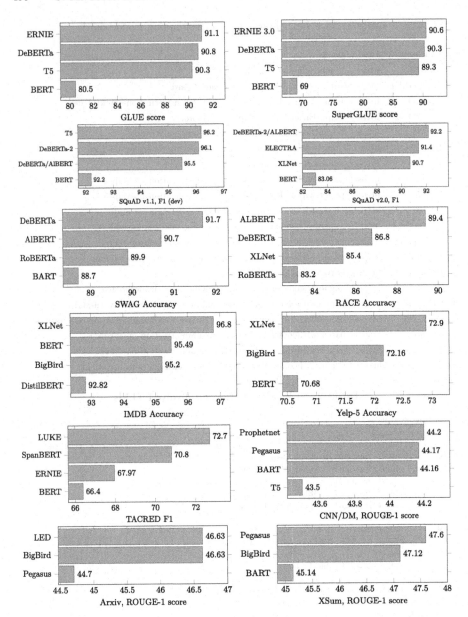

Fig. 1. Best-performing TLMs on selected NLP benchmarks

the next level achieving impressive results. A similar scenario can be found in SuperGLUE, where ERNIE 3.0, DeBERTa and T5 represent the top-3 TLMs, with even a larger score-gap to BERT than in GLUE. In absolute terms, ERNIE 3.0 obtains the 3rd position among all NLP methods in the leaderboard. Notably, DeBERTa is able to beat the SuperGLUE human baselines, thus marking a milestone toward the general-purpose language models performance [10].

The GLGE benchmarks provide scores of BART and ProphetNet as strong baselines and available on the leaderboard. In GLGE-Easy, ProphetNet outperforms BART and is ranked absolute 3rd, while in GLGE-Medium and GLGE-Hard settings, ProphetNet and BART are respectively ranked first.

In SQuAD v1.1, the majority of TLMs have been evaluated on development set (for short, dev set), since the test set was not released to the public. Largest T5 (11B parameters) achieves the best F1 score, improved only by a model based on XLNet [18]. The original papers of RoBERTa, AlBERT, DeBERTa and ELECTRA present dev F1 scores on the benchmark not shown in the SQuAD leaderboard, while the T5 paper shows a higher score than that reported in the leaderboard, which may be due to an earlier version of the paper reporting a score of 95.64. According to the scores reported in the papers, the leaderboard on dev F1 would change to the following order: T5 (96.22), DeBERTa/AlBERT (95.5), and XLNet (95.1), but recent versions of DeBERTa[3] enhance performance on SQuAD reaching a dev F1 score of 96.1. Test set of SQuAD v2.0 is not public too, but various TLMs have been submitted for evaluation on test set with scores available on the leaderboard. Also in this case, recent versions of DeBERTa reach AlBERT in the first position (92.2), followed by ELECTRA and XLNet. In the leaderboard, we notice a large use of ensemble models for this task.

The SWAG leaderboard presents scores for TLMs that are not included in the original papers. DeBERTa is ranked first among all NLP methods on SWAG. In the absolute ranking, AlBERT also obtains the third position after a modified version of RoBERTa, called ALUM-RoBERTa-large [20]. From the leaderboard, we notice the predominant use of TLMs for this task.

According to the original papers, the top three TLMs in RACE are AlBERT (89.4), DeBERTa (86.8) and XLNet (85.4). In the leaderboard, top positions are taken by ensemble of TLMs, while AlBERT score from [16] is not reported in the leaderboard, and the same holds for the XLNet score.

From the leaderboards of Yelp-5 and Yelp-2, we retrieve the XLNet accuracy scores, whereas the XLNet paper reports the error rates. On XLNet paper it is also reported the error rate of BERT on Yelp-2 and Yelp-5, from which the accuracy scores can be calculated. The leaderboard of Yelp-5 shows also the accuracy score of BigBird (which matches the F1 micro-averaged score reported in the original paper). Performance on Yelp-2 is not reported, since the only available accuracy score refers to XLNet and it is shown in the relative leaderboard.

On IMDB, two leaderboards are available (cf. Table 1), which report different accuracy scores for XLNet, with the one matching the performances of XLNet and BigBird shown in their respective papers (for the latter, the original paper reports the micro-averaged F1 for both BigBird and RoBERTa), and the other one including the accuracy scores of BERT and DistilBERT. In TACRED, the top-3 TLMs are LUKE, SpanBERT and ERNIE. According to the available leaderboard, the best absolute method uses SpanBERT. The BERT score is from the SpanBERT work [12].

---

[3] https://github.com/microsoft/DeBERTa.

As regards HotpotQA, results are known from the original papers of Long-former [2] and BigBird [39], both using the distractor setting of the benchmark and F1 metric. BigBird achieves better performance on test set, with a score of 73.6 against 73.2 by Longformer. In the current leaderboard, we observe that the method in the top position (submitted on 28 Jan 2022) is based on AlBERT and achieves a score of 76.54, while BigBird and Longformer are ranked 20th and 21th, respectively. Analogously, BigBird and Longformer are tested on WikiHop benchmark. From the original papers and the available leaderboard, BigBird outperforms Longformer (82.3 against 81.9). Bigbird is also the best absolute method according to the leaderboard. In NQ, BigBird achieves in the current leaderboard the 6th position for long answer setting (77.78 on test F1) and the 24th position in short answer setting (57.85 on test F1).

Concerning semantic textual similarity, S-BERT and S-RoBERTa were tested on STS-2016 without using any specific STS training data [29]. From the reported performance, S-RoBERTa achieves the best score against S-BERT and the competitors. In the current leaderboard, S-RoBERTA is ranked 9th.

In AS tasks, we notice the predominant presence of Pegasus in the top-3 TLMs. From the available leaderboard of CNN/DM, the current top model w.r.t. ROUGE-1 metric is a recent TLM called *GLM* [7]. On Arxiv, XSum and BigPatent, best performance of BigBird is obtained by leveraging Pegasus; this version is known as BigBird-Pegasus [39]. In [2] BigBird and LED are ranked the same for Arxiv on ROUGE-1 metric, but LED outperforms BigBird on ROUGE-2 and ROUGE-L; however, in the Arxiv leaderboard, the LED score is missing. On XSum, the "Mixed and Stochastic" version of Pegasus outperforms BigBird and BART with a score of 47.6. In the leaderboard of XSum, the score of BigBird-Pegasus is missing, while the reported Pegasus score refers to the version of the model trained on HugeNews. As regards BigPatent, BigBird-Pegasus and Pegasus achieve ROUGE-1 score of 60.64 and 53.63, respectively. In the BigPatent leaderboard, it is just reported BigBird-Pegasus, with no competitors.

It should be emphasized that it is not always possible to compare all the models applied to the same benchmark, due to different choices adopted by researchers in the experimental settings. In NewsQA, SearchQA, HotpotQA and NQ, the authors of SpanBERT use a simplified version of the benchmarks taken from the MRQA shared task [9]; for example, in NQ, only the short answers (SA) are considered, and long answers (LA) are used as context, while in NewsQA unanswerable questions or without annotator agreement are discarded. The authors experimented also with BERT on those MRQA tasks highlighting the superior performance of SpanBERT. In [24], we can observe a fair comparison of BERT, XLNet, RoBERTa, AlBERT and BART on NewsQA in terms of F1 score and using the base version of all of them. RoBERTa achieved the best results, followed by BART, XLNet, BERT and AlBERT.

Main Findings, Limitations and Further Perspectives. In this paper, we have discussed how most existing TLMs perform on well-known NLP benchmarks. Our general objective was to provide a short guide on the ability of

TLMs to achieve significant performance on fundamental NLP tasks. We believe this can be useful not only to practitioners who may want to know which TLM should be preferred on given tasks, but also to NLP specialists looking for baselines and competitors for their own methods, or for methods that can inspire new solutions for the NLP problems.

In the attempt of answering about the extent to which TLMs are able to perform well, or even close to human level, we have ascertained that TLMs can achieve very high or near-optimal performance in some tasks (e.g., IMDB and SQuAD v1.1), whereas others (e.g., Yelp-5 and TACRED) indicate that the margins of improvement for TLMs are still large.

Nonetheless, our major findings in this work go beyond the TLM performance cases. In fact, we have noticed that the picture on NLP benchmark scores cannot always be complete or totally certain, which depends on various factors. For instance, the benchmark leaderboards can report methods' scores that are not present in the original works (sometimes due to the unavailability of test sets during the benchmark competition, or simply because others than the method's authors applied the method to the benchmark data). It also happens that the benchmark leaderboards are not up-to-date w.r.t. all relevant TLM scores (e.g., T5 in SQuAD v1.1 on the dev set), or they can miss new emerging TLMs. Overall, for benchmarks like GLUE and SQuAD, the involved methods turn out to be comparable and we have indeed shown the top performers, but for other benchmarks, such as NewsQA and NQ, it is difficult to get a fair comparison due to differences between the benchmark and the method in terms of experimental setup (e.g., open-domain vs. closed-domain), dataset modifications or simplifications, and variations in the assessment criteria.

Our study has also a number of limitations. First, the length constraints of this paper forced us to make a selection from all existing TLMs and benchmarks; in this respect, our preference went to most popular and/or relevant models and tasks, although we had to leave out of consideration challenging problems such as coreference resolution, or machine translation and related multi-/cross-lingual tasks, as well as emerging TLMs such as REALM, ProphetNet-X and MASS. Second, we restricted our analysis to the original versions of TLMs, although existing variants (in terms of architecture components, training procedures, and parameter settings) could have also been used on NLP benchmarks. Third, our study discarded tasks for specific domains, such as the legal and biomedical ones, which have their own competitions and benchmarks. Therefore, we recognize the need for further investigating the performance of TLMs on NLP benchmarks to fill the lack of knowledge on the above points.

References

1. Agirre, E., et al.: SemEval-2016 task 1: semantic textual similarity, monolingual and cross-lingual evaluation. In: Proceedings of SemEval@NAACL-HLT, pp. 497–511 (2016)
2. Beltagy, I., Peters, M.E., Cohan, A.: Longformer: the long-document transformer. CoRR arXiv:2004.05150 (2020)

3. Brown, T., et al.: Language models are few-shot learners. In: Proceedings of NeurIPS, pp. 1877–1901 (2020)
4. Clark, K., Luong, M., Le, Q.V., Manning, C.D.: ELECTRA: pre-training text encoders as discriminators rather than generators. In: Proceedings of ICLR (2020)
5. Cohan, A., et al.: A discourse-aware attention model for abstractive summarization of long documents. In: Proceedings of NAACL-HTL, pp. 615–621 (2018)
6. Devlin, J., Chang, M., Lee, K., Toutanova, K.: BERT: pre-training of deep bidirectional transformers for language understanding. In: Proceedings of NAACL-HLT, pp. 4171–4186 (2019)
7. Du, Z., et al.: GLM: general language model pretraining with autoregressive blank infilling. In: Proceedings of ACL (2022)
8. Dunn, M., Sagun, L., Higgins, M., Güney, V.U., Cirik, V., Cho, K.: SearchQA: a new Q&A dataset augmented with context from a search engine. CoRR arXiv:1704.05179 (2017)
9. Fisch, A., et al.: MRQA 2019 shared task: evaluating generalization in reading comprehension. In: Proceedings of MRQA@EMNLP, pp. 1–13 (2019)
10. He, P., Liu, X., Gao, J., Chen, W.: DeBERTa: decoding-enhanced BERT with disentangled attention. In: Proceedings of ICLR (2021)
11. Hermann, K.M., et al.: Teaching machines to read and comprehend. In: Proceedings of NIPS, pp. 1693–1701 (2015)
12. Joshi, M., Chen, D., Liu, Y., Weld, D.S., Zettlemoyer, L., Levy, O.: SpanBERT: improving pre-training by representing and predicting spans. Trans. Assoc. Comput. Linguist. **8**, 64–77 (2020)
13. Karpukhin, V., et al.: Dense passage retrieval for open-domain question answering. In: Proceedings of EMNLP, pp. 6769–6781 (2020)
14. Kwiatkowski, T., et al.: Natural questions: a benchmark for question answering research. Trans. Assoc. Comput. Linguist. **7**, 452–466 (2019)
15. Lai, G., Xie, Q., Liu, H., Yang, Y., Hovy, E.H.: RACE: large-scale reading comprehension dataset from examinations. In: Proceedings of EMNLP, pp. 785–794 (2017)
16. Lan, Z., Chen, M., Goodman, S., Gimpel, K., Sharma, P., Soricut, R.: ALBERT: a lite BERT for self-supervised learning of language representations. In: Proceedings of ICLR (2020)
17. Lewis, M., et al.: BART: denoising sequence-to-sequence pre-training for natural language generation, translation, and comprehension. In: Proceedings of ACL, pp. 7871–7880 (2020)
18. Li, X., Sun, X., Meng, Y., Liang, J., Wu, F., Li, J.: Dice loss for data-imbalanced NLP tasks. In: Proceedings of ACL, pp. 465–476 (2020)
19. Liu, D., et al.: GLGE: a new general language generation evaluation benchmark. In: Proceedings of ACL/IJCNLP, pp. 408–420 (2021)
20. Liu, X., et al.: Adversarial training for large neural language models. CoRR arXiv:2004.08994 (2020)
21. Liu, Y., et al.: RoBERTa: a robustly optimized BERT pretraining approach. CoRR arXiv:1907.11692 (2019)
22. Nallapati, R., Zhou, B., dos Santos, C.N., Gülçehre, Ç., Xiang, B.: Abstractive text summarization using sequence-to-sequence RNNs and beyond. In: Proceedings of CoNLL, pp. 280–290 (2016)
23. Narayan, S., Cohen, S.B., Lapata, M.: Don't give me the details, just the summary! Topic-aware convolutional neural networks for extreme summarization. In: Proceedings of EMNLP, pp. 1797–1807 (2018)

24. Pearce, K., Zhan, T., Komanduri, A., Zhan, J.: A comparative study of transformer-based language models on extractive question answering. CoRR arXiv:2110.03142 (2021)
25. Qi, W., et al.: ProphetNet: predicting future n-gram for sequence-to-sequence pre-training. In: Proceedings of EMNLP, pp. 2401–2410 (2020)
26. Radford, A., et al.: Language models are unsupervised multitask learners. OpenAI Blog **1**(8), 9 (2019)
27. Raffel, C., et al.: Exploring the limits of transfer learning with a unified text-to-text transformer. J. Mach. Learn. Res. **21**, 140:1–140:67 (2020)
28. Rajpurkar, P., Zhang, J., Lopyrev, K., Liang, P.: SQuAD: 100, 000+ questions for machine comprehension of text. In: Proceedings of EMNLP, pp. 2383–2392 (2016)
29. Reimers, N., Gurevych, I.: Sentence-BERT: sentence embeddings using Siamese BERT-networks. In: Proceedings of EMNLP-IJCNLP, pp. 3980–3990 (2019)
30. Sanh, V., Debut, L., Chaumond, J., Wolf, T.: DistilBERT, a distilled version of BERT: smaller, faster, cheaper and lighter. CoRR arXiv:1910.01108 (2019)
31. See, A., Liu, P.J., Manning, C.D.: Get to the point: summarization with pointer-generator networks. In: Proceedings of ACL, pp. 1073–1083 (2017)
32. Sharma, E., Li, C., Wang, L.: BIGPATENT: a large-scale dataset for abstractive and coherent summarization. In: Proceedings of ACL, pp. 2204–2213 (2019)
33. Sun, Y., et al.: ERNIE 3.0: large-scale knowledge enhanced pre-training for language understanding and generation. CoRR arXiv:2107.02137 (2021)
34. Trischler, A., et al.: NewsQA: a machine comprehension dataset. In: Proceedings of Rep4NLP@ACL Workshop, pp. 191–200 (2017)
35. Welbl, J., Stenetorp, P., Riedel, S.: Constructing datasets for multi-hop reading comprehension across documents. Trans. Assoc. Comput. Linguist. **6**, 287–302 (2018)
36. Yamada, I., Asai, A., Shindo, H., Takeda, H., Matsumoto, Y.: LUKE: deep contextualized entity representations with entity-aware self-attention. In: Proceedings of EMNLP, pp. 6442–6454 (2020)
37. Yang, Z., Dai, Z., Yang, Y., Carbonell, J.G., Salakhutdinov, R., Le, Q.V.: XLNet: generalized autoregressive pretraining for language understanding. In: Proceedings of NeurIPS, pp. 5754–5764 (2019)
38. Yang, Z., et al.: HotpotQA: a dataset for diverse, explainable multi-hop question answering. In: Proceedings of EMNLP, pp. 2369–2380 (2018)
39. Zaheer, M., et al.: Big Bird: transformers for longer sequences. In: Proceedings of NeurIPS (2020)
40. Zellers, R., Bisk, Y., Schwartz, R., Choi, Y.: SWAG: a large-scale adversarial dataset for grounded commonsense inference. In: Proceedings of EMNLP, pp. 93–104 (2018)
41. Zhang, J., Zhao, Y., Saleh, M., Liu, P.J.: PEGASUS: pre-training with extracted gap-sentences for abstractive summarization. In: Proceedings of ICML, pp. 11328–11339 (2020)
42. Zhang, Y., Zhong, V., Chen, D., Angeli, G., Manning, C.D.: Position-aware attention and supervised data improve slot filling. In: Proceedings of EMNLP, pp. 35–45 (2017)
43. Zhang, Z., Han, X., Liu, Z., Jiang, X., Sun, M., Liu, Q.: ERNIE: enhanced language representation with informative entities. In: Proceedings of ACL, pp. 1441–1451 (2019)

Kern: A Labeling Environment for Large-Scale, High-Quality Training Data

Johannes Hötter[(⊠)], Henrik Wenck, Moritz Feuerpfeil, and Simon Witzke

kern.ai, Gerhart-Hauptmann-Allee 71, 15732 Eichwalde, Germany
{johannes.hoetter,henrik.wenck,moritz.feuerpfeil,simon.witzke}@kern.ai
https://www.kern.ai

Abstract. The lack of large-scale, high-quality training data is a significant bottleneck in supervised learning. We introduce `kern`, a labeling environment used by machine learning experts and subject matter experts to create training data and find manual labeling errors powered by weak supervision, active transfer learning, and confident learning. We explain the current workflow and system overview and showcase the benefits of our system in an intent classification experiment, where we reduce the labeling error rate of a given dataset by an absolute 4.9% while improving the F_1 score of a baseline classifier by a total of 9.7%.

Keywords: Data labeling · Data management · Supervised learning

1 Introduction

In recent years, the unreasonable effectiveness of data enabled breakthroughs in supervised learning areas such as natural language processing or computer vision [7,16]. With large amounts of labeled training data, deep learning techniques can learn task-specific representations even for unstructured data, which are in general characterized by their high dimensionality and diversity [2].

However, such labeled training data is a scarce resource for many real-world applications, making it the very bottleneck during implementation [13]. Depending on the task at hand, manual labeling can require weeks or months of repetitive work, making it both expensive and impractical. Thus, further research is needed into methods that obtain *necessary amounts* of labeled training data with *sufficient quality* at a *reasonable effort*.

Efficiently obtaining more labeled data is researched in the open-source libraries *Snorkel* [11] and *modAL* [3]. *Snorkel* offers weak supervision, a framework to automate data labeling by integrating noisy and limited information sources such as labeling functions [12].[1] *modAL* provides active learning via continuous model training in the labeling process to support the annotator.[2]

---

[1] *Snorkel* is available under https://github.com/snorkel-team/snorkel.
[2] *modAL* is available under https://github.com/modAL-python/modAL.

© The Author(s), under exclusive license to Springer Nature Switzerland AG 2022
P. Rosso et al. (Eds.): NLDB 2022, LNCS 13286, pp. 502–507, 2022.
https://doi.org/10.1007/978-3-031-08473-7_46

Increasing the quality of labeled data is researched in the open-source library *cleanlab* [9].[3] *cleanlab* aims to identify label errors in datasets such as ImageNet [4] via likelihoods estimated through inconsistencies in ground truth and model prediction.

We introduce our system `kern`, which *combines* concepts applied in named libraries to enable *both* large-scale *and* high-quality data labeling at a reasonable effort.[4] In `kern`, large-scale data labeling is achieved through weak supervision and active transfer learning, whereas confident learning, extensive data management, and monitoring capabilities ensure high-quality data. `kern` uses JSON as its data model (which makes it applicable e.g. for tabular and textual data) and is designed to be used by both machine learning experts and subject matter experts and aims to engage their collaboration further to address practical challenges. Ultimately, it seeks to shorten the data preparation cycle while improving supervised learning applications.

2   Conceptual Background

The features of `kern` consist of mainly three areas which are explained below.

2.1   Weak Supervision

Weak supervision is a unifying framework for integrating noisy labels of imprecise and limited information sources, aiming to synthesize "denoised" labels on large-scale [12]. In general, information sources - such as labeling functions, machine learning models, third-party applications (via API), or crowd workers - must fit the interface of weak supervision in that they produce noisy label vectors.

Weak supervision does not define the specific algorithm used to synthesize the noisy label matrix. Common approaches include majority voting, bayesian expectation-maximization [1,8], or closed-form solutions to model parameters such as proposed by Fu et al. [6].

2.2   Active Transfer Learning

In *active learning*, supervised learning models are trained continuously during the labeling procedure to support the annotator with inferred information from unlabeled data, e.g., deriving priority queues from low-confidence predictions or converting high-confidence forecasts into ground truth labels [14].

The first layers of neural networks generally recognize basic patterns shared across domains, whereas only the final layers are task-specific [17]. *Transfer learning* modifies the last k layers of a pre-trained neural network to efficiently transfer knowledge from a given domain to the task at hand [18].

---

[3] *cleanlab* is available under https://github.com/cleanlab/cleanlab.

[4] We chose this name to allude that training data is the "core" of modern supervised learning applications, both in research and applied systems.

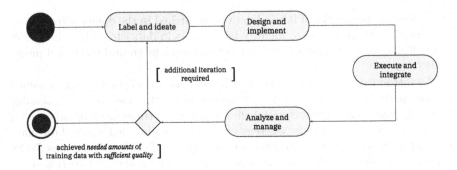

Fig. 1. Simplified workflow of the `kern` system.

Shi et al. [15] initially combined those concepts in an *active transfer learning* framework. As active learning models "borrow" knowledge from a pre-trained model, they converge faster, reducing the amount of manual effort to label data.

2.3 Confident Learning

As shown by Northcutt et al. [9], even well-researched datasets such as ImageNet [4] contain significant amounts of labeling errors. *Confident learning* finds such manual labeling errors by comparing the given ground truth with the prediction distribution of an estimator further to improve the data quality of a given labeled dataset.

3 Workflow and System Overview

`kern` is designed to be used by both *machine learning experts* (MLE) and *subject matter experts* (SME). We explain the workflow of `kern` in Fig. 1 and highlight which step includes MLEs or SMEs supported by a system overview in Fig. 2.

Label and Ideate. Both MLEs and SMEs start to manually label *some* data using the `kern` user interface during the first step. This phase aims to help gain a better understanding of the dataset characteristics.

Design and Implement. In doing so, SMEs and MLEs find and discuss patterns. `kern` comes with an integrated heuristics editor for labeling functions and active transfer learning.[5] External sources such as crowd workers or third-party applications are integrated via API (e.g., RapidAPI endpoints such as Symanto's psychology AI[6]). Information sources implicitly document the data.

---

[5] Models are implemented using the embedding store, and standard machine learning libraries such as *Scikit-Learn* [10].

[6] Accessible under https://rapidapi.com/organization/symanto.

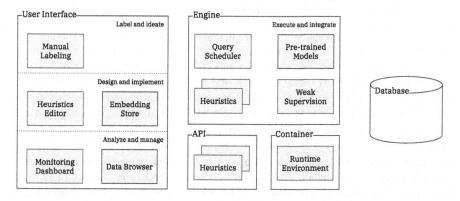

Fig. 2. Simplified overview of the kern system.

Execute and Integrate. The third step is to create the noisy label matrix by running the information sources.[7] kern provides multiple strategies to derive the weakly supervised label, e.g., by analyzing metadata such as precision, counts, conflicts, and overlaps, or by computing a closed-form solution to model parameters as proposed by Fu et al. [6]. The goal of this step is to achieve high-coverage, high-precision data labeling.

Analyze and Manage. Lastly, the results can be analyzed by SMEs and MLEs to improve the data quality continuously. The kern data browser provides extensive scheduling capabilities, e.g., validating selected information sources, identifying mismatches in labels, determining label error likelihoods, or finding outliers using diversity sampling. MLEs can use existing metadata to slice the data for new labeling sessions, making manual labeling more efficient.

Once sufficient data has been labeled, MLEs can export the existing data.

4   Evaluation

In this experiment, the intents of external emails of a customer service department are classified to either forward messages to the best potential responder or to answer messages automatically based on the extracted data of such emails.[8] The department collected intents of past emails via their ticket system workflow, resulting in more than 100,000 labeled emails (called *legacy* data hereafter). However, in data exploration, SMEs found that intents were partially mislabeled.

With kern, we create weakly supervised labeling corrections selected via confident learning for the full *legacy* data (called *iterated* data). In three workshops, we collect 20 information sources, e.g., regular expressions and active transfer

---

[7] Information sources are run containerized due to security and scalability.

[8] For instance, if the intent is to cancel an order, a system can automatically do so if it can find the order reference number within the given text message.

Table 1. We evaluate implications of improving the data quality.

Label	Ratio	Legacy			Prediction[a]			Iterated			Prediction		
		P	R	F_1	P	R	F_1	P	R	F_1	P	R	F_1
Purchases	68.2	97	95	96	92.7	91.8	92.2	99.1	98.3	98.7	94.4	93.6	94
Cancellations	10.9	79	88.2	83.3	57.4	60.8	59.1	90.9	98.0	94.3	65.5	70.6	67.9
Complaints	10.1	82.3	92.7	87.2	67.9	69.1	68.5	96.4	96.4	96.4	82	74.6	78.1
Questions	5.2	57.1	53.3	55.2	53.3	53.3	53.3	81.3	86.7	83.9	75	80	77.4
Instructions	2.9	100	69.2	81.8	61.5	61.5	61.5	100	92.3	96	66.7	92.3	77.4
Reportings	2.6	100	96.2	98	100	96.2	98	100	96.2	98	100	92.3	96
Macro F_1 (Lift)		83.6			72.1			94.6 (11)			81.8 (9.7)		
Accuracy (Lift)		92.3			84.5			97.4 (5.1)			88.7 (4.2)		

[a] The prediction columns represent a logistic regression trained on BERT embeddings.

learning modules. We validate the quality improvement by manually and randomly relabeling 500 emails as test ground truths. We train a logistic regression with BERT embeddings [5] for both versions. The results are shown in Table 1.

As observable, the *legacy* data has a labeling error rate of 7.7%. The *iterated* version reduces the error rate to 2.6%. The implications can be seen in the model training, as the classifier trained on the *iterated* data has a 9.7% higher F_1 than the one trained on the *legacy* data, making it a significant improvement based solely on improving the quality of the data using `kern`.

5   Conclusion

We combine weak supervision, active transfer learning, and confident learning for large-scale, high-quality training data and demonstrate `kern`'s workflow and system overview. We showcase how `kern` can be applied to increase the performance of a model solely by improving the training data quality using weakly supervised labeling corrections. We thus address the issue of obtaining *necessary amounts* of labeled training data with *sufficient quality* with *reasonable effort*.

References

1. Basile, A., Pérez-Torró, G., Franco-Salvador, M.: Probabilistic ensembles of zero- and few-shot learning models for emotion classification. In: Proceedings of the International Conference on Recent Advances in Natural Language Processing (RANLP 2021), pp. 128–137. INCOMA Ltd., September 2021
2. Bengio, Y., Courville, A., Vincent, P.: Representation learning: a review and new perspectives. IEEE Trans. Pattern Anal. Mach. Intell. **35**, 1798–1828 (2013)
3. Danka, T., Horvath, P.: modAL: a modular active learning framework for Python. https://github.com/modAL-python/modAL, arXiv:1805.00979
4. Deng, J., Dong, W., Socher, R., Li, L.J., Li, K., Fei-Fei, L.: ImageNet: a large-scale hierarchical image database. In: 2009 IEEE Conference on Computer Vision and Pattern Recognition, pp. 248–255 (2009)

5. Devlin, J., Chang, M., Lee, K., Toutanova, K.: BERT: pre-training of deep bidirectional transformers for language understanding. In: Proceedings of the 2019 Conference of the North American Chapter of the Association for Computational Linguistics: Human Language Technologies, NAACL-HLT 2019, Minneapolis, MN, USA, 2–7 June 2019, Volume 1 (Long and Short Papers), pp. 4171–4186. Association for Computational Linguistics (2019)
6. Fu, D.Y., Chen, M.F., Sala, F., Hooper, S.M., Fatahalian, K., Ré, C.: Fast and three-rious: speeding up weak supervision with triplet methods. In: Proceedings of the 37th International Conference on Machine Learning (ICML 2020) (2020)
7. Halevy, A., Norvig, P., Fernando, N.: The unreasonable effectiveness of data. IEEE Intell. Syst. **24**, 8–12 (2009)
8. Hovy, D., Berg-Kirkpatrick, T., Vaswani, A., Hovy, E.: Learning whom to trust with MACE. In: Proceedings of the 2013 Conference of the North American Chapter of the Association for Computational Linguistics: Human Language Technologies, Atlanta, Georgia, pp. 1120–1130. Association for Computational Linguistics, June 2013
9. Northcutt, C., Jiang, L., Chuang, I.: Confident learning: estimating uncertainty in dataset labels. J. Artif. Intell. Res. **70**, 1373–1411 (2021)
10. Pedregosa, F., et al.: Scikit-learn: machine learning in Python. J. Mach. Learn. Res. **12**, 2825–2830 (2011)
11. Ratner, A., Bach, S.H., Ehrenberg, H., Fries, J., Wu, S., Ré, C.: Snorkel. Proc. VLDB Endow. **11**(3), 269–282 (2017)
12. Ratner, A., Sa, C.D., Wu, S., Selsam, D., Ré, C.: Data programming: creating large training sets, quickly. In: Proceedings of the 30th International Conference on Neural Information Processing Systems, NIPS 2016, pp. 3574–3582. Curran Associates Inc., Red Hook (2016)
13. Roh, Y., Heo, G., Whang, S.E.: A survey on data collection for machine learning: a big data - AI integration perspective. IEEE Trans. Knowl. Data Eng. **33**(4), 1328–1347 (2021)
14. Settles, B.: Active learning literature survey. Computer Sciences Technical Report 1648, University of Wisconsin-Madison (2009)
15. Shi, X., Fan, W., Ren, J.: Actively transfer domain knowledge. In: Daelemans, W., Goethals, B., Morik, K. (eds.) ECML PKDD 2008. LNCS (LNAI), vol. 5212, pp. 342–357. Springer, Heidelberg (2008). https://doi.org/10.1007/978-3-540-87481-2_23
16. Sun, C., Shrivastava, A., Singh, S., Gupta, A.K.: Revisiting unreasonable effectiveness of data in deep learning era. In: 2017 IEEE International Conference on Computer Vision (ICCV) (2017)
17. Vaswani, A., et al.: Attention is all you need. In: Guyon, I., et al. (eds.) Advances in Neural Information Processing Systems, vol. 30. Curran Associates, Inc. (2017)
18. Zhuang, F., et al.: A comprehensive survey on transfer learning. Proc. IEEE **109**(1), 43–76 (2020)

Selective Word Substitution
for Contextualized Data Augmentation

Kyriaki Pantelidou, Despoina Chatzakou$^{(\boxtimes)}$, Theodora Tsikrika,
Stefanos Vrochidis, and Ioannis Kompatsiaris

Information Technologies Institute, Centre for Research and Technology Hellas,
Thessaloniki, Greece
{kpantelidou,dchatzakou,theodora.tsikrika,stefanos,ikom}@iti.gr

Abstract. The often observed unavailability of large amounts of training data typically required by deep learning models to perform well in the
context of NLP tasks has given rise to the exploration of data augmentation techniques. Originally, such techniques mainly focused on rule-based
methods (e.g. random insertion/deletion of words) or synonym replacement with the help of lexicons. More recently, model-based techniques
which involve the use of non-contextual (e.g. Word2Vec, GloVe) or contextual (e.g. BERT) embeddings seem to be gaining ground as a more
effective way of word replacement. For BERT, in particular, which has
been employed successfully in various NLP tasks, data augmentation is
typically performed by applying a masking approach where an arbitrary
number of word positions is selected to replace words with others of the
same meaning. Considering that the words selected for substitution are
bound to affect the final outcome, this work examines different ways of
selecting the words to be replaced by emphasizing different parts of a
sentence, namely specific parts of speech or words that carry more sentiment information. Our goal is to study the effect of selecting the words
to be substituted during data augmentation on the final performance
of a classification model. Evaluation experiments performed for binary
classification tasks on two benchmark datasets indicate improvements in
the effectiveness against state-of-the-art baselines.

Keywords: Contextual data augmentation · Word substitution ·
Binary classification

1 Introduction

Due to the large amount of text data available in the wild, natural language
processing (NLP) techniques have been developed to automatically understand
and represent human language. To this end, machine learning models are often
built, with deep neural networks being among the most prominent. However,
the performance of deep learning models depends significantly on the size of
the ground truth dataset [3]; creating though a large ground truth dataset is
a rather expensive and time consuming process. To overcome the lack of large

© The Author(s), under exclusive license to Springer Nature Switzerland AG 2022
P. Rosso et al. (Eds.): NLDB 2022, LNCS 13286, pp. 508–516, 2022.
https://doi.org/10.1007/978-3-031-08473-7_47

annotated datasets, data augmentation methods have emerged to artificially expand the size of such datasets, primarily in the areas of computer vision [6,16] and speech [9], with recent works focusing also on textual data [10,15,19,21]. E.g., multi-granularity text-oriented data augmentation was recently proposed, including word-, phrase-, and sentence-level data augmentation [19]. Moreover, the "Easy Data Augmentation" method suggested four operations towards data augmentation: synonym replacement, random insertion, swap, and deletion [21].

As an alternative, contextualized data augmentation techniques have arisen due to their ability to better capture the contextual relations between words in a sentence, thus resulting in a more effective word suggestion for substitution. For instance, the so-called Contextual Augmentation follows a contextual prediction approach to suggest words that have paradigmatic relations with the original words [10]. More recent studies on data augmentation utilize BERT (Bidirectional Encoder Representations from Transformers) [7], a pre-trained deep bidirectional representation that jointly conditions on both left and right context in all layers. For example, the proposed "masked language model" (MLM) randomly masks a certain percentage of input tokens to finally predict such masked words based on their context for the formation of new sentences [4]. A complementary approach is the so-called "Conditional BERT Contextual Augmentation", a variant of the BERT-based model aimed at predicting label-compatible words based on both their context and the sentence label [22]; however, its close tie with the BERT architecture somewhat prevents its direct use in other pre-trained language models. As a countermeasure, a solution that prepends the class label to text sequences has been suggested, resulting in a simple but yet effective way to condition the pre-trained models for data augmentation [11]. Finally, more recently, the "Generative pre-training" (GPT-2) model has been used as a basis for artificially generating new labeled data [1].

Thus far, contextualized BERT-based methods have only considered random selections of words for replacement in order to generate new synthetic sentences. As intuitively expected, the words selected for replacement can play a decisive role in the quality of the new generated sentences that are subsequently used as input for training a neural network model. In this regard, this work proposes more targeted word replacements, by paying attention to specific and potentially more significant and/or informative parts of a sequence. In particular, this work proposes that specific part-of-speech tags, such as adjectives and adverbs that can be seen as modifiers of other words (e.g. nouns, pronouns and verbs), are considered for replacement, as well as words that carry sentiment information. Our intuition is that focusing only on such words for substitution will lead to new sentences that will provide more variability in a deep learning model for better adaptation to different ways of expressing the same thing; methods adopted so far in most of cases lead to the substitution of words that are not always sufficiently distinctive and therefore may not result in substantially different sentences. Evaluation is performed for binary classification tasks on two well-established datasets, the SST-2 [17] and the SUBJ [13], which comprise of short sentences characterized as either positive/negative or subjective/objective, respectively. Overall, the experimental results underscore the contribution and positive affect of proper selection of words for replacement in data augmentation.

2 Methodology

This section outlines: (i) the methods considered for word substitution; (ii) the applied contextualized data augmentation method that follows label-compatible or label-independent replacement; and finally (iii) the deep neural network model used for evaluating the proposed approaches for word selection and substitution.

2.1 Substitution of Words: Target Masked Words

In this work, BERT-based models are used for data augmentation. Before feeding word sequences into BERT-based models, part of words in a sequence is replaced with a [MASK] token. The model then attempts to predict the original value of the masked words, based on the context provided by the rest, non-masked, words in the sequence, thus resulting to the creation of new sentences with the same meaning but different words. So, the first step involves the selection of words to be masked. To this end, we first describe the baseline (i.e. Random) and then the three proposed approaches (i.e. Word modifiers (all), Word modifiers (15%), and Sentiment-related words) for word selection and substitution.

- **Random:** we randomly mask at maximum the 15% of all word tokens in a sequence. We iterate over all tokens in a sequence and when the i-th token is chosen, we replace it with (i) the [MASK] token 80% of the time and (ii) the unchanged i-th token 20% of the time. We repeat this process until the 15% of the tokens are masked or when all the tokens have been checked. This typical approach for contextual data augmentation [4] is our baseline.
- **Word modifiers (all):** we obtain the part-of-speech (POS) tag of each token in a sequence using the spaCy library [18]. Then, we choose to mask all tokens characterized as ADJ (adjectives) and ADV (adverbs), since these function as word modifiers for nouns and verbs, respectively, and could therefore influence and have a greater impact on the actual meaning of a sentence.
- **Word modifiers (15%):** we follow the same process as before, with the difference being the selection of a maximum of 15% of ADJ and ADV tokens to be masked. Similar to the baseline method, 80% of the times the token is marked with [MASK] and 20% it remains unchanged.
- **Sentiment-related words:** we utilize SentiWordNet [5], a lexical resource in which each word is associated with three numerical scores Obj, Pos, and Neg, describing how objective, positive, and negative the word is. The sum of these scores equals to 1.0. We choose to mask all the words that have a positive or negative score > 0.0, excluding this way the more "neutral" terms that have no-influence on the sentiment of a sentence.

At the end of each of the aforementioned words selection processes, we obtain a list with the target masked words to be predicted by the BERT-based models.

2.2   Contextualized Data Augmentation

For data augmentation, we considered both BERT and conditional BERT.

BERT-Based Approach. To predict the target masked words, we first proceed with BERT [4], and in particular with the "bert-base-uncased" model [2], a pretrained model on English language using a masked language modeling (MLM) objective, which does not consider the label of each sequence during replacement.

Conditional BERT-Based Approach (CBERT). The conditional BERT-based contextual augmentation [22] considers the label of the original sequence for artificially generating new labeled data. CBERT shares the same model architecture with the original BERT. The main differences lay on the input representation and training procedure. The input embeddings of BERT are the sum of the token embeddings, the segmentation embeddings, and the position embeddings. However, these embeddings have no connection to the actual annotated labels of a sentence, thus the predicted word is not always compatible with the annotated label. To build a conditional MLM, CBERT finetunes on the pre-trained BERT (i.e. "bert-base-uncased") by altering the segmentation embeddings to label embeddings, which are learned corresponding to their annotated labels on labeled datasets. In the end, the model is expected to be able to predict words in masked position by considering both the context and the label.

2.3   Deep Neural Network Model

To evaluate the proposed word substitution approaches in contextualized data augmentation, we focus on a binary classification task. In this respect, and in the same direction as similar works [10,21,22], a Convolutional Neural Network (CNN) based architecture is built, given CNNs' proven usefulness for NLP tasks.

Text Input. Before feeding any text to the network, a set of preprocessing steps takes place to reduce noise. Specifically, URLs, digits, and single character words are removed, as well as punctuation and special characters. In addition, as neural networks are trained in mini-batches, each batch in the sample should have the same sequence length; we set the sequence length to 100.

Embedding Layer. The first layer of the neural network architecture is the embedding layer, which maps each word to a high-dimensional layer. We opted for pre-trained word embeddings from GloVe [14] of 100 dimensions.

Neural Network Layer. The CNN architecture is as follows: one 1D convolutional layer of 50 filters and kernel size 3, 1D average pool layer, and one dense layer of 20 hidden units. To avoid over-fitting, we use a spatial dropout of $p = 0.6$. This architecture was chosen as it leads to fair performance across the two datasets considered.

Classification Layer. Since in our case the objective is to classify texts into two classes, *sigmoid* is used as activation function.

3 Experimental Setup and Results

3.1 Datasets

We conducted experiments on two benchmark datasets: (i) the **SST-2**: Stanford Sentiment Treebank [17], which includes one-sentence movie reviews labeled positive or negative. The dataset contains $8,741$ samples and is split in (train, test, validation) sets with size $(6,228, 1,821, 692)$, respectively; and (ii) the **SUBJ**: Subjectivity Dataset [13] which includes $5,000$ subjective and $5,000$ objective processed sentences of movie reviews and it is split in $(9,000, 900, 100)$ samples for (train, test, validation), respectively. After data augmentation, we doubled the size of the training sets, while keeping the test and validation sets intact.

3.2 Experimental Setup

For our implementation, we use Keras [8] with TensorFlow [20]. We run the experiments on a server with one GeForce RTX 2080 GPU of 12GB memory.

In terms of training, we use binary cross-entropy as loss function. As for the learning rate, which is a very important hyper-parameter when it comes to training a neural network, a scheduler-based approach is followed. Specifically, cosine annealing is used which initiates with a large learning rate that decreases relatively quickly to a minimum value before increasing rapidly again. For such an implementation, AdamW [12] is used. Finally, a maximum of 150 epochs is allowed, while also the validation set is used to perform early stopping. Training is interrupted if the validation loss does not drop in 3 consecutive epochs.

Experimentation Phases. Overall, we consider two experimentation phases: (i) BERT-based contextual augmentation, and (ii) Conditional BERT-based contextual augmentation. For both phases, the four methods for words substitution presented in Sect. 2.1 are examined. For evaluation purposes, standard metrics are considered, namely accuracy (Acc), precision (Prec), recall (Rec), weighted area under the ROC curve (AUC), and the loss/accuracy curves.

3.3 Experimental Results

Tables 1 and 2 present the results obtained with the classification model described in Sect. 2.3 before and after data augmentation is applied, for the SST-2 and SUBJ datasets, respectively. In all cases, the classification performance is better when an augmented dataset is used compared to when the original dataset is used, which highlights the overall usefulness of data augmentation.

BERT-Based Augmentation: In the first experimentation phase, we observe that the best performance in both datasets is achieved when specific (rather than random) words are selected for replacement.

Table 1. Classification results for the **SST-2** dataset

	Before data augmentation			
	Acc	Prec	Rec	AUC
	80.79	81.19	80.80	89.45

	After data augmentation							
	BERT				Conditional BERT			
	Acc	Prec	Rec	AUC	Acc	Prec	Rec	AUC
Random (baseline)	81.85	81.92	81.85	90.50	81.58	81.95	81.59	90.28
Modifiers (all)	81.75	82.02	81.76	90.42	82.58	82.73	82.58	90.62
Modifiers (15%)	**82.12**	**82.46**	**82.13**	**90.76**	81.26	81.73	81.27	90.30
Sentiment-related words	81.61	81.84	81.62	90.34	**82.61**	**82.88**	**82.62**	**90.91**

For the SST-2 dataset, the best performance is obtained when only the 15% of the word modifiers is selected for replacement (acc: 82.12%, prec: 82.46%, rec: 82.13%, AUC: 90.76%); the differences between the Modifiers (15%) and the baseline are statistically significant ($p < 0.05$) for all evaluation metrics.

By analyzing the content of the augmented sentences produced by the different word substitution methods, we observe that the Random method replaces in most cases general words (such as pronouns and nouns) that do not affect the actual meaning and sentiment of a sentence. On the contrary, the Modifiers (all) and Sentiment-related words methods in many cases suggest words for replacement that change the overall sentiment of the sentence, resulting in lower performance compared to the random-based replacement approach (but still better than the non-augmented case). On the other hand, manual inspection of the sentences generated by the Modifiers (15%) method indicates that the number of cases where the sentiment changes is smaller compared to the other two proposed methods, while at the same time more informative words (of the same meaning) are replaced, thus resulting in the best overall performance.

Overall, it appears that the addition of sentences that have the same sentiment with the original ones and at the same time differ somehow in the way of expressing the same opinion and attitude in relation to an event (e.g. opinion about a movie as in our case) can probably make the model more capable of locating the correctly expressed sentiment on new data as it has learned to better interpret different ways of expressing the same or similar opinions and notions.

For the SUBJ dataset, we observe that in relation to accuracy, precision, and recall the selection of sentiment words for substitution allows for the generation of an augmented dataset that leads to a better performance ($p < 0.05$ when compared to the Random baseline). A slightly better performance in terms of AUC is achieved by the Modifiers (15%); compared though to the rest of the proposed methods their differences are not statistically significant ($p > 0.05$).

Table 2. Classification results for the **SUBJ** dataset

	Before data augmentation			
	Acc	Prec	Rec	AUC
	90.53	90.54	90.53	96.38
	After data augmentation							

	BERT				Conditional BERT			
	Acc	Prec	Rec	AUC	Acc	Prec	Rec	AUC
Random (baseline)	91.18	91.19	91.18	96.49	90.78	90.80	90.78	96.81
Modifiers (all)	91.37	91.38	91.37	96.89	91.00	91.00	91.00	**96.83**
Modifiers (15%)	91.24	91.24	91.24	**96.91**	91.06	91.06	91.06	**96.83**
Sentiment-related words	**91.56**	**91.57**	**91.56**	96.88	**91.14**	**91.15**	**91.14**	**96.83**

Contrary to the SST-2 dataset, in the SUBJ dataset, we observe that the selection of sentiment words for substitution leads to a better performance. As the SUBJ dataset is oriented towards the characterization of texts as either objective or subjective, it is quite expected that in subjective sentences the expression of sentiments/emotions will be more intense compared to the objective ones. Therefore, in this case, the presence of sentiment words alone in a sentence can be an important indication of the subsequent characterization of a text as subjective or objective, even without the consideration of labels during augmentation, which is examined next.

Conditional BERT-Based Augmentation: The aim in this experimental setup is to assess whether and how the inclusion of the label during augmentation will affect the overall performance in terms of the different word substitution approaches examined in this work. The results in both Tables 1 and 2 indicate that when we focus on specific words for replacement we achieve better performance in most cases compared to the baseline (random replacement). The best performance is obtained when only the sentiment words are considered for substitution. In Table 1, the Sentiment-related words method achieves acc: 82.61%, prec: 82.88%, rec: 82.62%, AUC: 90.91%, with the differences to the baseline being statistically significant ($p<0.05$) for all the evaluation metrics. In Table 2, the Sentiment-related words method achieves acc: 91.14%, prec: 91.15%, rec: 91.14%, AUC: 96.83%, with the differences to the baseline being statistically significant ($p<0.05$) for all evaluation metrics except AUC. These results highlight the importance of focusing on sentiment words for substitution (probably due to such words conveying more useful information to the classification model), considering also the label of the original sequence.

4   Conclusions and Future Work

In this work we studied how the performance of a neural network model is affected when a more focused (rather than random) word substitution approach is adopted during contextualized data augmentation. The focus was on specific

POS tags, as well as on words that reflect sentiments, following either a label-compatible or a label-independent replacement approach. Overall, the results indicate that a careful selection of words for substitution is beneficial. In the future, we intend to conduct a similar study by using alternative and more recent contextualized data augmentation methods, such as XLNet [23], which are able to capture the semantic relations between the masked tokens of a sequence.

Acknowledgements. This research is part of projects that have received funding from the European Union's H2020 research and innovation programme under CON-NEXIONs (GA No 786731), CREST (GA No 833464), and STARLIGHT (GA No 101021797).

References

1. Anaby-Tavor, A., et al.: Do not have enough data? deep learning to the rescue! In: AAAI Conference on Artificial Intelligence, vol. 34, pp. 7383–7390 (2020)
2. BERT base model. https://huggingface.co/bert-base-uncased, (accessed 2021)
3. Brownlee, J.: (2019).https://bit.ly/2SB0n5G
4. Devlin, J., Chang, M.W., Lee, K., Toutanova, K.: Bert: Pre-training of deep bidirectional transformers for language understanding. In: NAACL (2019)
5. Esuli, A., Sebastiani, F.: Sentiwordnet: a publicly available lexical resource for opinion mining. In: LREC (2006)
6. Frid-Adar, M., Klang, E., Amitai, M., Goldberger, J., Greenspan, H.: Synthetic data augmentation using GAN for improved liver lesion classification. In: 15th International Symposium on Biomedical Imaging, ISBI 2018, pp. 289–293. IEEE (2018)
7. Kenton, J.D.M.W.C., Toutanova, L.K.: Bert: Pre-training of deep bidirectional transformers for language understanding. In: NAACL-HLT, pp. 4171–4186 (2019)
8. Keras: (2020). https://keras.io/
9. Ko, T., Peddinti, V., Povey, D., Khudanpur, S.: Audio augmentation for speech recognition. In: International Speech Communication Association (2015)
10. Kobayashi, S.: Contextual augmentation: data augmentation by words with paradigmatic relations. In: Proceedings of the 2018 Conference of the North American Chapter of the Association for Computational Linguistics: Human Language Technologies, vol. 2 (Short Papers), pp. 452–457 (2018)
11. Kumar, V., Choudhary, A., Cho, E.: Data augmentation using pre-trained transformer models. In: Proceedings of the 2nd Workshop on Life-long Learning for Spoken Language Systems, ACL, pp. 18–26 (2020)
12. OverLordGoldDragon: Keras adamw. GitHub. Note: (2019).https://github.com/OverLordGoldDragon/keras-adamw/
13. Pang, B., Lee, L.: A sentimental education: sentiment analysis using subjectivity summarization based on minimum cuts. In: Proceedings of the 42nd Annual Meeting on Association for Computational Linguistics, pp. 271-es (2004)
14. Pennington, J., Socher, R., Manning, C.D.: Glove: global vectors for word representation. In: EMNLP, pp. 1532–1543 (2014)
15. Sennrich, R., Haddow, B., Birch, A.: Improving neural machine translation models with monolingual data. In: Proceedings of the 54th Annual Meeting of the Association for Computational Linguistics, vol. 1 (Long Papers), pp. 86–96 (2016)

16. Simard, P.Y., LeCun, Y.A., Denker, J.S., Victorri, B.: Transformation invariance in pattern recognition – tangent distance and tangent propagation. In: Montavon, G., Orr, G.B., Müller, K.-R. (eds.) Neural Networks: Tricks of the Trade. LNCS, vol. 7700, pp. 235–269. Springer, Heidelberg (2012). https://doi.org/10.1007/978-3-642-35289-8_17

17. Socher, R., et al.: Recursive deep models for semantic compositionality over a sentiment treebank. In: EMNLP, pp. 1631–1642 (2013)

18. SpaCy: https://spacy.io/, (accessed 2021)

19. Sun, X., He, J.: A novel approach to generate a large scale of supervised data for short text sentiment analysis. Multimedia Tools Appli. **79**(1), 5439–5459 (2018). https://doi.org/10.1007/s11042-018-5748-4

20. TensorFlow: https://www.tensorflow.org/, (accessed 2021)

21. Wei, J., Zou, K.: EDA: Easy data augmentation techniques for boosting performance on text classification tasks. In: EMNLP-IJCNLP, pp. 6383–6389 (2019)

22. Wu, X., Lv, S., Zang, L., Han, J., Hu, S.: Conditional BERT contextual augmentation. In: Rodrigues, J.M.F., et al. (eds.) ICCS 2019. LNCS, vol. 11539, pp. 84–95. Springer, Cham (2019). https://doi.org/10.1007/978-3-030-22747-0_7

23. Yang, Z., Dai, Z., Yang, Y., Carbonell, J., Salakhutdinov, R.R., Le, Q.V.: Xlnet: generalized autoregressive pretraining for language understanding. In: Advances in Neural Information Processing Systems, vol. 32. Curran Associates, Inc. (2019)

Data to Value: An 'Evaluation-First' Methodology for Natural Language Projects

Jochen L. Leidner[1,2,3](✉)

[1] Coburg University of Applied Sciences, Friedrich-Streib-Str. 2, 96450 Coburg, Germany
[2] University of Sheffield, Regents Court, 211 Portobello, Sheffield S1 5DP, England, UK
[3] KnowledgeSpaces UG (haftungsbeschr.), Erfurter Straße 25a, 96450 Coburg, Germany
leidner@acm.org

Abstract. While for data mining projects (for example in the context of e-commerce) some methodologies have already been developed (e.g. CRISP-DM, SEMMA, KDD), these do *not* account for (1) early evaluation in order to de-risk a project (2) dealing with text corpora ("unstructured" data) and associated natural language processing processes, and (3) non-technical considerations (e.g. legal, ethical, project management aspects). To address these three shortcomings, a new methodology, called *"Data to Value"*, is introduced, which is guided by a detailed catalog of questions in order to avoid a disconnect of large-scale NLP project teams with the topic when facing rather abstract box-and-arrow diagrams commonly associated with methodologies.

Keywords: Methodology · Process model · Supervised learning · Natural language processing · Data science · Unstructured data

1 Introduction

Engineering has been defined as "the application of scientific, economic, social, and practical knowledge in order to design, build, and maintain structures, machines, devices, systems, materials and processes." (Wikipedia) or the "[t]he creative application of scientific principles to design or develop structures, machines, apparatus, or manufacturing processes, or works utilizing them singly or in combination; or to construct or operate the same with full cognizance of their design; or to forecast their behavior under specific operating conditions; all as respects an intended function, economics of operation or safety to life and property" (American Engineers' Council for Professional Development). In Natural Language Engineering (NLE), like in all engineering, we should adhere to a *principled approach* following *best practices* (methodology) and

---

This paper was written in part while the author spent time as a guest lecturer at the University of Zurich, Institute for Computational Linguistics. The author gratefully acknowledges the support of Martin Volk for extending the invitation to teach and for his hospitality, to Khalid Al-Kofahi (Thomson Reuters) for supporting this visit, and to Maria Fassli for the invitation to present a preliminary version at the Essex University Big Data Summer School. Thanks to Beatriz De La Iglesia for useful discussions.

P. Rosso et al. (Eds.): NLDB 2022, LNCS 13286, pp. 517–523, 2022.
https://doi.org/10.1007/978-3-031-08473-7_48

generate a *predictable outcome*, namely: (1) forecasting observed runtime (2) forecasting memory requirements (3) forecasting delivery time, i.e. a time at which a successful project can be concluded; and (4) forecasting output quality (e.g. F1-score). At the time of writing, there is no theory that permits us to forecast even one of these factors; in this paper, as a first step towards this end, we present a methodology that addresses the point of delivery as 'predictable outcome": our methodology aims to deliver projects more consistently, and with less time wasted. This is achieved by a finer-grained sequence of phases, and by additional guidance in the form of guiding questions. The unique characteristics of our methodology, named D2V (for "Data to Value" process) are: it is *evaluation-first*, which means that the construction of a system and proceeding between the various phases itself is driven by quantitative metrics; it is intended for projects involving *unstructured* data (text content), as it fills a gap in the space of existing methodologies; it is *question-informed*, as it benefits from a catalog of questions associated with particular process phases.

2 Related Work

According to the PMI [9], a project is completed successfully if it is completed (1) on *time* (2) on *budget* (3) *to specification* and (4) with *customer acceptance*. In the area of software engineering, the waterfall model and the agile model have been the most popular process models for constructing general software systems [12]. Working with data has a slightly different focus compared to traditional software development: systems for mining rules, classifying documents, tagging texts and extracting information are also software artifacts, but the software co-evolves with various data sets and linguistic resources that are used by it. While we are not aware of prior work on any methodologies specifically for processing large quantities of text, in the context of developing data mining projects, three popular methodologies have been developed, which shall be reviewed here. The **KDD Process** [4–6] grew out of the Knowledge Discovery in Databases research community, which in 1995 had its first of a series of workshops. It proposes a sequence of five [6, p. 30–31] to nine [6, p. 29, Fig. 1] steps to get from raw data to knowledge: Selection, Pre-Processing, Transformation, Data Mining and Interpretation/Evaluation. Each of these steps is seen as depending on the previous steps, yet its proponents suggest a certain flexibility in applying the steps was vital, and left to the discretion of the experienced researcher. For example, at any stage could one consider going back to a any previous stage and repeat the steps from there, and multiple iterations were considered likely. private company SAS Institute, Inc. The name is an acronym, which stands for "Sample, Explore, Modify, Model, and Assess. SAS Enterprise Miner nodes "are arranged on tabs with the same names." [10, p. 5] In SEMMA, a cycle with five process stages is applied: "Sample – extracting a portion of a large data set big enough to contain the significant information, yet small enough to manipulate quickly. This stage is pointed out as being optional. Explore – exploring the data by searching for unanticipated trends and anomalies in order to gain understanding and ideas. Modify –This stage consists on the modification of the data by creating, selecting, and transforming the variables to focus the model selection process. Model – This stage consists on modeling the data by allowing the software to search automatically for a combination of data that reliably predicts a desired outcome. Assess – for assessing the data by evaluating the usefulness and reliability of the findings from the data mining process and estimate how well it performs." [2]. The **CRISP-DM** methodology [1,3,11], short for "CRoss Industry Standard Process for Data Mining", which was developed by a consortium comprising DamilerChrysler, SPSS, NCR and OHRA, can be looked at from four different levels of abstraction: phases, generic tasks, specialized task and process instances. The reference model defines the transitions between phases, and a user guide describes how-to information in more detail. It comprises six loose phases: Business Understanding, Data Understanding, Data Preparation, Modeling, Evaluation and Deployment. See [1,2,7] for more detail on the similarities and differences between KDD, SEMMA and CRISP-DM.

We point to the shortcomings with regards to detail about a number of areas of past work: 1. working with text data in particular, is not specifically accommodated by either approach; 2. supervised learning, which is the approach of choice in scenario where quality matters, is not specifically catered for; 3. ethical questions are not part of previously proposed processes; 4. the scale aspects of big data influences the process and day-to-day work; 5. most importantly, we are first to strongly advocate an "evaluation first" approach.

Evaluation design: one of the earliest steps in a project following our methodology is to determine how the output of the system is to be evaluated. This step is a peculiarity of the D2V process, and makes it "evaluation-first". An implenmentation of said evaluation's test harness typically goes hand in hand with the design.

3   Data to Value (D2V)

Figure 1 shows the high-level process model behind the Data-to-Value development methodology: in the beginning, the Project Planning and Initiation stage is used to draft a project charter, and to formally launch the project. A significant part of the planning process is the specification of success, the planning of automatic or manual evaluation procedures, and the budgeting of evaluation resources.

Once a business case is made (i.e., the value of a new product, service or feature has been established, the *Project Planning and Initiation* (1) phase aims to author a project charter and project plan, and initiate the project formally. Before, after, or during this activity, an *Ethics Review I* (2) is conducted to answer the question of whether the project and its output are morally objectionable. Assuming no ethical obstacles, the *Requirements Elicitation* (3) phase seeks to obtain more detailed formal requirements, both functional and non-functional. In the *Data Acquisition* (4) phase, autorization and access to any prerequisite data-sets are obtained. The *Feasibility Study* (5) phase, shown as a "sub-process" because it could be seen as a light-weight version of the Fig. 1 as a whole, is used to re-risk the project, by conducting some preliminary experiments on a static data sample drawn from the full data-set(s) to be used by the project. Although optional, it is highly recommended for all complex projects. Very early in the process, in the *Evaluation Design* (6) phase, an experimental design is worked out and an evaluation protocol is committed to. In the *Data Pre-Processing and Cleansing* (7)

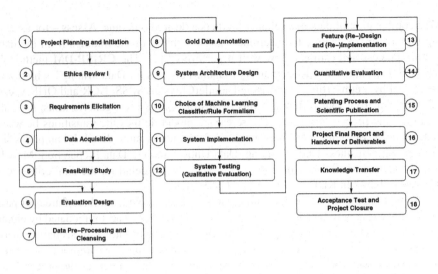

Fig. 1. Data-to-value process model. note two steps contain sub-processes.

phase, all data sets are brought in the right formats suitable for the project. In particular, eliminating noise elements (data irrelevant to the project, or data that may be relevant that violates formatting specifications), translating elements into a canonical form, and linking data sets together where appropriate happens here. In some projects, 80% of the project time gets spent in this phase, and it is not uncommon that this phase needs to be repeated due to the late recognition that more work is required. The *Gold Data Annotation* (8) phase is a sub-process explained in [8]) creating data that gets used to train classifiers if a supervised training regime is used; a second purpose is to create a ground truth for regular automatic evaluation runs. The annotation of gold data requires care, patience, resources and foresight, and if all of these are committed, the medium-term payback can be huge. In contrast, if conducted sloppily or omitted, projects can fail entirely or at least significant waste is likely to occur. The longer version of this paper, the technical report [8], describes the process, which typically takes a few weeks or months, divided into multiple iterations. After that, the *System Architecture Design* (9) phase produces the architecture of the software system. Then a particular paradigm is chosen in the *Choice of Machine Learning Classifier/Rule Formalism* (10) phase: if the system is going to be a rule based system, the kind of rule processing technology or framework, and if machine learning is to be used, which type of model. The framing in terms of choice of classifier or rule formalism may impact the detailed architecture, so in practice, the *System Architecture Design* (9) and *Choice of Machine Learning Classifier/Rule Formalism* (10) phases are intertwined more often than not. Then the *System Implementation* (11) phase targets the actual software development of the processing engine, which comprises most of the software but not any rules or features, which are separately devised, and often by different team members. The *System Testing* (12) phase, which includes both manual tests and automated (unit) tests, is dedicated to the qualitative evaluation; in other words, either the system is working to specification or there are still known bugs. With entering the *Feature Design and Implementation* (13) phase, a series of iterations begins that ultimately only terminates for one of two reasons: either the projected time dedicated to this phase is used up, or the targeted quality level has already been reached. Sometimes we may want to stop earlier if no further progress seems possible, and additional efforts show diminishing returns. Each iteration begins with feature brainstorming sessions and includes studying data from the training set, implementation sprints, and *Quantitative Evaluation I* (14) steps to try out new features and their effectiveness. Ultimately, the loop exits, and four concluding phases wrap up the project (*Patenting and Publication* (15) to document the work and secure the intellectual property rights to novel invented methods, authoring the *Final Report Authoring* (16), handing over the deliverables in the form of data, software and documentation and the *Knowledge Transfer* (17) phase, which verbally communicates the findings to stakeholders and ascertains a full understanding at the receiving end; finally, a successful *Acceptance and Closure* (18) leads to the formal project closure). While technically, our model for conducting *research* projects could end (*Research Project* (1-18)), industrial real-life systems get used in production, and modern systems require recurring activities to update statistical model after deployment. Therefore, it is advisable to have a look at what happens around the launch: before we launch the system in the *Deployment* (20*) phase, we again conduct an *Ethics Review II* (19*) to assess potential moral objections, this time paying attention to morally questionable system functions and emergent properties (e.g. discrimination or unfairness). Once the system is running, a *Monitoring* (21*) phase watches the system perform its function whilst logging interesting events (system decisions, user activities). At regular intervals, a *Quantitative Evaluation II* (22*) phase is followed by *Model Re-Training* (23*), depending on its findings, in order to keep statistical models "fresh". Note that Fig. 1 shows only the process for *development* of a system as a project. In real-life settings, this is interleaved with deploying and operating the result of the development *process*. This short paper does not include it but see [8] for more detail on this important part. Finally, each process phase has a set of *guidance questions* assigned to it (cf. Appendix A in the longer version of this paper [8] for some examples), which help junior workers to get start and to increase outcome consistency for experience professionals.

4   Discussion

The D2V methodology is quite a rich model, considering the number of distinct phases. It was not aimed to be easily memorable, but was designed to give the practitioner comprehensive guidance, which may or may not be required for each project: a detailed question catalog Experienced project managers will adjust the process to the complexity and nature of project; for example, bigger or more complex projects need more rigid processes and detailed formal documentation than small studies conducted by teams of two. A poll conducted twice within seven years in-between suggests that CRISM-DM is consistently the most popular process by a large margin (Table 1); however, neither of the processes listed are actually potential substitutes for D2V, since none of them have provisions for working with text. Indeed, since most data falls into the unstructured category, it is suprising that no process has previously been proposed. our subsequent work will focus on software tool support.

Table 1. An Internet poll conducted by the data mining portal in the years 2007 and 2014 (total $N = 200$). Remarkably, relative popularity has not changed much in 7 years.

Methodology	Used	by	Respondents
CRISP-DM	42%	–	43%
SEMMA	8%	–	13%
KDD	7%	–	8%

Table 2 shows a summary comparison between D2V and previous methodologies. One limitation of D2V methodology is that its dedication to unstructured projects makes it less suitable for structured data mining projects, but that domain is sufficiently addressed by the CRISP-DM model. Another shortcoming of D2V, in the version presented here, and also of all other models is that they do not permit a prediction of the time spent in each phase, and of the duration of the project overall; we will re-visit this in future work.

Table 2. Evaluative Ccmparison between CRISP-DM, SEMMA, KDD and D2V: D2V provides more fine-grained phases and more substantial guidance with around one hundred process-supporting questions.

Process model	Phases	Structured data	Unstructured data	Rule-based approaches	Learning-based approaches	Guidance questions	"Evaluation-first?"
CRISP-DM	6	yes	no	yes	(yes)	n/a	no
SEMMA	4–5	yes	no	yes	(yes)	n/a	no
KDD	5–9	yes	no	yes	(yes)	n/a	no
Marr. Strat. Board	7	yes	no	no	no	6	no
D2V	**30**	**no**	**yes**	**yes**	**yes**	**96**	**yes**

5 Summary, Conclusion and Future Work

D2v, a new process model for the systematic pursuit of text analytics projects has been described. It is different from past work in that is not concerned with data mining;

instead, supervised learning of textual structures are the main focus. Importantly, it can be characterized as "evaluation-first", not just because it de-risks projects by prioritizing the scrutinizing of success criteria, but also because it includes provisions for gold standard annotation and an overall iterative approach that terminates based on diminishing returns informed by repeat evaluations. It is also informed by a catalog of guiding questions. We believe this model has merit to improve awareness of the best practices for professionals in projects using unstructured data. The D2V methodology can also aid the teaching of data science. In future work, data collection exercises should be attempted to measure typical absolute and relative resources spend in each phase, in order to permit forecasting-oriented modeling towards cost and quality estimation. Another avenue for future work is the predictive modeling of quality as it relates to time and cost.

References

1. Anand, S.S., et al.: Knowledge discovery standards. Artif. Intell. Rev. **27**(1), 21–56 (2007)
2. Azevedo, A., Santos, M.F.: KDD, SEMMA and CRISP-DM: a parallel overview. In: Proceedings of the IADIS European Conference on Data Mining 2008, pp. 182–185 (2008)
3. Chapman, P.: CRISP-DM 1.0 - step-by-step data mining guide. Technical report The CRISP-DM Consortium (2000). http://www.crisp-dm.org/CRISPWP-0800.pdf. Accessed 05 Jan 2008
4. Debuse, J.C.W., de la Iglesia, B., Howard, C.M., Rayward-Smith, V.J.: Building the KDD roadmap: a methodology for knowledge discovery. In: Roy, R. (ed.) Industrial Knowledge Management, pp. 179–196. Springer, London (2001). https://doi.org/10.1007/978-1-4471-0351-6_12
5. Fayyad, U.M., Piatetsky-Shapiro, G., Smyth, P.: From data mining to knowledge discovery: an overview. In: Fayyad, U.M., et al. (eds.) Adv. Knowl. Dis. Data Min. MIT Press, Cambridge, MA, USA (1996)
6. Fayyad, U., Piatetsky-Shapiro, G., Smyth, P.: The KDD process for extracting useful knowledge from volumes of data. Commun. ACM **39**(11), 27–34 (1996)
7. Kurgan, L., Musilek, P.: A survey of knowledge discovery and data mining process models. Knowl. Eng. Rev. **21**(1), 1–24 (2006)
8. Leidner, J.L.: Data-to-value: an 'evaluation-first' methodology for natural language projects. Technical report (2022). https://arxiv.org/abs/2201.07725, available from the Cornell University ArXiV pre-print server, cited 20 April 2022
9. PMI (ed.): A Guide to the Project Management Body of Knowledge Project (PMBOK Guide), 5th edn. The Project Management Institute Inc., New York (2013)
10. SAS Institute Inc.: Data Mining Using SAS Enterprise Miner: A Case Study Approach, 3rd edn. SAS Institute Inc., Cary (2013)
11. Shearer, C.: The CRISP-DM model: the new blueprint for data mining. J. Data Warehous. **5**(4), 13–22 (2000)
12. Sommerville, I.: Software Engineering, 10th edn. Addison-Wesley, Boston (2015)

Author Index